Lecture Notes in Computer Science 14346

The series Lecture Notes in Computer Science (LNCS), including its subseries Lecture Notes in Artificial Intelligence (LNAI) and Lecture Notes in Bioinformatics (LNBI), has established itself as a medium for the publication of new developments in computer science and information technology research, teaching, and education.

LNCS enjoys close cooperation with the computer science R & D community, the series counts many renowned academics among its volume editors and paper authors, and collaborates with prestigious societies. Its mission is to serve this international community by providing an invaluable service, mainly focused on the publication of conference and workshop proceedings and postproceedings. LNCS commenced publication in 1973.

Gene Tsudik · Mauro Conti · Kaitai Liang ·
Georgios Smaragdakis
Editors

Computer Security – ESORICS 2023

28th European Symposium
on Research in Computer Security
The Hague, The Netherlands, September 25–29, 2023
Proceedings, Part III

 Springer

Editors
Gene Tsudik
University of California
Irvine, CA, USA

Mauro Conti 🆔
University of Padua
Padua, Italy

Kaitai Liang 🆔
Delft University of Technology
Delft, The Netherlands

Georgios Smaragdakis
Delft University of Technology
Delft, The Netherlands

ISSN 0302-9743   ISSN 1611-3349 (electronic)
Lecture Notes in Computer Science
ISBN 978-3-031-51478-4   ISBN 978-3-031-51479-1 (eBook)
https://doi.org/10.1007/978-3-031-51479-1

This Springer imprint is published by the registered company Springer Nature Switzerland AG
The registered company address is: Gewerbestrasse 11, 6330 Cham, Switzerland

Paper in this product is recyclable.

Preface

We are honoured and pleased to have served as PC Co-Chairs of ESORICS 2023. As one of the longest-running reputable conferences focused on security research, ESORICS 2023 attracted numerous high-quality submissions from all over the world, with authors affiliated with diverse academic, non-profit, governmental, and industrial entities.

After two rounds of submissions, each followed by an extensive reviewing period, we wound up with an excellent program, covering a broad range of timely and interesting topics. A total of 478 submissions were received: 150 in the first round and 328 in the second. 3–4 reviewers per submission in a single blind review driven by selfless and dedicated PC members (and external reviewers) who collectively did an amazing job providing thorough and insightful reviews. Some PC members even "went the extra mile" by reviewing more than their share. The end-result was 93 accepted submissions: 28 and 65, in the first and second rounds, respectively.

The 18-session ESORICS 2023 technical program included: (1) 93 talks corresponding to accepted papers, (2) a poster session, and (3) 3 impressive keynote talks by internationally prominent and active researchers: Virgil Gligor, Carmela Troncoso, and Mathias Payer. The program testifies to the level of excellence and stature of ESORICS.

We offer our deepest gratitude to:

- **Authors** of all submissions, whether accepted or not. We thank them for supporting ESORICS and for their trust in us and the PC to fairly evaluate their research results.
- **General Chairs:** Kaitai Liang and Georgios Smaragdakis, who dealt with (and addressed) numerous logistical and organisational issues. We very much appreciate it!
- **Submission Chairs:** Gabriele Costa and Letterio Galletta, for their super-human efforts and invaluable support during the submission and reviewing processes. We could not have done it without them!
- **Publication Chairs:** Florian Hahn and Giovanni Apruzzese, for handling the proceedings. We are especially grateful to them for handling numerous requests from the authors.
- **Web Chair:** Yury Zhauniarovich for creating and maintaining the conference website.
- **Poster Chair:** Bala Chandrasekaran, for taking care of the poster track.
- **All PC members** and their delegated reviewers, who were the main engine of success of ESORICS 2023 and whose hard work yielded an excellent program.

  - Special thanks to the recipients of the *Outstanding Reviewer Award*: Ferdinand Brasser and Brendan Saltaformaggio, for their exceptional reviewing quality.

In closing, though clearly biased, we believe that ESOIRCS 2023 was an overall success and we hope that all attendees enjoyed the conference.

September 2023   Mauro Conti
                                                                Gene Tsudik

Organization

General Chairs

Kaitai Liang   Delft University of Technology, The Netherlands
Georgios Smaragdakis   Delft University of Technology, The Netherlands

Program Committee Chairs

Mauro Conti   University of Padua, Italy & Delft University of
     Technology, The Netherlands
Gene Tsudik   University of California, Irvine, USA

Submission Chairs

Gabriele Costa   IMT School for Advanced Studies Lucca, Italy
Letterio Galletta   IMT School for Advanced Studies Lucca, Italy

Workshops Chairs

Jérémie Decouchant   Delft University of Technology, The Netherlands
Stjepan Picek   Radboud University & Delft University of
     Technology, The Netherlands

Posters Chair

Bala Chandrasekaran   Vrije Universiteit Amsterdam, The Netherlands

Publication Chairs

Florian Hahn   University of Twente, The Netherlands
Giovanni Apruzzese   University of Liechtenstein, Liechtenstein

Publicity Chair

Savvas Zannettou   Delft University of Technology, The Netherlands

Sponsorship Chair

Giovane Moura   SIDN/Delft University of Technology,
                                     The Netherlands

Web Chair

Yury Zhauniarovich   Delft University of Technology, The Netherlands

Programme Committee

Gergely Acs	Budapest University of Technology and Economics, Hungary
Massimiliano Albanese	George Mason University, USA
Cristina Alcaraz (only Round 2)	University of Malaga, Spain
Alejandro Cabrera Aldaya	Tampere University of Technology, Finland
Mark Allman	International Computer Science Institute, USA
Elli Androulaki	IBM Zurich, Switzerland
Giovanni Apruzzese	University of Liechtenstein, Liechtenstein
Mikael Asplund	Linköping University, Sweden
Ahmad Atamli	Nvidia, UK
Vijay Atluri	Rutgers University, USA
Kiran Balagani	New York Institute of Technology, USA
Giampaolo Bella (only Round 2)	University of Catania, Italy
Antonio Bianchi	Purdue University, USA
Giuseppe Bianchi	Università di Roma Tor Vergata, Italy
Jorge Blasco	Royal Holloway, University of London, UK
Ferdinand Brasser	SANCTUARY Systems GmbH, Germany
Alessandro Brighente	University of Padua, Italy
Ileana Buhan	Radboud University, The Netherlands
Alvaro Cardenas	University of California Santa Cruz, USA
Xavier Carpent	University of Nottingham, UK
Anrin Chakraborti	Stony Brook University, USA
Sze Yiu Chau	Chinese University of Hong Kong, China
Liqun Chen	University of Surrey, UK

Scott Coull	Mandiant, USA
Bruno Crispo	University of Trento, Italy
Michel Cukier (only Round 1)	University of Maryland, USA
Sanchari Das	University of Denver, USA
Lucas Davi	University of Duisburg-Essen, Germany
Fabio De Gaspari	Sapienza University of Rome, Italy
Ivan De Oliveira Nunes	Rochester Institute of Technology, USA
Roberto Di Pietro	Hamad Bin Khalifa University, Qatar
Xuhua Ding	Singapore Management University, Singapore
Shlomi Dolev	Ben-Gurion University of the Negev, Israel
Anna Lisa Ferrara	University of Molise, Italy
Barbara Fila	INSA Rennes, IRISA, France
Simone Fischer-Hübner	Karlstad University, Sweden
Olga Gadyatskaya	University of Leiden, The Netherlands
Ankit Gangwal	International Institute of Information Technology, Hyderabad, India
Siddharth Garg	NYU Tandon, USA
Giorgio Giacinto	University of Cagliari, Italy
Alberto Giaretta	Örebro University, Sweden
Devashish Gosain	KU Leuven, Belgium
Matteo Große-Kampmann (only Round 2)	Ruhr-Universität Bochum, Germany
Berk Gulmezoglu	Iowa State University, USA
Thomas Haines	Norwegian University of Science and Technology, Norway
Hugo Jonker	Open University of the Netherlands, The Netherlands
Sokratis Katsikas	Norwegian University of Science and Technology, Norway
Stefan Katzenbeisser	University of Passau, Germany
Jihye Kim	Kookmin University, South Korea
Hyoungshick Kim	Sungkyunkwan University, South Korea
Hyungsub Kim	Purdue University, USA
Marina Krotofil	European Commission, Switzerland
Juliane Krämer	University of Regensburg, Germany
Alptekin Küpçü	Koç University, Turkey
Katsiaryna Labunets (only Round 2)	Utrecht University, The Netherlands
Peeter Laud	Cybernetica AS, Estonia
Adam Lee	University of Pittsburgh, USA
Kyu Hyung Lee	University of Georgia, USA
Valeria Loscrì	Inria, France

Contents – Part III

Blockchain

Miscellaneous

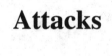

Attacks

Layered Symbolic Security Analysis in DY*

Karthikeyan Bhargavan[1,2], Abhishek Bichhawat[3], Pedram Hosseyni[4],
Ralf Küsters[4], Klaas Pruiksma[4(✉)], Guido Schmitz[5],
Clara Waldmann[4], and Tim Würtele[4]

[1] INRIA Paris, Paris, France
karthikeyan.bhargavan@inria.fr
[2] Cryspen, Paris, France
[3] IIT Gandhinagar, Gandhinagar, India
abhishek.b@iitgn.ac.in
[4] University of Stuttgart, Stuttgart, Germany
{pedram.hosseyni,ralf.kuesters,klaas.pruiksma,
clara.waldmann,tim.wuertele}@sec.uni-stuttgart.de
[5] Royal Holloway University of London, Egham, UK
guido.schmitz@rhul.ac.uk

Abstract. While cryptographic protocols are often analyzed in isolation, they are typically deployed within a stack of protocols, where each layer relies on the security guarantees provided by the protocol layer below it, and in turn provides its own security functionality to the layer above. Formally analyzing the whole stack in one go is infeasible even for semi-automated verification tools, and impossible for pen-and-paper proofs. The DY* protocol verification framework offers a modular and scalable technique that can reason about large protocols, specified as a set of F* modules. However, it does not support the *compositional* verification of layered protocols since it treats the global security invariants monolithically. In this paper, we extend DY* with a new methodology that allows analysts to modularly analyze each layer in a way that compose to provide security for a protocol stack. Importantly, our technique allows a layer to be replaced by another implementation, without affecting the proofs of other layers. We demonstrate this methodology on two case studies. We also present a verified library of generic authenticated and confidential communication patterns that can be used in future protocol analyses and is of independent interest.

1 Introduction

Modern Web applications combine a variety of cryptographic mechanisms and protocols to achieve their security goals. For example, to log in to a banking website or code repository, a user typically first enters a username and password over HTTPS. The server may then ask for a second-factor authentication via an independent secure channel with the user's phone. Only when both authentication mechanisms succeed is the user allowed to access any sensitive resource. Each such security mechanism may in turn rely on a whole stack of cryptographic protocols underneath it, each with its own security assumptions and guarantees.

© The Author(s), under exclusive license to Springer Nature Switzerland AG 2024
G. Tsudik et al. (Eds.): ESORICS 2023, LNCS 14346, pp. 3–21, 2024.
https://doi.org/10.1007/978-3-031-51479-1_1

Consider the password-based login mechanism, where the user sends a username and secret password to a website over the HTTPS protocol, which implements a confidential request-response communication pattern between an unauthenticated client and authenticated server. The HTTPS exchange is encoded within the duplex encrypted data streams provided by the Record sub-protocol of Transport Layer Security (TLS); the keys encrypting these streams are set up by an authenticated key exchange implemented by the TLS Handshake sub-protocol. TLS itself relies on the X.509 public key infrastructure (PKI) for server authentication, a trusted cryptographic library, and an untrusted TCP/IP networking stack for communication.

Consequently, the security and functionality of the password-based login mechanism relies on the correct design and implementation of the stack of protocols depicted on the right. Each layer depends on the security guarantees provided by the layer below and offers new functionality and guarantees to the layer above. The protocol at each layer may well be secure in isolation, but if it is used incorrectly by the layers above it, or if there is any secret value or state shared between two layers, the composite stack may well be insecure. For example, the Triple Handshake attacks [13] demonstrated how three different key exchange protocols that are secure on their own break when composed together. Hence, it is important to analyze the stack as a whole, proving security for the green layers, under precise security assumptions on the crypto, treating the untrusted network as controlled by the adversary.

One option would be to model all the green layers together and prove them secure in a single proof, but this effort can quickly become too large and untenable for pen-and-paper proofs and even automated protocol verification tools. The problem is that although many protocol analysis approaches are effective on small protocols, they are not modular, compositional, or scalable enough to analyze large and complex protocol stacks.

We say that a protocol specification methodology is *modular* when each protocol can be modeled in its own module(s) with a succinct interface that describes its assumptions, functionality, and security guarantees. Further, we say that a protocol analysis framework is *compositional* if it allows different protocols to also be verified independently and then composed without needing to redo the analysis. Finally, we say that a protocol analysis tool is *scalable* if the verification time and effort grows proportionately with the size and complexity of the protocol. We believe that all three properties are needed to cleanly model and feasibly analyze stacks of layered real-world protocols.

Automated whole-protocol analysis tools like ProVerif [15] and Tamarin [31] work well for small-to-medium protocols, but suffer from not having these three properties. Indeed, it can take hours to analyze a monolithic model of TLS 1.3 using these tools [10,20], without even considering the PKI or the application. Recognizing this drawback, a line of work on symbolic protocol composition studies conditions under which protocol proofs built with such tools can be composed (see e.g. [18,27]). Computational cryptographic provers like EasyCrypt [3], SSProve [1], CryptoVerif [14] model cryptography more precisely but are less effective than symbolic tools and have only been applied to constructions and small protocols. For these tools, composability is even more important to enable the analysis of large protocols by breaking them into sub-protocols.

In this work, we adopt the type-based machine-checked protocol analysis methodology of DY* [5], which natively supports modular specification and enables proofs that are scalable, since proofs can be type-checked in time linear in the size of the protocol. We observe, however, that the DY* framework is not compositional in that it requires the security invariants for all protocols in a stack to first be specified together, and then each protocol can be independently analyzed with respect to these monolithic security predicates. Changing any protocol layer requires the full stack to be verified again.

Contributions. We design and implement an extension to DY* that enables compositional protocol verification. We use this extension to develop verified implementations of several generic layers, including PKI, TLS, and a library of communication patterns that includes HTTPS-style request-response exchanges, all of which are designed to be easily reused and built upon in future analyses. We use these verified libraries to build and analyze protocol stacks for two case studies.[1] We show how each layer can be verified independently and safely composed. We also show how one implementation of a layer can be replaced by another, without re-verifying all other layers. We believe our extension to DY* to be the first symbolic protocol verification methodology that applies to executable protocols and allows for mechanized analysis in a modular, scalable, and compositional way, thereby producing machine-checked proofs.

Paper Structure. We first briefly recall the DY* framework. We then, in Sect. 3, present the two mentioned simple case studies, which we use as running examples through the paper. We outline our general approach of layered analysis in DY* in Sect. 4, with instantiations for a generic PKI layer and a communication layer, built on top of the PKI layer, presented in Sect. 5. The analysis of our case studies based on the latter two layers is given in Sect. 6. Related work is discussed in Sect. 7, and Sect. 8 concludes.

2 The DY* Framework

DY* is a framework for symbolic security analysis of protocol code written in the F* [36] programming language. DY* has been successfully used to verify a variety of cryptographic protocols, including classic protocols like Needham-Schroeder-Lowe and ISO [7], ratcheted key exchange protocols like Signal [5], modern standards like ACME [6], secure channel frameworks like Noise [28], and group protocols like TreeSync [37]. Proofs in DY* are not fully automated

---

[1] Code for all of these implementations can be found in [8].

and require manual annotations, but in return, DY* offers many advantages over fully automated symbolic analysis frameworks like ProVerif and Tamarin.

First, DY* proofs have access to the full F* proof assistant, and hence can handle arbitrary recursion in protocols using inductive proofs, unlike Tamarin and ProVerif, which only have limited support for induction. Second, DY* supports executable protocol specifications that can be tested to simulate full protocol runs and attacks. Third, DY* uses a type-based proof methodology that scales linearly in the size of the protocol, since every protocol function is analyzed independently. While automated tools are more effective and convenient than DY* for small protocols, they tend to blow up on large protocols like ACME, Signal, and Noise, which is where DY* starts to shine.

In the following, we briefly describe DY* focusing on the aspects that are relevant for the rest of the paper. We refer to [5] for details on the design of DY* and to [7] for a tutorial-style introduction to this framework.

Trace-Based Semantics. DY* explicitly encodes the global run-time semantics of distributed protocol executions in terms of a *global trace* and the symbolic security analysis is proved sound with respect to this semantics *within* the verification framework itself.

DY* models the global interleaved execution of a set of protocol participants (or *principals*) as a trace of observable protocol actions (or *entries*). As a principal executes a role in some run of a protocol, it can send and receive messages, generate random values, log security events, and store and retrieve its state (consisting of sessions), and each of these operations either reads from or extends the global trace. The protocol code for each principal cannot directly read from or write to the trace, but instead must use a typed trace API that enforces an append-only discipline on the global trace.

Symbolic Cryptographic Library. DY* also provides a library for the manipulation of bytes. The interface of this library treats bytes abstractly and provides functions for creating constants, concatenating and splitting bytes, and applying various cryptographic primitives such as public-key encryption and signatures, symmetric encryption and message authentication codes, hashing, Diffie-Hellman, and key derivation, which are treated as black-boxes.

The library interface also provides a series of lemmas relating to these functions that effectively form an equational theory, stating, for example, that decryption is an inverse of encryption, or that splitting concatenated bytes returns its components, or that signature verification always succeeds on a validly generated signature. Bytes can only be manipulated by using the functions of this cryptographic API. This ensures that all byte manipulations adhere to the equational theory. For example, signing keys cannot be extracted from a signature and hash functions cannot be inverted, in particular by the attacker.

Dolev-Yao Adversary. The standard attacker model captured by DY* is the symbolic Dolev-Yao active network attacker [22]. This adversary is modeled as an (arbitrary) F* program that is given full access to the cryptographic API and limited access to the global trace API. That is, it can call functions to generate its own random values, send a message from any principal to any principal, and read any message from the trace. Notably, it cannot read any random values or logged security events from the trace, and *a priori* it cannot read the session states stored by any principal. However, the attacker is given a special function that it can call at any time to compromise other principals' states (fully or partly), which marks the respective state as compromised in the trace and unlocks access to its contents. DY* defines a predicate that captures the knowledge that the adversary can possibly gain at any point in a trace, and we can use this predicate to reason about fine-grained confidentiality guarantees.

Symbolic Execution and Testing. The code for protocol models in DY* can be executed symbolically to obtain traces that can be printed and inspected for debugging. This feature is invaluable to test the model and ensure that it behaves as expected. For example, we can ensure that there isn't a bug in the protocol code that prevents protocol runs from finishing, or we can write example attacker code and test potential attacks against our protocol.

Authentication and Confidentiality Goals. The security goals of a protocol are stated as predicates over all reachable global traces. The trace predicate has full visibility over all entries in the global trace, including sent messages, logged events, and states stored at any principal. To specify an authentication goal, we typically state that certain events must be recorded in a certain order with matching parameters (e.g., when principal B accepts a session with A, then A needs to have initiated this session). To specify confidentiality, we state conditions on the attacker's knowledge at specific points in the trace.

Proof Methodology. The main proof technique in DY* is to establish an invariant over all reachable traces that capture relevant aspects of the modeled protocol and prove that this invariant implies the desired goals. In particular, we need to prove that all functions that can modify the trace, either on behalf of honest protocol code or the attacker, preserve the invariant. To this end, DY* offers a modular proof methodology, where programmers only need to define and prove local protocol-specific state invariants and security goals, and the framework completes the proof by filling in generic security invariants that are proved once-and-for-all for all protocols.

DY* defines a library of *labeled* APIs that enforce a labeling discipline on the usage of cryptography to simplify reasoning about secrecy. The labels explicitly capture the intended set of principals that may know certain bytes, and the labeled APIs enforce that only this set of principals can access the bytes. This library defines a computational effect LCrypto that enforces a global trace invariant called valid_trace. The labeled APIs have valid_trace as both pre- and post-condition for all functions by using the LCrypto effect. The global trace invariant consists of several components, some generic invariants and some predicates that have to be defined for each protocol.

Protocol-Specific Predicates. For each protocol, we specify predicates on the usage of cryptographic functions, pre-conditions for logged events, and invariants on the session states stored by protocol participants. The predicates on the usage of cryptographic functions restrict the application of cryptographic functions to certain messages and keys. For example, the usage predicate for public key encryption (can_pke_enc) may state that honest principals encrypt only messages of a certain form, if certain events have occurred on the global trace, or nonces have a certain label, which in turn gives other honest principals decrypting such messages these guarantees. We note that the attacker/dishonest principals are not restricted in any way.

3   Motivating Examples

In the rest of this paper, we use two high-level security protocols to illustrate our key concepts and our compositional verification methodology. These case studies do not themselves use much cryptography, but they rely on lower-layer cryptographic protocols to provide various kinds of secure channels. Consequently, the analysis of these examples should depend only on the guarantees of the underlying channels but not on the details of how these channels are implemented.

Basic Authentication (BA). The first example, depicted below, is a *basic authentication* protocol, inspired by the Basic HTTP Authentication scheme [33].

A client can send two different kinds of requests to a server. First, a request to register an account at the server, containing a password (Step ①). When receiving such a request, the server generates a long-term secret (essentially a resource) and stores the secret along with the password (Step ②). The client can send a second type of request (access request) to retrieve the long-term secret, which needs to include the password used for account generation (Step ④). Upon receiving such a request, the server checks whether an account identified by the password exists and returns the corresponding long-term secret (Step ⑤).

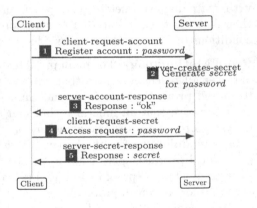

The security guarantee we want to show for this example is that if an honest (i.e. uncorrupted) Client and Server communicate via a server-authenticated confidential channel (like TLS), then the long-term secret stays confidential.

Source Routing (SR). Our second example is a simple *source routing* protocol where a message is to be sent along a pre-specified path of participants.

On the right, we show the protocol for three participants where the message m should take the path $[A, B, C]$. (Note that the protocol itself works for paths of any length.) A initiates the flow by sending the message and the planned path to B, the next participant on the path. B processes the message and sends it on to the next participant C. Once C receives the message the protocol ends.

The security guarantees of the source routing example depend on the types of channels that are used. For example, if all principals send the messages over authenticated channels, then we would like to show that the message indeed took the specified path, as long as none of the participants on the path gets corrupted. Similarly, we would like to prove confidentiality guarantees for the message if the channels are also confidential.

4 Layered Symbolic Protocol Analysis

As mentioned in Sect. 2, DY* enables the modular and scalable analysis of protocols by relying on the expressiveness of F*, like inductive reasoning and type-based proofs. However, there remain some limitations that make proofs of large protocols in DY* difficult and fragile. For example, consider the BA example described above. The security of this protocol relies on a server-authenticated confidential request-response channel between a client and a server. In practice, this channel is implemented by HTTPS, which in turn relies on TLS, the X.509 PKI, and a crypto library. To fully verify the security of this protocol, we have to model all these layers. Doing so in a monolithic proof framework like ProVerif or Tamarin is infeasible, both due to the effort involved and the verification time.

In DY*, we can rely on the modularity provided by F* to put the modeling *code* for each layer into a separate module and verify them separately. However, even if the code for different layers is independent, the *predicates* that are used in the security proof are shared between all layers. Consequently, we have to globally define the state invariants, event preconditions, the predicates for cryptographic primitives, such as encryption, signatures, and MACs, all in once place. If any two layers use the same cryptographic construction, e.g. public key encryption, we have to instantiate the predicate for public-key encryption, can_pke_enc (see also Sect. 2), in a way that both layers still typecheck, which in turn requires a proof that the uses of this predicate in the two layers are disjoint, i.e. they do not conflict with each other. These kinds of proofs are not just unpleasant, but also non-compositional. If we wanted to change (say) the channel implementation from TLS to some other protocol with the same guarantees, we would have to change the predicates and reverify the full stack.

In short, DY* offers a scalable proof methodology and a modular specification technique, but does not support composable proofs for sub-protocols or protocol layers. Even to prove simple protocols like our case studies, the analyst must read, edit, and verify a set of global predicates that include details of lower-level protocols and higher-layer applications that they may not be familiar with.

The Layered Predicates Approach. In this paper, we propose a new methodology for the *layered analysis* of protocols modeled in DY*. Our key insight is to separately model both the code and the predicates of each protocol layer in its own module, and specify rules on how these predicates are composed. Essentially, each lower layer takes the higher-layer predicates as opaque parameters and incorporates them in its analysis. Consequently, the security proof of the lower layer is done only once for *all* instantiations of the higher-layer predicates. Unlike in classic DY*, this proof does not need to be redone even if the higher-layer protocol changes. Conversely, each higher-layer protocol is aware of the lower-layer it depends upon. If the lower layer changes, the higher layer may need to be re-verified but we carefully restrict the new proofs to a minimal set of properties about overlapping cryptographic usage.

We illustrate the general concept using state invariants. In DY*, each principal stores and maintains local state for every protocol session it participates in. For example, both participants in a confidential channel protocol usually store a symmetric key that is used to encrypt messages between them. In addition, they may store session state, such as passwords, used by higher-layer protocols. For the security proof, we need to show that this stored data satisfies certain properties, which are captured by state invariants. For example, the symmetric key (and the password) must have a secrecy label that ensures that it can only be read by the principal and its peer. In DY*, these invariants are so far defined monolithically for all protocol layers in a global state invariant.

In contrast, in our layered approach the state invariant of each layer is defined independently, only taking higher_layer_preds as parameter, as illustrated below:

```
let state_invariant higher_layer_preds principal state = match state with
  | CommunicationState sym_key responder → (*Communication layer invariants*)
  | HigherLayerState higher_layer_state → (*must satisfy higher−layer invariants*)
    higher_layer_preds.state_invariant principal higher_layer_state
  | _ → ⊥
```

Here, the state invariant for the communication layer (of Sect. 5) says that the stored state is structured in two disjoint parts, one part for itself and one for all higher layers. Each part enforces its own state invariant. This style allows us to easily compose multiple layers in a stack. Indeed, the communication layer invariant itself serves as a higher-layer predicate for the layers below it.

Lifting Cryptographic Functions. If different layers overlap in the cryptographic functions and keys they use, this can, in principle, result in an insecure composition, even if both layers are secure by themselves. For example, if a secure channel protocol makes its internal encryption key available also to higher layers, then it may be possible for the attacker to inject messages encrypted by the higher layer into the secure channel, undermining the integrity of the channel. If two layers do not conflict in this way, we say that they satisfy *implicit disjointness*, reusing a term from the setting of Universal Composability [29].

To verify a stack of protocols, we therefore need to prove that every pair of protocols is pairwise disjoint. Using our layered approach, we turn this global property into a local condition at every layer. Each layer redefines (or *lifts*) all the cryptographic functions it uses, defines local predicates specifying its own usage of these functions, and specifies disjointness conditions for the safe usage of these functions in higher layers. For any crypto function not used in a layer, these functions and predicates are simply passed through to the next layer.

As an example of the simplest case, consider a layer that does not use MACs. The local MAC usage predicate of this layer is equivalent to the higher-layer predicate, without any additional local conditions. Its MAC disjointness condition for higher layers is the same as the disjointness predicate for its lower layer.

The lifted MAC function provided by this layer has mac_disjoint and the higher-layer mac_predicate as preconditions, which means that any higher layer is free to use this MAC function, in accordance with its own local MAC usage predicate, as long as it ensures disjointness with the layers below.

Suppose a layer does use a cryptographic function, say AEAD encryption, but defines its own local keys which are not shared with any other layer. This is the most common (and most advisable) design pattern. In DY*, each key is associated with a usage string. For example, the communication layer creates symmetric keys with the usage string CommunicationLayerSymKey, and uses this key to encrypt requests and responses (see Sect. 5 for details). If this key usage is not used in any other layer, then the AEAD predicate of this layer can cleanly distinguish between its own usage and that of higher layers. No additional disjointness condition is needed, only those imposed by lower layers (as in MAC).

Implicit Disjointness in the General Case. The most complicated case is when the same cryptographic function and key may be used in multiple layers. This failure of key independence between protocol layers is tricky to handle in security proofs, but can unfortunately often occur in real-world protocols.

In our approach, we use the disjointness predicate to ensure that if a higher layer uses a key that is also used by some lower layer, then the messages that it uses (e.g., encrypts) with this key are disjoint from (e.g., have different formats than) those used in lower layers. For example, the communication layer's AEAD disjointness predicate requires that the higher layer only encrypts messages with keys or formats that do not conflict with this or lower layers:

```
let aead_disjoint key_usage key plaintext =
   key_usage == "CommunicationLayerSymKey" ⟹
   match split plaintext with
   | Success ("CommunicationLayerRequest", message) → ⊥
   | Success ("CommunicationLayerResponse", message) → ⊥
   | _ → Lower_layer.aead_disjoint key_usage key plaintext
```

As long as the higher layer meets this condition, it can freely use the AEAD key and enforce its own local AEAD usage predicate.

The communication layer then defines its own local AEAD usage predicate, encompassing all the ways that AEAD may be used by this or higher layers:

```
let aead_predicate higher_layer_preds key_usage key plaintext =
  if key_usage == "CommunicationLayerSymKey" then
    (match split plaintext with
     | Success ("CommunicationLayerRequest", message) →
       communication_layer_request_predicate higher_layer_preds message
     | Success ("CommunicationLayerResponse", message) →
       communication_layer_response_predicate higher_layer_preds message
     | _ → higher_layer_preds.aead_predicate key_usage key plaintext)
  else higher_layer_preds.aead_predicate key_usage key plaintext
```

This predicate states that if the key usage is CommunicationLayerSymKey, and the plaintext matches the format of the communication layer's request or response, then the inner message must satisfy the communication layer's request_predicate or response_predicate, which may in turn take into account additional conditions specified in the higher layer predicates. If the key has a different usage or the plaintext has a different format, then they must satisfy the higher layer's AEAD encryption predicate. Hence, the higher layer may either (1) call the communication layer to encrypt plaintexts, by obeying its request or response API, or (2) use independent keys to encrypt its own plaintexts, or (3) use the same key but with a disjoint message format. In the latter two cases, the key and message must satisfy the higher-layer usage predicate.

Compositional Verification. Importantly, when verifying the higher layer, we do not need to understand the possibly complex details of the lower-layer protocol implementation encoded in its usage predicate; we only need to prove the lower-layer disjointness predicate and the higher-layer usage predicate. We also note that these predicate definitions are verified, not trusted. If a protocol designer incorrectly makes them too strong or too weak, then typechecking will fail at the lower layer or at the higher layer.

Altogether, our changes extend DY* to a fully compositional layered protocol verification framework. Each layer only needs to be verified once, and changes to any layer implementation affect only those higher layers that reuse the same crypto functions and keys. So far, we have only considered vertical and sequential compositions of layers into a protocol stack. In future work, we intend to extend this framework to account for other composition patterns, such as horizontal compositions. Note that such composite protocols are already verifiable in DY*, but they can not benefit from the compositional proof technique in this paper.

5   Instantiation: Generic PKI and Communication Layers

We now illustrate how to instantiate the approach presented in the previous section by two layers, a simple PKI and a communication layer that uses it. These layers provide a basic library for these common protocol components that can be reused in future analyses.

5.1   A Layer for Public-Key Infrastructure

The PKI layer models the functionality of a certificate authority, and hence, the correct distribution of public keys, but, importantly, also the generation of public/private key-pairs and their management/storage at principals. Keys can have different types (public-key encryption, Diffie-Hellman key exchange, signing, MACing, etc.) and usages. The PKI layer exposes APIs to generate and retrieve keys of the desired type with an intended usage. Using labels, it additionally guarantees that the private keys of principals indeed belong to (and are only known by) the respective principals, and that the predicates that hold true at the higher layer, in particular, regarding the state of principals, also hold true in the PKI layer, following the principle outlined in Sect. 4.

5.2   A Layer for Confidential and Authenticated Communication

As a second instance of our layering approach, we design a communication layer providing APIs to exchange messages with different types of security guarantees. We model sending *authenticated* and/or *confidential* (single) messages as well as *request-response pairs*. This layer is built on top of the PKI layer.

For all functions in the interface of the communication layer we give *implementations*, showing that the pre- and post-conditions can be realized based on cryptographic primitives. For some functions/channel types, we even have multiple implementations, including one inspired by TLS 1.3., showing that our guarantees can be achieved by real-world protocols.

Interface and Guarantees. At a high level, the sender of a message using the communication layer can convey not just the message itself, but also some proof information, using new predicates exposed by the layer for applications to define. The guarantees that the receiver of the message gets depend on the type of communication (e.g. authenticated). These guarantees may talk about the contents of the message, but also may convey information about the state of the sender or about past events in the trace, which greatly facilitates scalable and composable analysis of protocols.

We now examine specific examples of the guarantees provided by the communication layer, in the context of our source routing protocol from Sect. 3.

Intuitively, the receiver of an *authenticated* message should be guaranteed that the sender of the message, if honest, followed the protocol when creating the message. Since the details of message creation depend on the specific application being modeled, the application may specify the exact properties that should hold for an honest sender, by defining the predicate authenticated_send_pred exposed by the communication layer. In the source routing example, this predicate states that .if all participants on the path are honest, then the previous participant processed the message.

Similarly, a *confidential* message should guarantee the receiver that its contents do not leak to the attacker in transit. As in the authenticated case, the details of what parties should be allowed to know are application-specific, and

can be defined in the confidential_send_pred exposed by the communication layer.
We note that while secrecy properties are natural candidates for this predicate,
we can also include more general guarantees, as in the authenticated case. In the
source routing example, the predicate says that the content of the message can
only be known by the participants on the path.

We can also send messages that are both authenticated and confidential,
using the authenticated_confidential_send_pred predicate to specify the guarantees
the application expects, which are a combination of those for authenticated-
only and confidential-only messages. Similarly, we can send request/response
pairs, which resemble a confidential (and optionally authenticated) message,
responded to by an authenticated and confidential message. These pairs use
their own predicates request_pred and response_pred, which are similar to the
other predicates, but have slightly more expressive power, e.g., the response
predicate can refer to both the request and the response.

In addition to the communication functions, the layer also exposes lifted
versions of the cryptographic functions provided by DY^*, as described in Sect. 4.
The communication layer uses a symmetric key for securing request/response
pairs (as is common in practice), and exposes this key to the higher layer, which
may freely use this key as long as it does not interfere with the communication
layer, as already discussed in Sect. 4.

Implementation. As a sanity check and to prove that the interface of the
communication layer, and the guarantees that come with it, can be realized, we
provide implementations of the interface for the various channels and prove (in
DY^*) that these typecheck against the interface, and hence, provide the desired
guarantees. Our implementations are rather straightforward and are based on
public-key cryptography, which is why they are based on the PKI layer. However,
as mentioned, we also provide a simplified implementation of TLS 1.3 (see below).

The implementation for sending authenticated messages adds a signature
to the original message, while confidential messages simply encrypt the original
message with the public key of the receiver. Messages which are both confidential
and authenticated use an encrypt-then-sign scheme. For request/response pairs,
we use a hybrid encryption scheme where the request contains a fresh symmetric
key, encrypted asymmetrically with the public key of the receiver. We provide
two variants for the encryption of the request body, one using this symmetric
key, and one using the public key of the receiver. In either case, the receiver then
uses the symmetric key from the request to encrypt the response.

The guarantees of the communication layer can then be derived (internally
to the communication layer) from the guarantees of the cryptographic functions
used. In this way, we implement the predicates exposed by the communication
layer (e.g. request_pred) from the lower-level predicates exposed by the PKI layer
to the communication layer.

TLS Implementation. The Transport Layer Security Protocol [34,35] is a
widely used cryptographic protocol ensuring end-to-end security of messages
exchanged by applications running on top of it. Various prior works [10,12,20,21]
have identified flaws and presented proofs and verified implementations of TLS.

We provide a second implementation of the request/response pattern of the communication layer based on a simplified version of the latest TLS version, namely TLS 1.3, which illustrates that our communication layer can have multiple, including real-word, implementations. Importantly, as explained in Sect. 4, typically higher layers, e.g., those using the communication layer, can be analyzed independently of the specific implementations of lower layers.

Our model of TLS is itself modularized into two layers: one for the *handshake* protocol for key-exchange (TLS AKE in Sect. 1), and the other is the *record* layer for the transmission of messages (TLS Stream in Sect. 1). The handshake layer involves the exchange of three messages: (1) the initiator/client generates a Diffie-Hellman (DH) key pair and sends their public key to the server; (2) the responder/server generates its own DH keypair and shares the public key with the client signed with the server's signature key; (3) the client acknowledges the receipt of the server's public key signed with their signature key. At the end of the protocol, both client and server share a secret alongside authenticating themselves with each other. The guarantees for the keys used in the three steps are obtained from the PKI layer on top of which this layer is implemented.

6   Analysis of BA Example

Next, we present our security analysis of the BA example from Sect. 3, showing how the communication layer greatly facilitates this analysis and makes it independent of the concrete implementation of that layer; the analysis of the source routing example can be found in our technical report [9].

Obviously, we model the BA example on top of the communication layer: The client has two functions for creating and sending the requests, and two for receiving the corresponding responses. The client stores the secret it receives from the server in its state. Further, there is a function for the server to receive and respond to each request. When it receives an account registration request it generates a new secret and stores this secret next to the password in its state.

The main property that we want to prove for this example is that the secret received by the client is only known to the client and server, provided neither is corrupted. By stating this property from the perspective of the client receiving the secret, we provide security guarantees to such clients.

The core of the proof of this property is a set of global trace invariants, which we show are preserved by each protocol participant, and which are strong enough to imply our security property. Our main invariant is an invariant on the state of clients, which tells us that if a client stores in its state a secret received through the BA protocol, along with the server from whom the secret was received, then either the client or the server is corrupt, or the secret is labelled with exactly these two parties. The security property follows immediately from this invariant together with the preconditions of the property, in particular that the client stores the secret in its state, and the soundness of the DY* labeling system, which guarantees that secrets are only known to the parties in their labels.[2]

The bulk of the work then lies in proving that the protocol functions preserve this property, so it is indeed an invariant of valid traces. The secret is only written into the state of a client in the function where a client receives a response to an access request. If both parties are honest at that time, the communication layer guarantees that the predicate response_pred holds. This predicate states that the label of the received secret is the same as that of the password sent in the corresponding request.

Note how the communication layer makes it simple to convey information from one principal to another—in this particular case, the server needs to prove the response_pred before it can send a response containing a secret, and the client can then make use of this same predicate upon receiving the message. This means that the server, who does not know the label of the password, can still convey to the client that the labels of the secret and the password are the same (trivially so, since the server generates the secret with this property).

Another part of a client's state invariant states that the password is labeled with exactly the client and the server it interacts with. The client, knowing the label of the password, is then able to determine precisely the label of the secret, allowing us to establish the state invariant for the client.

Simplicity of Analysis and Independence from Channel Implementations. This case study highlights several benefits of the layered approach. First, the higher-level interface of the communication layer makes it quite natural to model the BA example, just as secure communication libraries simplify protocol implementation by abstracting away from cryptographic primitives. Moreover, the security of the BA example can also be proven at a much higher level of abstraction, using the guarantees provided by the communication layer (and customizable by higher layers via predicates), again hiding fine details of cryptography. Since the BA example does not directly use any cryptography, implicit disjointness with the communication layer comes for free, as described in Sect. 4. In particular, this means that we can switch our implementation of the communication layer (e.g. between our simple and TLS implementations) without changes to the analysis of the BA example.

Implicit Disjointness. We also implemented and analyzed a variant of the BA example where the server uses the symmetric key exposed by the communication layer to encrypt the secret, in addition to the underlying encryption used by the communication layer. This illustrates the flexibility of our layered approach. As outlined in Sect. 4, the server must then prove that it satisfies the implicit disjointness predicate whenever it encrypts messages using the exposed symmetric key. Since the definition of this predicate depends on the underlying implementation of the communication channel, the analysis of the BA example may need to be adjusted when this implementation changes, but only in this

---

[2] The soundness of the labeling system has been mechanically proved once and for all in DY* itself.

specific aspect. This dependence on the implementation is inherent if the same key material is used across layers, as implicit disjointness properties need to be established, and depend on the specific format of messages.

Informal Benchmark. While we do not have an unlayered version of this example to compare to, we can approximate it by looking at each component of the BA example's stack individually. The verification time for an unlayered version would be at least as long as the sum of the times for the components, and likely longer, as the predicates involved would be more complex. This lets us get a rough idea of the time savings of being able to recheck changes to the example without needing to reverify the full stack. Here, the BA example in isolation takes only about 19% of the verification time of the full stack of layers (see Table 1). With more layers or added complexity, we expect that this full-stack verification time would increase even more relative to the single-component verification time, further increasing the benefits of the layering approach.

Table 1. Size and verification time of components of the BA example

	Size (LoC)	Verif. Time (s)
BA example	1216	117
Comm. Layer	2125	142
PKI Layer and Core DY*	4736	358

7 Related Work

This paper presents a symbolic protocol analysis methodology that extends an existing semi-automated verification framework (DY*), in order to enable modular, scalable, and compositional protocol proofs. Many prior and concurrent works present related results. In this section, we compare our approach with closely related work on developing machine-checked compositional protocol proofs. A wider survey of the area may be found in [2].

Symbolic Protocol Analysis. Tools that verify protocols in the symbolic or Dolev-Yao model [22] rely on a simplified abstraction of cryptography that makes it easier to automate security proofs and to find logical flaws and attacks on protocols. In particular, tools like ProVerif [15] and Tamarin [31] have been successful in performing fully automated proofs of protocols like TLS 1.3 [10, 20]. However, these tools do not support modular specifications or compositional proofs, do not allow inductive proofs, and do not scale well to larger protocols.

Type-based approaches like DY* [5] and its predecessors [4, 11] have been used for the modular proofs of large protocols like ACME [6] and Signal [5]. This paper represents a substantial extension to DY* that enables layered analysis by changing the way security predicates are defined and composed. An early idea for an authenticated channel layer appeared in the ACME analysis but our treatment in this paper extends it with a full set of communication patterns (confidential channels, request-response exchanges) and implementations of these patterns by multiple protocols, including TLS.

Symbolic Protocol Composition. Prior works [18,19,25–27,32] have explored conditions under which symbolic security proofs of two cryptographic protocols can be safely composed. The composition patterns considered include parallel composition of unrelated protocols, sequential composition—where one protocol uses a secret generated by another, and vertical composition of protocols that are layered one above another. In all these works, the key idea is to limit the interactions between composed protocols or to characterize under what conditions protocols can safely be composed; along with the analysis of individual protocols, the conditions for their secure composition need to be checked.

Most of these prior works do not support machine-checked proofs. [27] formalizes the composition proof in Isabelle but the individual protocol proofs are usually done using a different tool (PSPSP) and protocols are not expressed in a full-fledged programming language, rather in a much simpler domain specific language. In contrast, in our work, the full development, including soundness proofs, composition proofs, and individual protocol proofs are all in the same framework (F*), and by this, come with all the benefits of such a fully-fledged programming environment (see also Sect. 2). Furthermore, by extending an existing expressive tool, we automatically support all the cryptographic primitives one can express in DY*, including Diffie-Hellman, which are essential for protocols like TLS, but are not modeled in prior works like [27].

Compositional Cryptographic Proofs. Modularity and composability have long been guiding principles for provable security, perhaps best exemplified by the line of work on universal composability (UC) [16,30]. More recently, a series of tools [1,17,23] seek to apply modular design principles to mechanized cryptographic proofs. One of the most recent works is Owl [24], which produces proofs of protocols using information flow types, and unlike, DY* aims at full automation for protocols specified in a domain-specific language and restricted to static corruption, as the framework is based on UC.

In contrast to these works on computational cryptographic proofs, our work is in the symbolic model, and hence makes less precise assumptions about cryptographic primitives. In return, our framework is capable of analyzing large protocols with ease, which still remains a challenge for computational tools.

8   Conclusion

In this paper, we presented a layered approach to symbolic protocol analysis, as an extension to DY*. This approach allows us to *compositionally* analyze stacks of layered protocols, looking at each layer individually. While DY* already allows for modular and scalable analyses, it does not enable compositional proofs. So, when any layer changed, the entire protocol stack had to be re-proved. In our approach, lower layer proofs never have to be redone if higher layers are modified. Furthermore, if a higher layer does not use the same cryptographic primitives or the same key material as its lower layers, then it does not have to be reproved if the lower layer implementation changes.

Our approach also accounts for cases where different layers use the same cryptographic functions and key material. By lifting cryptographic functions at each layer and explicitly expressing sufficient disjointness conditions, dependencies between layers are kept to a minimal set of predicates. Only these disjointness conditions need to be re-proved when a lower-layer implementation changes, while the rest of the proof remains unchanged.

We highlight the utility of this approach by means of two independently useful layers for security protocols, namely a PKI and a secure communication layer. The communication layer allows for the analysis of applications based on abstract secure communication, without the need to consider or verify details of the underlying cryptographic primitives and communication. We use these layers to implement two case studies that use various communication patterns. While it takes around 10 min to verify the entire stack of one of our examples, each example takes only around 2 min to verify on its own, illustrating the time savings of being able to verify layers independently.

As pointed out in Sect. 4, so far, we have only considered vertical and sequential compositions of layers into a protocol stack. In future work, we intend to extend this approach to horizontal compositions, where the main challenge lies in determining how predicates from different protocols at the same layer of the protocol stack can be safely merged. Furthermore, all our analysis is in the symbolic model. Investigating whether our layered approach can also be applied to computational verification tools is an interesting topic for future research.

Acknowledgements. We would like to thank the anonymous reviewers for their feedback on our paper. This work was supported in part by the DFG through grants KU 1434/10-2 and KU 1434/12-1, and the DST-INSPIRE Faculty grant.

References

1. Abate, C., et al.: SSProve: a foundational framework for modular cryptographic proofs in Coq. In: 2021 IEEE 34th Computer Security Foundations Symposium (CSF), pp. 1–15. IEEE Computer Society (2021)
2. Barbosa, M., et al.: SoK: computer-aided cryptography. In: 2021 IEEE Symposium on Security and Privacy (SP), pp. 777–795 (2021). https://doi.ieeecomputersociety.org/10.1109/SP40001.2021.00008
3. Barthe, G., Grégoire, B., Heraud, S., Béguelin, S.Z.: Computer-aided security proofs for the working cryptographer. In: Rogaway, P. (ed.) CRYPTO 2011. LNCS, vol. 6841, pp. 71–90. Springer, Heidelberg (2011). https://doi.org/10.1007/978-3-642-22792-9_5
4. Bengtson, J., Bhargavan, K., Fournet, C., Gordon, A.D., Maffeis, S.: Refinement types for secure implementations. ACM Trans. Program. Lang. Syst. (TOPLAS) **33**(2), 1–45 (2011)

5. Bhargavan, K., et al.: DY*: a modular symbolic verification framework for executable cryptographic protocol code. In: IEEE European Symposium on Security and Privacy (EuroS&P), pp. 523–542 (2021)
6. Bhargavan, K., et al.: An in-depth symbolic security analysis of the ACME standard. In: Kim, Y., Kim, J., Vigna, G., Shi, E. (eds.) CCS 2021: 2021 ACM SIGSAC Conference on Computer and Communications Security, Virtual Event, Republic of Korea, 15–19 November 2021, pp. 2601–2617. ACM (2021)
7. Bhargavan, K., et al.: A tutorial-style introduction to DY*. In: Dougherty, D., Meseguer, J., Mödersheim, S.A., Rowe, P. (eds.) Protocols, Strands, and Logic. LNCS, vol. 13066, pp. 77–97. Springer, Cham (2021). https://doi.org/10.1007/978-3-030-91631-2_4
8. Bhargavan, K., et al.: DY* layering source code (2023). https://publ.sec.uni-stuttgart.de/esorics23-layered-symbolic-security-analysis-in-dystar-code.zip
9. Bhargavan, K., et al.: Layered symbolic security analysis in DY*. Technical report (2023). https://eprint.iacr.org/2023/1329
10. Bhargavan, K., Blanchet, B., Kobeissi, N.: Verified models and reference implementations for the TLS 1.3 standard candidate. In: IEEE S&P, pp. 483–502 (2017)
11. Bhargavan, K., Fournet, C., Gordon, A.D.: Modular verification of security protocol code by typing. In: Proceedings of the 37th Annual ACM SIGPLAN-SIGACT Symposium on Principles of Programming Languages, pp. 445–456 (2010)
12. Bhargavan, K., Fournet, C., Kohlweiss, M., Pironti, A., Strub, P.-Y., Zanella-Béguelin, S.: Proving the TLS handshake secure (as it is). In: Garay, J.A., Gennaro, R. (eds.) CRYPTO 2014. LNCS, vol. 8617, pp. 235–255. Springer, Heidelberg (2014). https://doi.org/10.1007/978-3-662-44381-1_14
13. Bhargavan, K., Lavaud, A.D., Fournet, C., Pironti, A., Strub, P.Y.: Triple handshakes and cookie cutters: breaking and fixing authentication over TLS. In: 2014 IEEE Symposium on Security and Privacy (2014)
14. Blanchet, B.: CryptoVerif: computationally sound mechanized prover for cryptographic protocols. In: Dagstuhl Seminar "Formal Protocol Verification Applied, vol. 117, p. 156 (2007)
15. Blanchet, B.: Modeling and verifying security protocols with the applied pi calculus and ProVerif. Found. Trends Priv. Secur. 1, 1–135 (2016)
16. Canetti, R.: Universally composable security: a new paradigm for cryptographic protocols. In: Proceedings of the 42nd Annual Symposium on Foundations of Computer Science (FOCS 2001), pp. 136–145. IEEE Computer Society (2001)
17. Canetti, R., Stoughton, A., Varia, M.: EasyUC: using EasyCrypt to mechanize proofs of universally composable security. In: 2019 IEEE 32th Computer Security Foundations Symposium (CSF), pp. 167–183. IEEE Computer Society (2019)
18. Cheval, V., Cortier, V., Warinschi, B.: Secure composition of PKIs with public key protocols. In: 30th IEEE Computer Security Foundations Symposium, CSF 2017, Santa Barbara, CA, USA, 21–25 August 2017, pp. 144–158. IEEE Computer Society (2017)
19. Ciobâca, S., Cortier, V.: Protocol composition for arbitrary primitives. In: 23rd IEEE Computer Security Foundations Symposium, pp. 322–336 (2010)
20. Cremers, C., Horvat, M., Hoyland, J., Scott, S., van der Merwe, T.: A comprehensive symbolic analysis of TLS 1.3. In: ACM CCS, pp. 1773–1788 (2017)
21. Delignat-Lavaud, A., et al.: Implementing and proving the TLS 1.3 record layer. In: IEEE S&P, pp. 463–482 (2017)
22. Dolev, D., Yao, A.C.: On the security of public-key protocols. IEEE Trans. Inf. Theory 29(2), 198–208 (1983)

23. Fournet, C., Kohlweiss, M., Strub, P.: Modular code-based cryptographic verification. In: Chen, Y., Danezis, G., Shmatikov, V. (eds.) Proceedings of the 18th ACM Conference on Computer and Communications Security, CCS 2011, Chicago, Illinois, USA, 17–21 October 2011, pp. 341–350. ACM (2011)
24. Gancher, J., Gibson, S., Singh, P., Dharanikota, S., Parno, B.: Owl: compositional verification of security protocols via an information-flow type system. In: 2023 IEEE Symposium on Security and Privacy (SP), pp. 1130–1147. IEEE Computer Society (2023). https://doi.ieeecomputersociety.org/10.1109/SP46215.2023.10179477
25. Gondron, S., Mödersheim, S.: Vertical composition and sound payload abstraction for stateful protocols. In: 34th IEEE Computer Security Foundations Symposium, CSF 2021, Dubrovnik, Croatia, 21–25 June 2021, pp. 1–16. IEEE (2021)
26. Groß, T., Mödersheim, S.: Vertical protocol composition. In: Proceedings of the 24th IEEE Computer Security Foundations Symposium, CSF 2011, Cernay-la-Ville, France, 27–29 June 2011, pp. 235–250. IEEE Computer Society (2011)
27. Hess, A.V., Mödersheim, S.A., Brucker, A.D.: Stateful protocol composition in Isabelle/HOL. ACM Trans. Priv. Secur. **26**(3), 1–36 (2023)
28. Ho, S., Protzenko, J., Bichhawat, A., Bhargavan, K.: Noise*: a library of verified high-performance secure channel protocol implementations. In: 43rd IEEE Symposium on Security and Privacy, SP 2022, San Francisco, CA, USA, 22–26 May 2022, pp. 107–124. IEEE (2022)
29. Küsters, R., Tuengerthal, M.: Composition theorems without pre-established session identifiers. In: Chen, Y., Danezis, G., Shmatikov, V. (eds.) Proceedings of the 18th ACM Conference on Computer and Communications Security (CCS 2011), pp. 41–50. ACM Press (2011). https://doi.org/10.1145/2046707.2046715
30. Küsters, R., Tuengerthal, M., Rausch, D.: The IITM model: a simple and expressive model for universal composability. J. Cryptol. **33**(4), 1461–1584 (2020). https://doi.org/10.1007/s00145-020-09352-1
31. Meier, S., Schmidt, B., Cremers, C., Basin, D.: The TAMARIN prover for the symbolic analysis of security protocols. In: Sharygina, N., Veith, H. (eds.) CAV 2013. LNCS, vol. 8044, pp. 696–701. Springer, Heidelberg (2013). https://doi.org/10.1007/978-3-642-39799-8_48
32. Mödersheim, S., Viganò, L.: Sufficient conditions for vertical composition of security protocols. In: Moriai, S., Jaeger, T., Sakurai, K. (eds.) 9th ACM Symposium on Information, Computer and Communications Security, ASIA CCS 2014, Kyoto, Japan, 03–06 June 2014, pp. 435–446. ACM (2014)
33. Reschke, J.: The 'basic' HTTP authentication scheme. RFC 7617 (2015). https://www.rfc-editor.org/info/rfc7617
34. Rescorla, E.: The transport layer security (TLS) protocol version 1.3. RFC 8446 (2018). https://www.rfc-editor.org/info/rfc8446
35. Rescorla, E., Dierks, T.: The transport layer security (TLS) protocol version 1.2. RFC 5246 (2008). https://www.rfc-editor.org/info/rfc5246
36. Swamy, N., et al.: Dependent types and multi-monadic effects in F*. In: Proceedings of the 43rd Annual ACM SIGPLAN-SIGACT Symposium on Principles of Programming Languages, POPL 2016, St. Petersburg, FL, USA, 20–22 January 2016, pp. 256–270 (2016)
37. Wallez, T., Protzenko, J., Beurdouche, B., Bhargavan, K.: {TreeSync}: authenticated group management for messaging layer security. In: 32nd USENIX Security Symposium (USENIX Security 23), pp. 1217–1233 (2023)

Indirect Meltdown: Building Novel Side-Channel Attacks from Transient-Execution Attacks

Daniel Weber[(✉)], Fabian Thomas, Lukas Gerlach, Ruiyi Zhang,
and Michael Schwarz

CISPA Helmholtz Center for Information Security, Saarbrücken, Saarland, Germany
{daniel.weber,fabian.thomas,lukas.gerlach,ruiyi.zhang,
michael.schwarz}@cispa.de

Abstract. The transient-execution attack Meltdown leaks sensitive information by transiently accessing inaccessible data during out-of-order execution. Although Meltdown is fixed in hardware for recent CPU generations, most currently-deployed CPUs have to rely on software mitigations, such as KPTI. Still, Meltdown is considered non-exploitable on current systems.

In this paper, we show that adding another layer of indirection to Meltdown transforms a transient-execution attack into a side-channel attack, leaking metadata instead of data. We show that despite software mitigations, attackers can still leak metadata from other security domains by observing the success rate of Meltdown on non-secret data. With LeakIDT, we present the first cache-line granular monitoring of kernel addresses. LeakIDT allows an attacker to obtain cycle-accurate timestamps for attacker-chosen interrupts.

We use our attack to get accurate inter-keystroke timings and fingerprint visited websites. While we propose a low-overhead software mitigation to prevent the exploitation of LeakIDT, we emphasize that the side-channel aspect of transient-execution attacks should not be underestimated.

1 Introduction

Microarchitectural side-channel attacks have been known for several years [27]. These attacks exploit the side effects of CPU implementations to infer metadata about processed data. Well-known examples of microarchitectural side-channel attacks include cache attacks, e.g., Flush+Reload [64] or Prime+Probe [40], which have been used to leak cryptographic secrets [2,64] or violate the privacy of users, e.g., by spying on user input [17,39,48]. The discovery of transient-execution attacks, such as Meltdown [35] and Spectre [26], was a game changer for microarchitectural attacks, as these directly leak data instead of metadata. Hence, even best practices for side-channel-resistant software [11,23] do not protect secrets anymore. In Meltdown attacks, architecturally inaccessible data is accessed during out-of-order execution and encoded into a microarchitectural element, e.g., the cache, protected from the pipeline flush [35,44]. A subsequent

© The Author(s), under exclusive license to Springer Nature Switzerland AG 2024
G. Tsudik et al. (Eds.): ESORICS 2023, LNCS 14346, pp. 22–42, 2024.
https://doi.org/10.1007/978-3-031-51479-1_2

side-channel attack, e.g., Flush+Reload, converts the microarchitectural into an architectural state, revealing the data.

As only new CPU generations contain hardware fixes for Meltdown-type attacks, short- and mid-term mitigations rely on software workarounds. These workarounds ensure that no confidential data is stored in affected buffers when untrusted code is executed [21,49,57] or that the victim data is not address-able [14,54]. For Meltdown-US-L1 [35], i.e., the original Meltdown attack, the OS unmaps the majority of its address space while running in user space, making sensitive data non-addressable [15]. The remaining mapped pages are not consid-ered confidential, such that Meltdown-US-L1 is considered not exploitable. On Linux, this technique is implemented as kernel page-table isolation (KPTI) [12].

In this paper, we show that even with state-of-the-art mitigations, Meltdown can be transformed from a transient-execution attack into a side-channel attack. The main idea is based on two properties. First, while KPTI unmaps most kernel pages, several kernel pages with non-secret content are necessary on x86 CPUs and cannot be unmapped in user space. Second, Meltdown [35] can only leak data if it is cached in the L1D cache, making it usable as a cache-state oracle. Combining these two properties leaks the meta information on whether (non-confidential) kernel data was accessed. Hence, Meltdown can be used as a high-resolution cache attack with cache-line granularity on the kernel. This side channel is superior to state-of-the-art cache attacks on the kernel, which only achieve page [32] or cache-set granularity [48].

We gain an interesting insight from this attack:

While a layer of indirection is necessary for Meltdown to leak data, another layer of indirection transforms the attack to leak metadata of architecturally inac-cessible data.

In other words, exploiting a modified version of the Meltdown attack enables the leakage of metadata that cannot be leaked in this granularity with a tradi-tional side-channel attack.

Based on this, we present LeakIDT, a side-channel attack able to spy on interrupts. We exploit that the interrupt descriptor table (IDT) must always be mapped on x86 [15,19]. Hence, despite software mitigations such as KPTI, an attacker can use the side channel to monitor interrupt activity. In contrast to previous works that exploit interrupts as a side channel [33,48,56], LeakIDT can target specific interrupts, e.g., network or keyboard interrupts, instead of just observing that *any* interrupt occurred and works for unprivileged attack-ers. We identify which website a user visits from the Alexa top 15 and top 100 websites with a precision of 80% and 55%, respectively. Furthermore, we reliably observe keystroke timings with an average F-score of 0.89. We propose to miti-gate LeakIDT by marking the IDT uncachable, preventing any entry from being cached. This mitigation is practical, with an average performance overhead of less than 0.5% in 5 different benchmarks simulating real-world workloads.

Our attacks show that while mitigating data leakage is essential, the side-channel aspect of such fixes can be overlooked. We show that adding additional layers of indirection to existing attacks can change their properties. As a result, we create a new side-channel attack from a CPU vulnerability commonly considered unexploitable when applying state-of-the-art software mitigations. Hence, we argue that future software workarounds should consider the side-channel aspect to prevent such attack vectors. Thus, we encourage researchers to look at other mitigations for hardware vulnerabilities to determine whether they can be circumvented to repurpose the underlying vulnerability as a side channel. For this purpose and to ease reproducibility, we open-source the code of our findings on GitHub[1].

To summarize, we make the following contributions:

1. We show that adding another layer of indirection to Meltdown transforms Meltdown into a side channel that infers the cache state of non-sensitive kernel pages with cache line granularity, leaking details about, e.g., interrupts.
2. We use our side channel to detect the visited websites of a user and spy on their keystroke timings.
3. We present a practical mitigation that stops our attack, while introducing an average overhead of less than 0.5% for real-world workloads.

Responsible Disclosure. We disclosed our findings to Intel on February 15, 2023 and AMD on February 16, 2023. Despite both vendors acknowledging our findings, they informed us that they do not plan to roll out further mitigations.

2   Background

In this section, we provide the background for this paper. We introduce side channels, transient-execution attacks, and the interrupt descriptor table.

2.1   Side Channels

Side channels leak metadata of (secret) information. In a side-channel attack, an attacker infers secrets from this metadata. For leaking metadata, secret-dependent observable differences must exist, e.g., response time or power consumption that depends on the bits of a cryptographic key. Previous research showed that side channels can be practical tools in an attacker's repertoire [27,38], especially for attacking cryptographic implementation [27,38]. In recent years, researchers have shown various side-channel attacks exploiting microarchitectural components [38,39,41,60,61]. These components include CPU caches [40,64], branch predictors [3,4], execution units [13,61], DRAM components [41], and power usage [63]. The fundamental property that enables such microarchitectural side-channel attacks is that different processes share many hardware components. Hence, the resource usage of one process affects the possible resource usage of another process, leaking meta information between the processes.

---

[1] https://github.com/cispa/indirect-meltdown.

2.2   Transient-Execution Attacks

Two important performance optimizations in modern CPUs are out-of-order execution and speculative execution. Out-of-order execution allows the CPU to reorder or parallelize the execution of instructions in the instruction stream. Speculative execution predicts the outcome of branch and memory load instructions, reducing pipeline stalls. Executed instructions that never commit their state changes to the architecture due to a misspeculation or preceding fault are called transient instructions [8,24]. Transient-execution attacks [8] exploit transient instructions to read otherwise inaccessible memory [26,35]. While transient instructions do not have an architectural effect, they can influence microarchitectural states, such as cache states. These traces can be converted to architectural states using a microarchitectural side channel, e.g., Flush+Reload. In recent years, researchers and CPU vendors discovered a variety of transient-execution attacks [6,8,26,28,35–37,44–46,49,55,57].

One category of transient-execution attacks are Meltdown-type attacks [8]. The first discovered Meltdown-type attack, later referred to as Meltdown-US-L1 [8], allows unprivileged attackers to leak cached kernel memory. After a faulting load to a kernel address, the value is transiently available and can be encoded in the microarchitecture, e.g., in the cache. The attacker decodes the encoded value using a side channel, e.g., using Flush+Reload. Meltdown-type attacks, and especially Meltdown-US-L1, affect a variety of modern CPUs [22].

2.3   Interrupt Descriptor Table (IDT)

Devices, such as network interface controllers or keyboards, use interrupts to notify the OS of events, e.g., incoming network packets or key presses. On an interrupt, the CPU switches to ring 0 and looks up the corresponding interrupt service routine (ISR) for the specific interrupt in the interrupt descriptor table (IDT). The CPU interrupts the current execution and jumps to the ISR to handle the interrupt. After handling the interrupt, the CPU continues executing the previous instruction stream. We only consider the 64-bit x86 IDT. Each core can have its own IDT containing 256 interrupt vectors [20, Chapter 6.10 & 6.14]. Each interrupt vector is 16 bytes in size and represents one device [20, Chapter 6.10 & 6.14]. Hence, the IDT has a total size of 4 kB, i.e., one memory page, and is stored in the main memory. Each of these interrupt vectors essentially consists of a 64-bit (8-byte) pointer to its ISR in the kernel. The remaining 8 bytes store additional meta-information about the interrupt, such as the type and the privilege level of the interrupt [20, Chapter 6.14]. The base pointer to the IDT is stored in a CPU-internal register, which can be read with the sidt instruction. On modern Linux systems, the IDT is hard-coded to 0xffffffe0000000000 [31].

3   Meltdown as a Side Channel

In this section, we introduce the concept of transforming the transient-execution attack Meltdown into a side channel. The main idea is that the success rate of

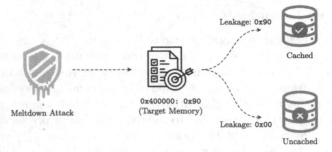

Fig. 1. Meltdown as a side channel. The Meltdown attack only leaks data if the target address is in the L1D cache. Otherwise, the value 0x00 is leaked.

```
1 ; rax = kernel address, rcx/rbx= probe page 1/2,
2 cmp     [rax], 0x0
3 cmovne  rcx, rbx
4 mov     rax, [rcx]
```

Listing 1. Using Meltdown-US-L1 as a side channel. If the target kernel address is cached, the user address stored in RBX is cached. Otherwise, the user address stored in RCX is cached.

Meltdown-US-L1 reveals the cache state of the target memory address. We discuss which kernel memory ranges are still mapped despite the KPTI mitigation and how Meltdown-US-L1 can be used to leak metadata about these memory pages. For a list of CPUs affected by Meltdown-US-L1 and thus affected by our attack, we refer the reader to the Intel's list of vulnerable CPUs [22].

While Lipp et al. [35] discussed that Meltdown-US-L1 works best if the target address is stored in the L1D cache, Xiao et al. [62] and Schwarzl et al. [50] show that Meltdown-US-L1 is limited to the L1D cache. Leakage from other cache levels is only caused by prefetching the data into the L1 cache, e.g., via speculative execution. We exploit this requirement to use Meltdown as a side channel: If data is leaked via Meltdown-US-L1, it is in the L1D cache. An illustration of this concept is given in Fig. 1.

By detecting whether the target memory address can be leaked, we learn whether it was previously accessed. If the cache-line content can be leaked, the cache line is cached in the L1D, which is only the case if the cache line was recently accessed. As this attack can be applied to any mapped memory address, we can also use it on kernel memory pages that are mapped while in userspace. This converts Meltdown-US-L1 into an Evict+Reload-style side channel for kernel memory.

Attack Details. Listing 1 shows the implementation of the encoding step when using Meltdown-US-L1 as a side channel. We compare the content of the kernel address to zero (Line 2) and, based on the result, select (Line 3) and access (Line 4) one out of two different pages. This works as the access transiently results in a zero if no value can be leaked by Meltdown-US-L1. Otherwise, the result is non-zero if the targeted memory address is non-zero. This code sequence is simpler than the Meltdown-US-L1 code [35] that transiently loads the value at the kernel address into a register and accesses one out of 256 pages based on the loaded value, since we only need to consider two cases, i.e., cached and non-cached. This means that instead of monitoring 256 cache lines, our attack only has to monitor a single cache line. In line with the Meltdown-US-L1 attack, this code snippet raises an exception that has to be handled, e.g., with fault handling, TSX, or fault suppression via speculation [35]. For the decoding, i.e., transferring the information encoded in the microarchitecture to an architectural state, any side channel can be used. For simplicity and in line with related work [6,35,49,54,57], we rely on Flush+Reload to recover the encoded information. In case of a recent access by the victim, the target address is stored in the L1D cache. Thus, to monitor further cache accesses, we need to remove the target address from the L1D cache. As the target memory address cannot be accessed, we need to rely on eviction. However, as the L1D cache is virtually-indexed, evicting from it is straightforward and can be achieved by accessing virtual memory addresses falling into the same cache line as the target address. Note that we only need to evict the target address when an access occurred, as the Meltdown attack itself does not cache the target address.

Attack Surface. We investigate the attack surface of using Meltdown-US-L1 as a side channel by analyzing which kernel pages are mapped in user space when KPTI is active. As Meltdown-US-L1 cannot be fixed via microcode on affected hardware, KPTI [14] is used as a software workaround on Meltdown-US-L1-affected CPUs. KPTI ensures that while an application runs in user space, no kernel page containing sensitive information is mapped into the address space. For this, KPTI relies on a second set of page tables [15]. However, while this works theoretically, x86 always requires some kernel pages to be mapped, even when running in user space. Luckily, the content of these pages, e.g., the IDT, can be chosen such that they do not contain secrets.

We investigate which pages are still mapped in userspace by iterating through the user page tables using the kernel module PTEditor [47]. For the user-page-table root, we set bit 11 of the physical address stored in the kernel CR3 register [15]. We iterate through the mappings in the upper half of the address space for kernel addresses mapped in user space. We discover between 198 and 394 4 kB kernel pages mapped in user space, depending on the CPU. However, these pages can be classified into only 3 distinct ranges. The first range is the kernel entry. This range has been exploited for microarchitectural KASLR breaks [7,46,61]. The second range is used for descriptor tables, such as the interrupt-descriptor table or the global-descriptor table. Finally, the third range is within the range of the direct physical map [31], mapping 4 physical pages. One of these mappings is to the task state segment, which is also mapped directly. We cannot explain the reason for these remaining mappings, as the target is already mapped in user space. Still, this does at least not increase the attack surface. The most interesting target for using Meltdown-US-L1 as a side channel is the IDT (cf. Sect. 4).

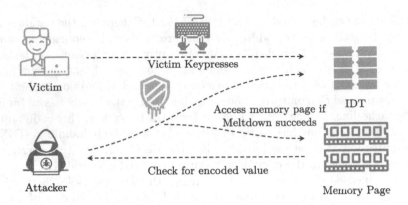

Fig. 2. Using LeakIDT to leak interrupts, such as keystrokes.

4   LeakIDT

In this section, we introduce LeakIDT, a side-channel attack that precisely detects when an attacker-chosen interrupt occurs. LeakIDT achieves that by observing the cache state of the IDT entries of the targeted interrupts.

Linux uses one IDT per core that always resides at the same location (cf. Sect. 2.3). This IDT is mapped in all processes, even with KPTI. Hence, our attack can target the IDT despite applied software-based Meltdown-US-L1 mitigations. Note that a different operating system could randomize the location of the IDT upon booting and thus harden the system against our attack.

Attack Overview. Figure 2 shows an overview of LeakIDT. We use Meltdown-US-L1 to read a specific IDT entry corresponding to a targeted interrupt. IDT entries are accessed—and thus cached in L1D—if the CPU core handles an interrupt. Hence, if the leakage of the entry is successful, we infer that the interrupt was triggered; otherwise, it was not. Consequently, with LeakIDT we know the timestamp when the interrupt occurred. Note that due to the CPU's hardware prefetchers the actual accuracy of our attack is reduced to blocks of 8 adjacent IDT entries. Further details on this are discussed later in this section. When detecting an interrupt, LeakIDT uses eviction to remove the targeted IDT entry from the L1D cache again. This is crucial for the attack as after every observed interrupt, the attacker must ensure that the IDT entry is removed from the cache as quickly as possible. Otherwise, subsequent accesses to that memory address, i.e., subsequent interrupts of the same type, cannot be detected.

Threat Model. Our attack requires a victim application that leaks information by having secret or data-dependent interrupts. Such a victim can, e.g., receive keystrokes [17,33], issue secret-dependant legacy syscalls [65], or communicate over the network [66]. Besides this, we assume a bug-free software containing no logical vulnerabilities. We further consider the attacker and victim both executing unprivileged native code on the same Meltdown-US-L1-affected CPU. The attack does not assume any disabled mitigations, i.e., it works with state-of-the-art software-based Meltdown mitigations.

Implementation. For inferring the cache state of the IDT entry, we use the code from Listing 1. Note that each IDT entry is 16 bytes in size. Thus, there are 4 IDT entries per cache line that are all cached when an interrupt occurs. The exact offset of the IDT entry we are targeting with LeakIDT is irrelevant, as every interrupt corresponding to that entry caches the entire cache line. One should note that the granularity of our attack in a normal environment is restricted to blocks of 8 IDT entries. The reason is that upon receiving an interrupt, the CPU's adjacent cache-line prefetcher puts two adjacent cache lines, i.e., 8 adjacent IDT entries, into the L1D cache at once.

To detect the correct entry in the IDT, we template the IDT entries. First, we record the number of interrupts for every IDT entry over a fixed time window, e.g., 100 ms. Second, we repeat this recording step while inducing the interrupt in parallel. Depending on the type of interrupt, this can be done in soft- or hardware. Some interrupts can be triggered the same way the victim triggers the interrupt, e.g., sending a network packet for network interrupts. If this is not possible, e.g., for keyboard interrupts, an attacker can induce the same interrupt as a software interrupt, using the `int` instruction. If the difference in the number of interrupts correlates with the induced interrupts, the correct IDT entry is identified. As we do not require fine-grained measurements for this step, we can take the information exposed by the Linux interface, i.e., the file `/proc/interrupts`.

As discussed in Sect. 3, to ensure that LeakIDT can detect more than the first interrupt, the IDT entry has to be evicted again from the L1D cache. The cache replacement policy on our machines is Tree-PLRU [1], and the cache is virtually indexed using bits 6 to 11. Thus, we access memory addresses falling into the same L1D cache set by accessing pages at the same offset as IDT entry offset, which performs well enough for the attacks.

5   Evaluation

In this section, we evaluate the performance and reliability of LeakIDT. All experiments are executed on an Intel Core i7-6600U running Ubuntu 20.04 with Linux kernel 5.4.0. On a general level, LeakIDT allows observing the cache state of an inaccessible but mapped memory page. More precisely, we can distinguish between a memory address that is cached in the L1D cache and a memory address that is not cached in the L1D.

First, we evaluate how precisely we can distinguish between such two memory addresses. We mount our exploit on two memory addresses, one being cached in the L1D cache and one not being cached. Note that distinguishing between an address cached in L1D and not cached at all is enough for an attacker to mount side-channel attacks. Our tests show that for a memory address cached in L1D, we have a successful leak in 99.6% of cases and no leakage in 100% of cases for uncached memory addresses. We observe that for the uncached target byte, we only see the byte 0x0 encoded in our lookup array. This observation

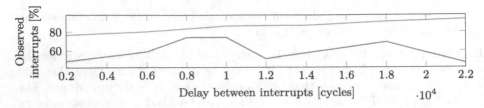

Fig. 3. Delay between interrupts and number of interrupts missed by LeakIDT (upper line) and Prime+Probe (lower line).

is in line with previous work [35,62]. These results show that an attacker can reliably infer the cache state of the target kernel memory address by observing whether the Meltdown-US-L1 leakage exists.

Figure 3 shows how different delays between interrupts interfere with the observation rate of our attack, i.e., the number of interrupts successfully detected. More precisely, we trigger 10 000 interrupts with an artificial busy wait of n cycles between them. This allows us to measure the success rate of our attack when the victim triggers interrupts at a high frequency. We observe that if the interrupts are more closely spaced than 25 000 cycles, our detection rate decreases. We further observe that for interrupts happening at a slower rate, we have success rates of up to 99.5%. Thus, attackers can exploit LeakIDT to reliably leak interrupts up until this frequency.

Comparison to Related Kernel Attacks. To the best of our knowledge, LeakIDT is the first cache-line-granular side-channel attack on the kernel. LeakIDT does not require read- or writable shared memory, which is typical for cache attacks [16,34,64], preventing their use on kernel memory. While there are also cache attacks not requiring shared memory [5,10,40,43], LeakIDT yields a better granularity as it allows targeting specific cache lines of the kernel. Additionally, cache attacks without shared memory often require knowledge of physical addresses to construct reliable and efficient eviction sets [53]. As we do not assume that knowledge in our threat model, we compare LeakIDT with Prime+Probe on the L1D, as this attack has the same threat model.

Not only does LeakIDT have a finer granularity, but it also outperforms Prime+Probe in terms of reliability. Figure 3 shows the number of interrupts missed by our Prime+Probe implementation. Note that our implementation only counts an interrupt if two probe steps show higher access timing. While this may not be optimal, it significantly reduces the number of false positives and shows the best performance during our evaluation. We suspect that the reason for this is that the probes execute fast enough to measure the activity on the IDT entry multiple times during the interrupt handling. To further compare the two side channels, we compare their performance in a more artifical scenario. We take 100 000 measurements for each attack while the victim accesses the targeted cache line 50 000 times per attack. Finally, we compare the results of our side-channel attacks to the ground truth of victim accesses. For LeakIDT, we get a recall of 0.999 and a precision of 1.0, yielding an F-score of 0.999. For Prime+ Probe on the L1D, we measure a recall of 1.0 and a precision of 0.834, yielding an F-score of 0.91.

6   Case Studies

In this section, we introduce 2 case studies demonstrating LeakIDT. Leveraging LeakIDT, we show that an attacker can spy on websites visited by a victim on the same system (cf. Sect. 6.1). Furthermore, we show that fine-grained timing measurements of interrupts leak information about the keystrokes entered by a user (cf. Sect. 6.2).

6.1   Website Fingerprinting

In this section, we use LeakIDT to detect which website a user opens by monitoring network interrupts. For this purpose, we perform the website fingerprinting attack on an Intel Xeon E3-1505M v5, with Ubuntu 20.04 and Linux kernel 5.4.0.

Threat Model. In line with previous work [18,25,29,52,65], we assume an unprivileged attacker with native code execution on the victim system. In contrast to these works, we do not rely on OS interfaces, as they are nowadays only available to privileged users. We assume the attacker application runs on the physical core that handles the network interrupts, which the unprivileged `pthread_setaffinity_np` Linux API can achieve.

Attack Overview. We do not assume prior knowledge of the IDT entry that the attacker needs to probe. Thus, the first step of the attack is to find the specific IDT entry that handles the network interrupts. To do that, we use LeakIDT on all IDT entries while introducing additional network traffic. For each entry, we record the number of accesses during a short fixed period, e.g., 1 s. Next, we repeat the measurement without generating additional network interrupts. As the network interrupts bring the specific IDT entries into the cache, entries with the most significant differences in the number of accesses are likely related to the network interrupts.

In line with previous work [66], we rely on a coarse-grained timer, e.g., `clock_gettime` or `setitimer`, to record the number of interrupts per 5 ms interval when a user opens a website. We then train a random forest classifier to fingerprint the opened website.

Results. We collect 100 interrupt traces for each of the Alexa 100 most-visited websites. Each trace collects the number of interrupts in a 5 ms interval 400 times (2 s in total). The dataset is split into a training set of 7000 and a test set of 3000 examples, and the `n_estimators` for the random forest classification are set to the default of 100. For the top 15 websites, we achieve a precision of 80% and a recall of 81%, as illustrated in the confusion matrix in Fig. 4. For the top 100 websites, we achieve an overall precision of 55% and a recall of 56%. Note

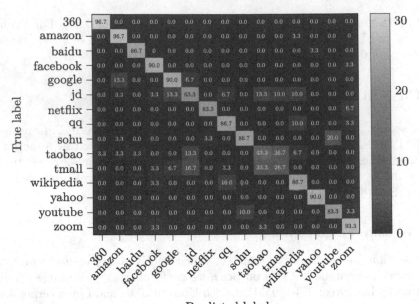

Fig. 4. The confusion matrix for the website classification. Given the Alexa top 15 websites, the trace is classified correctly with an overall probability of 80%.

that a more precise timer, i.e., with a better accuracy than 5 ms would likely improve these results.

Comparison to Related Work. While Spreitzer et al. [52] report 89% accuracy on 100 sites on Android, the attack requires the unprivileged interface for sampling data-usage statistics. Zhang et al. [66] report 71% accuracy on 100 sites on Intel, relying on the new `umwait` instructions only available on the latest Intel microarchitectures. The interrupt attack by Lipp et al. [33] correctly classifies a website in 81.75% of cases inside the browser when only looking at 10 websites. Lee et al. [29] exploit GPU vulnerabilities and report 69.4% and 60.9% with two different techniques on 100 sites randomly chosen from Alexa Top 1000.

6.2   Keystroke Timings via LeakIDT

In this section, we show that LeakIDT can be used for keystroke-timing attacks, as first discussed by Song et al. [51]. We show that LeakIDT reliably recovers keystroke timings on USB keyboards on an Intel Xeon E3-1505M v5, with Ubuntu 20.04 and Linux kernel 5.4.0.

Threat Model. We assume an unprivileged attacker with native code execution on a system vulnerable to LeakIDT. We further assume that the attacker application can be pinned to specific physical cores by unprivileged APIs.

Experiment Setup. In line with the first case study, we do not assume knowledge of the IDT entry. Thus, an attacker trying to locate the core responsible for

Table 1. Results for the inter-keystroke timing attack.

Run	Noise	Recall	Precision	F-score	Delay (std dev.)
1	no	0.93	0.89	0.91	$-323\,\mu s$ $(35.66\,\mu s)$
2	no	0.91	0.95	0.93	$-334.5\,\mu s$ $(29.71\,\mu s)$
3	no	0.90	0.90	0.90	$-324\,\mu s$ $(34.11\,\mu s)$
1	yes	0.89	0.87	0.88	$-573\,\mu s$ $(64.25\,\mu s)$
2	yes	0.88	0.88	0.88	$-568\,\mu s$ $(49.46\,\mu s)$
3	yes	0.86	0.86	0.86	$-551\,\mu s$ $(56.28\,\mu s)$

handling keyboard interrupts can probe all interrupts on all cores for a short and fixed time interval. Afterward, when the attacker knows that the victim is likely pressing keys, e.g., by checking for interactive applications in the list of running processes, the attacker can probe these interrupts again and check for significant differences. To optimize the measurements for this case study, the attacker pins the spy process on the sibling of the previously identified core.

We perform our experiments in two settings. In the first setting, a lab environment, the eXtensible Host Controller Interface (xHCI) interrupts are handled by an isolated core. In the second setting, a realistic environment, we boot the system without any preparations and simulate heavy system load with the stress utility (`stress -m 2 -c 2`). The kernel distributes the interrupts over the available 4 cores. xHCI interrupts share their core only with peripheral network interrupts in our experiments. These interrupts occur every 2 s.

We spawn two processes. The first one reads characters from `stdin` and logs microsecond timestamps of the keystrokes. This process can be spawned on any core and provides ground-truth data. The second process is pinned to the physical core handling xHCI interrupts. This process logs microsecond timestamps of leaked interrupts via LeakIDT.

We perform 3 runs of typing 200 random keys on the keyboard for both setups. In our case study, all inputs are entered by a single person. We record the timestamp traces of both processes. We then match every recorded interrupt timestamp to the nearest ground truth timestamp. Since xHCIs generate two interrupts for USB keyboards, i.e., key down and key up, we assume two captured interrupts per actual timestamp. Even though the difference between key down and key up events can improve the results of keystroke attacks [42], we choose to ignore their impact in this case study to focus on the concept. Any missing timestamp from the expected 2 interrupts for each actual timestamp is counted as a false negative. Any detected interrupt matching with more than one uniquely identifiable key-up and key-down event is counted as a false positive.

Results. Table 1 shows the results for the 3 runs for both setups. We calculate recall, precision, and F-score with the data acquired from matching recorded interrupts to ground truth timestamps. We measure the median and the standard deviation of the delay when we detect the interrupts, showing that we detect keystroke interrupts around half a microsecond before they can be read from stdin in the victim application. As expected, LeakIDT performs slightly worse in the realistic setup compared to the isolated lab setup. In the isolated setup, we observe an F-score of 0.91, and for the realistic setup an F-score of 0.87. In comparison, the Android-based keystroke timing attacks from Schwarz et al. [48] achieve an F-score of 0.94 and 0.81. Similar attacks from Vila et al. [58] and Wang et al. [59] achieve a recall of 0.98 and 0.57, respectively. Thus, our results are comparable to previous work. Note that depending on the goal of an attacker, further steps are required for an end-to-end attack, such as machine-learning-based password recovery or user classification.

7 Mitigations

In this section, we propose a mitigation against LeakIDT. We evaluate the mitigation and show that it only introduces a minimal performance overhead.

Although the root cause of LeakIDT cannot be mitigated in software, we propose a software mitigation to prevent exploitation. The main idea is to ensure that the cache state of an IDT entry cannot be inferred by marking the IDT as uncachable, ensuring that the cache state is always the same.

Implementation. Linux uses a shared IDT across all CPU cores. This single IDT is allocated once by the OS and keeps its physical location until reboot. We rely on memory-type range registers (MTRRs) to mark the physical range of the IDT as uncachable. While the number of MTRRs is limited [20, Chapter 11.11], we only require a single MTRR due to the shared IDT. MTRRs have the advantage that the memory type defined by them cannot be overwritten.

Alternatively, if no MTRR can be spared, the IDT mapping can be marked as uncachable via the memory type in the corresponding page-table entry. Care has to be taken that this is done in every single user-space process, as well as in the kernel. This requires more changes to the kernel and introduces a startup overhead for every application. Thus, we opted for the MTRR-based approach, requiring only a minimal overhead at boot for the configuration and allowing the implementation as a kernel module.

Evaluation. We evaluate the security and performance of our approach. All evaluations are run on an Intel Xeon E3-1505M v5, with Ubuntu 20.04.1 and kernel 5.4.0. For the security evaluation, we mount LeakIDT with our active mitigation. As expected, we do not see any leakage. With the uncachable IDT, LeakIDT can never leak an entry of the IDT, preventing LeakIDT.

To evaluate the overhead of our mitigation, we execute benchmarks generating both high CPU loads and a large number of interrupts. We execute SPEC CPU 2017, which resembles generic real-world workloads, and additionally, Kraken and JetStream, two JavaScript benchmarks, to see the impact on web services. For the baseline, we run the benchmarks on the unmodified system. As marking the IDT as uncachable is implemented as a kernel module, we can

Table 2. Performance of uncachable IDT on the SPEC CPU 2017 benchmark.

Benchmark	SPEC Score		Overhead
	Baseline	Uncachable	[%]
600.perlbench_s	1.88	1.88	0.00%
602.gcc_s	1.11	1.11	0.00%
605.mcf_s	1.91	1.91	0.00%
620.omnetpp_s	1.50	1.52	+1.33%
623.xalancbmk_s	1.55	1.58	+1.94%
625.x264_s	1.54	1.54	0.00%
631.deepsjcng_s	1.33	1.33	0.00%
641.leela_s	1.20	1.20	0.00%
648.exchange2_s	3.50	3.52	+0.57%
657.xz_s	0.91	0.91	0.00%
Average			+0.65%

run the benchmark on precisely the same kernel without even rebooting. Hence, with this setup, there should not be any other factors influencing the benchmark results. Table 2 shows the results of the SPEC CPU benchmark. The details of the JavaScript benchmarks can be found in Appendix A. On average, we only measure a minimal performance overhead of 0.65% with SPEC CPU 2017, 0.57% with Kraken (cf. Table 3), and 0.32% with JetStream. We further test the impact on two interrupt-heavy benchmarks. We execute the YCSB benchmark [9] to evaluate the overhead for databases. We test against a MongoDB instance and configure YCSB for 4 500 000 operations. We observe an increase in interrupts of 2326.29%, i.e., 52 853.62 interrupts (on average over the 8 cores of the system), compared to the system idling for the same amount of time, i.e., 2326.29 interrupts. As these benchmarks have a shorter execution time than the previous ones, we repeat this measurement 10 times on the baseline system and 10 times on the same system with the applied mitigation, thus ensuring a stable result. We observe a median runtime of 155 155 ms with a standard deviation of 243.01 for the baseline system and a median runtime of 155 181.5 ms with a standard deviation of 286.99, i.e., an overhead of 0.02%. To test the performance of a network-based key-value store, we evaluate the impact on a Memcached instance using the benchmarking framework mutilate [30]. We configure mutilate to execute 16 connections spanned over 8 threads. Table 4 shows the results. Hereby, we observe an increase in interrupts of 2630.30%, i.e., 69 892.38 interrupts (on average over the 8 cores of the system), compared to the system idling for the same amount of time, i.e., 2559.88 interrupts. We execute this benchmark 10 times with and without the mitigation applied. We observe a slowdown of the receive rate, the transmission rate, and the QPS of 0.14% each.

Table 3. Kraken benchmark results.

Test Case	Baseline	Uncacheable IDT	Overhead
ai	164.8 ms (± 6.0%)	169.6 ms (± 6.0%)	+2.91%
astar	164.8 ms (± 6.0%)	169.6 ms (± 6.0%)	+2.91%
audio	532.8 ms (± 2.6%)	540.8 ms (± 2.1%)	+1.50%
beat-detection	141.2 ms (± 3.6%)	141.7 ms (± 3.0%)	+0.28%
dft	115.8 ms (± 3.7%)	117.9 ms (± 5.2%)	+1.81%
fft	125.2 ms (± 2.9%)	125.8 ms (± 3.3%)	+0.48%
oscillator	150.6 ms (± 6.6%)	155.5 ms (± 5.3%)	+3.25%
imaging	406.2 ms (± 2.1%)	400.3 ms (± 2.4%)	−1.45%
gaussian-blur	158.3 ms (± 4.0%)	154.0 ms (± 2.3%)	−2.72%
darkroom	80.1 ms (± 0.8%)	79.6 ms (± 0.9%)	−0.62%
desaturate	167.8 ms (± 4.4%)	166.7 ms (± 5.9%)	−0.66%
json	73.9 ms (± 7.0%)	76.7 ms (± 5.0%)	+3.79%
parse-financial	37.0 ms (± 13.7%)	37.7 ms (± 9.6%)	+1.89%
stringify-tinderbox	36.9 ms (± 2.7%)	39.0 ms (± 4.5%)	+5.69%
stanford	288.3 ms (± 2.3%)	287.0 ms (± 1.6%)	−0.45%
crypto-aes	73.9 ms (± 3.2%)	74.1 ms (± 3.2%)	+0.27%
crypto-ccm	65.6 ms (± 4.1%)	63.6 ms (± 2.4%)	−3.05%
crypto-pbkdf2	100.0 ms (± 1.9%)	101.1 ms (± 1.7%)	+1.10%
crypto-sha256-iterative	48.8 ms (± 5.6%)	48.2 ms (± 3.0%)	−1.23%
Total	1466.0 ms (± 0.9%)	1474.4 ms (± 0.7%)	+0.57%

Table 4. Mutilate benchmark results.

Attribute	Baseline score	UC IDT score	Slowdown
QPS	176 238.35 (std: 1376.41)	175 987.5 (std: 1407.86)	0.14%
RX	7 759 664 293 B (std: 60 596 022.33)	7 748 550 743.5 B (std: 62 033 777.92)	0.14%
TX	1 208 593 212 B (std: 9 439 659.48)	1 206 927 213 B (std: 9 614 344.61)	0.14%

8   Discussion

In this section, we discuss Meltdown mitigations, their remaining leakage, and their applicability to other Meltdown variants, OS, and architectures.

Meltdown Mitigations. Gruss et al. [15] showed that unmapping the kernel when possible mitigates several side-channel attacks on it. This has become the state-of-the-art mitigation against Meltdown-US-L1 [14,35]. However, a limitation of the x86 architecture is that specific kernel structures, such as the IDT, must always be mapped. While related work used these mappings to break KASLR [7,46,61], such attacks can be prevented by using a different randomization offset for the pages that remain mapped. However, this would not prevent LeakIDT. The reason is that LeakIDT exploits the metadata of the data stored on kernel pages and not the content [35] or the location [7, 46, 61].

We show that uncachable memory eliminates the remaining leakage of KPTI. Restricting the uncachable memory to the IDT ensures that the performance impact is minimal. Hence, combining two incomplete mitigations for orthogonal problems hardens a system against side-channel attacks.

Ideally, vulnerabilities are mitigated in the hardware. Still, despite hardware fixes, Canella et al. [7] showed that they leak metadata about the mapping of a virtual address. While the leakage is much more limited than in our attack, it also shows that side-channel leakage can be overlooked when designing mitigations.

Applicability to other Meltdown-Type Attacks. Our attack is not limited to attacking the kernel. While we convert Meltdown-US-L1 into a side channel, the same technique can also be applied to other Meltdown variants. For example, on CPUs affected by Foreshadow [54], our technique could be used to implement an Evict+Reload-style attack on Intel SGX enclaves. For this, only the Meltdown attack has to be replaced with the related Foreshadow attack. However, in contrast to the Meltdown-US-L1 mitigations in the OS, the Foreshadow mitigations for SGX entirely prevent Foreshadow. Hence, an enclave that can be attacked with Foreshadow as a side channel could also be attacked directly with Foreshadow. We leave it to future work to investigate whether other Meltdown-type attacks, such as RIDL [57], ZombieLoad [49], or Fallout [6], could also be transformed into practical side-channel attacks.

Other OS and Architectures. The underlying effects exploited in this paper are OS-agnostic. While this paper targets Linux, we do not require any Linux-specific functionality. For example, while the interrupt numbers differ on Windows, the mechanism is still the same. The IDT is also mapped, as this is required by the x86 architecture, enabling LeakIDT.

As LeakIDT fundamentally relies on the Meltdown-US-L1 CPU vulnerability, it does not apply to Meltdown-unaffected CPUs. Hence, AMD and most Arm CPUs are not affected [35]. While there are Arm CPUs affected by Meltdown-US-L1 [35], the interrupt handling is different, which would require adapting LeakIDT to work with the IDT-equivalent, the Interrupt Vector Table (IVT).

9 Conclusion

We showed that Meltdown cannot only act as a transient-execution attack but can also be exploited as a side-channel attack by adding another layer of indirection, despite active software mitigations. We presented LeakIDT, a side-channel attack that allows an attacker to monitor mapped kernel pages with cache-line granularity, enabling attackers to spy on chosen interrupts. We showed that attackers can exploit this primitive to spy on websites visited by a user. We analyzed that this fine-granular information leakage also reveals valuable insights into the typing behavior of a user by allowing to spy on their keystroke timings.

Hence, we conclude that even though Meltdown-US-L1 is considered no longer exploitable, it still threatens the security of modern systems.

Acknowledgment. We want to thank our anonymous reviewers for their comments and suggestions. We also want to thank Leon Trampert and Niklas Flentje for providing their help with running the experiments. This work was partly supported by the Semiconductor Research Corporation (SRC) Hardware Security Program (HWS).

A   JavaScript Benchmark Results

Table 5 shows the impact of our mitigations measured using the JetStream JavaScript benchmark. The total overhead is 0.23%.

Table 5. JetStream benchmark results.

Test Case	Baseline	UC IDT	Overhead
3d-cube-SP	142.229	142.101	−0.09%
3d-raytrace-SP	120.536	130.642	+8.38%
acorn-wtb	14.267	13.714	−3.88%
ai-astar	335.52	330.153	−1.60%
Air	186.75	195.861	+4.88%
async-fs	73.995	68.635	−7.24%
Babylon	180.118	169.655	−5.81%
babylon-wtb	14.468	16.173	+11.78%
base64-SP	218.656	236.194	+8.02%
Basic	195.428	168.823	−13.61%
bomb-workers	20.826	17.721	−14.91%
Box2D	120.487	144.29	+19.76%
cdjs	32.632	28.819	−11.68%
chai-wtb	42.27	42.068	−0.48%
coffeescript-wtb	21.964	18.937	−13.78%
crypto	279.665	341.319	+22.05%
crypto-aes-SP	179.095	146.226	−18.35%
crypto-md5-SP	113.45	106.569	−6.07%
delta-blue	226.869	176.9	−22.03%
earley-boyer	199.003	201.622	+1.32%
espree-wtb	15.742	14.141	−10.17%
first-inspector-code-load	102.469	99.755	−2.65%
FlightPlanner	176.477	176.196	−0.16%
float-mm.c	7.474	7.497	+0.31%
gaussian-blur	225.208	230.45	+2.33%
gbemu	62.156	57.95	−6.77%
gcc-loops-wasm	21.568	22.449	+4.08%
hash-map	94.658	124.756	+31.80%
HashSet-wasm	27.422	29.125	+6.21%
jshint-wtb	21.484	20.658	−3.84%
json-parse-inspector	111.78	108.445	−2.98%
json-stringify-inspector	122.419	120.712	−1.39%
lebab-wtb	24.557	24.599	+0.17%
mandreel	32.562	32.546	−0.05%
ML	13.853	13.274	−4.18%
multi-inspector-code-load	109.236	92.512	−15.31%
n-body-SP	466.978	459.006	−1.71%
navier-stokes	400.438	409.595	+2.29%
octane-code-load	502.996	460.544	−8.44%
octane-zlib	14.938	15.063	+0.84%
offineAssembler	36.527	33.54	−8.18%
pdfjs	75.934	78.712	+3.66%
prepack-wtb	20.974	20.541	−2.06%
quicksort-wasm	215.166	217.597	+1.13%
raytrace	202.931	222.117	+9.45%
regex-dna-SP	255.332	249.183	−2.41%
regexp	281.028	279.361	−0.59%
richards	196.298	189.976	−3.22%
richards-wasm	37.949	33.478	−11.78%
segmentation	11.835	12.609	+6.54%
splay	88.279	85.402	−3.26%
stanford-crypto-aes	173.872	188.774	+8.57%
stanford-crypto-pbkdf2	213.472	258.864	+21.26%
stanford-crypto-sha256	322.22	317.002	−1.62%
string-unpack-code-SP	168.69	141.399	−16.18%
tagcloud-SP	77.685	99.776	+28.44%
tsf-wasm	42.163	67.481	+60.05%
typescript	6.67	6.598	−1.08%
uglify-js-wtb	12.796	13.636	+6.56%
UniPoker	196.529	195.398	−0.58%
WSL	0.411	0.405	−1.46%
Total	7909.404	7927.544	+0.23%

References

1. Abel, A., Reineke, J.: uops.info: characterizing latency, throughput, and port usage of instructions on intel microarchitectures. In: ASPLOS (2019)
2. Acıiçmez, O., Schindler, W.: A vulnerability in RSA implementations due to instruction cache analysis and its demonstration on OpenSSL. In: Malkin, T. (ed.) CT-RSA 2008. LNCS, vol. 4964, pp. 256–273. Springer, Heidelberg (2008). https://doi.org/10.1007/978-3-540-79263-5_16
3. Acıiçmez, O., Koç, Ç.K., Seifert, J.-P.: Predicting secret keys via branch prediction. In: Abe, M. (ed.) CT-RSA 2007. LNCS, vol. 4377, pp. 225–242. Springer, Heidelberg (2006). https://doi.org/10.1007/11967668_15
4. Bhattacharya, S., Mukhopadhyay, D.: Who watches the watchmen?: utilizing performance monitors for compromising keys of RSA on intel platforms. Cryptology ePrint Archive, Report 2015/621 (2015)
5. Briongos, S., Malagón, P., Moya, J.M., Eisenbarth, T.: RELOAD+REFRESH: abusing cache replacement policies to perform stealthy cache attacks. In: USENIX Security Symposium (2020)
6. Canella, C., et al.: Fallout: leaking data on meltdown-resistant CPUs. In: CCS (2019)
7. Canella, C., Schwarz, M., Haubenwallner, M., Schwarzl, M., Gruss, D.: KASLR: break it, fix it, repeat. In: AsiaCCS (2020)
8. Canella, C., et al.: A systematic evaluation of transient execution attacks and defenses. In: USENIX Security Symposium (2019). Extended classification tree and PoCs at https://transient.fail/
9. Cooper, B.F., Silberstein, A., Tam, E., Ramakrishnan, R., Sears, R.: Benchmarking cloud serving systems with YCSB. In: ACM Symposium on Cloud Computing (2010)
10. Disselkoen, C., Kohlbrenner, D., Porter, L., Tullsen, D.: Prime+Abort: a timer-free high-precision L3 cache attack using Intel TSX. In: USENIX Security Symposium (2017)
11. Federal Office for Information Security. Minimum requirements of evaluating side-channel attack resistance of RSA, DSA, and Diffie-Hellman key exchange implementations (2013). https://www.bsi.bund.de/SharedDocs/Downloads/DE/BSI/Zertifizierung/Interpretationen/AIS_46_BSI_guidelines_SCA_RSA_V1_0_e_pdf.pdf
12. Gleixner, T.: x86/KPTI: kernel page table isolation (was KAISER) (2017). https://lkml.org/lkml/2017/12/4/709
13. Gras, B., Giuffrida, C., Kurth, M., Bos, H., Razavi, K.: ABSynthe: automatic blackbox side-channel synthesis on commodity microarchitectures. In: NDSS (2020)
14. Gruss, D., Hansen, D., Gregg, B.: Kernel isolation: from an academic idea to an efficient patch for every computer. In: USENIX (2018)
15. Gruss, D., Lipp, M., Schwarz, M., Fellner, R., Maurice, C., Mangard, S.: KASLR is dead: long live KASLR. In: Bodden, E., Payer, M., Athanasopoulos, E. (eds.) ESSoS 2017. LNCS, vol. 10379, pp. 161–176. Springer, Cham (2017). https://doi.org/10.1007/978-3-319-62105-0_11
16. Gruss, D., Maurice, C., Wagner, K., Mangard, S.: Flush+flush: a fast and stealthy cache attack. In: Caballero, J., Zurutuza, U., Rodríguez, R.J. (eds.) DIMVA 2016. LNCS, vol. 9721, pp. 279–299. Springer, Cham (2016). https://doi.org/10.1007/978-3-319-40667-1_14

17. Gruss, D., Spreitzer, R., Mangard, S.: Cache template attacks: automating attacks on inclusive last-level caches. In: USENIX Security Symposium (2015)
18. Gulmezoglu, B., Zankl, A., Eisenbarth, T., Sunar, B.: PerfWeb: how to violate web privacy with hardware performance events. In: Foley, S.N., Gollmann, D., Snekkenes, E. (eds.) ESORICS 2017. LNCS, vol. 10493, pp. 80–97. Springer, Cham (2017). https://doi.org/10.1007/978-3-319-66399-9_5
19. Intel. Intel®64 and IA-32 Architectures Software Developer's Manual, Volume 1: Basic Architecture, vol. 253665 (2016)
20. Intel. Intel®64 and IA-32 Architectures Software Developer's Manual, Volume 3 (3A, 3B & 3C): System Programming Guide (2019)
21. Intel. Intel-SA-00233 Microarchitectural Data Sampling Advisory (2019). https://www.intel.com/content/www/us/en/security-center/advisory/intel-sa-00233.html
22. Intel. Affected Processors: Transient Execution Attacks (2023). https://www.intel.com/content/www/us/en/developer/topic-technology/software-security-guidance/processors-affected-consolidated-product-cpu-model.html
23. Intel Corporation. Guidelines for Mitigating Timing Side Channels Against Cryptographic Implementations (2020). https://www.intel.com/content/www/us/en/developer/articles/technical/software-security-guidance/secure-coding/mitigate-timing-side-channel-crypto-implementation.html
24. Intel Corporation. Refined Speculative Execution Terminology (2020). https://software.intel.com/security-software-guidance/insights/refined-speculative-execution-terminology
25. Jana, S., Shmatikov, V.: Memento: learning secrets from process footprints. In: S&P 2012 (2012)
26. Kocher, P., et al.: Spectre attacks: exploiting speculative execution. In: S&P (2019)
27. Kocher, P.C.: Timing attacks on implementations of Diffie-Hellman, RSA, DSS, and other systems. In: Koblitz, N. (ed.) CRYPTO 1996. LNCS, vol. 1109, pp. 104–113. Springer, Heidelberg (1996). https://doi.org/10.1007/3-540-68697-5_9
28. Koruyeh, E.M., Khasawneh, K., Song, C., Abu-Ghazaleh, N.: Spectre returns! Speculation attacks using the return stack buffer. In: WOOT (2018)
29. Lee, S., Kim, Y., Kim, J., Kim, J.: Stealing webpages rendered on your browser by exploiting GPU vulnerabilities. In: S&P (2014)
30. Leverich, J.: Mutilate: high-performance memcached load generator (2014). https://github.com/leverich/mutilate
31. Linux. Complete virtual memory map with 4-level page tables (2019). https://www.kernel.org/doc/Documentation/x86/x86_64/mm.txt
32. Lipp, M., Gruss, D., Schwarz, M.: AMD prefetch attacks through power and time. In: USENIX Security (2022)
33. Lipp, M., Gruss, D., Schwarz, M., Bidner, D., Maurice, C., Mangard, S.: Practical keystroke timing attacks in sandboxed JavaScript. In: Foley, S.N., Gollmann, D., Snekkenes, E. (eds.) ESORICS 2017. LNCS, vol. 10493, pp. 191–209. Springer, Cham (2017). https://doi.org/10.1007/978-3-319-66399-9_11
34. Lipp, M., Gruss, D., Spreitzer, R., Maurice, C., Mangard, S.: ARMageddon: cache attacks on mobile devices. In: USENIX Security Symposium (2016)
35. Lipp, M., et al.: Meltdown: reading kernel memory from user space. In: USENIX Security Symposium (2018)
36. Maisuradze, G., Rossow, C.: ret2spec: speculative execution using return stack buffers. In: CCS (2018)
37. Moghimi, D., Lipp, M., Sunar, B., Schwarz, M.: Medusa: microarchitectural data leakage via automated attack synthesis. In: USENIX Security Symposium (2020)

38. Monaco, J.: SoK: keylogging side channels. In: S&P (2018)

39. Oren, Y., Kemerlis, V.P., Sethumadhavan, S., Keromytis, A.D.: The spy in the sandbox: practical cache attacks in javascript and their implications. In: CCS (2015)

40. Percival, C.: Cache missing for fun and profit. In: BSDCan (2005)

41. Pessl, P., Gruss, D., Maurice, C., Schwarz, M., Mangard, S.: DRAMA: exploiting DRAM addressing for cross-CPU attacks. In: USENIX Security Symposium (2016)

42. Pinet, S., Ziegler, J.C., Alario, F.-X.: Typing is writing: linguistic properties modulate typing execution. Psychon. Bull. Rev. **23**(6), 1898–1906 (2016)

43. Purnal, A., Turan, F., Verbauwhede, I.: Prime+scope: overcoming the observer effect for high-precision cache contention attacks. In: CCS (2021)

44. Ragab, H., Barberis, E., Bos, H., Giuffrida, C.: Rage against the machine clear: a systematic analysis of machine clears and their implications for transient execution attacks. In: USENIX Security (2021)

45. Ragab, H., Milburn, A., Razavi, K., Bos, H., Giuffrida, C.: CrossTalk: speculative data leaks across cores are real. In: S&P (2021)

46. Schwarz, M., Canella, C., Giner, L., Gruss, D.: Store-to-leak forwarding: leaking data on meltdown-resistant CPUs. arXiv:1905.05725 (2019)

47. Schwarz, M., Lipp, M., Canella, C.: misc0110/PTEditor: a small library to modify all page-table levels of all processes from user space for x86_64 and ARMv8 (2018). https://github.com/misc0110/PTEditor

48. Schwarz, M., et al.: KeyDrown: eliminating software-based keystroke timing side-channel attacks. In: NDSS (2018)

49. Schwarz, M., et al.: ZombieLoad: cross-privilege-boundary data sampling. In: CCS (2019)

50. Schwarzl, M., Schuster, T., Schwarz, M., Gruss, D.: Speculative dereferencing of registers: reviving foreshadow. In: FC (2021)

51. Song, D.X., Wagner, D., Tian, X.: Timing analysis of keystrokes and timing attacks on SSH. In: USENIX Security Symposium (2001)

52. Spreitzer, R., Griesmayr, S., Korak, T., Mangard, S.: Exploiting data-usage statistics for website fingerprinting attacks on android. In: WiSec (2016)

53. Tromer, E., Osvik, D.A., Shamir, A.: Efficient cache attacks on AES, and countermeasures. J. Cryptol. **23**(1), 37–71 (2010)

54. Van Bulck, J.,et al.: Foreshadow: extracting the keys to the Intel SGX kingdom with transient out-of-order execution. In: USENIX Security Symposium (2018)

55. Van Bulck, J., et al.: LVI: hijacking transient execution through microarchitectural load value injection. In: S&P (2020)

56. Van Bulck, J., Piessens, F., Strackx, R.: Nemesis: studying microarchitectural timing leaks in rudimentary CPU interrupt logic. In: CCS (2018)

57. van Schaik, S., et al.: RIDL: rogue in-flight data load. In: S&P (2019)

58. Vila, P., Köpf, B.: Loophole: timing attacks on shared event loops in chrome. In: USENIX Security Symposium (2017)

59. Wang, H., Lai, T.T.-T., Roy Choudhury, R.: MoLe: motion leaks through smartwatch sensors. In: Proceedings of the International Conference on Mobile Computing and Networking (2015)

60. Wang, Y., Paccagnella, R., He, E., Shacham, H., Fletcher, C.W., Kohlbrenner, D.: Hertzbleed: turning power side-channel attacks into remote timing attacks on x86. In: USENIX Security Symposium (2022)

61. Weber, D., Ibrahim, A., Nemati, H., Schwarz, M., Rossow, C.: Osiris: automated discovery of microarchitectural side channels. In: USENIX Security (2021)

62. Xiao, Y., Zhang, Y., Teodorescu, R.: SPEECHMINER: a framework for investigating and measuring speculative execution vulnerabilities. In: NDSS (2020)
63. Yan, L., Guo, Y., Chen, X., Mei, H.: A study on power side channels on mobile devices. In: Symposium on Internetware (2015)
64. Yarom, Y., Falkner, K.: Flush+Reload: a high resolution, low noise, L3 cache side-channel attack. In: USENIX Security Symposium (2014)
65. Zhang, K., Wang, X.: Peeping Tom in the neighborhood: keystroke eavesdropping on multi-user systems. In: USENIX Security Symposium (2009)
66. Zhang, R., Kim, T., Weber, D., Schwarz, M.: (M)WAIT for it: bridging the gap between microarchitectural and architectural side channels. In: USENIX Security (2023)

Accessorize in the Dark: A Security Analysis of Near-Infrared Face Recognition

Amit Cohen and Mahmood Sharif[✉]

Tel Aviv University, Tel Aviv, Israel
mahmoods@tauex.tau.ac.il

Abstract. Prior work showed that face-recognition systems ingesting RGB images captured via visible-light (VIS) cameras are susceptible to real-world evasion attacks. Face-recognition systems in near-infrared (NIR) are widely deployed for critical tasks (e.g., access control), and are hypothesized to be more secure due to the lower variability and dimensionality of NIR images compared to VIS ones. However, the actual robustness of NIR-based face recognition remains unknown. This work puts the hypothesis to the test by offering attacks well-suited for NIR-based face recognition and adapting them to facilitate physical realizability. The outcome of the attack is an adversarial accessory the adversary can wear to mislead NIR-based face-recognition systems. We tested the attack against six models, both defended and undefended, with varied numbers of subjects in the digital and physical domains. We found that face recognition in NIR is highly susceptible to real-world attacks. For example, $\geq 96.66\%$ of physically realized attack attempts seeking arbitrary misclassification succeeded, including against defended models. Overall, our work highlights the need to defend NIR-based face recognition, especially when deployed in high-stakes domains.

1 Introduction

Face-recognition technology has become increasingly popular in recent years, with applications ranging from border security [7] and surveillance [41] to access control [1,2]. Among others, face recognition based on near infrared (NIR) imaging has received wide adoption (e.g., [1,2]) due to its near-invariance to changes in ambient illumination and its ability to capture facial features in dark environments [17]. Because such NIR-based face-recognition systems are deployed to address security-critical problems, it is crucial to analyze their integrity against adversaries seeking to mislead them (e.g., to circumvent surveillance or receive unauthorized access).

Recent work in adversarial machine learning (ML) has demonstrated that ML models in general, and ones for face-recognition in particular, are vulnerable to evasion attacks at deployment time (e.g., [20,32,33,36,37]). Specifically, adversaries generating so-called adversarial examples—minimally but strategically modified variants of benign inputs—can lead ML models to misclassify. These adversarial examples can also be realized in the problem space to mislead

G. Tsudik et al. (Eds.): ESORICS 2023, LNCS 14346, pp. 43–61, 2024.
https://doi.org/10.1007/978-3-031-51479-1_3

systems [29]. For example, adversaries can physically realize and wear accessories such as eyeglasses to impersonate others against face recognition in visible light (VIS) [32,33]. Still, prior work demonstrating evasion attacks against image classification chiefly focused on systems relying on VIS sensors, and the susceptibility of NIR-based face recognition to evasion attacks has yet to be determined. Indeed, because NIR images vary less under changes in imaging conditions [17] and have lower dimensionality (shown to be correlated with susceptibility to attacks [31]) than VIS images, it is plausible that NIR-based face-recognition systems could be less susceptible to evasion than their VIS counterparts.

Our work fills the gap by developing and evaluating attacks against state-of-the-art NIR-based face-recognition models, enabling us to determine whether and to what extent these systems are vulnerable to evasion attacks in the digital and physical domains. We design attacks that enable adversaries to mislead NIR-based face recognition according to different attack objectives (namely, dodging to attain arbitrary misclassifications or impersonation), and further extend them to facilitate realizing adversarial examples in the physical world. For example, among others, we ensure attacks are robust to real-world transformations, such as changes in pose and camera sampling noise. The attacks result in accessories (namely, eyeglasses) adversaries can wear to mislead face recognition.

We extensively tested attacks against six state-of-the-art NIR-based face-recognition models in the digital and physical domains. Our experiments involved varied numbers of subjects, and both undefended and defended [42] models. We found that the models were highly vulnerable to evasion, with a mean of 98.33% of dodging attempts and 77.77% of impersonation attempts succeeding in the physical domain. The defense hindered impersonation attacks to some extent (36.66% mean attack success rate), but was still vulnerable to dodging (96.66% mean attack success rate). Overall, our work highlights that NIR-based face recognition-systems are not inherently more robust than their VIS counterparts, and that defenses to advance their integrity in adversarial settings are crucial.

The paper is structured as follows. Next, we present necessary background (Sect. 2) and the threat model (Sect. 3). Then, we introduce our methodology (Sect. 4), followed by an evaluation of NIR-based face recognition's robustness (Sect. 5). Lastly, we close the paper by discussing its limitations (Sect. 6) and concluding (Sect. 7).

2   Background and Related Work

2.1   Face Recognition in NIR

NIR is a portion of the electromagnetic spectrum falling between visible light and mid-infrared, with wavelengths ranging between ~700 and ~2500 nm. As NIR light can penetrate certain material, such as clothing and wood, it is particularly useful for imaging such objects. Consequently, NIR is commonly used in various applications, ranging from gaze detection in challenging conditions [24] to the analysis of food and agricultural products [25]. In the biometrics field,

NIR has been used for face recognition, including in widely deployed commercial systems (e.g., [1,2]), due to its ability to capture facial features that may not be otherwise visible. Notably, NIR cameras can capture images in low-light conditions, rendering them useful for settings with limited (VIS) illumination, such as surveillance and biometric authentication in the dark.

Leading NIR-based face-recognition systems rely on deep learning [9,10, 12,14,15,23,43,44,49]. For example, Lezama et al. presented a deep-learning-based face-recognition system to identify individuals based on their NIR facial images [18]. They attained high recognition performance by leveraging generative models mapping NIR to VIS and an off-the-shelf feature-extraction network as a backbone, and tuning the representations using generated images. Later on, Wu et al. presented a deep convolutional neural network, named LightCNN, designed to be light-weight and effective on multiple tasks [43]. Among others, LightCNN achieves high accuracy on NIR-based face recognition. In a follow-up work, Fu et al. proposed an LightCNN variant, LightCNN-DVG [12], achieving the highest face-recognition accuracy in NIR to date. The primary difference between LightCNN and LightCNN-DVG is that the latter is fine-tuned with NIR-VIS data. During fine-tuning, LightCNN-DVG was trained to map NIR and VIS image pairs of the same person (resp., different people) into feature vectors that are close together (resp., further away) in the feature space. We evaluate our proposed attack against a representative set of such top performing models.

2.2 Attacking ML

Attacks against ML models can be categorized based on attacker objectives and capabilities. Several attack types against ML have been proposed, including, but not limited to, training-time attacks, where adversaries partially control the training data or process to harm model performance (e.g., [5,16]); privacy attacks, where adversaries aims to extract sensitive information about the training data from access to the model or training process (e.g., [34]); and availability attacks, where attackers seek to craft inputs that increase prediction or training latency (e.g., [35]). By contrast, our work studies evasion attacks in which adversaries have no control over the trained model but can manipulate inputs at inference time to induce misclassifications (e.g., [20,36]).

Evasion attacks were first popularized by Biggio et al. [4] and Szegedy et al. [36], who demonstrated the vulnerability of ML models to small perturbations of their inputs. Since then, evasion attacks have been studied extensively, with numerous techniques proposed for generating and defending against adversarial examples (e.g., [6,13,20,27]). Formally, evasion attacks seek to find a solution to some variation of the following optimization problem:

$$\arg\max_{\delta} L\big(f(x + \delta), c_x\big)$$

where f is an ML model, x is the input, δ is an adversarial perturbation, c_x is the input's class (i.e., label), and L is the loss function. Often, the optimization is constrained by requiring that δ's ℓ_p-norm is bounded by a constant ϵ, (i.e., $||\delta||_p = \left(\sum_i |\delta_i|^p \right)^{1/p} \leq \epsilon$, commonly for $p \in \{2, \infty\}$). By solving the optimization, attacks aim to find perturbations increasing the loss, leading f to misclassify. Several first-order (i.e., gradient-based) optimization methods have been proposed to solve the optimization (e.g., [6,13]), many of which are slight variants of the popular Projected Gradient Descent (PGD) attack [20]. Given a model and a sample input, PGD generates adversarial perturbations in an iterative manner—it calculates the input gradients w.r.t. the loss, and updates the input in the direction maximizing the model's error. More formally, PGD computes the perturbed sample x^{t+1} at iteration $t+1$ by:

$$x^{t+1} = \Pi_S(x^t + \alpha \; sign(\nabla_{x^t} L(f(x^t), c_x)))$$

where α is the step size, and Π_S projects samples into a set of allowed perturbations S (e.g., ϵ-ball around x), and x^0 is set to x or randomly initialized within S. The attack we design (Sect. 4) is a variant of PGD in which δ's max-norm is unbounded, but the perturbation can be applied to a specific region in the image covered by an accessory, as defined by a mask.

Attackers performing evasion can vary in their capabilities. In *white-box* settings, attackers have full access to the model parameters and architectures, allowing them to design powerful attacks using their knowledge about the model (e.g. gradients [20]). By contrast, in *black-box* settings, attackers have no access to the model internals, and may only query models [27]. Thus, intuitively, black-box attacks are more challenging than white-box attacks. Attacker goals may also vary. An attacker may aim to produce any misclassification—i.e., conduct an *untargeted* attack—or induce a misclassification to a particular class—i.e., perform a *targeted* attack [28]. Intuitively, targeted attacks impose more constraints and are hence more challenging.

Early evasion attacks primarily explored adversarial perturbations constrained in ℓ_p-norms. While in those settings the adversarial sample is close to the original benign example, ℓ_p-norm-bounded attacks are challenging to realize in the problem space (i.e., as an artifact whose corresponding features are misclassified by a model) [29]. By contrast, realizable attacks incorporate domain constraints to produce problem-space artifacts that lead to evasion (e.g., [3,11,29,30,32].) For example, Sharif et al. showed how to produce eyeglass frames that adversaries can don to evade VIS-based face recognition [32]. The attack was effective under real-world circumstances, allowing adversaries to mislead recognition by wearing eyeglass frames with specific color patterns. Differently than Sharif et al., we develop attacks suited for NIR-based face recognition.

2.3   Defending ML

Defending models' integrity against evasion attacks is crucial for ensuring safe and secure deployment. Adversarial training—the process of augmenting the training data with correctly labeled adversarial examples—is one of the most effective techniques for enhancing model robustness (e.g., [13,20]).

Other defenses offer methods to detect adversarial inputs (e.g., [22]), sanitize adversarial perturbations (e.g., [48]), and certify robustness within certain regions (e.g., [8]). Researchers have also published defenses against patch-based attacks [45–47], however these are either limited to models with small receptive fields or significantly increase inference time. Wu et al. presented a defense method called Defense against Occlusion Attacks (DOA) to defend against physically realizable attacks in the image domain [42]. They suggest adversarially training models with an abstract adversary perturbing a rectangular patch and show this enhances robustness against adversaries using eyeglasses to evade face recognition and ones producing stickers to evade traffic-sign recognition. We evaluate our attack against a model defended via DOA.

3 Threat Model

In this paper, we primarily study white-box evasion attacks against NIR-based face-recognition models. Studying white-box attacks is critical, as *(1)* it can help us assess systems' vulnerability when relying on publicly available models (e.g., [43]) or when proprietary models are stolen [38]; *(2)* they help assess the effectiveness of defenses against worst-case adversaries with complete knowledge of the system, and inform means to enhance them; and *(3)* these attacks serve as the basis for black-box attacks using queries to estimate gradients [27] or via transferability [26]. Indeed, we attempt to transfer attacks created against surrogate models to target models, thus simulating black-box attacks, and find that evasion attempts often transfer between NIR-based face-recognition models. We implement both untargeted (dodging) and targeted (impersonation) attacks, and test them both in digital and physical domains against state-of-the-art models.

To maintain stealth and plausible deniability, we consider attacks using everyday accessories (mainly eyeglasses, but also face masks and stickers), in line with prior work [32,37]. By using accessories, the adversary aims to remain inconspicuous and avoid raising suspicion by observers. Additionally, we aim for the attacks to be (physically) realizable, such that adversaries would be able to mislead the system by slightly changing their own appearance, without altering their surroundings or manipulating the digital representation of their image.

4 Methodology

We now present our attacks against NIR-based face recognition, starting with how to evade models before describing how to enable physical realizability.

4.1 Evading Recognizers

The face-recognition systems we study classify NIR face images by finding the most similar VIS image from within an image gallery. The process is enabled by neural networks that extract feature vectors of both NIR and VIS images.

For classification, the systems compute the cosine similarity $cos(\cdot, \cdot)$ between the NIR features and each of gallery images' features. Eventually, the gallery subject with the highest similarity is selected as the classification result. After exploring numerous directions (see Sect. 5.2), we identified techniques that were most effective at producing dodging and impersonation attacks.

Dodging. In dodging, the adversary's goal is to produce an arbitrary misclassification to any class other than the true class. We find that evading classification by increasing the similarity w.r.t. the closest incorrect class (in a given attack iteration) and decreasing it w.r.t. the true class is most effective (Sect. 5.2). Given an input x pertaining to class (i.e., gallery subject) c_x, we denote the feature array of the gallery images by $G \in \mathbb{R}^{k \times d}$, where k is the number of classes, and d is the dimensionality of the features extracted by the model f, and by $max_{c \neq c_x}(cos(f(x), G[c]))$ the closest class to x which is not c_x. To produce a misclassification, we find a perturbation δ that maximizes the dodging loss:

$$L_{dodge}(x, c_x) = -\alpha cos(f(x + \delta), G[c_x]) + \beta max_{c \neq c_x}(cos(f(x + \delta), G[c]))$$

where α and β are two non-negative constants, aiming to balance the first objective (decreasing the distance from c_x) and the second objective (increasing similarity with the most similar class $c \neq c_x$), respectively. After running a grid search, we found that setting both α and β to one led to the highest success.

Impersonation. In impersonation, the adversary selects a target class (i.e., subject) c_t to impersonate. To achieve this objective, besides increasing similarity with c_t and decreasing similarity with c_x, we found that it is crucial to decrease similarity with all gallery subjects that are more similar to the input than the target, or are less similar to the input than the target but only slightly so. Said differently, our attack aims to ensure that the similarity with c_t is higher than all other classes by a significant margin, increasing the confidence that the (adversarial) input pertains to c_t. In doing so, we could increase the likelihood that attacks would succeed when realized, even when similarity with c_t is decreased after realization (e.g., due to imperfect fabrication of the accessory). To this end, we define the high-margin (hm) loss:

$$L_{hm} = \frac{1}{k} \sum_c ReLU(cos(f(x + \delta), G[c]) - cos(f(x + \delta), G[c_t]) + \tau)$$

where τ is a small non-negative constant set to ensure that the perturbation decreases the similarity w.r.t. classes sufficiently similar to x (i.e., with similarity higher or up to a small margin of c_t). We empirically found that $\tau = 0.2$ leads to successful attacks (see Sect. 5). Accordingly, the impersonation attacks aim to maximize the impersonation loss, defined by:

$$L_{imp}(x, c_x) = \alpha cos(f(x + \delta), G[c_t]) - \beta cos(f(x + \delta), G[c_x]) - \gamma * L_{hm}$$

where α, β, and γ are non-negative constants to balance between the attack goals, of increasing similarity with c_t, decreasing similarity with c_x, and decreasing L_{hm}. We set α and β to 6, and γ to 15, as we found these to work best after performing a grid search.

(a)   (b)

Fig. 1. Attacks generated with (a) and without (b) minimizing TV.

4.2 Realizing Attacks

To implement attacks in the physical world, measures to aid in fabricating the adversarial artifacts and improve their robustness to varying imaging conditions (e.g., scale and pose) are necessary [32]. We address this by adding constraints to the attack to encourage the creation of objects that resemble their digital counterpart when printed and photographed with an NIR camera, and are robust to transformations encountered in the real world, as elaborated below.

Total Variation (TV). When not restricted, the attack may produce sharp, unnatural transitions between neighboring pixels. Such transitions would be challenging to realize, as they would require high-resolution printers and cameras to produce and capture them [21,32]. Thus, to facilitate realizability and promote inconspicuousness, we use TV as part of the loss, similarly to Sharif et al.'s work [32]. Given an input $x \in \mathbb{R}^{d \times d}$, TV measures the distance between neighboring pixels via the following formula:

$$TV(x) = \sum_{i,j} [(x_{i,j} - x_{i+1,j})^2 + (x_{i,j} - x_{i,j+1})^2]^\beta$$

where β is a configurable parameter that we set to 1, in line with prior work [32]. Figure 1 shows artifacts produced with and without TV—by minimizing TV, attacks produce artifacts with smooth textures more amenable for realization.

Printability. To produce adversarial artifacts containing colors that can be physically realized via printing, we define and use a Non-Printability Score (NPS) metric tailored for the NIR domain. To define NPS, we first identify the color ranges our printer can produce and model how they are captured by cameras. Empirically, this works by printing a grayscale palette covering the entire [0, 255] range and photographing it (see Fig. 2a).[1] Doing so showed that the range of printable colors is a consecutive sub-range $[v_{lb}, v_{ub}] = [40,180]$ of the full [0,255] range (see Fig. 2b). Moreover, we observe a roughly linear relationship between printed colors an their captured counterparts, enabling us to pre-process the accessories' colors prior to printing to preserve similarity between the printed

---

[1] We use grayscale as NIR contains a single channel and we found grayscale covers the value range more comprehensively than RGB.

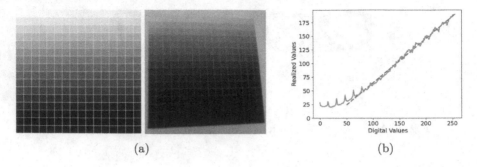

(a)   (b)

Fig. 2. (a) Digital grey-scale palette (left) compared to a printed and photographed palette (right). (b) Comparison of digital colors and their realized counterparts (after being printed and recaptured via an NIR camera). A dotted line is added to emphasize the roughly linear relationship.

and captured colors (Sect. 5.3). Accordingly, we defined the NPS formula as follows:

$$NPS(x) = \sum_{i,j}[ReLU(v_{lb} - x_{i,j}) + ReLU(x_{i,j} - v_{ub})].$$

Intuitively, the NPS accumulates a penalty for each pixel that is lower than the lower bound or higher than the upper bound color we could realize. Therefore, by minimizing NPS, our attack pushes colors on the adversarial artifacts to become printable, thus aiding in realizability.

Expectation Over Transformation (EOT). is a measure aiming to enhance robustness against changes likely to be encountered in the physical world [3]. For instance, when an attacker wears accessories (e.g., eyeglasses), we cannot assume they will be located exactly as intended on the face, that the attacker pose will be completely frontal, or that they will stand at a fixed distance w.r.t. the camera. To ensure that attacks succeed across input variations, we adapt EOT to face recognition such that we maximize the expected impersonation and dodging losses over potential variations. Formally, given an image x and a perturbation δ, instead of maximizing $L_{\{dodge|imp\}}$ over $x + \delta$, we maximize it over $t_1(x + t_2(\delta))$ for $t_1 \sim T_1$ and $t_2 \sim T_2$, where T_1 are transformations applied to the face and accessory combined (e.g., changes in pose or distance), and T_2 are transformations applied to accessory alone (e.g., slight translation due to dislocation and noise due to sampling errors). Specifically, for T_2, we use slight rotations ($\in [-2,2]$ degrees), scaling ($\times[0.98,1.02]$), and translations along the x- and y-axes ($\in \{-2,\ldots,2\}$), to account for potential variations that might occur when attackers wear the accessory. Furthermore, we add small amount of zero-centered Gaussian noise ($\sigma = 0.04$) to δ to account for slight color noise during sampling. To simulate transformations of the face and accessory (i.e., T_1), we take multiple images per attacker with slight variations in pose, distance, and lighting and attach the accessories to them via perspective transformation.

Overall Objective. To physically realize attacks we find δ that maximizing

$$\arg\max_\delta E_{t_1,t_2 \sim T_1,T_2} \left[L_{\{dodge|imp\}} \left(f(t_1(x + t_2(\delta))), c_{\{x|t\}} \right) \right] - \omega_1 TV(\delta) - \omega_2 NPS(\delta).$$

The optimization process searches for a perturbation δ maximizing L_{dodge} or L_{imp} (depending on the attack objective) over expected input transformations, while minimizing the TV and NPS of δ. ω_1 and ω_2 are non-negative constants for balancing the objectives tuned to maximize the success of realized attacks.

Implementation Details. We solve the optimization using PGD, after initializing the accessory colors to a uniform grayscale value of 76/255, allowing the accessory's values to range $\in [0,1]$ while not perturbing values not covered by the accessory. We run PGD for 400 iterations and set its step size to 1/255. To enable a more direct comparison with prior work, we use Sharif et al.'s eyeglasses covering 8% of the image [32] as the adversarial accessory. We tested other accessories (e.g., face masks and stickers) in the digital domain and found they led to relatively lower success than eyeglasses (Sect. 6). We implemented attacks using PyTorch and published our code to aid in reproducibility.[2]

5   Evaluation

Our experiments examined the vulnerability of several NIR-based face-recognition systems to dodging and impersonation attacks in the digital and physical domains. Next, we describe our experimental setup before reporting the results of attacks in the digital (Sect. 5.2) and physical (Sect. 5.3) domains.

5.1   Experimental Setup

Data. For our evaluation, we relied on the CASIA NIR-VIS 2.0 dataset [19]. This dataset consists of frontal face images of 725 subjects collected using NIR and VIS sensors. The VIS images were collected in visual light, while NIR images were collected in complete darkness, using an NIR camera surrounded by 850 nm NIR light-emitting diodes (LEDs). Figure 3 presents samples from the dataset. The number of VIS images per subject varies between one and 22 while that of NIR images varies between five and 50. For testing, the dataset contains a gallery of 358 VIS images, one per subject, and a probe set consisting of 6,000 NIR images for the same 358 subjects. The objective is to map the NIR images from the probe set to the correct identity from the gallery. The dimensionality of the images is 480×640, and we aligned them to a fixed pose and cropped them to 224×224 centered around the face, per standard practice [32].

To conduct experiments in the physical domains, we further augmented the dataset by enrolling three additional subjects—two males and a female 28–31 years of age. We refer to them by S_1–S_3. For each subject enrolled, we captured

---

[2] Code available at https://github.com/AmitCohen3/Accessorize-in-the-dark.

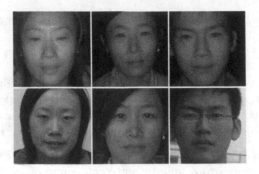

Fig. 3. NIR (top) and VIS (bottom) images of three subjects (columns) from the CASIA NIR-VIS 2.0 dataset.

a VIS image and 20 NIR images, all using an Intel RealSense D415 camera. Similarly to CASIA NIR-VIS 2.0 dataset [19], both VIS and NIR images were taken with the subject's face positioned in the middle of the frame with a frontal pose. When capturing images in NIR, the subjects were wearing eyeglasses frames and were asked to slightly move their faces in a circular motion. All images were taken in a dark room, with closed window blinds to prevent external light, while turning on NIR LEDs positioned around the camera to faithfully simulate CASIA NIR-VIS 2.0's conditions. For printing, we used a Xerox B230 printer.

Models. We evaluated attacks against state-of-the-art architectures for NIR-VIS face-recognition: LightCNN, LightCNN-DVG, LightCNN-Rob, and ResNeSt. Wu et al. proposed LightCNN and trained it using multiple VIS datasets after converting inputs to one-dimensional (i.e., grayscale) images [43]. They showed that, by training model on noisy labels, LightCNN can attain high performance on the NIR-VIS face-recognition task. We acquired the LightCNN weights published by the authors. LightCNN-DVG was proposed in a follow-up work by the same group, in which they fine-tuned LightCNN using generated pairs of NIR-VIS face images to further improve the model's accuracy [12]. We trained a LightCNN-DVG model on our dataset using the official code. To enhance model robustness against attacks, we also followed Wu et al.'s protocol to adversarially train a model [42]. In particular, we fine-tuned LightCNN-DVG using the DOA method, running 10 epochs of adversarial training.[3] Finally, because some NIR-based face recognition systems leverage typical VIS models receiving three channels as input (e.g., [18]), we complemented the LightCNN variants with a Residual Neural Network with Split Attention (ResNeSt) model [50]. We acquired pre-trained ResNeSt weights through Wang et al.'s project [39], and found it was markedly more accurate than other 11 models ingesting three channels Wang et al. offer (including ResNet and VGG models). Lastly, to assess how the number of subjects affects attack success, we evaluated variants of LightCNN-DVG, LightCNN-DVG-10 and LightCNN-DVG-100, on a subset of

---

[3] We used the Adam optimizer with a 1e-5 learning rate for best performance.

Table 1. The models' benign accuracy with the enrolled subjects included. The standard deviation is negligible ($<1e-4$), thus excluded.

Model	Benign accuracy
LightCNN	98.27%
LightCNN-DVG	99.80%
LightCNN-DVG-100	99.84%
LightCNN-DVG-10	99.85%
LightCNN-Rob	99.56%
ResNeSt	91.10%

ten and 100 subjects, respectively, both of which include the three subjects we enrolled.

To measure benign accuracy, we followed CASIA's protocol [19]: we divided the data into ten folds while adding the enrolled subjects to each of the folds and measured the mean accuracy over the folds. For models with ten or 100 subjects, we randomly chose the subjects from the dataset to compute benign accuracy, and calculated the mean over ten repetitions. Table 1 reports the benign accuracy of all models. All models were highly accurate, and, as expected, the most advanced model, LightCNN-DVG, was most accurate, with an increasing accuracy as the number of subjects decreased.

Metrics. We measured attack performance by their success rate (SR) and margin. SR estimates how often the attack achieves its objective—i.e., the percentage of time the attacker is misclassified as someone else (resp. target class) in dodging (resp. impersonation) attacks. The margin is a proxy for the confidence in the (mis)classification result. We measured it by the difference between similarity with the top prediction (resp. target class) and the true class in dodging (resp. impersonation) attacks.

5.2   Digital Attacks

We tested attacks in the digital domain to find loss functions that maximize attack success and assess the security of NIR-based face recognition in ideal settings, where adversaries can precisely produce adversarial accessories. In these attacks we ignored the TV, printability, and EOT objectives, and mainly focused on misclassifications using a single adversary image. We evaluated both dodging and impersonation attacks, selecting the impersonation targets at random. We ran each attack type ten times, each time with different 1,024 NIR images (or all images available for the subjects, if less than 1,024), and measured the average and standard deviation (std) of the SR and margin over these repetitions. Lastly, we tested the transferability of attacks—i.e., how often attacks created against one model succeed against other models—to simulate black-box attacks.

Table 2. Comparison between dodging losses against LightCNN-DVG.

Loss	SR	Margin (std)
$L_{dodge}^1 = -\alpha cos\big(f(x+\delta), G[c_x]\big)$	100.00%	0.38 (0.13)
$L_{dodge}^2 = -\alpha cos\big(f(x+\delta), G[c_x]\big) + \beta \max_{c \neq c_x}\big(cos(f(x), G[c])\big)$	100.00%	0.30 (0.11)
$L_{dodge}^3 = -\alpha cos\big(f(x+\delta), G[c_x]\big) + \beta \max_{c \neq c_x}\big(cos(f(x+\delta), G[c])\big)$	**100.00%**	**0.50 (0.13)**

Table 3. Comparison between impersonation losses against LightCNN-DVG.

Loss	SR	Margin (std)
$L_{imp}^1 = cos\big(f(x+\delta), G[c_t]\big)$	84.37%	0.20 (0.15)
$L_{imp}^2 = \alpha cos\big(f(x+\delta), G[c_t]\big) - \beta cos\big(f(x+\delta), G[c_x]\big)$	72.07%	0.40 (0.16)
$L_{imp}^3 = \alpha cos\big(f(x+\delta), G[c_t]\big) - \beta \max_c(cos(f(x+\delta), G[c]))$	87.07%	0.02 (0.02)
$L_{imp}^4 = \alpha cos\big(f(x+\delta), G[c_t]\big) - \beta cos\big(f(x+\delta), G[c_x]\big) - \gamma \max_c(cos(f(x+\delta), G[c]))$	80.23%	0.40 (0.16)
$L_{imp}^5 = \alpha cos\big(f(x+\delta), G[c_t]\big) - \beta cos\big(f(x+\delta), G[c_x]\big) - \gamma \max_{c \neq c_x}(cos(f(x+\delta), G[c]))$	85.89%	0.34 (0.15)
$L_{imp}^6 = \alpha cos\big(f(x+\delta), G[c_t]\big) - \beta cos\big(f(x+\delta), G[c_x]\big) - \gamma * L_{hm}$	**91.01%**	**0.34 (0.17)**

Table 4. SRs and margins for digital-domain dodging and impersonation attacks.

Model	Dodging		Impersonation	
	SR	Margin (std)	SR	Margin (std)
LightCNN	100.00%	0.48 (0.15)	90.92%	0.30 (0.17)
LightCNN-DVG	100.00%	0.50 (0.13)	91.01%	0.34 (0.17)
LightCNN-DVG-100	100.00%	0.50 (0.12)	94.95%	0.39 (0.17)
LightCNN-DVG-10	100.00%	0.47 (0.12)	98.78%	0.35 (0.17)
LightCNN-Rob	100.00%	0.36 (0.13)	52.66%	0.09 (0.19)
ResNeSt	100.00%	0.35 (0.10)	89.05%	0.20 (0.11)

Loss-Function Selection. We evaluated various loss function for dodging and impersonation to identify the ones maximizing attack success. In these experiments, we ran attacks against LightCNN-DVG, as it was the most robust amongst the undefended models. Table 2 presents the three dodging losses considered and their corresponding SRs and margins. L_{dodge}^1 aims to decrease the similarity with the true class; L_{dodge}^2 extends L_{dodge}^1 by increasing similarity with the closest subject (excluding c_x) prior to running the attack; and L_{dodge}^3 (L_{dodge} in Sect. 4.1) extends L_{dodge}^1 by increasing similarity with the closest subject to $x + \delta$ in the current iteration. L_{dodge}^3 led to markedly higher margins, hence we used it in subsequent attacks. Table 3 lists the six impersonation losses we tested and their respective SRs and margins. L_{imp}^1 seeks to increase similarity with c_t; L_{imp}^2 also aims to decrease similarity with c_x; L_{imp}^3 extends L_{imp}^1 by decreasing similarity with the current top prediction; L_{imp}^4 combines L_{imp}^2 and L_{imp}^3; L_{imp}^5 refines L_{imp}^4 by excluding c_x when decreasing similarity with the top prediction; and L_{imp}^6 is equivalent to L_{imp} described in Sect. 4.1. It can be immediately seen

Table 5. Transferability of digital dodging (left) and impersonations (right).

Surrogate \ Target	LightCNN-DVG	LightCNN	LightCNN-Rob	ResNeSt
LightCNN-DVG	100.00%	98.82%	76.95%	38.67%
LightCNN	100.00%	100.00%	68.93%	41.28%
LightCNN-Rob	96.24%	89.52%	100.00%	40.31%
ResNeSt	1.32%	11.45%	20.04%	100.00%

Surrogate \ Target	LightCNN-DVG	LightCNN	LightCNN-Rob	ResNeSt
LightCNN-DVG	91.02%	66.99%	25.00%	0.00%
LightCNN	65.42%	90.9%	37.10%	0.00%
LightCNN-Rob	41.30%	26.48%	52.56%	0.39%
ResNeSt	0.16%	0.17%	0.22%	89.04%

that L_{imp}^6 reached remarkably higher SR than other losses. Thus, we used L_{imp}^6 to perform impersonations in the following experiments.

Attack Evaluation. Table 4 reports the performance of digital-domain dodging and impersonation attacks against all models, using L_{dodge} and L_{imp}, respectively. It can be observed that all dodging attempts against all models succeeded. Impersonation attacks' SRs, on the other hand, ranged between 52.66% and 98.78%. The defended model, LightCNN-Rob, was the most challenging to mislead, with 52.66% impersonation SR and a 0.09 margin, compared to $\geq$89.05% and $\geq$0.20 margins for the undefended models. Moreover, perhaps intuitively, impersonation attacks against models with fewer subjects (i.e., LightCNN-DVG-10 and LightCNN-DVG-100) were relatively more successful than the model with all subjects (i.e., LightCNN-DVG).

Although attacks were not optimized for transferability, we found that they often transfer successfully, especially between the LightCNN variants (Table 5). Between different LightCNN models, the mean SR of transferred attacks ranged between 68.93%–100.00% for dodging and 25.00%–65.42% for impersonation. Impersonation attacks transferred from and to ResNeSt had low SRs ($\leq$0.39%), but dodging attacks against LightCNN variants often misled ResNeSt (38.67%–41.28% mean SR). We expect higher SRs would be achievable by integrating techniques to promote transferability (e.g., [40]).

5.3 Physical Attacks

We tested physical-domain attacks against all models. In these experiments, the three subjects introduced to the dataset simulated attackers. For each subject, we ran dodging and impersonation attacks against each model, for a total of 3 × 2 × 6 = 36 attack attempts. As in the digital-domain, we randomly chose the target in each impersonation attack. For each attack, we solved the corresponding optimization with all objectives (Sect. 4.2) to generate eyeglass textures, which we then printed, cut, and affixed to 3D frames. To this end, we used all NIR images available for the subject to estimate the EOT of the loss and solve the optimization. Prior to printing, we increased the accessory's pixels' brightness by 40/255 to ensure the printed value of each pixel corresponds to its digital counterpart (per Fig. 2b). We then collected ten images of the person simulating the attacker while wearing the adversarial eyeglasses to measure attack SR. Besides white-box attacks, we again evaluated the transferability of attacks between models to simulate black-box settings. Next, we report how we weighted each term in the overall attack objective, followed by the attack performance.

Table 6. Digital-domain impersonation SR against LightCNN-DVG for varied TV and NPS weights.

TV w.	NPS w.			
	0	1e−4	1e−3	1e−2
0	92.18%	91.60%	91.01%	85.54%
2e−4	91.99%	91.99%	**91.99%**	90.82%
2e−3	85.15%	90.62%	90.62%	90.42%
2e−2	85.74%	87.69%	87.5%	87.69%

Table 7. Mean NPS (left) and TV (right) values for varied TV and NPS weights.

TV w. \ NPS w.	0	1e−4	1e−3	1e−2
0	319.24	273.99	165.10	32.4481
2e−4	263.72	263.72	**244.79**	157.34
2e−3	32.24	182.62	175.07	128.75
2e−2	30.03	116.12	112.13	90.14

TV w. \ NPS w.	0	1e−4	1e−3	1e−2
0	347.33	295.46	201.50	112.38
2e−4	229.74	229.74	**217.67**	167.73
2e−3	100.15	95.20	93.62	83.04
2e−2	61.34	23.04	22.96	22.27

Fig. 4. S_1 physically dodging (left) and impersonating (middle) target ID 00041 (right) against LightCNN-DVG.

Setting TV's and NPS' Weights. In our preliminary experiments, we found that adversarial eyeglasses with a TV value of ∼200 and an NPS value of ∼250 preserve the digital-domain SR best when realized. To this end, to appropriately tune the TV and NPS weights and attain values in the desirable range while maximizing attack SRs, we performed a grid search, evaluating attack SRs in the digital domain with different weights assigned to the TV and NPS objectives. Specifically, we conducted digital-domain impersonation attacks against LightCNN-DVG, using a single adversary image at a time. We repeated the experiment 512 times, each time with different attacker image and a target selected at random. Tables 6–7 report the mean attack SRs, and the mean TV and NPS scores. Per these results, we set the TV and NPS weights to 2e−4 and 1e−3, respectively, as they resulted in the highest attack SRs while attaining TV and NPS conducive for faithful realization.

Table 8. SRs of physical attacks. For each model, we report the dodging and impersonation attack SRs per subject simulating the attacker out of ten attempts, as well as the mean SR across attackers. In the interest of reproducibility, we also report the randomly selected impersonation targets.

Model	Attacker	Dodging		Impersonation		
		SR	Mean(SR)	Target	SR	Mean(SR)
LightCNN	S_1	10/10	93.33%	10047	10/10	100.00%
	S_2	9/10		20476	10/10	
	S_3	9/10		20361	10/10	
LightCNN-DVG	S_1	10/10	100.00%	20370	9/10	96.66%
	S_2	10/10		20389	10/10	
	S_3	10/10		00050	10/10	
LightCNN-DVG-100	S_1	10/10	100.00%	10123	0/10	66.66%
	S_2	10/10		20472	10/10	
	S_3	10/10		00140	10/10	
LightCNN-DVG-10	S_1	10/10	100.00%	20387	10/10	76.66%
	S_2	10/10		20364	10/10	
	S_3	10/10		30565	3/10	
LightCNN-Rob	S_1	9/10	96.66%	00041	10/10	36.66%
	S_2	10/10		30778	0/10	
	S_3	10/10		10210	1/10	
ResNeSt	S_1	10/10	100.00%	20349	10/10	90.00%
	S_2	10/10		00202	7/10	
	S_3	10/10		00122	10/10	

Table 9. Transferability of physical dodging (left) and impersonations (right).

Surrogate \ Target	LightCNN-DVG	LightCNN	LightCNN-Rob	ResNeSt
LightCNN-DVG	100.00%	63.33%	63.33%	0.00%
LightCNN	43.33%	100.00%	40.00%	13.33%
LightCNN-Rob	30.00%	23.33%	96.66%	0.00%
ResNeSt	0.00%	3.33%	33.33%	100.00%

Surrogate \ Target	LightCNN-DVG	LightCNN	LightCNN-Rob	ResNeSt
LightCNN-DVG	100.00%	36.66%	30.00%	0.00%
LightCNN	33.33%	96.66%	26.66%	0.00%
LightCNN-Rob	23.33%	0.00%	36.66%	0.00%
ResNeSt	0.00%	0.00%	0.00%	90.00%

Attack Evaluation. Table 8 reports the attack SRs against all models. Dodging attacks were highly successful, with $\geq 9/10$ attempts leading to misclassification in all cases, and all attempts being misclassified for most subject and model pairs. The models were also relatively susceptible to impersonation attacks, with $\geq 1/10$ attempts succeeding in 16 of the 18 impersonation attacks, and 36.66%–100.00% mean SR across the six models. Naturally, the adversarially trained model, LightCNN-Rob, was the most challenging to mislead, however, even against it, two of the three impersonation attacks succeeded in at least $1/10$ attempts, with one attack succeeding in all attempts. An example of a physical attack is depicted in Fig. 4.

Similarly to the digital domain, attacks exhibited strong transferability between LightCNN variants (Table 9)—mean SRs ranged between 30.00%–

63.33% for transferred physical-world dodging attempts and reached up to 36.66% for impersonation. However, despite 33.33% mean SR for dodging attempts transferred from ResNeSt to LightCNN-Rob, physical-world attacks transferred between ResNeSt and other models had limited SRs (0.00%–13.33% in all other cases). Overall, the SRs of transferred attacks were non-negligible, but we expect they could be further improved via techniques geared to enhance transferability.

6   Limitations

Our findings should be interpreted in light of certain limitations. We evaluated physical attacks in relatively controlled settings, in a single room, with three subjects acting as adversaries. Hence, the generalizability of the results to more settings with other attackers remains to be determined. Still, we expect our results to inform us about the susceptibility of NIR-based face recognition systems in real-world deployments, where imaging variations may resemble those in our experiments (e.g., internal deployment in airports). We also primarily studied evasion attacks using eyeglasses. However, when testing other accessories, such as face masks and stickers [37], we found that attack SRs in the digital environment were significantly lower than with eyeglasses (e.g., 58.43% impersonation SR with stickers against LightCNN-DVG) or that attacks were conspicuous (e.g., attacks with face masks added odd facial features to masks).

7   Conclusion

Prior work has shown VIS-based face-recognition systems to be vulnerable to evasion attacks (e.g., [32,33,37]). To the best of our knowledge, we are the first to demonstrate realizable evasion attacks against NIR-based face recognition. As those systems are widely employed in security-critical settings (e.g., [1,2]), our work highlights the need for enhancing their robustness, especially as existing defenses [42] remain vulnerable to attacks (Sect. 5). Relatively expensive defense techniques, such as human supervision to ascertain the absence of facial accessories, can be implemented immediately. However, further research is needed to establish technical means to enhance NIR-based face recognition's adversarial robustness. We hope that the attacks presented in this work can help inform the design of such defenses and aid in evaluating them.

Acknowledgments. We thank Amir Barda and Amit Bermano for their help printing the 3D frames, and the PLUS research group's members for helpful feedback. This work was supported in part by Len Blavatnik and the Blavatnik Family foundation; by a Maof prize for outstanding young scientists; by a scholarship from the the Shlomo Shmeltzer Institute for Smart Transportation at Tel-Aviv University; and by the Neubauer Family foundation.

References

1. Face ID security. https://help.apple.com/pdf/security/en_US/apple-platform-security-guide.pdf
2. Windows Hello. https://docs.microsoft.com/en-us/windows/security/identity-protection/hello-for-business/hello-overview
3. Athalye, A., Engstrom, L., Ilyas, A., Kwok, K.: Synthesizing robust adversarial examples. In: Proceedings ICML (2018)
4. Biggio, B., et al.: Evasion attacks against machine learning at test time. In: Proceedings ECML PKDD (2013)
5. Biggio, B., Roli, F.: Wild patterns: ten years after the rise of adversarial machine learning. Pattern Recogn. **84**, 317–331 (2018)
6. Carlini, N., Wagner, D.: Towards evaluating the robustness of neural networks. In: Proceedings IEEE S&P (2017)
7. Carlos-Roca, L.R., Torres, I.H., Tena, C.F.: Facial recognition application for border control. In: Proceedings IJCNN (2018)
8. Cohen, J., Rosenfeld, E., Kolter, Z.: Certified adversarial robustness via randomized smoothing. In: Proceedings ICML (2019)
9. Deng, Z., Peng, X., Li, Z., Qiao, Y.: Mutual component convolutional neural networks for heterogeneous face recognition. IEEE Trans. Image Process. **28**(6), 3102–3114 (2019)
10. Duan, B., Fu, C., Li, Y., Song, X., He, R.: Cross-spectral face hallucination via disentangling independent factors. In: Proceedings CVPR (2020)
11. Eykholt, K., et al.: Robust physical-world attacks on deep learning visual classification. In: Proceedings CVPR (2018)
12. Fu, C., Wu, X., Hu, Y., Huang, H., He, R.: DVG-face: dual variational generation for heterogeneous face recognition. IEEE Trans. Pattern Anal. Mach. Intell. (PAMI) **44**, 2938–2952 (2021)
13. Goodfellow, I.J., Shlens, J., Szegedy, C.: Explaining and harnessing adversarial examples. In: Proceedings ICLR (2015)
14. Hu, W., Hu, H.: Orthogonal modality disentanglement and representation alignment network for NIR-VIS face recognition. IEEE Trans. Circuits Syst. Video Technol. **32**(6), 3630–3643 (2021)
15. Hu, W., Yan, W., Hu, H.: Dual face alignment learning network for NIR-VIS face recognition. IEEE Trans. Circuits Syst. Video Technol. **32**(4), 2411–2424 (2021)
16. Huang, H., Mu, J., Gong, N.Z., Li, Q., Liu, B., Xu, M.: Data poisoning attacks to deep learning based recommender systems. In: Proceedings NDSS (2021)
17. Kong, S.G., Heo, J., Abidi, B.R., Paik, J., Abidi, M.A.: Recent advances in visual and infrared face recognition-a review. Comput. Vis. Image Underst. **97**(1), 103–135 (2005)
18. Lezama, J., Qiu, Q., Sapiro, G.: Not afraid of the dark: NIR-VIS face recognition via cross-spectral hallucination and low-rank embedding. In: Proceedings CVPR (2017)
19. Li, S., Yi, D., Lei, Z., Liao, S.: The CASIA NIR-VIS 2.0 face database. In: Proceedings CVPRW (2013)
20. Madry, A., Makelov, A., Schmidt, L., Tsipras, D., Vladu, A.: Towards deep learning models resistant to adversarial attacks. In: Proceedings ICLR (2018)
21. Mahendran, A., Vedaldi, A.: Understanding deep image representations by inverting them. In: Proceedings CVPR (2015)

22. Metzen, J.H., Genewein, T., Fischer, V., Bischoff, B.: On detecting adversarial perturbations. In: Proceedings ICLR (2017)
23. Miao, Y., Lattas, A., Deng, J., Han, J., Zafeiriou, S.: Physically-based face rendering for NIR-VIS face recognition. In: Proceedings NeurIPS (2022)
24. Naqvi, R.A., Arsalan, M., Batchuluun, G., Yoon, H.S., Park, K.R.: Deep learning-based gaze detection system for automobile drivers using a NIR camera sensor. Sensors 18(2), 456 (2018)
25. Osborne, B.G.: Near-infrared spectroscopy in food analysis. Encyclopedia of analytical chemistry: Applications, theory and instrumentation (2006)
26. Papernot, N., McDaniel, P., Goodfellow, I.: Transferability in machine learning: from phenomena to black-box attacks using adversarial samples. arXiv preprint (2016)
27. Papernot, N., McDaniel, P., Goodfellow, I., Jha, S., Celik, Z.B., Swami, A.: Practical black-box attacks against machine learning. In: Proceedings AsiaCCS (2017)
28. Papernot, N., McDaniel, P., Jha, S., Fredrikson, M., Celik, Z.B., Swami, A.: The limitations of deep learning in adversarial settings. In: Proceedings IEEE EuroS&P (2016)
29. Pierazzi, F., Pendlebury, F., Cortellazzi, J., Cavallaro, L.: Intriguing properties of adversarial ml attacks in the problem space. In: Proceedings S&P (2020)
30. Schönherr, L., Kohls, K., Zeiler, S., Holz, T., Kolossa, D.: Adversarial attacks against automatic speech recognition systems via psychoacoustic hiding (2019)
31. Shamir, A., Safran, I., Ronen, E., Dunkelman, O.: A simple explanation for the existence of adversarial examples with small hamming distance. arXiv preprint (2019)
32. Sharif, M., Bhagavatula, S., Bauer, L., Reiter, M.K.: Accessorize to a crime: real and stealthy attacks on state-of-the-art face recognition. In: Proceedings CCS (2016)
33. Sharif, M., Bhagavatula, S., Bauer, L., Reiter, M.K.: A general framework for adversarial examples with objectives. ACM Trans. Priv. Secur. (TOPS) 22(3), 16:1–16:30 (2019)
34. Shokri, R., Stronati, M., Song, C., Shmatikov, V.: Membership inference attacks against machine learning models. In: Proceedings IEEE S&P (2017)
35. Shumailov, I., Zhao, Y., Bates, D., Papernot, N., Mullins, R., Anderson, R.: Sponge examples: energy-latency attacks on neural networks. In: Proceedings IEEE EuroS&P (2021)
36. Szegedy, C., et al.: Intriguing properties of neural networks. In: Proceedings ICLR (2014)
37. Tong, L., et al.: FaceSec: A fine-grained robustness evaluation framework for face recognition systems. In: Proceedings CVPR (2021)
38. Tramèr, F., Zhang, F., Juels, A., Reiter, M.K., Ristenpart, T.: Stealing machine learning models via prediction APIs. In: Proceedings USENIX Security (2016)
39. Wang, J., Liu, Y., Hu, Y., Shi, H., Mei, T.: FaceX-Zoo: a PyTorch toolbox for face recognition. In: Proceedings MM (2021)
40. Wang, X., He, X., Wang, J., He, K.: Admix: enhancing the transferability of adversarial attacks. In: Proceedings ICCV (2021)
41. Wang, Y., Bao, T., Ding, C., Zhu, M.: Face recognition in real-world surveillance videos with deep learning method. In: Proceedings ICIVC (2017)
42. Wu, T., Tong, L., Vorobeychik, Y.: Defending against physically realizable attacks on image classification. In: Proceedings ICLR (2020)
43. Wu, X., He, R., Sun, Z., Tan, T.: A light CNN for deep face representation with noisy labels. IEEE Trans. Inf. Forensics Secur. 13(11), 2884–2896 (2018)

44. Wu, X., Huang, H., Patel, V.M., He, R., Sun, Z.: Disentangled variational representation for heterogeneous face recognition. In: Proceedings AAAI (2019)
45. Xiang, C., Bhagoji, A.N., Sehwag, V., Mittal, P.: PatchGuard: a provably robust defense against adversarial patches via small receptive fields and masking. In: Proceedings USENIX Security (2021)
46. Xiang, C., Mahloujifar, S., Mittal, P.: PatchCleanser: certifiably robust defense against adversarial patches for any image classifier. In: Proceedings USENIX Security (2022)
47. Xiang, C., Mittal, P.: PatchGuard++: efficient provable attack detection against adversarial patches. In: Proceedings ICLRW (2021)
48. Xu, W., Evans, D., Qi, Y.: Feature squeezing: detecting adversarial examples in deep neural networks. In: Proceedings NDSS (2018)
49. Yu, A., Wu, H., Huang, H., Lei, Z., He, R.: LAMP-HQ: a large-scale multi-pose high-quality database and benchmark for NIR-VIS recognition. Int. J. Comp. Vision (IJCV) **129**(5), 1467–1483 (2021)
50. Zhang, H., et al.: ResNeSt: split-attention networks. In: Proceedings CVPR (2022)

A Rowhammer Reproduction Study Using the Blacksmith Fuzzer

Lukas Gerlach[✉], Fabian Thomas, Robert Pietsch, and Michael Schwarz

CISPA Helmholtz Center for Information Security, Saarbrücken, Saarland, Germany
{lukas.gerlach,fabian.thomas,robert.pietsch,michael.schwarz}@cispa.de

Abstract. Rowhammer is a hardware vulnerability that can be exploited to induce bit flips in dynamic random access memory (DRAM), compromising the security of a computer system. Multiple ways of exploiting Rowhammer have been shown and even in the presence of mitigations such as target row refresh (TRR), DRAM modules remain partially vulnerable. In this paper, we present a large-scale reproduction study on the Rowhammer vulnerability using the Blacksmith Rowhammer fuzzer. The main focus of our study is the impact of the fuzzing environment. Our study uses a diverse set of 10 DRAM chips from various manufacturers, with different capacities and memory frequencies. We show that the runtime, used seeds, and DRAM coverage of the fuzzer have been underestimated in previous work. Additionally, we study the entire hardware setup's impact on the transferability of Rowhammer by fuzzing the same DRAM on 4 identical machines. The transferability study heavily relates to Rowhammer-based physically unclonable functions (PUFs) which rely on the stability of Rowhammer-induced bit flips. Our results confirm the findings of the Blacksmith fuzzer, showing that even modern DRAM chips are vulnerable to Rowhammer. In addition, we show that PUFs are challenging to achieve on commodity systems due to the high variability of Rowhammer bit flips.

1 Introduction

The Rowhammer effect was first documented in 2014 [15]. With this effect, bit flips can be induced in the DRAM by rapidly accessing adjacent memory cells in the DRAM. While first deemed unexploitable, multiple exploitation techniques [2,8,22,23,27–29] have been presented, making Rowhammer a threat to the security of systems. Consequently, in addition to multiple academic mitigations [12,15,18,20,25,26,30,31], industry also tried to prevent the exploitation of this effect [13]. However, some implemented mitigations have been bypassed using new hammering techniques [6,9,11,17]. Mounting Rowhammer with countermeasures such as target row refresh (TRR) or error correction code (ECC) memory in place requires sophisticated techniques often discovered using specialized fuzzers to search for hammering patterns automatically [3,6,11].

These fuzzers were evaluated on a large set of different DRAM modules (up to 42 DIMMS) where they report impressive results [6]. However, in contrast to

G. Tsudik et al. (Eds.): ESORICS 2023, LNCS 14346, pp. 62–79, 2024.
https://doi.org/10.1007/978-3-031-51479-1_4

fuzzing papers on software [16], these results are often not reproduced. One reason is that microarchitectural attacks, particularly Rowhammer, require specific expertise [5]. There is a non-trivial configuration phase of the system. In the case of Rowhammer, it is necessary to reverse engineer the DRAM memory addressing function before an attack can be mounted [7,10,21]. As this function depends on the CPU's memory controller, this step adds additional complexity to a rowhammer attack. In addition, attack parameters that work for the specific DRAM module under test must be found. Moreover, multiple DIMMs are required for statistically significant results, making these experiments more expensive than fuzzing software. Hence, even given open-source Rowhammer fuzzers [6,11], it is not trivial to reproduce the results.

In this paper, we evaluate the *reproducibility* of Rowhammer fuzzing runs, showing that the current metric of flips in 12 h is not ideal for comparing fuzzers. For the results, we focus on the *transferability* of Rowhammer patterns across *identical* machines and *identical* DIMMs. More precisely, our analysis focuses on the following research question: *Does the same DIMM show different bit flips on different but identical machines?*

For our setup, we rely on the state-of-the-art open-source Rowhammer fuzzer Blacksmith [11]. Our analysis with 10 DIMMs on 4 *identical* machines shows that the reported results are reproducible on a wide range of commonly-available DIMMs and desktop computers without requiring any special hardware setup or software configuration. Surprisingly, our non-optimized setup discovers 5397 bit flips on average, which aligns with the original paper [11]. However, as the default configuration of the fuzzer only uses 1 GB of randomly mapped memory, the number of discovered flips in 12 h varies significantly, from 0 to 18 142 on the same DIMM. Hence, this shows that the number of bit flips in such a short time frame and over such a comparatively small memory region is not the ideal metric to compare the performance of fuzzers.

To further analyze the *transferability* of the discovered bit flips, we rely on 3 identical DIMMs and 4 identical desktop setups. We analyze both the difference in bit flip between the identical DIMMs on the same machine, and the same DIMM on identical machines. To enable such an analysis, we modify Blacksmith to deterministically map and sweep hammering patterns over a defined memory area. In line with previous work, we show that bit flips are unique to DIMMs, even if they are of the same model. However, we show that the used machine also has a significant impact. When we used a fixed 256 MB memory region and hammering pattern, in the most extreme case, we achieve on average 13 282 bit flips on 3 machines, but no bit flip on the 4th machine. This insight that even identical setups significantly impact bit flips directly affects proposals that rely on Rowhammer as a physical-unclonable function [1,24].

Contributions. The contributions of this paper are:

1. Reproducing the results of Jattke et al. [11] on 4 identical machines and 10 DIMMs, showing that current metrics for comparing Rowhammer fuzzers are not ideal.

2. Study of the transferability of bit flips between identical machines, showing that the impact of the used hardware was underestimated in previous work.
3. Evaluation of DRAM as a physically unclonable function, showing that such constructions suffer from practical issues.

Outline. Sect. 2 provides the necessary background. Section 3 introduces our evaluation methodology. Section 4 presents our results. Section 5 evaluates the usability of Rowhammer as a PUF. Section 6 discusses the implications of our study and potential future work. Section 7 concludes.

2   Background

In the following, we introduce the necessary background to understand the remainder of this paper.

2.1   Rowhammer

Rowhammer is a vulnerability that affects modern DRAM modules, allowing attackers to induce bit flips. Modern DRAM modules are physically organized into rows containing memory cells. Each memory cell can hold a single bit, represented by a capacitor's charge level. Because the capacitor constantly discharges, it must be regularly refreshed to prevent data loss. By design of the DRAM module, data can only be accessed in rows, discharging all capacitors in the addressed row. Therefore, after both read and write accesses, the entire row must be refilled with both the changed and unchanged data. Rowhammer attacks abuse this effect by repeatedly rapidly accessing one or more DRAM rows ("aggressor" rows) to influence neighboring DRAM rows ("victim" rows). Capacitors in neighboring rows then lose their charge more quickly, up to a point where the charge decreases below a threshold necessary to reliable detect the bit's value. This behavior allows an attacker to corrupt memory, thereby creating a potential security threat. As demonstrated by previous research [15,22,23], Rowhammer attacks can reliably flip bits at attacker-chosen addresses by accessing DRAM rows in fixed patterns. Such targeted bit flips can be used for sandbox escapes and privilege-escalation attacks on various systems, including desktop computers [8,15], mobile devices [28], and cloud servers [29], even by a remote attacker [19,27]. In an attempt to prevent Rowhammer attacks, a class of hardware mitigations called Target Row Refresh (TRR) [6] was proposed. These mitigations detect frequently-accessed rows and refresh them and other rows in proximity. While TRR prevents Rowhammer attacks relying on simple hammering patterns, it has been shown that the majority of TRR implementations is still vulnerable to more sophisticated Rowhammer attacks [6,11,17].

2.2   Blacksmith Rowhammer Fuzzer

Blacksmith [11] is a state-of-the-art Rowhammer fuzzer aiming to find memory access patterns that yield particularly high rates of Rowhammer-induced bit flips. It improves on previous Rowhammer attacks by not only considering patterns with a uniform distribution of accesses onto the aggressor rows, but also allowing non-uniform patterns. Moreover, the fuzzer considers patterns that span over multiple refresh intervals, as these significantly improve the number of induced bit flips. Because the search space for non-uniform fuzzing patterns of varying lengths is large, Blacksmith uses a heuristic (called fuzzing in the frequency domain by the authors) to efficiently explore promising hammering patterns. This method has been shown to be highly effective in finding patterns with a high rate of Rowhammer-induced bit flips. In addition, the generated patterns have been shown to be able to bypass mitigations like TRR. TRR is bypassed by particular hammering patterns that are outside the detection scope of current hardware countermeasures [6,11,17].

2.3 Rowhammer as Physically-Unclonable Function (PUF)

Rowhammer can be leveraged as a Physically-unclonable Function (PUF) [1,24], a security primitive that uses the physical variations specific to individual hardware components to generate unique and unpredictable cryptographic keys. For Rowhammer, the physical variation in DRAM cells can be used to generate a unique bit flip sequence that can be used as a basis for further cryptographic operations. As the variations in susceptibility to bit flips vary between DRAM modules, even ones from an identical manufacturing run, the bit flips of each module are unique. However, the reliability of this approach is still an active area of research, as the stability and predictability of the bit sequence can be affected by various factors, such as temperature and voltage fluctuations and the quality of the DRAM module itself. Therefore, PUFs based on Rowhammer require a fuzzy extractor construction [4] to deal with the underlying unstableness of Rowhammer bit flips. In addition, attacks against Rowhammer-based PUF constructions have been proposed [32]. It was shown that given enough observations of a PUF scheme using Rowhammer, an attacker can predict the subsequent PUF response, allowing an attacker to imitate the PUF generated, therefore breaking its security guarantees. In addition, a denial of service attack was shown. While not directly undermining the security guarantees of Rowhammer-based PUFs, this attack renders a PUF based on Rowhammer unusable.

3 Evaluation Methodology

In this section, we describe our methodology for reproducing the Blacksmith Rowhammer fuzzer as well as the impact of the remaining computing system on the presence and frequency of Rowhammer bit flips. By reproducing the results found with the Blacksmith fuzzer, we gain valuable insight into the intricacies in the evaluation of Rowhammer fuzzers. In addition, we further characterize the distribution of Rowhammer bit flips in the tested DRAM modules. To combine both our evaluation goals, we use the Blacksmith fuzzer to find flips on 10 different DDR4 modules and repeat the process on 4 identical machines (Sect. 3.2). As the Blacksmith fuzzer heavily relies on randomization, it depends heavily on the desired property one wants to validate or falsify whether the data it produces is useful. We modify Blacksmith to be deterministic for reproducible runs by employing a fixed seed and ensuring that the same physical memory is mapped between runs. Based on the performed fuzzing runs, we create a data set that we also use for our analysis in Sect. 4.

3.1 Testing Setup

This section describes our testing setup regarding both hardware and methodology. We provide details about the machines and DRAM modules used during our evaluation and introduce the testing setup for the Blacksmith fuzzer.

Tested Machines. We conduct our tests using 4 identical machines, each with an Intel Core i7 9700K CPU, HP 8591 mainboard, and HP HQ-TRE 71025 power supply. All machines run a freshly-installed stock Ubuntu 22.04 using the 5.19.0 Linux kernel. We verify that each machine uses microcode version 0xf0 from May 10, 2022, which is the default microcode with the installed Linux distribution. We reset the BIOS settings to eliminate the influence of BIOS settings on the fuzzing runs to factory default settings. In addition, all machines are placed in one room to minimize the impact of different temperature environments. In the remainder of the paper, we refer to these machines as machine $\mathcal{A}$ to machine $\mathcal{D}$.

Tested DRAM Modules We use 10 different DDR4 DRAM modules of varying memory sizes from 3 different manufacturers. The tested modules range in memory sizes from 8 GB to 32 GB. In addition, they cover a wide range of memory speeds from 2133 MHz up to 3200 MHz. The manufacturing date of the DRAM modules ranges from 2016 to 2022. Further information on the tested DRAM modules is provided in Table 1.

3.2 Fuzzing and Memory Sweep

We set up Blacksmith to run for 12 h, consistent with the evaluation by Jattke et al. [11]. For each module, we perform one run on machines $\mathcal{A}$ to $\mathcal{D}$. We label each run with a combination of DRAM module and machine, e.g., $\mathcal{A}_1$ for machine $\mathcal{A}$ and DRAM module 1. During each fuzzing run, Blacksmith searches for patterns that produce bit flips. We label a fuzzing run successful if it produces at least one bit flip. When a successful fuzzing run is found, it is followed by a memory sweep, where a randomly-mapped 256 MB memory range is tested again using the pattern that produced the most bit flips in the initial run. This configuration is consistent with the Blacksmith paper and allows for a more thorough inspection of bit flips in a smaller chunk of memory.

To study the transferability of the bit flips between the different machines, we rely on the best fuzzing patterns, i.e., the ones producing the most bit flips in our initial runs. To ensure that we always test the same physical memory cells on the DRAM module, we modify Blacksmith to always map the same memory

Table 1. Module information of our tested DIMMs.

Manufacturer	Module Id	Manufactured	Size	Ranks	Frequency	Flips Observed
A	Module 1	2018 Q2	32 GB	2	2666 MHz	✓
	Module 2	2018 Q2	32 GB	2	2666 MHz	✓
	Module 3	2018 Q2	32 GB	2	2666 MHz	✓
	Module 4	2018 Q2	32 GB	2	2666 MHz	✓
	Module 5	2021	8 GB	1	3200 MHz	✓
	Module 6	2021	8 GB	1	3200 MHz	✓
B	Module 7	2017	8 GB	2	3200 MHz	✓
	Module 8	2022	16 GB	2	3200 MHz	✓
C	Module 9	2016	8 GB	2	2133 MHz	✗
	Module 10	2016	8 GB	2	2133 MHz	✗

region when sweeping a fuzzing pattern. We test the best fuzzing patterns found on the identical modules 1, 2 and 4[1] on each of the 4 identical machines, allowing us to study the transferability of bit flips under an identical setup.

4   Results

We present the results of the fuzzing evaluation with regard to the individual runs performed with the unmodified Blacksmith fuzzer. By analyzing the distribution of the found bit flips, we gain additional insights into the bit-flip characteristic of the analyzed DRAM modules. We make several interesting observations. First, 8 out of the 10 tested modules are affected by Rowhammer bit flips on at least one of the test machines, confirming claims from prior work that most modules are affected. Second, Sect. 4.1 shows potential areas for improvement when using simple evaluation criteria such as the number of bit flips or bit flips over time. Third, Sect. 4.2 shows that the bit flips are not uniformly distributed across rows but instead localized within a smaller subset of the rows, and that bit flips with lower hamming weight are more likely, i.e., bit flips where only a few memory cells change their value. Finally, a factor that was previously not analyzed and has considerable influence is the machine used during Rowhammer testing, as we show in Sect. 4.3. As a result, we gain valuable insights into the specifics of Rowhammer fuzzer evaluation that show that current evaluations are not ideal for comparing fuzzers. Building on the result that Rowhammer depends on the entire underlying system, we perform a case study in Sect. 5 showing that its use as a PUF, as proposed by previous work [1,24], is very challenging on a commodity system.

---

[1] DRAM module 3 broke during testing and is therefore excluded in the transferability study.

4.1   Temporal Distribution of Bit Flips

Two standard time-based metrics when evaluating software fuzzers are crashes and coverage over time [16]. While these metrics originate from software fuzzing, they can also find application in evaluating more specialized fuzzers such as Blacksmith. However, as Blacksmith does not produce crashes, we use the number of bit flips over time reported during each fuzzing run.

A common methodology in software fuzzing is dedicating crashes to isolate a unique trigger for each crash [16]. Deduplication, when used in the practical context of vulnerability discovery, simplifies the analysis of crash root causes. Further, deduplication eases the evaluation of a software fuzzer as one crash may have many different root causes, which, when not deduplicated, can also complicate the comparison between different fuzzers. Similarly to the deduplication of crashes in software fuzzing, we also deduplicate the bit flips and count the number of unique bit flips over time. While multiple deduplication granularities are possible as the DRAM is hierarchically organized, we decided to duplicate on a per-row basis. We experimentally evaluated multiple deduplication strategies and found that a per-row deduplication is an effective middle ground allowing for interesting observations. This means that we only count the new rows where a bit flip occurs not the position inside a row. As observed in Sect. 4.2, up to 75 % of all memory cells are vulnerable when hammering long enough.

As seen in Fig. 1, Blacksmith finds bit flips quickly. On average, the time to the first bit flip is 47.78 min, excluding runs that do not produce flips. The higher time to first bit flip is easily explained by two outlier samples where the time to the first bit flip takes multiple hours. This also reflects in the much lower median time to the first bit flip of 3.78 min. Similar differences between the time to first bit flip have been observed by Jattke et al. [11]. In addition, once the first bit flip occurred, further bit flips are consistently found. These observations highlight that Blacksmith's fuzzing strategy can consistently produce patterns that induce bit flips. Overall, a linear relationship exists between time and the number of bit flips, both when considering unique and non-unique bit flips, as seen in Fig. 1. We also calculate the factor with which unique bit flips occur less than general bit flips. We observe that unique bit flips occur around 3 orders of magnitude less often than just any observed bit flip (to be more precise, general bit flips occur 1694 times more often than unique ones). While this factor is comparatively high, the high number of overall bit flips also implies a high number of unique bit flips. Even more interesting, the factor with which unique vs. non-unique bit flips occur, stabilizes quickly after starting a fuzzing run. It also remains stable during the 12 h duration of the run. The fact that this factor stays constant over the time of the fuzzing run indicates that there are still new bit flips found at the end of the run. Therefore, the 12 h duration for each fuzzing run is likely too short to exhaust all unique bit flips in the 1 GB memory area under test by fuzzing. Future work could evaluate similar fuzzers based on the time until no unique flips are found. This strategy can lead to two potentially interesting metrics.

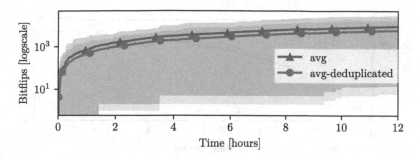

Fig. 1. Flips over time observed by the fuzzing runs. Both duplicated and non-deduplicated bit flips are plotted with the minimum and maximum flips at the current time point as well as the average.

First, the time until no more unique bit flips are found indicates how long a fuzzer needs to reach its optimal coverage, after which point fuzzing for longer produces diminishing returns. The number of unique bit flips yields insight into the maximum reachable performance of the fuzzer. Combining these metrics by dividing the total number of unique bit flips by the time needed to reach a point where little to no new bit flips are found gives a combined metric for the fuzzing performance. Intuitively, one wants many unique bit flips as fast as possible, favoring fuzzers that efficiently explore the DRAM to produce new ones. In addition, this metric enables comparing long-running fuzzers that try to scan the memory thoroughly for a maximum amount of bit flips with ones that are optimized to produce bit flips as quickly as possible.

> **Takeaway** Simply evaluating Rowhammer fuzzers by the number of bit flips they produce in a fixed time interval oversimplifies the comparison.

Second, the coverage, again similar to classic software fuzzers, is another interesting metric. In contrast to coverage metrics from software testing, a much simpler coverage metric suffices for Rowhammer. We monitor how many of the total DRAM rows in the 1 GB memory interval are accessed by Blacksmith during its 12 h fuzzing campaign. As illustrated in Fig. 2, during each of the 12 h fuzzing runs, a coverage of over 90.5 % is reached. Due to the randomized fuzzing strategy that Blacksmith employs, the coverage differs between fuzzing runs, with different runs producing different minimal and maximal coverage. We also see that the increase in global coverage slows down over time as Blacksmith randomly picks addresses in the DRAM. This leads to a situation where the more prolonged the fuzzing is, the more the DRAM has been covered, and the less likely it is to uncover new DRAM locations randomly. This observation can be valuable if a fuzzer should reach maximal global coverage quickly, in which case the design employed by Blacksmith is not ideal. Instead, already

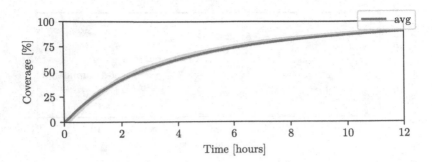

Fig. 2. Coverage of the 1 GB memory region over the time of the 12 h fuzzing run. The margins show the minimum and maximum coverage achieved over all runs at each point in time.

tested DRAM locations could be blocklisted in favor of new untested locations, therefore enabling rapid exploration of the provided memory.

> **Takeaway** Coverage of current Rowhammer fuzzers can be improved by avoiding already fuzzed DRAM cells.

4.2 Spatial Distribution of Bit Flips

In addition to the temporal resolution, i.e., how long it takes to find bit flips, the spatial distribution of the bit flips is a relevant metric. An important starting point is the distribution of Rowhammer-susceptible DRAM rows over the analyzed DRAM module.

We compute the distribution of bit flips among the tested DRAM rows. In the interest of keeping the results readable, we compute a histogram over the rows where we group 256 rows into one bucket. The results of this evaluation are shown in Fig. 3, where it can be observed that the bit flips are not uniformly distributed across the DRAM rows but are concentrated in a small subset of rows. In addition, we observe that this effect is consistent over multiple machines and DRAM modules as well as over the random memory ranges picked by Blacksmith for each fuzzing run. As we observe this effect on independent fuzzing runs, we hypothesize it is more a property of the DRAM itself and not one of the fuzzing patterns generated by Blacksmith. In addition, we observe the same effect even if the memory ranges used for fuzzing reside at a fixed physical address, implying that this effect is not due to the specifics of address allocation from the OS. Our current hypothesis is that the physical memory layout of the DRAM chip is reflected in the observed bit flips. As the physical layout does not need to match the physical addresses, we assume that a more vulnerable DRAM integrated circuit on the DRAM module is indexed at regular intervals yielding the observed patterns. While this effect has to be better understood to determine its root

	0-256	256-512	512-768	768-1024	1024-1280	1280-1536	1536-1792	1792-2048	2048-2304	2304-2560	2560-2816	2816-3072	3072-3328	3328-3584	3584-3840	3840-4096
$\mathcal{A}_1$	243	1575	1092	507	792	899	497	990	1043	1155	457	412	282	955	570	443
$\mathcal{A}_2$	1192	1106	1941	1219	608	753	959	1196	813	288	623	615	334	491	552	666
$\mathcal{A}_3$	1532	1037	1641	1244	2394	1009	1767	932	1702	686	95	885	967	742	757	849
$\mathcal{A}_4$	2745	3138	2129	1792	1476	1939	1550	2265	997	408	1695	794	572	861	708	227
$\mathcal{B}_1$	1088	1429	1952	1057	986	2289	1519	1670	1802	526	407	880	673	604	785	295
$\mathcal{B}_2$	863	1339	1372	1280	789	1177	660	777	573	148	94	602	891	666	111	656
$\mathcal{B}_3$	1287	1769	3264	2908	4338	2063	1755	2977	2041	772	678	965	630	2025	156	1705
$\mathcal{B}_4$	1110	1086	2754	1594	978	942	1047	1544	1062	1230	596	947	461	632	116	1024
$\mathcal{C}_1$	427	364	679	671	1556	989	814	1072	494	534	336	228	239	263	155	403
$\mathcal{C}_2$	210	1504	529	2122	1183	1179	755	1426	668	1121	127	572	446	859	378	38
$\mathcal{C}_3$	739	508	1058	963	1262	843	1100	466	364	389	355	438	856	398	344	127
$\mathcal{C}_4$	301	536	265	128	112	72	173	134	239	198	121	65	64	29	21	180
$\mathcal{D}_1$	14	34	20	20	15	21	28	9	19	4	8	18	2	3	6	8
$\mathcal{D}_2$	6	22	14	5	13	16	13	4	2	4	5	5	4	2	20	9
$\mathcal{D}_3$	15	9	53	40	10	19	19	7	10	7	5	4	12	8	8	2
$\mathcal{D}_4$	36	31	24	19	28	41	34	36	42	20	4	10	10	5	26	8

Fig. 3. Accumulated bit flips per row range on $\mathcal{A}_1$ to $\mathcal{D}_4$ averaged over all banks. It can be seen that flips are not evenly distributed across rows.

cause, we can see potential consequences. A fuzzer searching for Rowhammer bit flips could employ a search strategy favoring memory regions where bit flips already occurred to target the localized bit flips. In addition, an attacker can employ a similar strategy to scan the memory for the required bit flip patterns.

> **Takeaway** Bit flips are not uniformly distributed across DRAM rows. Instead, they are local, mostly occurring in a smaller subset of the rows.

In addition to analyzing the distribution of bit flips across different DRAM rows, we analyze the Hamming weight of bit-flip patterns induced during each fuzzing run. A pattern is a 64-bit bitmask representing the difference between the original and flipped data, i.e., the location of bit flips. Figure 4 shows the results of summing up the occurrences of Hamming weights per machine-DRAM pair. Note that we accumulate the data of all patterns by summing the Hamming weights of the patterns. While most patterns have a Hamming weight of 1, we find up to 5 bit flips per quadword, i.e., a Hamming weight of 5, on $\mathcal{C}_1$ and $\mathcal{C}_4$. This is in line with work by Kim et al. [14,15]. They report up to 4 bit flips. Further, we analyze the maximum flip rate per row. We find up to 364 bit flips per row ($8\,KiB = 65536$ bits) on $\mathcal{C}_4$ with pattern $\mathcal{A}$, giving a maximum flip rate of 0.56 %. This is again in line with Kim et al. [14] who report a maximum flip rate between 0.1 % and 1 % for new DDR4 chips. When analyzing the distribution of bits in the bit-flip patterns, we find that the flipped bits are uniformly distributed in a

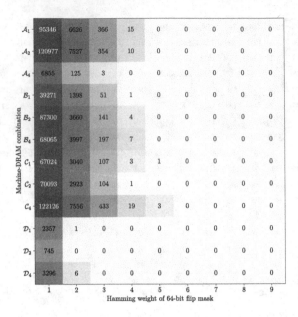

Machine-DRAM combination

	1	2	3	4	5	6	7	8	9
A_1	95346	6626	366	15	0	0	0	0	0
A_2	120977	7527	354	10	0	0	0	0	0
A_4	6855	125	3	0	0	0	0	0	0
B_1	39271	1398	51	1	0	0	0	0	0
B_2	87300	3660	141	4	0	0	0	0	0
B_4	68065	3997	197	7	0	0	0	0	0
C_1	67024	3040	107	3	1	0	0	0	0
C_2	70093	2923	104	1	0	0	0	0	0
C_4	122126	7556	433	19	3	0	0	0	0
D_1	2357	1	0	0	0	0	0	0	0
D_2	745	0	0	0	0	0	0	0	0
D_4	3296	6	0	0	0	0	0	0	0

Hamming weight of 64-bit flip mask

Fig. 4. Distribution of Hamming weights per quadword on machine-DRAM combinations accumulated over all patterns that produce bit flips. The distribution is close to a normal distribution with a mean at around 32.

quadword. This aligns with results by Gruss et al. [8], who report that bit-flip locations are uniformly distributed when averaging over multiple pages.

> **Takeaway** In rare cases, Blacksmith finds patterns that induce up to 5 bit flips per quadword. Further, Blacksmith reaches a maximum flip rate of 0.56 % per hammering run. As reported by related work, the bit-flip locations are uniformly distributed in a quadword.

4.3 Transferability

A key goal of our study is to analyze the transferability of Rowhammer bit flips on the same DRAM module but on different, identical machines. For this, we analyze the observed bit flips induced by a hammering pattern between different machines. The vital difference to the transferability study of Jattke et al. [11] is that we examine the transferability of hammering patterns between machines and not DRAM modules.

We perform the memory sweep on all machines with the best pattern found for the DRAM module on one machine. Each pattern is replayed over the *exact same* physical memory range in the *exact same* order. We take the above steps to eliminate side effects caused by the choice of memory region. As seen in Fig. 3, bit flips are not uniformly distributed across rows. Therefore, picking a different memory and row range could bias the results.

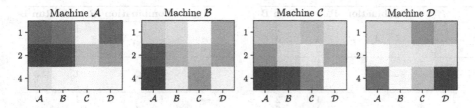

Fig. 5. Transferability of patterns between different machines. Each heatmap illustrates fuzzing runs on one machine over the 3 tested DIMMs with patterns found on all other machines. Darker colors indicate more observed bit flips.

Figure 5 illustrates our results. We observe that the occurrence and count of bit flips depend on the machine. In the most extreme cases, this can lead to cases where we do observe bit flips on one machine but not the other using the same hammering pattern and DRAM module. We suspect that manufacturing differences in non-DRAM parts of the system could induce these differences. One example could be the different frequency scaling behavior of CPUs depending on minor manufacturing differences. Similar differences could also influence the mainboard components and power supply, leading to a different number of observed bit flips.

> **Takeaway** The combination of the machine, hammering pattern and DRAM module impacts the presence and count of bit flips.

5 Case Study: Rowhammer as Physically Unclonable Function

In this section, we further quantify the extent to which the machine in that a DRAM module is installed influences the observed bit flips. This effect directly impacts not only the evaluation of Rowhammer fuzzers but also the use of DRAM as a physically-unclonable function (PUF) [1,24]. Assuming that the bit flips are randomly distributed and dependent on manufacturing differences unique to each DRAM module, a random and unique bit stream can be obtained. This bit stream can then be used as an entropy source for further operations, such as serving as a seed in cryptographic operations. We experimentally quantify the additional error induced by manufacturing differences in the same model of different CPUs.

Schaller et al. [24] conclude that an error rate of 5 % achieved in their experiments is acceptable when using a fuzzy extractor construction [4]. To stay comparable to the work of Schaller et al. [24], we also use the Jaccard index as a measurement of error. The Jaccard index J can be computed between two sets of measurements H_1 and H_2, obtained during two hammering runs, using the formula $J = \frac{|H_1 \cap H_1|}{|H_1 \cup H_2|}$. We store the rows index of the rows that produced bit flips in these

d_J	Combination	Run A	Run B
0.18		1	2
0.11	$\mathcal{A}_1$	1	3
0.16		2	3
0.78		1	2
1.00	$\mathcal{A}_2$	1	3
1.00		2	3
0.39		1	2
0.35	$\mathcal{A}_4$	1	3
0.18		2	3
1.00		1	2
0.30	$\mathcal{B}_1$	1	3
1.00		2	3
0.47		1	2
0.33	$\mathcal{B}_2$	1	3
0.43		2	3
1.00		1	2
1.00	$\mathcal{B}_4$	1	3
1.00		2	3

d_J	Combination	Run A	Run B
1.00		1	2
0.18	$\mathcal{C}_1$	1	3
1.00		2	3
0.39		1	2
0.35	$\mathcal{C}_2$	1	3
0.41		2	3
1.00		1	2
1.00	$\mathcal{C}_4$	1	3
0.35		2	3
1.00		1	2
0.82	$\mathcal{D}_1$	1	3
1.00		2	3
0.78		1	2
0.53	$\mathcal{D}_2$	1	3
0.76		2	3
1.00		1	2
0.50	$\mathcal{D}_4$	1	3
1.00		2	3

Fig. 6. Comparison of three deterministic runs (same machine, same DRAM, same pattern) on machines $\mathcal{A}$-$\mathcal{D}$. The jackard index d_j shows how consistent the runs are, with $d_j = 0$ we observe the same bitflips between two different runs.

sets H_1 and H_2. We focus on the error rate between different machine-DRAM pairs, which is the Jaccard distance computed as $d_J = 1 - J$, where J is the Jaccard index between two fuzzing runs using the same pattern and memory range.

5.1 Reliability

To ensure that machine-DRAM pairs can be used as PUF, we analyze 3 repeated fuzzing runs on the same machine-DRAM pair. Figure 6 illustrates the results. For $\mathcal{A}$, both DRAM modules 1 and 4 give low error rates between the 3 runs, while DRAM 2 has a high error rate. Consequently, modules 1 and 4 could be used as PUF with $\mathcal{A}$, while module 2 cannot be used. On $\mathcal{B}$ to $\mathcal{D}$, we see contrary results. While DRAM module 2 performs best, both modules 1 and 4 cannot be used on any of the 3 machines. On $\mathcal{D}$ we even see that no module works reliably, with error rates above 50 %.

We conclude that DRAM modules may work perfectly with one machine while inducing high error rates on another machine. Further, we conclude that some machines induce bit flips less reliably than others and, therefore, are not suitable for usage as PUFs. Additionally, we conclude that multiple hammering runs are needed for reliable results as can be seen with the runs on $\mathcal{C}_1$, where two runs compared well, while the others had no common flipped rows. Multiple reasons can potentially explain the high error rates on some machines:

– **More diverse hardware**: Our experiments are performed on DRAM modules from multiple vendors. In addition, additional variations could be introduced as we use commodity computers instead of a specialized testing setup.

- **System noise**: We perform our experiments under a normal Linux setup introducing additional unrelated noise on the DRAM modules.
- **Hammering patterns**: We use complex hammering patterns generated by Blacksmith, which could introduce additional noise.

Quantifying if and to which extent the above points change the occurrence of bit flips requires further studies. Especially the relationship between the complexity of a hammering pattern and the determinism of the induced bit flips is important for both the usage of Rowhammer as a PUF and also the reliability of Rowhammer exploits.

> **Takeaway** System noise, hardware differences, and different hammering patterns make it unlikely to trigger identical bit flips reliably on the same DIMM.

5.2   Uniqueness

In this section, we investigate on which parameters the uniqueness of Rowhammer as PUF depends. For that, we evaluate both pairs of the same machine and differing DRAM and differing machine and the same DRAM.

Table 2 gives an overview of the best (lowest error rate) 15 pairs of combinations of machine, DRAM, and pattern. While most pairs result in error rates above 40 %, we find 3 cases with lower error rates. In all of these cases, both memory sweeps that are compared are performed with the same DRAM module, only the machine changes. Further, we see no cases of low error rates when using a different machine as well as a different DRAM module from our test pool. From these observations, we draw the following conclusions:

1. **DRAM has more impact on the error rate than the machine**: The pairs with the lowest error rate all have in common that they share the same DRAM module. Thus, we conclude that DRAM has a higher impact on a low error rate than the machine. This further leads us to the next conclusion.
2. **Uniqueness is guaranteed when DRAM is secret, i.e., not shared**: We see no pair of machine-DRAM combinations with error rates below 50 %, where only the machine matches. Thus, we argue that a secret DRAM module, i.e., a non-shared one, already fulfills the uniqueness guarantees of a PUF. Section 5.1 in contrast shows that the machine has a high impact on the reliability and applicability of Rowhammer as PUF.

> **Takeaway** PUFs with Rowhammer are difficult to achieve on commodity systems. While there are no false positives (no combination of DRAM and machines is the same), the false positive rate is high as it heavily depends on the machine (minor change in the environment leads to non-reproducible output of the PUF).

Table 2. The 15 combinations of machine, DRAM, and pattern, whith the lowest error rate. At least one of the three parameters is different in between the runs. We compute the jackard distance d_j for each of the tested combinations.

d_J	Combination A	Combination B	Same machine	Same DRAM	Pattern
0.21	B_1	C_1	✗	✓	B
0.29	A_1	B_1	✗	✓	A
0.35	A_2	B_2	✗	✓	B
0.40	B_2	C_2	✗	✓	C
0.42	A_2	C_2	✗	✓	A
0.43	A_4	C_4	✗	✓	A
0.52	A_2	C_2	✗	✓	C
0.55	A_2	C_1	✗	✗	C
0.59	B_2	C_1	✗	✗	C
0.60	B_4	C_4	✗	✓	C
0.62	C_1	C_2	✓	✗	C
0.62	C_1	C_2	✓	✗	C
0.62	C_2	C_1	✓	✗	C
0.62	C_2	C_1	✓	✗	C
0.67	C_4	D_4	✗	✓	D

6   Discussion

In this section we discuss the implications of our work and the potential for future work building on our research.

6.1   Implications

In this paper we reproduced the results presented in the Blacksmith paper and quantified the impact of hardware other than the DRAM module on the presence of Rowhammer bit flips. Our results show that Blacksmith effectively finds bit flips in 8 of the 10 tested DRAM modules. However, our results also show that the hardware, beyond the DRAM module, significantly impacts the occurrence and distribution of bit flips. These results do not only have implications on the evaluation of Rowhammer fuzzers but also on the usage of DRAM as a PUF. We show that depending on the machine, even if they have identical hardware, the change in bit flips and therefore the error rate of a Rowhammer-based PUF can reach over 80 %.

Our results confirm the ongoing threat of Rowhammer as an attack vector. The fact that Blacksmith can find bit flips in 8 of the 10 tested DRAM modules again underlines the need for effective Rowhammer countermeasures. Our results also show that the spatial distribution of bit flips is an important metric to consider when evaluating a Rowhammer attack's effectiveness.

6.2 Future Work

Future work could include evaluating the performance of Blacksmith against other Rowhammer fuzzers. Our study shows that Blacksmith is effective in finding bit flips in various DRAM modules, but it is unclear how it compares to other search strategies employed in other fuzzers. Our analysis also shows that a simple metric such as bit flips in a 12 % run can be misleading when comparing Rowhammer fuzzers. Therefore, future work should explore methods to fairly and reliably compare fuzzers, which is challenging given that the amount of Rowhammer bit flips strongly depends on the tested DRAM module.

Another avenue for future research is to analyze the impact of further factors, such as specific CPU and mainboard features, on the occurrence and distribution of bit flips. In addition, a study with more diverse hardware and uniform DRAM modules could be performed, further quantifying the impact of hardware other than the DRAM module on Rowhammer. This information could aid the design of better Rowhammer countermeasures and more effective Rowhammer attacks.

Lastly, fundamental observations regarding the Rowhammer effect could be further quantified. We observed that the bit flips found by Blacksmith were not uniformly distributed across DRAM. In addition, further characterizing the bit flip patterns found by Blacksmith beyond the hamming weight of the bit flips could reveal insights about the distribution of bit flips inside a single row.

7 Conclusion

In this paper, we presented a reproduction study on the Rowhammer security vulnerability using the Blacksmith Rowhammer fuzzer. We also investigated the impact of the entire hardware setup on the transferability of Rowhammer flips across different but identical machines. With 8 out of 10 DDR4 DIMMs showing bit flips, the findings revealed that the Rowhammer vulnerability is still prevalent in modern DRAM chips and could be easily reproduced using the correct tools. Additionally, identical machines were utilized to determine the transferability and variability of the Rowhammer effect between different system setups. This transferability study was closely related to Rowhammer-based physically unclonable functions (PUF), which depend on the stability of Rowhammer-induced bit flips. In conclusion, the results confirmed the findings of the Blacksmith fuzzer, demonstrating that even modern DRAM chips were vulnerable to Rowhammer. However, we also showed that the fair comparison of Rowhammer fuzzers is difficult due to the hardware-dependent fuzzing environment. Finally, our results indicate that achieving PUF on commodity systems is challenging due to the high variability of Rowhammer bit flips.

Acknowledgment. We thank our anonymous reviewers for their valuable feedback. We thank Michele Marazzi for fruitful discussions.

References

1. Anagnostopoulos, N.A., et al.: Intrinsic run-time row hammer PUFs: leveraging the row hammer effect for run-time cryptography and improved security. In: Cryptography (2018)
2. Bosman, E., Razavi, K., Bos, H., Giuffrida, C.: Dedup est machina: memory deduplication as an advanced exploitation vector. In: S&P (2016)
3. Cojocar, L., Razavi, K., Giuffrida, C., Bos, H.: Exploiting correcting codes: on the effectiveness of ECC memory against rowhammer attacks. In: S&P (2019)
4. Dodis, Y., Reyzin, L., Smith, A.: Fuzzy extractors: how to generate strong keys from biometrics and other noisy data. In: Cachin, C., Camenisch, J.L. (eds.) EUROCRYPT 2004. LNCS, vol. 3027, pp. 523–540. Springer, Heidelberg (2004). https://doi.org/10.1007/978-3-540-24676-3_31
5. Easdon, C., Schwarz, M., Schwarzl, M., Gruss, D.: Rapid prototyping for microarchitectural attacks. In: USENIX Security (2022)
6. Frigo, P., et al.: TRRespass: exploiting the many sides of target row refresh. In: S&P (2020)
7. Gerlach, L., Schwarz, S., Faroß, N., Schwarz, M.: Efficient and generic microarchitectural hash-function recovery. In: S&P (2024)
8. Gruss, D., et al.: Another flip in the wall of Rowhammer defenses. In: S&P (2018)
9. Hassan, H., Can Tuğrul, Y., Kim, J.S., Van der Veen, V., Razavi, K., Mutlu, O.: Uncovering In-DRAM RowHammer protection mechanisms: a new methodology, custom RowHammer patterns, and implications. In: IEE MICRO, 2021, extended classification tree and PoCs at https://transient.fail/
10. Helm, C., Akiyama, S., Taura, K.: Reliable reverse engineering of intel dram addressing using performance counters. In: International Symposium on Modeling, Analysis, and Simulation of Computer and Telecommunication Systems (MASCOTS) (2020)
11. Jattke, P., van der Veen, V., Frigo, P., Gunter, S., Razavi, K.: Blacksmith: scalable rowhammering in the frequency domain. In: S&P (2022)
12. Juffinger, J., Lamster, L., Kogler, A., Eichlseder, M., Lipp, M., Gruss, D.: CSI: Rowhammer-cryptographic security and integrity against rowhammer. In: IEEE S&P (2022)
13. Kaczmarski, M.: Thoughts on Intel ® Xeon ® E5-2600 v2 product family performance optimisation – component selection guidelines, August 2014. http://infobazy.gda.pl/2014/pliki/prezentacje/d2s2e4-Kaczmarski-Optymalna.pdf
14. Kim, J.S., et al.: Revisiting RowHammer: an experimental analysis of modern DRAM devices and mitigation techniques. In: ISCA (2020)
15. Kim, Y., et al.: Flipping bits in memory without accessing them: an experimental study of DRAM disturbance errors. In: ISCA (2014)
16. Klees, G., Ruef, A., Cooper, B., Wei, S., Hicks, M.: Evaluating fuzz testing. In: SIGSAC (2018)
17. Kogler, A., et al.: Half-double: hammering from the next row over. In: USENIX Security Symposium (2022)
18. Lee, E., Kang, I., Lee, S., Suh, G.E., Ahn, J.H.: Twice: preventing row-hammering by exploiting time window counters. In: ISACA (2019)
19. Lipp, M.et al.: Nethammer: inducing Rowhammer faults through network requests. In: SILM Workshop (2020)
20. Park, Y., Kwon, W., Lee, E., Ham, T.J., Ahn, J.H., Lee, J.W.: Graphene: strong yet lightweight row hammer protection. In; MICRO (2020)

21. Pessl, P., Gruss, D., Maurice, C., Schwarz, M., Mangard, S.: DRAMA: exploiting DRAM addressing for cross-CPU attacks. In: USENIX Security Symposium (2016)
22. Qiao, R., Seaborn, M.: A new approach for Rowhammer attacks. In: International Symposium on Hardware Oriented Security and Trust (2016)
23. Razavi, K., Gras, B., Bosman, E., Preneel, B., Giuffrida, C., Bos, H.: Flip feng shui: hammering a needle in the software stack. In: USENIX Security Symposium (2016)
24. Schaller, A., et al.: Intrinsic Rowhammer PUFs: leveraging the Rowhammer effect for improved security. In: Hardware Oriented Security and Trust (HOST) (2017)
25. Seyedzadeh, S.M., Jones, A.K., Melhem, R.: Mitigating wordline crosstalk using adaptive trees of counters. In: ISCA. IEEE (2018)
26. Son, M., Park, H., Ahn, J., Yoo, S.: Making dram stronger against row hammering. In: DAC (2017)
27. Tatar, A., Krishnan, R., Athanasopoulos, E., Giuffrida, C., Bos, H., Razavi, K.: Throwhammer: Rowhammer attacks over the network and defenses. In: USENIX ATC (2018)
28. van der Veen, V., et al.: Drammer: deterministic Rowhammer attacks on mobile platforms. In: CCS (2016)
29. Xiao, Y., Zhang, X., Zhang, Y., Teodorescu, R.: One bit flips, one cloud flops: cross-VM row hammer attacks and privilege escalation. In: USENIX Security Symposium (2016)
30. Yağlıkçı, A.G., et al.: BlockHammer: preventing RowHammer at low cost by black-listing rapidly-accessed DRAM rows. In: HPCA (2021)
31. You, J.M., Yang, J.-S.: MRLoc: mitigating row-hammering based on memory locality. In: DAC (2019)
32. Zeitouni, S., Gens, D., Sadeghi, A.-R.: It's hammer time: how to attack (rowhammer-based) dram-PUFs. In: DAC (2018)

Reviving Meltdown 3a

Daniel Weber[✉], Fabian Thomas, Lukas Gerlach, Ruiyi Zhang,
and Michael Schwarz

CISPA Helmholtz Center for Information Security, Saarbrücken, Saarland, Germany
{daniel.weber,fabian.thomas,lukas.gerlach,ruiyi.zhang,
michael.schwarz}@cispa.de

Abstract. Since the initial discovery of Meltdown and Spectre in 2017, different variants of these attacks have been discovered. One often overlooked variant is Meltdown 3a, also known as Meltdown-CPL-REG. Even though Meltdown-CPL-REG was initially discovered in 2018, the available information regarding the vulnerability is still sparse.

In this paper, we analyze Meltdown-CPL-REG on 19 different CPUs from different vendors using an automated tool. We observe that the impact is more diverse than documented and differs from CPU to CPU. Surprisingly, while the newest Intel CPUs do not seem affected by Meltdown-CPL-REG, the newest available AMD CPUs (Zen3+) are still affected by the vulnerability. Furthermore, given our attack primitive CounterLeak, we show that besides up-to-date patches, Meltdown-CPL-REG can still be exploited as we reenable performance-counter-based attacks on cryptographic algorithms, break KASLR, and mount Spectre attacks. Although Meltdown-CPL-REG is not as powerful as other transient-execution attacks, its attack surface should not be underestimated.

1 Introduction

Microarchitectural side-channel attacks have been known for several decades [31]. These attacks exploit the side effects of CPU implementations to infer metadata about actual data being processed by the CPU. Well-known examples of microarchitectural side-channel attacks include cache attacks, e.g., Flush+Reload [67] or Prime+Probe [47], which have been used to leak cryptographic secrets [4,37,67] or violate the privacy of users, e.g., by spying on user input [19,34,44,55]. Another example of side-channel attacks are attacks based on the CPUs performance counters [8,12,58]. However, these attacks are considered mitigated as access to performance counters is restricted on modern CPUs [12].

In 2017, transient execution attacks were first discovered in the form of Meltdown [36] and Spectre [30]. Shortly afterward, a variety of transient execution attacks were discovered [10,32,40,50,51,56,61,65]. One attack that is often considered less powerful than other variations, and thus easily overshadowed by the discovery of other variants, is Meltdown 3a [6,10], later on, referred to as Meltdown-CPL-REG in the extended transient-execution attack classification by Canella et al. [10]. Meltdown-CPL-REG allows an unprivileged attacker to leak

G. Tsudik et al. (Eds.): ESORICS 2023, LNCS 14346, pp. 80–99, 2024.
https://doi.org/10.1007/978-3-031-51479-1_5

the content of system registers restricted to privileged access. After the discovery of the attack, CPU vendors reacted with microcode updates to fix the vulnerabilities [6,25]. More precisely, CPU vendors fixed the vulnerability for system registers containing confidential information, such as model-specific registers.

In this paper, we show that Meltdown-CPL-REG exposes a more complex attack surface than originally thought, which allows an attacker to exploit it, even 5 years after the initial discovery of the attack. Although the Meltdown variant itself is known, there is no systematic analysis yet. Thus, we introduce RegCheck, an automated tool to test x86 CPUs for various Meltdown-CPL-REG variants. Our analysis using RegCheck reveals two main insights. First, CPUs that are vulnerable to Meltdown-CPL-REG do not show the same leakage for all system registers. Instead, the analysis shows that different CPUs expose leakage of different system registers. Hence, the category Meltdown-CPL-REG is too coarse-grained to determine if a CPU is affected. The official tables published by Intel [25] comment only on the leakage of the rdmsr instruction. Nevertheless, RegCheck shows that for some of these CPUs, there is at least one system register that can be leaked. Second, the fact that a CPU is unaffected by the original Meltdown attack, i.e., Meltdown-US-L1 [10,36], does not imply that the CPU is also unaffected by Meltdown-CPL-REG as we observe leakage until the newest tested AMD CPUs. Our analysis shows that while Meltdown-CPL-REG was mitigated using microcode updates for system registers containing confidential data, Meltdown-CPL-REG is still possible on modern CPUs for those privileged registers that are not considered confidential, including registers containing only metadata about a program, such as performance counters.

Based on these observations, we introduce the attack primitive Counter-Leak. CounterLeak allows unprivileged attackers to read performance counters, thereby leaking performance monitoring metadata about applications running on a system. This shows that the state-of-the-art Meltdown-CPL-REG mitigations are insufficient for protecting against side-channel leakage. In our proof-of-concept attack, we read the performance counters to leak meta information about applications. We encode transiently-read data in the form of a Spectre attack with 66.7bit/s, but with a generic encoding gadget. We also break the security mitigation Kernel Address Space Layout Randomization (KASLR) by leaking meta information of the page-table walker when accessing potential kernel pages. Furthermore, CounterLeak re-enables attacks that rely on performance counters [3,7]. These attacks are considered mitigated because the required performance interface was made privileged. Our attack extracts an RSA key from a square-and-multiply implementation based on MbedTLS. We demonstrate a full key recovery of a 2048-bit key within 15min. We also show that CounterLeak can be used to break the Zigzagger branch-shadowing mitigation [33]. While all these attacks require that the underlying system has performance counters enabled, this is the case for various performance-counter-based defenses that were proposed [11,29,42,43,46,63,64,69,71,72]. Thus, we stress that when designing defense tools, it is crucial to evaluate the additional attack surface introduced by these tools.

To summarize, we make the following contributions:

1. We analyze 19 CPUs of different vendors using an automated tool, showing that Meltdown-CPL-REG was never fully mitigated and can still be exploited. The analysis tool is open-source and can be found on GitHub[1].
2. We use our side channel for a novel Spectre attack using performance counters and to bypass KASLR based on the performance characteristics of the page-table walker.
3. We re-enable attacks on cryptographic libraries.

Outline. Section 2 provides background. Section 3 discusses our analysis of Meltdown-CPL-REG across different Intel and AMD CPUs. Section 4 presents the CounterLeak primitive, and Sect. 5 evaluates the primitive. Section 6 shows 4 case studies based on the attack primitive. Section 7 discusses mitigations to prevent the exploitation of Meltdown-CPL-REG and CounterLeak. Section 8 discusses related work and the generalization of our insights. Section 9 concludes.

Responsible Disclosure. We disclosed our findings to Intel on February 15, 2023 and AMD on February 16, 2023. While both vendors got back to us, neither plan to roll out mitigations for the new findings.

2   Background

In this section, we provide the background for this paper. We introduce performance counters as we attack this interface in the remainder of the paper. We introduce side channels and transient-execution attacks, as these concepts are crucial for the understanding of our attack implementation.

2.1   Performance Counters

Modern CPUs expose performance counters to help developers analyze and benchmark their programs. Performance counters keep track of different microarchitectural events, such as the number of issued micro-operations or the number of evicted cache lines from the L1D cache. Performance counters are programmed to record a specific event. The current count of the event can be read using the x86 instruction `rdpmc`. The privilege level needed to execute `rdpmc` can be configured by the operating system. For example, Linux exposes this configuration via the file `/sys/devices/cpu/rdpmc`. In the past, unprivileged access to performance counters was exploited to mount side-channel attacks and break KASLR [12,58]. Thus, modern operating systems, such as Debian 11, Ubuntu 20.04, or Fedora 35, disallow the access to the performance monitoring interface.

---

[1] https://github.com/cispa/regcheck.

2.2   Side Channels

The term side channel refers to a meta information leaking from a system that can be used to reason about the actual inaccessible data being processed by the system. In CPU microarchitectures, this meta information occurs in various forms, including power usage [35], access timings [18,47], and contention [5,16,45]. An attack exploiting observable meta information is referred to as a side-channel attack. Microarchitectural software-based side-channel attacks (in the remainder of this paper just referred to as "side-channel attacks") have been demonstrated against cryptographic algorithms and libraries [8,38,47,67], to spy on users [55], and to break security boundaries [12,13,17]. Over the last few decades, researchers have demonstrated side-channel attacks based on several microarchitectural components, such as the CPU caches [18,47,48,67], the execution units [5,52], or the component's power consumption [35].

2.3   Transient-Execution Attacks

Transient-execution attacks exploit performance optimizations of the microarchitecture. They are split into two major categories, namely Meltdown-type and Spectre-type attacks, based on the type of performance optimization they exploit [10,27]. While Spectre-type attacks exploit branch predictors, Meltdown-type attacks exploit faulting instructions for which the processor continues to execute depending instructions. These instructions can compute with the values of the faulting instructions until the fault is recognized by the CPU and the instruction stream is rolled back to before the faulting instruction. These instructions that were executed but never architecturally visible because of the roll-back, are called transient instructions [10,27]. One Meltdown-type attack that is typically considered less critical, is Meltdown-CPL-REG (initially called Meltdown 3a) [6,10,23]. Meltdown-CPL-REG allows an unprivileged attacker to leak the content of privileged system registers. Hereby, the attacker reads the system registers via a designated instruction such as rdmsr and encodes the content into a microarchitectural element before the roll-back occurs. Afterward, the attacker can decode this information using a side-channel attack, thus leaking the system register's content. To mitigate the impact of Meltdown-CPL-REG, CPU vendors provide microcode updates for affected systems [6,25].

3   Analysis of Meltdown-CPL-REG

For Meltdown-CPL-REG, microcode prevents the leakage of system registers containing sensitive values. However, other registers containing meta-data about applications can still be leaked, enabling another source of side-channel leakage. We present the first systematic analysis of Meltdown-CPL-REG [6,10,23] to analyze the remaining attack surface after applying state-of-the-art microcode patches. To systematically analyze CPUs, we design RegCheck to test a CPU for different Meltdown-CPL-REG variants automatically. Our analysis of 19 systems leads to two main insights. First, if a system is vulnerable to Meltdown-CPL-REG, this does not mean that *all* system registers are affected. Second, even fully patched recent CPUs unaffected by the original Meltdown attack (Meltdown-US-L1) [36] can be vulnerable to Meltdown-CPL-REG.

Design and Implementation. Our prototype of RegCheck is developed for Intel and AMD CPUs running Linux. Note that the same approach can be ported to other architectures, e.g., to support Arm CPUs, as this is purely an engineering task. RegCheck tests a list of different system registers that are either only accessible for privileged users or can be configured to only allow privileged access. The list is based on Intel's list of affected registers [23]. We provide a complete list of analyzed system registers in Table 1. The inner workings of RegCheck can be broken down into two steps:

First, RegCheck changes the kernel parameters to a consistent state for the measurements. More precisely, one CPU core is isolated using the isolcpus kernel parameter, and unprivileged access to rdfsbase and rdgsbase is disabled using the nofsgsbase kernel parameter. Similarly, the access to further system registers which are not permanently restricted to privileged access, e.g., performance counters (cf. Sect. 2.1), is configured to prevent unprivileged access to these registers before testing. After applying these settings, RegCheck executes on the isolated CPU core to reduce the system noise for its measurements. Next, for each system register, RegCheck tries to reason about its exploitability. To do so, RegCheck tries to exploit Meltdown-CPL-REG and encode 8 bits of the system register into a lookup array. The encoding is done by transiently accessing the corresponding index of the array, e.g., if the leaked bits form the value 7, then an access to array[7 * N] is performed. The resulting fault can either be suppressed or handled. For RegCheck we choose to handle the fault using a signal handler as this approach is portable to all modern CPUs. Our implementation varies N from 1024 to 4096 bytes to find a good tradeoff between the size of memory pages needed to encode the values while still preventing different accessing from either directly going into the same cache line or prefetching other array entries. Note that we choose to encode 8 bits instead of only 1 bit to distinguish actual leakage from system noise better. After encoding these bits, the tool checks whether a transient access to any index has taken place by iterating over the array and performing Flush+Reload, i.e., timing the memory access to each array index. If RegCheck succeeds at leaking the target system register multiple times, it flags it as vulnerable. We test our tool on Intel and AMD CPUs from different generations. All tests use the latest microcode available in the Ubuntu repositories. For further details on the specific microcode version used we refer the reader to Table 2.

Affected Registers. The main insight from our analysis is that not all privileged registers are affected in the same way by Meltdown-CPL-REG. This is especially interesting because Intel's list of CPUs affected by certain vulnerabilities [25] (accessed May 2023) only lists CPUs where the rdmsr instruction can be exploited by Meltdown-CPL-REG. However, our results in Table 2 show that some CPUs that Intel flags as unaffected by the Meltdown-CPL-REG rdmsr

Table 1. System registers and their access instructions tested by RegCheck.

Access Instruction	Details
rdpmc	Reads the specified Performance counter
rdtsc	Reads the CPU timestamp counter
rdtscp	Reads the CPU timestamp counter
mov CRx	Loads the Control registers 0–8
mov DRx	Loads the Debug registers 0–7
rdfsbase	Retrieves segment selector of the FS segment base register
rdgsbase	Retrieves segment selector of the GS segment base register
rdmsr	Model Specific Registers
str	Loads the segment selector of the Task register
sldt	Loads the segment selector from the Local Descriptor Table register
sidt	Loads the segment selector from the Interrupt Descriptor Table register
sgdt	Loads the segment selector from the Global Descriptor Table register
smsw	Loads the Machine status word

leakage can still be exploited to leak the contents of other system registers, such as the performance counters using rdpmc. This, for example, is the case for the Intel Celeron J4005 and the Intel Celeron N3350. The results in Table 2 show that the instruction rdfsbase leaks on 8 out of 14 CPUs affected by Meltdown-CPL-REG. The CPU timestamp counter accessed via rdtsc or rdtscp leaks on 2 out of 14 affected CPUs. Performance counter leak on 3 of the affected CPUs via rdpmc. A possible explanation for these different leakage rates could be that for executing rdpmc, the CPU has to decode an argument of the instruction, i.e., the index of the access performance counter stored in RCX, while for rdtsc, rdtscp, and rdfsbase all required information to fetch the requested data is available, leading to a potentially simpler execution path. Nevertheless, the CPUs where rdpmc is vulnerable do not show a superset of the vulnerable instructions compared to the other systems. Even though these systems show vulnerable rdpmc implementations, we could not verify further leakage.

Affected CPUs. Our second insight is that the fact that CPUs are vulnerable to Meltdown-US-L1 is not related to whether a CPU is also vulnerable to Meltdown-CPL-REG, as shown in Table 2. In other words, we can leak from system registers of CPUs that are affected by Meltdown-US-L1 and of CPUs not affected by Meltdown-US-L1. This is especially surprising for recently released CPUs, such as the Ryzen 9 6900HX. We observe that the tested Intel CPUs from Alder Lake onward do not show leakage, while newer AMD CPUs do.

RegCheck Limitations. The current proof-of-concept implementation of our tool RegCheck comes with different limitations. We do not check for the leakage of swapgs as previous work has already analyzed this instruction and its leakage potential [39]. We neither check the xgetbv instruction. The reason for the latter is that to prevent unprivileged access to xgetbv, RegCheck needs to set the OSXSAVE bit of CR4, which crashes the tested OS. A detailed list of the analyzed system registers is shown in Table 1.

Table 2. CPUs tested by RegCheck for Meltdown-CPL-REG. "U" means we could not verify if an actual timestamp is leaked. "ZF" means that only the value 0 is returned transiently. Additionally, we annotate machines that are vulnerable to the original Meltdown attack.

CPU	μcode	μarch	Release	MD-US	Leaking Instructions
Intel Core i5-2520M	0x2f	Sandy Bridge	2011	Yes	rdtsc, rdtscp
Intel Core i5-3230M	0x21	Ivy Bridge	2013	Yes	rdtsc, rdtscp, sldt
Intel Core i3-4160T	0x28	Haswell	2014	Yes	rdfsbase, rdgsbase
Intel Core i3-5010U	0x2f	Broadwell	2015	Yes	rdfsbase, rdgsbase, rdtsc (U), rdtscp (U)
Intel Atom x5-Z8350	0x411	Cherry Trail	2016	Yes	rdpmc
Intel Celeron N3550	0x28	Apollo Lake	2016	No	rdpmc
Intel Celeron J4005	0x3c	Gemini Lake	2017	Yes	rdpmc
Intel Core i3-7100T	0xf0	Kaby Lake	2017	Yes	rdfsbase, rdgsbase
Intel Core i3-1005G1	0xb2	Ice Lake	2019	No	–
Intel Core i7-10510U	0xf0	Comet Lake	2019	No	rdfsbase, rdgsbase
Intel Core i7-1185G7	0xa4	Tiger Lake	2020	No	–
Intel Celeron N4500	0x240000023	Jasper Lake	2021	No	rdfsbase (ZF), rdgsbase (ZF), sldt (ZF)
Intel Core i9-12900K	0x22	Alder Lake	2021	No	–
Intel Atom x6425E	0x17	Elkhart Lake	2021	No	–
AMD GX-415GA	0x700010f	Jaguar	2013	No	–
AMD Ryzen 5 2500U	0x810100b	Zen	2017	No	rdfsbase, rdgsbase
AMD Ryzen 5 3550H	0x8108102	Zen+	2019	No	rdfsbase, rdgsbase
AMD Epyc 7252	0x8301055	Rome	2019	No	rdfsbase, rdgsbase, str (ZF)
AMD Ryzen 9 6900HX	0xa404102	Zen 3+	2022	No	rdfsbase, rdgsbase

Table 2 flags rdtsc and rdtscp for certain instances with an "U" (short for "unverified"). On these systems, we observed leakage from the system registers, but could not verify that the leakage stems from the CPU timestamp counter. The reason for this is that RegCheck uses a counting thread as a timer for analyzing the instructions rdtsc and rdtscp. However, this timer does not work reliably on CPUs not supporting hyperthreading, as the counting and attacker thread yield a more accurate timer when both threads execute on co-located hyperthreads. Table 2 also has system registers flagged with "ZF" (short for "zero forwarding"). For these registers, an access always returns the value 0 instead of the actual value. While such behavior intuitively sounds invulnerable, instructions forwarding zero values already led to microarchitectural attacks [9,60].

4   Attack Primitive

In this section, we introduce our attack primitive CounterLeak. CounterLeak exploits Meltdown-CPL-REG to leak performance-counter values using rdpmc to infer side-channel information about program executions.

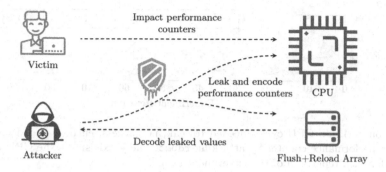

Fig. 1. Meltdown-CPL-REG leaking system registers, such as performance counters.

4.1   Threat Model

We assume an unprivileged attacker with native code execution. We further assume bug-free victim software, e.g., the absence of memory corruption or logical vulnerabilities. However, our attacker model relies on side-channel vulnerabilities, i.e., we assume secret-dependent control or data flow in the victim application. Even though our attacks are, in theory, mountable from inside virtual machines, we did not explicitly test this, and attackers could only target victims inside their own virtual machine and not the hypervisor or other virtual machines. While this weakens the attack surface, intra-VM attacks are still a realistic scenario, e.g., in container-based environments. We target only Intel and AMD CPUs in this work. Note that Meltdown-CPL-REG is also exploitable on Arm [6] but we consider further architectures out of scope for the experiments conducted in this paper and only discuss them in Sect. 8.

4.2   CounterLeak

The CounterLeak attack primitive relies on Meltdown-CPL-REG. We use Meltdown-CPL-REG to infer side-channel information about a victim program. Based on our systematic analysis using RegCheck, and the publicly-available information regarding Meltdown-CPL-REG by Intel [23], we build our attack primitive on top of rdpmc. rdpmc provides a generic but privileged interface to performance counters. Access to these performance counters leaks information about the program execution that can be exploited for side-channel attacks [8,12,58].

Attack Overview. CounterLeak relies on Meltdown-CPL-REG to leak the content of a performance counter. We assume that the system already has a performance counter programmed. This is the case if the system uses performance counters for attack detection, as suggested by previous work [20,28,46,69]. For example, Cloudflare relies on performance counters to detect Spectre attacks [62]. An attacker leaks the performance-counter values by encoding the transiently-read return value of the rdpmc instruction into the microarchitecture and recovers it using a side channel.

Implementation. In line with previous Meltdown-type attacks [10,30,36,41, 56,59,61], we use the CPU cache to encode the transiently-leaked values and

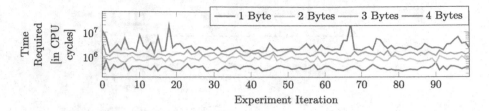

Fig. 2. CounterLeak: CPU cycles needed to leak, i.e., access, encode, and decode, n bytes of a performance counter by attacking `rdpmc`. The y-axis shows the CPU cycles required for each repetition of the experiment (x-axis).

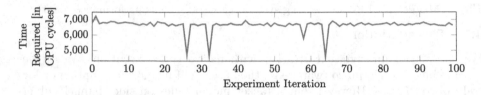

Fig. 3. CounterLeak: CPU cycles needed to transiently encode 4 bytes of the CPU timestamp counter. The y-axis shows the CPU cycles required for each repetition of the experiment (x-axis).

Flush+Reload as the covert channel to make the values architecturally visible. We support leakage of 1 to 4 bytes per `rdpmc` invocation by encoding each byte into the cache state of an array consisting of 256 pages. The more data is encoded into the microarchitecture, the better the resolution of the underlying performance counter value. However, this also leads to a slower decoding phase, as more Flush+Reload attacks are required. For leaking a single byte, at most 256 Flush+Reload attacks are necessary, while for leaking 4 bytes, at most 1024 Flush+Reload attacks are necessary. We evaluate this trade-off in Sect. 5.

5   Evaluation

In this section, we evaluate the attack primitive CounterLeak which is based on Meltdown-CPL-REG. All evaluations use our proof-of-concept implementation on an Intel Celeron J4005 running Ubuntu 20.04 with Linux kernel 5.4.0.

The most important property in our evaluation is the temporal resolution of CounterLeak, i.e., the time between two measurements. This property reflects how fine-grained the information can be leaked by the exploit. We evaluate the time it takes to leak n bytes of a system register. This measurement directly gives us the temporal resolution of the attack. We observe that the implementation leaks 1 byte of a system register in, on average, 348 257 cycles ($n = 100$). Figure 2 summarizes the time an attacker needs to leak the content of a performance counter when leaking n bytes within one transient window. We emphasize that this is a good indication of the theoretical performance of this attack, as an attacker can likely mount exploits by only leaking parts of the system register.

We also require only partial leakage for our attacks discussed in Sect. 6. Note that the temporal resolution mostly affects the execution time of an attack but does not prevent an attack. An attacker can often compensate for a lower temporal resolution by averaging over repeated measurements [35].

Still, whereas our complete attack primitive takes millions of CPU cycles for one iteration (cf. Fig. 2), the actual time spent encoding multiple bytes of a system register is significantly shorter. While the time needed to leak n bytes of a performance counter, i.e., the attack's temporal resolution, is important for repeated measurements, another critical metric is the time that an attacker needs to encode a value in the CPU cache. This metric is especially important for event-driven attack scenario, i.e., whenever the attacker wants to take a measurement after a certain event has happened. To evaluate the time it takes to encode a value, we record the time needed to encode the value of the timestamp register over 100 runs. Figure 3 shows the results. We observe that the average time between the faulting access and the first subsequent attacker-controlled instruction when encoding 4 bytes simultaneously is 6655 cycles. Whereas the effective blindspot of our attack is higher, this time yields the offset between an event triggering a measurement in the attacker code and the measurement itself.

6 Case Studies

In this section, we introduce 4 case studies demonstrating CounterLeak. We demonstrate a Spectre proof-of-concept (PoC) (Sect. 6.1) and break KASLR by monitoring the behavior of page walks (Sect. 6.2). To demonstrate that our side channels re-enable mitigated attacks, we leak a 2048-bit RSA private key from a square-and-multiply implementation found in MbedTLS using CounterLeak (Sect. 6.3). Lastly, we show that we can break the branch-shadowing mitigation proposed by Lee et al. [33] using CounterLeak (Sect. 6.4).

6.1 Spectre with CounterLeak

In this case study, we demonstrate a Spectre-type attack [10,30] with our CounterLeak primitive to leak otherwise inaccessible data. We build a Spectre-PHT [10,30] PoC with a performance counter as covert channel.

Target Performance Counter. We target a performance counter that tracks speculative events [49], such as CYCLES_DIV_BUSY.ALL and assume that it is either activated or can be enabled by the attacker. Note that depending on the victim's code, the discussed attack can also be mounted with a different performance counter. The only requirement is that the accessed secret can be encoded in branches that can be distinguished based on any performance counter.

Attack Overview. We attack a Spectre gadget of the form

```
1 if (i >= 0 && i < array_size) {
2     int tmp = (array[i] >> offset);
3     if ((tmp & 1))  x / y;
4 }
```

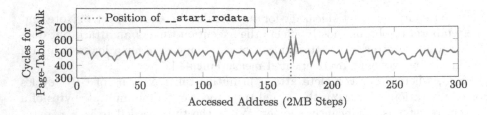

Fig. 4. The leaked values of `DTLB_LOAD_MISSES.WALK_COMPLETED_2M_4M` when iterating over the potential locations where the Linux kernel could be mapped. The page-table walk needs longer when the address is the actual start of the kernel, i.e., the position of the kernel symbol `__start_rodata`.

The attacker controls the variables i and `offset`. Note that even though the inner `if` branch is only doing an operation that should not result in any state change, it still affects related performance counters and hence suffices to enable our attack. The attacker starts by mistraining the outer `if` branch such that its subsequent execution is misspeculated to be taken. The simplest way to achieve this is by in-place mistraining [10], i.e., executing the branch multiple times with i being a valid offset for the array. As a baseline, the attacker leaks the value of the performance counter `CYCLES_DIV_BUSY.ALL` using CounterLeak. This performance counter keeps track of the number of cycles the CPU's divider units are used. The attacker executes the victim function with an index i that is outside the bounds of the array and corresponds to the targeted memory address. Afterward, the attacker again leaks the performance counter of `CYCLES_DIV_BUSY.ALL` using CounterLeak and subtracts the previously leaked value. As the divider is only used when the inner `if` branch is (speculatively) taken, the delta is slightly higher if the transiently-accessed bit is '1'.

Results. We measure each bit 50 times and set a threshold on the median to distinguish between '1' and '0' bits based on the value of the performance counter. Our PoC achieves a leakage rate of 66.7 bit/s with an accuracy of 99.6%. While not the fastest covert channel, we argue that it is still fast enough to pose a threat when such an attack is mounted.

Comparison to Similar Attacks. Our attack only relies on a control flow that is distinguishable by observing performance counters. Common covert channels used in Spectre-type attacks require cache accesses to encode data from transient execution [21,30,32,40]. Finding such code paths that can be exploited by Spectre-type attacks, also referred to as Spectre gadgets, is a challenging task. While our attack is limited to a CPU vulnerable to CounterLeak and providing a usable performance counter, it can use both traditional Spectre gadgets and novel types of gadgets. Hence, with the combination of Spectre and CounterLeak, the number of potential gadgets increases.

6.2 Breaking KASLR with CounterLeak

We demonstrate that unprivileged access to performance counters breaks Kernel Space Address Layout Randomization (KASLR). KASLR randomizes the base address of the operating system kernel upon booting. As precise knowledge of the memory layout is a requirement for many attacks, KASLR adds an additional barrier that attackers have to overcome for a successful kernel exploit. We show that we can derandomize the location of the Linux kernel on an Intel Celeron N3350 running Ubuntu 22.04 with Linux kernel 5.15.0 and thus bypass KASLR.

Target Performance Counter. We target a performance counter influenced by page-table walks, such as DTLB_LOAD_MISSES.WALK_COMPLETED_2M_4M and assume that is already programmed or can be programmed by the attacker. A scenario in which this is the case is if the system is protected using the approach of Wang et al. [63].

Attack Overview. For derandomizing the kernel location, we rely on the property that non-present pages are not stored in the TLB [9]. Thus, a memory load request to a non-present page always leads to a page-table walk, whereas a memory load request to a present page leads to a TLB hit, resulting in no page-table walk if the page was recently accessed. The attack iterates over each potential location of the kernel and accesses it. The resulting fault caused by the access is suppressed using speculative execution, TSX transactions, or fault handling. For each memory access, the attacker leaks the performance counter DTLB_LOAD_MISSES.WALK_COMPLETED_2M_4M, or an alternative one correlating to the number of or the cycles spent for page-table walks, using CounterLeak. Based on the leaked value, the attacker can observe whether a memory page is present and was recently accessed. The first page of the kernel's .rodata section is frequently accessed. Thus, the first address showing an abnormal timing difference is the location of the kernel symbol __start_rodata. Note that a more advanced version of this attack can also be used to actively monitor the access to kernel memory pages, similar to the work of Schwarz et al. [53].

Results. Figure 4 shows the cycle difference iterating over the kernel address space. The kernel location is easily distinguishable from non-present pages due to the change in cycles spent for page table walks. We tested our KASLR break on an Intel Celeron J4005 running Ubuntu 20.04 with Linux kernel 5.4.0 observing a success rate of 98% (n = 100) and a median execution time of 4.7 s.

6.3 Attacking RSA with CounterLeak

In this case study, we attack the RSA implementation based on the MbedTLS version 1.3.10 running on an Intel Celeron J4005 with Ubuntu 20.04 and Linux kernel 5.4.0. This MbedTLS version implements RSA by using a window-based square-and-multiply algorithm. We configure the window size to 1. Previous work [37] showed that all window sizes are vulnerable if window size 1 is vulnerable. While such square-and-multiply implementations are known to be vulnerable to side-channel attacks, we choose this target as it is a common target

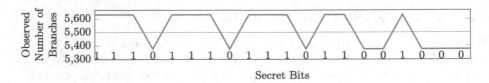

Secret Bits

Fig. 5. The leaked value of the performance counter `BR_INST_RETIRED.NEAR_TAKEN` and its correlation to the secret bits of the exponent.

for related attacks [14,22,33,54,66]. Hence, we ease comparison with other side-channel attacks.

Target Performance Counter. We target the performance counter `BR_INST_RETIRED.NEAR_TAKEN` and assume that it is either already programmed or can be programmed by the attacker. This performance counter keeps track of the number of taken near-branch instructions. An example for a realistic scenario in which this performance counter would be programmed is a system protected by the rootkit detection of Singh et al. [57].

Attack Overview. The victim application consists of a branch only taken when the currently-processed secret bit is '1'. Thus, the secret bit correlates with the number of branches taken. The attacker gains oracle access to the signing routine of the application to sign arbitrary messages. We assume that the attacker and victim are synchronized, i.e., the attacker either knows when the victim processes each iteration of the exponentiation loop, or the attacker can influence this by, e.g., interrupting the victim. During the execution of the victim, the attacker repeatedly leaks the value of the performance counter and, thereby, the number of branches taken. The attacker leaks the performance counter once per key bit. Afterward, the attacker stores the delta of two consecutive performance counter leaks, i.e., the approximation of the victim's taken branches for the processing of a specific secret bit. The attacker repeats this procedure for the decryption of 10000 different messages, averaging out the noise of branches taken by CounterLeak itself and the unrelated branches of the victim application.

Results. By averaging over 10 000 traces, we extract a clear indication of the secret bits. Figure 5 visualizes the correlation between the number of branches taken and the secret bits. Using a simple threshold, we recover 99.9% of the 2048-bit RSA keys ($n = 10$) in around 15 min. Compared to previous work, there are both faster attacks requiring fewer encryptions [2,37] and attacks requiring a similar number of decryptions or more time to execute [68,70]. We conclude that CounterLeak yields a strong primitive for leaking secrets from, for example, cryptographic implementations.

6.4   Breaking Zigzagger with CounterLeak

In this case study, we explore how CounterLeak breaks the Zigzagger branch-shadowing mitigation. Branch-shadowing attacks exploit the shared branch history between processes, allowing attackers to reason about the direction of a branch. For example, Lee et al. [33] demonstrate that a branch-shadowing attack can leak confidential data from Intel SGX enclaves. To prevent branch-shadowing attacks, Lee et al. [33] proposed a software mitigation called Zigzagger. Zigzagger replaces a set of branches with a single indirect branch. Thus, the attacker can only infer whether the branch was executed but cannot infer the branch direction anymore. To compute the address of the indirect jump, additional conditional-move instructions are used. In line with Gerlach et al. [15], we exploit the number of retired instructions to break the Zigzagger mitigation. While Gerlach et al. used an architectural interface to this information, we show that we can recover the same information using CounterLeak. This information allows an attacker again to distinguish the branches taken by the victim.

Target Performance Counter. We target the INSTR_RETIRED performance counter that is either already programmed or can be programmed by the attacker. A realistic scenario for this would be if the defense approach of Wang et al. [63] is in use on the system.

Attack Overview. The victim process contains secret-dependent branches and is hardened against branch-shadowing attacks using Zigzagger [33]. The attacker leaks the INSTR_RETIRED performance counter before and after the Zigzagger-hardened victim executes. The delta between these measurements yields the number of retired instructions. The attacker correlates this number with a baseline measurement for all branches.

Results. For the case study, we use an Intel Celeron J4005 running Ubuntu 20.04 with Linux kernel 5.4.0. For each of the 3 different possible arguments of the sample function, there is a unique number of retired instructions after the Zigzagger modification was applied. Hence, by observing the number of retired instructions, an attacker can directly infer the arguments. We observe a success rate of 100% using 10 000 recorded measurements.

7   Countermeasures

In this section, we discuss countermeasures against CounterLeak and Meltdown-CPL-REG. The fundamental problem is that an unprivileged attacker can transiently access the metadata of an application in the form of performance counters. The exploited vulnerability is rooted deep inside the CPU. As the information stem from a CPU register, no software is involved. Nevertheless, operating systems can still defend against the impact of the attack whereas the victim application itself can be hardened against the attack.

Firmware. Several CPUs received microcode updates to prevent the leakage of system registers [1]. While CPU vendors do not disclose internals of these updates, it is likely that a similar patch can also mitigate the remaining leakage. Thus, the most efficient and effective mitigation is likely via microcode updates.

Kernel. CounterLeak fundamentally relies on performance counters that are either already programmed or that can be programmed by an attacker-accessible

API. A common scenario for this are performance-counter-based detection approaches [11,29,42,43,46,63,64,69,71,72]. As the absence of programmed or programmable performance counter prevents CounterLeak, a carefully designed system that does not use performance counters at all or only in the absense of untrusted parties and code can also prevent the exploitation of CounterLeak. As performance counters and their programming requires kernel privileges, the kernel could, in theory, completely prevent the programming of performance counters. However, this decision comes with the drawback that it would break existing software like the performance-counter-based detection approaches or monitoring utilities such as `perf`. In contrast, an operating system can prevent attacks on KASLR without breaking existing software. Canella et al. [9] proposed mapping dummy pages in the kernel such that all kernel addresses are mapped. Consequently, an attacker cannot infer the real location of the kernel.

Userspace Software. As CounterLeak is a side-channel attack, it is fundamentally limited to leaking data from an application with secret-dependent branches or data-flow edges. However, an application can generally be implemented without any secret-dependent accesses [26]. Applications implemented in such a way are not susceptible to CounterLeak. Especially for cryptographic algorithms, such implementations are state-of-the-art.

8   Discussion

In this section, we discuss related work. Furthermore, we show how the presented attack primitive behaves on different operating systems and architectures. As the building blocks of CounterLeak are OS-agnostic and also exist on other architectures, we assume that similar attacks are also possible there.

8.1   Related Work

In 2018, Intel and Arm disclosed the vulnerability and assigned it CVE-2018-3640 [6,24]. While Intel released a security advisory and added a new category to their list of CPUs affected by vulnerabilities [24,25], Arm added a section about the vulnerability in their Cache-Speculation Side-Channel whitepaper [6]. Our work builds on this initial disclosure by analyzing the leakage of different system registers on 19 CPUs with applied vendor mitigations. We further demonstrate that it is still possible to exploit Meltdown-CPL-REG in different scenarios.

While we focus our work on Meltdown-CPL-REG, Canella et al. [10] analyzed the landscape of transient-execution attacks with a broader focus. Furthermore, they first introduced the split into Meltdown- and Spectre-type attacks. In contrast, our work focuses on the specific variant Meltdown-CPL-REG and analyzes further details about it, including how widespread the issue itself is.

Attacks exploiting performance counters have been shown when the interface was accessible to unprivileged users. In 2008, Uhsadel et al. [58] first exploited performance counters to leak information about the CPU caches. With information similar to a cache attack, they showed that the information can be exploited to recover confidential values from a victim program. They also demonstrated their attack on an OpenSSL AES implementation. Bhattacharya et al. [8] further demonstrated that performance counters expose even more information than just the cache state and thus allow reasoning about the branch-predictor state. Their work discusses an exploit on a square-and-multiply implementation of RSA using the Montgomery-ladder algorithm. Since then, the access to performance counters is privileged by default, preventing these attacks on modern systems [12]. Dixon et al. [12] further stresses the importance of disabling unprivileged access to performance counters by showing that it allows derandomizing the kernel location. Gerlach et al. [15] exploit the unprivileged access to performance counters on RISC-V CPUs to break KASLR, leak the presence of inaccessible files, and detect interrupts. Our work mainly differs from these previous ones by demonstrating these and similar attacks on modern systems where performance-counter access is restricted to privileged users.

8.2   Other OS and Architectures

The underlying effects exploited in this paper are OS-agnostic. While this paper targets Linux, we do not require any Linux-specific functionality. CounterLeak interacts with the hardware directly without requiring any OS support. If any application legitimately enables performance counters, they can be leaked.

CounterLeak requires systems that are vulnerable to Meltdown-CPL-REG. While Meltdown-CPL-REG was also shown on Arm CPUs [6], we leave it for future work to systematically analyze Arm CPUs for their Meltdown-CPL-REG attack surface. Nevertheless, as all strict requirements for CounterLeak are also given on Arm CPUs, we suspect that the issue also affects these systems.

9   Conclusion

In this paper, we analyzed the attack surface of Meltdown-CPL-REG. For this, we developed an automated approach using RegCheck (open-sourced on GitHub) to analyze 19 Intel and AMD CPUs based on different microarchitectures. In our analysis, we observe that the privileged system registers that can be leaked by Meltdown-CPL-REG differ from CPU to CPU. Furthermore, we observe that the FS and GS segment base registers can be leaked even on recent AMD CPUs (Zen 3+). We further show that our attack primitive CounterLeak can exploit side-channel information by leaking the values of performance counters using Meltdown-CPL-REG. We demonstrated CounterLeak in 4 different case studies. We showed that the primitive allows us to break KASLR by monitoring the page-table walker and can break the Zigzagger branch-shadowing mitigation [33]. Additionally, we demonstrated the applicability of CounterLeak as a flexible covert channel for Spectre attacks and leaked a 2048 bit RSA key from a square-and-multiply implementation in MbedTLS, verifying that our primitive reenables previously mitigated attacks. In conclusion, our work shows that Meltdown-CPL-REG should not be underestimated and still poses a threat to modern and fully patched systems.

Acknowledgment. We want to thank our anonymous reviewers for their comments and suggestions. We also want to thank Leon Trampert and Niklas Flentje for providing their help with running the experiments. This work was partly supported by the Semiconductor Research Corporation (SRC) Hardware Security Program (HWS).

References

1. Rogue system register read (2018). https://www.intel.com/content/www/us/en/developer/articles/technical/software-security-guidance/advisory-guidance/rogue-system-register-read.html
2. Acıiçmez, O.: Yet another microarchitecutral attack: exploiting I-cache. In: ASPLOS (2007)
3. Acıiçmez, O., Koç, Ç.K., Seifert, J.-P.: Predicting secret keys via branch prediction. In: Abe, M. (ed.) CT-RSA 2007. LNCS, vol. 4377, pp. 225–242. Springer, Heidelberg (2006). https://doi.org/10.1007/11967668_15
4. Acıiçmez, O., Schindler, W.: A vulnerability in RSA implementations due to instruction cache analysis and its demonstration on OpenSSL. In: Malkin, T. (ed.) CT-RSA 2008. LNCS, vol. 4964, pp. 256–273. Springer, Heidelberg (2008). https://doi.org/10.1007/978-3-540-79263-5_16
5. Aldaya, A.C., Brumley, B.B., ul Hassan, S., García, C.P., Tuveri, N.: Port contention for fun and profit. In: S&P (2018)
6. ARM: Cache Speculation Side-channels, version 2.5 (2020)
7. Bhattacharya, S., Maurice, C., Bhasin, S., Mukhopadhyay, D.: Template attack on blinded scalar multiplication with asynchronous perf-ioctl calls. Cryptology ePrint Archive, Report 2017/968 (2017)
8. Bhattacharya, S., Mukhopadhyay, D.: Who watches the watchmen?: Utilizing performance monitors for compromising keys of RSA on Intel platforms. Cryptology ePrint Archive, Report 2015/621 (2015)
9. Canella, C., Schwarz, M., Haubenwallner, M., Schwarzl, M., Gruss, D.: KASLR: break it, fix it, repeat. In: Asia CCS (2020)
10. Canella, C., et al.: A systematic evaluation of transient execution attacks and defenses. In: USENIX Security Symposium (2019). Extended classification tree and PoCs at https://transient.fail/
11. Chiappetta, M., Savas, E., Yilmaz, C.: Real time detection of cache-based side-channel attacks using hardware performance counters. ePrint 2015/1034 (2015)
12. Dixon, L.: Breaking KASLR with perf (2017). https://blog.lizzie.io/kaslr-and-perf.html
13. Frisk, U.: Windows 10 KASLR Recovery with TSX (2016). https://blog.frizk.net/2016/11/windows-10-kaslr-recovery-with-tsx.html
14. García, C.P., Ul Hassan, S., Tuveri, N., Gridin, I., Aldaya, A.C., Brumley, B.B.: Certified side channels. In: USENIX Security Symposium (2020)
15. Gerlach, L., Weber, D., Zhang, R., Schwarz, M.: A security RISC: microarchitectural attacks on hardware RISC-V CPUs. In: S&P (2023)
16. Gras, B., Giuffrida, C., Kurth, M., Bos, H., Razavi, K.: ABSynthe: automatic blackbox side-channel synthesis on commodity microarchitectures. In: NDSS (2020)
17. Gruss, D., Lipp, M., Schwarz, M., Fellner, R., Maurice, C., Mangard, S.: KASLR is dead: long live KASLR. In: Bodden, E., Payer, M., Athanasopoulos, E. (eds.) ESSoS 2017. LNCS, vol. 10379, pp. 161–176. Springer, Cham (2017). https://doi.org/10.1007/978-3-319-62105-0_11

18. Gruss, D., Maurice, C., Wagner, K., Mangard, S.: Flush+Flush: a fast and stealthy cache attack. In: Caballero, J., Zurutuza, U., Rodríguez, R.J. (eds.) DIMVA 2016. LNCS, vol. 9721, pp. 279–299. Springer, Cham (2016). https://doi.org/10.1007/978-3-319-40667-1_14

19. Gruss, D., Spreitzer, R., Mangard, S.: Cache template attacks: automating attacks on inclusive last-level caches. In: USENIX Security Symposium (2015)

20. Herath, N., Fogh, A.: These are not your grand Daddys CPU performance counters - CPU hardware performance counters for security. In: Black Hat Briefings (2015)

21. Hetterich, L., Schwarz, M.: Branch different - spectre attacks on apple silicon. In: Cavallaro, L., Gruss, D., Pellegrino, G., Giacinto, G. (eds.) DIMVA 2022. LNCS, vol. 13358, pp. 116–135. Springer, Cham (2022). https://doi.org/10.1007/978-3-031-09484-2_7

22. Huo, T., et al.: Bluethunder: a 2-level directional predictor based side-channel attack against SGX. In: CHES (2020)

23. Intel: Instructions affected by rogue system register read (2018). https://www.intel.com/content/www/us/en/developer/articles/technical/software-security-guidance/resources/instructions-affected-rogue-system-register-read.html

24. Intel: Intel-SA-00115 Q2 2018 Speculative Execution Side Channel Update (2019). https://www.intel.com/content/www/us/en/security-center/advisory/intel-sa-00115.html

25. Intel: Affected Processors: Transient Execution Attacks (2023). https://www.intel.com/content/www/us/en/developer/topic-technology/software-security-guidance/processors-affected-consolidated-product-cpu-model.html

26. Intel Corporation: Guidelines for Mitigating Timing Side Channels Against Cryptographic Implementations (2020). https://www.intel.com/content/www/us/en/developer/articles/technical/software-security-guidance/secure-coding/mitigate-timing-side-channel-crypto-implementation.html

27. Intel Corporation: Refined Speculative Execution Terminology (2020). https://software.intel.com/security-software-guidance/insights/refined-speculative-execution-terminology

28. Irazoqui, G., Eisenbarth, T., Sunar, B.: MASCAT: stopping microarchitectural attacks before execution. ePrint 2016/1196 (2017)

29. Irazoqui, G., Eisenbarth, T., Sunar, B.: MASCAT: preventing microarchitectural attacks before distribution. In: CODASPY (2018)

30. Kocher, P., et al.: Spectre attacks: exploiting speculative execution. In: S&P (2019)

31. Kocher, P.C.: Timing attacks on implementations of Diffie-Hellman, RSA, DSS, and other systems. In: Koblitz, N. (ed.) CRYPTO 1996. LNCS, vol. 1109, pp. 104–113. Springer, Heidelberg (1996). https://doi.org/10.1007/3-540-68697-5_9

32. Koruyeh, E.M., Khasawneh, K., Song, C., Abu-Ghazaleh, N.: Spectre returns! Speculation attacks using the return stack buffer. In: WOOT (2018)

33. Lee, S., Shih, M., Gera, P., Kim, T., Kim, H., Peinado, M.: Inferring fine-grained control flow inside SGX enclaves with branch shadowing. In: USENIX Security Symposium (2017)

34. Lipp, M., Gruss, D., Spreitzer, R., Maurice, C., Mangard, S.: ARMageddon: cache attacks on mobile devices. In: USENIX Security Symposium (2016)

35. Lipp, M., et al.: PLATYPUS: software-based power side-channel attacks on x86. In: S&P (2020)

36. Lipp, M., et al.: Meltdown: reading kernel memory from user space. In: USENIX Security Symposium (2018)

37. Liu, F., Yarom, Y., Ge, Q., Heiser, G., Lee, R.B.: Last-level cache side-channel attacks are practical. In: S&P (2015)

38. Lou, X., Zhang, T., Jiang, J., Zhang, Y.: A survey of microarchitectural side-channel vulnerabilities, attacks, and defenses in cryptography. In: ACM CSUR (2021)
39. Lutas, A., Lutas, D.: Bypassing KPTI using the speculative behavior of the SWAPGS instruction. In: BlackHat Europe (2019)
40. Maisuradze, G., Rossow, C.: ret2spec: speculative execution using return stack buffers. In: CCS (2018)
41. Moghimi, D., Lipp, M., Sunar, B., Schwarz, M.: Medusa: microarchitectural data leakage via automated attack synthesis. In: USENIX Security Symposium (2020)
42. Mushtaq, M., Akram, A., Bhatti, M.K., Chaudhry, M., Lapotre, V., Gogniat, G.: Nights-watch: a cache-based side-channel intrusion detector using hardware performance counters. In: HASP (2018)
43. Mushtaq, M., et al.: WHISPER: a tool for run-time detection of side-channel attacks. IEEE Access 8, 83871–83900 (2020)
44. Oren, Y., Kemerlis, V.P., Sethumadhavan, S., Keromytis, A.D.: The spy in the sandbox: practical cache attacks in JavaScript and their implications. In: CCS (2015)
45. Paccagnella, R., Luo, L., Fletcher, C.W.: Lord of the ring (s): side channel attacks on the CPU on-chip ring interconnect are practical. In: USENIX Security Symposium (2021)
46. Payer, M.: HexPADS: a platform to detect "stealth" attacks. In: Caballero, J., Bodden, E., Athanasopoulos, E. (eds.) ESSoS 2016. LNCS, vol. 9639, pp. 138–154. Springer, Cham (2016). https://doi.org/10.1007/978-3-319-30806-7_9
47. Percival, C.: Cache missing for fun and profit. In: BSDCan (2005)
48. Purnal, A., Turan, F., Verbauwhede, I.: Prime+Scope: overcoming the observer effect for high-precision cache contention attacks. In: CCS (2021)
49. Qiu, P., et al.: PMUSpill: the counters in performance monitor unit that leak SGX-protected secrets. arXiv:2207.11689 (2022)
50. Ragab, H., Barberis, E., Bos, H., Giuffrida, C.: Rage against the machine clear: a systematic analysis of machine clears and their implications for transient execution attacks. In: USENIX Security (2021)
51. Ragab, H., Milburn, A., Razavi, K., Bos, H., Giuffrida, C.: CrossTalk: speculative data leaks across cores are real. In: S&P (2021)
52. Rokicki, T., Maurice, C., Schwarz, M.: CPU port contention without SMT. In: Atluri, V., Di Pietro, R., Jensen, C.D., Meng, W. (eds.) ESORICS 2022. LNCS, vol. 13556, pp. 209–228. Springer, Cham (2022). https://doi.org/10.1007/978-3-031-17143-7_11
53. Schwarz, M., Canella, C., Giner, L., Gruss, D.: Store-to-leak forwarding: leaking data on meltdown-resistant CPUs. arXiv:1905.05725 (2019)
54. Schwarz, M., Weiser, S., Gruss, D., Maurice, C., Mangard, S.: Malware guard extension: using SGX to conceal cache attacks. In: Polychronakis, M., Meier, M. (eds.) DIMVA 2017. LNCS, vol. 10327, pp. 3–24. Springer, Cham (2017). https://doi.org/10.1007/978-3-319-60876-1_1
55. Schwarz, M., et al.: KeyDrown: eliminating software-based keystroke timing side-channel attacks. In: NDSS (2018)
56. Schwarz, M., et al.: ZombieLoad: cross-privilege-boundary data sampling. In: CCS (2019)
57. Singh, B., Evtyushkin, D., Elwell, J., Riley, R., Cervesato, I.: On the detection of kernel-level rootkits using hardware performance counters. In: Asia CCS (2017)

58. Uhsadel, L., Georges, A., Verbauwhede, I.: Exploiting hardware performance counters. In: 5th Workshop on Fault Diagnosis and Tolerance in Cryptography (FDTC 2008) (2008)
59. Van Bulck, J., et al.: Foreshadow: extracting the keys to the Intel SGX kingdom with transient out-of-order execution. In: USENIX Security Symposium (2018)
60. Van Bulck, J., et al.: LVI: Hijacking transient execution through microarchitectural load value injection. In: S&P (2020)
61. van Schaik, S., et al.: RIDL: rogue in-flight data load. In: S&P (2019)
62. Varda, K.: Dynamic process isolation: research by cloudflare and TU Graz (2021). https://blog.cloudflare.com/spectre-research-with-tu-graz/
63. Wang, H., Sayadi, H., Sasan, A., Rafatirad, S., Homayoun, H.: Hybrid-shield: accurate and efficient cross-layer countermeasure for run-time detection and mitigation of cache-based side-channel attacks. In: ICCAD (2020)
64. Wang, H., Sayadi, H., Sasan, A., Rafatirad, S., Mohsenin, T., Homayoun, H.: Comprehensive evaluation of machine learning countermeasures for detecting microarchitectural side-channel attacks. In: GLSVLSI (2020)
65. Weisse, O., et al.: Foreshadow-NG: Breaking the Virtual Memory Abstraction with Transient Out-of-Order Execution (2018). https://foreshadowattack.eu/foreshadow-NG.pdf
66. Xiao, Y., Li, M., Chen, S., Zhang, Y.: STACCO: differentially analyzing side-channel traces for detecting SSL/TLS vulnerabilities in secure enclaves. In: CCS (2017)
67. Yarom, Y., Falkner, K.: Flush+Reload: a high resolution, low noise, L3 cache side-channel attack. In: USENIX Security Symposium (2014)
68. Yarom, Y., Genkin, D., Heninger, N.: CacheBleed: a timing attack on OpenSSL constant-time RSA. JCEN **7**, 99–112 (2017). https://doi.org/10.1007/s13389-017-0152-y
69. Zhang, T., Zhang, Y., Lee, R.B.: CloudRadar: a real-time side-channel attack detection system in clouds. In: Monrose, F., Dacier, M., Blanc, G., Garcia-Alfaro, J. (eds.) RAID 2016. LNCS, vol. 9854, pp. 118–140. Springer, Cham (2016). https://doi.org/10.1007/978-3-319-45719-2_6
70. Zhang, Y., Juels, A., Reiter, M.K., Ristenpart, T.: Cross-VM side channels and their use to extract private keys. In: CCS (2012)
71. Zhang, Y., Reiter, M.: Düppel: retrofitting commodity operating systems to mitigate cache side channels in the cloud. In: CCS (2013)
72. Zhang, Z., et al.: See through walls: detecting malware in SGX enclaves with SGX-bouncer. In: Asia CCS (2021)

Tamarin-Based Analysis of Bluetooth Uncovers Two Practical Pairing Confusion Attacks

Tristan Claverie[1,2,3(✉)], Gildas Avoine[2,3], Stéphanie Delaune[3], and José Lopes Esteves[1]

[1] Agence Nationale de la Sécurité des Systèmes d'Information (ANSSI), Paris, France
[2] INSA de Rennes, Rennes, France
[3] Univ Rennes, CNRS, IRISA, Rennes, France
tristan.claverie@irisa.fr

Abstract. This paper provides a Tamarin-based formal analysis of all key-agreement protocols available in Bluetooth technologies, *i.e.*, Bluetooth BR/EDR, Bluetooth Low Energy, and Bluetooth Mesh. The automated analysis found several unreported attacks, including two attacks that exploit the confusion of Pairing modes, which occurs when a communicating party uses the Secure Pairing mode while the other one uses the Legacy Pairing mode. They have been validated in practice using off-the-shelf implementations for the genuine communicating parties, and a custom BR/EDR machine-in-the-middle framework for the attacker. Our attacks have been reported by Bluetooth SIG as CVEs.

1 Introduction

Bluetooth technologies are increasingly used worldwide as ways to transmit data over-the-air. In 2021, 4.7 billion Bluetooth devices were shipped according to the Bluetooth Special Interest Group (SIG) [24]. There are actually three distinct Bluetooth technologies: Bluetooth Basic Rate/Enhanced Data Rate (BR/EDR), Bluetooth Low Energy (BLE), and Bluetooth Mesh (BM). While the details differ, all of them aim at providing confidentiality, integrity, and authentication.

Many flaws have been discovered over the years in Bluetooth standards. Some of them are related to the use of improper cryptographic primitives [30–32], others are purely protocol-level flaws [1,2,15,37,40], and a few ones rely on incorrect implementations of cryptographic primitives [7,18,35]. The behaviour of Bluetooth stacks was also studied, especially on mobile platforms [3,41,42], revealing some vulnerabilities in implementations.

Bluetooth communication security mostly relies on the key agreement step, which can be performed using many different protocols and sub-protocols. This makes the security analysis highly complex. The *pairing confusion* introduced in [37] is an attack that exploits the interaction of two key-agreement protocols in Bluetooth. It consists in a scenario where an entity uses Protocol A while

This work received funding from the France 2030 program managed by the French National Research Agency under grant agreement No. ANR-22-PECY-0006.

G. Tsudik et al. (Eds.): ESORICS 2023, LNCS 14346, pp. 100–119, 2024.
https://doi.org/10.1007/978-3-031-51479-1_6

the other entity uses Protocol B, such that they are not aware of this protocol mismatch. Usually, such a mismatched interaction ends with a failure. However, for some protocol pairs, the attacker can exploit messages sent in Protocol A to break the security properties of Protocol B, and conversely.

Formal protocol verification is the process of abstracting a protocol to prove that the considered security properties hold. Tamarin [28] and ProVerif [8] are state-of-the-art tools that automatically perform this formal protocol verification. They have been used for verifying complex protocols such as TLS 1.3 [6,17] and 5G-AKA [16]. When their analyses complete, they grant either a formal proof that the considered security property hold, or an attack.

Several studies of protocol confusion have been performed for Bluetooth key agreements [23,33,40] using automated formal tools, but not in a systematic way. Although [23] and [33] consider some form of imperfect primitives, those representations are not accurate with regards to the current knowledge about Bluetooth protocols. As a result, most known attacks are not identified by those analyses.

Contributions. In this paper, comprehensive Tamarin models of all Bluetooth key-agreement protocols defined in BR/EDR, BLE, and BM are detailed. Those models are enhanced with representations of cryptographic imperfections that affect Bluetooth. In particular, they are used to systematically analyse pairing confusions in Bluetooth key agreements. Tamarin automatically identifies previously published attacks and identifies five new attacks, including four novel cases of protocol confusion. We highlight that the Bluetooth SIG assigned two CVEs for two of those attacks that defeat currently known mitigations against pairing confusions. To explore the practicality of these attacks, a BLE and a BR/EDR Machine-in-the-Middle (MitM) are implemented on the respective pairing methods of those technologies. To the best of our knowledge, this is the first practical MitM implementation on the BR/EDR pairing. Two additional attacks defeat proposed patches of BM Provisioning from the literature. A detailed research report of the presented work, including our Tamarin models, can be found in [14].

Outline. Section 2 provides an introduction to Bluetooth key-agreement protocols and their known flaws. Section 3 details the Tamarin formal models developed for this study. The results, including new attacks and their implementations are described in Sect. 4 before being compared to the literature.

2 Background

In this section, we introduce two distinct Bluetooth technologies: Bluetooth Basic Rate/Enhanced Data Rate (BR/EDR) and Bluetooth Low Energy (BLE), respectively standardised in 1999 and 2010 [9]. Bluetooth Mesh (BM) is not described in this section, but a description can be found in [14]. BR/EDR is routinely used in audio devices (*e.g.*, earbuds, speakers) while BLE is commonly used in other smart devices (*e.g.*, watches). They have a similar security architecture. Both technologies try to grant confidentiality, integrity and authenticity of communications. Those properties rely on symmetric keys that are exchanged during a key agreement.

2.1 Key Agreement

In BR/EDR and BLE, the key agreement step is called *Pairing* and is performed between devices respectively called *Initiator* and *Responder*. To uniquely identify each protocol, two concepts are introduced. The term *Pairing mode* refers to the type of Pairing, it can be Legacy or Secure. The term *Pairing method* refers to the protocol name as standardized in the specification. The differences between the methods lie in the messages required to complete them and input/output capabilities of devices. Table 1 lists the Pairing protocols standardised. In this paper, a protocol is identified by a mode and a method, *e.g.*, Legacy JustWorks, Secure Out-of-Band (OOB), etc.

Table 1. BR/EDR and BLE Pairing protocols

Pairing Mode	BR/EDR		BLE	
	Legacy	Secure	Legacy	Secure
Pairing Method	PIN Pairing	JustWorks Passkey Entry Numeric Comparison Out-of-Band	JustWorks Passkey Entry Out of Band	JustWorks Passkey Entry Numeric Comparison Out-of-Band

For illustration purposes, we detailed below two protocols, the Legacy PIN Pairing protocol in BR/EDR, and the Legacy Passkey Entry protocol in BLE.

Legacy PIN Pairing for BR/EDR (Fig. 1). Functions E_1, E_{21}, and E_{22} are defined in the specification [9] (Vol 2, Part H, §6). The key agreement starts when the Initiator sends a nonce *in_rand* to the Responder (1). The user has to exchange a numeric code between devices, called the *PIN* (2). This *PIN* is used alongside *in_rand* and the Initiator address to derive K_{init}. K_{init} is used to mask two nonces *comb_key$_i$* and *comb_key$_r$* (3) which are used to derive the *Link Key (LK)* (4). According to the specification, the Pairing process is over once *LK* is created, but a mutual authentication procedure has to follow (5).

Legacy Passkey Entry for BLE (Fig. 2). Functions c_1 and s_1 are defined in the specification [9] (Vol 3, Part H, §2.2). The protocol starts with a Feature Exchange step (1), that is used to provide information about input-output capabilities, key size to use, etc. Then, the user has to exchange a numeric code between the devices (2). Typically, one device displays a code that the user enters in the other one. This code is used as a symmetric key in a commitment scheme (3). This step is used to authenticate the capabilities and respective addresses of the devices. Finally, nonces exchanged in step (3) are used to derive a *Short-Term Key (STK)* that is then used to encrypt the communication.

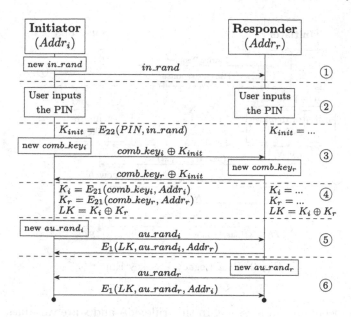

Fig. 1. BR/EDR Legacy PIN Pairing and Mutual Legacy Authentication

2.2 Tamarin Prover

The Tamarin prover [28] is a security protocol verification tool that supports both falsification and verification in the *symbolic model*. As usual in symbolic models, Tamarin represents the messages exchanged and computations as algebraic terms. Tamarin has already been successfully used to analyse many protocols, *e.g.*, TLS [17], WPA2 [19], and EMV [5]. Compared to similar tools like ProVerif [8] or AVISPA [38], Tamarin comes with a better user interface and more refined models for some primitives like Diffie-Hellman and XOR.

Modelling Protocols. At its core, Tamarin is based on multiset rewriting. This means a protocol is represented using a series of multiset rewriting rules. A rule essentially dictates the labelled transition from one set of facts to another.

rule Resp: [Resp1(idA), In(x)] ─[Label(idA,x)]→ [Resp2(idA, x), Out(h(x))]

Example 1. Tamarin rewriting rule

A Tamarin rule is composed of four elements, namely its *name*, the set of *facts* that are input to the rule, the set of *labels* that are produced by the rule, and the set of facts that are output by the rule. In Example 1, if there exists a fact Resp1(idA) and there is an input message x in Tamarin's state, applying this rule will consume the fact Resp1, and produce the fact Resp2. The label Label is generated by the application of this rule. Out(...) is a special fact that represents the emission of a message over a public channel. In(...) is also a special fact that

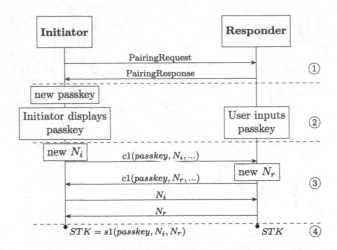

Fig. 2. BLE Legacy Passkey Entry

denotes the reception of a message. In this rule, idA and x are variables that can *a priori* be terms of any form or type.

Modelling Attacker. Tamarin analyses protocols in the Dolev-Yao model [20] where the attacker has full control over the communication channel: it is able to receive, intercept, modify, and forge messages. Tamarin automatically generates rules for the attacker, which enables it to perform common operations, like splitting and concatenating messages, etc. The attacker's knowledge is updated with each message sent on the public channel, hence with each Out(...) produced. Similarly, each message known to the attacker can be sent over the public channel, hence received in any In(...) fact.

In order to represent cryptographic operations, Tamarin enables to define function symbols and their relations through equations. It comes with existing symbols such as XOR, symmetric encryption, Diffie-Hellman, etc. The set of equations that relate functions together is called an *equational theory*.

Modelling Properties. To gain insight and knowledge about protocols, Tamarin allows encoding mathematical properties, called *lemmas*. They are expressed using labels that are produced by rewriting rules.

---

lemma InitKeySecrecy:
"$\forall$ *id, stk* #i. InitEndPairing(*id, stk*) @#i $\implies$ $\nexists$ #j . K(*stk*) @#j"

Example 2. Tamarin lemma

Example 2 expresses a simple weak secrecy claim: if an Initiator ends the protocol with a certain key *stk* at time #i, the attacker is unable to retrieve it at any point in time. The lemmas are expressed as logical formulas, using quantifiers and negations, and the attacker knowledge is represented with fact K.

When provided with a lemma, Tamarin tries to prove it is true in all cases or provide an execution trace. This execution trace illustrates the different rules that are applied and the actions the attacker took to contradict the lemma. From this trace, it is possible to manually identify the messages and computations an attacker does to invalidate the property studied. An other possibility is that Tamarin may not finish the proof within the allocated resources (time, memory). When Tamarin does not finish, it is possible to use an interactive mode and to prove the property manually by guiding Tamarin about the states to explore. Because Tamarin is, at its core, a prover, it does not yield all counterexamples of a lemma for a model. This means that when knowingly studying a flawed protocol, Tamarin is not able to enumerate all the attacks on this protocol. Furthermore, by default Tamarin considers cryptographic primitives to be perfect. However, some primitives have known weaknesses and some protocols use primitives in an incorrect way. Representing cryptographic imperfections requires an extra modelling step so Tamarin can include them in the model.

2.3 Related Work

Bluetooth technologies have been subject to many attacks over the years. A survey of those affecting BLE can be found in [10]. Some studies have focused on the security of the reconnection step: BIAS [1] considers the authentication protocol during reconnection in BR/EDR, KNOB [4] the key size reduction in BR/EDR, and BLESA [39] the reconnection in BLE.

There are also passive attacks on Bluetooth technologies. In BR/EDR, Legacy Pairing is vulnerable to offline key recovery from a capture of exchanged messages [32]. Legacy Pairing in BLE has the same flaw although the details differ [31]. In a Secure Pairing protocol, Lindell showed the possibility to retrieve passively an authentication secret [25], which applies to BLE and BR/EDR.

Rosa [30] proposed an active attack on Legacy Pairing in BLE that relies on a flawed cryptographic primitive. Researchers studied the use of ECDH in the Pairing protocols [7,18], found flaws in the authentication of public keys and discussed possible attacks. Key size reduction is also studied in BLE [2], which proved to be vulnerable to some extent.

BlueMirror [15] proposed an extensive study of reflection attacks in Bluetooth technologies and showed their applicability to all of them. In [37], the authors define the concept of *pairing confusion*, where the attacker forces two devices to use two different Pairing protocols. In their attack, an attacker forces device A to complete Secure Passkey Entry while device B completes Secure Numeric Comparison. They show that in this setup, implementations do not allow the user to distinguish between both protocols. As a result, the attacker can complete them and retrieve the encryption key derived by each device.

Bluetooth was also studied from a formal perspective. Some studies performed manual proofs of some parts of Bluetooth. In [26], a proof of Secure Numeric Comparison is done. A formal analysis of Secure Passkey Entry is proposed in [36]. The security of the reconnection step in BR/EDR and BLE is studied in [21]. Formal studies using automated tools are also detailed in [12,13,18,23,29,40] and [33]. They are discussed in depth in Sect. 4.3.

3   Formal Models

This section details the choices made to model Bluetooth key agreements. We list in Sect. 3.2 all the cryptographic weaknesses that the attacker can exploit and explain how they are modelled in Tamarin. Then, the approach taken for modelling Bluetooth key agreements is presented.

3.1   Security Model

Security Properties. We study three kinds of security goals that are defined in the specification: confidentiality, authentication, and MitM protection.

Confidentiality and authentication are defined in this paper similarly to what is done in other Bluetooth formal analyses [33,40]. For each Bluetooth technology, confidentiality comes from the secrecy of the keys derived at the end of the key agreement. Secrecy is modelled per participant, that is the secrecy of the keys derived by each participant is verified. To model authentication, we use the definition of *non-injective agreement* from Lowe's [27] taxonomy. Again, this property is modelled per participant, to ensure that no device has unknowingly completed a key agreement with an attacker.

Finally, the MitM protection [9] (Vol 1, Part A, §5.2.3) is formalized. It represents the fact that an attacker should not be able to complete a key agreement with both participants at the same time and yet know the keys derived by each side. This property is also studied in [33] for BLE Secure Pairing.

Attacker Model. There are three kinds of communication channels that are used in Bluetooth specifications. The first channel is the Bluetooth channel, which carries Bluetooth messages over the radio between devices. It is considered that the attacker has Dolev-Yao capabilities over the channel. The attacker is able to forge, modify, block, and relay messages over the radio.

The second kind of channel is the one used to model user interactions, because the user needs to perform some actions to complete most key agreements. In this model, the user is considered honest and performs actions as required by the specification. The attacker is supposed to have no access to the output/input of legitimate devices. When two devices output an information, the user verifies they match and confirms to continue the key agreement. When two devices expect an input, the user chooses a random number and fills it on both devices. When one device outputs an information and the other expects an input, the user enters the output information on the other device.

The third kind of channel is the OOB channel, that is used to transport information between two devices. This OOB channel is unspecified, but it is assumed that the attacker has no access to this channel given that this would break the security of the OOB protocols.

3.2   Representing Cryptographic Imperfections

By default, Tamarin assumes that cryptography is perfect, but primitives used in Bluetooth are known to have some weaknesses. This paragraph details how these imperfections are modelled in Tamarin.

Brute-Force of Low-Entropy Secrets. Some protocols rely on low-entropy secrets, which can be brute-forced by an attacker. Tis kind of vulnerability has various shapes depending on the technology and key agreement [2,15,25,31,32].

In Tamarin, the names used to represent nonces/passwords are unguessable by default: if there is a generated value $secret$ and the attacker has access to $h(secret)$, without further rule the attacker is unable to retrieve the value of $secret$. While this assumption is correct for some protocols (*e.g.*, if the secret value is 128-bit long), Bluetooth uses several low-entropy secrets that can be brute-forced in a practical time. To model this capability, special rules are created to output the targeted secret when the attacker has provided enough information.

---

rule Oracle_f4:
   [LowEntropyf4($pk1$, $pk2$, n, s), In($pk1$), In($pk2$), In(n), In(f4($pk1$, $pk2$, n, s))]
  −[AttackerRecoveredPasskey(s)]→ [Out(s)]

Example 3. Oracle rule in Tamarin

The implementation of the passkey recovery [25] from BLE Secure Passkey Entry protocol is done with the rule depicted in Example 1. The function f4 is defined in the specification and is common to several Pairing methods. The methods that use a low-entropy secret generate the fact LowEntropyf4 $(pk1, pk2, n, s)$ that allows to enter this rule. The attacker also needs to prove knowledge of all the elements by sending them on the public channel. When used, this rule outputs the secret. The use of an explicit "oracle" rule makes it appear in Tamarin's execution traces, therefore one may follow easily whether such a rule occurs in a Tamarin attack trace. The ability of the attacker to brute-force downgraded keys, discussed in [2,33] is also modelled using such an oracle.

Malleable Commitment. This issue is present in BLE Legacy Pairing [30] and in BM Provisioning [15]. While both instances of commitment functions in Bluetooth have different cryptographic details, they are conceptually very similar. In BLE, the commitment protocol is displayed in step ③ of Fig. 2: both devices exchange a commitment value computed from a key, a nonce, an authentication secret, and additional data. Device A sends the first commitment, followed by B. Then both devices exchange their nonces.

The vulnerabilities rely on the attacker posing as device B. Upon reception of A's commitment, the attacker replies to A with an arbitrary value. Then, A sends its nonce. From A's nonce and commitment, the attacker is able to recover an authentication secret. The attacker then crafts a nonce from the sent commitment and recovered authentication secret.

---

functions:
   aes_cmac/2, // *Representation of cmac*
   get_b1/3, // *Used to retrieve first block*
equations:
   get_b1(aes_cmac(k, <$b1$, $b2$>), k, $b2$) = $b1$,
   aes_cmac(k, <get_b1(c, k, $b2$), $b2$>) = c.

Example 4. Representing malleability in Tamarin

To implement the *malleable commitment* weakness, a specific equational theory is used. In Example 2, one can see the implementation for BM. In particular, it is necessary to define an equation to craft a nonce, represented here with get_b1. Then, one has to explicitly state that a confirmation that is used in this way is equal to a proper aes_cmac term. With this representation, Tamarin is able to find this class of attacks on the studied protocols.

This type of cryptographic problem strongly depends on the underlying cryptographic specification, and those equations are not suitable for all protocols. In Tamarin, it is impossible to state that this equation holds only if $b1$ and $b2$ have a specific size. As a result, those equations give the attacker more power than it has in practice and are not a generic representation of this kind of problem.

Small Subgroup Attack on ECDH Implementation. In Bluetooth, incorrect ECDH implementations have led to some attacks on implementations [7,18]. This attack is a type of small subgroup attack that affects BR/EDR and BLE when the validity of received public keys is not verified. The representation of this type of attacks and more generally of incorrect implementations of the Diffie-Hellman protocol with Tamarin is extensively discussed in [18]. The authors provide a model of Secure Numeric Comparison with their representation.

In all Bluetooth technologies, the elliptic curves used are P-192 or/and P-256, which are defined over a field of prime order. Therefore, we adapted the representation of ECDH provided in their model to all Bluetooth technologies. Basically, each public key is represented as a group identifier, the neutral element of the group and the group element. When deriving a Diffie-Hellman key, if the attacker has managed to modify the group of an element, the key is considered leaked to the attacker. This is representative of elliptic curve cryptography on the groups used in Bluetooth, because an appropriate modification of a public key yields a Diffie-Hellman secret that is on a group of low order (as low as 2). In that case, the secret becomes easily retrievable using brute-force.

3.3   Modelling Bluetooth Key Agreement Protocols

When modelling key agreements in Bluetooth, one needs to tackle the diversity of protocols. In order to model them accurately, one needs to model the user interaction required to complete each of them. In the specification, a single protocol may have several user interaction variations, depending on the input/output capabilities of both devices. For example, in BLE Legacy Passkey Entry, a device may have an input, an output or both. Whether the device outputs or waits for a numeric code depends on the other device's input-output capabilities. To address this variation, Legacy Passkey Entry is modelled as three sub-protocols to represent the different user interactions required. This also applies to other Pairing protocols, and increases the number of protocols that are represented. In total, there are 13 BLE protocols, 11 BR/EDR protocols, and 8 BM protocols to consider all the identified variations.

In practice, the choice of the protocol to use between two legitimate devices is done in the very first step, which is the Feature Exchange. An active attacker has the ability to modify the features sent by each device, and therefore the ability to force the protocol used on each side of the connection. Therefore, studying each pair of protocols makes sense from a Bluetooth's point of view. Studying the interaction of all possible pairs of protocols for each technology requires studying 354 ($13^2 + 11^2 + 8^2$) distinct cases, each case containing several properties to analyse. This forms the baseline of the models presented in this paper.

In total, there is one model per technology, containing all sub-protocols identified for this technology. Their respective size is detailed in Table 2. Although the models are large, the analysis of all lemmas of all protocols is efficient. The analysed configurations completed in less than 77 h of CPU time.

Table 2. Sizes of the Tamarin models

Model	# rules	# restrictions	# macros	# lemmas	# lines
BR/EDR	117	13	165	605	~11000
BLE	123	12	220	845	~14400
BM	57	8	100	640	~6600

Using the Models. The Tamarin preprocessor is used to prevent Tamarin from processing parts of the models that are irrelevant for an interaction. For this study, the use of macros yielded a speedup of two to three orders of magnitude for Tamarin. As a result all interactions can be studied in practical time.

Moreover, to gain more insight into the strengths and weaknesses of each protocol, one may want to study the effects of specific imperfections. Similarly, to study the effects of a patch, one may want to study the impact if only one of the two devices is patched. For example, in [18] the authors analyse the outcome of having one device with a patched ECDH implementation and another with a flawed one. The proposed models support this type of configuration. For example, it is possible to study all the mentioned protocols while preventing the attacker to brute-force low-entropy secrets using a simple command-line flag. Likewise, it is possible to study all the relevant protocols where one device has a patched version of ECDH using another flag. Overall, there are different flag combinations that allow to study different configurations of a model, from the same source file.

4   Security Analysis

The results of our study are presented in this section, and then compared with existing results from the literature.

4.1 Analysis of the Results

Various configurations of imperfections and patches are analysed. Each study requires to run Tamarin on the models to try to prove all lemmas, yielding a proof or an attack trace for each lemma. For example, when ECDH problems are patched and devices are not vulnerable to keysize reduction, Tamarin identifies 659 attack traces. Each attack trace is manually analysed to identify to which result it is linked to. Complete annotated result tables are released along with the models, this section only displays a synthesis of the results.

Table 3. Attacks identified by presented formal models on Bluetooth key agreements

Label	Attack	Technology BR/EDR	BLE	BM	This paper	Wu et al. [40]	Cremers et al. [18]	Jangid et al. [23]	Shi et al. [33]
A1	Reflection attack on Legacy PIN Pairing	X			✓				
A2	Brute-force PIN from protocol	X			✓				
A3	JustWorks is not authenticated	X	X		✓	✓			
A4	Pairing Method confusion	X	X		✓	✓		✓	✓
A5	Reflection attack in Secure Passkey Entry	X	X		✓			✓	
A6	(new) Extension to Pairing Method confusion	X			✓				
A7	(new) Pairing Mode confusion	X			✓				
A8	Invalid Curve attack	X	X		✓		✓		
A9	Reflection attack in Legacy Pairing		X		✓				
A10	Brute-force passkey from protocol		X		✓				
A11	Malleable commitment in Legacy Passkey Entry		X		✓				
A12	(new) Extension to Pairing Method confusion		X		✓				
A13	(new) Pairing Mode confusion		X		✓				
A14	Keysize downgrade in BLE-SC		X		✓				✓
A15	OOBno is not authenticated			X	✓	✓			
A16	Reflection attack in Provisioning			X	✓	✓			
A17	Brute-force AuthData from protocol			X	✓				
A18	(new) Lack of key confirmation in Provisioning			X	✓				
A19	(combination) Reflection and AuthData brute-force			X	✓				
A20	(combination) Reflection and AuthData retrieval			X	✓				
A21	(combination) AuthData retrieval and malleable commitment			X	✓				

Table 3 summarizes the attacks identified by the presented models. Moreover, attacks relying on different core assumptions, like semi-compromised devices, are not displayed. Most attacks were discovered across the years through manual analysis, and are accurately picked up by our Tamarin models. We only detail below the new attacks obtained.

In BM, we identify a lack of key confirmation at the end of the protocol (A18): an attacker can prevent a new device from joining the network, while making the network believe that the device has successfully joined. This leads to a Denial of Service (DoS), which exact effects are implementation-dependent.

Several protocol confusions attacks are picked up. The original attack [37] (A4), describes a confusion between Secure Passkey Entry and Secure Numeric

Comparison that affects BR/EDR and BLE. Tamarin identifies four novel confusion attacks for other pairs of protocols, that break all studied security properties.

- A6: Legacy PIN Pairing/Secure Numeric Comparison (BR/EDR)
- A7: Legacy PIN Pairing/Secure Passkey Entry (BR/EDR)
- A12: Legacy Passkey Entry/Secure Numeric Comparison (BLE)
- A13: Legacy Passkey Entry/Secure Passkey Entry (BLE)

The original attack is a Pairing confusion regarding the method, whereas the new ones are Pairing confusions regarding the mode. More importantly, the original attack, as well as attacks A6 and A12 can be mitigated by improving the display of expected user actions. In Numeric Comparison, the expected action is for the user to confirm that two numeric codes are equal, while for Passkey Entry the expected action is that the user inputs a numeric code displayed by one device on the other. Some implementations do not have a correct display of expected user actions, which leads to the possible confusion: users input the confirmation code into another device [37].

By contrast, attacks A7 and A13 bypass this mitigation because all involved protocols have identical user actions. They have been attributed CVE identifiers by the Bluetooth SIG and are described in more details below. Both attacks share a similar setup, but rely on different cryptographic weaknesses. The attacker forces one device to use a Legacy protocol which has the same user interaction as Secure Passkey Entry. The attacker uses a cryptographic issue to complete the Legacy protocol, retrieving the encryption key and the passkey/PIN used. Then, the attacker uses the gained knowledge of the passkey to complete the Secure Passkey Entry protocol.

Attack A7: Pairing Mode Confusion in BR/EDR - CVE-2022-25837. The attack is depicted in Fig. 3. The attacker forces the Initiator to use the Secure Passkey Entry protocol and the Responder to use the PIN Pairing protocol. To do so, the attacker sends the first message of the PIN Pairing protocol to the Responder which forces it to use this protocol. Then, upon connection of the Initiator, the attacker announces support for Secure Pairing in its features. By modifying its input-output capabilities, the attacker forces a valid user interaction between PIN Pairing and Secure Passkey Entry, for example the Initiator may display a numeric code (the passkey) and the Responder asks the user to input a numeric code (the PIN). The PIN can be recovered from the values exchanged in the PIN Pairing protocol and the authentication protocol which serves as key confirmation [32]. Because the PIN is the passkey in the Secure Passkey Entry protocol, the attacker completes the key agreement with the Initiator. In the end, the attacker has successfully completed Pairing with both devices and shares a different encryption key with each of them.

Attack A13: Pairing Mode Confusion in BLE - CVE-2022-25836. The attack is depicted in Fig. 4. Function $c1$ is defined in the specification, function get_n computes a correct nonce given a confirmation value. This results in the

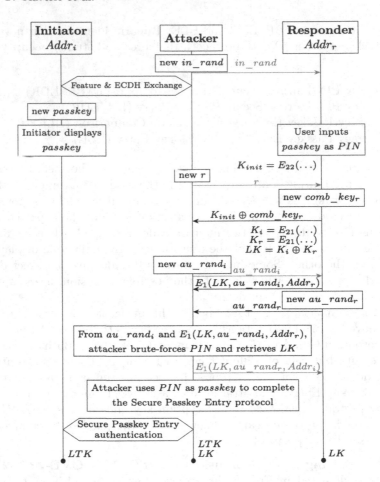

Fig. 3. Pairing Mode Confusion in BR/EDR **A7**

malleability of the commitment function in Legacy Passkey Entry protocol, as found by Rosa [30]. The attacker can force the Initiator to use the Legacy Passkey Entry protocol and the Responder to use the Secure Passkey Entry protocol by modifying the input-output capabilities and the *Secure* flag during Feature Exchange. The attacker then completes the protocol on the Legacy side, which makes use of the ability to brute-force the passkey and of the malleability of the commitment in Legacy Pairing. This enables the attacker to recover the passkey, thus to have a legitimate Secure Passkey Entry interaction with the Responder. In the end, the attacker has completed Pairing with both devices while sharing a different encryption key with each of them.

4.2   Practical Implementation

To assess their applicability, Pairing Mode confusion attacks have been tested on off-the-shelf devices. In BR/EDR and BLE, the specification defines a complete

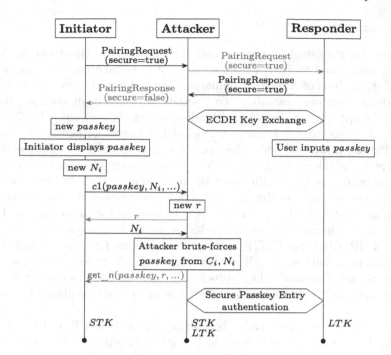

Fig. 4. Pairing Mode Confusion in BLE A13

protocol stack, from the physical layer to the application layer. Pairing happens in the intermediate layers of the protocol stack. Both Pairing Mode confusions require the attacker to implement a custom Pairing procedure. Hence, to perform the attack one needs the ability to receive and craft Pairing messages.

To implement the attack in BR/EDR, the research-oriented firmware Brak-Tooth [22] is used. It is to be noted that the core feature necessary to implement this attack, namely message injection in the layer handling Pairing messages in BR/EDR, is an undocumented component of the firmware. Thus, a custom driver is developed to create a MitM framework out of two dongles flashed with this firmware. Then, the handling of Pairing messages is reimplemented to implement both sides of the attacks. To the best of the authors knowledge, this is the first practical implementation of BR/EDR MitM on a Pairing protocol.

To implement the attack in BLE, the framework Mirage [11] that has built-in support of BLE MitM is used. As with BR/EDR, the handling of Pairing messages is reimplemented to implement both sides of the attacks.

For each technology, two Android phones are used as targets. The attack is successful in both cases, meaning that the attacker is able to retrieve the encryption key with both devices. It is important to raise that the user interaction is the same for both the Legacy and the Secure modes. Finally, it is noted that the user interaction on Android is identical between BR/EDR and BLE. Though it was not tested, it could be used to create Pairing Technology confusion attacks, by using a different technology with each target.

4.3   Related Work

There are few published formal symbolic analyses of the Bluetooth protocols involving automated tools. For completeness, it is noted that [13] performed a ProVerif [8] analysis of Numeric Comparison but did not identify any weakness. In [12] the authors demonstrated that injective key agreement does not hold in Numeric Comparison. A study of misbinding attacks is performed in [29] using ProVerif. All those studies focus on various definitions of authentication for one or two Pairing protocols, while the present paper considers all Bluetooth key agreements. The relevance of our model and results are discussed with respect to more accurate models of Bluetooth key agreements: [18, 23, 40] and [33].

In [18], the authors use Tamarin to study the security of the Secure Numeric Comparison protocol with regards to small subgroup attacks on the Diffie-Hellman key exchange, extending results from [7]. In the present study, the analysis of BR/EDR and BLE is also done considering two, one or none of the devices patched. This allows identifying more possible attack scenarios where some attacks are combined. The results for those configurations are not reported in this paper due to size constraints, but the models are available for further study.

In [40], the authors also study the Pairing protocols in BR/EDR and BLE. However, they do not take into account Legacy protocols, and do not perform a systematic study of possible confusion attacks. Also, their model of Secure protocols considers perfect cryptographic primitives, this makes them miss attacks on ECDH and the reflection attack on Secure Passkey Entry, which are correctly identified by our models. In Bluetooth Mesh, the authors propose a patch for the reflection attack identified (A15). However, those patches were analysed with our models and proven insecure, as they still allow an attacker to compromise communications. The attacks on the patches rely on a known weakness of Bluetooth Mesh in the use of a malleable commitment function based on AES-CMAC. As a result, the attacks on the patches are similar to the attacks on the original Provisioning protocol described in [15].

In [23], the authors analyse Secure Passkey Entry in Tamarin. Among the attacks they identified, there are Pairing Confusion [37] and the reflection attack [15]. These attacks were known before and also retrieved by our analysis. The other attacks they identified rely on the hypothesis that the attacker gains the passkey in other ways, due to implementation problems (e.g., bad randomness). In our model we decided not to make any implementation-related assumptions, meaning that we do not catch these attacks. Furthermore, their study tackles only one Pairing protocol, while ours encompasses all Bluetooth key agreements and considers more cryptographic imperfections.

The authors of [33] study protocol confusion, but only for BLE Secure Pairing. They did neither model BR/EDR Secure Pairing nor Legacy protocols. They also study the possibility of keysize downgrade in BLE Secure Pairing, but do not model any other cryptographic weakness. They identify another type of attack that may lead to a DoS called keysize confusion attack. The keysize downgrade is accurately picked up by our analysis, but the keysize confusion is not caught because DoS attacks are out of scope of this paper. It is worth noting that our work confirms that the keysize downgrade attack is valid in BLE Secure Pairing, but it shows that it does not affect BLE Legacy Pairing. Upon verification, the reason is that the bytes containing the key size are part of the authentication protocol in all Legacy Pairing protocols, but are not in any Secure Pairing protocol. As a result, an attacker can modify the keysize bytes without affecting the protocol in BLE Secure Pairing, but cannot do so in BLE Legacy Pairing.

5   Conclusion

Bluetooth has a security mode in BLE and BR/EDR that forces connections to use Secure Pairing modes only and 128-bit keys. For example, this mode can be used for critical applications. Whether it is implemented and enforced remains an implementation and configuration matter.

The attacks presented in this paper demonstrate that the knowledge of the configuration of one of the two devices is not enough to have complete security guarantees. If one device is configured to use only Secure Pairing but the peer device still allows Legacy Pairing, then the communication between them is not immune to attacks. Moreover, the user is not able to detect the attack because the mode confusion keeps an identical user interaction as a legitimate exchange.

In its statement about the original Pairing Method confusion from [37], the Bluetooth SIG [34] recommends device manufacturers to make it more obvious which interaction is expected from users, to avoid confusions. They did not modify the underlying protocols, hence no patch is enforced for this problem. The confusions presented in this paper bypass this mitigation because the user interaction is not only similar but identical for both protocols.

For the Pairing Mode confusion, weaknesses in Legacy modes are used to break a Secure mode. Because Legacy Pairing protocols are structurally broken, they cannot be patched while remaining compatible with older devices. Security-wise, the only definitive technical solution consists in removing Legacy Pairing from implementations and specifications to make devices compliant with Legacy Pairing gradually disappearing. However, removing Legacy Pairing would prevent communication with devices that do not support Secure Pairing.

In its statements about those vulnerabilities, the Bluetooth SIG recommends to disable Legacy Pairing and to implement better user interaction to indicate if Legacy mode is being used. However, this is not always possible, as not all devices possess a screen to accurately inform the user. Overall, for an informed user, the best way to remain protected from such attacks is to verify that both communicating devices are up to date and have disabled Legacy Pairing.

Acknowledgements. We kindly thank the authors of [40] for their insightful remarks about Bluetooth formal modelling and Bluetooth Mesh Provisioning.

References

1. Antonioli, D., Tippenhauer, N.O., Rasmussen, K.: BIAS: Bluetooth Impersonation AttackS. In: 41st IEEE Symposium on Security and Privacy, SP 2020, San Francisco, CA, USA, 18–21 May 2020, pp. 549–562. IEEE Computer Society (2020). https://doi.org/10.1109/SP40000.2020.00093
2. Antonioli, D., Tippenhauer, N.O., Rasmussen, K.: Key negotiation downgrade attacks on Bluetooth and Bluetooth low energy. ACM Trans. Priv. Secur. **23**(3), 1–28 (2020). https://doi.org/10.1145/3394497
3. Antonioli, D., Tippenhauer, N.O., Rasmussen, K., Payer, M.: BLURtooth: exploiting cross-transport key derivation in Bluetooth classic and Bluetooth low energy. In: ASIA CCS 2022: ACM Asia Conference on Computer and Communications Security, Nagasaki, Japan, 30 May 2022–3 June 2022, pp. 196–207. ACM (2022). https://doi.org/10.1145/3488932.3523258
4. Antonioli, D., Tippenhauer, N.O., Rasmussen, K.B.: The KNOB is broken: exploiting low entropy in the encryption key negotiation of Bluetooth BR/EDR. In: 28th USENIX Security Symposium, USENIX Security 2019, Santa Clara, CA, USA, 14–16 August 2019, pp. 1047–1061. USENIX Association (2019)
5. Basin, D.A., Sasse, R., Toro-Pozo, J.: The EMV standard: break, fix, verify. In: 2021 IEEE Symposium on Security and Privacy (SP), San Francisco, CA, US, 23–27 May 2021, pp. 1766–1781. IEEE (2021). https://doi.org/10.1109/SP40001.2021.00037
6. Bhargavan, K., Blanchet, B., Kobeissi, N.: Verified models and reference implementations for the TLS 1.3 standard candidate. In: 38th IEEE Symposium on Security and Privacy, SP 2017, San Jose, CA, USA, 22–26 May 2017, pp. 483–502. IEEE Computer Society (2017). https://doi.org/10.1109/SP.2017.26
7. Biham, E., Neumann, L.: Breaking the Bluetooth pairing – the fixed coordinate invalid curve attack. In: Paterson, K.G., Stebila, D. (eds.) SAC 2019. LNCS, vol. 11959, pp. 250–273. Springer, Cham (2020). https://doi.org/10.1007/978-3-030-38471-5_11
8. Blanchet, B.: Automatic verification of security protocols in the symbolic model: the verifier ProVerif. In: Aldini, A., Lopez, J., Martinelli, F. (eds.) FOSAD 2012-2013. LNCS, vol. 8604, pp. 54–87. Springer, Cham (2014). https://doi.org/10.1007/978-3-319-10082-1_3
9. Bluetooth SIG: Bluetooth Core Specification, v5.4 (2023)
10. Cäsar, M., Pawelke, T., Steffan, J., Terhorst, G.: A survey on Bluetooth low energy security and privacy. Comput. Netw. **205**, 108712 (2022). https://doi.org/10.1016/j.comnet.2021.108712
11. Cayre, R., Nicomette, V., Auriol, G., Alata, E., Kaâniche, M., Marconato, G.V.: Mirage: towards a metasploit-like framework for IoT. In: 30th IEEE International Symposium on Software Reliability Engineering, ISSRE 2019, Berlin, Germany, 28–31 October 2019, pp. 261–270. IEEE Computer Society (2019). https://doi.org/10.1109/ISSRE.2019.00034
12. Chang, R., Shmatikov, V.: Formal analysis of authentication in Bluetooth device pairing. In: Proceedings of the Joint Workshop on Foundations of Computer Security and Automated Reasoning for Security Protocol Analysis, FCS-ARSPA 2007, pp. 45–62 (2007)
13. Chothia, T., Smyth, B., Staite, C.: Automatically checking commitment protocols in ProVerif without false attacks. In: Focardi, R., Myers, A. (eds.) POST 2015. LNCS, vol. 9036, pp. 137–155. Springer, Heidelberg (2015). https://doi.org/10.1007/978-3-662-46666-7_8

14. Claverie, T., Avoine, G., Delaune, S., Lopes Esteves, J.: Extended version: tamarin-based analysis of Bluetooth uncovers two practical pairing confusion attacks. https://hal.science/hal-04079883

15. Claverie, T., Lopes Esteves, J.: BlueMirror: reflections on Bluetooth pairing and provisioning protocols. In: 15th IEEE Workshop on Offensive Technologies, WOOT 2021, San Francisco, CA, USA, 27 May 2021, pp. 339–351. IEEE Computer Society (2021). https://doi.org/10.1109/SPW53761.2021.00054

16. Cremers, C., Dehnel-Wild, M.: Component-based formal analysis of 5G-AKA: channel assumptions and session confusion. In: 26th Annual Network and Distributed System Security Symposium, NDSS 2019, San Diego, California, USA, 24–27 February 2019. The Internet Society (2019)

17. Cremers, C., Horvat, M., Scott, S., van der Merwe, T.: Automated analysis and verification of TLS 1.3: 0-RTT, resumption and delayed authentication. In: 37th IEEE Symposium on Security and Privacy, SP 2016, San Jose, CA, USA, 22–26 May 2016, pp. 470–485. IEEE Computer Society (2016). https://doi.org/10.1109/SP.2016.35

18. Cremers, C., Jackson, D.: Prime, order please! Revisiting small subgroup and invalid curve attacks on protocols using Diffie-Hellman. In: 32nd IEEE Computer Security Foundations Symposium, CSF 2019, Hoboken, NJ, USA, 25–28 June 2019, pp. 78–93. IEEE Computer Society (2019). https://doi.org/10.1109/CSF.2019.00013

19. Cremers, C., Kiesl, B., Medinger, N.: A formal analysis of IEEE 802.11's WPA2: countering the kracks caused by cracking the counters. In: 29th USENIX Security Symposium, USENIX Security 2020, 12–14 August 2020, pp. 1–17. USENIX Association (2020)

20. Dolev, D., Yao, A.C.: On the security of public key protocols. IEEE Trans. Inf. Theory **29**(2), 198–207 (1983). https://doi.org/10.1109/TIT.1983.1056650

21. Fischlin, M., Sanina, O.: Cryptographic analysis of the Bluetooth secure connection protocol suite. In: Tibouchi, M., Wang, H. (eds.) ASIACRYPT 2021. LNCS, vol. 13091, pp. 696–725. Springer, Cham (2021). https://doi.org/10.1007/978-3-030-92075-3_24

22. Garbelini, M.E., Bedi, V., Chattopadhyay, S., Sun, S., Kurniawan, E.: BrakTooth: causing havoc on Bluetooth link manager via directed fuzzing. In: 31st USENIX Security Symposium, USENIX Security 2022, Boston, MA, USA, 10–12 August 2022, pp. 1025–1042. USENIX Association (2022)

23. Jangid, M.K., Zhang, Y., Lin, Z.: Extrapolating formal analysis to uncover attacks in Bluetooth passkey entry pairing. In: 30th Annual Network and Distributed System Security Symposium, NDSS 2023, San Diego, California, USA, 27 February–3 March 2023. The Internet Society (2023)

24. Jason, M.: New wireless trends and forecasts for the next 5 years. https://www.bluetooth.com/blog/new-trends-and-forecasts-for-the-next-5-years/

25. Lindell, A.Y.: Attacks on the pairing protocol of Bluetooth v2.1. BlackHat, USA (2008). https://www.blackhat.com/presentations/bh-usa-08/Lindell/BH_US_08_Lindell_Bluetooth_2.1_New_Vulnerabilities.pdf

26. Lindell, A.Y.: Comparison-based key exchange and the security of the numeric comparison mode in Bluetooth v2.1. In: Fischlin, M. (ed.) CT-RSA 2009. LNCS, vol. 5473, pp. 66–83. Springer, Heidelberg (2009). https://doi.org/10.1007/978-3-642-00862-7_5

27. Lowe, G.: A hierarchy of authentication specification. In: Computer Security Foundations Workshop 1997. IEEE Computer Society (1997). https://doi.org/10.1109/CSFW.1997.596782

28. Meier, S., Schmidt, B., Cremers, C., Basin, D.: The TAMARIN prover for the symbolic analysis of security protocols. In: Sharygina, N., Veith, H. (eds.) CAV 2013. LNCS, vol. 8044, pp. 696–701. Springer, Heidelberg (2013). https://doi.org/10.1007/978-3-642-39799-8_48

29. Peltonen, A., Sethi, M., Aura, T.: Formal verification of misbinding attacks on secure device pairing and bootstrapping. J. Inf. Secur. Appl. **51**, 102461 (2020). https://doi.org/10.1016/j.jisa.2020.102461

30. Rosa, T.: Bypassing passkey authentication in Bluetooth low energy. IACR Cryptology ePrint Archive, p. 309 (2013). http://eprint.iacr.org/2013/309

31. Ryan, M.: Bluetooth: with low energy comes low security. In: 7th USENIX Workshop on Offensive Technologies, WOOT 2013, Washington, D.C., USA, 13 August 2013. USENIX Association (2013)

32. Shaked, Y., Wool, A.: Cracking the Bluetooth PIN. In: Proceedings of the 3rd International Conference on Mobile Systems, Applications, and Services, MobiSys 2005, Seattle, Washington, USA, 6–8 June 2005, pp. 39–50. ACM (2005). https://doi.org/10.1145/1067170.1067176

33. Shi, M., Chen, J., He, K., Zhao, H., Jia, M., Du, R.: Formal analysis and patching of BLE-SC pairing. In: 32nd USENIX Security Symposium, USENIX Security 2023, Anaheim, CA, USA, 9–11 August 2023. USENIX Association (2023)

34. Bluetooth SIG: Bluetooth SIG Statement Regarding the Method-Confusion Pairing Vulnerability. https://www.bluetooth.com/learn-about-bluetooth/key-attributes/bluetooth-security/method-vulnerability/

35. Tillmanns, J., Classen, J., Rohrbach, F., Hollick, M.: Firmware insider: Bluetooth randomness is mostly random. In: 14th USENIX Workshop on Offensive Technologies, WOOT 2020, 11 August 2020. USENIX Association (2020). https://www.usenix.org/conference/woot20/presentation/tillmanns

36. Troncoso, M., Hale, B.: The Bluetooth CYBORG: analysis of the full human-machine passkey entry AKE protocol. In: 28th Annual Network and Distributed System Security Symposium, NDSS 2021, 21–25 February 2021. The Internet Society (2021)

37. von Tschirschnitz, M., Peuckert, L., Franzen, F., Grossklags, J.: Method confusion attack on Bluetooth pairing. In: 42nd IEEE Symposium on Security and Privacy, SP 2021, San Francisco, CA, USA, 24–27 May 2021, pp. 1332–1347. IEEE Computer Society (2021). https://doi.org/10.1109/SP40001.2021.00013

38. Viganò, L.: Automated security protocol analysis with the AVISPA tool. In: Annual Conference on Mathematical Foundations of Programming Semantics 2005. Elsevier (2005). https://doi.org/10.1016/j.entcs.2005.11.052

39. Wu, J., et al.: BLESA: spoofing attacks against reconnections in Bluetooth low energy. In: 14th USENIX Workshop on Offensive Technologies, WOOT 2020, 11 August 2020. USENIX Association (2020). https://www.usenix.org/conference/woot20/presentation/wu

40. Wu, J., Wu, R., Xu, D., Tian, D.J., Bianchi, A.: Formal model-driven discovery of Bluetooth protocol design vulnerabilities. In: 43rd IEEE Symposium on Security and Privacy, SP 2022, San Francisco, CA, USA, 22–26 May 2022, pp. 2285–2303. IEEE Computer Society (2022). https://doi.org/10.1109/SP46214.2022.9833777

41. Xu, F., Diao, W., Li, Z., Chen, J., Zhang, K.: BadBluetooth: breaking Android security mechanisms via malicious Bluetooth peripherals. In: 26th Annual Network and Distributed System Security Symposium, NDSS 2019, San Diego, California, USA, 24–27 February 2019. The Internet Society (2019)

42. Zhang, Y., Weng, J., Dey, R., Jin, Y., Lin, Z., Fu, X.: Breaking secure pairing of Bluetooth low energy using downgrade attacks. In: 29th USENIX Security Symposium, USENIX Security 2020, pp. 37–54. USENIX Association (2020). https://www.usenix.org/conference/usenixsecurity20/presentation/zhang-yue

MARF: A Memory-Aware
CLFLUSH-Based Intra- and Inter-CPU
Side-Channel Attack

Sowoong Kim, Myeonggyun Han, and Woongki Baek[✉]

UNIST, Ulsan, Republic of Korea
{bioloid,hmg0228,wbaek}@unist.ac.kr

Abstract. In this work, we conduct in-depth characterization to quantify the impact of DRAM refresh, the location of the target memory object within a non-uniform memory access (NUMA) node, and task and page placement across NUMA nodes and identify a set of the patterns in the `clflush` latency data. Based on characterization results, we propose MARF, a novel memory-aware `clflush`-based intra- and inter-CPU side-channel attack on NUMA systems. Our case studies on three real NUMA systems demonstrate that MARF can robustly be used to attack applications that use widely-used cryptographic and user-interface libraries. We also present potential countermeasures against MARF.

1 Introduction

The wide adoption of NUMA systems and workload consolidation [3,24] has both positive and negative aspects in terms of security. With workload consolidation, malicious users can deploy attacks that exploit the side channels available through various hardware components such as caches [7,8,13,15–17,20,23,29,34], translation look-aside buffers (TLBs) [8,12,19], branch target buffers (BTBs) [8,9,16,17], and directories [21,33] against other applications consolidated on the same physical servers. The attacker can monitor the states of security-critical hardware components, infer the activities (e.g., memory accesses) of the victim based on the changes in the hardware states, and discover security-sensitive information (e.g., the private key of a cryptographic service) based on the inferred activities of the victim.

Most of the prior works on micro-architectural side-channel attacks assume single CPU scenarios in which consolidated workloads are placed on the same multi-core CPU [7–9,12,13,15–17,19,21,23,29,33,34]. With the widespread use of NUMA systems, security-sensitive applications can be isolated on the dedicated CPU among the multiple CPUs in order to defeat single CPU-based micro-architectural side-channel attacks.

Irazoqui et al. propose a `clflush`-based side-channel attack for multi-CPU scenarios [20]. However, the attack proposed in [20] has two major limitations – (1) unawareness of DRAM refresh and (2) use of the `load` instruction. The attack proposed in [20] is oblivious of DRAM refresh. Therefore, it suffers from

© The Author(s), under exclusive license to Springer Nature Switzerland AG 2024
G. Tsudik et al. (Eds.): ESORICS 2023, LNCS 14346, pp. 120–140, 2024.
https://doi.org/10.1007/978-3-031-51479-1_7

low accuracy because a considerable portion of the latency data samples collected by the attacker are significantly affected by DRAM refresh. In addition, since the attack proposed in [20] frequently executes the load instruction to probe the activities of the victim, it can be mitigated or defeated by the existing defense techniques that identify suspicious applications that incur high cache miss rates through hardware performance counters [2,5]. To bridge this gap, this paper makes the following contributions:

- We quantify the impact of DRAM refresh, the location of the target memory object in a NUMA node, and task and page placement on the clflush latency on three real NUMA systems and identify a set of the clflush latency data patterns with respect to the aforementioned factors.
- Guided by the characterization results, we propose MARF, a memory-aware clflush-based intra- and inter-CPU side-channel attack.
- We present case studies where MARF is used to attack applications that use widely-used cryptographic and user-interface libraries (i.e., GnuPG [31], OpenSSL's T-table implementation of Advanced Encryption Standard [28], and GIMP Drawing Kit (Appendix B) [10]) on NUMA systems. We also demonstrate that the DRAM refresh interval detection and avoidance algorithms of MARF significantly improve the attack accuracy (Appendix C).
- We present potential countermeasures against MARF and discuss their advantages and disadvantages (Appendix D).

2 Background

2.1 NUMA, Cache Coherence, and CLFLUSH

A *memory node* is defined as a group of dual in-line memory modules (DIMMs) locally attached to a CPU. A NUMA system is a system with two or more memory nodes. The local memory node of a CPU is directly connected to the CPU. In contrast, remote memory nodes of a CPU are directly connected to the other CPUs and the CPU accesses the remote memory nodes via the interconnection network (ICN) that connects the CPUs. Because of the extra delay incurred in the ICN, remote memory accesses incur longer latency than local accesses.

Modern NUMA systems provide cache coherence, which is an architectural mechanism that ensures that cores that share a memory object observe the same value when the shared memory object is dynamically cached and modified. Cache coherence is usually provided at the cache line granularity.

With the directory-based cache coherence protocol, the coherence information is stored in hardware components called *directories* [18]. Each directory dynamically tracks the coherence information on its associated cache lines. When a core is about to execute an instruction that changes the coherence state of a cache line, it first queries the corresponding directory and identifies the caches currently holding the cache line. A coherence message is then generated and selectively sent to the associated caches to maintain cache coherence. Because of its high scalability, it is widely used in NUMA systems [20,26].

Recent Intel CPUs employ hierarchical directory structures that consist of two types of directories – in-cache and in-memory directories [25,33]. The in-cache directory is located in the last-level cache and stores the coherence information on the cache lines in the private and shared caches in the corresponding CPU. Since the coherence information on the cache lines stored in a CPU can directly be obtained from the in-cache directory, the performance of NUMA systems can significantly be improved by reducing the inter-CPU coherence traffic.

Recent Intel CPUs use the MOESI protocol to maintain the cache coherence states within a NUMA node [25]. With the MOESI protocol, a cache line can be in one of the five states (i.e., modified, owned, exclusive, shared, and invalid).

In contrast, recent Intel CPUs employ a simpler protocol which consists of three states (i.e., A, S, and I) for inter-CPU cache coherence [25]. In-memory directories store the inter-CPU cache coherence information. If a memory object is in the A state, it indicates that the memory object may currently be cached in a remote CPU and the corresponding cache line is dirty. If a memory object is in the S state, it indicates that the memory object may currently be cached in one or more remote CPUs and the corresponding cache lines are clean. If a memory object is in the I state, it indicates that no remote CPU is currently caching the memory object.

Modern CPUs provide the clflush instruction. clflush writes back the content of the cache line holding the target memory object if it is dirty and invalidates all the cache lines holding the object. It is used for programming models such as memory mapped I/O and persistent memory programming [22] that require that the main memory to hold the up-to-date data for correctness.

2.2   DRAM Refresh

A DIMM consists of a group of DRAM chips mounted on a printed circuit board (PCB) [18]. A DRAM rank in a DIMM is defined as a group of DRAM chips that are connected to the same chip select pins and simultaneously accessible. For example, the DIMMs evaluated in this work comprise two ranks, each of which is equipped with 9 1 GB DRAM chips, and provide the error correction code (ECC) functionality.

DRAM cells may gradually lose its stored data because of the leakage current [4]. Memory cells are periodically refreshed to prevent data loss. The JEDEC Solid State Technology Association formally specifies the details of DRAM refresh. Specifically, the DRAM refresh period is 7.8 ms and the time spent for each DRAM refresh (i.e., the DRAM refresh duration) for 1 GB DRAM chips is 350 ns [4]. Each DRAM rank independently performs DRAM refresh without coordinating with others.

We define the DRAM refresh interval as the time interval between the beginning and end of DRAM refresh. While a DRAM rank is being refreshed, all the incoming memory requests to the rank are queued and remain unprocessed until the on-going DRAM refresh finishes. DRAM refresh poses critical challenges to timing-based side-channel attacks against the memory hierarchy including the clflush-based attacks as follows. First, a considerable portion of the latency data samples collected by the attacker is affected by DRAM refresh. Specifically, since the DRAM refresh duration is 350 ns and it occurs in every 7.8 ms, 4.5% (i.e., $\frac{0.35}{7.8} \times 100 = 4.5\%$) of the latency data samples collected by the attacker are affected by DRAM refresh.

Second, it is challenging for the attacker to precisely determine whether a latency data sample has been affected by DRAM refresh or not. This is mainly because the extra latency incurred by DRAM refresh can significantly vary (from 0 to 350 ns with a uniform distribution) depending on when the memory request generated by the attacker arrives at the target DRAM rank that is being refreshed. For instance, if the memory request arrives at the rank when the progress of DRAM refresh is 0% and 50%, the extra latency incurred by DRAM refresh is 350 and 175 ns. These noises make the attacker hard to infer whether the latency differences have been caused by the activities of the victim or DRAM refresh.

3 Methodology

We use three NUMA systems equipped with recent Intel CPUs. We refer the NUMA systems installed with Intel Xeon Gold 6242 (16 cores per CPU), 5318H (18 cores per CPU), and 6338 (32 cores per CPU) CPUs that implement the Cascade Lake, Cooper Lake, and Ice Lake architectures to the CCL, CPL, and ICL systems. The evaluated NUMA systems are equipped with four 16 GB DDR4 memory DIMMs per NUMA node. Each DIMM is connected to a separate memory channel. While, for conciseness, we report the experimental results that are collected on the ICL system, similar data trends are observed on the CCL and CPL systems.

Ubuntu 20.04 and the Linux kernel 5.4.0 are installed on the evaluated NUMA systems. For all the experiments, the CPUfreq governor is set to the performance governor. The rdtsc instruction is used to measure the time.

4 Characterization

In this section, we quantify the impact of DRAM refresh, the location of the target memory object within a NUMA node, and the task and page placement on NUMA systems on the clflush latency. For our characterization studies, we use a simple microbenchmark that consists of two processes – the attacker and the victim. The two processes share a read-only 64-byte memory object, which we refer to the target memory object. The attacker executes clflush against the memory object. The victim accesses (i.e., reads or executes) the memory object or performs no operation depending on the configuration of each experiment.

In each experiment, the two processes periodically repeat the following steps in a synchronized manner. First, the victim accesses the target memory object or performs no operation depending on the configuration for the experiment. Second, the attacker executes clflush against the memory object and measures the clflush latency.

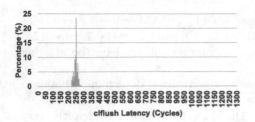

Fig. 1. clflush latency measured when the attacker periodically executes clflush with no delay

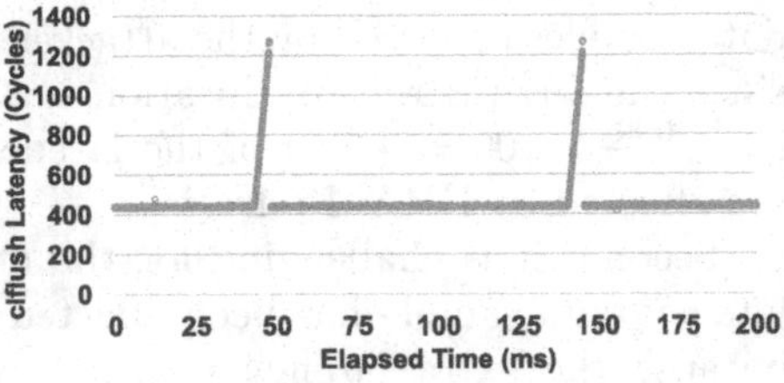

Fig. 2. clflush latency measured when the attacker executes clflush with a period of 7.8 ms

The microbenchmark has the key configuration parameters (i.e., the NUMA nodes where the attacker and the victim are placed, the address and the NUMA node where the target memory object is located). These configuration parameters are used to create various scenarios in terms of the location of the memory object in a NUMA node and task and page placement on NUMA systems.

For brevity, we refer the NUMA nodes where the attacker, the victim, and the target memory object to N_A, N_V, and N_O, respectively. We indicate whether the victim has accessed the target memory object (and the memory object is in the hardware caches on N_V) as a boolean variable A_V.

4.1   DRAM Refresh

We quantify the impact of DRAM refresh on the clflush latency. To this end, we use the following configuration for the microbenchmark – $N_O = N_A$ and $A_V =$ False. In this configuration, every execution of clflush triggers a query to the corresponding in-memory directory in N_O to retrieve the coherence information on the target memory object. If the query request arrives at the rank where DRAM refresh is being performed, the clflush latency will be increased because of the delay in processing the query request.

Figure 1 shows the clflush latency measured when the target memory object is placed at different locations within the same NUMA node and the attacker periodically executes clflush against the memory object with no delay. First, a significant portion (i.e., 95.2%) of the data samples are clustered at 250 cycles. These data samples are collected when the DRAM rank where the memory object is placed is not in the DRAM refresh mode.

Second, a non-negligible portion (i.e., 4.8%) of the data samples are distributed from 285 to 1054 cycles. These data samples are collected when the target DRAM rank is performing DRAM refresh. Since the DRAM refresh period and duration are 7.8 ms (or 15,600 CPU cycles on the ICL system) and 350 ns (or 700 CPU cycles) [4], the theoretically estimated portion of the data samples that would be affected by DRAM refresh is 4.5%, which is in line with the experimentally measured portion (i.e., 4.8%).

In addition, since the `clflush` request may arrive at the target DRAM rank at any time within the DRAM refresh interval, the extra latency caused by DRAM refresh widely varies (i.e., from 0 to 700 cycles). Our experimental results show that the attacker must be capable of reliably detecting and avoiding the DRAM refresh interval because DRAM refresh affects a considerable portion of the `clflush` latency data samples and adds unpredictable widely-varying noises.

Figure 2 shows the `clflush` latency measured when the attacker executes `clflush` with a period of 7.8 ms. First, the `clflush` latency varies over the time, which indicates that the DRAM refresh period is not precisely 7.8 ms. If the DRAM refresh period was exactly 7.8 ms, the measured `clflush` latency would be always same. Second, the `clflush` latency drifting rate is low and predictable (i.e., 5 cycles every 31.2 ms). This indicates that DRAM refresh is periodically performed at a period slightly longer than 7.8 ms. Our experimental results indicate that the attacker must consider the drifting issue when predicting the DRAM refresh interval.

4.2 Location of the Target Memory Object

We quantify the impact of the location of the target memory object within a NUMA node on the `clflush` latency. To this end, we conduct two sets of experiments based on the microbenchmark. In the first set of experiments, we use the following configuration for the microbenchmark – $N_A \neq N_V$, $N_O = N_V$, and $A_V =$ False. In each experiment, we vary the location of the memory object in the corresponding NUMA node and measure the `clflush` latency.

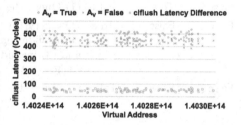

Fig. 3. `clflush` latency measured when the target memory object is placed at various locations in a NUMA node

Figure 3 shows the `clflush` latency when the memory object is placed at different locations within the same NUMA node.

First, the `clflush` latency widely varies with different locations of the target memory object. We conjecture that the large variance of the `clflush` latency is caused by various factors such as the location of the memory controller and DIMM associated with the memory object. Since the attacker has no control over the location of the memory object, the large variance of the `clflush` latency poses a critical challenge. Second, there is no clear data pattern between the location of the memory object and the `clflush` latency. We conjecture that this complicated data trend is mainly due to the sophisticated undisclosed hardware functions that map an address to a memory controller and a DIMM [30,32,35].

In the second set of experiments, we use the following configuration – $N_A \neq N_V$, $N_O = N_V$ and $A_V =$ True (i.e., same as the first set of experiments except that the victim accesses the target memory object). We also configure the microbenchmark to place the memory object at the same set of locations as the first set of experiments. Figure 3 shows the `clflush` latency differences

Table 1. Possible scenarios with respect to task and page placement and the memory access of the victim and the actions performed with `clflush`

$N_A = N_V$	$N_O = N_A$	A_V	Actions performed
True	True	True	If the victim reads the target memory object, (1) invalidate the cache line in N_A. If the victim executes the memory object, (1) invalidate the cache line in N_A and (2) query the in-memory directory in N_A.
True	True	False	(1) Query the in-memory directory in N_A.
True	False	True	If the victim reads the target memory object, (1) invalidate the cache line in N_A. If the victim executes the memory object, (1) invalidate the cache line in N_A and (2) query the in-memory directory in N_O.
True	False	False	(1) Query the in-memory directory in N_O.
False	True	True	(1) Query the in-memory directory in N_A, (2) send an invalidation request to N_V, and (3) invalidate the target cache lines in the local caches in N_V.
False	True	False	(1) Query the in-memory directory in N_A.
False	False	True	(1) Query the in-memory directory in N_V, (2) send an invalidation request to the local caches in N_V, and (3) invalidate the target cache lines in the local caches in N_V.
False	False	False	(1) Query the in-memory directory in N_V

measured when the memory object is accessed by the victim and the memory object is not accessed by the victim.

We observe that the variance of the `clflush` latency difference is small when the target memory object is placed at different locations. Since a portion of the `clflush` latency for a given location of the memory object is affected by the same factors (e.g., memory controller and DIMM locations) regardless of whether the victim has accessed the memory object or not, the portion of the `clflush` latency caused by the location of the memory object is cancelled in the `clflush` latency difference. This data trend indicates that the attacker can robustly infer the activities of the victim regardless of the location of the memory object within a NUMA node by computing the `clflush` latency difference measured when $A_V = \text{True}$ and $A_V = \text{False}$.

4.3   Task and Page Placement

We quantify the impact of task and page placement on NUMA systems on the `clflush` latency. Table 1 summarizes all the possible scenarios with respect to N_A, N_V, N_O, and A_V and the actions performed in each scenario during the execution of clflush. The clflush latency in each scenario is primarily determined by the set of actions performed during the execution of clflush.

For example, when $N_A = N_V$ and $A_V =$ True and the access performed by the victim is "read", clflush only incurs the invalidation of the cache line holding the target memory object because the cache line is in the exclusive (E) state [6]. In this scenario, the clflush latency is expected to be relatively short in comparison with other scenarios.

Interestingly, when $N_A = N_V$ and $A_V =$ True and the access performed by the victim is "execute", our experimental results indicate that clflush causes a query to the in-memory directory in the DIMM where the target memory object is stored. We are unaware of its exact cause and conjecture that in-cache directories do not need to track the coherence information on cache lines that contain instructions, which are write-protected.

For another example, when $N_A \neq N_V$, $N_O = N_A$, and $A_V =$ True, clflush triggers the following actions – (1) querying the in-memory directory in N_A because the target memory object is not cached in the local caches of N_A, (2) sending an invalidation request to N_V, (3) invalidating the cache lines in the local caches in N_V. In this scenario, the clflush latency is expected to be longer than other scenarios.

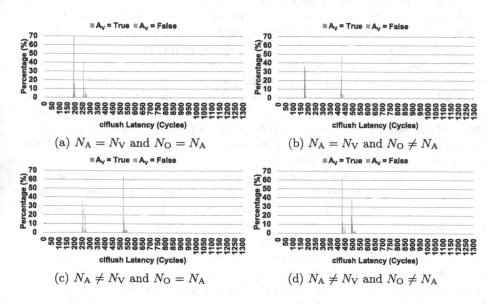

(a) $N_A = N_V$ and $N_O = N_A$

(b) $N_A = N_V$ and $N_O \neq N_A$

(c) $N_A \neq N_V$ and $N_O = N_A$

(d) $N_A \neq N_V$ and $N_O \neq N_A$

Fig. 4. Impact of task and page placement

We quantify the impact of task and page placement on the clflush latency by configuring the microbenchmark to generate all the aforementioned eight scenarios. We measure the clflush latency without varying its location within the NUMA node in each scenario because the similar data trends are observed across various locations as discussed in Sect. 4.2. Figure 4 shows the experimental results with the following data trends.

First, most of the distributions of the clflush latency data collected across the scenarios are distinct. This is because clflush generates a unique set of actions in each of the most scenarios. This data trend indicates that the attacker can infer the placement of the victim and the target memory object and whether the victim has accessed the memory object by measuring the clflush latency.

Figures 4a and 4b show that the clflush latency is same regardless of the placement of the target memory object when $N_A = N_V$, $A_V =$ True, and the access performed by the victim is "read". Since clflush only triggers an action that invalidates the cache line in N_A without querying the in-memory directory in these scenarios, the same clflush latency is observed regardless of the placement of the memory object. However, it is acceptable because the attacker can still infer that the victim has accessed the memory object in both scenarios.

While omitted for brevity, when $N_A = N_V$, $A_V =$ True, and the access performed by the victim is "execute", the clflush latency differs depending on whether $N_O = N_A$ (i.e., 308 cycles) or $N_O \neq N_A$ (i.e., 516 cycles). When the victim executes the target memory object, clflush executed by the attacker triggers a query to the in-memory directory in the local or remote NUMA node, resulting in the difference in the clflush latency.

Second, when the victim has not accessed the target memory object, the clflush latency is significantly longer when $N_O \neq N_A$ than $N_O = N_A$. This is due to the difference between the latency for accessing the remote in-memory directory (i.e., $N_O \neq N_A$) and the latency for accessing the local in-memory directory (i.e., $N_O = N_A$). This data trend indicates that the attacker can determine whether the memory object is located in N_A or not by measuring the clflush latency when the victim has not accessed the memory object. We refer the clflush latency measure when $N_O = N_A$ and $A_V =$ False to $L_{A_V=F,s}$ (i.e., 258 cycles) and the clflush latency measure when $N_O \neq N_A$ and $A_V =$ False to $L_{A_V=F,l}$ (i.e., 428 cycles), respectively.

Third, as shown in Figs. 4a and 4c, when $N_O = N_A$, $A_V =$ True, and the access performed by the victim is "read", the clflush latency measured with $N_A = N_V$ is shorter than $L_{A_V=F,s}$ by 65 cycles (i.e., $\delta_{N_A=N_V,N_O=N_A}$) and the clflush latency measured with $N_A \neq N_V$ is longer than $L_{A_V=F,s}$ by 268 cycles (i.e., $\delta_{N_A\neq N_V,N_O=N_A}$), respectively. Similarly, as shown in Figs. 4b and 4d, when $N_O = N_V$, $A_V =$ True, and the access performed by the victim is "read", the clflush latency measured with $N_A = N_V$ is shorter than $L_{A_V=F,l}$ by 249 cycles (i.e., $\delta_{N_A=N_V,N_O\neq N_A}$) and the clflush latency measured with $N_A \neq N_V$ is longer than $L_{A_V=F,l}$ by 70 cycles (i.e., $\delta_{N_A\neq N_V,N_O\neq N_A}$), which is in line with the data trend reported in [6]. While omitted for conciseness, when the access performed by the victim is "execute", we can find $L_{A_V=F,s}$ or $L_{A_V=F,l}$ in a similar manner. This data trend suggests that the attacker can precisely determine whether the victim has accessed the target memory object when the measured clflush latency differs from $L_{A_V=F,s}$ or $L_{A_V=F,l}$.

5   The MARF Attack

MARF is a `clflush`-based intra- and inter-CPU side-channel attack on NUMA systems.[1] It exploits the difference in the `clflush` latency depending on whether the victim has accessed the target memory object or not. It works even with varying `clflush` latency because of DRAM refresh, the location of the target memory object within a NUMA node, and task and page placement. It consists of four phases – (1) DRAM refresh interval detection, (2) threshold determination, (3) refresh-aware flush and inference, and (4) recalibration phases.

DRAM Refresh Interval Detection: The first phase of MARF is the DRAM refresh interval detection phase, which aims to empirically find the beginning and end time of DRAM refresh in each DRAM refresh period for the DRAM rank where the target memory object is placed. Since there is no direct way to retrieve the information on the DRAM refresh interval of the target DRAM rank, the attacker detects the DRAM refresh interval based on the `clflush` latency data.

The attacker begins the DRAM refresh interval detection process by sampling the *baseline time* defined as the time at which the attacker starts detecting the DRAM refresh interval. We define the *offset* as an amount of time added to the baseline time. The attacker periodically executes `clflush` at the time computed using Eq. 1, where t_{base}, n, $p_{refresh}$, and o denote the baseline time, a non-negative integer, the DRAM refresh period, and the offset, respectively. The attacker then measures the `clflush` latency to determine whether the target DRAM rank was performing DRAM refresh during the execution of `clflush`.

$$t_{refresh} = t_{base} + n \times p_{refresh} + o \tag{1}$$

The goal of the DRAM refresh interval detection algorithm is to find the offset value with which the attacker observes DRAM refresh if it executes `clflush` at the time computed using Eq. 1. Algorithm 1 shows the pseudocode for the `detectRefInterval` function, which implements the proposed algorithm.

`detectRefInterval` takes three parameters – `addr`, τ_{min}, and τ_{max}. `addr` is the address of the target memory object. τ_{min} and τ_{max} denote the minimum and maximum values used to construct a time window. The values of τ_{min} and τ_{max} are empirically determined in a way that if the measured `clflush` latency is within the time window (i.e., $[\tau_{min}, \tau_{max}]$), the corresponding execution of `clflush` has been performed while the target DRAM rank was being refreshed. In this work, τ_{min} and τ_{max} are set to 700 and 1300 cycles.

`detectRefInterval` iteratively finds the offset value with which the attacker would encounter DRAM refresh at the target DRAM rank if it executed `clflush` at the time computed based on Eq. 1 (Lines 4–27). Specifically, for a given offset value, `detectRefInterval` executes `clflush` $N_{sampling}$ times (Lines 11–21) and considers that the offset value is aligned with the DRAM refresh interval if there are at least $N_{threshold}$ data samples that show that the measured `clflush` latency is within the time window (Lines 22–25).

---

[1] The threat model of MARF is described in Appendix A.

Algorithm 1. The detectRefInterval function

1: **procedure** DETECTREFINTERVAL(addr, τ_{min}, τ_{max})
2:      stride ← $(\tau_{max} - \tau_{min}) \times 0.5$
3:      t_{base} ← rdtsc()
4:      **while true do**
5:          offset ← 0
6:          **while** offset < refPeriod **do**
7:              $N_{refresh}$ ← 0
8:              t_{now} ← rdtsc()
9:              δ_{offset} ← offset − $((t_{now} - t_{base})$ % refPeriod$)$
10:             t_{next} ← t_{now} + $(\delta_{offset}$ % refPeriod$)$ + refPeriod
11:             **for** i ← 1 **to** $N_{sampling}$ **do**
12:                 t_{curr} ← rdtsc()
13:                 **while** t_{curr} < t_{next} **do**
14:                     | t_{curr} ← rdtsc()
15:                 t_{begin} ← rdtsc()
16:                 clflush(addr)
17:                 t_{end} ← rdtsc()
18:                 δ_{flush} ← t_{end} − t_{begin}
19:                 **if** $\delta_{flush} \in [\tau_{min}, \tau_{max}]$ **then**
20:                     | $N_{refresh}$ ← $N_{refresh}$ + 1
21:                 t_{next} ← t_{next} + refPeriod
22:             **if** $N_{refresh} \geq N_{threshold}$ **then**
23:                 $t_{refresh}$ ← t_{base} + offset
24:                 $t_{refresh}$ ← $t_{refresh}$ + δ_{flush} − $(\tau_{max} + \tau_{min}) \times 0.5$
25:                 **return** $t_{refresh}$
26:             offset ← offset + stride
27:         t_{base} ← t_{base} + $(\tau_{max} - \tau_{min}) \times 0.1$

If the current offset value is not aligned with the DRAM refresh period, detectRefInterval increments the offset with a stride of $\frac{\tau_{max} - \tau_{min}}{2}$ and repeats the aforementioned process (Line 26). We use this stride value to execute detectRefInterval at least once during the time window.

Finally, if the offset value that is aligned with the DRAM refresh interval still remains undiscovered after checking all the possible offset values, detectRefInterval slightly increments the baseline time and repeats the aforementioned process (Line 27). While we add this code segment to handle rare cases in which the DRAM refresh interval remains undiscovered even after iterating all the possible offset values for a given baseline time, our experimental results show that detectRefInterval robustly detects the DRAM refresh interval without the need for executing it.

Threshold Determination: The second phase of MARF is the threshold determination phase, which aims to determine thresholds that are used to classify whether the victim has accessed the target memory object or not. The threshold determination algorithm collects the clflush latency data and determines

---

Algorithm 2. The determineThresholds function

1: **procedure** DETERMINETHRESHOLDS(addr, t_{nxtRef})
2:     data $\leftarrow$ sampleFlushLat(addr, t_{nxtRef})
3:     $L \leftarrow \min(\text{data})$; $L_{\text{maxSample}} \leftarrow L$; $N_{\text{maxSample}} \leftarrow 0$
4:     **while** $L + \tau_{\text{window}} \leq \max(\text{data})$ **do**
5:         $N_{\text{sample}} \leftarrow \text{partialSum}(\text{data}, L, L + \tau_{\text{window}})$
6:         **if** $N_{\text{sample}} > N_{\text{maxSample}}$ **then**
7:             $L_{\text{maxSample}} \leftarrow L$; $N_{\text{maxSample}} \leftarrow N_{\text{sample}}$
8:         $L \leftarrow L + 1$
9:     $L_{A_V=F} \leftarrow \text{avg}(\text{data}, L_{\text{maxSample}}, L_{\text{maxSample}} + \tau_{\text{window}})$
10:    **if** isAttackerHomeNode($L_{A_V=F}$) **then**
11:        $L_{N_A=N_V, A_V=T} \leftarrow L_{A_V=F} - \delta_{N_A=N_V, N_O=N_A}$
12:        $L_{N_A \neq N_V, A_V=T} \leftarrow L_{A_V=F} + \delta_{N_A \neq N_V, N_O=N_A}$
13:    **else**
14:        $L_{N_A=N_V, A_V=T} \leftarrow L_{A_V=F} - \delta_{N_A=N_V, N_O \neq N_A}$
15:        $L_{N_A \neq N_V, A_V=T} \leftarrow L_{A_V=F} + \delta_{N_A \neq N_V, N_O \neq N_A}$
16:    $\theta_{\text{low}} \leftarrow (L_{A_V=F} + L_{N_A=N_V, A_V=T}) \times 0.5$
17:    $\theta_{\text{high}} \leftarrow (L_{A_V=F} + L_{N_A \neq N_V, A_V=T}) \times 0.5$
18:    **return** $\theta_{\text{low}}, \theta_{\text{high}}$

---

the average `clflush` latency (i.e., $L_{A_V=F}$) measured when the victim has not accessed the target memory object.

Based on the empirical evidence discussed in Sect. 4.3, for given $L_{A_V=F}$, the attacker can determine whether the target memory object is located at the same NUMA node or not. The attacker can then determine $L_{N_A=N_V, A_V=T}$ and $L_{N_A \neq N_V, A_V=T}$, which denote the `clflush` latency measured when (1) $N_A = N_V$ and $A_V = \text{True}$ and (2) $N_A \neq N_V$ and $A_V = \text{True}$, respectively. The attacker then determines the thresholds using Eqs. 2 and 3.

$$\theta_{\text{low}} = (L_{A_V=F} + L_{N_A=N_V, A_V=T}) \times 0.5 \qquad (2)$$

$$\theta_{\text{high}} = (L_{A_V=F} + L_{N_A \neq N_V, A_V=T}) \times 0.5 \qquad (3)$$

If the target memory object is part of data and the measured `clflush` latency is within $(\theta_{\text{low}}, \theta_{\text{high}})$, the attacker infers that the victim has not accessed (i.e., read) the target memory object. Otherwise, the attacker determines that the victim has accessed (i.e., read) the target memory object.

In contrast, if the target memory object is part of code and the measured `clflush` latency is shorter than θ_{low}, the attacker infers that the victim has not accessed (i.e., executed) the target memory object. Otherwise, the attacker determines that the victim has accessed (i.e., executed) the target memory object.

Algorithm 2 shows the pseudocode for the `determineThresholds` function, which implements the proposed threshold determination algorithm. It collects the `clflush` latency data by repeatedly executing `clflush` (Line 2). It uses a time window whose width is set to a sufficiently large value to capture most of the `clflush` latency data samples measured when the victim has not accessed

---

Algorithm 3. The flushAndInfer function

1: **procedure** FLUSHANDINFER(addr, t_{refresh}, $\tau_{\min}$, $\tau_{\max}$)
2:     $t_{\text{nxtRef}} \leftarrow t_{\text{refresh}} + \text{refPeriod}$; $N_{\text{refresh}} \leftarrow 0$
3:     **while** rdtsc() > t_{nxtRef} **do**
4:         $t_{\text{nxtRef}} \leftarrow t_{\text{nxtRef}} + \text{refPeriod}$; $N_{\text{refresh}} \leftarrow N_{\text{refresh}} + 1$
5:         **if** $N_{\text{refresh}} = \eta$ **then**
6:             $t_{\text{nxtRef}} \leftarrow t_{\text{nxtRef}} + \tau_{\text{delay}} \times \eta$; $N_{\text{refresh}} \leftarrow 0$
7:     **while true do**
8:         $t_{\text{curr}} \leftarrow$ rdtsc()
9:         **if** $t_{\text{curr}} \in [t_{\text{nxtRef}} - \text{refDuration}, t_{\text{nxtRef}} + \text{refDuration}]$ **then**
10:             **while** $t_{\text{curr}} \leq t_{\text{nxtRef}} + \text{refDuration}$ **do**
11:                 $t_{\text{curr}} \leftarrow$ rdtsc()
12:         $t_{\text{begin}} \leftarrow$ rdtsc()
13:         clflush(addr)
14:         $t_{\text{end}} \leftarrow$ rdtsc()
15:         $\delta_{\text{flush}} \leftarrow t_{\text{end}} - t_{\text{begin}}$
16:         **if** $\delta_{\text{flush}} \notin [\tau_{\min}, \tau_{\max}]$ **then**
17:             infer(δ_{flush})
18:             **if** $t_{\text{begin}} \geq t_{\text{nxtRef}} + \text{refDuration}$ **then**
19:                 $t_{\text{nxtRef}} \leftarrow t_{\text{nxtRef}} + \text{refPeriod}$; $N_{\text{refresh}} \leftarrow N_{\text{refresh}} + 1$
20:                 **if** $N_{\text{refresh}} = \eta$ **then**
21:                     $t_{\text{nxtRef}} \leftarrow t_{\text{nxtRef}} + \tau_{\text{delay}} \times \eta$; $N_{\text{refresh}} \leftarrow 0$
22:         **else**
23:             $t_{\text{newRef}} \leftarrow t_{\text{begin}} + (\delta_{\text{flush}} - (\tau_{\max} + \tau_{\min}) \times 0.5)$
24:             $t_{\text{nxtRef}} \leftarrow t_{\text{newRef}} + \text{refPeriod}$; $N_{\text{refresh}} \leftarrow 0$

---

the target memory object. It iteratively moves the time window to find the location of the time window at which the largest number of the data samples are captured (Lines 4–8). It then computes the average clflush latency based on the data samples within the time window with the largest number of the data samples and sets $L_{A_V=F}$ to the computed average clflush latency (Line 9).

It determines whether the target memory object is located in the NUMA node of the attacker based on the value of $L_{A_V=F}$ (Line 10). It then computes the two threshold values (i.e., θ_{low}, θ_{high}) using Eqs. 2 and 3 (Lines 10–17).

Refresh-Aware Flush and Inference: The third phase of MARF is the refresh-aware flush and inference phase. To understand the need for detecting and avoiding the DRAM refresh interval, let us consider a case in which the victim accesses the target memory object during the DRAM refresh interval. If the attacker immediately executes clflush without waiting during the DRAM refresh interval, the corresponding clflush latency data sample would be inaccurate because it is likely to have been affected by DRAM refresh. Further, the side effect (i.e., the cache line holding the target memory object) made by the victim would completely be lost by clflush. In contrast, if the attacker waits until the on-going DRAM refresh finishes, it prevents collecting inaccurate clflush latency data and preserves the side effect made by the victim.

Algorithm 3 shows the `flushAndInfer` function, which implements the refresh-aware flush and inference phase. `flushAndInfer` determines when to execute `clflush`. To this end, it predicts whether the target DRAM rank is currently performing DRAM refresh based on the current time and the offset. If the target DRAM rank is expected to be in the DRAM refresh interval, `flushAndInfer` waits until the on-going DRAM refresh finishes (Lines 9–11).

The target DRAM rank is expected not to be currently in the DRAM refresh interval, `flushAndInfer` executes `clflush` and measures the `clflush` latency (Lines 12–15). It then determines whether the victim has accessed the target memory object by invoking the `infer` function, which compares the measured `clflush` latency with the thresholds derived in the threshold determination phase and infers the victim's memory access pattern (Line 17).

In addition, `flushAndInfer` periodically adjusts the offset value used to estimate the DRAM refresh interval (Lines 20–21) by 5 cycles every 31.2 ms (i.e., $\eta \times 7.8$ ms, where η is 4). This is to address the DRAM refresh interval drifting issue caused by the fact that the DRAM refresh period is not exactly 7.8 ms. It then repeats the aforementioned process.

Recalibration: MARF transitions to the recalibration phase if the measured `clflush` latency is within time window (i.e., $[\tau_{\min}, \tau_{\max}]$) used for DRAM refresh interval detection, which indicates that the offset value used to predict the DRAM refresh interval might have become out of phase (Lines 22–24 in Algorithm 3). In this case, it restarts from the DRAM refresh interval detection phase for recalibration.

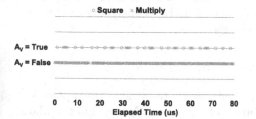

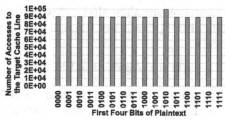

Fig. 5. MARF against GnuPG   Fig. 6. MARF against O-AES

6   Evaluation

We evaluate the effectiveness of MARF by presenting case studies where it is deployed to attack applications that use widely-used cryptographic and user-interface (Appendix B) libraries [10,28,31] and quantifying the effectiveness of its DRAM refresh detection and avoidance algorithms (Appendix C).

We report experimental results collected using the configuration in which the attacker and the victim are placed on different NUMA nodes and the target memory object is located on the same node as the victim (i.e., $N_A \neq N_V$ and

$N_O = N_V$), which closely represents common scenarios in cluster, cloud, and datacenter computing and defeats all the side-channel attacks that are designed only for single-CPU scenarios.

6.1   Attack Against GnuPG

We present a case study where MARF is deployed to infer the private key of the victim that executes an application based on GnuPG, a widely-used cryptographic library [31]. The GnuPG version 1.4.13 used in this work is vulnerable to timing-based side-channel attacks [16,21,23,33,34].

GnuPG uses the square-and-multiply exponentiation algorithm [11]. It iterates every exponent bit in the private key and performs a different set of computations based on the exponent bit value. Specifically, if the value of the currently-iterated exponent bit is zero, it calls the `square` function. Otherwise, it calls the `square` and `multiply` functions. If the attacker can precisely infer the victim's call sequence to `square` and `multiply` through a side channel, it can reconstruct the private key.

We deploy MARF against GnuPG as follows. The attacker selects an instruction within `square` and an instruction within `multiply` as the target memory objects. The attacker periodically executes `clflush` against the target memory objects and measures the `clflush` latency without requiring any synchronization with the victim, infers the victim's call sequence to the two functions based on the measured `clflush` latency, and reconstructs the private key.

Figure 5 shows the first 16 bits (i.e., "1000011010111000") of the private key and the call sequence to `square` and `multiply` identified by MARF. Our experimental results show that MARF precisely and robustly reconstructs the first 16 bits of the private key through the side channel.

6.2   Attack Against AES

We present a case study where MARF is deployed to attack an application based on OpenSSL's T-table implementation of Advanced Encryption Standard (`O-AES`), a widely-used cryptographic library [28]. The `O-AES` version 0.9.8 used in this work is vulnerable to timing-based side-channel attacks [7,13,21].

`O-AES` employs *T-tables* for encrypting and decrypting data. The index of the entry of the first T-table, which is accessed by `O-AES`, is computed by XORing the first byte of the plaintext and the first byte of the secret key. If the four-bit prefix (i.e., the first four bits) of the plaintext and the four-bit prefix of the secret key are identical, it accesses the cache line (i.e., $CL_{1,1}$) that holds the first 64 bytes of the first T-table.

We deploy MARF against `O-AES` as follows. The attacker keeps sending encryption requests to the victim that executes an application based on `O-AES`. For each request, the attacker sets the four-bit plaintext prefix to one of the 16 possible values and the remaining bits to a random value and checks whether the victim has accessed $CL_{1,1}$ by executing `clflush` against $CL_{1,1}$ and measuring the `clflush` latency. If the attacker discovers that the victim has accessed $CL_{1,1}$ with the corresponding plaintext, the attacker can identify the four-bit prefix of the victim's secret key.

We use a secret key whose four-bit prefix is "1010" for experiments. Figure 6 shows the number of accesses of the victim to $CL_{1,1}$, which is inferred by the attacker when the attacker deploys MARF with each of the 16 possible four-bit plaintext prefixes. The attacker can robustly identify the four-bit prefix of the secret key by inferring that the victim has accessed $CL_{1,1}$ for all the encryption requests when the four-bit plaintext prefix is set to 1010. Note that the percentage of encryption requests that access $CL_{1,1}$ is non-zero even when the four-bit plaintext prefix is set to a value other than 1010 because $CL_{1,1}$ can still be accessed during the encryption of the rest of the plaintext depending on what value is randomly assigned to the rest of the plaintext.

7   Related Work

Prior works have extensively proposed micro-architectural side-channel attacks and defenses [7–9,12,13,15–17,19,21,23,29,33,34]. The micro-architectural side-channel attacks and defenses proposed in the prior works focus on various hardware components such as caches [7,8,13,15–17,23,29,34], translation look-aside buffers (TLBs) [8,12,19], branch target buffers (BTBs) [8,9,16,17], and directories [21,33]. However, since these attacks assume a single-CPU scenario, they cannot be applied in multi-CPU scenarios in which the attacker and the victim are placed on different CPUs. Our work significantly differs in that we propose a micro-architectural side-channel attack that robustly works in both single- and multi-CPU scenarios and quantify the impact of task and page placement on the `clflush` latency on NUMA systems.

Prior works have investigated `clflush`-based side-channel attacks [13,20,34]. While the attacks proposed in the prior works have a similarity to MARF in that they exploit `clflush`, they, except for the one proposed in [20], focus on a single-CPU scenario.

Irazoqui et al. propose a `clflush`-based inter-CPU side-channel attack [20]. The prior work observes that the `load` latency against the target memory object is different depending on whether the victim has accessed it or not [20]. The attack proposed in [20] repeatedly executes the `clflush` and `load` instructions and measures the `load` latency to infer the activities of the victim.

However, the attack proposed in [20] has the following limitations. First, it suffers from low accuracy because it is oblivious of DRAM refresh, which affects a non-negligible portion of the latency data samples with significant noises on NUMA systems. Second, it uses the `load` instruction, which incurs a high cache miss rate. Defense techniques have been proposed to detect `load`-based attacks by identifying processes that incur high cache miss rates based on hardware performance counters [2,5].

Our work is significantly different in that it investigates the impact of DRAM refresh on the `clflush` latency and proposes the novel DRAM refresh interval detection and avoidance algorithms to considerably improve the accuracy of MARF. Further, MARF effectively nullifies the existing defense techniques based on cache miss-related hardware performance counters by eliminating the use of the load instruction that makes the attacker generate frequent cache misses.

8   Conclusions

In this work, we present in-depth characterization to quantify the impact of DRAM refresh, the location of the target memory object within a NUMA node, and task and page placement on the clflush latency on NUMA systems and identify a set of the patterns in the clflush latency data. Based on the characterization results, we propose MARF, a novel memory-aware clflush-based intra- and inter-CPU side-channel attack. We design and implement MARF in a way that it robustly and accurately infers the activities of the victim even with the noise caused by DRAM refresh in all the possible scenarios with respect to task and page placement on NUMA systems. Our experimental results collected on three real NUMA systems demonstrate that MARF can robustly be used to attack applications that employ widely-used cryptographic and user-interface libraries. In addition, we discuss potential countermeasures against MARF.

Acknowledgements. This research was partly supported by NRF (NRF-2021R1A2C1011482) and IITP (No. 2020-0-01336, No. 2021-0-01817). Woongki Baek is the corresponding author.

Appendix A   Threat Model

The threat model of MARF is as follows. First, the attacker and the victim are located on the same physical server. Since maximizing resource utilization is highly crucial in cluster, cloud, and datacenter computing, multiple workloads are often consolidated on the same physical server [3,24].

Second, the attacker has permission to execute clflush in line with other side-channel attacks (e.g., the FLUSH+RELOAD attack [34]) based on clflush. In particular, clflush is a non-privileged instruction on the x86-64 architecture, which user-level processes can directly execute.

Third, the attacker has access to a timer to measure the time difference between two events of interest in line with other timing-based attacks such as PRIME+PROBE [23,29]. For example, the x86-64 architecture supports the rdtsc instruction that can be used to measure time differences at the granularity of CPU cycles as a non-privileged instruction.

Fourth, the attacker and the victim share one or more read-only data memory object(s) and/or executable code memory object(s) and the victim's access pattern to the shared memory object(s) may reveal security-sensitive information, which is a widely-used assumption in a large body of prior works on attacks (including clflush-based attacks) and defenses [1,8,13,15,20,27,34]. For example, the attacker and the victim may execute the same code implemented in a shared library.

Appendix B   Attack against GDK

The GIMP Drawing Kit (GDK) library is a wrapper around the windowing and graphics systems on various Linux distributions [10]. The latest old stable version (i.e., 3.24.34) of the GDK library has a vulnerability to timing-based side-channel attacks [13,14]. Specifically, key presses on a group of keys (e.g., the keys 0–8 on the keypad) generate accesses to their corresponding 64-byte memory object. Therefore, if the attacker can accurately observe the victim's memory access pattern through a side channel, the attacker can infer whether such keys have been pressed by the victim. We deploy MARF against GDK to detect key presses on the keypad. While omitted for brevity, our experimental results demonstrate that the attacker can robustly detect key presses on the keypad through MARF.

Appendix C   Refresh Interval Detection and Avoidance

We evaluate the effectiveness of the DRAM refresh interval detection and avoidance algorithms of MARF. To this end, we create two synthetic versions – refresh-oblivious and non-adjusting versions. The refresh-oblivious version is oblivious of DRAM refresh and executes `clflush` without considering the DRAM refresh interval. The non-adjusting version initially detects the DRAM refresh interval and estimates the upcoming DRAM refresh interval based on Eq. 1 and the initially detected offset value. However, it is oblivious of the DRAM refresh interval drifting issue.

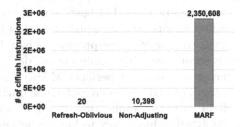

Fig. 7. Effectiveness of the DRAM refresh interval detection and avoidance algorithms

We configure the two versions and the full version of MARF to repeatedly execute `clflush` and measure the number of the consecutive executions of `clflush` without encountering DRAM refresh. Figure 7 shows that each of the proposed techniques for DRAM refresh interval detection and avoidance constructively compose, allowing MARF to keep executing `clflush` without encountering DRAM refresh.

Further, we deploy the refresh-oblivious version against GnuPG with the same private key evaluated in Sect. 6.1. The refresh-oblivious version fails to correctly identify the first 16 bits (i.e., incorrectly identified as "1000001010010011" instead of "1000011010111000") of the private key because of the noises caused by DRAM refresh, demonstrating the effectiveness of the proposed techniques.

Appendix D   Countermeasures

D.1   Memory Duplication

One of the fundamental assumptions for MARF is that the attacker and the victim have a shared memory object based on memory deduplication techniques such as shared libraries [1,27]. One of the simplest countermeasures against MARF is to disallow the sharing of memory objects among processes. The major advantage of this approach is that it is applicable to a wide range of existing systems and applications because it requires no special hardware functionalities or code changes. However, this approach has disadvantages such as the increase in memory footprints and the less effective use of hardware caches and TLBs.

D.2   Hardware Transactional Memory

Hardware transactional memory (HTM) guarantees that when any code block marked as a *transaction* is successfully executed, no cache line has been evicted during its execution. Prior work employs this property to construct a counter-measure against cache-based side-channel attacks [14].

Specifically, the HTM-based countermeasure works as follows. The programmer first marks security-sensitive code blocks as transactions. In the prologue of each transaction, the programmer or the compiler adds the code that pre-loads security-sensitive code and/or data to transactionally access them. If the attacker attempts to perform MARF against the application annotated with transactions and triggers a cache miss during the execution of a security-sensitive code block of the application, it will abort the corresponding transaction. Even if the attacker has a way to know whether the transaction has been aborted, it reveals no secret information because the attacker cannot distinguish whether the victim has accessed the target memory object in the pre-loading code or the rest of the code of the transaction.

However, in this case, MARF essentially becomes the denial-of-service (DoS) attack. This is because the attacker can prevent the victim from making any forward progress by repeatedly aborting the transactions of the victim through the execution of `clflush` [21].

References

1. Bosman, E., et al.: Dedup Est machina: memory deduplication as an advanced exploitation vector. In: IEEE Symposium on Security and Privacy (SP) (2016)
2. Briongos, S., et al.: CacheShield: Detecting cache attacks through self-observation. In: Proceedings of the Eighth ACM Conference on Data and Application Security and Privacy (2018)
3. Chen, S., Delimitrou, C., Martínez, J.F.: PARTIES: QoS- aware resource partitioning for multiple interactive services. In: Proceedings of the Twenty- Fourth International Conference on Architectural Support for Programming Languages and Operating Systems (2019)

4. DDR4 SDRAM STANDARD

5. Demme, J., et al.: On the feasibility of online malware detection with performance counters. In: Proceedings of the 40th Annual International Symposium on Computer Architecture (2013)

6. Didier, G., Maurice, C.: Calibration done right: noiseless flush+flush attacks. In: Detection of Intrusions and Malware, and Vulnerability Assessment: 18th International Conference, DIMVA 2021, Proceedings (2021)

7. Disselkoen, C., et al.: Prime+abort: a timer-free high-precision L3 cache attack using Intel TSX. In: 26th USENIX Security Symposium (2017)

8. Easdon, C., et al.: Rapid prototyping for microarchitectural attacks. In: 31st USENIX Security Symposium (2022)

9. Evtyushkin, D., Ponomarev, D., Abu-Ghazaleh, N.: Jump over ASLR: attacking branch predictors to bypass ASLR. In: International Symposium on Microarchitecture (MICRO) (2016)

10. GDK-3.0. https://docs.gtk.org/gdk3/

11. Gordon, D.M.: A survey of fast exponentiation methods. J. Algorithms (1998)

12. Gras, B., et al.: Translation leak-aside buffer: defeating cache side-channel protections with TLB attacks. In: 27th USENIX Security Symposium (2018)

13. Gruss, D., et al.: Flush+Flush: a fast and stealthy cache attack. In: Proceedings of the 13th International Conference on Detection of Intrusions and Malware, and Vulnerability Assessment - Volume 9721 (2016)

14. Gruss, D., et al.: Strong and efficient cache side-channel protection using hardware transactional memory. In: 26th USENIX Security Symposium (2017)

15. Guo, Y., et al.: Adversarial prefetch: new cross-core cache side channel attacks. In: 43rd IEEE Symposium on Security and Privacy (SP) (2022)

16. Han, M., Baek, W.: SDRP: safe, efficient, and SLO-aware workload consolidation through secure and dynamic resource partitioning. In: IEEE Transactions on Services Computing (2022)

17. Han, M., Yu, S., Baek, W.: Secure and dynamic core and cache partitioning for safe and efficient server consolidation. In: 2018 18th IEEE/ACM International Symposium on Cluster, Cloud and Grid Computing (CCGRID) (2018)

18. Hennessy, J.L., Patterson, D.A.: Computer Architecture, 6th edn.: A Quantitative Approach (2017)

19. Hund, R., Willems, C., Holz, T.: Practical timing side channel attacks against kernel space ASLR. In: Proceedings of the IEEE Symposium on Security and Privacy (2013)

20. Irazoqui, G., Eisenbarth, T., Sunar, B.: Cross processor cache attacks. In: Proceedings of the 11th ACM on Asia Conference on Computer and Communications Security (2016)

21. Kim, S., Han, M., Baek, W.: DPrime+DAbort: a high-precision and timer- free directory-based side-channel attack in non-inclusive cache hierarchies using Intel TSX. In: 2022 IEEE International Symposium on High-Performance Computer Architecture (HPCA) (2022)

22. Kim, W.-H., et al.: PACTree: a high performance persistent range index using PAC guidelines. In: 28th Symposium on Operating Systems Principles (2021)

23. Liu, F., et al.: Last-level cache side-channel attacks are practical. In: 2015 IEEE Symposium on Security and Privacy (2015)

24. Lo, D., et al.: Heracles: improving resource efficiency at scale. In: Proceedings of the 42Nd Annual International Symposium on Computer Architecture (2015)

25. Loughlin, K., et al.: MOESI-prime: preventing coherence-induced hammering in commodity workloads. In: 49th International Symposium on Computer Architecture (2022)
26. Molka, D., et al.: Cache coherence protocol and memory performance of the intel Haswell-EP architecture. In: 2015 44th International Conference on Parallel Processing (2015)
27. Oliverio, M., et al.: Secure page fusion with VUsion. In: Proceedings of the 26th Symposium on Operating Systems Principles (2017)
28. OpenSSL. https://www.openssl.org/
29. Osvik, D.A., Shamir, A., Tromer, E.: Cache attacks and countermeasures: the case of AES. In: Proceedings of the RSA Conference on Topics in Cryptology (2006)
30. Pessl, P., et al.: DRAMA: exploiting dram addressing for cross-CPU attacks. In: 25th USENIX Security Symposium (2016)
31. The GNU Privacy Guard. https://gnupg.org/
32. Wang, M., et al.: DRAMDig: a knowledge-assisted tool to uncover DRAM address mapping. In: Proceedings of the Design Automation Conference (2020)
33. Yan, M., et al.: Attack directories, not caches: side channel attacks in a non-InclusiveWorld. In: 2019 IEEE Symposium on Security and Privacy (SP) (2019)
34. Yarom, Y., Falkner, K.: FLUSH+RELOAD: a high resolution, low noise, L3 cache side-channel attack. In: 23rd USENIX Security Symposium (2014)
35. Zhang, Z., et al.: SoftTRR: protect page tables against Rowhammer attacks using software-only target row refresh. In: USENIX Annual Technical Conference (2022)

You Reset I Attack! A Master Password Guessing Attack Against Honey Password Vaults

Tingting Rao[1,2], Yixin Su[1,2], Peng Xu[1,2(✉)], Yubo Zheng[1,2], Wei Wang[3(✉)], and Hai Jin[1,4]

[1] National Engineering Research Center for Big Data Technology and System, Services Computing Technology and System Lab, Huazhong University of Science and Technology, Wuhan 430074, China
{raott,yxsu,xupeng,zhengyubo,hjin}@mail.hust.edu.cn

[2] Hubei Key Laboratory of Distributed System Security, Hubei Engineering Research Center on Big Data Security, School of Cyber Science and Engineering, Huazhong University of Science and Technology, Wuhan 430074, China

[3] Cyber-Physical-Social Systems Lab, School of Computer Science and Technology, Huazhong University of Science and Technology, Wuhan 430074, China
viviawangwei@mail.hust.edu.cn

[4] Cluster and Grid Computing Lab, School of Computer Science and Technology, Huazhong University of Science and Technology, Wuhan 430074, China

Abstract. It is natural for Internet users to use a password vault to encrypt and manage numerous passwords with a master password. Using one to rule all that is handy but attackers can focus on breaking the vault by brute-force attacking the master password. The honey password vault is proposed to handle the above security concern. It traps the attacker by generating a plausible decoy vault when decrypting the password vault with a "guessing" master password, such that it is hard for the attacker to obtain the real vault. Following the seminal work (S&P'15), many schemes have been proposed to counter advanced attacks, e.g., the Kullback-Leibler divergence attack (CCS'16), encoding attack (USENIX Security'19), and intersection attack (USENIX Security'21). But we find that they barely capture the security after the master password is reset. Once the reset is completed, the attacker can identify the decoy vault by decrypting and comparing the old and new versions of a password vault. To prove this, we propose a new master password guessing attack (MPGA) to break all the existing honey password vault schemes. Experimental results show that MPGA can easily distinguish real and decoy vaults with 99.12%–100.00% accuracy. We further design a secure master-password-updatable honey password vault scheme, named SMART, to resist MPGA. SMART guarantees that the MPGA attacker decrypts out similar decoy vaults from the old and new versions of a password vault. We demonstrate that SMART restricts the attack performance of the MPGA to 49.88% (close to the ideal value 50.00%).

Keywords: Honey password vault · Master password guessing attack · Master password reset

© The Author(s), under exclusive license to Springer Nature Switzerland AG 2024
G. Tsudik et al. (Eds.): ESORICS 2023, LNCS 14346, pp. 141–161, 2024.
https://doi.org/10.1007/978-3-031-51479-1_8

1   Introduction

Password-based authentication is one of the most widely-used online services for Internet users [2,11,22]. However, it is hard for users to memorize a large number of passwords for various online services. To alleviate this issue, *password vault*, a convenient tool, is proposed to manage users' passwords [8,19,21]. It enables a user to encrypt passwords by password-based encryption (PBE) with a single master password and manage passwords in the setting of ciphertext. The user just needs to memorize the master password instead of all passwords. However, the user is prone to choose the weak master password, which makes an attacker easy to guess by a brute-force way [15,25]. The attacker can repeat decrypting the password vault of the user with all candidate master passwords until obtaining reasonable (not random) passwords, as shown in Fig. 1(a). In practice, real-world incidents have demonstrated this security risk. For example, the traditional PBE-based password vaults (e.g., Lastpass [17], Enpass [7], 1password [1]) leak master passwords because a significant number of users tend to choose weak master passwords.

Honey password vault is a promising technique to mitigate the above issue [3]. The core component of honey password vaults is the distribution transforming encoder (DTE), as shown in Fig. 1(b). Such an encoder converts the plaintext password vault to a seed, then PBE encrypts the seed to ciphertext. Under the above brute-force guessing attack, the attacker always decrypts out a plausible decoy vault even with any candidate master password. This feature makes the attacker hard to identify if a candidate master password is a real one. One may note that the attacker can verify the validity of a candidate master password by logging in an online service with the decrypted decoy vault. This method is impractical as some existing techniques, like restricting malicious login attempts, have been widely adopted as an effective countermeasure [9,23,24]. For example, when the Google website detects suspicious login attempts, it will notify users and block their accounts [12].

Despite the promising feature of the honey vault, prior schemes are vulnerable to various practical attacks due to the weaknesses of DTEs [4,6,10] and the update of the vault [5], as shown in Fig. 1(c). Chatterjee et al. designed the first DTE-based honey password vault scheme (denote as *Chatterjee-PCFG*) [4]. They utilized a PCFG model to construct DTE. Later, Golla et al. [10] discovered the distribution differences between the decoy and real vaults in Chatterjee-PCFG and designed the Kullback-Leibler (KL) divergence attack. Meanwhile, they proposed an adaptive encoder scheme (denote as *Golla-Markov*) to resist the attack. Cheng et al. [6] found that previous DTEs [4,10] generate different encoding paths for the decoy and real vaults. From that, they proposed the encoding attack. As a countermeasure, they exploited the generative probability model to construct a new type of DTE. On the other hand, due to Chatterjee-PCFG and Golla-Markov did not consider the update of password vaults, Cheng et al. [5] also launched the intersection attack by overlapping password vaults before and after updating. Furthermore, they proposed an incrementally updatable honey password vault (denote as *Cheng-IUV*) to resist both the encoding

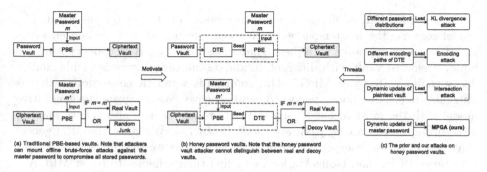

Fig. 1. Overview: The differences between the traditional PBE-based vault and the honey password vault. Moreover, we show the prior threats and our MPGA on honey password vaults. Note the password vault, real and decoy vaults mentioned in this paper are in plaintext.

and the intersection attacks. Thus, Cheng-IUV does enhance the security of the honey password vault.

The aforementioned works [4–6,10] do not consider the security for master password reset[1]. It is inevitable that a user has to reset the long-term-used master password periodically, which could be required by the vault applications (especially after the disclosure of leaked passwords). After the master password is reset, the honey password vault scheme fully re-encrypts the vault. In detail, the scheme must first decrypt the ciphertext vault to the seed with the old master password and decode the seed to plaintext password vault. Then, it re-encodes plaintext password vault to a new seed and re-encrypts the seed with a new master password. We find out that various encryption versions[2] of a vault can cause a severe threat of leaking the new master password. This paper aims to answer: *"Given different encryption versions, could attackers break honey password vault via some well-designed strategies?"* and if so, *"Are there any practical-but-not-trivial countermeasures for the attack?"*

Our Contributions. To answer the first question, we propose a *Master Password Guessing Attack (MPGA)* against existing honey password vault schemes. Given two encryption versions of the honey password vault, the attacker can distinguish the real vault from decoy ones. For example, if the attacker guesses correct master passwords to decrypt two encryption versions of a vault, he can obtain two fully same real vaults; otherwise, he obtains two totally different decoy vaults with a significant probability. We state that MPGA works effectively in all existing honey password vault schemes.

---

[1] To avoid ambiguity, hereafter, "reset" a master password, we mean a user updates or modifies the master password and we also note that this action could be fully or partially on the password based on the user's habits.

[2] In this work, we only focus on the reset of master password, in which the plaintext password vault remains unchanged. Note we will also discuss the case where users modify proportions of the password vault in Appendix B.1.

To resist MPGA, we design a generative model for the master password. The model converts the master password to a cognate password and then encrypts plaintext password vaults with the cognate password. In this case, decrypting the honey password vault with different candidate master passwords yields similar decoy vaults, so to resist MPGA. Our solution is a generic construction that is pluggable to existing honey password vault schemes. We integrate the generative model with the most recent Cheng-IUV to produce a new and *secure master-password-updatable honey password vault (SMART)*. We state that the generative model is also compatible with other honey password vault schemes, e.g., Chatterjee-PCFG and Golla-Markov, enabling their schemes to resist MPGA.

We conduct empirical experiments to evaluate the effectiveness of the proposed MPGA and SMART. The results show that MPGA can achieve remarkable attack accuracy 99.12%–100.00%. It yields the best attack performance against honey password vault schemes compared to previous attacks (i.e., KL divergence attack [10], encoding attack [6], and intersection attack [5]). As a countermeasure, SMART substantially restrains the performance of MPGA to 49.88% (where the ideal is 50.00%). We further evaluate SMART against prior attacks [5,6,10]. The experimental results illustrate that the attack accuracy is restricted to 56.41% (close to the best-reported result 53.22%). This confirms that our design achieves a significant improvement in security.

2   Master Password Guessing Attack

A secure honey password vault scheme must ensure security after the master password is reset. Any scheme without considering the above security is vulnerable to our proposed attack MPGA, in which the attacker can obtain significant advantages from different encryption versions of the password vault so as to guess the corresponding master passwords.

2.1   Attack Model

The MPGA attacker is allowed to access the old and new encryption versions of a vault after the master password is reset and aims to recover the new master password. Without loss of generality, suppose that the algorithm of honey password vault schemes, including DTE and PBE, is public. The MPGA attacker can guess the new master password with high accuracy even without knowing any additional information, such as the distribution or encoding paths of the passwords.

Let p_M and p_V be two priority functions. Both functions will be used to rank the candidate master passwords according to the different rules. More details about those two functions will be given in Sect. 2.2. The attack process of MPGA (see Algorithm 1) consists of the following main parts: 1) Generate candidate master password lists $\mathcal{M}_{ca}^o$ and $\mathcal{M}_{ca}^n$ for the (stolen) old and new ciphertext vaults respectively, order the candidate master passwords in $\mathcal{M}_{ca}^o$ and $\mathcal{M}_{ca}^n$ according to the priority function p_M, and let the ordered lists be $\mathcal{M}_{ord}^o$ and

---

Algorithm 1. The Attack Process of MPGA

$\text{MPGA}(C^o, C^n)$

1: Generate candidate master password lists $\mathcal{M}_{ca}^o$ and $\mathcal{M}_{ca}^n$ (both of size N) for the (stolen) old and new ciphertext vaults C^o and C^n, respectively
2: Sort the lists $\mathcal{M}_{ca}^o$ and $\mathcal{M}_{ca}^n$ in ascending order of $p_M(\mathcal{M}_{ca}^o, \mathcal{M}_{ca}^n)$ respectively and let $\mathcal{M}_{ord}^o$ and $\mathcal{M}_{ord}^n$ be the two corresponding sorted lists
3: **for** $i = 1$ **to** N **do**
4:     Decrypt C^o and C^n with the i-th candidate master passwords $mpw_i^o \in \mathcal{M}_{ord}^o$ and $mpw_i^n \in \mathcal{M}_{ord}^n$, respectively
5:     Add the decrypted password vaults v^o and v^n into $\mathcal{V}_{ca}^o$ and $\mathcal{V}_{ca}^n$, respectively
6: **end for**
7: Sort the list $\mathcal{M}_{ord}^n$ in ascending order of $p_V(\mathcal{V}_{ca}^o, \mathcal{V}_{ca}^n)$ and let $\mathcal{M}_{res}^n$ be the sorted list
8: **return** $\mathcal{M}_{res}^n$

$p_M(\mathcal{M}_{ca}^o, \mathcal{M}_{ca}^n)$

1: **for** $i = 1$ **to** N **do**
2:     Calculate the Levenshtein Distance d_i between $mpw_i^o \in \mathcal{M}_{ca}^o$ and $mpw_i^n \in \mathcal{M}_{ca}^n$ /* More details about Levenshtein Distance will be given in Section 2.2 */
3: **end for**
4: **return** $\{d_i | i \in [1, N]\}$

$p_V(\mathcal{V}_{ca}^o, \mathcal{V}_{ca}^n)$

1: Given a plaintext password vault v and a seed s, let $\Pr(s|v)$ be the probability of encoding v to s using DTE
2: Let s^o and s^n be two seeds decrypted from C^o and C^n, respectively
3: **for** $i = 1$ **to** N **do**
4:     **for** $j = 1$ **to** N **do**
5:         $k_j = \left| 1 - \frac{\Pr(s_j^o | v_j^o)}{\Pr(s_i^n | v_i^n)} \right|$, where s_j^o and s_i^n are the corresponding seeds of v_j^o and v_i^n during decryption, respectively, $v_j^o \in \mathcal{V}_{ca}^o$, and $v_i^n \in \mathcal{V}_{ca}^n$
6:     **end for**
7:     Find the minimum value $r_i = \min\{k_j | j \in [1, N]\}$
8: **end for**
9: **return** $\{r_i | i \in [1, N]\}$

$\mathcal{M}_{ord}^n$; 2) Decrypt the (stolen) old and new ciphertext vaults with the candidate master passwords in $\mathcal{M}_{ord}^o$ and $\mathcal{M}_{ord}^n$ respectively and let the decrypted password vaults be $\mathcal{V}_{ca}^o$ and $\mathcal{V}_{ca}^n$; 3) Rank the candidate master passwords in $\mathcal{M}_{ord}^n$ according to the priority function p_V and let $\mathcal{M}_{res}^n$ be the resulted list. Finally, the master password with a lower index in $\mathcal{M}_{res}^n$ has a higher possibility of being correct.

The effectiveness of MPGA depends on those two priority functions. We design the priority function p_M according to the fact that a pair of the old and new candidate master passwords is more likely to be real if they have a stronger correlation. The priority function p_V implies the fact that a pair of the old and new candidate master passwords is more likely to be real if the decrypted vaults from C^o and C^n have more similarity.

2.2   Priority Functions p_M and p_V

We propose two priority functions p_M and p_V, as the core strategies for the MPGA attacker, to choose the most-probable-real master password from candidate master passwords. The attacker can construct priority functions using all available information to obtain optimal ranked lists of candidate master passwords and candidate vaults.

The Priority Function p_M. This function is based on the similarity between the old and new master passwords, as shown in Algorithm 1. It allows the attacker to focus on the promising master passwords and reduce the time and resources required to decrypt the ciphertext vault. Thus, the priority function p_M plays a crucial role in MPGA. In Algorithm 1 (p_M), each master password in $\mathcal{M}_{ca}^n$ is compared to $\mathcal{M}_{ca}^o$ and assigned a ranking value by *Levenshtein Distance* [26]. As a commonly used method to calculate the similarity between two passwords, the Levenshtein Distance measures the minimum number of edit operations required to transform an old master password into a new one. Most users prefer to obtain the new master password by directly modifying some characters in the old master password for convenience. Therefore, there is a high probability that the two passwords are similar. The lower the ranking value, the more likely the candidate master password is real. Hence, the priority function p_M is defined as

$$p_M(\mathcal{M}_{ca}^o, \mathcal{M}_{ca}^n) = \left\{ d_i \,\middle|\, \begin{array}{l} d_i \text{ is the Levenshtein Distance between} \\ mpw_i^o \in \mathcal{M}_{ca}^o \text{ and } mpw_i^n \in \mathcal{M}_{ca}^n, i \in [1, N] \end{array} \right\}.$$

The Priority Function p_V. This function is used to rank the master passwords by decrypted candidate vaults. To facilitate description, we let $mpw_i \in \mathcal{M}$, $v_i \in \mathcal{V}$, $s_i \in \mathcal{S}$ and $c_i \in \mathcal{C}$ denote a master password, a plaintext vault, a seed, and a ciphertext vault, respectively, where the s_i is decrypted from c_i with mpw_i, and v_i is decoded from s_i. We define the random variable $mpw_i = MPW$ as the event that the master password is correct. Meanwhile, the real password vault, real seed and the ciphertext vault denote as V, S, and C, respectively. In order to get the correct password vault, the optimal strategy is to rank v_i in the descending order of $\Pr\left(mpw_i = MPW \mid c_i = C\right)$.

Recall that a vault scheme may leak the old and new ciphertexts of the same vault v_i after resetting the master password. Let the v_i^o and v_i^n denote the decrypted old and new password vaults with candidate master passwords. Like Cheng-IUV's encoder, we extend the probability $\Pr(mpw_i = MPW|c_i = C) = \epsilon \cdot \Pr(s_i|v_i)$, where $\epsilon = \Pr(mpw_i = MPW) \cdot \Pr(v_i = V)$ is a constant independent of i, and $\Pr(s_i|v_i)$ is the probability of encoding v_i to s_i. We further capture the ratio of $\Pr(s_i^o|v_i^o)$ and $\Pr(s_i^n|v_i^n)$ for the old and new versions. Given the two encryption versions of a vault, we distinguish real and decoy based on the similarity of them. The priority function p_V is defined as

$$p_V(\mathcal{V}_{ca}^o, \mathcal{V}_{ca}^n) = \left\{ r_i \,\middle|\, r_i = \min \left\{ k_j \,\middle|\, \begin{array}{l} k_j = \left| 1 - \frac{\Pr(s_j^o|v_j^o)}{\Pr(s_i^n|v_i^n)} \right|, \\ v_j^o \in \mathcal{V}_{ca}^o, v_i^n \in \mathcal{V}_{ca}^n, j \in [1, N] \end{array} \right\}, i \in [1, N] \right\},$$

where s_j^o and s_i^n are the corresponding seeds of v_j^o and v_i^n during decryption, respectively. If v_j^o and v_i^n are real vaults, the probability $\Pr(s_j^o|v_j^o)$ will be identical with $\Pr(s_i^n|v_i^n)$, namely the corresponding value k_j is the minimum one. Hence, the priority function p_V aims to find the most similar vault $v_j^o \in \mathcal{V}_{ca}^o$ for each $v_i^n \in \mathcal{V}_{ca}^n$ and guides MPGA to distinguish the real vault from decoy vaults.

2.3 MPGA on the Existing Honey Password Vaults

In practice, the honey password vault could leak multiple encryption versions after the user resets the master password. Hence, all existing honey password vault schemes suffer from MPGA. We will conduct further empirical experiments to show MPGA against Chatterjee-PCFG, Golla-Markov, and Cheng-IUV in Sect. 4. The experiment results show that MPGA achieves 100% attack accuracy. Here, we explain why MPGA is effective for the different schemes as follows.

MPGA on Chatterjee-PCFG. MPGA can distinguish the real password vault from the decoy ones according to their differences in sub-grammar. After resetting the master password, Chatterjee-PCFG re-encodes the vault. The new encoding result (i.e., sub-grammar) still remains the same. When the attacker decrypts different versions of the vault with incorrect master passwords, he will produce distinct sub-grammars and decode to distinct decoy vaults. The correct master passwords will result in identical sub-grammar and identical password vaults. Hence, the attacker can rank those "identical" password vaults at the top of the candidate vault list, according to the priority function p_V.

MPGA on Golla-Markov. MPGA digs out the differences between the real vault and decoy vault generated from the reuse approach. The reuse approach of Golla-Markov encodes the vault by selecting a base password and using the base to encode each password. For example, in order to encode a vault $v = $ (abcdef, abcdef, abcdef@), the reuse approach chooses "abcdef" as the base of the vault. Then, the Markov model encodes passwords in the vault using the base as a part of the passwords. However, the decoder randomly selects the base password upon decrypting the old and new versions of the vault. Hence, the new password vault differs from the old one under the incorrect master password decryption.

MPGA on Cheng-IUV. MPGA provides insight into the vulnerability in the incrementally updatable honey password vault after the master password is reset. When adding, deleting, and modifying a password in the password vault, the scheme keeps old passwords unchanged and incrementally pads the new password pw_{i+1} to the end of the vault v. Accordingly, the Cheng-IUV encodes the new password to sub-seed s_{i+1} and concatenates the s_{i+1} to the end of s. After resetting the master password, the scheme re-encodes the whole vault by the conditional probability model to obtain the new seed s'. However, when decrypting the old and new vault versions using incorrect master passwords, the model generates completely different conditional probabilities of the whole passwords in the vault. Therefore, the old and new decoy password vaults are not exactly identical after decrypting with incorrect master passwords.

3 Secure Master-Password-Updatable Honey Password Vault

We design a generic countermeasure against the MPGA and further develop a secure master-password-updatable honey password vault named *SMART*. In our scheme, we construct the generative model to produce a cognate password for encrypting the password vault, as shown in Fig. 2. By implementing this construction, SMART effectively produces a more extensive list of identical decoy vaults during the decryption process. Thus, our countermeasure increases the difficulty for potential attackers to distinguish the real vault from the decoy ones, thereby enhancing the overall security of the honey password vault scheme.

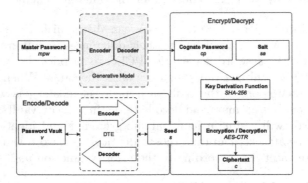

Fig. 2. The simplified architecture of our secure master-password-updatable honey password vault (SMART). At the encoding stage, the DTE encodes the vault v to a seed s. Then, in the encrypting process, the seed s is encrypted with the cognate password generated by the generative model. Note that everytime the master password mpw is reset, SMART will choose a new salt sa. Thus, the old master password could not decrypt the new ciphertext vault.

3.1   A Generic Solution Against MPGA

Recall that the attacker's primary challenge is to generate a ranked list of master passwords after obtaining the old/new encryption versions of a vault. The correct master password is more likely to be ranked higher on this list. Existing schemes barely generate identical decoy password vaults when decrypting the old and new versions with incorrect master passwords. On the contrary, when decrypting both versions with the correct master password, the same password vaults are obtained. Thus, the attacker can easily distinguish the real master password. Based on this fact, we construct the generative model for the master password that can generate a cognate password to encrypt the vault. By utilizing the model, the honey password vault scheme can resist MPGA.

The generative model aims to convert the master password to a cognate password by the conditional probability of a master password. In the following, we will describe how to construct the generative model that estimates the conditional probability $\Pr(m|\tilde{m})$ for a cognate password m under the master password $\tilde{m}$. Since a password is composed of a sequence of characters, we let $\tilde{m} = \tilde{c}_1, \ldots, \tilde{c}_{l'}$ and $m = c_1, \ldots, c_l$. For a pair of passwords $(\tilde{m}, m)$, we define all possible transformation paths from $\tilde{m}$ to m as $\mathcal{T}_{\tilde{m} \to m}$; each path $T_{\tilde{m} \to m} \in \mathcal{T}_{\tilde{m} \to m}$ consists of several regular edit operations (insert, replace, and delete); and the size of $T_{\tilde{m} \to m}$ is defined as the corresponding edit distance. In order to obtain the shortest edit distance, we prioritize the delete operation. The conditional probability of the transformations for the pair $(\tilde{m}, m)$ is defined as $\Pr(T_{\tilde{m} \to m} \mid \tilde{m}) = \prod_{i=1}^{t} \Pr(\tau_i \mid \tilde{m}, \tau_1, \ldots, \tau_{i-1})$, where t is the edit distance between m and $\tilde{m}$, and the transformation path is $T_{\tilde{m} \to m} = \tau_1, \ldots, \tau_t$.

We design the encoder and decoder functions using recurrent neural networks to instantiate the generative model. The encoder function maps the input character sequence of a master password onto a real value vector $w \in \mathbb{R}^d$ for hyperparameter dimension d. Then, the decoder function takes the vector w as the input, and outputs a cognate password. The cognate password has the maximum conditional probability in the transformation. Accordingly, we further extend above conditional probability as $\Pr(T_{\tilde{m} \to m} \mid \tilde{m}) = \prod_{i=1}^{t} \Pr(\tau_i \mid w_0, \tau_1, \ldots, \tau_{i-1}) =$ $\prod_{i=1}^{t} \Pr(\tau_i \mid w_{i-1}, \tau_{i-1})$, where w_0 is the output weight of the encoder function with input $\tilde{m}$, and w_{i+1} is the output weight of the decoder function with inputs w_i and τ_i. We set up the learning process of the generative model as a supervised learning task. The training objective is to find the parameter θ that maximizes the log probability of the proper edit path between the password pairs. Denote D as the password pairs set. The generative model training objective as $\operatorname{argmax}_{\theta} \frac{1}{|D|} \sum_{(\tilde{m},m) \in D} \log \Pr(T_{\tilde{m} \to m} \mid \tilde{m}; \theta)$.

The generative model converts similar passwords generated by a user into the same cognate password with high probability. Moreover, the cognate password yields the same seed decrypted from different master passwords, and then obtains the same decoy password vaults. Through the generative model, converting the master password to the cognate password is concise. Firstly, the encoder transforms the master password $\tilde{m}$ into a d-dimension vector $w_{\tilde{m}} \in \mathbb{R}^d$, and feeds it to the decoder. Then, the decoder receives the hyperparameters from the encoder and calculates the probability distribution over the transform set. The model chooses the most probable output w_i in each iteration and utilizes them in the following invocation until reaching the end symbol of the sequence. At last, it combines the sequence with the master password $\tilde{m}$ to output a cognate password.

3.2   Training the Generative Model

Training Dataset. The leaked passwords we use for the training were published on the Internet between 2009 and 2017. They contain 14,000 million email-password pairs with 11,000 million unique emails and 463 million unique passwords from Twitter, Facebook, Myspace, Yahoo, and other websites. For simplicity, we only focus on the characteristics of the password without considering the different website password policies (e.g. [18]). Hence, we only select the password pairs in which the passwords contain ≥ 4 but ≤ 20 characters. We also delete the non-printable characters and reduce valid passwords to 460,400,000.

The datasets are not harmful to current users, and the experiment's results contribute to devising a more secure honey password vault scheme.

Training Process. We construct the generative model with the encoder-decoder neural network. Firstly, we initialize the model network using the method introduced in [20]. The embedding layers are initialized with uniform random values in $[-\sqrt{3}, \sqrt{3}]$ and the rest layers of the neural network with the values in $[-\sqrt{6}/(d_i + d_{i+1}), \sqrt{6}/(d_i + d_{i+1})]$, where the d_i is the dimension of the i-th layer. After that, we train the model by reducing the cross-entropy loss between the predicted outputs of the network and the expected outputs. This training process utilizes the stochastic gradient descent method and the Adam optimizer [16] to learn the conditional probability of the output given hyperparameters. For the training dataset, we randomly select 80.00% of the above dataset (as the training set) to train the generative model and the rest as the test set. As for the training setup, we set the layer as 3-hidden layers with 128 hidden units in each layer. The learning rate is set as 0.001, which provides high conversion accuracy. The above neural network settings are consistent with [20]. The experimental environment of the training is given in Sect. 4.1.

3.3 Instantiation with Incrementally Updatable Scheme

To instantiate SMART, we integrate the generative model with Cheng-IUV. Like general honey vault schemes (see Appendix A), SMART comprises two parts: DTE and PBE. For the DTE construction, we use a conditional probability model transforming encoder from Cheng-IUV to generate the seed. The conditional probability model transforming encoder chooses one path from the existing generating paths. Meanwhile, the conditional encoder is seed-uniform, and the encoding path is unfixed. Our DTE is able to adjust the decoy vault distribution by assigning a higher probability to the existing passwords in the vault and then normalizing the decoy distribution. Based on the above facts, SMART resists the encoding and KL divergence attacks.

For the part of PBE, the generative model converts the master password to a cognate password. PBE utilizes the key derivation function (PBKDF) to generate the encryption key with the cognate password. Then, it encrypts the seed s by AES in CTR-mode with the encryption key. Our SMART naturally brings the incrementally updatable mechanism. The core consideration on updating the vault is to completely maintain the old password vault and increment the new password to the end of the vault. Whilst updating the vault, SMART decrypts the vault to the seed first. Then, it adds the new sub-seed to the end of the seed if users add or modify passwords. If users request to delete some passwords, it records these passwords' positions as none in plaintext. With the incrementally updatable mechanism, SMART ensures security after password vault updates.

Compatibility with Other Schemes. We state that our generative model can also be effectively and efficiently applied to other existing honey password vault schemes, such as Chatterjee-PCFG and Golla-Markov. In Chatterjee-PCFG scheme, our generative model is compatible with the encryption process. The generative model generates the same cognate passwords for enough amount of incorrect candidate master passwords. When decrypting the old and new versions of vaults with cognate passwords, Chatterjee-PCFG obtains the completely identical sub-grammar. With the same sub-grammar, the decoder outputs identical password vaults. Furthermore, our generative model is also compatible with Golla-Markov. Similarly, when decrypting with the same cognate passwords, Golla-Markov obtains the identical base password and then decodes to the same decoy vaults.

4 Evaluation

We implement our proposed attack, MPGA, against prior schemes Chatterjee-PCFG, Golla-Markov, and Cheng-IUV. The results demonstrate that MPGA achieved exceptional attack accuracy. Furthermore, we evaluate and compare SMART with prior schemes under the well-studied attacks and MPGA via real-world datasets. Our solution is practical and effective with a remarkable improvement in security.

4.1 Experimental Environment

We implement the honey password vaults [4,5,10] and the instantiated SMART in the same experimental environment of python-3.6.6 with Cryptography-37.02. For the encryption process, we use AES within CTR-mode encryption and SHA-256 within PBKDF for the key derivation function by following the setting defined in previous works. The generative model training and the DTE training are performed on an Nvidia Tesla V100. All implementation and evaluation experiments are on an Intel Core-i7 with 16 GB of Linux RAM.

4.2 Dataset

We consider the most-widely used datasets to yield a fair comparison with previous works [4,5,10]. To evaluate MPGA, we conduct tests on the real-world password vault dataset Pastebin and leaked password datasets RockYou, Yahoo, Gmail, and Myspace. We state that Pastebin is currently the only real-world leaked plaintext password vault dataset comprising 276 password vaults (where each vault is with the size of 2–50). On the other hand, RockYou is one of the most extensive leaked plaintext password datasets. It provides 32 million password samples with around 14 million unique passwords. The Yahoo dataset leaked in the server vulnerability incident includes approximately 442,800 password samples. The Gmail dataset contains 5 million passwords. The Myspace dataset contains 41,500 passwords. It is worth noting that previous research works [4,5,10] also leverage the above datasets to demonstrate the potential risks of existing schemes and the effectiveness of countermeasures. The datasets used in our experiments do not imperil the privacy and security of current password users. We randomly split the password datasets (RockYou, Yahoo, Gmail, and Myspace) into two sets: training (90.00%) and testing (10.00%). As for the Pastebin dataset, we randomly divide it into five parts, with one portion serving as the test set and the union of the rest as the training set.

4.3   Security Metrics

We define two crucial security metrics, the real vault average rank $\bar{r}$ and the attack accuracy α. To provide a fair comparison, we use Cheng et al.'s method [5] to estimate the real vault's rank cumulative distribution function (RCDF) $F(x) = \Pr(\bar{r} \leq x)$. The function $F(x)$ is a comprehensive presentation of the attack results. If the scheme is entirely secure, the ranks are uniformly distributed. Specifically, we define the rank $\bar{r}$ as the ratio of the real vault to the number of decoy vaults, and $\bar{r} \in [0,1]$. This rank serves as a quantitative measure that indicates the relative position of the real vault in the online verification order. When the $\bar{r}$ is lower, the real vault is more likely to be ranked at the top of the verification order. On the other hand, a higher $\bar{r}$ implies that the real vault is positioned further down the verification order. For example, when $\bar{r} = 0.10$, the attacker could confirm the real password vault after verifying 10.00% of the decoy password vaults. We further set the accuracy α as the metric to distinguish the real vault from decoy vaults, and $\alpha \in [0,1]$. We state that $\bar{r}$ and α can be calculated from $F(x)$ as $\bar{r} = 1 - \int_0^1 F(x)dx$, and $\alpha = 1 - \bar{r}$. We set the uniform distribution U as the baseline, and the $\bar{r} = \alpha = 0.5$. We also use $F(0)$, $F(1/4)$, $F(1/2)$, and $F(3/4)$ as the rank proportion of real vaults rank of 0, 1/4, 1/2, and 3/4. Since the cumulative distribution function of U is linear, the ideal values of $F(0)$, $F(1/4)$, $F(1/2)$, and $F(3/4)$ are 0, 0.25, 0.5, and 0.75, respectively.

4.4   Implementation and Evaluation on MPGA

Implementation of MPGA. The attack implementation follows the process given in Sect. 2.1. Here are the details:

1. Generate and rank the candidate master passwords. Firstly the attacker generates candidate master passwords to form $\mathcal{M}^o$ and $\mathcal{M}^n$. And the two real master passwords are in $\mathcal{M}^o$ and $\mathcal{M}^n$, respectively. Instead of blind guessing, the attacker combines users' additional behavior information and possible reuse habits to derive a list of candidate master passwords. Then, the attacker ranks the guessed master passwords by the similarity of old and new master passwords calculated with the Levenshtein Distance.
2. Obtain ciphertext vaults after resetting the master password. Denote the old ciphertext vault as C^o. The attacker obtains the new ciphertext vault C^n after the master password is reset. The plaintext passwords in the vault are

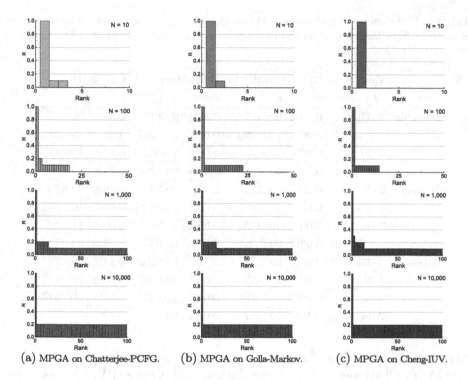

(a) MPGA on Chatterjee-PCFG.   (b) MPGA on Golla-Markov.   (c) MPGA on Cheng-IUV.

Fig. 3. The rank results of MPGA: The real vault is a sample from Pastebin, and the decoy vaults are generated from Chatterjee-PCFG, Golla-Markov, and Cheng-IUV. MPGA ranks password vaults in descending order of the similarity rate R. The real password vault with a 100% similarity rate are always ranked 1st. The candidate list size $N \in \{10, 100, 1000, 10000\}$.

unchanged. Namely, the old password vault v^o is exactly the same as the new v^n. In practice, there exists a scenario where users may prefer to update both the master password and passwords stored in the vault. We will discuss this case and show the experimental results in Appendix B.1.

3. Decrypt the ciphertext vaults to generate candidate vaults. The attacker obtains N candidate vaults by repeatedly decrypting ciphertext vaults C^o and C^n using the ranked master passwords $\mathcal{M}^o$ and $\mathcal{M}^n$, respectively. Note that the decoy vaults' size is identical to real vaults. Finally, the attacker obtains N candidate vaults consisting of a real vault v^o_{real} and $N - 1$ decoy vaults v^o_{decoy}. In the same way, the attacker obtains a v^n_{real} and $N - 1$ v^n_{decoy}.

4. Rank the candidate vaults and get the ranked candidate master passwords according to ranked candidate vaults. The attacker can rank the candidate vaults in the descending order of the R, where R is the proportion of the same passwords in the two versions of password vaults. Note we set $N \in \{10, 100, 1000, 10000\}$.

Table 1. Performance of MPGA against existing honey password vaults. The real vault is sampled from Pastebin, Rockyou and Myspace. The vault size $M \in [2, 50]$, and the candidate size $N = 1,000$.

	Vault Size	Chatterjee-PCFG		Golla-Markov		Cheng-IUV	
	M	$\bar{r}$	α	$\bar{r}$	α	$\bar{r}$	α
Pastebin	2–3	0.30%	99.70%	0.86%	99.14%	0.88%	99.12%
	4–8	0.00%	100.00%	0.00%	100.00%	0.00%	100.00%
	9–50	0.00%	100.00%	0.00%	100.00%	0.00%	100.00%
	All (2–50)	0.10%	99.90%	0.28%	99.72%	0.29%	99.71%
Rockyou	2–3	0.10%	99.90%	0.22%	99.78%	0.16%	99.84%
	4–8	0.00%	100.00%	0.00%	100.00%	0.00%	100.00%
	9–50	0.00%	100.00%	0.00%	100.00%	0.00%	100.00%
	All (2–50)	0.03%	99.97%	0.07%	99.93%	0.05%	99.95%
Myspace	2–3	0.18%	99.82%	0.17%	99.83%	0.11%	99.89%
	4–8	0.00%	100.00%	0.00%	100.00%	0.00%	100.00%
	9–50	0.00%	100.00%	0.00%	100.00%	0.00%	100.00%
	All (2–50)	0.10%	99.90%	0.05%	99.95%	0.03%	99.97%

MPGA's Performance with Pastebin. We compare the performance of MPGA on Chatterjee-PCFG, Golla-Markov, and Cheng-IUV schemes. The experimental results are summarized in Table 1 and Fig. 3. As shown in Table 1, we evaluate previous works using various sizes M of the real-world vaults in Pastebin. The average rank $\bar{r}$ is between 0.00%–0.88%, achieving 99.12%–100.00% accuracy, which reduces approx. 85.33%–100.00% of online guessing as compared to the best-reported attack in Cheng-IUV. When the M is set to 2–3, there are about 0.30%–0.88% of the old and new versions of vaults that are identical. Moreover, this experiment shows that only the real password vaults can be identical, when $M > 3$, shown in Table 1. Recall that we denote the proportion of identical passwords in the two password vaults as R. The larger the vault size we have, the smaller the R we obtain. This indicates that there are more different passwords between the old and new vaults. Therefore, increasing the number of passwords in the password vault will hardly increase the similarity rate R.

In Fig. 3, we conduct the experiments for the candidate size $N \in \{10, 100, 1000, 10000\}$ to evaluate the influence of candidate set size on the ranking. The results prove that MPGA can effectively rank the real vault on the top with 100.00% accuracy under previous honey password vault schemes. When the $N \in \{10, 100\}$, the R of the real vault is still 100.00%, but that of the decoy vaults drops to 10.00%. When the candidate size climbs to 1,000 and 10,000, the R of most decoy vaults increases to 20.00%. And a few pairs of password vault R is 30.00%. The number of identical passwords can be scaled up with the increase in the number of decoy password vaults. But experiment results show that their schemes still do not produce the entirely same decoy password vaults.

Table 2. Evaluation: our SMART and existing schemes against MPGA and previous attacks. The security metrics $\bar{r}, \alpha, F(0), F(1/4), F(1/2)$, and $F(3/4)$ are defined in Sect. 4.3. The real vaults are chosen from Pastebin, where the vault size $M \in [2, 50]$, and the candidate list size $N = 1,000$.

Scheme	Attack	$\bar{r}$	α	$F(0)$	$F(1/4)$	$F(1/2)$	$F(3/4)$
Chatterjee-PCFG [4]	KL divergence attack	11.91%	88.09%	61.22%	82.82%	88.61%	93.71%
	Encoding attack	12.18%	87.82%	47.96%	82.48%	90.10%	95.75%
	Intersection attack	0.00%	100.00%	100.00%	100.00%	100.00%	100.00%
	MPGA	**0.00%**	**100.00%**	100.00%	100.00%	100.00%	100.00%
Golla-Markov [10]	KL divergence attack	51.19%	48.81%	0.00%	22.45%	50.34%	75.34%
	Encoding attack	15.10%	84.90%	5.44%	75.34%	95.58%	100.00%
	Intersection attack	0.00%	100.00%	100.00%	100.00%	100.00%	100.00%
	MPGA	**0.00%**	**100.00%**	100.00%	100.00%	100.00%	100.00%
Cheng-IUV [5]	KL divergence attack	44.59%	55.41%	0.85%	31.29%	56.80%	78.91%
	Encoding attack	39.82%	60.18%	0.63%	38.78%	62.24%	81.97%
	Intersection attack	46.78%	53.22%	0.88%	27.89%	54.08%	77.38%
	MPGA	**0.00%**	**100.00%**	100.00%	100.00%	100.00%	100.00%
SMART [Sect. 3]	KL divergence attack	44.39%	55.61%	0.76%	28.57%	54.76%	82.82%
	Encoding attack	46.32%	53.68%	0.34%	33.33%	63.10%	89.80%
	Intersection attack	43.59%	56.41%	0.17%	30.10%	58.84%	83.16%
	MPGA	**50.12%**	**49.88%**	0.00%	22.45%	50.34%	75.34%

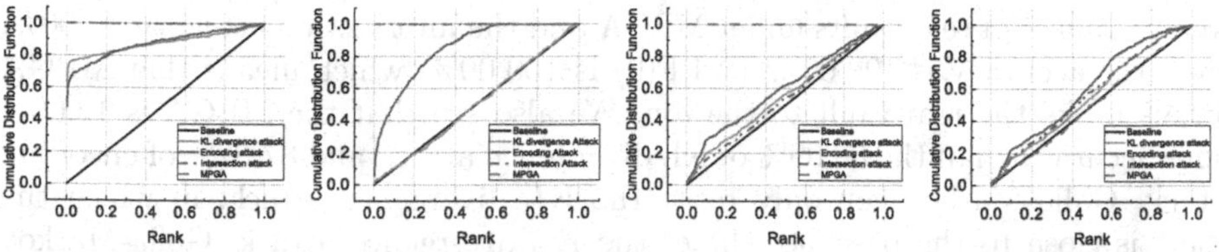

(a) Chatterjee-PCFG.   (b) Golla-Markov.   (c) Cheng-IUV.   (d) SMART.

Fig. 4. Comparison: honey password vault schemes under previous attacks and MPGA. We use the vaults with sizes $M \in [2, 50]$ in Pastebin, and the candidate size $N = 1,000$.

MPGA's Performance with Other Datasets. Previous works [4,5,10] performed practical simulations in Pastebin. However, the scale of Pastebin is relatively small. To test MPGA on large-scale datasets, we construct password vaults with passwords from Rockyou and Myspace. We set the vault size as M and randomly chose M passwords from Rockyou and Myspace to form the real vaults, respectively. The rest of the attack setup and settings are the same as the above evaluation with Pastebin. In Table 1, we show the performance of Chatterjee-PCFG, Golla-Markov, and Cheng-IUV honey password schemes in Rockyou and Myspace. The average rank $\bar{r}$ is 0.00%–0.22%, and accuracy is 99.78%–100.00% under MPGA. When M is 2–3, MPGA can achieve 99.78%–99.90% accuracy, which is very close to the experimental result using Pastebin.

4.5 Evaluation on SMART and Prior Schemes

Our SMART achieves stronger security than prior schemes. In the multi-leakage case, we significantly improve the resistance to MPGA. As shown in Fig. 4(d)

Table 3. The time cost of handling a vault.

Vault size	2	20	200	2,000
Encrypt	2.96 ms	37.06 ms	1,296.62 ms	94,665.23 ms
Decrypt	1.56 ms	4.88 ms	26.24 ms	736.96 ms
Encode	1.38 ms	15.60 ms	636.88 ms	48,553.66 ms
Decode	0.69 ms	1.70 ms	10.34 ms	255.69 ms
Vault storage file	0.55 KB	5.50 KB	55.00 KB	550.00 KB

and Table 2, SMART can mitigate MPGA since $\bar{r}$ and α are only 49.88% and 50.12%, respectively. SMART also maintains security in the case where only a single version of the password vault is exposed to attackers. The results show that attackers must verify at least 44.39%, 46.32%, and 43.59% of decoy vaults online under the KL divergence, encoding, and intersection attacks, respectively. We have shown that SMART resists MPGA and previous attacks effectively. In the following, we compare the performance of SMART to previous works. The results show that Chatterjee-PCFG cannot resist KL divergence attack, encoding attack, intersection attack, and MPGA. As shown in Fig. 4(a) and Table 2, the average rank $\bar{r}$ of real vaults under MPGA and the intersection attack are 0.00%, when the accuracy is 100.00%; and F(0) is 100.00%, which means that MPGA always ranks the real vault to the top. We also see that the MPGA is 12.00% more accuracy than the 88.09% of KL divergence attack and 87.82% of encoding attack. Golla-Markov can only resist the KL divergence attack, in which the result is close to the baseline. Under the KL divergence attack, Golla-Markov captures 51.19% average rank and 48.81% attack accuracy. Compared to the KL divergence attack, MPGA has a significant improvement, where the average rank $\bar{r}$ is 0.00%. Both the encoding attack and the intersection attack exclude all decoy vaults with 100.00% attack accuracy. Cheng-IUV also cannot resist MPGA. In Fig. 4(c) and Table 2, the $\bar{r}$ of real vaults under MPGA is 0.00%, and the accuracy is 100.00%. Our evaluations confirm that Cheng-IUV indeed resists KL divergence, encoding, and intersection attacks, decreasing the accuracy α to 55.41%, 60.18%, and 53.22%, respectively. We also evaluate the impact of different vault sizes and password datasets in Appendix B.2.

Implementation and Efficiency. We conduct the performance on "encrypt", "decrypt", "encode", and "decode" processes. Following previous works [4,5], we set the vault size $M \in \{2, 20, 200, 2000\}$, and the vault storage file $f \in \{0.55\,\text{KB}, 5.50\,\text{KB}, 55.00\,\text{KB}, 550.00\,\text{KB}\}$. In practice, a password vault usually stores at least two passwords. Therefore, we choose two passwords as the smallest unit for our experiments. As shown in Table 3, encrypting a vault of size 200 increases the time cost by approximately 10.00% compared to Cheng-IUV [5]. Because SMART involves the conversion of the master password into the cognate password, which contributes to the slightly increased computational overhead.

5   Conclusion

To the best of our knowledge, this work is the first to study the security of honey vault schemes after the master password is reset. We propose MPGA against existing honey password vault schemes. Our experiments with MPGA provide excellent attack performance in scenarios where multiple versions of the honey password vault are leaked. We design a secure master-password-updatable honey password vault called SMART. The evaluations on the real-world datasets show that SMART significantly improves security against previous attacks and MPGA.

Acknowledgements. We would like to thank the anonymous reviewers for their insightful comments and valuable suggestions. This work was supported in part by the National Key Research and Development Program of China under Grant No. 2021YFB3101304, in part by the National Natural Science Foundation of China under Grant No. 62272186 and No. 62372201.

A   Honey Password Vaults

The concept of decoy vaults comes from Bojinov et al.'s password vault Kamouflage [3]. However, their scheme is based on a static amount (e.g., 1,000) of decoy vaults pre-generated and is incompatible with the *honey encryption (HE)* [13,14] scheme. In this work, we deal with HE-based schemes, e.g., [4–6,10]. HE encodes the vault to the bit string called seed through DTE and then encrypts the seed to ciphertext using PBE. DTE consists of an encoder and a decoder. At the encoding stage, encode passwords in a vault to obtain the bit string s called the seed. Then, the string s is encrypted with the master password in the PBE scheme. In the encrypting process, HE derives a key $K = KDF(mpw, sa)$, where sa is the generated uniform salt, and mpw is the master password. Here, KDF is a password-based key derivation function with SHA-256. Then, encrypt s using AES in CTR-mode with key K and generate the ciphertext C. The decryption works reversely as compared to the above process. Take the master password as input from the user, then derive K as the decryption key. Then, decrypt the C with the K and decode the decrypted s to the plaintext password vault. Existing honey password vault schemes store passwords in the form of ciphertext through the HE scheme. The metadata (i.e., Domain, Username, Computer-generated, Password position) in the password vault is stored in plaintext. The computer-generated passwords are encoded into uniformly distributed seed. In contrast, the user-generated passwords are encoded by the DTE. In this work, we only focus on user-generated passwords. The existing popular password vault systems can remind users to reset the passwords that may have been leaked. To update the vault, incrementally add the updated password to the end of the vault and modify the password position. If the master password is reset, the old vault will be "re-encrypted" accordingly.

B   Extended Evaluations

B.1   MPGA's Performance on Updated Vault

We test the security of honey password vault schemes against a *hybrid attack* where the master password and the vault (i.e., the passwords stored in the vault) are updated simultaneously. The process of resetting the master password is relatively straightforward from the user's perspective. The user only needs to authenticate once to do so. However, updating the passwords in the vault is complicated, as each password corresponds to a different website policy, and the user has to execute various authentication steps. In addition, since the user probably cannot update the entire password vault (i.e., all the passwords) at the same time, the vault service provider may back up multiple historical versions of the vault. Hence, the attacker could obtain multi-leakage versions.

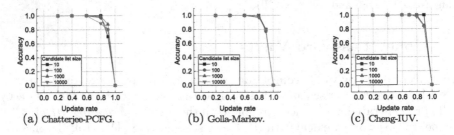

(a) Chatterjee-PCFG.   (b) Golla-Markov.   (c) Cheng-IUV.

Fig. 5. Performance: hybrid attack on honey password vault schemes under the update rate $ur \in \{20.00\%, 40.00\%, 60.00\%, 80.00\%, 100.00\%\}$. The candidate list size $N \in \{10, 100, 1000, 10000\}$.

We choose the vaults with size $M \geq 10$ from Pastebin. Then, we randomly shuffle the passwords in each vault and denote the last $ur \in \{20.00\%, 40.00\%, 60.00\%, 80.00\%, 100.00\%\}$ password as the newly added passwords. In the old version of a vault, we remove the last ur of passwords. We use this simplified approach to simulate the old and new versions of a vault after the user updates both the master password and the vault (i.e., all the passwords). The candidate list size $N \in \{10, 100, 1000, 10000\}$. Given the old/new plaintext password vaults v^o, v^n, the priority function $p_{HA}(v^o, v^n)$ of the hybrid attack is equal to 1 if v^o is the same as v^n except for the update passwords; otherwise, the $p_{HA}(v^o, v^n)$ is equal to 0. We have

$$p_{HA}(v^o, v^n) = \begin{cases} 1, & v^o \text{ is the front part of } v^n, \\ 0, & \text{otherwise.} \end{cases}$$

As shown in Fig. 5, the accuracy of the hybrid attack can reach 100.00%, when the update rate is < 80.00%. If the rate is > 80.00%, the accuracy reduces accordingly, and the attack fails when there is a 100.00% update. Note that the user cannot update the entire password vault at the same time. Moreover, every

Table 4. Performance: hybrid attack on our scheme under the update rate $ur \in$ $\{20.00\%, 40.00\%, 60.00\%, 80.00\%, 100.00\%\}$. We set the candidate list size $N = 1,000$.

Vault update rate	20.00%	40.00%	60.00%	80.00%	100.00%
$\overline{r}$	50.00%	50.00%	50.00%	50.00%	50.00%
α	50.00%	50.00%	50.00%	50.00%	50.00%

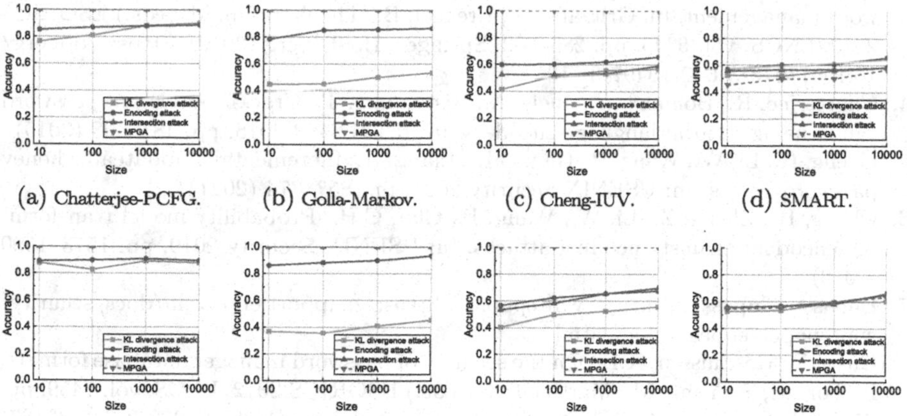

(a) Chatterjee-PCFG.   (b) Golla-Markov.   (c) Cheng-IUV.   (d) SMART.

(e) Chatterjee-PCFG.   (f) Golla-Markov.   (g) Cheng-IUV.   (h) SMART.

Fig. 6. Evaluation: attacking different vault sizes $M \in \{10, 100, 1000, 10000\}$ of honey password vaults, and the candidate size $N = 1,000$. We used the leaked password datasets Yahoo (subfig. a–d) and Gmail (subfig. e–h) to train DTEs.

modification cannot update too many passwords. The hybrid attack is effective if the difference rate between the old and new versions is less than 80%. We state that our SMART is resistant to the hybrid attack, and the accuracy rate remains at 50.00% after various vault updates, see Table 4.

B.2   Experimental Parameters Evaluation

In this evaluation, we randomly select 90.00% of passwords from the Yahoo dataset as the training set to train the DTE and the other 10.00% as the real password vault. In the real password vault, we set up the same size $M \in \{10, 100, 1000, 10000\}$. The experiments on Gmail follow the same settings. In Fig. 6, we show the accuracy of the four attacks (i.e., KL divergence attack, encoding attack, intersection attack, and MPGA) by increasing the number of passwords in the vault. MPGA maintains 100.00% accuracy against previous schemes (i.e., Chatterjee-PCFG, Golla-Markov, and Cheng-IUV). SMART still has great resistance to above attacks. We also see that different password datasets produce similar results, and the vault size has a minor effect on the results.

References

1. 1password: 1password security design. https://1passwordstatic.com/files/security/1password-white-paper.pdf
2. Bohuk, M.S., Islam, M., Ahmad, S., Swift, M., Ristenpart, T., Chatterjee, R.: Gossamer: securely measuring password-based logins. In: USENIX Security 2022, pp. 1867–1884 (2022)
3. Bojinov, H., Bursztein, E., Boyen, X., Boneh, D.: Kamouflage: loss-resistant password management. In: Gritzalis, D., Preneel, B., Theoharidou, M. (eds.) ESORICS 2010. LNCS, vol. 6345, pp. 286–302. Springer, Heidelberg (2010). https://doi.org/10.1007/978-3-642-15497-3_18
4. Chatterjee, R., Bonneau, J., Juels, A., Ristenpart, T.: Cracking-resistant password vaults using natural language encoders. In: IEEE S&P 2015, pp. 481–498 (2015)
5. Cheng, H., Li, W., Wang, P., Chu, C.H., Liang, K.: Incrementally updateable honey password vaults. In: USENIX Security 2021, pp. 857–874 (2021)
6. Cheng, H., Zheng, Z., Li, W., Wang, P., Chu, C.H.: Probability model transforming encoders against encoding attacks. In: USENIX Security 2019, pp. 1573–1590 (2019)
7. Enpass: Enpass security whitepaper. https://support.enpass.io/docs/security-whitepaper-enpass/index.html
8. Gasti, P., Rasmussen, K.B.: On the security of password manager database formats. In: Foresti, S., Yung, M., Martinelli, F. (eds.) ESORICS 2012. LNCS, vol. 7459, pp. 770–787. Springer, Heidelberg (2012). https://doi.org/10.1007/978-3-642-33167-1_44
9. Gelernter, N., Kalma, S., Magnezi, B., Porcilan, H.: The password reset MitM attack. In: IEEE S&P 2017, pp. 251–267 (2017)
10. Golla, M., Beuscher, B., Dürmuth, M.: On the security of cracking-resistant password vaults. In: ACM CCS 2016, pp. 1230–1241 (2016)
11. Golla, M., Dürmuth, M.: On the accuracy of password strength meters. In: ACM CCS 2018, pp. 1567–1582 (2018)
12. Google: Google chrome privacy whitepaper. https://www.google.com/chrome/privacy/whitepaper.html
13. Jaeger, J., Ristenpart, T., Tang, Q.: Honey encryption beyond message recovery security. In: Fischlin, M., Coron, J.-S. (eds.) EUROCRYPT 2016. LNCS, vol. 9665, pp. 758–788. Springer, Heidelberg (2016). https://doi.org/10.1007/978-3-662-49890-3_29
14. Juels, A., Ristenpart, T.: Honey encryption: security beyond the Brute-Force bound. In: Nguyen, P.Q., Oswald, E. (eds.) EUROCRYPT 2014. LNCS, vol. 8441, pp. 293–310. Springer, Heidelberg (2014). https://doi.org/10.1007/978-3-642-55220-5_17
15. Juels, A., Rivest, R.L.: Honeywords: making password-cracking detectable. In: ACM CCS 2013, pp. 145–160 (2013)
16. Kingma, D.P., Ba, J.: Adam: a method for stochastic optimization. arXiv preprint arXiv:1412.6980 (2014)
17. Lastpass: Lastpass technical whitepaper. https://support.lastpass.com/help/lastpass-technical-whitepaper
18. Lastpass: Master password policy. https://support.lastpass.com/help/what-is-the-lastpass-master-password-lp070014
19. Mayer, P., Munyendo, C.W., Mazurek, M.L., Aviv, A.J.: Why users (don't) use password managers at a large educational institution. In: USENIX Security 2022, pp. 1849–1866 (2022)

20. Pal, B., Daniel, T., Chatterjee, R., Ristenpart, T.: Beyond credential stuffing: Password similarity models using neural networks. In: IEEE S&P 2019, pp. 417–434 (2019)

21. Ray, H., Wolf, F., Kuber, R., Aviv, A.J.: Why older adults (don't) use password managers. In: USENIX Security 2021, pp. 73–90 (2021)

22. Ur, B., et al.: How does your password measure up? The effect of strength meters on password creation. In: USENIX Security 2012, pp. 65–80 (2012)

23. Wang, D., Zhang, Z., Wang, P., Yan, J., Huang, X.: Targeted online password guessing: an underestimated threat. In: ACM CCS 2016, pp. 1242–1254 (2016)

24. Wang, D., Zou, Y., Dong, Q., Song, Y., Huang, X.: How to attack and generate honeywords. In: IEEE S&P 2022, pp. 489–506 (2022)

25. Weir, M., Aggarwal, S., De Medeiros, B., Glodek, B.: Password cracking using probabilistic context-free grammars. In: IEEE S&P 2009, pp. 391–405 (2009)

26. Yujian, L., Bo, L.: A normalized Levenshtein distance metric. IEEE Trans. Pattern Anal. Mach. Intell. **29**(6), 1091–1095 (2007)

Attacking Logo-Based Phishing Website Detectors with Adversarial Perturbations

Jehyun Lee[1]([✉]), Zhe Xin[2], Melanie Ng Pei See[2], Kanav Sabharwal[2],
Giovanni Apruzzese[3], and Dinil Mon Divakaran[2,4]

[1] Trustwave, Singapore, Singapore
jehyun.lee@trustwave.com
[2] National University of Singapore, Singapore, Singapore
[3] Liechtenstein Business School, University of Liechtenstein, Vaduz, Liechtenstein
[4] Acronis Research, Singapore, Singapore

Abstract. Recent times have witnessed the rise of anti-phishing schemes powered by deep learning (DL). In particular, logo-based phishing detectors rely on DL models from Computer Vision to identify logos of well-known brands on webpages, to detect malicious webpages that imitate a given brand. For instance, Siamese networks have demonstrated notable performance for these tasks, enabling the corresponding anti-phishing solutions to detect even "zero-day" phishing webpages. In this work, we take the next step of studying the robustness of logo-based phishing detectors against adversarial ML attacks. We propose a novel attack leveraging generative adversarial perturbations to craft "adversarial logos" that, with no knowledge of phishing detection models, can successfully evade the detectors. We evaluate our attacks through: (i) experiments on datasets containing real logos, to evaluate the robustness of state-of-the-art phishing detectors; and (ii) user studies to gauge whether our adversarial logos can deceive human eyes. The results show that our proposed attack is capable of crafting perturbed logos subtle enough to evade various DL models—achieving an evasion rate of up to 95%. Moreover, users are not able to spot significant differences between generated adversarial logos and original ones.

Keywords: Phishing · Adversarial Machine Learning · Deep Learning

1 Introduction

Phishing attacks are on the rise [2], and they represent a serious threat to both organizations and individuals alike. While there have been numerous research efforts to counter this long-running security problem [25,30,31,56], a universal solution against phishing has yet to be found, as new ways to lure unaware victims keep emerging [3]. We focus on the problem of detecting phishing *websites*, which has witnessed 61% increase in 2022 [6].

The first line of defense against phishing websites is represented by blocklists, which are nowadays leveraged at scale [29]. Unfortunately, such rule-based countermeasures only work against the phishing entries in the blocklist, and attackers are well-aware of this (for a recent report, see [4]). To protect users against evolving phishing websites, current anti-phishing schemes are now equipped with data-driven methods that detect malicious webpages by leveraging some heuristics [5]. In particular, the constant progress and successes of *machine learning* (ML) algorithms in research [51,57] led to the integration of ML-based phishing detectors also in popular browsers [33].

There are various ways in which ML is used to identify phishing websites, depending on the input analyzed by the ML model [22]: URL (e.g., [30,53]), HTML contents (e.g., [32,56,57]), or visual representations (e.g., [7,20]) of a webpage. Detection methods based on visual analytics are now receiving much attention (e.g., [7,19,20,28,34,35]), likely due to the tremendous advancements in deep learning (DL). In this work, we delve into the application of DL for *logo-based* phishing website detection—a state-of-the-art approach[1] that is *(i)* considered in recent researches (e.g., [19,28,34,35]), and *(ii)* deployed in practice [11].

In logo-based detection, the first task is to extract the logo(s) from a webpage (typically from its screenshot); the subsequent task is to identify the brand of the logo. The latter task can be accomplished by means of DL today, as demonstrated by recent works, e.g., by employing Siamese neural networks [34,35]. Given the relevance of these solutions in anti-phishing schemes, we scrutinize the robustness of DL models for logo identification against subtle adversarial perturbations. Even though many efforts in the DL community reveal the vulnerability of image classification models to adversarial examples [26,38,43,50], to the best of our knowledge, there exists no work that studies the vulnerability of logo-based phishing detectors against such sophisticated attacks. Therefore, besides the Siamese models proposed by prior work, we also develop two new logo-identification solutions based on state-of-the-art transformer models from Computer Vision—namely, Vision Transformer ViT [23] and Swin [36].

Subsequently, we propose a novel attack using *generative adversarial perturbations* (GAP) [43], to craft adversarial logos that simultaneously deceive *(i)* DL models for logo identification, and *(ii)* human users, i.e., potential victims. Through a comprehensive experimental study based on datasets of real logos, we demonstrate the quality of our proposed DL models for logo identification and the efficacy of the adversarial logos generated by our GAP attack to evade all three powerful models for logo identification (Siamese, ViT and Swin).

Finally, we carry out two user studies to assess the impact of our attack on real humans. We summarise our three major contributions:

1. We propose *a novel attack*, based on generative adversarial perturbations (GAP), against logo-based anti-phishing schemes (Sect. 4). Our proposed

---

[1] **Background:** in simple terms, logo-based phishing detection seeks to identify those (malicious) webpages that attempt to imitate a well-known brand. Intuitively, if a given webpage has the logo of a well-known brand (e.g., PayPal), but the domain does not correspond to the same brand (e.g., www.p4y-p4l.com), the webpage is classified as phishing. Though these approaches require maintenance of a database of logos for brands, such a task is not impractical given that the number of brands targeted by attackers is typically small ($\approx$ 200) [7,18,34].

attack treats a phishing detection (specifically, logo-identification) model as a black-box and does not require any model-specific information.

2. We propose *two new logo-identification solutions* leveraging transformer-based DL models: `ViT` and `Swin` (Sect. 3). We empirically demonstrate that both `ViT` and `Swin` achieve performance comparable to the state-of-the-art solutions relying on `Siamese` models [34,35] (Sect. 5.3).

3. Through a reproducible evaluation on real data, we *evaluate the robustness of three DL models for logo-identification* (`ViT`, `Swin`, `Siamese`) against our GAP-based attack (Sect. 5.4). We further validate the *impact of our attack on real humans* through a user study entailing ∼250 people (Sect. 6).

We suggest potential countermeasures against our attack, and also discuss ways that attackers can use to circumvent such countermeasures (Sect. 7). Finally, we publicly release our resources to the scientific community [1].

2   Threat Model

We describe the threat model by first summarizing the functionality of the target system, and then presenting the characteristic of our envisioned attacker.

2.1   Target System: Logo-Based Phishing Website Detectors

Fig. 1 presents the general workflow of logo-based phishing detection systems. From a given webpage, the detection system first extracts the logo as an image; then, it identifies the brand the logo belongs to by using a discriminator. Such a discriminator can be implemented in various ways, e.g., earlier works employed methods based on SIFT (scale-invariant feature transformation) [9,54]; however, current state-of-the-art methods use DL models [16,34,35], and we focus on these. Upon identifying the brand of a logo, the system determines if the webpage is legitimate or not by comparing the webpage's domain with the domain of the brand associated with the logo.

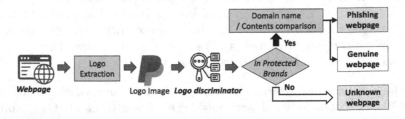

Fig. 1. Detection process of logo-based phishing detection systems

Since logo-identification is a multi-class classification problem, the DL model is trained on a static set of classes, i.e., the brands of the logos. Such a set of *protected brands* determines the size of the prediction classes; one brand may have multiple logos. Previous research has shown that 99% of the attacks target less than 200 brands [7,34,35].

In practice, phishing detectors must exhibit low false-positive rates (FPR), typically below 10^{-3} [31,44]. To successfully detect phishing webpages while maintaining low FPR, logo-based detectors follow two principles [34]: *(a)* the highest predicted class is decided as the target brand *if and only if* the prediction probability is greater than a predefined *decision threshold* (say, θ); *(b)* if the identified logo does not belong to any brand in the protected set, the webpage is considered benign to avoid triggering false positives (see Fig. 1). Unfortunately, these principles can be maliciously exploited: by lowering the prediction probability, it is possible to evade logo-based phishing detectors.

2.2 Attack: Adversarial Logos

The basic intuition behind our attack is to create an *adversarial logo* that is *(i)* minimally altered w.r.t. its original variant (to deceive the human eye); and that *(ii)* misleads the phishing detector. Let us describe our attacker by using the well-known notion of adversarial ML attacks [11,17].

- Goal: The attacker wants to craft an adversarial logo related to brand b which evades the phishing detector (at inference) while deceiving human eyes.
- Knowledge and Capabilities: To train a model for evasion, an attacker can collect authentic logos of any brand (e.g., of PayPal), via crawling or from public datasets (e.g., *Logo2K+* [55]). The attacker knows that their victims are protected by a logo-based phishing detector powered by ML. The attacker has a way to infer the decision result of the phishing detector (this is doable even if the detector is "invisible" [11], e.g., by inspecting visits to the hosted phishing webpage). The attacker does not i) require knowledge of the logo-identification model employed by the phishing detector, ii) manipulate the data used to train the ML model. In other words, it's neither a white-box attack nor performs data poisoning.
  Note, the attacker targets a set of brands for phishing; if the targeted brand is not within the protected set, then that is already favorable for an attacker—there is no perturbation required! Finally, the attacker naturally has control on their phishing webpages.
- Strategy: The attacker manipulates the logo(s) of brand b in their phishing webpages by introducing perturbations so that the logo-identification model predicts with lower confidence, i.e., the probability of the logo being of any brand is lower than the decision threshold (θ). This way, the phishing detector decides the logo *not* to be one of the protected brands, which makes way for successful evasion.

Scope of Attack. In our threat model, the attacker exploits the vulnerability of *logo-identification* methods integrated into phishing detectors. We focus on logo-identification DL models because they are i) state-of-the-art research with phishing detecting capability in the wild ('zero-day' phishing) [34,35], and ii) used in commercial phishing detectors [11]. Threats against logo extraction from a webpage, however interesting, are not within the scope of our current work. Lastly, we do not consider attacks to make an unknown logo be identified as one of the protected logos, as that is not beneficial for the attacker.

3 Deep Learning for Logo-Based Phishing Detection

Development of the transformer architecture [52] paved the way for various state-of-the-art language models, such as BERT, ChatGPT, and PaLM. Dosovitskiy et al. [23] applied transformer to Computer Vision tasks with the introduction of Vision Transformer (ViT), demonstrating state-of-the-art performance on benchmark datasets [23]. The attention mechanism in transformers allows them to capture local and global contextual information effectively, resulting in superior performance on large-scale image classification tasks. This capability is also beneficial for logo identification, since logos of the same brand, while being visually distinct, share the same inherent design structure. Therefore, in this work, we propose, develop and evaluate two transformer-based models, ViT and Swin, for logo identification. To the best of our knowledge, we are the first to leverage transformers for logo-based phishing detection.

We now describe our proposed ViT (Sect. 3.1) and Swin (Sect. 3.2), for which we provide an overview in Figs 2 and 3. Then, we present our own implementation of Siamese (Sect. 3.3) neural networks. Altogether, these three DL models will represent the target of our attacks (Sect. 5).

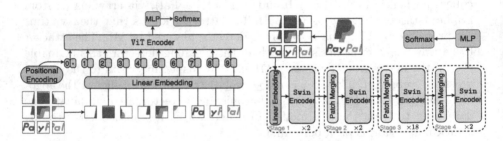

Fig. 2. ViT-based Model Architecture   **Fig. 3.** Swin-based Model Architecture

3.1 ViT for Logo Identification

As illustrated in Fig. 2, we develop a logo-identification model by fine-tuning a pre-trained ViT-base model [23] on our dataset (which we discuss in Sect. 5.1). The model takes as input an image of size $3 \times 224 \times 224$. The image is then split into patches, each of size 16×16, for further processing. Each patch is then linearly embedded into a vector of size 1×768. An additional classification token is then added to the linear embedding to form an embedded vector of size 197×768. The embeddings are positionally encoded before being fed into the transformer encoder. Finally, a fully connected layer takes the output from the encoder and maps it to a 2-dimensional space. The resulting logits are passed through a softmax layer to produce the final prediction probabilities for each class (logo). We denote this new logo-identification model as $\mathcal{D}_{\texttt{ViT}}$.

3.2 Swin for Logo Identification

Next, we propose Swin-based logo-identification model that utilizes the Swin transformer, a hierarchical transformer architecture introduced by Liu et al. [36]. Unlike ViT, Swin uses shifted windows to efficiently compute local self-attentions and build hierarchical feature maps through patch merging techniques. As illustrated in Fig. 3, each window contains multiple non-overlapping patches, and each transformer block in the Swin architecture contains two attention layers: a window-based multi-head self-attention (W-MSA) layer that calculates local attention within a specific window, and a shifted window-based multi-head self-attention (SW-MSA) layer that introduces cross-window connections. This approach allows for more efficient computation while still extracting both local and global contextual information.

In our implementation, we use the Swin-Transformer-Small architecture proposed by Liu et al. [36]. The model takes an input image of size $3 \times 224 \times 224$, which is split into patches of size 4×4. As depicted in Fig. 3, the patches are fed sequentially into four encoding stages consisting of 2, 2, 18, and 2 encoder blocks. Each encoding stage merges and downsamples the size of the feature maps by a factor of two, while doubling the number of channels.

The final feature map of size is 7×7 is transformed by a fully connected and softmax layer to obtain the output logits. We denote this model as $\mathcal{D}_{\text{Swin}}$.

3.3 Siamese and Siamese^{++} for Logo Identification

The Siamese neural network is a state-of-the-art for image-based phishing detection, both for comparing screenshots [7] and logos [16,34,35]. In logo-based phishing detectors, Siamese models measure the similarity of a given logo to those in the protected set. We train a Siamese model as proposed in Phishpedia [34] and PhishIntention [35], utilizing a transfer learning approach. Specifically, we train a logo classification model with the ResNetV2 network as the backbone, which effectively extracts different features from various logo variants. We then connect the trained ResNetV2 network to a Global Average Pooling layer to output a vector for any given logo. The learned vector representation is compared to those of the logos of protected brands using cosine similarity; the target with the highest similarity is identified as the brand the logo is trying to imitate.

We refer to our implementation of the Siamese model as $\mathcal{D}_{\text{Siamese}}$. Additionally, Phishpedia [34] proposed an adversary-aware detector by replacing the ReLU activation function with a variant called step-ReLU (Appendix A). We also consider this robust version of Siamese, which we refer to as $\mathcal{D}_{\text{Siamese}^{++}}$.

4 Our Attack: Adversarial Logos

While recent logo-based phishing detection systems [34,35] have demonstrated robustness against generic gradient-based attacks such as FGSM [26] and Deep-

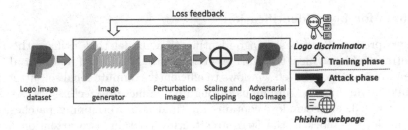

Fig. 4. Generative adversarial perturbation workflow

Fool [39],[2] their resilience against more sophisticated adversarial attacks proposed in the literature [38,43] remains unexplored. To this end, we propose a DL-based generative framework inspired by Generative Adversarial Perturbations (GAP) [43], that specifically trains against logo identification models. This framework generates perturbation vectors that can be added to a target logo image, allowing the perturbed logo to evade phishing detection while remaining imperceptible to the human eye. We now describe our framework at a high-level (Sect. 4.1), for which we provide an overview in Fig. 4; and then provide low-level details on how to practically implement our attacks (Sect. 4.2).

4.1 Framework: Generative Adversarial Perturbations for Logos

As illustrated in Fig. 4, our framework involves training a `Generator` that learns to generate perturbations. When added to a logo image, these perturbations can mislead a logo-identification model, which acts as the `Discriminator`, into lowering its prediction probability below the decision threshold. During the training process, the weights of the `Discriminator` are frozen, treating it as a black box to guide the training of the `Generator`.

Generator. We employ a Deep Residual Network with six residual blocks (ResNet-6) [27] as the core architecture of our `Generator`. Given a legitimate logo image as input, the `Generator` is trained to generate a *perturbation vector*. The generated perturbations undergo a *Scaling and Clipping* stage. In this stage, the perturbation vector is first scaled and normalized based on the L_∞ norm to control the magnitude of the perturbations, so that they remain imperceptible to human viewers. Subsequently, the normalized perturbations are added pixel-wise to the legitimate logo image, resulting in the adversarial logo.

Discriminator. The `Discriminator` is a pre-trained multi-class classifier designed to process a logo image and estimate the probability that the image

---

[2] FGSM and DeepFool assume an adversary with complete knowledge of the target classifier, which is much stronger (and less realistic [11]) than the attacker envisioned in our threat model.

belongs to a target brand in the protected set. In our framework, we select one of the logo-identification models described in Sect. 3 to serve as the `Discriminator`.

4.2 Implementation

We utilize the pre-trained `Discriminator` as a black box to assess the effectiveness of the `Generator` in crafting adversarial logo images. The `Discriminator` predicts the probability of a given logo belonging to each of the k protected brands; $\mathbf{V}_{\text{true}} : [p_1, p_2, p_3....p_k]$, where $\sum_{i=1}^{k} p_i = 1$. As mentioned in Sect. 2.1, for a webpage to be classified as phishing, the logo-identification model must confidently identify the logo as one of the target brands i from the protected set, with a probability p_i greater than the phishing detector's decision threshold θ.

Hence, to devise our `Generator`, we introduce a target probability $p_{\text{adversarial}}$, such that $p_{\text{adversarial}} < \theta$. The `Generator` is trained to craft adversarial logos that are classified with probabilities lower than $p_{\text{adversarial}}$ for all of the protected brands, so as to evade phishing detection. Empirically, we observe that θ is very high (above 0.8) for all discriminators, and for our attacks, $p_{\text{adversarial}}$ can be much lower (in our experiments, it is 0.5; see Table 3 in Appendix B).

To guide the training process, the `Generator` is trained with a target probability vector $\mathbf{V}_{\text{target}} : [p'_1, p'_2, p'_3....p'_k]$, where each element p'_i is defined such that $p'_i = \min(p_i, p_{\text{adversarial}})$. This ensures that the generated adversarial logos are classified with probabilities below the θ for all protected brands.

The loss function is defined as a decreasing function of the cross entropy $\mathcal{H}(V_{\text{true}}, V_{\text{target}})$ between the target probability vector $\mathbf{V}_{\text{target}}$ and $\mathbf{V}_{\text{true}}$. The specific form of the loss function can be expressed as follows:

$$\text{loss} = \log\left(\mathcal{H}\left(\mathbf{V}_{\text{true}}, \mathbf{V}_{\text{target}}\right)\right) \tag{1}$$

Minimizing this loss, the `Generator` learns to craft adversarial logos that evade phishing detection[3]; furthermore, perturbations preserve the visual similarity with the original logo, thereby facilitating deception to the human eye.

5 Experimental Evaluations

We now empirically assess the quality of our contributions. We begin by describing the datasets used for our experiments (Sect. 5.1), and introduce the metrics used for our performance assessment (Sect. 5.2). Then, we first show that our two DL models for logo-identification achieve state-of-the-art performance (Sect. 5.3), and then demonstrate that our attacks can evade all our considered logo-identification models (Sect. 5.4). Our code, dataset used, as well as generated perturbed logos are available at [1].

---

[3] **Remark:** Our attack relies on the logos generated by the `Generator`, which in turn depend on a `Discriminator`, i.e., a DL model for identifying logos. However, the `Discriminator` *does not* necessarily have to be the identical one used in the targeted phishing detection system: as our experiments show, our adversarial logos evade even DL models that have not been used to develop the `Generator` (by leveraging the well-known transferability property of adversarial examples [21]).

5.1 Dataset

To evaluate the performance of logo-based phishing detectors and their robustness against generative adversarial perturbations, we use two sets of logo images:

- **L, Protected brands:** The logo image set of protected brands, **L**, consists of images of 181 brands which are identical to the brands used in Phishpedia [34]. According to the empirical observation in [34], 99% of phishing pages target one of these 181 brands. For these protected brands, we collected 28 263 public logo images from search engines and Pawar's logo image dataset [42]. Each brand's logo has 100–200 variants.
- **L̄, Unprotected brands:** Logo image set **L̄** is the set of 2 045 images from 2 000 brands that do not belong to the brands in **L**. The image samples are from the *Logo2K+* dataset, which is publicly available [55].

The data was collected in the second half of January 2023.

5.2 Performance Metrics

In what follows, we denote the logo-identification models as `discriminators`; the attack `generators` also use the discriminators in their training phase.

<u>Logo Identification Performance:</u> We provide the definitions of metrics for logo-based phishing webpage detection. Note that, for a discriminator used for phishing detection, the positives are the logos in **L**, the protected brand list, that need to be identified. If the highest prediction probability of a logo is below a certain decision threshold, it is classified as an unknown brand.

- *True positive (TP):* A TP in our evaluation denotes the case of correct brand identification of the given logo (of a protected brand) by the discriminator.
- *False positive (FP):* An FP denotes the case when the given logo image is wrongly identified as one of the protected brands when in reality, the given logo image does not belong to the protected brand set.
- *True negative (TN):* A TN occurs when the brand of the given logo is not in the protected brand set and gets correctly classified as an unknown brand.
- *False negative (FN):* An FN denotes when the brand of the given logo belonging to the protected brand set is classified as any other brand.

Denoting the actual brand of a given logo l as l_b, and the predicted brand by the discriminator as l_p, we define the True Positive Rate (TPR) and False Positive Rate (FPR):

$$\text{TPR} = \frac{|(l_b = l_p) \wedge (l_p \in \mathbf{L})|}{|l_b \in \mathbf{L}|}; \qquad \text{FPR} = \frac{|(l_p \in \mathbf{L}) \wedge (l_b \in \bar{\mathbf{L}})|}{|l_b \in \bar{\mathbf{L}}|} \quad (2)$$

<u>Impact of the Attacks:</u> Recall that our attacker aims to fool the discriminator into classifying a protected brand logo as an unknown brand. Hence, we introduce

the *Fooling ratio*, which is the rate of adversarial logos classified as being of an unknown brand (out of all the phishing logos). Formally:

$$\text{Fooling ratio} = \frac{|l_p \notin \mathbf{L} \wedge l_b \in \mathbf{L}|}{|l_b \in \mathbf{L}|} \tag{3}$$

Intuitively, a higher fooling ratio denotes an attack with a higher impact.

5.3   Baseline: Analysis of Logo-Identification Models

We assess the performance of the four DL models for logo-identification presented in Sect. 3. Specifically, we first measure the TPR and FPR of the state-of-the-art discriminators (i.e., `Siamese` and its robust version `Siamese`++ [34]), and compare them with the transformer-based discriminators that we proposed in this work (i.e., `ViT` and `Swin`).

Setup. We use the datasets $\mathbf{L}$ and $\bar{\mathbf{L}}$ (see Sect. 5.1), with a train:test split of 85:15. For `ViT` and `Swin`, we apply the common model head fine-tuning for 50 epochs and then transfer training on the entire networks for the next 150 epochs, reducing computational time while improving performance. We provide hyper-parameters configurations of our discriminators in Table 2 (in the appendix).

Results. Figure 5a shows the ROC curves of the four discriminators (the x-axis denoting FPR is in log-scale for visibility). Overall, `Siamese` and `Siamese`++ show the best performance in terms of logo identification. All four models show comparable TPRs at FPR above 10^{-2}. For practical purposes, however, we have to evaluate the detection capability at low FPRs [22, 44]. Observe that, the TPR values of the discriminators `ViT` and `Swin` at FPR below 10^{-2} are worse than the `Siamese` models. Figure 5b shows the gap in TPR between the discriminators at the more practical FPR value of 10^{-3}; `Siamese` and `Siamese`++ show around six and twelve percent-point higher TPR than the `ViT` and `Swin`, respectively.

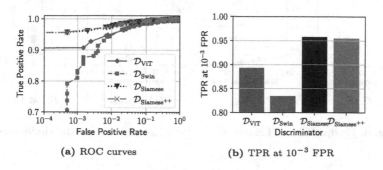

(a) ROC curves

(b) TPR at 10^{-3} FPR

Fig. 5. Comparing discriminators for logo identification

Although `Swin` and `ViT` are not better than `Siamese`, they still achieve an appreciable degree of performance, and hence are used to evaluate our attacks.

5.4   Attack: Evasiveness of Adversarial Logos, and Computational Cost

We quantitatively analyze the effects of adversarial logos generated by our attack against DL models for logo identification. We do this through a cross-evaluation that captures both 'white-box' and 'black-box' adversarial settings. At the end of this section, we also discuss the computational cost of our attacks.

Setup. Recall that our attack (Sect. 4) entails training a generator by using a given discriminator (i.e., DL models for identifying logos). For our experiments, we consider three discriminators: ViT, Swin and Siamese, thereby yielding three corresponding generators: $\mathcal{G}_{\text{ViT}}$, $\mathcal{G}_{\text{Swin}}$ and $\mathcal{G}_{\text{Siamese}}$. After training each generator, we assess the adversarial logos against *all our discriminators*. Such an evaluation protocol allows one to analyze the effects of our attacks when the adversary does not know the DL model used for the defense.

For evaluations, we train our generators on the dataset **L**; we provide the hyperparameters of our generators in Table 3 (Appendix B). Subsequently, we test the discriminators with the adversarial logos crafted by each generator.

Results. The results are plotted in Fig. 6, where we compare the fooling ratio of discriminators against the different attacker models for varying FPRs (in log-scale). It stands out that each discriminator is much weaker against the adversarial logos created by the 'matching' generator compared to those created by generators trained on different discriminators. For instance, from Fig. 6a, we observe that the adversarial logos generated by $\mathcal{G}_{\text{ViT}}$ are more effective against ViT (blue line) than against Swin (green line). We observe from Fig. 6b and Fig. 6c that, if the attacker's generator model is not trained with ViT, the fooling ratio drops significantly for the defender with the ViT discriminator.

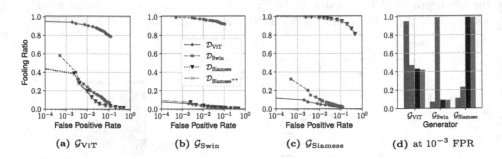

(a) $\mathcal{G}_{\text{ViT}}$ (b) $\mathcal{G}_{\text{Swin}}$ (c) $\mathcal{G}_{\text{Siamese}}$ (d) at 10^{-3} FPR

Fig. 6. Comparison of different generators against different discriminators

From the adversary's perspective, ViT is the most effective generator against all discriminators. Figure 6d compares the fooling ratios of the four discriminators at a fixed FPR of 10^{-3}; note, **fooling ratios against $\mathcal{G}_{\text{ViT}}$ are high, ranging from 42% to 95%**. In other words, with $\mathcal{G}_{\text{ViT}}$, at least 42% of attacker generated logos can evade phishing detectors, independent of the discriminator deployed. Against such an attacker, the defender might prefer to use Siamese (or Siamese^{++}) as it achieves the lowest fooling ratio (of around 42% at 10^{-3} FPR). Interestingly, the most robust model for the defender against an *arbitrary* generator model would be ViT, since, on average, ViT achieves a lower fooling ratio against all generator models.

Computational Cost. Two factors contribute to the computation time to realize our adversarial logos: i) generator training and ii) perturbed logo generation. We measure the generator training time with the three models, i.e., ViT, Swin, and Siamese, for each training epoch and the required epochs till reaching a compelling performance, i.e., 0.9 of fooling ratio against the discriminator with the corresponding model. The experiments are performed on a system with NVIDIA RTX3090 GPU, 2.8 GHz 32-core AMD CPU, 80GB RAM with Python 3.8.10, and PyTorch 1.2.0 on Ubuntu 20.04 OS. We report the results in Table 1.

Table 1. Training time for the perturbation generators

	$\mathcal{G}_{ViT}$	$\mathcal{G}_{Swin}$	$\mathcal{G}_{Siamese}$
Avg. training time per epoch (min.)	12	23	8
No. of epochs for 0.9 fooling ratio	62	12	1
Training time for 0.9 fooling ratio (min.)	744	277	8

From this table, we observe an apparent gap between the models in their training time. While the ViT-based generator, $\mathcal{G}_{ViT}$, takes only half the training time per epoch in comparison to $\mathcal{G}_{Swin}$, it requires five times more training epochs to reach the same level of performance, (i.e., 0.9 fooling ratio). $\mathcal{G}_{Siamese}$ shows significantly less overhead than the other two, in both, training time per epoch and the required epoch. $\mathcal{G}_{Siamese}$ accomplishes a fooling ratio of 0.9 against $\mathcal{D}_{Siamese}$ after just one epoch of training which takes only eight minutes. Overall, training $\mathcal{G}_{ViT}$ takes 744 min to have 0.9 fooling ratio, which is around 2.8 and 93 times longer training time than $\mathcal{G}_{Swin}$ and $\mathcal{G}_{Siamese}$, respectively. Although there are significant differences in training times, when it comes to generating perturbed logos, all three generators take only around 0.7 s per image on average; this negligible cost allows an attacker to generate a large number of samples to test against a deployed phishing detector.

Takeaways. i) An attacker with knowledge of the discriminator used for defense achieves more than 95% fooling ratio with our adversarial generator. ii) In the absence of knowledge of the discriminator (i.e., independent of the discriminator), an attacker choosing $\mathcal{G}_{ViT}$ as the generator achieves a fooling ratio of at least 42% against the defender (see Fig. 6d).

6   User Study: Do Adversarial Logos Trick Humans?

We now provide a complementary evaluation of our proposed attack. Specifically, we seek to investigate *if our adversarial logos can be spotted by humans*. Indeed, even if a phishing detector can be evaded, this would be useless if the human, the actual target of the phishing attack, can clearly see that something is "phishy". Hence, we carry out **two user-studies**, which we describe (Sect. 6.1) and discuss (Sect. 6.2) in the remainder of this section.

6.1   Methodology

Our goal is to assess if the perturbations entailed in an adversarial logo can be recognized by humans. There are many ways to perform such an assessment through a user-study, each with its own pros and cons[4].

We build our user-studies around a central research question (RQ): *given a pair of logos (i.e., an 'original' one, and an 'adversarial' one), can the human spot any difference?* Our idea is to design a questionnaire containing multiple pairs of logos, and ask the participants to rate (through a 1–5 Linkert scale) the similarity of the logos in each pair. Intuitively, if the results reveal that users perceive the logos to be "different", then it would mean that our adversarial logos are not effective against humans.

To account for the fact that the responses we would receive are entirely subjective, we carry out (in April 2023) two quantitative user studies:

1. *Vertical Study* (VS), which entails a small population ($N = 30$) of similar users (students of a large university, aged 20–30). The questionnaire has ten questions (each being a pair of logos to rate), wherein each participant is shown a different set of questions. The purpose of VS is to capture the responses of a specific group of humans across a large set of adversarial logos.
2. *Horizontal Study* (HS), which entails a large population ($N = 287$) of users with diverse backgrounds (Amazon Turk Workers with 95+% hit-rate, aged 18–70). The questionnaire includes 21 questions, which are always the same for each participant. The purpose of HS is to capture the response of various humans to a small set of adversarial logos.

For both VS and HS, participants were asked to provide a response within 5 s of seeing the pair of logos (because, realistically, users do not spend much time looking at the logo on a website). We also included control questions (e.g., pairs of identical logos, and pairs of clearly different logos) as a form of attention mechanism[5]. Finally, we shuffled the questions to further reduce bias. For transparency, we provide our questionnaire at [1].

For VS (resp. HS), we included 2 (resp. 3) "identical" pairs as baseline; and 5 (resp. 12) "original-adversarial" pairs to answer our RQ.

---

[4] Designing bias-free user-studies in the phishing context is an open problem [10,48].
[5] For HS, we received 322 responses, but we removed 35 because some users took too little time to answer the entire questionnaire, or did not pass our attention checks.

6.2   Results

We present the results of both of our user studies in Fig. 7. Specifically, Fig. 7a shows the cumulative distribution of the scores for the three 'identical' pairs, and the five 'original-adversarial' pairs in VS. Whereas the boxplots in Fig. 7b show how the participants of HS rated the 12 "original-adversarial" pairs; the rightmost boxplot aggregates all results. In our rating definition, 5 means 'similar', and 1 means 'different'.

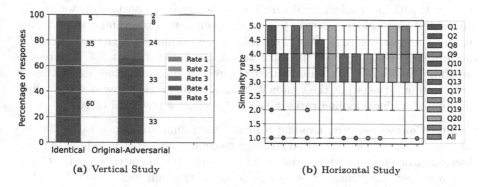

(a) Vertical Study   (b) Horizontal Study

Fig. 7. Results of our two user-studies: vertical study and horizontal study

From Fig. 7a, we observe that 95% of all responses (30 users × 10 questions) rated all 'identical' pairs (left bin) between 4 and 5 (only 5% answered with a 3). That is to say; they correctly guessed that all identical pairs were indeed very similar, thereby also confirming that this population was very reliable. For this reason, we find it noteworthy that **our adversarial logos are able to deceive them**: in the right bin, 66% rated the 'original-adversarial' pairs with either 4 or 5, and only 10% rated them with a 1 or 2.

Figure 7b shows the results for the 'adversarial-original' pairs (we already removed some clearly noisy answers, as stated in Sect. 6.1). We observe that the wide majority of HS population rated the pairs as similar (the average is always below the middle point, 3). Hence, we can conclude: HS also reveals that **our adversarial logos are barely detected by humans as perturbed**.

7   Countermeasures (and Counter-Countermeasures)

Given that our adversarial logos can simultaneously fool state-of-the-art DL models for logo-identification and human eyes, we ask ourselves: *how can adversarial logos be countered?* One potential mitigation is to leverage *adversarial learning* by injecting evasive logos in the training set [12], thereby realizing an *adversarially robust* discriminator. However, an expert attacker may anticipate this and can hence attempt to circumvent such a robust discriminator by developing a new generator, thereby crafting more evasive adversarial logos (e.g., as demonstrated in other domains [45,49]). We now investigate both of these scenarios through additional proof-of-concept experiments, which involve the strongest discriminator of our evaluation: ViT.

Countermeasure: Building Robust Discriminator. Adversarial training is one of the most well-known techniques to defend against adversarial examples [12,46]. The idea is to update a given ML model by training it on adversarial examples that can mislead its predictions. We build our robust discriminators, $\mathcal{D}'^{0.3}_{\text{ViT}}$, $\mathcal{D}'^{0.5}_{\text{ViT}}$, and $\mathcal{D}'^{0.7}_{\text{ViT}}$, by replacing 30%, 50%, and 70% of the logos in the training dataset $\mathbf{L}$ with their adversarial variants, respectively. In particular, we use the adversarial logos generated with $\mathcal{G}_{\text{ViT}}$, i.e., trained with the vanilla ViT discriminator. Then, we compare these three robust discriminators with the vanilla ViT discriminator $\mathcal{D}_{\text{ViT}}$, against the same attack presented in Sect. 5.4. The results are shown in Fig. 8a. We observe that the robust discriminators exhibit much lower fooling ratios: while the vanilla ViT has a fooling ratio above 0.8, the robust discriminators have fooling ratios below 0.2 even at a low FPR of 10^{-3}.

Counter-Countermeasure: Evading Robust Discriminators. An attacker is also capable of taking a sophisticated strategy to counter a robust logo-identification discriminator built via adversarial training. To do this, the attacker must obtain such a robust discriminator—this can be done through well-known black-box strategies [15,41], or the attacker could even build one on their own. The attacker must then use the robust discriminator to train an 'adaptive' generator that can yield more evasive perturbations. For this experiment, we consider the case wherein the attacker trains the adaptive generator by using $\mathcal{D}'^{0.3}_{\text{ViT}}$, $\mathcal{D}'^{0.5}_{\text{ViT}}$, and $\mathcal{D}'^{0.7}_{\text{ViT}}$, thereby realizing $\mathcal{G}'^{0.3}_{\text{ViT}}$, $\mathcal{G}'^{0.5}_{\text{ViT}}$, and $\mathcal{G}'^{0.7}_{\text{ViT}}$, respectively. The results are shown in Fig. 8b, which plots the fooling ratio of the *adaptive* generator against the corresponding *robust* discriminator.

Compared to the attacks from the 'vanilla' generator $\mathcal{G}_{ViT}$ in Fig. 8a (which achieves below 20% of fooling ratio at 10^{-3} FPR), the adaptive generators in Fig. 8b are much more effective. Yet, we observe that discriminators trained with more adversarial logos tend to be more robust: at 10^{-3} FPR, $\mathcal{D}'^{0.3}_{\text{ViT}}$ has a fooling ratio of 0.9, whereas $\mathcal{D}'^{0.5}_{\text{ViT}}$ and $\mathcal{D}'^{0.7}_{\text{ViT}}$ have 0.8 and 0.6, respectively.

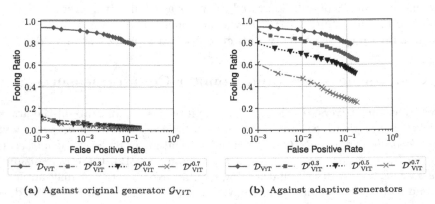

(a) Against original generator $\mathcal{G}_{\text{ViT}}$ (b) Against adaptive generators

Fig. 8. Performance of discriminator and generator due to adversarial training

We find it enticing that this continuous game between attacker and defender, reflected in the generator (attacker) and discriminator (defender), eventually forms the concept of the Generative Adversarial Network (GAN). Indeed, a question rises: "what happens if this process is repeated many times?" We plan to address this intriguing research question in our future work.

8   Related Works

Phishing Website Detection via ML. Many works leveraged statistical models, including ML, for phishing website detection (e.g., [8,37,51,56,57]). Typically, these models are trained on labeled datasets to learn to discriminate between phishing and benign webpages. There also exists an orthogonal family of countermeasures, referred to as reference-based phishing detectors, that identify visually similar webpages. This is based on the notion that phishing webpages are more successful when they imitate a legitimate website. This characteristic has been extensively scrutinized by prior literature [7,9,19,24,28,34,35,54]. For example, VisualPhishNet trains a Siamese model to detect visually similar *screenshots* between a given webpage and those in a set of well-known brands [7]. Other works (e.g., [9,19,34,35,54]) focus on identifying visually invariant *logos*.

Attacks Against ML-Based Phishing Website Detectors. Expert attackers are aware of the development of anti-phishing solutions and constantly refine their techniques to avoid being taken down. For instance, phishers can use cloaking to evade automated crawlers often used by security vendors [59]; alternatively, they can exploit 'squatting' to evade detectors analyzing the URL [51]. It is also easy to change the HTML contents to evade HTML-based phishing detectors [13,32]. Researchers have also examined the impact of adversarial perturbations on image-based phishing detectors [7,20,34,35]. However, these attacks assume that the attacker possesses complete knowledge of the deployed model and can access the model gradients, enabling manipulations in the feature-space (for further details, refer to [13]). We demonstrate a successful attack conducted by an attacker lacking both knowledge of and access to the deployed model. Furthermore, none of the prior works have conducted user studies to validate the practicality of their attacks.

Adversarial Perturbations. Moving away from gradient-based perturbations, Moosavi et al. introduced Universal Adversarial Perturbations [38], a framework for learning perturbations that are image-agnostic and generalized across various image classification models. This work sparked further proposals [40,47,58] aiming to enhance universal perturbations. Subsequently, Poursaeed et al. proposed Generative Adversarial Perturbations [43]. The generative model achieved state-of-the-art performance, unifying the framework for image-agnostic and image-dependent perturbations and considering both targeted and non-targeted attacks. We draw inspiration from their framework to develop a generative network specifically for crafting adversarial logos.

Summary. While prior works have investigated gradient-based attacks [34,35] against image classifiers, to the best of our knowledge, we are the first to show the feasibility of attacks using a generative neural network model trained to craft adversarial logos, and comprehensively evaluate the impact of such attacks on state-of-the-art methods for logo-identification.

9   Conclusions

Logo-based phishing detectors have shown significant capabilities with the employment of DL models. In this work, we developed and presented a novel attack against logo-based phishing detection systems. Our experiments demonstrate the capability of an attacker equipped with a generative adversarial model in defeating the detection systems as well as human users. We hope this will trigger further research and development of phishing detection solutions that are robust to adversarial ML attacks.

Acknowledgment. We thank the Hilti Corporation, Trustwave, NUS (National University of Singapore) and Acronis, for supporting this research.

Ethical Statement. Our institutions do not require any formal IRB approval to carry out the research discussed herein. We always followed the guidelines of the Menlo report [14]. For our user-studies, we never asked for sensitive data or PII. Finally, although we publicly release our code for the sake of science, as mentioned on the GitHub page [1], such code should not be used for any unethical or illegal purposes.

Appendix

A   Step-ReLu activation Function

The step-ReLU function utilised in training the robust `Siamese` model $\mathcal{D}_{\text{Siamese}++}$ (Sect. 3.3) is expressed as:

$$f(x) = \max(0, \alpha \cdot \lceil \frac{x}{\alpha} \rceil) \tag{4}$$

B   Discriminator and generator configurations

Table 2. Hyperparameter configurations for discriminators

Parameters	$\mathcal{D}_{\text{ViT}}$	$\mathcal{D}_{\text{Swin}}$	$\mathcal{D}_{\text{Siamese}}$
Backbone	ViT	Swin	ResNetV2
Pre-trained Model	ViT-b/16	Swin-S	BiT-M-R50x1
No. of params	85.9M	49.0M	23.9M
Batch size	32	32	32
Optimizer	SGD	SGD	SGD
Momentum	0.9	0.9	0.9
Weight decay	0.0005	0.0005	–
Epochs (Steps)	200	200	10000 (Steps)
Learning rate	0.01	0.01	0.003 (Staircase decay)
λ (value clipping)	2.5	2.5	–

Table 3. Hyperparameter configurations for generators

Parameters	$\mathcal{G}_{\text{ViT}}$	$\mathcal{G}_{\text{Swin}}$	$\mathcal{G}_{\text{Siamese}}$
Batch size	32	16	32
Optimizer	Adam	Adam	Adam
β_1 & β_2 for Adam	0.5 & 0.999	0.5 & 0.999	0.5 & 0.999
Magnitude of perturbations	10	10	10
Epochs	200	200	100
Learning rate	0.0002	0.0002	0.0002
Target probability, $p_{\text{adversarial}}$	0.5	0.5	0.5

References

1. Adversarial logos against phishing detection systems: Code repository. https://github.com/JehLeeKR/Adversarial-phishing-logos
2. APWG: Phishing activity trends report, 4th quarter 2022. https://docs.apwg.org//reports/apwg_trends_report_q4_2022.pdf
3. Browser In The Browser (BITB) Attack. https://mrd0x.com/browser-in-the-browser-phishing-attack/ (2022)
4. COFENSE: Phishing URLs 4x more likely than attachments to reach users. https://cofense.com/blog/urls-4x-more-likely-than-phishing-attachments-to-reach-users/ (2023)
5. Google Safe Browsing. https://developers.google.com/safe-browsing/ (2023)

6. Phishing attacks jump 61% in 2022. https://venturebeat.com/security/report-phishing-attacks-jump-61-in-2022-with-255m-attacks-detected/ (2023)
7. Abdelnabi, S., Krombholz, K., Fritz, M.: VisualphishNet: zero-day phishing website detection by visual similarity. In: Proceedings ACM CCS, pp. 1681–1698 (2020)
8. Abu-Nimeh, S., Nappa, D., Wang, X., Nair, S.: A comparison of machine learning techniques for phishing detection. In: Proceedings of the Anti-Phishing Working Groups, 2nd Annual eCrime Researchers Summit. eCrime '07 (2007)
9. Afroz, S., Greenstadt, R.: Phishzoo: detecting phishing websites by looking at them. In: IEEE International Conference on Semantic Computing (2011)
10. Alsharnouby, M., Alaca, F., Chiasson, S.: Why phishing still works: user strategies for combating phishing attacks. Int. J. Hum Comput Stud. **82**, 69–82 (2015)
11. Apruzzese, G., Anderson, H., Dambra, S., Freeman, D., Pierazzi, F., Roundy, K.: Position:"Real Attackers Don't Compute Gradients": Bridging the Gap Between Adversarial ML Research and Practice. In: IEEE Conference on Secure and Trustworthy Machine Learning (2023)
12. Apruzzese, G., Andreolini, M., Marchetti, M., Venturi, A., Colajanni, M.: Deep reinforcement adversarial learning against botnet evasion attacks. IEEE Trans. Netw. Serv. Manage. **17**, 1975–1987 (2020)
13. Apruzzese, G., Conti, M., Yuan, Y.: SpacePhish: the evasion-space of adversarial attacks against phishing website detectors using machine learning. In: Proceedings ACSAC (2022)
14. Bailey, M., Dittrich, D., Kenneally, E., Maughan, D.: The Menlo Report. IEEE S&P (2012)
15. Bhagoji, A.N., He, W., Li, B., Song, D.: Practical black-box attacks on deep neural networks using efficient query mechanisms. In: Ferrari, V., Hebert, M., Sminchisescu, C., Weiss, Y. (eds.) ECCV 2018. LNCS, vol. 11216, pp. 158–174. Springer, Cham (2018). https://doi.org/10.1007/978-3-030-01258-8_10
16. Bhurtel, M., Siwakoti, Y.R., Rawat, D.B.: Phishing attack detection with ML-based siamese empowered ORB logo recognition and IP mapper. In: Proceedings IEEE Conference on Computer Communications Workshops (INFOCOM WKSHPS) (2022)
17. Biggio, B., Roli, F.: Wild patterns: ten years after the rise of adversarial machine learning. Pattern Recogn. **84**, 317–331 (2018)
18. Bitaab, M., et al.: Scam pandemic: how attackers exploit public fear through phishing. In: Proceedings APWG Symposium on Electronic Crime Research (eCrime), pp. 1–10. IEEE (2020)
19. Bozkir, A.S., Aydos, M.: LogoSENSE: a companion HOG based logo detection scheme for phishing web page and e-mail brand recognition. Comput. Secur. **95**, 101855 (2020)
20. Corona, I., et al.: DeltaPhish: detecting phishing webpages in compromised websites. In: Proceedings ESORICS (2017)
21. Demontis, A., et al.: Why do adversarial attacks transfer? Explaining transferability of evasion and poisoning attacks. In: USENIX Security Symposium (2019)
22. Divakaran, D.M., Oest, A.: Phishing detection leveraging machine learning and deep learning: a review. IEEE Secur. Priv. **20**(5), 86–95 (2022)
23. Dosovitskiy, A., et al.: An image is worth 16 × 16 words: transformers for image recognition at scale. arXiv preprint arXiv:2010.11929 (2020)
24. Fu, A.Y., Wenyin, L., Deng, X.: Detecting phishing web pages with visual similarity assessment based on earth mover's distance (EMD). IEEE Trans. Dependable Secure Comput. **3**(4), 301–311 (2006)

25. Garera, S., Provos, N., Chew, M., Rubin, A.D.: A framework for detection and measurement of phishing attacks. In: Proceedings ACM Workshop on Recurring Malcode (2007)
26. Goodfellow, I.J., Shlens, J., Szegedy, C.: Explaining and harnessing adversarial examples. In: International Conference on Learning Representations (Poster) (2015)
27. He, K., Zhang, X., Ren, S., Sun, J.: Deep residual learning for image recognition. In: Proceedings IEEE CVPR, pp. 770–778 (2016)
28. Hout, T.v.d., Wabeke, T., Moura, G.C.M., Hesselman, C.: LogoMotive: detecting logos on websites to identify online scams - a TLD case study. In: Proceedings of PAM (2022)
29. Kondracki, B., Azad, B.A., Starov, O., Nikiforakis, N.: Catching transparent phish: analyzing and detecting MITM phishing toolkits. In: Proceedings of ACM CCS (2021)
30. Le, H., Pham, Q., Sahoo, D., Hoi, S.C.: URLNet: learning a URL representation with deep learning for malicious URL detection. arXiv preprint arXiv:1802.03162 (2018)
31. Lee, J., Tang, F., Ye, P., Abbasi, F., Hay, P., Divakaran, D.M.: D-Fence: a flexible, efficient, and comprehensive phishing email detection system. In: Proceedings IEEE EuroS&P (2021)
32. Lee, J., Ye, P., Liu, R., Divakaran, D.M., Choon, C.M.: Building robust phishing detection system: an empirical analysis. In: Proceedings NDSS MADWeb (2020)
33. Liang, B., Su, M., You, W., Shi, W., Yang, G.: Cracking classifiers for evasion: a case study on the Google's phishing pages filter. In: Proceedings WWW (2016)
34. Lin, Y., et al.: Phishpedia: a hybrid deep learning based approach to visually identify phishing webpages. In: Proceedings USENIX Security Symposium (2021)
35. Liu, R., Lin, Y., Yang, X., Ng, S.H., Divakaran, D.M., Dong, J.S.: Inferring phishing intention via webpage appearance and dynamics: a deep vision based approach. In: Proceedings USENIX Security Symposium (2022)
36. Liu, Z., et al.: Swin transformer: hierarchical vision transformer using shifted windows. In: Proceedings the IEEE/CVF International Conference on Computer Vision, pp. 10012–10022 (2021)
37. Ma, J., Saul, L.K., Savage, S., Voelker, G.M.: Identifying suspicious URLs: an application of large-scale online learning. In: Proceedings ICML (2009)
38. Moosavi-Dezfooli, S.M., Fawzi, A., Fawzi, O., Frossard, P.: Universal adversarial perturbations. In: Proceedings IEEE CVPR, pp. 1765–1773 (2017)
39. Moosavi-Dezfooli, S.M., Fawzi, A., Frossard, P.: DeepFool: a simple and accurate method to fool deep neural networks. In: Proceedings IEEE CVPR, pp. 2574–2582 (2016)
40. Mopuri, K.R., Ganeshan, A., Babu, R.V.: Generalizable data-free objective for crafting universal adversarial perturbations. IEEE Trans. Pattern Anal. Mach. Intell. **41**(10), 2452–2465 (2018)
41. Papernot, N., McDaniel, P., Goodfellow, I., Jha, S., Celik, Z.B., Swami, A.: Practical black-box attacks against machine learning. In: Proceedings ACM ASIACCS (2017)
42. Pawar, R.: Logo images dataset. https://github.com/revanks/logo-images-dataset (2021), gitHub repository
43. Poursaeed, O., Katsman, I., Gao, B., Belongie, S.: Generative adversarial perturbations. In: Proceedings IEEE CVPR, pp. 4422–4431 (2018)
44. Quiring, E., et al.: Do's and don'ts of machine learning in computer security. In: Proceedings USENIX Security Symposium (2022)

45. Rahman, M.S., Imani, M., Mathews, N., Wright, M.: Mockingbird: defending against deep-learning-based website fingerprinting attacks with adversarial traces. IEEE Trans. Inf. Forensics Secur. **16**, 1594–1609 (2020)
46. Shafahi, A., et al.: Adversarial training for free! In: Advances in Neural Information Processing Systems (2019)
47. Shafahi, A., Najibi, M., Xu, Z., Dickerson, J., Davis, L.S., Goldstein, T.: Universal adversarial training. In: Proceedings of the AAAI Conference on Artificial Intelligence, vol. 34, pp. 5636–5643 (2020)
48. Sharma, K., Zhan, X., Nah, F.F.H., Siau, K., Cheng, M.X.: Impact of digital nudging on information security behavior: an experimental study on framing and priming in cybersecurity. Organ. Cybersecur. J. Pract. Process People **1**(1), 69–91 (2021)
49. Shenoi, A., Vairam, P.K., Sabharwal, K., Li, J., Divakaran, D.M.: iPET: privacy enhancing traffic perturbations for secure IoT communications. Proce. Priv. Enhan. Technol. **2**, 206–220 (2023)
50. Szegedy, C., et al.: Intriguing Properties of Neural Networks. CoRR (2014)
51. Tian, K., Jan, S.T., Hu, H., Yao, D., Wang, G.: Needle in a haystack: tracking down elite phishing domains in the wild. In: Internet Measurement Conference (2018)
52. Vaswani, A., et al.: Attention is all you need. In: Advances in Neural Information Processing Systems 30 (2017)
53. Verma, R., Dyer, K.: On the character of phishing URLs: accurate and robust statistical learning classifiers. In: Proceedings ACM Conference Data Application Security Privacy (2015)
54. Wang, G., et al.: Verilogo: Proactive phishing detection via logo recognition, Department of Computer Science and Engineering. University of California, San Diego (2011)
55. Wang, J., et al.: Logo-2K+: a large-scale logo dataset for scalable logo classification. In: Proceedings AAAI, pp. 6194–6201 (2020)
56. Whittaker, C., Ryner, B., Nazif, M.: Large-scale automatic classification of phishing pages. In: Proceedings NDSS (2010)
57. Xiang, G., Hong, J., Rose, C.P., Cranor, L.: CANTINA+: a feature-rich machine learning framework for detecting phishing web sites. ACM Trans. Inform. Syst. Secur. **14**(2), 1–28 (2011)
58. Zhang, C., Benz, P., Imtiaz, T., Kweon, I.S.: CD-UAP: class discriminative universal adversarial perturbation. In: Proceedings AAAI Conference on Artificial Intelligence, vol. 34, pp. 6754–6761 (2020)
59. Zhang, P., et al.: CrawlPhish: large-scale analysis of client-side cloaking techniques in phishing. In: Proceedings IEEE S&P (2021)

Hiding Your Signals: A Security Analysis of PPG-Based Biometric Authentication

Lin Li[1]($\boxtimes$), Chao Chen[2], Lei Pan[3], Yonghang Tai[4], Jun Zhang[1], and Yang Xiang[1]

[1] Swinburne University of Technology, Melbourne, Australia
linli@swin.edu.au
[2] RMIT University, Melbourne, Australia
[3] Deakin University, Melbourne, Australia
[4] Yunnan Normal University, Kunming, China

Abstract. Recently, physiological signal-based biometric systems have received wide attention. Photoplethysmogram (PPG) signal is easy to measure, making it more attractive than many other physiological signals for biometric authentication. However, with the advent of remote PPG, unobservability has been challenged when the attacker can remotely steal the PPG signals by monitoring the victim's face, subsequently posing a threat to PPG-based biometrics. In this paper, we firstly analyze the security of PPG-based biometrics, including user authentication and communication protocols. We evaluate the signal waveforms and inter-pulse-interval information extracted by five rPPG methods. Our empirical studies on five datasets show that rPPG poses a serious threat to the authentication system. The success rate of the rPPG signal spoofing attack in the user authentication system reached 35%. The bit hit rate is 60% in inter-pulse-interval-based security protocols. Further, we propose an active defence strategy to hide the physiological signals of the face to resist the attack. It reduces the success rate of rPPG spoofing attacks in user authentication to 5%. The bit hit rate was reduced to 50%, which is at the level of a random guess. Our strategy effectively prevents the exposure of PPG signals to protect users' sensitive physiological data.

Keywords: Biometrics · Spoofing Attack · Signal Hiding · PPG · User Authentication · Key Exchange Protocol

1 Introduction

Over the past decade, biometric systems have provided high authentication accuracy and user convenience, driving widespread deployment. However, with the popularity of biometrics, researchers have found that traditional biometric authentication is vulnerable to spoofing attacks. Traditional biometric features like face and fingerprint recognition can be directly observed with the human eye, and an attacker can compromise the authentication system without strong technical knowledge. Researchers are turning to a potentially reliable and unobservable biological feature, the physiological signal.

© The Author(s), under exclusive license to Springer Nature Switzerland AG 2024
G. Tsudik et al. (Eds.): ESORICS 2023, LNCS 14346, pp. 183–202, 2024.
https://doi.org/10.1007/978-3-031-51479-1_10

Common physiological signals, including Electrocardiogram, Electroencephalogram, and Photoplethysmogram (PPG) are widely used as biometric features [18,20,36,42]. A light source and a light sensor is sufficient to obtain PPG signals without other complicated devices required by other physiological signals, making them more widely used in life. For example, popular wearable devices use PPG sensors for health monitoring—Apple and Samsung. Therefore, PPG signals are considered to be more practical and attractive than other physiological signals in real-world applications [20].

Currently, known threats against PPG-based biometric authentication require the collection of the victim's PPG signal. This attack requires close contact with the victim, which significantly limits the possibility of an attack. Some attacks targeting specific protocol vulnerabilities typically cannot be directly applied to other protocols without modification [30]. However, the emergence of remote PPG (rPPG) signals has challenged the unobservable property of PPG signals, which means that PPG-based biometric authentication will lose the advantage of unobservability. rPPG attempts to capture PPG-like signals by monitoring subtle changes in the color of a person's facial skin in the video. The rPPG signal has been successfully applied to infer biometric signals, such as monitoring heart rate [10,17] and predicting blood pressure.

Although some studies explore using rPPG signals to attack inter-pulse interval (IPI)-based security protocols [6,21,37], they do not discuss viable defence strategies. In addition, there is still a research gap between rPPG signals and PPG-based biometric authentication. In an existing rPPG method, its validity is assessed mainly by heart rate, but signal morphological characteristics are often neglected. In PPG-based biometric authentication, the morphological characteristics of the signal are the main contributors to the uniqueness of the user. In addition, the rPPG signal is extracted from the human face, and the PPG signal is from the fingertips or wrist. Different skin tissues and distances from the heart can lead to differences in shape and phase between PPG signals. Thus, it is crucial to explore the potential of rPPG-based attacks to evaluate the security of PPG-based biometrics, which is one of the aims of this work.

In this paper, we analyze the security of PPG-based biometric authentication, particularly in user authentication and communication protocols. Current methods only require access to video clips of the victim's face to achieve a remote attack, increasing the likelihood of the attack in reality. We first analyze rPPG-based spoofing attacks and some common defence strategies to reduce the threat. We further propose an effective defence strategy and evaluate the defence performance. The main contributions of this paper are as follows:

1. We analyze the potential threats of rPPG to PPG-based biometrics using five methods (CHROM [11], POS [43], LGI [34], PCA [26], CL_rPPG [13]) on five datasets (PURE [38], UBFC_rPPG [4], UBFC_Phys [32], LGI_PPGI [34], COHFACE [15]). The success rate of the spoofing attack on user authentication reached 35%. The bit hit rate in the IPI-based security protocols reached 60%.

2. We analyze a series of defence strategies to mitigate the threat of rPPG-based spoofing attacks on biometrics. Existing passive defence strategies of spoofing attacks can significantly degrade the performance of the user authentication model.

3. We propose a signal hiding method (SigHid) by injecting an arbitrary waveform into the face of the video. Our active defence strategy reduces the success rate of spoofing attacks on user authentication to 5%. And it will not affect the performance of the authentication model. The bit hit rate in the IPI-based security protocols was reduced to 50%.

The rest of the paper is organized as follows: Sect. 2 reviews related work, including PPG-based biometric authentication methods, existing attacks, and rPPG methods. Section 3 and 5 describe the attack and defence strategies we used. In Sect. 4 and 6, experimental results are provided along with a discussion on the performance of the attack and defence strategy, respectively. Finally, Sect. 7 concludes this work.

2   Related Work

2.1   PPG-Based Biometrics

In the context of biometrics, PPG signals are mainly used in user authentication and communication protocols.

User Authentication: The PPG signal contains a wealth of personal cardiac data. The earliest studies used clinical features commonly existed in PPG signals as biometric features [14,23]. For example, as shown in Fig. 1, the ratio of b to a is related to arterial stiffness [39]. $A1$ and $A2$ areas are related to systemic vascular resistance [1]. However, some characteristics of these features are sensitive to changes over time. For example, ΔT changes with an individual's age [33]. Thus, researchers have applied a few techniques to get stable features, such as transforming robust features by leveraging wavelet transform [45], short-time Fourier transform [12], and GAN [19].

After constituting an individual template using the extracted signal features, identifying the individual template is similar to other biometric authentication systems. The early generations of authentication systems match individuals by calculating the distance between features and templates [14]. Gradually, machine learning models replace simple distance calculations to improve template matching performance. However, many machine learning models require manual feature extraction so that the system designer and engineers may introduce bias. Recently, deep learning methods have provided an end-to-end authentication strategy, for example, CNN and LSTM are used to learn features from raw data automatically in the context of user recognition [3,20].

Communication Protocols: In body area sensor networks (BASN) with strict computational resource constraints, traditional encryption schemes for information transmission are difficult to apply because PPG signals can get similar measurements in different body parts. When used as an entity identifier

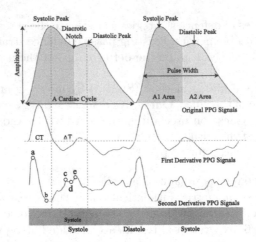

Fig. 1. Features of the PPG signal (including the original waveform, the first-/second-order derivatives of the waveform) that are related to heart health.

in a BASN symmetric encryption scheme, the distribution of pre key-agreement could be avoided [47]. IPI information extracted from the PPG signal is the most prevalent entity identifier. IPI indicates the time difference between two consecutive heartbeats, while PPG signal is usually regarded as the time difference between two pulse peaks. The timing of systolic peaks in the PPG signal is sympathetically related and influenced by various physiological factors. This characteristic allows the researcher to extract entity identifiers from the IPI information [9].

After obtaining the IPI, the randomness of the entity identifier needs to be extracted by quantization algorithms. A quantization algorithm encodes the signal into a binary representation. Two quantization methods exist. The first method was proposed in [29] to extract a random value from the intermediate bits of IPI. However, this method suffers from inbalanced randomness, that is, the high bits of IPI are not random enough, while the low bits have too much noise. The second method was proposed in [9] to use the trend of the IPI sequence as a random source of information. The second method improves the randomness attribute at the cost of excessive processing time.

2.2   Remote Photoplethysmogram (rPPG)

Most rPPG signals are obtained by analyzing subtle differences in the facial color channels from a video clip. The green channel is more readily absorbed by hemoglobin than the red and blue channels. In most circumstances, the green channel contains the strongest PPG signal, providing a high signal-to-noise ratio solution for signal acquisition [41]. Two blind source separation methods, Independent Component Analysis and Principal Component Analysis were proposed in [26,35] to isolate the approximately clean signals from the RGB channels.

Unlike contact PPG measurements, the signal reflected by the skin in rPPG measurements includes the specular reflection of natural light, leading to unpredictable normalization errors. CHROM [11] introduces chromatic aberration to eliminate specular reflection effects, assuming that the facial region's pixels contribute equally to the rPPG signal. Nevertheless, different noise levels may affect pixels collected from the face region.

A recent research trend is to apply deep learning in rPPG acquisition for an end-to-end solution framework. DeepPhys [7] uses an attention network with CNN to capture the differences in the spatial and temporal distribution of signals between video frames. PhysNct [46] uses a spatio-temporal convolutional network to restore the rPPG signal from the video clip. Meta-rPPG [25] presents a transduction meta-learner that allows the deep learning model to adapt the data distribution during deployment. A fully self-supervised training method was introduced in [13] to acquire the rPPG signals. In addition to existing progress, deep learning-based methods have good research potential for rPPG signal acquisition. In summary, the research trend for rPPG signal acquisition is toward automated end-to-end solutions with high accuracy and resilience to noise.

2.3 Existing Attacks

The first attack against IPI-based authentication using rPPG was proposed by Calleja et al. [6] in 2015. IPI signals help derive secure random sequences in the key distribution component of IPI-based authentication systems whose security conditions rely on the assumption that IPI can be measured by contact devices only. In fact, most of the IPI information acquired by PPG signals could also be obtained by non-contact techniques (rPPG). By analyzing the face's color change information in the video clip, the rPPG signal can be extracted like PPG. The extracted rPPG signal can be used to generate IPI, violating the assumptions in IPI-based authentication protocols [37]. Although rPPG does not accurately describe IPI generated from ECG signals, it has similar accuracy to contact PPG. Currently, PPG-based biometric authentication is mainly based on the morphological characteristics of the PPG signal rather than the IPI information.

In previous attacks on PPG-based biometric authentication, researchers almost always assume that the victim's PPG signal has been compromised. Karimian et al. [21] utilized a non-linear dynamic model [31] to extract model parameters from the victim's PPG signal before transforming the model parameters using two Gaussian functions as mapping functions. Thereafter, a spoofing attack was launched using the forged victim's PPG signal. Another study involved stealing a victim's PPG signal stealthily by installing a malicious PPG sensor on a device that the victim would touch [16]. Based on the recorded signals, the attacker can use a waveform generator to simulate the victim's PPG signal and compromise the authentication. However, contact-based PPG signals are challenging to obtain without the victim's awareness, significantly limiting these attacks' application scenarios. Our previous work successfully attacked PPG-based PPG signals via facial recovery [28].

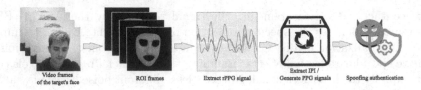

Fig. 2. Our proposed spoofing attack flow. We identify the ROI region from the target video frame before extracting the rPPG signal from the ROI. The rPPG signal is used to launch a spoofing attack on the authentication system.

3   Spoofing Attacks

In this work, we aim to conduct a comprehensive security analysis of PPG-based biometrics. First, Fig. 2 depicts our scheme that performs spoofing attacks on biometrics. We extracted the rPPG signal from the face video clip, then extracted the IPI and reconstructed the PPG signal from the rPPG signal. We consider various rPPG methods (CHROM, POS, LGI, PCA, CL_rPPG) to spoof biometric authentication and extract IPI information from the rPPG signal to spoof IPI-based security protocols.

3.1   Threat Model

PPG-based biometrics, including user authentication [49] and IPI-based security protocols [47], are vulnerable to spoofing attacks. This paper assumes that the attacker could obtain a video clip with the victim's face. In this age of social networking, it is easy to retrieve many videos with human faces on social media sites. For instance, YouTube and Facebook (Meta) host numerous HD video clips that are downloadable to the attacker. In contrast to the previous attack assumptions, our method requires no leaked PPG signals. In addition, we assume that the attacker knows the inputs to the user authentication model. For instance, a PPG signal with one heartbeat cycle is taken as input. The length of the signal is resampled to 60. The amplitude of the signal is normalized to 0–1.

3.2   rPPG Acquisition

Before acquiring the rPPG signal, we use MTCNN [48] to detect the face region in each video frame before isolation. Then the non-skin part of the face region is filtered by the skin detection algorithm proposed in [24]. For example, clothes, hair, and other parts that do not provide PPG signal information will be filtered. Each frame $F(n)$ is stored as a matrix of $w \times h \times 3$, where w and h represent the frame's width and height, and 3 is the number of color channels. The average value of RGB of the whole skin area is used as the R, G, B values of the current frame. A bandpass filter is applied to obtain the portion of the frame sequence with signal frequencies between 0.65 Hz and 4.0 Hz (i.e., between 39 and 240 bpm). The method in [40] was used to remove the breadth component of the signal. This preprocessing removes the signal's noise and breathing components (signal trend).

Upon removing noises, we extract the rPPG signal from the consecutive skin frames. As listed in Sect. 2.2, there are multiple methods for obtaining rPPG signals, including CHROM, POS, LGI, PCA, CL_rPPG. **CHROM** is based on the skin optical reflection model. The model assumes that the light reflected by the skin consists of diffuse and specular reflections, and the PPG signal is hidden in the diffuse reflection. CHROM eliminates the specular reflection component by using chrominance. CHROM uses simple mathematical operations to obtain the PPG signal quickly. Moreover, CHROM is resilient to motion artifacts. **POS** is similar to CHROM, which is also based on the skin reflection model assumption to obtain low signal-to-noise ratio PPG signals by removing specular reflections [43]. **LGI** introduces the Local Group Invariance features for estimating heart rate from face videos in complex environments. **PCA** (Principal component analysis) reduces features' dimensionality. PCA uses an orthogonal transformation to project the observed values of potentially correlated variables into a set of linearly uncorrelated variables. It separates the periodic pulse signals from the noisy signals. **CL_rPPG** is a deep learning-based rPPG signal extraction method. Traditional methods may lose vital information related to the heartbeat through manually designed features. The deep learning-based approach recovers the rPPG signal directly from the original face video. CL_rPPG has two versions: supervised learning (CL_P) and self-supervised learning (CL_F). For the supervised learning mode, the CL_P model is trained using the maximum cross-correlation between the ground truth PPG signal and the estimated PPG signal as the loss function. In the self-supervised learning model CL_F, negative samples with high heart rates are artificially generated by a frequency resampler for contrast training. The power spectral density means the squared error is used to measure the difference between two signals.

3.3 IPI Recovery and Quantification

To spoof IPI-based security protocols, we need to recover the IPI information from the signal. We mark the peak locations of the original signal before calculating the time difference between the peaks as IPI. As the standard heart rate in adults is 50–120 beats per minute [19], there are at most two heartbeats per second. To minimize sample loss, we exclude data where the distance between heartbeats is less than FPS/2.

For IPI sequences to be used in key exchange protocols, we need to quantize the IPI sequences. There are two mainstream quantification methods, trend-based and quantile function-based [47]. We use the Gray code as the quantization function for the quantile-based function. Firstly, we normalize the IPI time series to 0–1. Then, we multiply it by 256 and convert the result to an 8-bit Gray code.

For trend-based quantification, we divide each IPI value into 16 parts of an equal length following a normal distribution. Our setting is identical to IMD-Guard [44]. Subsequently, we encode the IPI sequence according to the trend of IPI values.

4   Attack Evaluation

In this section, we evaluate the effectiveness of spoofing attacks using rPPG signals. We select five common public datasets for our experiments. Experiments on spoofing user authentication were performed in UBFC-PHYS. We trained a state-of-the-art model as our user authentication target model (see Sect. 4.2). The threat of rPPG signals to IPI-based security protocols is explored on four datasets—PURE, UBFC_rPPG, LGI_PPGI, and COHFACE. We use trend-based and quantile function-based as our target model (see Sect. 3.3) for IPI-based security protocols. Then we use the rPPG signal (see Sect. 3.2) to perform a spoofing attack.

4.1   Datasets

UBFC-PHYS captures facial videos (1024 × 1024 resolution, 35 FPS, 227,474 Kbps) of 56 participants. Each participant recorded a one-minute video of the three states ('resting', 'talking', or 'calculating'). Meanwhile, the *Empatica E4* wristband was used to collect the PPG signal from the wrist synchronously with the sampling rate of 65 Hz. We perform repeated independent experiments for each user. Other users are treated as non-victims.

PURE captures 10 participants' facial videos. Each participant's videos were recorded in six states (Steady, Talking, Small/Medium Rotation, and Slow/Fast Translation). Each video clip is one-minute long with a resolution of 640 × 480 and a frame rate of 30 FPS. Meanwhile, the finger clip pulse oximeter acquired the PPG signal at a 65 Hz sampling rate.

UBFC_rPPG uses a webcam to record video (640 × 480 resolution, 30 FPS). Transmissive pulse oximetry (62 Hz) to obtain the PPG signal. It consists of two sub-datasets. In UBFC_1, participants were asked to remain stationary; in UBFC_2, participants played a mathematical game in front of a green screen.

LGI_PPGI records facial videos in four scenes (resting, head movement, fitness, and conversation in an urban background). The video clips were captured by a webcam (640 × 480 resolution, 25 FPS). The sampling rate of the pulse oximeter is 60 Hz.

COHFACE contains facial video clips (640 × 480 resolution, 20 FPS) of 40 subjects, including the simultaneous acquisition of PPG signals (256 Hz). Subjects were asked to sit still in front of the camera. The video was heavily compressed.

4.2   Experimental Implementation

We use Keras[1] to implement the most advanced PPG-based user authentication model [20]. We use the virtual heart rate pyVHR [5] to implement the different traditional rPPG methods (CHROM, POS, LGI, PCA). We choose to adopt the deep learning method in [13] for CL_rPPG.

---

[1] https://www.tensorflow.org/.

For the user authentication model, we mark the signals of the victims as class 1 and other users as 0. We aim to compare the threat of rPPG signals with other users' PPG signals for the user authentication system. We repeated the experiment separately with each user as a victim, and randomly select one-tenth of other users are used to train the user authentication model, which is realistic for authentication systems. It is possible to collect a large amount of data about the target user, but only a small amount of data from other users. The remaining data from other users were used as a random attack to evaluate the spoofing attack by rPPG signals. To explore the impact of signals collected in different states on spoofing attacks, we exclude the PPG signals in the 'talking' and 'calculating' states while training the user authentication model. The performance of the user authentication model is determined by the Equal Error Rate (EER). We regard the model for the false acceptance rate (FAR) of the rPPG signal as the success rate of spoofing. A higher success rate indicates that the authentication system is more vulnerable to spoofing attacks. Finally, we use the average results of all users.

For IPI-based security protocols, we evaluate them by using IPI. The primary metrics are mean absolute error (MAE) and root-mean-square deviation (RMSE). We also use Pearson's coefficient (PC) to compare the similarity between the PPG signal and the rPPG signal. Since IPI-based security protocols require multi-bit encoding from IPI, we use the bit hit rate (BHR) to show how many codes can be recovered by the rPPG signal. BHR is the percentage of recovered codes for all codes.

4.3   Attack in User Authentication

Among the different rPPG methods, we found that the signal waveform obtained by CHROM was the most similar to the contact PPG signal. Therefore in the user authentication we only show the results for CHROM. Table 1 shows the results of a random attack versus an attack using the victim's rPPG signal. The success rate of using the victim's rPPG signal is almost doubled compared to random attacks. The success rate of the Mean-treated signal is even higher, which is 34%. Although the success rate of rPPG signal is reduced in the Talking and Calculating states, the mean treatment can help mitigate this effect. It is a threat to the authentication model, since real-world authentication systems often allow users to make multiple attempts. By analyzing the results, we also found that individual differences were also evident in addition to the quality of the video, which significantly affected the attack's success rate. The highest success rate of rPPG signal can reach 98% for users. In contrast, some users' rPPGs cannot be used for spoofing attacks. We found a significant difference in the morphology of some users' rPPG and PPG signals, potentially caused by a variation in the user's facial expression.

Table 1. The success rate of spoofing attacks in UBFC-Phys. Mean indicates the average of the PPG signals over multiple cardiac cycles.

Status	Resting	Talking	Calculating
Random Attack	0.14	0.15	0.15
Victim rPPG Signal Attack	0.25	0.19	0.21
Mean rPPG Signal Attack	**0.34**	**0.35**	**0.35**

Table 2. Comparison of the video extracted IPIs with the PPG signal extracted IPIs in different datasets. PC: Pearson correlation coefficient. P: PURE. L: LGI_PPGI. U1: UBFC_1. U2: UBFC_2. C: COHFACE.

	CHROM	POS	LGI	PCA	CL_P	CL_F
MAE (P)	0.1153	0.0762	0.0721	0.0729	**0.0322**	0.0592
RMSE (P)	0.1564	0.1114	0.1045	0.1051	**0.0517**	0.0796
PC (P)	0.7764	0.7985	0.8275	0.8296	**0.9926**	0.9925
MAE (L)	0.1572	0.1019	**0.1001**	0.1162	–	–
RMSE (L)	0.2008	0.1452	**0.1419**	0.1598	–	–
PC (L)	**0.3597**	0.3132	0.3230	0.3212	–	–
MAE (U1)	0.0771	**0.0385**	0.0481	0.0816	–	–
RMSE (U1)	0.1207	**0.0694**	0.0906	0.1319	–	–
PC (U1)	0.6451	**0.7380**	0.6829	0.6099	–	–
MAE (U2)	0.1319	0.0776	0.0867	0.1131	**0.0457**	0.0753
RMSE (U2)	0.1849	0.1332	0.1508	0.1804	**0.1064**	0.1484
PC (U2)	0.7554	0.8474	0.6730	0.6018	**0.9248**	0.8787
MAE (C)	**0.1319**	0.2271	0.2166	0.2265	0.2167	0.2282
RMSE (C)	**0.1849**	0.2954	0.2836	0.2957	0.4252	0.3980
PC (C)	0.0110	0.0600	0.0340	0.0060	0.9850	**0.9880**

4.4   Attack in IPI-Based Security Protocols

We report MAE and RMSE for the video extracted IPIs with the PPG signal extracted IPI in Table 2. Since the data sets UBFC_1 and LGI_PPGI were not evaluated in the source code of CL_rPPG, we omit the results for these two datasets in the table. The MAE of the recovered IPI in the high-quality original video is below 0.1. CL_P reaches a minimum MAE of 0.03. It recovered an IPI that the Pearson correlation coefficient (PC) is as high as 0.99 with the IPI of PPG. Hence, the IPIs extracted by CL_P and PPG signals are very similar.

For quantile-based IPI coding, the randomness of the bit usually increases as the location of bits decreases. Because the performance of the original video extraction from COHFACE was poor in the previous experiments, we chose not to conduct the experiments on COHFACE. As shown in Fig. 3, the BHR of the encoding extracted from the original video varies with the position of bits. As the bit position decreases, so does BHR. In the LGI_PPGI and UBFC_1 datasets, BHR shows a decreasing trend from 70% to 50% with the decrease of bits. In UBFC_2, the CL_F high BHR reached above 80%, especially the overall BHR of CL_P is higher than 65%.

We observed that with the improvement of rPPG extraction methods, state-of-the-art methods have been able to recover the IPI from rPPG signals accurately. Both rPPG and PPG signals reflect individual cardiac information, making them contain a great deal of similar information. While this has facilitated the development of telemedicine, rPPG poses an actual threat to PPG-based biometrics.

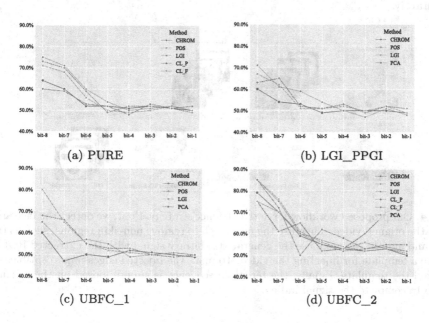

Fig. 3. The raw video quantile-based IPI coding bit hit rate in different datasets. Each figure shows the results of the different rPPG methods. The horizontal coordinate indicates the bit hit rate.

5   Defensive Strategies

In this section, we investigate passive and active defence strategies against the threats discussed in the previous section. Passive defence detects between regular and malicious access after an attacker has launched an attack. Active defence is a strategy taken before an attacker launches an attack. We hide the rPPG signal from the face of the video clip, making it difficult for the attacker to use the video to recover the PPG signal.

5.1 Passive Defence

Passive defence is primarily used for the scenario of user authentication. The input for user authentication is usually the fingertip or wrist PPG signal waveform. rPPG signals are collected from the human face, where there are phase differences and morphological differences between rPPG and PPG signals. The phase and morphological differences are measured to identify spoofing attacks.

Incremental Updating: When we have an attack sample, we can react to the attack instantly by incrementally updating the model. In practice, the attack sample can be obtained by pre-capturing the rPPG signal from the user's face. However, we may not be able to simulate the attack sample in this way accurately.

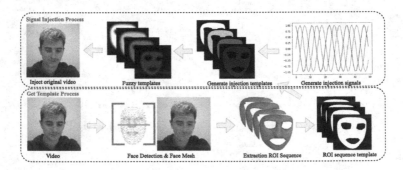

Fig. 4. Our proposed workflow for active defence strategy. First, we detect the face area from the original video. Then use the face mesh to remove non-skin regions, such as the eyes and mouth. Next, we use the generated arbitrary signal with the extracted ROI to create a template for injecting the video. To make the injected edges imperceptible, we blurred the template. Finally, the template sequence is superimposed on the original video to complete the signal hiding.

Anomaly Detection: It is also known as outlier analysis. It only needs to learn the user's samples before detecting malicious samples by excluding outliers. This paper uses Isolation Forest and One-Class SVM as anomaly detectors.

Passive defence usually follows the successful attack. Both incremental updates and anomaly detection can potentially affect the performance of the original user authentication model.

5.2 Active Defence

To solve the limitation of passive defence, we propose an active defence strategy, namely SigHid. As shown in Fig. 4, we hide the exposed rPPG signal by injecting the noise signal into the original video. It allows us to start our defence before being attacked, minimizing the impact on the original model. In contrast to [8], we hide the original signal by injecting a specific signal instead of eliminating it. Our active defence strategy consists of the following components:

Extraction of ROI Area: First we use BlazeFace [2] to detect the face area. It can detect faces quickly (200 to 1000 FPS) on a mobile GPU. Then, we apply the method in [22] to get the face landmarks. After that, we will get 468 3D face landmarks. These landmarks mark the locations of feature points in the face, such as the tip of the nose and the top of the left/right cheekbones.

Create Injection Template: For each frame $C(t)$ in the video, we use the facial region as the ROI and exclude the eye and mouth regions. As shown in the formula below, in the template, the RGB value of the ROI area is set to 1 and the rest of the area is set to 0.

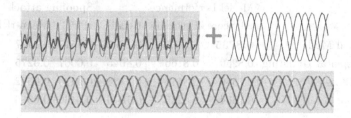

Fig. 5. An active defence example. The RGB sequence value extracted directly from the original video is in the upper left corner. The upper right corner is the injected signal. Below is the RGB sequence value extracted from the processed video.

$$C_{temp}(t) = \begin{cases} C_{ROI}(t) = 1 \\ C_O(t) = 0 \end{cases} \tag{1}$$

The sine signal is superimposed on the template.

$$Kernel = \frac{1}{30} \begin{bmatrix} 1 & \cdots & 1 \\ \cdots\cdots\cdots \\ 1 & \cdots & 1 \end{bmatrix}_{30 \times 30} \tag{2}$$

The template is fuzzed with a convolution kernel.

$$C_{final\_temp}(t) = C_{temp}(t) \times Sine(t) * Kernel \tag{3}$$

Finally, we superimpose the template sequence on the original video frames to complete the signal hiding. $Frame_f(t)$ represents the t-th frame of the processed video. $Frame_o(t)$ indicates the t-th frame of the original video clip.

$$Frame_f(t) = Frame_o(t) + C_{final\_temp}(t) \tag{4}$$

Figure 5 shows the results of our signal injection in the video. We observe that the injected signal is completely different from the original signal.

6   Defence Evaluation

We evaluate the performance of our defensive strategies (see Sect. 5) in this section. The same datasets as in the previous section are used in this section. We use MediaPipe[2] to obtain the face mesh for each video frame. Then the ROI template is extracted from the face mesh using OpenCV[3] before we perform signal injection to the templates.

Table 3. Performance of three passive defence strategies (Incremental Updating, One-Class SVM, and Isolation Forest). The left half shows the impact on the performance of the original model. The right half is the success rate of the victim rPPG signal attack authentication model.

	Model Performance			Spoofing attack	
	F1-Score	Precision	Recall	rPPG	Mean-rPPG
Original Model	**0.8735**	**0.9127**	**0.8548**	0.2517	0.3427
Incremental Updating	0.8269	0.8166	0.8645	0.0067	0.0275
One-Class SVM	0.7369	0.8141	0.7138	0.0420	0.0572
IsolationForest	0.7364	0.8265	0.7079	0.0430	0.0586

Table 4. Performance of active defence strategy in user authentication. SigHid: Our proposed signal hiding method.

Video Type	CHROM-rPPG	Mean-rPPG
Original Video	0.7005	1.0000
SigHid Video	0.0291	0.0577

6.1   Defence in User Authentication

Table 3 shows the performance of the passive defence strategy. These results show that all passive defence strategies significantly reduce the attack's success rate. The success rate of rPPG attacks has been reduced from 25% to at least 4%. Mean-treated rPPG was reduced to 5%. However, we observe that the passive defence strategy seriously affects the performance of the authentication model system. The incremental updating method has the least impact on the authentication system. The F1-Score of the model dropped from 87% to 82%. It reduces the success rate of rPPG attacks and makes the model less generalized. Isolation-Forest and One-Class SVM have a significant impact. The F1-Score of the model is around 73%. Unfortunately, it propagates the error rate to the authentication model while blocking the attack.

---

[2] https://google.github.io/mediapipe/.
[3] https://opencv.org/.

We propose an active defence strategy to solve the problems in passive defence. To maximize the active defence strategy's performance, we selected 13 video clips from the original videos with a success rate of being attacked greater than 50%. As shown in Table 4, the attack's success rate using the rPPG signal extracted from the original video reaches 70%, and the mean-treated rPPG signal even reaches 100%. The success rate of video rPPG attacks processed by the active defence strategy is reduced to 2%, and the mean-treated rPPG is decreased to 5%, almost achieving the same performance as the passive defence. Moreover, the active defence strategy does not affect the original model's performance.

6.2   Defence in IPI-Based Security Protocols

Compared to the best results (CL_P, PURE) of the original video extracted IPI, in our processed video, MAE increased to 0.2, PC was reduced to 0.28. In the other datasets, MSE increased to some extent. However, we found that the variation was minimal in COHFACE because the video clips in COHFACE are compressed. The MAE of the IPI recovered from COHFACE has reached 0.2 s. Their PC is around 0.05 for all methods except CL_P and CL_F. It indicates that the IPI recovered by other methods has a low correlation with the IPI of

Table 5. Comparison of the video extracted IPIs with the PPG signal extracted IPIs in different datasets. PC: Pearson correlation coefficient. P: PURE. L: LGI_PPGI. U1: UBFC_1. U2: UBFC_2. C: COHFACE. -S: Signal acquired from video processed using SigHid.

	CHROM	POS	LGI	PCA	CL_P	CL_F
MAE-S (P)	0.1729	0.2087	**0.1661**	0.1780	0.2039	0.1691
RMSE-S (P)	0.2222	0.2536	0.2153	0.2279	0.2422	**0.2086**
PC-S (P)	−0.046	−0.037	**−0.057**	−0.055	0.2897	0.3917
MAE-S (L)	0.2782	**0.2676**	0.2872	0.2899	–	–
RMSE-S (L)	0.3419	**0.3274**	0.3466	0.3509	–	–
PC-S (L)	0.0317	0.0112	**−0.009**	−0.005	–	–
MAE-S (U1)	0.3141	0.2481	**0.2472**	0.3417	–	–
RMSE-S (U1)	0.3687	0.3061	**0.3051**	0.3893	–	–
PC-S (U1)	0.0003	0.0115	0.0098	**−0.050**	–	–
MAE-S (U2)	0.3597	0.3063	0.3170	0.4012	0.3610	**0.2728**
RMSE-S (U2)	0.4077	0.3574	0.3689	0.4403	0.4045	**0.3200**
PC-S (U2)	0.0397	**0.0058**	0.0163	0.0447	0.4759	0.7647
MAE-S (C)	**0.2884**	0.2948	0.2943	0.2942	0.4112	0.4629
RMSE-S (C)	**0.3209**	0.3242	0.3237	0.3234	0.4873	0.5359
PC-S (C)	−0.007	**−0.033**	−0.025	−0.023	0.3360	0.2036

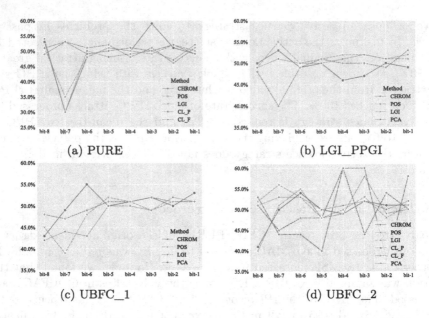

(a) PURE

(b) LGI_PPGI

(c) UBFC_1

(d) UBFC_2

Fig. 6. The processed video quantile-based IPI coding bit hit rate in different datasets. The horizontal coordinate indicates the bit hit rate. -S: Signal acquired from video processed using SigHid.

PPG. After processing the video, even the state-of-the-art method PC is reduced to approximately 0.3.

Contrary to the result in Sect. 4.4, In Fig. 6, in the processed video, BHR remains steady at approximately 0.5 with the bit position. For example, as shown in Fig. 3a, the LGI and POS methods gradually decrease in BHR from 0.7 to 0.5 as the bits go down. In contrast, as shown in Fig. 6a, BHR does not change with the bits. Hence, our proposed active defence method completely hides the PPG signal of the user in the video (Table 5).

6.3   Discussion

A common strategy to combat spoofing attacks is by introducing detection components. Nevertheless, the detection component is usually located in front of the recognition pipeline, and its errors will be propagated to the recognition model, affecting the overall model recognition performance. In particular, when the spoofed signal is similar to a real signal, the model's false-negative rate increases significantly. We observed that low-quality videos lower the success of spoofing attacks. For example, in the COHFACE dataset, the quality of the obtained rPPG signals is relatively poor, and the success rate of the attack is lower than in other datasets. Compared to other datasets, the video clips in COHFACE have a frame rate of 20 FPS, 640×480 resolution, and 255 Kbps bit rate. However, preventing attacks by sacrificing video quality is not always practical. Thus, we propose an active defence to prevent leaking the target's PPG signals by modifying the RGB pixel values of the facial skin in the video frame. Video hosting platforms like YouTube and TikTok can successfully prevent signal leakage by batch processing users' videos. Though an attacker may attempt to capture video of the victim using their own device from a distance, it is worth noting that in practical scenarios, the camera is typically situated in close proximity to the victim. It poses a significant challenge for the attacker to acquire the target signals without raising suspicion. Furthermore, future advancements could involve Challenge-Response authentication [27], for example, modifying the light source to augment the recognition process.

7 Conclusion

Recently, emerging biometric solutions using physiological signals have gained widespread attention. In particular, the PPG signal is easy to collect and unobservable to remote attackers. However, the rPPG signal breaks this unobservability. To comprehensively analyze the impact of the rPPG signal, we conducted experiments on five datasets (PURE, UBFC_rPPG, UBFC_Phys, LGI_PPGI, and COHFACE). We found that user authentication and IPI-based security protocols are vulnerable to rPPG signal spoofing attacks. To mitigate this spoofing attack, we propose an active defence scheme. It has the most negligible impact on the performance of the original model compared to the passive defence. Before releasing HD video, we recommend video platforms using active defence strategies in bulk to mitigate rPPG signal leakage.

References

1. Awad, A.A., et al.: The relationship between the photoplethysmographic waveform and systemic vascular resistance. J. Clin. Monit. Comput. **21**(6), 365–372 (2007)
2. Bazarevsky, V., Kartynnik, Y., Vakunov, A., Raveendran, K., Grundmann, M.: Blazeface: sub-millisecond neural face detection on mobile gpus. In: Proceedings of the IEEE/CVF Conference on Computer Vision and Pattern Recognition Workshops (CVPRW) (2019)
3. Biswas, D., et al.: CorNET: deep learning framework for PPG-based heart rate estimation and biometric identification in ambulant environment. IEEE Trans. Biomed. Circuits Syst. **13**(2), 282–291 (2019)
4. Bobbia, S., Macwan, R., Benezeth, Y., Mansouri, A., Dubois, J.: Unsupervised skin tissue segmentation for remote photoplethysmography. Pattern Recogn. Lett. **124**, 82–90 (2019)
5. Boccignone, G., Conte, D., Cuculo, V., D'Amelio, A., Grossi, G., Lanzarotti, R.: An open framework for remote-PPG methods and their assessment. IEEE Access **8**, 216083–216103 (2020)
6. Calleja, A., Peris-Lopez, P., Tapiador, J.E.: Electrical heart signals can be monitored from the moon: security implications for IPI-based protocols. In: Akram, R.N., Jajodia, S. (eds.) WISTP 2015. LNCS, vol. 9311, pp. 36–51. Springer, Cham (2015). https://doi.org/10.1007/978-3-319-24018-3_3

7. Chen, W., McDuff, D.: DeepPhys: video-based physiological measurement using convolutional attention networks. In: Ferrari, V., Hebert, M., Sminchisescu, C., Weiss, Y. (eds.) ECCV 2018. LNCS, vol. 11206, pp. 356–373. Springer, Cham (2018). https://doi.org/10.1007/978-3-030-01216-8_22

8. Chen, W., Picard, R.W.: Eliminating physiological information from facial videos. In: Proceedings of the IEEE International Conference on Automatic Face & Gesture Recognition, pp. 48–55 (2017)

9. Chizari, H., Lupu, E.: Extracting randomness from the trend of IPI for cryptographic operations in implantable medical devices. IEEE Trans. Dependable Secure Comput. **18**(2), 875–888 (2019)

10. Dasari, A., Prakash, S.K.A., Jeni, L.A., Tucker, C.S.: Evaluation of biases in remote photoplethysmography methods. NPJ Dig. Med. **4**(1), 1–13 (2021)

11. De Haan, G., Jeanne, V.: Robust pulse rate from chrominance-based rPPG. IEEE Trans. Biomed. Eng. **60**(10), 2878–2886 (2013)

12. Donida Labati, R., Piuri, V., Rundo, F., Scotti, F., Spampinato, C.: Biometric recognition of PPG cardiac signals using transformed spectrogram images. In: Del Bimbo, A., Cucchiara, R., Sclaroff, S., Farinella, G.M., Mei, T., Bertini, M., Escalante, H.J., Vezzani, R. (eds.) ICPR 2021. LNCS, vol. 12668, pp. 244–257. Springer, Cham (2021). https://doi.org/10.1007/978-3-030-68793-9_17

13. Gideon, J., Stent, S.: The way to my heart is through contrastive learning: Remote photoplethysmography from unlabelled video. In: Proceedings of the IEEE/CVF International Conference on Computer Vision (ICCV), pp. 3995–4004 (2021)

14. Gu, Y., Zhang, Y., Zhang, Y.: A novel biometric approach in human verification by photoplethysmographic signals. In: Proceedings of the International IEEE EMBS Special Topic Conference on Information Technology Applications in Biomedicine, pp. 13–14 (2003)

15. Heusch, G., Anjos, A., Marcel, S.: A reproducible study on remote heart rate measurement. arXiv preprint arXiv:1709.00962 (2017)

16. Hinatsu, S., Suzuki, D., Ishizuka, H., Ikeda, S., Oshiro, O.: Basic study on presentation attacks against biometric authentication using photoplethysmogram. Adv. Biomed. Eng. **10**, 101–112 (2021)

17. Hu, M., Qian, F., Guo, D., Wang, X., He, L., Ren, F.: ETA-rPPGNet: effective time-domain attention network for remote heart rate measurement. IEEE Trans. Instrum. Meas. **70**, 1–12 (2021)

18. Huang, Y., Yang, G., Wang, K., Liu, H., Yin, Y.: Learning joint and specific patterns: a unified sparse representation for off-the-person ECG biometric recognition. IEEE Trans. Inf. Forensics Secur. **16**, 147–160 (2021)

19. Hwang, D.Y., Taha, B., Hatzinakos, D.: PBGAN: learning PPG representations from GAN for time-stable and unique verification system. IEEE Trans. Inf. Forensics Secur. **16**, 5124–5137 (2021)

20. Hwang, D.Y., Taha, B., Lee, D.S., Hatzinakos, D.: Evaluation of the time stability and uniqueness in PPG-based biometric system. IEEE Trans. Inf. Forensics Secur. **16**, 116–130 (2021)

21. Karimian, N.: How to attack PPG biometric using adversarial machine learning. In: Proceedings of the Autonomous Systems: Sensors, Processing, and Security for Vehicles and Infrastructure. International Society for Optics and Photonics (2019)

22. Kartynnik, Y., Ablavatski, A., Grishchenko, I., Grundmann, M.: Real-time facial surface geometry from monocular video on mobile GPUs. In: Proceedings of the IEEE/CVF Conference on Computer Vision and Pattern Recognition Workshops (CVPRW) (2019)

23. Kavsaoğlu, A.R., Polat, K., Bozkurt, M.R.: A novel feature ranking algorithm for biometric recognition with PPG signals. Comput. Biol. Med. **49**, 1–14 (2014)

24. Kolkur, S., Kalbande, D., Shimpi, P., Bapat, C., Jatakia, J.: Human skin detection using RGB, HSV and YCbCr color models. In: Proceedings of the International Conference on Communication and Signal Processing, pp. 324–332. Atlantis Press (2016)

25. Lee, E., Chen, E., Lee, C.-Y.: Meta-rPPG: remote heart rate estimation using a transductive meta-learner. In: Vedaldi, A., Bischof, H., Brox, T., Frahm, J.-M. (eds.) ECCV 2020. LNCS, vol. 12372, pp. 392–409. Springer, Cham (2020). https://doi.org/10.1007/978-3-030-58583-9_24

26. Lewandowska, M., Rumiński, J., Kocejko, T., Nowak, J.: Measuring pulse rate with a webcam – a non-contact method for evaluating cardiac activity. In: Proceedings of the Federated Conference on Computer Science and Information Systems, pp. 405–410. IEEE (2011)

27. Li, J., Fawaz, K., Kim, Y.: Velody: nonlinear vibration challenge-response for resilient user authentication. In: Proceedings of the 2019 ACM SIGSAC Conference on Computer and Communications Security, pp. 1201–1213 (2019)

28. Li, L., Chen, C., Pan, L., Zhang, J., Xiang, Y.: Video is all you need: Attacking PPG-based biometric authentication. In: Proceedings of the 15th ACM Workshop on Artificial Intelligence and Security. AISec 2022, pp. 57–66, New York, NY, USA. Association for Computing Machinery(2022)

29. Lin, Q., et al.: H2B: heartbeat-based secret key generation using piezo vibration sensors. In: Proceedings of the International Conference on Information Processing in Sensor Networks, pp. 265–276 (2019)

30. Marin, E., Argones Rúa, E., Singelée, D., Preneel, B.: On the difficulty of using patient's physiological signals in cryptographic protocols. In: Proceedings of the 24th ACM Symposium on Access Control Models and Technologies, pp. 113–122 (2019)

31. McSharry, P.E., Clifford, G.D., Tarassenko, L., Smith, L.A.: A dynamical model for generating synthetic electrocardiogram signals. IEEE Trans. Biomed. Eng. **50**(3), 289–294 (2003)

32. Meziatisabour, R., Benezeth, Y., De Oliveira, P., Chappe, J., Yang, F.: UBFC-Phys: a multimodal database for psychophysiological studies of social stress. IEEE Trans. Affect. Comput. **14**, 622–636 (2021)

33. Millasseau, S.C., Kelly, R., Ritter, J., Chowienczyk, P.: Determination of age-related increases in large artery stiffness by digital pulse contour analysis. Clin. Sci. **103**(4), 371–377 (2002)

34. Pilz, C.S., Zaunseder, S., Krajewski, J., Blazek, V.: Local group invariance for heart rate estimation from face videos in the wild. In: Proceedings of the IEEE/CVF Conference on Computer Vision and Pattern Recognition Workshops (CVPRW), pp. 1254–1262 (2018)

35. Poh, M.Z., McDuff, D.J., Picard, R.W.: Non-contact, automated cardiac pulse measurements using video imaging and blind source separation. Opt. Express **18**(10), 10762–10774 (2010)

36. Rostami, M., Juels, A., Koushanfar, F.: Heart-to-heart (H2H) authentication for implanted medical devices. In: Proceedings of the 2013 ACM SIGSAC Conference on Computer & Communications Security, pp. 1099–1112 (2013)

37. Seepers, R.M., Wang, W., de Haan, G., Sourdis, I., Strydis, C.: Attacks on heartbeat-based security using remote photoplethysmography. IEEE J. Biomed. Health Inform. **22**(3), 714–721 (2018)

38. Stricker, R., Müller, S., Gross, H.M.: Non-contact video-based pulse rate measurement on a mobile service robot. In: Proceedings of the IEEE International Symposium on Robot and Human Interactive Communication, pp. 1056–1062. IEEE (2014)

39. Takazawa, K., et al.: Assessment of vasoactive agents and vascular aging by the second derivative of photoplethysmogram waveform. Hypertension **32**(2), 365–370 (1998)

40. Tarvainen, M.P., Ranta-Aho, P.O., Karjalainen, P.A.: An advanced detrending method with application to HRV analysis. IEEE Trans. Biomed. Eng. **49**(2), 172–175 (2002)

41. Verkruysse, W., Svaasand, L.O., Nelson, J.S.: Remote plethysmographic imaging using ambient light. Opt. Express **16**(26), 21434–21445 (2008)

42. Wang, M., Hu, J., Abbass, H.A.: BrainPrint: EEG biometric identification based on analyzing brain connectivity graphs. Pattern Recogn. **105**, 107381 (2020)

43. Wang, W., Den Brinker, A.C., Stuijk, S., De Haan, G.: Algorithmic principles of remote PPG. IEEE Trans. Biomed. Eng. **64**(7), 1479–1491 (2016)

44. Xu, F., Qin, Z., Tan, C.C., Wang, B., Li, Q.: Imdguard: Securing implantable medical devices with the external wearable guardian. In: Proceedings of the Annual IEEE International Conference on Computer Communications (INFOCOM), pp. 1862–1870. IEEE (2011)

45. Yadav, U., Abbas, S.N., Hatzinakos, D.: Evaluation of PPG biometrics for authentication in different states. In: Proceedings of the International Conference on Biometric, pp. 277–282 (2018)

46. Yu, Z., Peng, W., Li, X., Hong, X., Zhao, G.: Remote heart rate measurement from highly compressed facial videos: an end-to-end deep learning solution with video enhancement. In: Proceedings of the IEEE/CVF International Conference on Computer Vision (ICCV), pp. 151–160 (2019)

47. Zhang, J., Zheng, Y., Xu, W., Chen, Y.: H2K: a heartbeat-based key generation framework for ECG and PPG signals. IEEE Trans. Mob. Comput. (2021)

48. Zhang, K., Zhang, Z., Li, Z., Qiao, Y.: Joint face detection and alignment using multitask cascaded convolutional networks. IEEE Signal Process. Lett. **23**(10), 1499–1503 (2016)

49. Zhao, T., Wang, Y., Liu, J., Chen, Y., Cheng, J., Yu, J.: Trueheart: continuous authentication on wrist-worn wearables using PPG-based biometrics. In: Proceedings of the Annual IEEE International Conference on Computer Communications (INFOCOM), pp. 30–39. IEEE (2020)

Exploring Genomic Sequence Alignment for Improving Side-Channel Analysis

Heitor Uchoa[1,2], Vipul Arora[2], Dennis Vermoen[2], Marco Ottavi[1], and Nikolaos Alachiotis[1(✉)]

[1] University of Twente, Enschede, The Netherlands
n.alachiotis@utwente.nl
[2] Riscure B.V., Delft, The Netherlands

Abstract. Side-channel analysis (SCA) extracts sensitive information from a device by analyzing information that is leaked through side channels. These measurements are correlated with specific operations executed on the device, e.g., encryption or decryption, allowing to extract useful information from the data. Countermeasures, however, disrupt the synchronization between the device's operations and the corresponding side-channel data, yielding their alignment a prerequisite for successful SCA. In this work, we describe parallels between side-channel analysis and molecular biology, and propose a novel approach to align side-channel traces using genomic sequence alignment methods. We find that Multiple Sequence Alignment techniques can align power traces with higher quality than elastic alignment (based on Dynamic Time Warping), thereby enabling downstream SCA methods, e.g., Correlation Power Analysis, to extract cryptography keys with up to 44% less traces.

Keywords: Side Channel Analysis · Multiple Sequence Alignment

1 Introduction

Embedded devices collect, process, and exchange critical information on a daily basis. This information must be hidden from third parties to prevent being exploited by adversaries. To maintain secrecy, cryptography methods encrypt a plain text to a ciphertext using an encryption key. The ciphertext is transmitted to another device, which decrypts it using a decryption key. Cryptographic system vulnerabilities can be exploited using analytical attacks and side channels [1–3]. These channels can be power consumption, electromagnetic emissions, sound, temperature signatures, and timing information [4–6].

Side Channel Analysis (SCA) refers to the process of analyzing side channel leakage to extract useful information from a system. SCA exploits the fact that the physical behavior of electronic devices can reveal information about its internal state, such as information about secret keys used in cryptographic operations. Power variations, for instance, are exploited by techniques such as Differential Power Analysis (DPA [5]) and Correlation Power Analysis (CPA [7]) to extract the device's cryptography keys. Therefore, SCA approaches are widely employed to detect system vulnerabilities.

G. Tsudik et al. (Eds.): ESORICS 2023, LNCS 14346, pp. 203–221, 2024.
https://doi.org/10.1007/978-3-031-51479-1_11

SCA requires the acquisition of many traces from the same device while the device performs the same operation with different input. Various factors affect the trace acquisition process, such as triggering variations during traces collection or countermeasures that intentionally alter the measurements [8], resulting in the collected traces being misaligned in time. Countermeasures typically aim to make it more difficult for attackers to extract useful information, for example by introducing randomness (e.g., noise and random delays) to the traces [9]. Because time misalignments across traces reduce information leakage, it is of utmost importance to align side-channel traces to maximize data leakage.

This work describes analogies between biology and side channel analysis. We consider the device as a species and each trace as the genome of an individual within that species' population. We view countermeasures as the evolutionary forces that facilitate the adaptation of the species to a particular environment, e.g., natural selection. Additionally, we compare the impact of countermeasures on side-channel traces to the various alleles present at the same locus of different DNA sequences/genomes due to mutations accumulated over generations.

Motivated by the aforementioned parallels, we explore sequence alignment methods that have been traditionally used to align genomic sequences on side channel traces. Time variations across traces due to inaccurate triggering can be addressed using static alignment [4], which aligns traces by selecting a point in each trace that corresponds to the same operation and aligns all traces to that point. More profound alterations throughout the trace length require more complex methods such as Sliding-Window-DPA (SW-DPA) [8] or elastic alignment [10]; elastic alignment applies a warping function to the traces that stretches or compresses them in time to align all corresponding operations across the trace length. These methods typically use one of the traces as the reference, and iteratively align all other traces in the trace set with the reference trace on one-to-one basis with the goal to exploit the aligned regions across all traces for information leakage. Interestingly, genomic sequence alignment methods that align three or more sequences (Multiple Sequence Alignment, MSA [11]) are able to perform all-to-all alignments leveraging information from all sequences to align all sequences without the need for an arbitrary reference sequence.

We present a proof-of-concept framework for SCA that translates traces to DNA/protein sequences, employs MSA tools to produce an alignment, converts the genomic sequences back to traces, and performs the downstream SCA analysis to expose the secret key of the target device. We find that MSA-based trace alignment can successfully align traces that have been altered by countermeasures, leading to better alignments than both static and elastic alignment methods. Using a known-key analysis performed by a commercially available SCA tool [12], we observed that the higher quality trace alignment obtained using Bioinformatics alignment tools enables the successful application of CPA to expose the secret key with nearly half the number of traces that would otherwise be required for the same analysis if elastic alignment was used. To the best of the authors' knowledge, this is the first work that explores Bioinformatics methods for multiple sequence alignment to align side-channel traces.

2 Background

2.1 Side Channel Analysis (SCA)

Side channels are channels through which a device or application may unintentionally leak information (e.g., temperature, sound, power consumption, electromagnetic radiation, and time). Analyzing these leakages can potentially lead to the compromise of cryptography keys. The main goal of Side Channel Analysis (SCA) is to extract valuable information from these unintentional leakages.

In order to capture a trace from a device when a cryptography operation is performed, e.g., AES [13], a trigger signal is generated so that an oscilloscope can start collecting samples precisely at the beginning of the target operation. The computer that collects the traces provides input data to the device and receives the encrypted output data, which are associated with the power trace captured for this particular input-output pair.

Data leakage is possible when a data-dependent operation is captured within several traces. These traces typically need to be correctly aligned to facilitate SCA. A sufficiently good trace alignment maximizes the chances of successful attacks like DPA [5] or CPA [7]. Figure 1 shows a trace set without countermeasures (A) and its alignment using a static alignment approach (B).

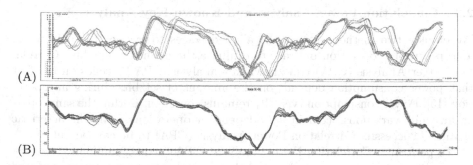

(A)

(B)

Fig. 1. A collection of power traces (A) and their static alignment (B). There were no countermeasures in place, so the collected traces were only shifted in time. Hence, static alignment, which aligns a single point across all traces, can be used.

2.2 Countermeasures

One of the main goals for employing countermeasures is to introduce disturbances [14] to the side channel so that the collected power traces are misaligned with respect to other power traces for the same operation, thereby presenting a challenge to the attacker to exploit data leakages; trace misalignment decreases the efficiency of an attack. While trace alignment, which is the focus of this work, improves the chances of a successful attack, several other preprocessing methods have been proposed for cases where trace alignment is not feasible, e.g., integration, convolution, and Fast Fourier Transform [4]. Figure 2A shows a trace set containing 10 traces with a countermeasure that creates process desynchronizations by injecting random delays [8]. This trace set requires elastic alignment

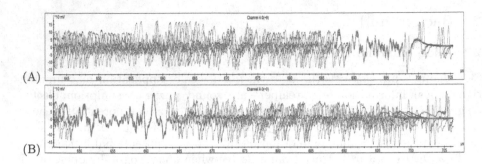

Fig. 2. A set of 10 power traces affected by a countermeasure that introduces random delays (A) and their static alignment (B). The static alignment aligns one region across all traces (samples 650–663) but the rest of the trace-set length remains unaligned.

methods because a static alignment approach will only align a single point across all traces, leaving the majority of the trace length unaligned, as shown in Fig. 2B. Examples of dynamically aligned traces using our proposed approach (discussed in Sect. 4) are shown in Fig. 8B.

2.3 Correlation Power Analysis and Known-Key Analysis

We employ two methods to use the aligned traces to extract the subkeys of a cryptographic operation in order to evaluate the alignment quality: Correlation Power Analysis (CPA) and known-key analysis. CPA [7] relies on the fact that power consumption depends on the amount of set bits during an operation [15]. Power consumption typically remains consistent during the same operation, while variations occur in data-dependent operations. This characteristic enables a successful Correlation Power Analysis (CPA) to be carried out.

To perform a Correlation Power Analysis (CPA) attack, random inputs are supplied to a cryptography device, and the corresponding outputs are captured while monitoring the power consumption. Keys are used to generate sub-keys, which are smaller and thus easier to attack. These sub-keys are then guessed to initiate an attack on the cryptography operation, such as AES, and the expected output is calculated. The resulting information provides a guessed output whose Hamming weight can be compared with the recorded power traces for correlation. The Pearson correlation between the guessed output Hamming weights and the power traces determines the key, with the key with the higher correlation being the correct one. Figure 3 shows an indicative physical setup for CPA.

Known-key analysis [12] was also used as an evaluation method for the quality of the sequence-based alignments. When the alignment is calculated, a first-order analysis employs statistical analysis methods to retrieve the key [16]. If it succeeds, the known-key analysis is used to obtain insights into the results. It shows the leakage strength related to every byte of the key at each data point of the input trace. Figure 4 provides an example of the outcome of a known-key analysis from a commercially available SCA tool [12]. The plot shows the rank evolution per sub key.

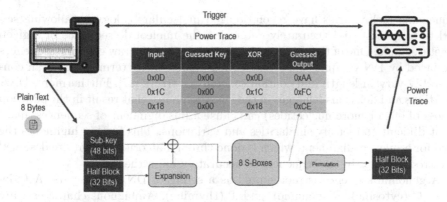

Fig. 3. A CPA (Correlation Power Analysis) to a specific cryptography operation based on guessing the keys.

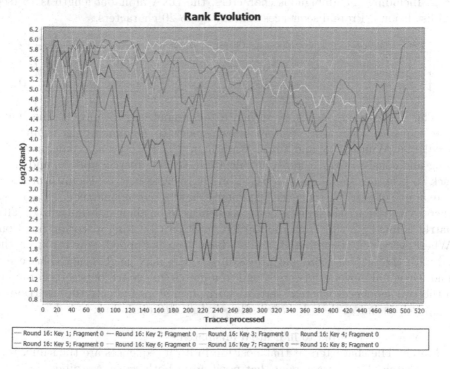

Fig. 4. The results of a known-key analysis using power traces.

2.4   Genomic Sequence Alignment

Sequence alignment methods identify similar regions between two or more biological sequences, such as DNA, RNA, or proteins. The goal is to understand the evolutionary relationships between different sequences and identify functional/structural motifs that are conserved (or not) across different species. DNA sequencing technologies have revolutionized molecular biology by allowing scientists to quickly and accurately determine the nucleotide sequence of a given genetic sample. One of the challenges, however, is that the raw genomic sequences produced by DNA sequencers ("reads" in Bioinformatics terminology) can considerably vary in length and contain sequencing errors [17]. Furthermore, DNA insertions and deletions (changes in the DNA sequence that result in the addition or loss of one or more nucleotides) can cause a misalignment of sequences, making it difficult to identify similarities and variations. This further highlights the need for sequence alignment, which is done through algorithms that are designed to introduce gaps in the sequences to accurately align them.

A genomic sequence is represented as a string of DNA characters: A (adenine), C (cytosine), G (guanine), and T (thymine). Ambiguous characters[1] are used to represent positions in DNA sequences where the nucleotide base cannot be determined with certainty, e.g., M to represent A or C, and S to represent C or G. Including the ambiguous characters, the DNA alphabet length is 15 (see full list below). Protein sequences contain up to 20 characters.

Character	Meaning
A	A
C	C
G	G
T/U	T

Character	Meaning
M	A or C
R	A or G
W	A or T
S	C or G

Character	Meaning
Y	C or T
K	G or T
V	A or C or G
H	A or C or T

Character	Meaning
D	A or G or T
B	C or G or T
N	A or C or G or T

The basic component in sequence alignment algorithms is the pairwise sequence alignment. Widely known pairwise alignment algorithms are Needleman-Wunsch [18] and Smith-Waterman [19]. Both use dynamic programming and consist of three steps: initialization, scoring matrix update, and trace back to generate the alignment based on the scoring matrix. Figure 5 provides an example of pairwise sequence alignment. First, a scoring matrix $C_{(N+1)(M+1)}$, where N and M are the lengths of the sequences to be aligned, is initialized. This matrix is filled starting from the top left position C_{00} using a scoring function.

When every cell is computed, a trace back step is applied, starting from the cell with the highest score and proceeding to the max neighboring value every time. Diagonal movements correspond to a match/mismatch between characters in the two sequences whereas vertical/horizontal steps indicate the insertion of a gap ('-') in one of the sequences. Three situations can occur:

- Gap: A '-' is inserted to indicate a mismatch.
- Match: The characters at that position in both sequences are the same.
- Mismatch: The characters at that position in both sequences differ.

The resulting alignment depends on the algorithm used and the scoring function. Key aspects of the scoring function are:

- Gap opening penalty: It lowers the frequency of opening gaps.
- Gap extension penalty: It lowers the chances of extending open gaps.

---

[1] https://genomevolution.org/wiki/index.php/Ambiguous_nucleotide.

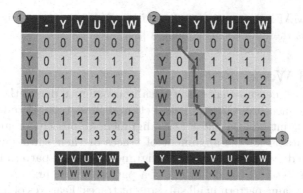

Fig. 5. Example of the three steps of pairwise sequence alignment: initialization (1), scoring matrix calculation (2), and trace back (3).

- Scoring matrix: It contains probabilistic relationships for all possible nucleotide substitutions derived from observations in nature (e.g., Blosum62 [20]).

A general description of a scoring function that can be used to fill the scoring matrix is given in Eq. 1 below,

$$C(i,j) = \max \begin{cases} C(i-1, j-1) + f(a_i, b_j), \\ \max_{k>0}\{C(i-k, j) - \text{Go} - (k-1)\text{Ge}\}, \\ \max_{k>0}\{C(i, j-k) - \text{Go} - (k-1)\text{Ge}\}, \end{cases} \quad (1)$$

where a_i and b_j are the ith and j^{th} characters in sequences a and b, respectively, $f(a,b)$ returns a similarity score for the two characters, and Go and Ge represent the gap opening and gap extension penalties, respectively. The notation $\max_{k>0}$ represents the maximum over all values of k greater than zero.

Multiple Sequence Alignment (MSA) is the alignment of three or more sequences. An example of an MSA of four sequences is illustrated in Fig. 6. Widely used methods that can align thousands of sequences are MAFFT [21] and CLUSTALW [22]. These methods align sequences by building tree structures that capture similarities through pairwise alignments. The process starts from the most similar pair and gradually includes more distant sequences. Sequences that have already been aligned can be realigned multiple times, each time including a larger sequence set to improve the quality of the alignment. The time com-

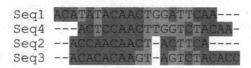

Fig. 6. An example of a multiple sequence alignment of four DNA sequences.

plexity of the MAFFT algorithm is $\mathcal{O}(N^2 L) + \mathcal{O}(NL^2)$, where L is the sequence length and N is the number of sequences [21].

3   Related Work

Raw side-channel measurements are typically misaligned due to the environment setup or countermeasures [23,24]. This section reviews trace alignment methods.

Mangard [4] introduced the static alignment approach for aligning power traces. It is suitable for the alignment of traces or their sub-regions that have not been affected by countermeasures. Alignment relies on pattern matching and consists of two steps: a) the definition of a pattern in the first trace, and b) the detection of the same pattern in all subsequent traces. Features of interest are the uniqueness of the pattern in the trace or trace set, the extent of data dependency of the corresponding operation, the length of the pattern, and the time distance to the point of interest (attack target). The author explains that length does not mean that the longest pattern is the best, and it requires a proper investigation to choose a pattern. Furthermore, if the time distance between the alignment point of the chosen pattern and the attacker's target is very large, it is highly likely that the region of interest will not be aligned as countermeasures might have acted and altered the traces. This work also discusses pattern matching techniques based on least squares and correlation.

van Woudenberg et al. [10] proposed a method called elastic alignment that relies on methods initially developed for speech recognition based on Dynamic Time Warping (DTW [25]). The authors explain that identifying speech is not a trivial task since the same spoken word can vary in timing every time it is repeated. Spoken words can not simply be compared to pre-recorded samples in a sample-to-sample approach. DTW is based on dynamic programming and it measures the distance between two utterances by elastically warping them in time. Due to the computational complexity of DTW, the authors use fast-DTW [26], an algorithmic optimization of DTW that reduces execution time by restricting the warp path. Elastic alignment is suitable for power trace alignment in the presence of countermeasures and it can also handle unstable clock cycles as it remains relatively unaffected by them.

Clavier et al. [8] propose a solution called SW-DPA to find the keys of cryptography operations when random process interrupts (RPIs) are used as countermeasures. The authors approach the problem under the assumptions that clock cycles have a fixed length and that RPIs occur with constant probability. Based on these two assumptions, SW-DPA integrates the leakage that is distributed over a number of clock cycles to facilitate DPA [5]. In comparison with static and elastic approaches, under the assumption of a fixed-length clock cycle, SW-DPA achieves a success rate close to 100% with only 160 traces, whereas static and elastic alignments achieve success rates of nearly 50% with 1,400 traces and nearly 100% with 270 traces, respectively.

Muijrers et al. [27] present an alignment method called RAM (Rapid Alignment Method) that is inspired by image processing algorithms, such as U-SURF [28], and is designed to perform continuous alignment faster than elastic alignment. U-SURF takes into account angle and light variations to recognize images that are similar (same scene/object) to a reference image. RAM is 20% faster than the previously discussed elastic alignment method [10] due to the use of block wavelets.

4   Methodology

An overview of our approach is depicted in Fig. 7. We first define the region of interest in the trace set (step 1) and then convert every trace to a genomic sequence (step 2). Thereafter, we define the MSA scoring scheme and construct the MSA (step 3). Finally, the aligned genomic sequences are converted to (aligned) traces (step 4) for downstream analysis.

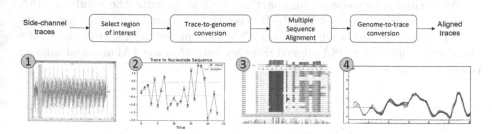

Fig. 7. Overview of the proposed side-channel trace alignment approach that relies on multiple sequence alignment.

Traces are converted to genomic sequences by dividing the total Y-axis range into subranges, the number of which being equal to the length of the alphabet (DNA or protein). For DNA, we use a 7-character alphabet that contains the four nucleotide bases A, C, G, T, and the three ambiguous characters M, S, and K to represent range values in-between A and C, C and G, and G and T, respectively. We implemented a conversion scheme that associates each nucleotide character to the corresponding sample value in order to reconstruct the exact same trace after alignment. The same DNA character, for instance, at different sequence positions corresponds to different sample values. When the alphabet is of a reasonable length, determined empirically to be at least four characters, the loss of information in the genomic-sequence representation of each trace is negligible. This is because the relative positions of neighboring characters across all sequences compensate for the loss of information. However, there is a need for an in-depth analysis to determine how many DNA/protein characters should be used for an SCA based on the minimum/maximum values in the traces.

An inherent feature of MSA methods is that they employ gap opening and extension penalties and scoring matrices, e.g., PAM40 [29] and Blosum62 [20]. A scoring matrix accounts for the fact that different amino acids can have similar phenotypic traits and thus need to be aligned differently than other amino acid combinations with unrelated functions. We exploit this observation by using the entire alphabet length for protein sequences and setting the probabilities in the scoring matrix in a way that they correspond to the proximity between the value ranges of the side-channel trace set that we associate with every character. We explored other trace-to-sequence conversion options as well, such as a custom adaptation of symbolic aggregate approximation [30], a widely used algorithm for data mining on time series data, as well as an assignment of variable-size trace segments to characters. However, we did not observe considerable advantages over the aforementioned Y-axis division approach. We also explored various MSA tools for performing the multiple sequence alignment, such as ClustalW [22], MAFFT [21], TCoffee [31], and MUSCLE [32]. We use MAFFT due to its capacity to handle a larger number of sequences and the ease of customizing the scoring scheme. To convert the resulting sequence alignment to traces, we represent every gap as a sample with value 0.0.

We devised a locus-based summary statistic to examine the result of MSA along the resulting trace-set length. By counting the number of gaps per alignment column, we obtain what we call an alignment profile. Figure 8 shows the alignment profile of an MSA aligned trace set with 15 traces (A) and four aligned traces from the same trace set (B).

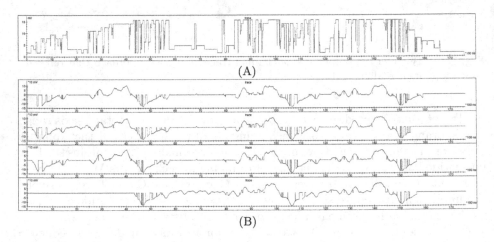

(A)

(B)

Fig. 8. A: An alignment profile based on a locus-based summary statistic that counts the number of gaps per alignment site. High-statistic values are indicative of aligned regions (through mostly matches and mismatches and considerably less gaps), while low-statistic values indicate the insertion of gaps in most of the sequences/traces. B: Four aligned traces from the same alignment. Notice the low value region 58–78 in the alignment profile with respect to the corresponding aligned regions in the traces.

Aligned trace regions for which our locus-based summary statistic assumes low values, such as region 58–78 in the figure, are likely to contain the result of countermeasures, since only one or a few traces contain samples in this region, and samples resulting from countermeasures can not be aligned with other traces.

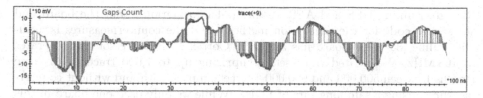

Fig. 9. MSA-based static alignment. The highlighted (green rectangular) well-aligned region has a high locus-based summary statistic value and the number of preceding gaps per trace is used to determine the amount of time shift required for each trace. (Color figure online)

Using this same summary statistic and focusing on aligned trace regions with high values allows us to perform MSA-based static alignment, which we henceforth refer to as MSA-based static-like alignment, by using a time shift amount per trace that is proportional to the number of gaps preceding the high-statistic-value trace-set region. Practically, an MSA-based static-like alignment aligns one single point across all traces (thus static) using the result of the MSA alignment. Figure 9 demonstrates the way MSA-based alignment can produce a static alignment. The trace set has been aligned using MAFFT and sequences have been converted to aligned traces by setting gaps equal to 0.0. The traces are overlapped in the figure and the longest high-statistic-value region across all traces is highlighted (green rectangular). By counting the number of gaps that have been inserted in each trace before the beginning of the highlighted well-aligned region, we can determine the time shift required for each trace in order to statically align the complete trace set. Notice that this method relies on the fact that at least one region of interest is identified (see green rectangular in the figure). This will be the case as long as countermeasures do not alter entire traces and traces are collected from the same devices under the same operation. Thus, at least one alignment point will exist across all traces given the considered countermeasures in this study. The length of this region, however, will change depending on the effect of these countermeasures.

5   Implementation

Our MSA-based trace alignment framework is developed in Python and is available for download at: https://github.com/pephco/MSA-based-trace-alignment. It converts side-channel traces (TRS format [33]) to genomic sequences (FASTA format [34]), invokes MAFFT [21] to construct the alignment, and converts the resulting alignment file (FASTA format) back to traces (TRS format) for downstream SCA analysis. We used a commercially available SCA tool, Riscure Inspector [12], for trace visualization and post-alignment SCA analysis, such as CPA, first-order analysis, and known-key analysis. We used the TRS library [33] provided by Riscure for storing and parsing side-channel traces to ensure compatibility with Inspector. We collected power traces using the pinãta board from

Riscure, running DES and AES. Additional information about the board and the source code for the encryption methods and the countermeasures is available online [35]. The board has an ARM Cortex-M4F processor that operates at 168 MHz. We created trace sets comprising up to 1,000 traces with trace lengths between 500,000 and 980,000 1-byte samples, with and without countermeasures, using a sampling rate of 1 GHz. While we only used one board in this proof-of-concept study, a variety of boards should be considered to assess the effectiveness of the proposed MSA-based trace alignment method.

6   Evaluation

6.1   Experimental Setup

We evaluated our proposed approach using two metrics: a) the highest correlation values obtained from CPA per output byte and b) the success-to-number-of-traces-ratio that was previously used by other studies as well [27]. For the latter, we report the number of traces required for revealing the key (based on known-key analysis). First, we empirically determined the intrinsic parameters of our method, such as the gap opening/extension penalties. To determine the alphabet length, we evaluated alignments obtained with all possible alphabet lengths (results not shown), from 2 characters (morphological data) to 20 characters (proteins). We observed that alphabet lengths of 5 characters or more achieved similar performance with respect to the ability of downstream SCA methods to extract the secret key. We opted to use the DNA alphabet with a length of 7 characters, using the four DNA characters and the three ambiguous characters that represent all possible pairwise combinations thereof to capture measurement uncertainty across measurement ranges. Thereafter, we compared the proposed MSA-based trace alignment method with the static alignment [4] and the elastic alignment [10] implementations of Inspector using trace sets without and with countermeasures, respectively.

6.2   Gap Opening Penalty

To examine the relationship between the amount of gaps inserted in an alignment and finding the cryptography key, we varied the gap opening penalty, from 0 to 26, and compared the resulting trace alignments with respect to the (aligned) trace-set length and the number of subkeys found by Inspector through CPA. Figure 10 shows the results of this comparison. All alignments were performed on the same trace set, which comprised 150 traces of length 6,000 samples. As can be observed in the figure, all alignments resulted in considerably longer traces due to the insertion of gaps, and, expectedly, lower gap penalties led to longer aligned traces than higher gap penalties. Increasing the gap penalty, however, did not benefit CPA as the number of found keys was reduced; a high gap penalty restricts the MSA tool's freedom to correctly align all possible positions along the sequences as it is being forced to accept more mismatches instead of introducing gaps for higher alignment quality.

Gap Opening Penalty	0	8	15	26
Trace size	19740	17932	17038	16163
Sub-Keys found (150 Traces)	8	8	6	5

Fig. 10. The effect of different gap opening penalties on the resulting trace-set length and the respective number of subkeys found by Inspector through CPA. The initial trace length (before alignment) was 6,000 samples.

6.3   Comparison with Static Alignment

To compare the MSA-based alignment with static alignment, we used a trace set comprising misaligned traces due to imprecise triggering start times, i.e., the acquired traces are only shifted in time with respect to each other. The trace set contains 1,000 traces with 400,000 samples each. The aim is to examine whether the proposed method can provide an alignment that can be used for CPA to detect data leakage. Figure 11 illustrates the results of CPA for 8 bytes of the key using static alignment (A), MSA-based static-like alignment (B), and MSA-based alignment (C). Recall that the difference between MSA-based alignment and MSA-based static-like alignment is that the former represents every gap as a sample with 0.0 value, while the latter uses the locus-based summary statistic described in Sect. 4 to calculate the shift amount per trace. As a result, the MSA-based static-like alignment aligns traces to a single point in each trace, which is related to the location of the well-aligned region with high locus-based summary statistic values (static alignment aligns traces by selecting a point in each trace that corresponds to the same operation and aligns all traces to that point).

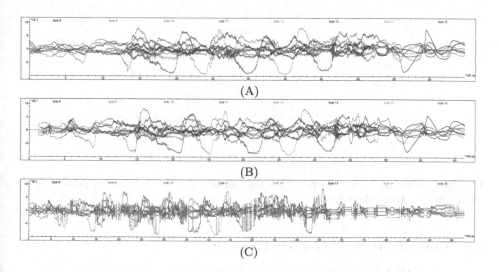

(A)

(B)

(C)

Fig. 11. CPA results obtained using different alignment methods: static alignment (A), MSA-based static-like alignment (B), and MSA-based alignment (C). The correlation lines for the 8 output bytes are overlapped in the plots.

Figure 12 summarizes the results of this comparison based on the maximum correlation value obtained for each byte with each alignment method. The plot additionally includes per-byte max correlation scores from CPA performed using the raw (unaligned) traces. As can be observed, MSA-based alignment can be used to align time-shifted traces in the absence of countermeasures as it produces comparable results with static alignment in this case.

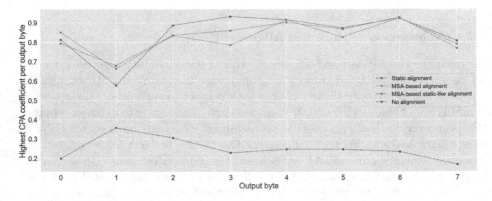

Fig. 12. Comparison of the highest CPA coefficients obtained by the alignment methods under comparison per byte.

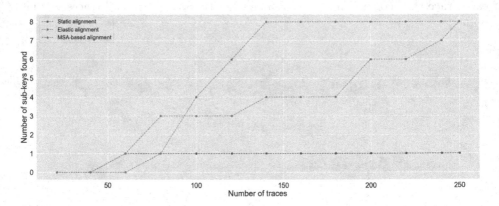

Fig. 13. Number of subkeys found as the number of traces increases using power traces containing random delays for SCA.

6.4   Comparison with Elastic Alignment

To compare MSA-based alignment with elastic alignment, we used power traces containing random delays as a countermeasure. We collected 500 traces with

400,000 samples each. For this comparison, we focused on the last round of encryption, and the resulting trace set contained 6,400 samples per trace. The same trace set was aligned with static, elastic, and MSA-based alignment. CPA was performed and the results were analyzed using known-key analysis. Figure 13 summarizes the results of this comparison. It shows the number of subkeys found by each of the alignment methods with an increasing number of traces. The individual known-key analysis results per method are shown in Fig. 14. The analysis was performed in fragments (parts of the trace) and the aligned trace sets were divided into the same number of fragments. It can be observed that our proposed method converges to rank 1 faster, allowing to find all subkeys with 140 traces. Using elastic alignment leads to finding only half of the subkeys with the same number of traces and requires 250 traces to find all subkeys. Thus, when MSA-based alignment is used instead of elastic alignment, up to 44% less traces are needed.

6.5 Time Complexity

Due to the need to compute pairwise alignments, the time complexity of MSA in practice is $\mathcal{O}(N^2L^2)$, where N is the number of sequences and L is the average length of the sequences. Note that the actual computational time required for MSA can vary depending on the complexity of the sequences. MAFFT experiments with several trace sets containing 100 to 250 traces with 6,000–10,000 samples took between 2,000 and 6,500 s. The table below reproduces a time comparison of previous alignment methods by Muijrers et al. [27]. These results are not directly comparable with the execution time of MAFFT, as they are based on different experimental setups. However, they highlight the need for further research to accelerate the alignment of side-channel traces, as, at this juncture, with post-quantum cryptography expected to replace public-key cryptography in the future, the increased key sizes and more complex mathematical principles of post-quantum cryptography will raise the data and computational complexity to analyze an implementation and evaluate side-channel leakage.

Method	Static Alignment	SW-DPA	RAM	Elastic Alignment
Run time (minutes)	12	18	76	3,115
Time per trace (ms)	1.44	2.16	9.1	373.8

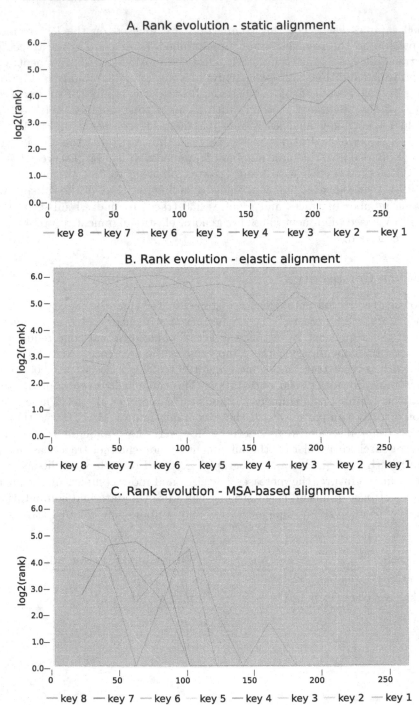

Fig. 14. The results of known-key analysis performed by Inspector: Static alignment (A), Elastic alignment (B), and MSA-based alignment (C). A faster convergence of all rank-evolution lines to rank 1 indicates higher performance, i.e., exposing the subkeys using less traces.

7   Conclusion

We presented a novel approach to align side-channel traces for improving SCA, drawing inspiration from the field of Bioinformatics, and more specifically the domain of multiple sequence alignment. We developed a proof-of-concept implementation and used a commercially available SCA tool for the evaluation of the resulting trace alignments. We obtained higher quality alignments than elastic alignment methods and we were able to almost halve the number of traces required by CPA to expose the secret key. While time performance was not the goal of this work, preliminary results showed that MSA-based alignment is slower than elastic alignment, thereby suggesting a trade-off between trace availability and alignment time. We are going to improve execution time performance of our approach as part of our future work. Furthermore, since recent research findings have shown that the use of MSA in conjunction with deep learning methods for genomics data results in enhanced classification accuracy, as a next step, we aim to investigate whether similar benefits can be observed for deep-learning-based SCA by incorporating MSA-based trace alignment.

References

1. Matsui, M.: Linear cryptanalysis method for DES cipher. In: Helleseth, T. (ed.) EUROCRYPT 1993. LNCS, vol. 765, pp. 386–397. Springer, Heidelberg (1994). https://doi.org/10.1007/3-540-48285-7_33
2. Jithendra, T., Shahana, K.B.: Enhancing the uncertainty of hardware efficient substitution box based on differential cryptanalysis. In: Proceedings of the 6th International Conference on Advances in Computing, Control, and Telecommunication Technologies (ACT 2015), Trivandrum, India, vol. 45-B, pp. 318–329, October (2015)
3. Courtois, N.T.: Feistel schemes and bi-linear cryptanalysis. In: Franklin, M. (ed.) CRYPTO 2004. LNCS, vol. 3152, pp. 23–40. Springer, Heidelberg (2004). https://doi.org/10.1007/978-3-540-28628-8_2
4. Mangard, S., Oswald, E., Popp, T.: Power analysis attacks: revealing the secrets of smart cards. Springer Science & Business Media, 2008, vol. 31 (2008)
5. Kocher, P., Jaffe, J., Jun, B.: Differential power analysis. In: Wiener, M. (ed.) CRYPTO 1999. LNCS, vol. 1666, pp. 388–397. Springer, Heidelberg (1999). https://doi.org/10.1007/3-540-48405-1_25
6. Brumley, D., Boneh, D.: Remote timing attacks are practical. Comput. Netw. 48(5), 701–716 (2005)
7. Brier, E., Clavier, C., Olivier, F.: Correlation power analysis with a leakage model. In: Joye, M., Quisquater, J.-J. (eds.) Cryptographic Hardware and Embedded Systems - CHES 2004: 6th International Workshop Cambridge, MA, USA, August 11-13, 2004. Proceedings, pp. 16–29. Springer Berlin Heidelberg, Berlin, Heidelberg (2004). https://doi.org/10.1007/978-3-540-28632-5_2
8. Clavier, C., Coron, J.-S., Dabbous, N.: Differential power analysis in the presence of hardware countermeasures. In: Koç, Ç.K., Paar, C. (eds.) Cryptographic Hardware and Embedded Systems — CHES 2000, pp. 252–263. Springer Berlin Heidelberg, Berlin, Heidelberg (2000). https://doi.org/10.1007/3-540-44499-8_20

9. Coron, J.-S., Kizhvatov, I.: Analysis and improvement of the random delay countermeasure of CHES 2009. In: Mangard, S., Standaert, F.-X. (eds.) CHES 2010. LNCS, vol. 6225, pp. 95–109. Springer, Heidelberg (2010). https://doi.org/10.1007/978-3-642-15031-9_7

10. van Woudenberg, J.G.J., Witteman, M.F., Bakker, B.: Improving differential power analysis by elastic alignment. In: Kiayias, A. (ed.) CT-RSA 2011. LNCS, vol. 6558, pp. 104–119. Springer, Heidelberg (2011). https://doi.org/10.1007/978-3-642-19074-2_8

11. Chatzou, M., Magis, C., Chang, J.-M., Kemena, C., Bussotti, G., Erb, I., Notredame, C.: Multiple sequence alignment modeling: methods and applications. Brief. Bioinform. **17**(6), 1009–1023 (2016)

12. "Riscure inspector." https://www.riscure.com/security-tools/inspector-sca/

13. Nechvatal, J., et al.: Report on the development of the advanced encryption standard (aes). J. Res. Nat. Inst. Stand. Technol. **106**(3), 511 (2001)

14. Shamir, A.: Protecting smart cards from passive power analysis with detached power supplies. In: Koç, Ç.K., Paar, C. (eds.) Cryptographic Hardware and Embedded Systems — CHES 2000, pp. 71–77. Springer Berlin Heidelberg, Berlin, Heidelberg (2000). https://doi.org/10.1007/3-540-44499-8_5

15. Messerges, T.S., Dabbish, E.A., Sloan, R.H.: Investigations of power analysis attacks on smartcards. Smartcard **99**, 151–161 (1999)

16. Whitnall, C., Oswald, E.: A fair evaluation framework for comparing side-channel distinguishers. J. Cryptogr. Eng. **1**(2), 145–160 (2011)

17. Alachiotis, N., Vogiatzi, E., Pavlidis, P., Stamatakis, A.: Chromatogate: a tool for detecting base mis-calls in multiple sequence alignments by semi-automatic chromatogram inspection. Comput. Struct. Biotechnol. J. **6**(7), e201303001 (2013)

18. Needleman, C.D., Saul, B., Wunsch: A general method applicable to the search for similarities in the amino acid sequence of two proteins. J. Molecular Biol. **48** (3), 443–453 (1970)

19. Smith, T.F., Waterman, M.S.: Identification of common molecular subsequences. J. Mol. Biol. **147**(1), 195–197 (1981)

20. Henikoff, S., Henikoff, J.G.: Amino acid substitution matrices from protein blocks. Proc. National Acad. Sci. **89**(22), 10 915–10 919 (1992)

21. Katoh, K., Toh, H.: Recent developments in the MAFFT multiple sequence alignment program. Brief. Bioinform. **9**(4), 286–298, (2008). https://doi.org/10.1093/bib/bbn013

22. Thompson, J.D., Higgins, D.G., Gibson, T.J.: CLUSTAL W: improving the sensitivity of progressive multiple sequence alignment through sequence weighting, position-specific gap penalties and weight matrix choice. Nucleic Acids Res. **22**(22), 4673–4680 (1994)

23. Cagli, E., Dumas, C., Prouff, E.: Convolutional neural networks with data augmentation against jitter-based countermeasures: profiling attacks without preprocessing. In: Fischer, W., Homma, N. (eds.) Cryptographic Hardware and Embedded Systems – CHES 2017: 19th International Conference, Taipei, Taiwan, September 25-28, 2017, Proceedings, pp. 45–68. Springer International Publishing, Cham (2017). https://doi.org/10.1007/978-3-319-66787-4_3

24. Picek, S., Perin, G., Mariot, L., Wu, L., Batina, L.: Sok: deep learning-based physical side-channel analysis. ACM Comput. Surv. **55**(11), 1–35 (2023)

25. Sakoe, H., Chiba, S.: Dynamic programming algorithm optimization for spoken word recognition. IEEE Trans. Acoust. Speech Signal Process. **26**(1), 43–49 (1978)

26. Salvador, S., Chan, P.: Fastdtw: Toward accurate dynamic time warping in linear time and space. In: KDD Workshop on Mining Temporal and Sequential Data. Citeseer (2004)

27. Muijrers, R.A., van Woudenberg, J.G.J., Batina, L.: RAM: rapid alignment method. In: Prouff, E. (ed.) CARDIS 2011. LNCS, vol. 7079, pp. 266–282. Springer, Heidelberg (2011). https://doi.org/10.1007/978-3-642-27257-8_17

28. Bay, H., Ess, A., Tuytelaars, T., Van Gool, L.: Speeded-up robust features (surf). Comp. Vision Image Understand. **110**(3), 346–359 (2008)

29. Dayhoff, M., Schwartz, R., Orcutt, B.: 22 a model of evolutionary change in proteins. Atlas Protein Seq. Struct. **5**, 345–352 (1978)

30. Yu, Y., Zhu, Y., Wan, D., Liu, H., Zhao, Q.: A novel symbolic aggregate approximation for time series. In: Lee, S., Ismail, R., Choo, H. (eds.) Proceedings of the 13th International Conference on Ubiquitous Information Management and Communication (IMCOM) 2019, pp. 805–822. Springer International Publishing, Cham (2019). https://doi.org/10.1007/978-3-030-19063-7_65

31. Notredame, C., Higgins, D.G., Heringa, J.: T-coffee: a novel method for fast and accurate multiple sequence alignment. J. Mol. Biol. **302**(1), 205–217 (2000)

32. Edgar, R.C.: Muscle: multiple sequence alignment with high accuracy and high throughput. Nucleic Acids Res. **32**(5), 1792–1797 (2004)

33. "Riscure trs library." https://trsfile.readthedocs.io/en/latest/

34. Lipman, D.J., Pearson, W.R.: Rapid and sensitive protein similarity searches. Science **227**(4693), 1435–1441 (1985)

35. "Piñata board: Manuals, software, hardware and source-codes." https://support.riscure.com/en/support/solutions/articles/15000022083-pinata-release-v2-3

The Grant Negotiation and Authorization Protocol: Attacking, Fixing, and Verifying an Emerging Standard

Florian Helmschmidt, Pedram Hosseyni[ID], Ralf Küsters[ID], Klaas Pruiksma[ID], Clara Waldmann[✉][ID], and Tim Würtele[ID]

University of Stuttgart, Stuttgart, Germany
flori@nhelmschmidt.de,
{pedram.hosseyni,ralf.kuesters,klaas.pruiksma,clara.waldmann,
tim.wuertele}@sec.uni-stuttgart.de

Abstract. The Grant Negotiation and Authorization Protocol (GNAP) is an emerging authorization and authentication protocol which aims to consolidate and unify several use-cases of OAuth 2.0 and many of its common extensions while providing a higher degree of security. OAuth 2.0 is an essential cornerstone of the security of authorization and authentication for the Web, IoT, and beyond, and is used, among others, by many global players, like Google, Facebook, and Microsoft. Historical limitations of OAuth 2.0 and its extensions have led prominent members of the OAuth community to create GNAP, a newly designed protocol for authorization and authentication. Given GNAP's advantages over OAuth 2.0 and its support within the OAuth community, GNAP is expected to become at least as important as OAuth 2.0.

In this work, we present the first formal security analysis of GNAP. We build a detailed formal model of GNAP, based on the Web Infrastructure Model (WIM) of Fett, Küsters, and Schmitz, and provide formal statements of the key security properties of GNAP, namely authorization, authentication, and session integrity. We discovered several attacks on GNAP in the process of trying to prove these properties. We present these attacks, as well as changes to the protocol that prevent them. These modifications have been incorporated into the GNAP specification after discussion with the GNAP working group. We give the first formal security guarantees for GNAP, by proving that GNAP, with our modifications applied, satisfies the mentioned security properties.

GNAP was still an early draft when we began our analysis, but is now on track to be adopted as an IETF standard. Hence, our analysis is just in time to help ensure the security of this important emerging standard.

1 Introduction

Delegated authorization is a common problem on the Web and beyond. With some service providers holding a large amount of data from their users, there are many cases where a user wants to allow some other service to use some (but

G. Tsudik et al. (Eds.): ESORICS 2023, LNCS 14346, pp. 222–242, 2024.
https://doi.org/10.1007/978-3-031-51479-1_12

not all) of this data. For example, a printing service may allow a user to directly print photos from the user's Google account. Authorization protocols provide a way for a user to grant access to data, via an API provided by the host of the data, without the user having to reveal credentials to the service. In the example, the printing service, called *client*, might send a request to Google (*authorization server (AS)*) asking to access the user's data (*resources*), and Google would then forward this request to the user (*resource owner (RO)*) for authorization.

The OAuth 2.0 framework [24],[1] developed by the IETF OAuth Working Group (OAuth WG), is an omnipresent standard for delegated authorization: in 2016, about 80% of the Alexa Top 500 websites for the US and China used OAuth [56]. For example, it is used by Google [23], Dropbox [12], Facebook [38], Github [21], by some financial institutions to provide third-party services access to initiate transactions [32], as well as for authorizing IoT devices [10,22].

Closely related is authentication: a user wants to use a single account for multiple services (single sign-on), e.g., on the many sites with "login with" buttons. While OAuth is primarily for authorization, the OpenID Connect (OIDC) [52] extension by the OpenID Foundation adds support for authentication.

A variety of other extensions of OAuth have been developed to improve its functionality in other ways. Some of these extensions improve the security of certain aspects of the protocol, e.g., by adding protection if specific tokens used in the protocol leak [8,53] or moving certain messages to direct server-to-server communication [34] instead of communication via the user's browser. Others, e.g. [48], add support for additional features like management of clients at ASs or new flows allowing input-constrained devices to be authorized [10].

Motivated by many limitations and shortcomings of OAuth and its extensions [42], both in terms of functionality and security, in 2019, members of the OAuth WG – several of them having worked on OAuth and its extensions for many years – started to create a new and completely redesigned protocol, the Grant Negotiation and Authorization Protocol (GNAP) [43].

Unlike OAuth, GNAP includes several ways that an RO can interact with an AS to authorize resource access. It also includes the ability for a client to renegotiate an ongoing request, and the ability for a client to participate in the protocol without being registered. In addition to the authorization use case, GNAP aims to also provide authentication.

Many details necessary for a typical use case are underspecified in OAuth, so extensions are needed to create a usable ecosystem. The high number of (historically grown) extensions of OAuth is a problem by itself. There are currently 27 standards and nine active drafts by the OAuth WG,[2] 16 standards and more than 20 drafts from the OpenID Foundation,[3] and even more standards related to OAuth, like User-Managed Access Grant (UMA) [35], which originate outside these two main standardization bodies. This makes it difficult for developers to choose the right set of extensions for their use case, especially if the use

---

[1] We will often refer to OAuth 2.0 as just OAuth.
[2] see https://datatracker.ietf.org/wg/oauth/documents/.
[3] see https://openid.net/developers/specs/.

case needs more security than provided by OAuth. For example, OAuth does not define the necessary details of security tokens (these are instead defined in extensions such as [6, 47]) or how third-party services can register at a service provider (e.g., [49]). Also, some of the OAuth extensions overlap in functionality, addressing similar problems in different ways. For example, cross-site request forgery (CSRF) protection can be achieved in multiple ways: using the OAuth state parameter, using the OIDC nonce value, or using the PKCE extension [53], to name just a few (see also [33, Sect. 2.1]). Using multiple extensions in the same deployment leads to increasing complexity, and unintended interactions between the extensions can lead to bugs, including security vulnerabilities. Diametrical to having too many options, some of the original OAuth flows are not recommended anymore: the OAuth Security Best Current Practice document [33] discourages the use of the implicit flow and the resource owner password credentials flow, two of the four original OAuth flows.

The GNAP project attempts to learn from OAuth and its extensions by creating a monolithic protocol that incorporates concepts of several existing OAuth extensions. Furthermore, GNAP aims to provide more flexibility and a higher degree of security than OAuth and allows for a uniform base for extensions. While GNAP is not designed to be backwards compatible with OAuth, and will not immediately replace it, its additional expressive power makes it likely to coexist with and gradually take over from OAuth.

In the past, several attacks on OAuth and its extensions, e.g., OIDC, FAPI 1.0 [50, 51], and PKCE [53], have been found [5, 14, 18, 19, 36, 39]. While GNAP is certainly inspired by OAuth and tries to cover features of various OAuth extensions, e.g., the Device Authorization Grant [10] and Pushed Authorization Requests [34], it is a freshly designed protocol, so the results of previous analyses of OAuth and its extensions do not carry over to GNAP. For example, GNAP allows for flexible flows by combining different methods for the interaction between parties, whereas OAuth defines a fixed set of grant flows. GNAP also mandates back-channel communication for sensitive information instead of sending it through users' browsers (which is required in most OAuth flows). Another major difference is that GNAP allows for an unlimited number of (re-)negotiations of details for a flow, i.e., the client can change the requested authorization and authentication details. Furthermore, GNAP considers use cases like input-constrained client devices, which in OAuth require extensions (e.g., the Device Grant [10]) that may have their own new security vulnerabilities [31].

Our Contributions. In this work, we present the first formal security analysis of GNAP. Our analysis has led to the discovery of several attacks. We propose changes to the specification to fix these issues and formally prove that these changes are sufficient to get strong security guarantees for GNAP. We have reported these issues and fixes to the GNAP working group, which resulted in several changes to the specifications, following our recommendations. Our work has greatly improved the security of this emerging protocol, which has the potential to become as widely used as OAuth and its extensions. More specifically, our contributions can be summarized as follows:

Formal Model of GNAP. We develop a formal model of GNAP, closely following its specification. Our GNAP model is built on top of the Web Infrastructure Model (WIM) [15], probably the most comprehensive model of web infrastructure to date. As a result, our GNAP model covers many details of real-world implementations of GNAP. We also extended the WIM with the ability to use codes for the authorization process and with HTTP Message Signatures [3], which is also useful for future analysis efforts and of independent interest.

Formal Security Properties. Based on our formal model, we precisely define what the aforementioned properties authorization and authentication mean in the context of GNAP. We also formalize two other common security properties for such protocols: session integrity for both authorization and authentication, which requires that the attacker cannot force the user to unintentionally access the attacker's resources or be logged in as the attacker.

Attacks and Fixes. While trying to prove that GNAP satisfies these security properties, we found several attacks that break these properties. We proposed to the working group specification changes that prevent these attacks, which have been adopted and included in the current version of the GNAP specification [43].

Proof of Security of GNAP. Finally, we prove that GNAP with the proposed fixes is secure w.r.t. the mentioned security properties. This is the first formal proof for GNAP, covering a wide range of attacks.

In this paper, we discuss the attacks and fixes and give a high-level explanation of our formal analysis. Full details, including the full formal GNAP model, formalizations of all security properties, full security proofs, as well as more details on and variants of the attacks, can be found in our technical report [27].

2   Grant Negotiation and Authorization Protocol

The Grant Negotiation and Authorization Protocol (GNAP) [43,44] specifies how an owner of some resources can give a piece of software access to their resources and how subject information about that owner can be conveyed to the software without the need for the owner to reveal login credentials to that software. Additionally, if the software lacks the rights to access the resources it initially requests, GNAP provides means for this request to be adjusted, via negotiations between the owner of the information and the receiving software. In what follows, we describe GNAP in more detail.

The GNAP specification consists of two documents: the *core* specification and the *resource server* specification. When we started our analysis, the most recent version of the core specification was version 8 [45] and version 2 for the resource server specification [46]. At the time of writing this paper, the current versions of these documents are 15 [43] and 3 [44], respectively, and the core specification is submitted to IESG for publication [55], indicating that it is in its final stages. Some of the (security-relevant) changes to the core specification introduced since version 8 result from suggestions we have proposed to the working group based on our analysis. We point those out in Sect. 3. In the following, we describe the originally analyzed version 8 of the core and version 2 of the resource server specifications. Note however that our final formal model (for which we proved security as explained below) incorporates the security-relevant changes introduced in versions 9-15 of the core specification.

Roles. In GNAP, there are five roles that participants can take. Firstly, there is the *resource owner (RO)* that authorizes access to their protected resources. Together with an *end user (EU)*, who wants to access some protected resource, they describe the two roles of non-software participants (for example natural persons). GNAP also defines two server roles. An *authorization server (AS)* delegates authorization of the resource owner by issuing access tokens. Protected resources are handled by a *resource server (RS)* that provides operations on these resources when presented with a valid access token. Finally, a *client instance (CI)* is the central piece of software that communicates with ASs to obtain access tokens and with RSs to obtain access to resources. In some settings, an end-user is present, interacting with the client instance (*end-user case*), but the client may also act on its own (*software-only case*).

Detailed Flow. We examine now a sample GNAP flow, shown in Fig. 1, stressing that this is only one example, and that GNAP allows for various other flows, for instance with different means of interaction between CI and AS. The details of communication with the EU and RO, who may represent natural persons, are out of scope for GNAP (see also "Interaction Methods"). The remainder of the flow, between the software participants CI, AS, and RS, can be grouped into four types of request-response pairs. For simplicity, we do not show here details of the messages, which contain assorted cryptographic information (e.g. nonces, hashes, signatures) to protect against attacks such as CSRF.

A *grant request* from a CI to an AS starts each GNAP flow (Step ☐2). In this initial request, the CI may request one or more access tokens and/or subject information about the RO, specifying information such as the type and access rights of the desired tokens, or the type of subject information. The CI additionally specifies what *interaction start* and *interaction finish* methods it supports for facilitating interaction between RO and AS (see "Interaction Methods"). Furthermore, the CI must identify itself to the AS so that the AS can relate future requests in this flow to the correct CI (see "Securing Client Requests").

The AS answers a grant request with a *grant response* (Step ☐3), which may contain the requested access tokens or subject information, and may also include a *continuation URI* and *continuation access token*, with which the CI can send *continuation requests*. If the request cannot immediately be granted (or denied), ·

the AS must interact with the RO to determine whether to grant the request (Steps ④, ⑤, and ⑥); see "Interaction Methods".

The CI may send a *continuation request* at any point after receiving the grant response (Step ③). These requests serve several purposes, allowing the client to negotiate details of the grant with the AS, as well to request an access token once interaction is complete (Step ⑦). In response, the AS sends a message with the same form as a grant response, including potentially providing a new continuation access token to allow further continuations. Negotiation of a grant may take arbitrarily many steps of communication at this stage before an access token is finally provided by the AS.

Once the CI receives an access token (Step ⑧), it can send a *resource request* to an RS (Step ⑨), including the token and proof that it is allowed to use the token (see "Presentation of Access Tokens"). When receiving an access token, the RS checks that it is valid and sufficient for the requested resource, and that the CI is entitled to use the token. The RS may be able to validate a token on its own (if the RS and AS agree on a structured token format, e.g., [6]), or may need to perform token introspection at the issuing AS. In the latter case, the RS sends an *introspection request* with the token to the AS (Step ⑩). The AS can

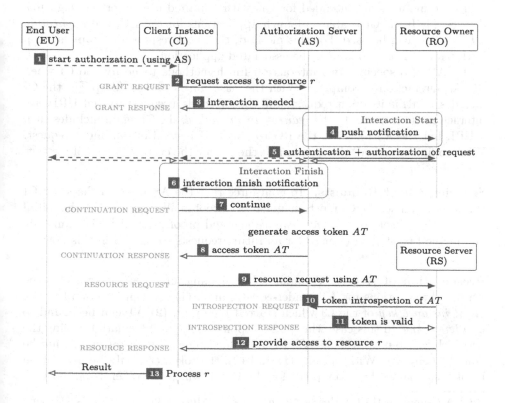

Fig. 1. Overview of a GNAP flow

then validate the token and send an *introspection response* to the RS (Step [11])
containing the necessary information for the RS to finish its checks. If all checks
succeed, the RS returns the resource to the CI in a *resource response* (Step [12]).

Interaction Methods. A central part of many GNAP flows is getting authorization from the RO (Step [5]). To facilitate interaction between AS and RO
and to inform the CI of completed interaction, GNAP defines several *interaction
start and finish methods*, marked by blue boxes in Fig. 1.

The AS may contact the RO directly, as shown in Fig. 1, but GNAP does
not specify details of this direct communication. If the RO and EU are the same
entity (which is often true in practice), the CI can assist the AS in contacting
the RO. GNAP defines four interaction start methods for this case. (1) With
the *redirect method*, the grant response contains an URI to which the CI then
redirects the RO, e.g., by displaying a QR code, or with an HTTP redirect. (2) In
the *user code URI method*, the grant response includes a short URI and user code.
The CI then communicates this URI and user code to the RO, who visits the
URI with a browser and enters the user code. (3) A simpler variant of (2) is the
user code method, which is similar, but uses a static URI which is assumed to be
known to the EU, e.g., by being printed onto a device implementing a CI. The
user code methods are intended for CIs with a limited user interface, e.g., IoT
devices. (4) If the CI is able to launch applications for the EU, the *application
URI method* can be used. For this method, the grant response contains an app
URI, which CI uses to launch the associated application.

GNAP also specifies two interaction finish methods to notify the CI when
RO-AS interaction is complete. With the *push finish method* (Step [6]), the CI
includes a URI in its grant request, and the AS sends a request to that URI once
interaction is complete. In the *redirect finish method*, the CI again includes such
a URI, but the AS redirects the RO to this URI instead of sending a request.
With no finish method, the CI can *poll* the AS for the current status of a grant.

Securing Client Requests. To guarantee that the AS talks to the same CI
throughout a flow, the CI must include a key proof in all requests. For the initial
request, the CI selects a *client instance key* and proof method.[4] The same key
and method must then be used for all future requests to the AS in this flow.

Presentation of Access Tokens. When issuing an access token (AT), the
AS has three options for AT sender-constraining: (1) AT can be bound to the
client instance key of the CI which started the grant. (2) AT can be bound to
a different key. In this case, the grant response includes information telling the
CI which key to use with this AT. (3) AT can also be a *bearer token*, i.e., not be
bound to any key. With options (1) and (2), the token can only be used at an
RS if accompanied by a key proof for the key to which the token is bound.

---

[4] GNAP supports HTTP Message Signatures [3], Mutual TLS certificates [41], and
JSON Web Signatures [30] as proof methods, where both symmetric and asymmetric
keys are allowed.

3 Attacks and Fixes

In this section, we first briefly and informally describe the security properties GNAP is expected to fulfill, including a short overview of our attacker model. We then present the attacks we found during our formal security analysis of GNAP and the fixes we propose to make GNAP satisfy the security properties.

3.1 Informal Security Properties

As noted before, GNAP is supposed to satisfy the following security properties:

Security W.r.t. Authorization. An attacker should not be able to access resources of an honest RO. This is a key property for any authorization protocol.

Session Integrity for Authorization. An honest end user should not unwillingly access resources of the attacker. More precisely, if the responsible AS is honest, end users should be able to access only the resources that they explicitly request.

Security W.r.t. Authentication. An attacker should not be able to log in at an honest CI under the identity (governed by an honest AS) of an honest user.

Session Integrity for Authentication. An honest user should only be logged in with an identity managed by an honest AS if they explicitly attempt to log in with this identity.

Attacker Model. These security properties should hold in the presence of a network attacker, which can also use Web features. For example, the browser of an honest user may also open websites of the attacker. Such an attacker website can deliver malicious scripts, use postMessage communication within the honest user's browser, or even include websites of honest parties in iframes, and try to exploit these and other Web features to launch attacks; similarly, honest websites may also include malicious websites. Additionally, we assume that the attacker can intercept sender-constrained access tokens. This is an implicit assumption when using token binding mechanisms, as otherwise, there is no need to use token binding. Such a leak of access tokens may happen for a number of reasons, e.g., due to a compromised RS (the token may be valid for multiple RSs), or through unsecured TLS intercepting proxy logs (considered, e.g., in [13]).

We refer to Sect. 4.4 for more details on the formalized security properties, and to Sect. 4.1 for more details on the attacker model.

3.2 Client Instance Mix-Up Attack

The client instance mix-up attack enables an attacker to access resources of an honest user, thus breaking the authorization property. We present three variants of this attack with different interaction start and finish methods using Fig. 2, but we also found variants with the user code start and push finish interaction, and with no interaction finish method used. Additionally, with the user code start methods, a variant of the attack based on social engineering rather than a man-in-the-middle is possible. Details on these versions of the attack can be found in our technical report [27].

Redirect/Redirect Interaction. In the first phase of the flow (up until Step 7 in Fig. 2), the attacker acts as a man-in-the-middle between an honest EU eu_h and an honest CI ci_h: eu_h starts a flow at the attacker's CI ci_a and wants to authorize ci_a to access a resource r managed by an honest AS as_h (Step 1). Instead of starting a grant with as_h, the attacker poses as an EU, starting a flow with as_h at ci_h to grant ci_h access to r (Step 2). Hence, ci_h sends a grant request to as_h (Step 3). Since the redirect interaction *finish* method is used, this grant request includes a URI *redirectUri$_{CI}$* to which the EU will be redirected by as_h once interaction between as_h and EU is completed. The grant response of as_h contains a URI *redirectUri$_{AS}$* which is associated with the ongoing grant (Step 4). This second URI is part of the redirect interaction *start* method. I.e., ci_h then instructs its end user (the attacker), to visit *redirectUri$_{AS}$* (Step 5).

The attacker, now again posing as ci_a to eu_h, does not visit *redirectUri$_{AS}$*, but instead instructs eu_h to do so (Step 6). Hence, eu_h authenticates and authorizes

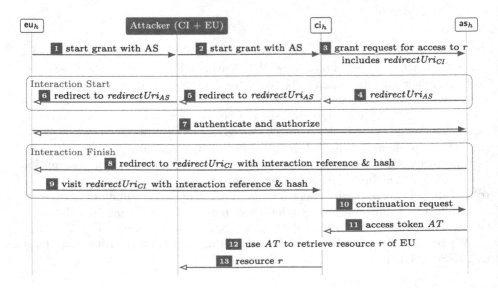

Fig. 2. Client Instance Mix-Up Attack (Redirect/Redirect interaction)

the request (Step $\boxed{7}$), as eu_h expected to be asked to authenticate and authorize access to r at that exact AS. However, from as_h's point of view, $redirectUri_{AS}$ is associated with the grant request sent by ci_h in Step $\boxed{3}$. Therefore, as_h now invokes the redirect interaction finish method and instructs eu_h to visit ci_h at $redirectUri_{CI}$, adding an interaction reference and interaction hash as URI parameters (Step $\boxed{8}$). Once again, eu_h complies, thus providing ci_h with interaction reference and interaction hash (Step $\boxed{9}$). Hence, ci_h can now request an access token (Step $\boxed{10}$). After receiving the access token in Step $\boxed{11}$, ci_h can access resource r of eu_h (Step $\boxed{12}$). However, from the point of view of ci_h, the access token, and thus r, are associated with the session between ci_h and the attacker posing as EU, hence giving the attacker access to r.

Redirect/Push Interaction. Similar problematic flows can occur with other interaction methods as well: If the *redirect* interaction start method is used with the *push* interaction finish method, the attack flow is identical to the one in Fig. 2 up to Step $\boxed{7}$—except for the grant request, which does not contain a redirect URI. Further, instead of redirecting the EU to ci_h (Steps $\boxed{8}$ and $\boxed{9}$), as_h sends a push notification with the interaction reference and hash directly to ci_h. Having received this push notification, ci_h sends a continuation request and the flow finishes as described above.

User Code/Redirect Interaction. When using the *user code* interaction start method with the *redirect* interaction finish method, the attack starts as before, but instead of including a redirection URI in its grant response (Step $\boxed{4}$), as_h includes a user code URI and a user code. Similar to the redirection URI shown in Fig. 2, these values are passed on to the attacker and from there to eu_h, who then visits the user code URI, enters the user code, authenticates, and authorizes the grant (similar to Step $\boxed{7}$). From there, the attack flow continues as depicted in Fig. 2: eu_h is redirected to ci_h, which sends a continuation request, receives an access token, and ultimately gives the attacker access to r.

Mitigations. There are conditions under which these attacks can be prevented: when using the *redirect* start and finish interaction methods with EUs which use a single browser for the whole interaction, the CI can establish a session with the EU's browser, e.g., by setting a session cookie, and verify that the browser initiating the flow is the same browser which is redirected to the CI by the AS. By implementing this fix for flows with browser-EUs using the *redirect* start and finish methods in our model, we were able to prove effectiveness of this fix.

In all other cases, the only reliable way to prevent this class of attacks is for the EU to only authorize CIs which the EU actually wants to authorize (see Step $\boxed{7}$ in Fig. 2), which requires the AS to provide enough (reliable) information about the CI, and the EU has to carefully inspect this information. We take this into account in our formal model, verifying that it is a sufficient check to prevent the attack.

We reported our findings, including the fix for the redirect/redirect case, to the GNAP WG [25], and helped to develop corresponding security guidance [26], which is now part of the GNAP specification [43, Sects. 13.22 & 13.23].

3.3 Further Attacks

During our formal analysis, we found further (classes of) attacks on GNAP, for which similar attack patterns are known from related protocols. We only mention these attacks here, but refer to our technical report [27] for full details.

We found one failure of authentication, where following a strict interpretation of the specification, the CI may not have enough information to uniquely identify user accounts. We also found a token replay attack, similar to the *Cuckoo's Token Attack* on the OpenID Financial-grade API [14], which can be mitigated by requiring clients to use different keys for each AS. A variant of the 307 redirect attack originally presented for OAuth [18] also applies to GNAP, which highlights the relevance of web-specific details to our analysis. It can be fixed by using the 303 redirect code in the redirect finish mode. All attacks and fixes were discussed with the GNAP WG and have been adopted as part of the GNAP specification [43, Sects. 3.4, 13.30, 13.16].

4   Formal Analysis

In this section, we present a high-level description of our formal security analysis of GNAP. Full details are provided in our technical report [27]. We first provide a brief overview of the WIM, which serves as a basis for our model of GNAP. We then describe our GNAP model in Sect. 4.2, which follows the latest version of the in-progress GNAP specifications for both the core protocol [43] and resource server behavior [44]. Our model includes the fixes presented in Sect. 3, which are now also part of the core GNAP specification. We then present formal definitions of the security properties sketched before (Sect. 4.4), followed by our main theorem, stating that GNAP is secure with respect to these properties.

4.1   Web Infrastructure Model (WIM)

Our model builds on the WIM of Fett, Küsters, and Schmitz, which was introduced in [15], and has since been extended and improved in later work (e.g. [11,14,16–19]). Our analysis is based on a consolidated version of the WIM [20]. We here only give a brief description of the WIM, sufficient to follow the paper, but all details can be found in [20]. We also note that in order to model GNAP, we have extended the WIM slightly to model the user-code interaction modes of GNAP, and by adding HTTP Message Signatures [3], including the Signature-Input and Signature HTTP headers. These extensions to the WIM are of independent interest, as they can be used for the analysis of other protocols.

The WIM is a formal model of the web infrastructure, designed to be general-purpose and allow for modelling various (web-based) applications. It closely follows published standards and specifications for the web, such as the HTTP/1.1

standard, for example. It provides a general communication model, which models, among other things, HTTP(S) requests and responses, including a variety of headers, such as Origin, Referer, Location, STS, Authorization, and Cookie headers. On top of this communication model, the WIM defines models for several types of processes, including web browsers, web servers, and DNS servers, as well as several forms of attacker processes. For example, the browser model covers the concepts of windows, documents, and iframes. It also has an abstract model of executable JavaScript, which can be sent between processes and executed by browsers, with access to a browser API, e.g., for postMessages, session and local storage, setting and reading headers, XMLHttpRequests, navigating and creating windows/iframes. Users interacting with a browser, e.g., clicking on a link or entering URLs, are modeled as non-deterministic actions of the browser that can be triggered by the attacker. In particular, this means that within our model, the GNAP end-user is subsumed by the browser.

4.2 Modeling GNAP

Since the WIM already formalizes the web infrastructure, to model applications we only need to specify application-specific processes, including scripts they use. Such application models are called *web systems* in the WIM.

Our model of GNAP therefore provides definitions of processes representing ASs, RSs, and CIs. Browsers are already specified in the core WIM – we only need to make some small modifications in order to model the user code interaction mode of GNAP and HTTP Message Signature. End-users are modelled by non-deterministic behaviour of browsers.

We call a web system a *GNAP web system*, denoted by $\mathcal{GWS}$, if it contains some arbitrary (but finite) number of instances of AS, RS, CI, and browser processes along with a network attacker process. Other than the attacker, all process instances are initially honest, i.e., they follow their given (GNAP) algorithms to take steps, but can become corrupted by the attacker at any time.

CIs and ASs are modeled in a straightforward way according to the specification of GNAP [43]. Our model includes a client script that initiates the protocol, and an AS script for authenticating the resource owner. For RSs we follow GNAP's resource server specification [44] for the pieces that are specified, and attempt to make minimal assumptions about RS behaviour otherwise in order to cover a wide variety of use cases.

As mentioned, the formal model presented in this section reflects the security considerations presented in the GNAP specification to avoid known attacks, particularly the fixes described in Sect. 3, which are necessary for our security properties to be provable.

In a real-world GNAP environment, participants may have diverse setups. For example, each CI has its own set of supported interaction methods. To account for all possible combinations of setups, we include them in two ways. Some parts are specified in the initial configuration of each process, e.g., private keys. Others are modeled by non-deterministic choices during the execution of processes. For example, for each new grant request, a CI chooses non-deterministically which interaction start and finish method to offer to the AS from the set of all available methods. We refer to our technical report [27] for our full formal model.

4.3 Modeling Considerations

While our model very closely follows the full GNAP specification, there are several places where we deviate from the GNAP specification. In some places we simplify and consider only a safe over-approximation. In others, we omit some pieces of the specification that are not security-relevant or are under-specified. Additionally, our model covers relevant security considerations recommended in the specification and all of our fixes to the attacks as described in Sect. 3. We will briefly discuss the key constraints and choices for our model (a full list can be found in our technical report [27, Appendix A.3]).

Simplifications. GNAP does not specify any particular resource access model, and so we use a simple model in which an access token issued for a given RO grants access to all of that owner's resources. This allows our model to avoid details of token management such as requests for multiple tokens, or requests to extend the rights of a token, while still being a safe over-approximation of real behavior. Since we use this simple resource access model, the RO does not need to be informed during interaction with the AS what access permissions it is being asked to authorize, and so our model does not need to include an explicit authorization step. As another safe over-approximation, we do not model token expiry or revocation — once a token is issued, it is valid forever.

Omissions Due to Under-Specification. While GNAP allows for both structured access tokens or opaque access tokens used in combination with token introspection, there is no specification for the format of structured access tokens, and so we have only modeled the case of opaque tokens together with token introspection.

Further, we only consider the case where the EU attempting to access a resource is the same as (or at least in direct out-of-band contact with) the RO. Otherwise, we have to model the case where an AS must get authorization from some third-party RO in order to complete a grant request. However, the details of such an interaction are out of scope of GNAP.

Security Considerations. We restrict the possible flows in our model by requiring the use of an interaction finish method. Allowing polling by the client instance can lead to AS mix-up attacks. To avoid this, we follow the recommendation of the corresponding security consideration [43, Sect. 13.22] and do not include polling in our model.

4.4 Definitions and Security Properties

This background is now sufficient to begin formalizing the security properties GNAP is supposed to satisfy. We focus here on the case of authorization, giving only a brief overview of authentication. We also, for simplicity of presentation, elide some of the technical details here. Full details can be found in our technical report [27].

Security with Respect to Authorization. As mentioned before, this property states that an attacker should not be able to access the resources of an honest resource owner. There are several immediate problems with this intuition.

Most obviously, if the RO stores its resources on an RS that is corrupted by the attacker, there is no hope of security, as the RS can simply give the attacker access to any resources it stores. Likewise, the RO and the AS responsible for the resource need to be honest. A few other simple problems can lead to security failures as well. If an RO authorizes a corrupt CI to access its resources, then the attacker naturally can learn those resources. Likewise, if the AS validly issues a bearer token (see Sect. 2) to a CI, and that CI then attempts to use the token at a corrupt RS, any security associated with that token is lost. Finally, and more subtly, if a CI shares a symmetric key with an honest AS and a corrupted RS, that RS can take over a session between the CI and AS, by impersonating the CI to the AS, and can thereby gain access to resources without permission.

A few definitions allowing us to relate ROs and ASs and to refer to the situation where a browser attempts to authorize a grant request at an AS (Step $\boxed{5}$ of Fig. 1) will be useful in stating our security properties:

Definition 1. *We identify resource owners by* identities. *An identity u consists of a name and a domain for some process. We think of this domain as indicating what AS manages an account, and the name as some identifier of that account at the manager. Given an identity u, we define* governor(u) *to be the AS responsible for that identity (and its resources). We also define* ownerOfID(u) *to be the browser controlling the identity u (i.e., the browser used by the end user to whom the identity corresponds). This can be formalized by requiring that each identity u has an associated secret credential, which is initially known only to the governor of u and some browser. That browser is then* ownerOfID(u).

Definition 2. *If, during step i of a run ρ (a sequence of configurations consisting of process states, waiting messages, and a pool of fresh nonces, see [20]), a browser b attempts to authenticate, i.e., log-in, using identity u at a process* as, *in order to authorize a client* ci, *we write* tryLogin$_\rho^i(b, \text{ci}, u, \text{as})$.

We can now define the authorization property for GNAP.

Definition 3 (Security w.r.t Authorization). *Let $\mathcal{GWS}$ be a GNAP web system. We say that $\mathcal{GWS}$ is secure w.r.t. authorization iff the following implication holds, where ρ denotes a run of $\mathcal{GWS}$, j is a timestamp within ρ, u is an identity (of some RO), and RS rs stores a resource r_u on behalf of u: Given conditions*

(1)–(5), the attacker cannot derive r_u from its knowledge at time j, where conditions (1)–(5) are defined as follows: (1) rs is honest at j; (2) governor(u) *is honest at j; (3)* ownerOfID(u) *is honest at j; (4) for every CI* ci *which is honest at j, a symmetric key shared between* ci *and* governor(u) *is not also shared with a corrupted RS rs'; (5) if for some $i \leq j$,* tryLogin$_\rho^i$(ownerOfID(u), ci, u, governor(u)), *then* ci *is honest at j and, if this login succeeds and grants* ci *a bearer token, then* ci *does not send this token to a corrupted RS rs'.*

Each of the five premises in the implication above corresponds to one of the situations described before where security would necessarily fail. This property then states that other than the simple, relatively apparent failures of security when some parties in the protocol are dishonest, there is no way for an attacker to derive a resource belonging to an honest user.

Security w.r.t. Authentication. This property is similar in many respects to security with respect to authorization. Informally, we want to ensure that an attacker is not able to log in to an honest client as an honest user. As with authorization, if certain parties are corrupt, this property immediately fails: A corrupt client can allow the attacker to log in as any user, a corrupt end user can log in on behalf of the attacker, and a corrupt AS can authenticate logins for any account it manages. Since these kinds of failures are unavoidable for any protocol, our formal security property needs to rule them out, only ensuring that an attacker is not logged in as an honest user at an honest client when the AS responsible for the account is also honest.

Session Integrity. In addition to these properties capturing that the attacker should not be able to access honest user's resources or accounts, session integrity (for both authorization and authentication) captures the intuitive idea that an honest user should not be forced to access the attacker's resources or accounts. Informally, if an honest user accesses a resource or is logged in with some account, then the user authorized that resource access or authenticated for that login. We formalize session integrity for authorization with the definition below, leaving the case of authentication to our technical report [27].

Definition 4. *Let $\mathcal{GWS}$ be a GNAP web system. We say that $\mathcal{GWS}$ has session integrity for authorization iff the following implication holds, where ρ is a run of $\mathcal{GWS}$, j is a timestamp in ρ, u is an identity (of some RO), and where we assume that an RS rs stores a resource r_u on behalf of u, and a client c sends r_u to a browser b: If c, rs,* governor(u), *and* ownerOfID(u) *are honest at j, then at some prior point, c began a GNAP flow at some as on behalf of b. Moreover, if as is honest, then there is some $i < j$ such that* tryLogin$_\rho^i(b, c, u,$ governor$(u))$.*

In this definition, we mention two potentially different authorization servers (*as* and governor(u)). This is because, in principle, nothing prevents a GNAP client from being directed from one AS to another over the course of a GNAP flow. Without this constraint that the initial AS in the flow is honest, some strange flows are possible, in which, for instance, an attacker may be able to force the end user to access resources which the attacker owns, but which are controlled by an honest AS. We discussed this problematic flow with the GNAP editors [9]. In their opinion, considering only cases where the initial AS is honest, is not a restriction. However, they will add a security consideration to the resource server specification explaining the problematic flow.

4.5   Results

Our key result is that the current GNAP specification including all our fixes satisfies the security properties set out in Sect. 4.4. We state the result in the following theorem, but as the proof is extensive (consisting of just under 30 separate lemmas), and obviously depends on details of the model, we leave it to our technical report [27].

Theorem 1. *Every GNAP web system $\mathcal{GWS}$ is secure with respect to authorization and authentication, and also has session integrity with respect to authorization and authentication.*

This means that even in the presence of a strong attacker which controls the network, observing all messages and determining when and to whom they are delivered, and which can corrupt other parties on the network, GNAP ensures that users are protected from a wide variety of attacks. In particular, attackers cannot access a user's resources or account unless some failure which is outside the scope of the protocol occurs (e.g. the user willingly gives their credentials to the attacker, or the attacker takes over a server on which the user's resources or account data is stored). Similarly, a user cannot be forced to access an attacker's resources or account through the GNAP protocol.

We highlight that our analysis accounts for many Web features that might possibly cause attacks, e.g., cookie management, in-browser communication using postMessages, HTTP redirect behavior, various headers, or the window and document structure of browsers, including iframes. The 307 redirect attack is an example where seemingly irrelevant details matter. Furthermore, the web system that our analysis considers can have an arbitrary number of CIs, ASs, and RSs, and parallel flows between them. Moreover, parties can be corrupted by the attacker at any time, and honest participants may communicate with corrupted ones, as the properties hold even if, for instance, an honest CI uses some corrupted ASs.

5   Related Work

To the best of our knowledge, our work is the first formal security analysis of GNAP. Axeland and Oueidat [2], informally analyze GNAP by testing the protocol against five attack classes known for OAuth 2.0 and conclude that most of those do not apply to GNAP, except for an AS mix-up attack [18]. They also only consider the redirect interaction modes.

To date, the WIM is the most detailed and expressive model of Web infrastructure, and as already mentioned, has successfully been used to analyze a variety of protocols, including several in the OAuth family [14,18,19], as well as Mozilla Browser ID [15,16] and the W3C Web Payment APIs [11]. All of the analyses using the WIM, including ours, rely on manual proofs. To the best of our knowledge, there is no mechanized model of the Web with a level of detail comparable to the WIM yet. Building such a model is a challenging future task. Existing tool-based analysis is based on far more limited models, mostly without taking web features into account or in an only very limited way: [4] use ProVerif [7] to analyze OAuth 2.0, considering some features of the Web infrastructure like cookies and origins. However, they focus on finding attacks and do not aim to provide security guarantees. In [40] the Alloy Analyzer [29] is used to analyze OAuth 2.0, [1] use Tamarin [37] to analyze an abstract model of ACE-OAuth [54] (a flow specifically designed for IoT devices), and Hofmeier [28] models OpenID Connect in Tamarin. The models created for these analyses, as well as the models of the underlying web infrastructure, are very limited.

6   Conclusion

We performed the first formal security analysis of GNAP. To this end, we built a detailed formal model of GNAP based on the WIM, which includes several start and finish interaction methods, both the software-only and end-user cases, arbitrary numbers of continuation requests, grant negotiation between CI and AS, token introspection, key-bound and bearer access tokens, subject information grants, different key proof methods, all while accounting for details of the Web infrastructure like different HTTP redirection codes, JavaScript running in browsers, important HTTP headers, and so on.

We formalized central security properties and tried to prove them, but discovered attacks that break them. These attacks were reported to the IETF's GNAP Working Group along with proposed fixes, which are now part of the specifications and which we incorporated into our formal model and proved that the fixed model fulfills the security properties. As our model accounts for many Web features, our security proof excludes large classes of attacks, even in the presence of a network attacker that can use all web features, e.g., provide malicious scripts, manipulate headers, etc., and can get hold of (sender-constrained) access tokens, and even if an unlimited number of users, CIs, ASs, and RSs, all of which the adversary can corrupt at any point, operate with an unlimited number of parallel sessions.

Considering GNAP's progress towards an IETF standard with the core specification being in the Working Group Last Call at the time of this writing, our analysis is just in time to support the standardization of an important protocol in terms of its security. Our work also shows that formal analysis in a meaningful and rich model is necessary for complex protocols, like GNAP, as even very experienced protocol designers easily overlook not only new attacks but also attacks previously found on related protocols.

Acknowledgements. This research was supported by the DFG through grant KU 1434/12-1.

References

1. Arnaboldi, L., Tschofenig, H.: A formal model for delegated authorization of IoT devices using ace-oauth. In: 4th OAuth Security Workshop (2019). https://homepages.inf.ed.ac.uk/larnibol/img/publications/Paper-03.pdf
2. Axeland, A., Oueidat, O.: Security analysis of attack surfaces on the grant negotiation and authorization protocol, Master's thesis, Chalmers University of Technology, University of Gothenburg (2021). https://odr.chalmers.se/items/7d36a5d4-c295-4270-886b-d5ed1154a8e8
3. Backman, A., Richer, J., Sporny, M.: HTTP message signatures. Internet-Draft draft-ietf-httpbis-message-signatures-15, Internet Engineering Task Force (2022). https://datatracker.ietf.org/doc/draft-ietf-httpbis-message-signatures/15/, work in Progress
4. Bansal, C., Bhargavan, K., Delignat-Lavaud, A., Maffeis, S.: Discovering concrete attacks on website authorization by formal analysis. J. Comput. Secur. **22**(4), 601–657 (2014)
5. Bansal, C., Bhargavan, K., Maffeis, S.: Discovering concrete attacks on website authorization by formal analysis. In: Chong, S. (ed.) 25th IEEE Computer Security Foundations Symposium, CSF 2012, pp. 247–262. IEEE Computer Society (2012)
6. Bertocci, V.: JSON Web Token (JWT) Profile for OAuth 2.0 Access Tokens. RFC 9068 (2021). https://doi.org/10.17487/RFC9068, https://www.rfc-editor.org/info/rfc9068
7. Blanchet, B.: An efficient cryptographic protocol verifier based on prolog rules. In: Proceedings of the 14th IEEE Computer Security Foundations Workshop (CSFW-14), pp. 82–96. IEEE Computer Society (2001)
8. Campbell, B., Bradley, J., Sakimura, N., Lodderstedt, T.: OAuth 2.0 mutual-TLS client authentication and certificate-bound access tokens. RFC 8705 (2020). https://doi.org/10.17487/RFC8705, https://www.rfc-editor.org/info/rfc8705
9. cwaldm: Issue 56 - RS validation of access token. GitHub Issue (2022). https://github.com/ietf-wg-gnap/gnap-resource-servers/issues/56
10. Denniss, W., Bradley, J., Jones, M., Tschofenig, H.: OAuth 2.0 device authorization grant. RFC 8628 (2019). https://doi.org/10.17487/RFC8628, https://rfc-editor.org/rfc/rfc8628.txt
11. Do, Q.H., Hosseyni, P., Küsters, R., Schmitz, G., Wenzler, N., Würtele, T.: A formal security analysis of the W3C web payment APIs: attacks and verification. In: 43rd IEEE Symposium on Security and Privacy (S&P 2022), vol. 1, pp. 134–153. IEEE Computer Society (2022). https://doi.org/10.1109/SP46214.2022.9833681
12. Dropbox Platform Team: Oauth guide. https://developers.dropbox.com/oauth-guide (2020)
13. Fett, D.: FAPI 2.0 attacker model, draft 02. OpenID Foundation (2022). https://openid.net/specs/fapi-2_0-attacker-model-02.html
14. Fett, D., Hosseyni, P., Küsters, R.: An extensive formal security analysis of the OpenID financial-grade API. In: 40th IEEE Symposium on Security and Privacy (S&P 2019), pp. 1054–1072. IEEE Computer Society, Los Alamitos, CA, USA (2019). https://doi.org/10.1109/SP.2019.00067, https://doi.ieeecomputersociety.org/10.1109/SP.2019.00067

15. Fett, D., Küsters, R., Schmitz, G.: An expressive model for the web infrastructure: definition and application to the BrowserID SSO system. In: 35th IEEE Symposium on Security and Privacy (S&P 2014), pp. 673–688. IEEE Computer Society (2014)

16. Fett, D., Küsters, R., Schmitz, G.: Analyzing the BrowserID SSO system with primary identity providers using an expressive model of the web. In: Pernul, G., Ryan, P.Y.A., Weippl, E. (eds.) ESORICS 2015. LNCS, vol. 9326, pp. 43–65. Springer, Cham (2015). https://doi.org/10.1007/978-3-319-24174-6_3

17. Fett, D., Küsters, R., Schmitz, G.: SPRESSO: a secure, privacy-respecting single sign-on system for the web. In: Proceedings of the 22nd ACM SIGSAC Conference on Computer and Communications Security, Denver, CO, USA, October 12–6, 2015, pp. 1358–1369. ACM (2015)

18. Fett, D., Küsters, R., Schmitz, G.: A comprehensive formal security analysis of OAuth 2.0. In: Proceedings of the 23nd ACM SIGSAC Conference on Computer and Communications Security (CCS 2016), pp. 1204–1215. ACM (2016)

19. Fett, D., Küsters, R., Schmitz, G.: The web SSO standard OpenID connect: in-depth formal security analysis and security guidelines. In: IEEE 30th Computer Security Foundations Symposium (CSF 2017). IEEE Computer Society (2017)

20. Fett, D., Küsters, R., Schmitz, G.: The web infrastructure model (WIM) (2022). https://www.sec.uni-stuttgart.de/research/wim/WIM_V1.0.pdf

21. GitHub docs: authorizing oauth apps (2023). https://docs.github.com/en/developers/apps/building-oauth-apps/authorizing-oauth-apps

22. Google: Oauth 2.0 for tv and limited-input device applications (2022). https://developers.google.com/identity/protocols/oauth2/limited-input-device

23. Google: using oauth 2.0 to access google APIs (2022). https://developers.google.com/identity/protocols/oauth2

24. Hardt (ed.), D.: The OAuth 2.0 authorization framework. RFC 6749 (2012). https://doi.org/10.17487/RFC6749, https://rfc-editor.org/rfc/rfc6749.txt

25. Helmschmidt, F.: Issue 364 - End user/client instance mix-up attack. GitHub Issue (2021). https://github.com/ietf-wg-gnap/gnap-core-protocol/issues/364

26. Helmschmidt, F.: Issue 390 - Clarified user presence on interaction finish methods. GitHub Commit (2022). https://github.com/ietf-wg-gnap/gnap-core-protocol/pull/390/commits/b028a1e363e90ad1c2711bd8244ea76e3957f935

27. Helmschmidt, F., Hosseyni, P., Kuesters, R., Pruiksma, K., Waldmann, C., Würtele, T.: The grant negotiation and authorization protocol: attacking, fixing, and verifying an emerging standard. Cryptology ePrint Archive, Paper 2023/1325 (2023). https://eprint.iacr.org/2023/1325

28. Hofmeier, X.: Formal analysis of web single-sign on protocols using TAMARIN. Bachelor's thesis, Swiss Federal Institute of Technology in Zurich, Switzerland (2019)

29. Jackson, D., Schechter, I., Shlyakhter, I.: Alcoa: the alloy constraint analyzer. In: Ghezzi, C., Jazayeri, M., Wolf, A.L. (eds.) Proceedings of the 22nd International Conference on on Software Engineering, ICSE 2000, Limerick Ireland, June 4–11, 2000, pp. 730–733. ACM (2000). https://doi.org/10.1145/337180.337616

30. Jones, M.B., Bradley, J., Sakimura, N.: JSON Web Signature (JWS). RFC 7515 (2015). https://doi.org/10.17487/RFC7515, https://www.rfc-editor.org/info/rfc7515

31. Kasselman, P., Fett, D., Skokan, F.: Cross-device flows: security best current practice. Internet-Draft draft-ietf-oauth-cross-device-security-00, Internet Engineering Task Force (2022). https://datatracker.ietf.org/doc/draft-ietf-oauth-cross-device-security/00/, work in Progress

32. Limited, O.B.: Open Banking UK (2022). https://www.openbanking.org.uk/
33. Lodderstedt, T., Bradley, J., Labunets, A., Fett, D.: OAuth 2.0 security best current practice. Internet-Draft draft-ietf-oauth-security-topics-21, Internet Engineering Task Force (2022). https://datatracker.ietf.org/doc/html/draft-ietf-oauth-security-topics-21, work in Progress
34. Lodderstedt, T., Campbell, B., Sakimura, N., Tonge, D., Skokan, F.: OAuth 2.0 pushed authorization requests. RFC 9126 (2021). https://doi.org/10.17487/RFC9126, https://www.rfc-editor.org/info/rfc9126
35. Machulak, M., Richer, J.: User-managed access (UMA) 2.0 grant for OAuth 2.0 authorization (2018). https://docs.kantarainitiative.org/uma/wg/rec-oauth-uma-grant-2.0.html
36. Mainka, C., Mladenov, V., Schwenk, J., Wich, T.: SoK: single sign-on security — an evaluation of OpenID connect. In: IEEE European Symposium on Security and Privacy, EuroS&P 2017, Paris, France, April 26–28, 2017 (2017)
37. Meier, S., Schmidt, B., Cremers, C., Basin, D.: The TAMARIN prover for the symbolic analysis of security protocols. In: Sharygina, N., Veith, H. (eds.) CAV 2013. LNCS, vol. 8044, pp. 696–701. Springer, Heidelberg (2013). https://doi.org/10.1007/978-3-642-39799-8_48
38. Meta for developers documents: facebook login for the web with the JavaScript SDK (2023). https://developers.facebook.com/docs/facebook-login/web/
39. Mladenov, V., Mainka, C., Krautwald, J., Feldmann, F., Schwenk, J.: On the security of modern single sign-on protocols: second-order vulnerabilities in OpenID connect. CoRR abs/1508.04324v2, http://arxiv.org/abs/1508.04324v2 (2016)
40. Pai, S., Sharma, Y., Kumar, S., Pai, R.M., Singh, S.: Formal verification of OAuth 2.0 using alloy framework. In: CSNT 2011 Proceedings of the 2011 International Conference on Communication Systems and Network Technologies, pp. 655–659. Proceedings of the International Conference on Communication Systems and Network Technologies (2011)
41. Rescorla, E.: The transport layer security (TLS) protocol version 1.3. RFC 8446 (2018). https://doi.org/10.17487/RFC8446, https://www.rfc-editor.org/info/rfc8446
42. Richer, J.: Moving on from OAuth 2: a proposal (2018). https://justinsecurity.medium.com/moving-on-from-oauth-2-629a00133ade
43. Richer, J., Imbault, F.: Grant negotiation and authorization protocol. Internet-Draft draft-ietf-gnap-core-protocol-15, Internet Engineering Task Force (2023). https://datatracker.ietf.org/doc/draft-ietf-gnap-core-protocol/15/, work in Progress
44. Richer, J., Imbault, F.: Grant negotiation and authorization protocol resource server connections. Internet-Draft draft-ietf-gnap-resource-servers-03, Internet Engineering Task Force (2023). https://datatracker.ietf.org/doc/draft-ietf-gnap-resource-servers/03/, work in Progress
45. Richer, J., Parecki, A., Imbault, F.: Grant negotiation and authorization protocol. Internet-Draft draft-ietf-gnap-core-protocol-08, Internet Engineering Task Force (2021). https://datatracker.ietf.org/doc/draft-ietf-gnap-core-protocol/08/, work in Progress
46. Richer, J., Parecki, A., Imbault, F.: Grant negotiation and authorization protocol resource server connections. Internet-Draft draft-ietf-gnap-resource-servers-02, Internet Engineering Task Force (2022). https://datatracker.ietf.org/doc/draft-ietf-gnap-resource-servers/02/, work in Progress
47. Richer (ed.), J.: OAuth 2.0 token introspection. RFC 7662 (2015). https://doi.org/10.17487/RFC7662, https://rfc-editor.org/rfc/rfc7662.txt

48. Richer (ed.), J., Jones, M., Bradley, J., Machulak, M.: OAuth 2.0 dynamic client registration management protocol. RFC 7592 (2015). https://doi.org/10.17487/RFC7592, https://rfc-editor.org/rfc/rfc7592.txt

49. Richer, J., Jones, M., Bradley, J., Machulak, M., Hunt, P.: OAuth 2.0 dynamic client registration protocol. RFC 7591 (2015). https://doi.org/10.17487/RFC7591, https://rfc-editor.org/rfc/rfc7591.txt

50. Sakimura, N., Bradley, J., Jay, E.: Financial-grade API security profile 1.0 - part 1: baseline (2021). https://openid.net/specs/openid-financial-api-part-1-1_0.html, openID Foundation

51. Sakimura, N., Bradley, J., Jay, E.: Financial-grade API security profile 1.0 - part 2: advanced (2021). https://openid.net/specs/openid-financial-api-part-2-1_0.html, openID Foundation

52. Sakimura, N., Bradley, J., Jones, M., de Medeiros, B., Mortimore, C.: OpenID connect core 1.0 incorporating errata set 1 (2014). http://openid.net/specs/openid-connect-core-1_0.html, openID Foundation

53. Sakimura (ed.), N., Bradley, J., Agarwal, N.: Proof key for code exchange by OAuth public clients. RFC 7636 (2015). https://doi.org/10.17487/RFC7636, https://rfc-editor.org/rfc/rfc7636.txt

54. Seitz, L., Selander, G., Wahlstroem, E., Erdtman, S., Tschofenig, H.: Authentication and authorization for constrained environments using the OAuth 2.0 framework (ACE-OAuth). RFC 9200 (2022). https://doi.org/10.17487/RFC9200, https://www.rfc-editor.org/info/rfc9200

55. Sheffer, Y.: GNAP core protocol - publication has been requested. GNAP Mailing List (2023). https://mailarchive.ietf.org/arch/msg/txauth/4q2W9cTho2chk4IunHKXztcorO0/

56. Yang, R., Li, G., Lau, W.C., Zhang, K., Hu, P.: Model-based security testing: an empirical study on OAuth 2.0 implementations. In: Proceedings of the 11th ACM on Asia Conference on Computer and Communications Security. ACM (2016). https://doi.org/10.1145/2897845.2897874

Everlasting ROBOT: The Marvin Attack

Hubert Kario[(⊠)] [iD]

Red Hat Czech S.r.o, Purkyňova 115, 61200 Brno, Czech Republic
hkario@redhat.com

Abstract. In this paper we show that Bleichenbacher-style attacks on RSA decryption are not only still possible, but also that vulnerable implementations are common. We have successfully attacked multiple implementations using only timing of decryption operation and shown that many others are vulnerable. To perform the attack we used more statistically rigorous techniques like the sign test, Wilcoxon signed-rank test, and bootstrapping of median of pairwise differences. We publish a set of tools for testing libraries that perform RSA decryption against timing side-channel attacks, including one that can test arbitrary TLS servers with no need to write a test harnesses. Finally, we propose a set of workarounds that implementations can employ if they can't avoid the use of RSA.

Keywords: Side-channel attacks · timing attacks · Bleichenbacher attack · RSA

1 Introduction

While the web traffic increasingly depends on the new ECDSA cryptosystem, majority of server certificates still use the RSA cryptosystem that was originally published in 1977. RSA saw first big use with the deployment of the Netscape Navigator 1.0 browser in 1994, as part of the SSL 2.0 protocol. Soon after that, in 1998, Daniel Bleichenbacher published a practical attack [2] on an SSL server due to both the faulty PKCS#1 v1.5 padding scheme and faults in the SSL protocol.

This was only the first of many attacks that followed. Large contributions to attacking RSA made by Manger [7] in 2001, Klíma, Pokorný, et al. [6] in 2003, Bardou et al. [1] in 2012, Meyer, Somorovsky, et al. [9] in 2014.

Despite those and other attacks being published, and an updated (also in 1998) version of the PKCS# 1 including the OAEP padding scheme, which is much more resistant against the attack published by Bleichenbacher, the vulnerable PKCS#1 v1.5 padding still remains in widespread use.

The SSL and TLS protocols never received an update to use the OAEP padding scheme for the RSA key exchange. It was only version 1.3 of the protocol, published in 2018, that completely removed support for this key exchange [15].

Many other widely used cryptographic protocols, like S/MIME or JSON Web Tokens (JWT) [13], still allow use of PKCS#1 v1.5 padding for encryption.

G. Tsudik et al. (Eds.): ESORICS 2023, LNCS 14346, pp. 243–262, 2024.
https://doi.org/10.1007/978-3-031-51479-1_13

Despite the original attack being nearly quarter of a century old, and the tested implementations (OpenSSL, NSS, GnuTLS) having been tested and included additional fixes in 2019 thanks to the work of Ronen et al. [16], we found them, and others, to be still vulnerable.

As it's a continuation of the ROBOT vulnerability [3], which we don't expect to get rid of any time soon, we've decided to name it after one everlasting "Paranoid Android".

1.1   Contributions

Our work makes the following contributions:

- We show that by using correct statistical methods and proper test setup, detection of side channels in RSA implementations is robust
- We show that multiple popular implementations, including ones previously tested, are still vulnerable to attacks utilising timing based oracles, both over loopback and over regular Ethernet networks.
- We publish a set of tools for testers of cryptographic libraries for checking the timing of APIs providing RSA decryption with minimal dependencies.
- For implementations which can't remove support for PKCS#1 v1.5 encryption, we propose an alternative decryption algorithm, which does not require side-channel free code on the application side.

2   Adaptive Chosen Ciphertext Attacks

The Bleichenbacher attack allows decrypting arbitrary RSA ciphertexts or forging signatures when the attacker can learn some information about specially crafted ciphertexts, related to the ciphertext they want to decrypt [2].

The attack works thanks to few properties of the RSA cryptosystem:

- the RSA encryption is homomorphic with regards to multiplication,
- the PKCS#1 v1.5 padding requires specific values of the two most significant bytes: 0 and 2, but not for the whole padding,
- learning about PKCS#1 v1.5 conformance of a related ciphertext provides specific bounds on the value of the plaintext we want to decrypt.

Homomorphism in RSA Cryptosystem. Let e and n be the RSA public key (with e representing the public exponent and n representing the modulus), and let d be the corresponding secret key (the private exponent).

The RSA encryption operation of a message m is equal to $m^e \mod n$, giving ciphertext c. The RSA decryption operation of the ciphertext c is equal to $c^d \mod n$.

See the PKCS#1 [14] specification for information on how n, d, and e are related to each-other, but it's not necessary to understand the attack.

Now, when we introduce some number s, then by calculating $c' = s^e c \mod n$ we effectively multiply the plaintext m by s, as $c' = s^e m^e = (sm)^e \mod n$. We can do that even when we don't know the value of m, just the value of it after encryption: c. Thus, we can multiply an arbitrary encrypted value by a value we know, just by having access to the public key.

PKCS#1 Padding. In the original attack [2], the attacker learns only whether or not a ciphertext decrypts to a correctly padded PKCS#1 v1.5 plaintext.

A plaintext is correctly padded when the number m converted to a big-endian representation of same size as the modulus n consists of 8-bit bytes as follows: 0x00, 0x02, PS, 0x00, P. Additionally the string PS consists of at least 8 bytes, none with value 0. The string P can include bytes of value 0 and can also be empty.

That means, that if a ciphertext is PKCS#1 conforming, we know that it decrypts to a value $2B \leq ms \bmod n < 3B$, where $B = 2^{8(k-2)}$ and k is the number of bytes necessary to represent n as as a big-endian integer (i.e. it's larger or equal to 0x000200...00, but smaller than 0x000300..00).

Bleichenbacher Attack. Note that if we know that $c \cdot s^e \bmod n$ is PKCS #1 conforming, it means that $m \cdot s \bmod n \in [2B, 3B)$. That implies that there is an integer r such that $2B \leq m \cdot s - r \cdot n < 3B$. Equivalently:

$$\frac{2B + rn}{s} \leq m < \frac{3B + rn}{s} \tag{1}$$

By finding multiple s numbers, we find multiple r values, which provide more and more restrictive ranges of m.

See the original analysis [2] for some optimisations on how to find values of s that are more likely to create PKCS conforming ciphertexts.

While the original paper required about one million calls to the oracle (checks if a message is PKCS#1 conforming or not), more recent analysis performed by Bardou et al. [1] shows that as few as 3800 oracle queries may be enough to decrypt a 1024 bit message.

RSA OAEP Encryption. PKCS#1 version 2.0 [10] specified a different padding format for RSA encryption intended to defeat attacks like the one proposed by Bleichenbacher.

While the standard specifies that the decryption needs to ignore the value of the most significant byte of plaintext, some implementations do not do that. This causes them to be vulnerable to a similar attack as the one with PKCS#1 v1.5 padding, as shown by Manger [7]. That attack requires as little as $\log_2 n$ oracle calls, where n is the RSA modulus, to perform a ciphertext decryption.

More General Plaintext Oracle. Meyer et al. [9] extended the attack algorithm to knowledge about arbitrary bytes of the message. In their example the oracle responds positively for any PKCS#1 plaintext that starts with arbitrary byte, not just 0x00, but still requires the second byte to be equal 0x02.

Attack Summary. The different attacks on RSA ciphertexts show that leaking any kind of information about the plaintext allows the attacker to decrypt ciphertexts or sign messages without access to the private key.

In particular, while alternative padding methods, like OAEP, help, they're not a panacea. Processing of any plaintext values, or variables directly related to the plaintext values, still must be performed in a way that does not leak information about the secret values.

3   Performed Attacks

As an attacker, we can easily create RSA ciphertexts that decrypt to specific plaintext: by simply encrypting the value we want the deblinding and depadding code to see. By sending such crafted ciphertexts to an implementation under test and measuring the times it takes to process them, we can tell if certain classes of plaintexts don't reveal different code paths taken.

By performing the measurements in double-blind fashion (making sure that the test runner is constant-time), where neither the test harness not the tested server can guess the PKCS#1 conformance of the decrypted plaintext, and by using paired difference tests (sign test or Wilcoxon signed rank test), which can be used with non-independent measurements, we can detect even very small differences in processing time compared to the observed noise and absolute measurement values.

3.1   M2Crypto

The M2Crypto library is a thin wrapper around the OpenSSL library. It allows easy access to some of the interfaces of the OpenSSL library from python applications.

One of the APIs supported is the `rsa_private_decrypt`, providing decryption of PKCS#1 v1.5 formatted ciphertexts. Unfortunately, when the underlying OpenSSL API returns an error, M2Crypto translates it to a Python exception (`M2Crypto.RSA.RSAError`). That means that PKCS#1 conforming and PKCS#1 non-conforming ciphertexts will have significantly different code paths executed.

In practical attack, with 1024 bit RSA keys, performed on a regular laptop computer (Lenovo T480s, Intel i7-8650U), with no special configuration and with regular desktop environment running, we were able to differentiate with extremely high confidence (sign test p-values smaller than 10^{-60}) conforming and non-conforming ciphertexts by measuring as little as 1000 decryptions of each. This is caused by fairly large median difference between conforming and non-conforming plaintexts, measuring around $0.6\,\mu s$, when the whole API call takes around $155\,\mu s$.

With this leak we were able to decrypt a ciphertext using an unoptimised algorithm (i.e. the original one published by Bleichenbacher) in 163 thousand oracle calls, or in about 9 h of real time on a regular machine.

The issue was reported to the M2Crypto maintainers in October of 2020 and was assigned the CVE-2020-25657. A partial fix to it was implemented[1] but it does not make the code paths of conforming and non-conforming ciphertexts identical. While we haven't tested this new code, we believe it to still be vulnerable.

3.2 pyca/cryptography

The pyca/cryptography is a newer wrapper library providing access to OpenSSL from Python. Similarly to M2Crypto, it too supports the RSA decryption with PKCS#1 v1.5 padding. For that we've used the decrypt() method of the RSAPrivateKey object.

Just like M2Crypto, pyca/cryptography raises an exception in case of malformed PKCS#1 plaintext. That means it is also vulnerable to timing attacks.

We've measured the difference between conforming and non-conforming ciphertexts of around 7.5 µs on an Intel 4790K @ 4.4 GHz when using 1024 bit RSA keys (with a processing time of about 105 µs). With such a huge difference, only 100 measurements were necessary to discern conforming ciphertexts from and non-conforming ones. In practice, on an unoptimised desktop system, with the original Bleichenbacher algorithm (median of 163 thousand oracle calls) the whole decryption took a bit under 4 h.

The issue was reported to the pyca/cryptography maintainers on 17th of October 2020 as being present in version 3.1.1 of the library. It was assigned the CVE-2020-25659. A partial workaround was developed[2] and shipped as part of version 3.2.

Given that the API throws an exception when OpenSSL returns an error, it's likely still vulnerable; it is now documented though as insecure[3].

3.3 Other High-Level Language Libraries

While we haven't tested other cryptographic library wrappers, we think that any libraries that return errors in fundamentally different way than a successful return from a call will provide a timing oracle for Bleichenbacher like attacks.

Similarly, CVE-2020-25659 and CVE-2020-25657 show that safe use of the RSA PKCS#1 v1.5 API is complex and error-prone.

3.4 NSS

Mozilla NSS is the cryptographic library used by the Firefox browser. As a general-purpose library, it provides support for both TLS ciphersuites that use

---

[1] https://gitlab.com/m2crypto/m2crypto/-/commit/84c53958def0f510e92119fca1 4d74f94215827a.

[2] https://github.com/pyca/cryptography/commit/58494b41d6ecb0f56b7c5f05d5f5e 3ca0320d494.

[3] https://cryptography.io/en/latest/limitations/#rsa-pkcs1-v1-5-constant-time-decryption.

RSA key exchange and a general purpose API for performing PKCS#1 v1.5 decryption.

One interesting aspect of this library is that it uses a PKCS#11 interface between the implementations of the cryptographic algorithms and rest of the library, like the TLS implementation. PKCS#11 is more commonly used as the API to communicate with cryptographic tokens (like smart cards and hardware security modules).

We've tested NSS on the TLS level, as that did not require creation of any test harness, effectively performing a black-box test. Additionally, that allowed us to perform an end-to-end test of the whole processing of the secret data: from reading the ciphertext, through decryption, depadding, derivation of the symmetric encryption keys to sending the TLS Alert message.

We've executed the test on a highly optimised machine, setup of which is described in appendix A, with an Intel i9-12900KS.

By running the test on such a system with a 2048 bit RSA key we found (see Fig. 2) that the NSS library has very significant leakage, providing 3 easily distinguishable classes of ciphertexts: ones that decrypt to PKCS#1 conforming plaintext with the message being correct size for TLS pre-master secret (48 bytes), ones that decrypt to PKCS#1 conforming plaintext but with incorrect message size (either shorter or longer than 48 bytes), and ones that decrypt to non-conforming plaintexts.

The statistical tests are providing statistically significant results (p-value for sign test smaller than 10^{-4}) for samples that have just 100 observations per class, with Friedman test p-values for the whole test with 31 classes being regularly smaller than 10^{-9} for the same data set.

Based on similar results against version 3.53 of NSS we've informed Mozilla on 16th of June 2020 that the bug #577498[4] is exploitable.

After discussing the possible causes, we've identified the PKCS#11 interface as the culprit. The fact of copying data vs returning an error was causing the significant differences in timing.

We've proposed implementation of an implicit rejection mechanism in the PKCS#11 token, so that it would return a pseudo-randomly generated message based on the received ciphertext and the used private key (the algorithm is described in detail in Sect. 4.2) instead of an error in case of PKCS#1 non-conforming plaintext. That algorithm was implemented in NSS[5] and shipped as part of version 3.61. That issue was later assigned CVE-2023-4421.

While this significantly reduced the observable side-channel (from around $5\,\mu s$ to $60\,ns$), it didn't eliminate it. We've informed NSS developers of this fact on 19th of January 2021.

After some discussions with upstream, we've come to conclusion that the remaining leak is most likely caused the numerical library performing "normalization": making sure that the most significant words of the internal multi-precision

---

[4] https://bugzilla.mozilla.org/show_bug.cgi?id=577498.
[5] https://phabricator.services.mozilla.com/rNSSfc05574c739947d615ab0b2b2b564f0 1c922eccd.

integer representation are non-zero after every fundamental operation (like addition or multiplication).

Note that with the Marvin workaround implemented, the testing script needs to have access to the private key to generate ciphertexts that can expose side-channels in the workaround or in the numerical library used for decryption. We describe the Marvin workaround in detail in Sect. 4.2. This is only a verification optimisation, as the test script is reusing the same RSA ciphertexts over and over, similar attack can be performed by randomising the ciphertexts while keeping specific property of plaintext (like zero most significant bytes) constant. That would require generating unique (or semi-unique) ciphertexts for every connection, which would be slow from the Python test runner we use.

We've executed the test against version 3.80 of the library and identified that plaintexts that have 8 or more zero bytes at the most significant positions have statistically significantly different behaviour (see Fig. 3). That confirmed the previous hypothesis about the leak coming from the numerical library. We've informed Mozilla of this on 20th of July 2022. We've also provided to Mozilla on 5th of October 2022 a simple pure C implementation of constant time multiplication and modulo operations (tested on x86_64, ppc64le, aarch64 and s390x architectures) to use for the deblinding operation. That being said, with this smaller side-channel, collecting even 400 thousand observations per class over 22 classes wasn't enough to consistently get statistically significant p-values (smaller than 10^{-5}) from the Freidman test.

As of the time of writing of this article, we're not aware of this, or any other code aiming at performing de-blinding in constant time, being added to NSS.

3.5 OpenSSL

For testing OpenSSL we've been using the same environment as for testing NSS.

Very quickly we've noticed that as few as 10 thousand observations per probe type are enough to have a statistically significant difference (p-values smaller than 10^{-5}) between a probe with many zero values at the most significant bytes and one with PKCS#1 conforming plaintext.

Issue in how BIGNUM is implemented was identified as the primary cause of the vulnerability. Which means that both OpenSSL and NSS suffer from fundamentally the same issue: using a general purpose numerical library to operate on cryptographically sensitive numbers.

Despite the numerical library in OpenSSL having smaller side channel than the one in NSS: OpenSSL is just under 30 ns while NSS is about 60 ns on the same i9-12900KS CPU; because the OpenSSL responses are quicker (median response of 381 µs vs 862 µs) and more consistent (MAD of inter-sample differences of 0.357 µs vs 13.7 µs), the side-channel leakage is easier to detect.

The fix for it (the history of which is described in appendix B) was merged and released as part of version 3.0.8 and 1.1.1t of the library on 7th of February 2023. It was assigned the ID of CVE-2022-4304. We've also verified that the merged patches don't show a side-channel leakage bigger than 10 ns when tested on x86_64, ppc64le, s390x and aarch64 architectures.

To fix CVE 2020-25659 in `pyca/cryptography` and CVE 2020-25657 in M2Crypto, we've also proposed to OpenSSL the implementation of the same Marvin workaround as the one implemented in NSS on 8th of January 2021[6]. That code was merged to the master branch (intended to become a future 3.2.0 release) on 12th of December 2022[7].

3.6   GnuTLS

While we've also suspected GnuTLS as vulnerable to timing side channels, and informed GnuTLS maintainers about it on 14th of July 2020, this happened before we had a side-channel free test harness, so identifying a cause from noisy results was difficult.

On 29th of July 2022 Alexander Sosedkin identified a logging function call[8] as likely responsible. We've tested a version of GnuTLS with those lines removed (they're useful only as a debugging aid) and found no side-channel after collecting timings for 34 million connections for each of the 31 types of probes on the highly optimised system with i9-12900KS. Calculated 95% confidence interval for median of differences was ± 2 ns (so about 10.5 CPU cycles). We've informed GnuTLS developers about this result on 11th of November 2022.

This fix was merged to GnuTLS master[9] and shipped as part of the 3.8.0 release on 10th of February 2023. The issue was assigned a CVE-2023-0361 identifier.

4   Proposed Countermeasures

Side-Channel Signals. The implementations of cryptographic algorithms need to both process and generate values in ways that do not leak information about the processed data. There are many different kinds of side-channels: timing, power, sound, light, etc. Generally, when we consider timing attacks, we mean the measurement of the time the whole operation took: how long it took to generate a shared secret, how long a signature operation took, and so on. This kind of side-channels provide only rough information about the processed data or used keys.

For example, a leaky implementation of modular exponentiation in RSA, when used together with ciphertext blinding will likely provide information about the Hamming weight of the private exponent or CRT exponents. But Hamming weight alone is insufficient for recovering the private key: Coppersmith method and derived algorithms require knowledge about consecutive bits of at least one private exponent.

---

[6] https://github.com/openssl/openssl/pull/13817.

[7] https://github.com/openssl/openssl/commit/7fc67e0a33102aa47bbaa56533eeecb98c 0450f7 and following patches.

[8] https://gitlab.com/gnutls/gnutls/-/blob/1f0183092125ac3c7449b8ee175f9c303cbab 384/lib/auth/rsa.c#L238-245.

[9] https://gitlab.com/gnutls/gnutls/-/merge_requests/1698.

Implementations of RSA should thus employ at least ciphertext blinding before performing private key operations. Though, this will only help against the simple timing attack with chosen ciphertexts. For protection against other kinds of side-channels, we recommended additionally use of exponent blinding.

RSA Implementation Decomposition. When implementing a generic RSA decryption algorithm, used for either RSA key exchange in TLS or called directly by other applications or libraries, multiple things need to happen before the data is securely processed.

1. Modular exponentiation using arbitrary precision integer arithmetic
2. Padding checks and secret extraction (PKCS#1 v1.5 or OAEP)
3. Secret value use and error handling

For RSA specifically, a popular workaround against leaks in the arbitrary precision arithmetic is the use of blinding. With blinding, the ciphertext is multiplied by a random value, the blinding factor. Then such blinded value undergoes modular exponentiation using a regular algorithm. Since the exact value exponentiated is unknown to the attacker, and different for every operation, even with the same ciphertext, they can't infer anything about actual value of it from the timing information alone. But to get access to the actual result of the operation (the encrypted message), the library needs to multiply the result of modular exponentiation by a multiplicative inverse of the blinding factor: the unblinding factor. While the inputs to the unblinding operation are uncorrelated with both the ciphertext and plaintext, and secret to the attacker, the output isn't.

Since CPUs commonly provide instructions to help in multiplication or addition, even if the result doesn't fit into a single register (like 64 bit multiply returning 128 bit result on 64bit CPUs), arbitrary precision implementations commonly store large integers as a list of word-sized integers (where word is the size of biggest general purpose register: 32 bit for 32 bit CPUs, 64 bit for 64 bit CPUs). For a generic purpose numerical library, storing additional words that specify zeros above the most significant digit is useless: it requires more memory and makes computation slower. So generic purpose libraries "clamp" or "normalize" the stored numbers: store only the significant non-zero words.

If that stored number is the result of RSA decryption operation, then difference in number of words used to store it will cause differences in time to convert it into a byte string (which is necessary to test padding, be it PKCS#1 v1.5 or RSA-OEAP, or to feed it into a KDF, like in case of RSASVE). So, by learning that the operation produced a smaller integer, the attacker knows that the high bits were all zero: exactly the information necessary to perform Bleichenbacher or Manger attacks.

4.1   Making Deblinding Constant-Time

Since the leak happens in the very last modular multiplication, the solution for implementations that employ blinding is to implement just that very last operation using constant time code.

While the inputs to that last multiplication come from a general purpose arbitrary precision arithmetic library and thus are clamped; since they are blinded, random, and secret, the conversion of them into constant size representations doesn't have to be side-channel free. Without knowledge of the used blinding factor, knowledge that a particular modular exponentiation provided a small output doesn't provide any information to the attacker.

Once the constant time modular multiplication result is calculated, it needs to be returned as a constant-sized (for a given modulus) list of integers. Converting that list into a byte string of constant size in side-channel free manner is simple.

We were able to implement both the arbitrary precision multiplication and Montgomery reduction algorithms for 64 bit CPUs in just 200 lines of portable C code. We've inspected the generated assembly by both LLVM and GCC compilers and didn't find any data-dependant instructions across code generate by multiple versions of the compilers. We've also tested it when compiled with GCC 11.3.1-2.1.el9, with -O3 optimisation level, on x86_64, aarch64, ppc64le, and s390x architectures and confirmed it to be side-channel free to the precision of TSC, cntvct_el0, mftb, and STCK time sources respectively.

As such, we believe that implementing side-channel free arbitrary precision integer arithmetic in pure C is possible. Given the speed of the algorithms used for typical cryptographic inputs, we also think that a simple regression test case, to protect against possible compiler optimisations introducing side-channels, executable in a CI environment, is also possible (the tests require less than half an hour of data collection to provide resolution down to single-digit CPU cycles).

4.2 Safe PKCS#1 V1.5 Decryption API

Application interfaces that implement the PKCS#1 v1.5 padding check are particularly vulnerable. This is caused by three things: the side-channel free check of the padding being complex, extraction and returning of the secret value in side-channel free way to the application being complex, and that handling of the returned error codes and secret value *in the application* needs to be performed in side-channel free manner.

Protocols like TLS work around this problem by performing implicit rejection: when the padding check fails, the size of the extracted secret is wrong, or the protocol version number in the extracted secret is wrong, instead of using extracted value as the secret, they need to use the previously generated random value as the input to the master secret generator function. Since the master secret is calculated from both the extracted pre-master secret and server-selected (outside the attacker's control) random value from the ServerHello message, the attacker is unable to differentiate the decryption failure caused by badly guessed, but actually extracted from PKCS#1 v1.5 ciphertext value, and a previously generated random value [11].

This kind of workaround doesn't work for a generic API, as a randomly generated value will cause a different behaviour of the calling application than a constant value, even if unknown to the attacker. But, since *by definition* the attacker doesn't know if the decrypted value has a PKCS#1 v1.5 conforming padding or not, we can make this signal useless as a Bleichenbacher oracle by making all ciphertexts decrypt to a value, as long as the same ciphertext will decrypt to the same plaintext every time.

One of the features of the PKCS#1 v1.5 padding is that it includes at least 8 bytes of random data as padding. That means that there are almost 2^{64} ciphertexts[10] that decode to one and same message, significantly more if the returned message is smaller. Thus an attacker that has access to the literal result of the decryption would need to encrypt this many ciphertexts to know if the decrypted value could be represented as the given ciphertext, and thus know if the real, padded plaintext starts with a zero byte.

This approach is particularly useful for implementations that expose only PKCS#11 interface, like smart-cards or hardware security modules, as those need to copy different amount of data to the calling application depending on whether the padding check was successful or not.

To calculate an unpredictable, but deterministic, message, we can use the private exponent and the literal ciphertext as the inputs to a key derivation function (similar to the deterministic nonce generation for (EC)DSA signatures [12]).

Note that, as two different implementations of this general idea that use the same key can be used to cross-check if the decrypted value is the result of valid or invalid padding, we strongly recommend to implement the following algorithm precisely as stated. If not done as such, attacks may still be possible against heterogeneous environments.

As such, we propose this alternative algorithm for PKCS#1 v1.5 depadding (the Marvin attack workaround, or implicit rejection for RSA decryption):

1. Check the length of input message according to step one of RFC 8017 Sect. 7.2.2 (since all inputs are public, this check doesn't have to be performed in side-channel free way and the processing can stop here).
2. Derive the Key Derivation Key (KDK) from the private exponent and public ciphertext
   (a) Convert the private exponent (d) to a big-endian integer, left-padded with zeros so that it has the same size the public modulus
   (b) Hash it using SHA-256, store that value (since it's constant you can reuse it, but it needs to be kept secret, just like the private exponent)
   (c) Use the hash of the exponent as an SHA-256 HMAC key and the provided ciphertext as a message to the HMAC. The output of the HMAC is the KDK.
3. Create a list of candidate lengths and a random message
   (a) Define a Pseudo Random Function that takes as input a key, label, and number of bytes to output. This function needs to generate sequential blocks of random data by calling SHA-256 HMAC with the provided key as the key, and message set to concatenation of an iterator (initialised to 0, increased by 1 for every HMAC call, encoded as a two-byte big-endian

---

[10] exactly it is equal to $(2^8 - 1)^8 \approx 2^{63.95}$, as every individual byte of the padding must not be equal 0 and there are 8 of them.

integer), the label (as-is, *without* C-like null byte termination) and the number of bits to output (i.e. 8 times the number of output bytes; encoded as two-byte big-endian integer). If output size is not a multiple of SHA-256 HMAC size, the output should be right-truncated to fit (i.e. only the most significant bytes of last HMAC output should be returned).

  (b) Using the PRF with KDK and "length" as six byte label encoded with UTF-8 generate 256 byte output. Interpret it as 128 two byte big-endian numbers.

  (c) Using the PRF with KDK and "message" as seven byte label encoded with UTF-8 generate as many bytes as are necessary to represent the modulus (k). This is the alternative decryption to use in case the padding check fails.

4. Select a length of the returned message in case the padding check fails (Note: this step needs to be performed in side-channel free way)

  (a) For each of the 128 possible lengths zero-out the high-order bits so that they have the same bit length as the length of the maximum acceptable message size ($k - 11$).

  (b) Select the last length that's not larger than $k - 11$, use 0 if none are.

5. Perform standard RSA decryption as described in step 2 of RFC 8017 Sect. 7.2.2. (Note: this step needs to use side-channel free code)

6. Verify the EM padding as described in step 3 of RFC 8017 Sect. 7.2.2, but instead of outputting "decryption error", return the last l bytes of the "message" PRF, where l is the selected length from step 4.. (Note: both selection of use of the generated message as well as the copy of it needs to be performed with side-channel free code).

Practical implementations as well as test vectors of this algorithm can be found in tlslite-ng (pure Python), Mozilla NSS, and OpenSSL PR #13817.

While this algorithm changes the semantics of error handling, so code that depends on "decryption error" to mean that the key used to decrypt the ciphertext was incorrect may misbehave, it should be noted that a plaintext returned by decrypting a ciphertext under a different key-pair that was used to encrypt it will be effectively random. Random plaintexts have a non irrelevant chance of being PKCS#1 v1.5 conforming. Thus the use of this alternative algorithm changes the *likelihood* of getting a message decryption by using a wrong key, it doesn't change the *possibility* of it. So any protocol that tries decryption of RSA ciphertexts with different keys needs to employ a different way to detect if the ciphertext matches the key than the absence of errors in RSA PKCS#1 v1.5 decryption.

4.3   Countermeasures Summary

While we provide an algorithm for more secure PKCS#1 v1.5 depadding, given the complexity of implementing and testing this algorithm, we strongly recommend for libraries to instead remove support for encryption using PKCS#1 v1.5 padding completely. The far simpler workaround described for TLS (Sect. 7.4.7.1

of RFC 5246 [11]) was previously found to be implemented incorrectly by over 20 different implementations [3]. That's on top of the fact that testing for correctness of the TLS-specific workaround is much easier than testing for correctness of the Marvin workaround. Thus, we would consider any use of generic PKCS#1 v1.5 API that doesn't use the Marvin workaround internally to be a case of CWE-242[11] ("Use of Inherently Dangerous Function") and, without a verified side-channel free code on the calling side, an automatic vulnerability for the calling code.

While we haven't tested any actual hardware PKCS#11 modules, based on results from NSS, we're afraid that most, if not all uses of PKCS#11 tokens and modules for PKCS#1 v1.5 decryption will be vulnerable to the Bleichenbacher oracle in practice. Simply transferring a different amount of data flowing between application and module in case of an error and a message that decrypts to very few or very many bytes would already provide enough of a side-channel to make it vulnerable.

We also recommend against the use of OAEP and RSASVE with libraries that don't have verified side-channel free arbitrary precision integer arithmetic library. Any library that uses general purpose integer arithmetic implementations should be considered suspect.

5 Test Framework

To conduct those tests we've used the `tlsfuzzer` test suite[12]. It's a TLS protocol conformity test suite able to generate different kind of arbitrary messages to send to the server and then to verify that the reply matches some expectations.

We've used it to send the pregenerated RSA ciphertexts to the TLS server in the TLS ClientKeyExchange messages.

For conducting the timing tests, the scripts first generate the test payloads in random order, write them to disk, together with information which payload corresponds to which probe. Such generated payloads are then read sequentially, send one by one to the server, and server response times are captured by the `tcpdump` running in the background.

This ensures that the payload generation, its name, placement in memory, or anything similar, doesn't influence the timing of probe sending, making the test harness effectively constant time. By using packet capture to collect timing data, we both provide larger separation between measuring server response times and ensure that the payloads sent by the test harness don't influence the measurement.

Only when the individual time measurements are interpreted according to the order in which they were originally generated do the patterns in server responses emerge.

---

[11] https://cwe.mitre.org/data/definitions/242.html.

[12] https://github.com/tlsfuzzer/tlsfuzzer.

The script we generally used to perform those tests is the `test-bleichenbacher-timing-pregenerate.py` in the `scripts` directory of the tls-fuzzer repo.

For servers that implement the Marvin workaround on the API level, we have prepared a script that generates ciphertexts decrypting to the same length of plaintext both for valid and invalid padding case: the `test-bleichenbacher-timing-marvin.py`.

See their `--help` messages and the documentation[13] on more tips on their execution.

Based on tlsfuzzer code we've also created a set of scripts for preparing test cases for testing generic RSA encryption functions as the `marvin-toolkit`[14]. It should be noted that it does not create random, single use ciphertexts, like the TLS script, so trying to measure decryption of the same ciphertexts over and over may report false positives if the numerical library is not fully constant time (as then the leak based on *ciphertext* may end up being detected, which is not security relevant).

6   Future Work

In this work, we have focused only on the simplest side-channel attack: a low granularity timing side channel. Higher granularity side-channels, like ones from microarchitectural sources, together with more robust statistical methods, are likely to show that fewer observations are necessary for statistically significant results. More advanced side-channel attacks, like ones that use power analysis, electromagnetic emissions, or sound are still likely possible.

We have tested just a handful of the popular cryptographic libraries. Larger scale testing of software and hardware implementing RSA encryption (of any kind) will likely reveal many more vulnerable implementations.

Only the Bleichenbacher attack against RSA decryption was tested. Performing similar tests against constant-timeness with regards to used private keys should also be possible with similar approach and a proper test harness.

Extending the presented approach should also be possible for testing other timing attacks in TLS, like the Lucky13 attack.

7   Summary and Recommendations

We've shown that by using correct statistical methods we can detect much smaller timing side-channels than previously expected to be possible.

With this new approach we've analysed multiple cryptographic libraries, both ones implementing the algorithms directly (OpenSSL, NSS, and GnuTLS), as well as higher-level language bindings (M2crypto, and pyca/cryptography).

---

[13] https://tlsfuzzer.readthedocs.io/en/latest/timing-analysis.html.
[14] https://github.com/tomato42/marvin-toolkit.

Every single one of them turned out to be vulnerable or exploitable to the Bleichenbacher attack against RSA encryption. Our recommendation is thus that RSA encryption shouldn't be used, as implementing it correctly is very hard, if not impossible. We especially recommend that the PKCS#1 v1.5 padding for RSA encryption should not be used, and any protocols that allow its use should deprecate, forbid its use completely.

For implementations that cannot deprecate and remove support for PKCS#1 v1.5 decryption we've proposed an algorithm to implement implicit rejection of ciphertexts that fail the padding check. We recommend its use in all general APIs that cannot remove support for PKCS#1 v1.5 decryption, including PKCS#11. We must stress though, that implementing it correctly and verifying correctness of that implementation is hard, so it should be employed as a last-ditch solution, when all other options to remove need for PKCS#1 v1.5 encryption have been exhausted.

We recommend that static code analysis scanners should mark any uses of PKCS#1 v1.5 decryption APIs as inherently unsafe.

We've also shown that while the use of mitigations such as (base) blinding for RSA decryption helps, it cannot be implemented blindly and steps that have access to real plaintext values, like the unblinding step and conversion from multi-precision integer to a byte string, must be implemented with special care and with verified side-channel free code. Because of the root cause of the vulnerabilities presented here in OpenSSL, NSS and a similar issue in GnuTLS (CVE-2018-16868), was the use of general-purpose numerical methods to implement cryptographic operations, and because other cryptographic primitives are similarly vulnerable to leaks related to high order bits, like the Minerva attack against ECDSA [5], the Raccoon attack against DHE [8] (and that the same hidden number problem applies to ECDHE [4]), we recommend to consider any implementation of cryptographic arithmetic that uses general-purpose multi-precision numerical methods to be vulnerable to side-channel attacks. In particular, any code that uses variable size internal representation of integers is, most likely, vulncrable to side-channel attacks.

Acknowledgments. I'd like to thank Jan Koscielniak for the initial test implementation and test results that were the inspiration for this research. Stefan Berger for discussions that led to the workaround on API level. Daniel J. Bernstein and Juraj Somorovsky for research pointers and sanity check of the workaround idea. Greg Sutcliffe for discussions about statistical methods for analysing the timing data.

A   System Tuning

To minimise amount and magnitude of the noise in measurements we found some changes to system configuration to be very effective.

The BIOS was configured to override the processor base power to the same level as the maximum turbo power (241 W), so as to remove the time limits on how long will the CPU run with turbo boost (run at elevated frequency). The BIOS was also configured to allow high frequency (high multiplier) operation even when multiple cores are active (we've noticed that this is important as the BIOS/CPU consider the core to be "active" when it's in the C2 power state or higher).

Hyper-Threading was disabled. The Linux kernel was configured using the `tuned` cpu-isolation profile with 4 of the 8 P-cores isolated. Tuned cpu-isolation profile sets the idle driver to keep all the CPU cores (not just the isolated ones) at the C1 power state. This is important because the test harness (`tlsfuzzer`) and the system under test (like NSS `selfserv` or openssl `s_server`) execute on separate cores and use a network protocol to communicate, so there are idle periods when they wait for a reply from the other side of the connection. During those idle periods, the CPU normally goes into a deeper idle state (lower power state): C2, C3, or higher. The problem is that going out of those idle states back to the state where the CPU can execute instructions (C0) takes different amounts of time, generally the deeper the C-state, the longer the transition to C0 state. C1 state is a bit special in that it's reported by the hardware as requiring just a single CPU cycle to transition to C0. In quick testing we haven't noticed qualitatively better results by disabling C-states completely and using just the Linux polling idle driver compared to the approach taken by `tuned`. At the same time, allowing the CPU to switch to C3 states did cause the results to be significantly worse, increasing the bootstrapped 95% confidence interval of the median of differences from 0.223 μs to 3.23 μs and the median absolute deviation[15] of inter-sample differences from 7 μs to 1.2 ms.

The machine also has configured aggressive fan curves and a large CPU heatsink installed, causing the CPU to stay under 50°C when running the tests, often around 40°C, making sure that the CPU does not employ thermal throttling.

The CPU was running at a stable 5.225 GHz when measuring the server response times. We also tested a configuration in which the two cores used for measurement were running at the maximum supported frequency of 5.5 GHz, but found it to provide lower quality results, not offset by the quicker execution.

Please note that while this configuration provides higher quality results, it's *not* necessary for the correct operation of the statistical tests.

B   OpenSSL Fix History

The development and integrations of the patches to the OpenSSL took a very long time.

We've originally informed the OpenSSL project that their implementation of RSA decryption in version 1.1.1c is vulnerable on 14th of July 2020.

Over the next few weeks (on 6th of August) we've identified the previously reported issue #6640[16] (in the way that BIGNUM code is implemented) as the primary cause of the timing side channel.

---

[15] Median absolute deviation (MAD) is a robust measure of the variability of the data, similar to standard deviation measure, but resilient against outliers.

[16] https://github.com/openssl/openssl/issues/6640.

On 15th of July 2022 we've informed OpenSSL that the implementation is most likely exploitable against a network attacker when non standard key sizes (2049 bit or 2056 bit) or 32 bit compiles are used. In that message we've also suggested workarounding the leakage in BIGNUM implementation by performing the deblinding step using a portable C implementation of multiplication and modulo operations. See Sect. 4.1 for details.

The code to perform that, including one that uses Montgomery reduction to calculate the mod was provided to OpenSSL in October 2022.

C   Graphs of Test Results

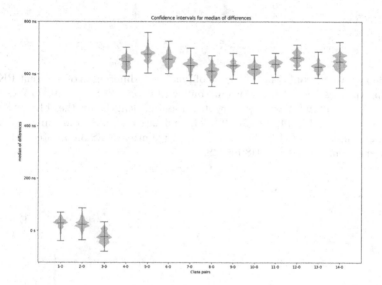

Fig. 1. Bootstrapped confidence intervals of median of differences of different PKCS#1 conforming (probes 1, 2, and 3) and non-conforming plaintexts (4 and larger) compared to a PKCS#1 conforming plaintext. M2Crypto 0.35.2, Intel i7-8650U, 1000 observations per class. 2048 bit RSA.

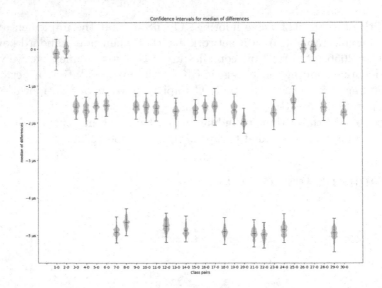

Fig. 2. Bootstrapped confidence intervals of median of differences of different PKCS#1 conforming (probes 1 and 2), conforming but with wrong TLS version (probes 26 and 27), conforming but with wrong encrypted message length for the TLS pre-master secret (probes 7, 8, 12, 14, 18, 21, 22, 24, and 29) and non-conforming plaintexts (remaining) compared to a PKCS#1 conforming plaintext. NSS 3.60, Intel i9-12900KS, 10000 observations per class. 2048 bit RSA

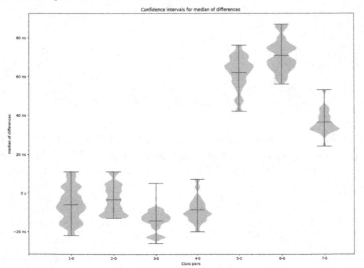

Fig. 3. Bootstrapped confidence intervals of median of differences of different PKCS#1 non-conforming probes compared to a PKCS#1 non-conforming plaintext. The probe 2 has all bytes non zero, probe 1 has one most significant byte set to zero, probe 3 has two, 4 has four, probe 5 has 8 zero bytes, probe 6 has 16, and 7 has 40 most significant bytes set to zero. NSS 3.80, Intel i9-12900KS, 33.5 million observations per class. 2048 bit RSA

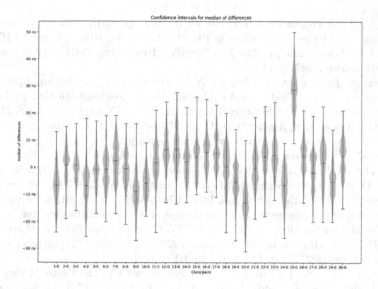

Fig. 4. Bootstrapped confidence intervals of median of differences of different probes compared to a PKCS#1 conforming plaintext. The probe 25 has forty of the most significant bytes set to zero. OpenSSL 1.1.1p, Intel i9-12900KS, 10 thousand observations per class. 2048 bit RSA

References

1. Bardou, R., Focardi, R., Kawamoto, Y., Simionato, L., Steel, G., Tsay, J.-K.: Efficient padding oracle attacks on cryptographic hardware. In: Safavi-Naini, R., Canetti, R. (eds.) Advances in Cryptology – CRYPTO 2012, pp. 608–625. Springer Berlin Heidelberg, Berlin, Heidelberg (2012). https://doi.org/10.1007/978-3-642-32009-5_36
2. Bleichenbacher, D.: Chosen ciphertext attacks against protocols based on the RSA encryption standard PKCS #1. In: Krawczyk, H. (ed.) CRYPTO 1998. LNCS, vol. 1462, pp. 1–12. Springer, Heidelberg (1998). https://doi.org/10.1007/BFb0055716
3. Böck, H., Somorovsky, J., Young, C.: Return of Bleichenbacher's oracle threat (ROBOT). In 27th USENIX Security Symposium (USENIX Security 18), pp. 817–849, Baltimore, MD, August 2018. USENIX Association. ISBN 978-1-939133-04-5. https://www.usenix.org/conference/usenixsecurity18/presentation/bock
4. Boneh, D., Halevi, S., Howgrave-Graham, N.: The modular inversion hidden number problem. In: Boyd, C. (ed.) ASIACRYPT 2001. LNCS, vol. 2248, pp. 36–51. Springer, Heidelberg (2001). https://doi.org/10.1007/3-540-45682-1_3
5. Jancar, J., Sedlacek, V., Svenda, P., Sys, M.: Minerva: The curse of ECDSA nonces: systematic analysis of lattice attacks on noisy leakage of bit-length of ECDSA nonces. IACR Trans. Cryptograph. Hardw. Embedded Syst. **26**, 281–308 (2020). https://doi.org/10.46586/tches.v2020.i4.281-308
6. Klíma, V., Pokorný, O., Rosa, T.: Attacking RSA-based sessions in SSL/TLS. In: Walter, C.D., Koç, Ç.K., Paar, C. (eds.) Cryptographic Hardware and Embedded Systems - CHES 2003, pp. 426–440. Springer Berlin Heidelberg, Berlin, Heidelberg (2003). https://doi.org/10.1007/978-3-540-45238-6_33

7. Manger, J.: A chosen ciphertext attack on rsa optimal asymmetric encryption padding (OAEP) as standardized in PKCS #1 v2.0. In: Kilian, J. (ed.) CRYPTO 2001. LNCS, vol. 2139, pp. 230–238. Springer, Heidelberg (2001). https://doi.org/10.1007/3-540-44647-8_14

8. Merget, R., Brinkmann, M., Aviram, N., Somorovsky, J., Mittmann, J., Schwenk, J.: Raccoon attack: Finding and exploiting Most-Significant-Bit-Oracles in TLS-DH(E). In 30th USENIX Security Symposium (USENIX Security 21), pp. 213–230. USENIX Association, August 2021. ISBN 978-1-939133-24-3. https://www.usenix.org/conference/usenixsecurity21/presentation/merget

9. Meyer, C., Somorovsky, J., Weiss, E., Schwenk, J., Schinzel, S., Tews, E.: Revisiting SSL/TLS implementations: New Bleichenbacher side channels and attacks. In 23rd USENIX Security Symposium (USENIX Security 14), pp. 733–748, San Diego, CA, August 2014. USENIX Association. ISBN 978-1-931971-15-7. https://www.usenix.org/conference/usenixsecurity14/technical-sessions/presentation/meyer

10. Kaliski, B. and Staddon, J.: PKCS #1: RSA Cryptography Specifications Version 2.0. RFC 2437 (Informational), October 1998. ISSN 2070–1721. https://www.rfc-editor.org/rfc/rfc2437.txt. Obsoleted by RFC 3447

11. Dierks, T., Rescorla, E.: The Transport Layer Security (TLS) Protocol Version 1.2. RFC 5246 (Proposed Standard), August 2008. ISSN 2070–1721. https://www.rfc-editor.org/rfc/rfc5246.txt. Obsoleted by RFC 8446, updated by RFCs 5746, 5878, 6176, 7465, 7507, 7568, 7627, 7685, 7905, 7919, 8447, 9155

12. Pornin, T.: Deterministic Usage of the Digital Signature Algorithm (DSA) and Elliptic Curve Digital Signature Algorithm (ECDSA). RFC 6979 (Informational), August 2013. ISSN 2070–1721. https://www.rfc-editor.org/rfc/rfc6979.txt

13. Jones, M., Hildebrand, J.: JSON Web Encryption (JWE). RFC 7516 (Proposed Standard), May 2015. ISSN 2070–1721. https://www.rfc-editor.org/rfc/rfc7516.txt

14. Moriarty, K., (Ed.), Kaliski, B., Jonsson, J., Rusch, A.: PKCS #1: RSA Cryptography Specifications Version 2.2. RFC 8017 (Informational), November 2016. ISSN 2070–1721. https://www.rfc-editor.org/rfc/rfc8017.txt

15. Rescorla, E.: The Transport Layer Security (TLS) Protocol Version 1.3. RFC 8446 (Proposed Standard). RFC. Fremont, CA, USA: RFC Editor, Aug. 2018. url: https://www.rfc-editor.org/rfc/rfc8446.txt. https://doi.org/10.17487/RFC8446

16. Ronen, E., Gillham, R., Genkin, D., Shamir, A., Wong, D., Yarom, Y.: The 9 lives of bleichenbacher's cat: New cache attacks on tls implementations. In: 2019 IEEE Symposium on Security and Privacy (SP), pp. 435–452, 2019. https://doi.org/10.1109/SP.2019.00062

JWTKey: Automatic Cryptographic Vulnerability Detection in JWT Applications

Bowen Xu[1,2], Shijie Jia[1,2(✉)], Jingqiang Lin[3], Fangyu Zheng[1,2], Yuan Ma[1,2], Limin Liu[1,2], Xiaozhuo Gu[1,2], and Li Song[1,2]

[1] State Key Laboratory of Information Security, Institute of Information Engineering, Chinese Academy of Sciences, Beijing, China
jiashijie@iie.ac.cn
[2] School of Cyber Security, University of Chinese Academy of Sciences, Beijing, China
[3] School of Cyber Security, University of Science and Technology of China, Hefei, China

Abstract. JSON Web Token (JWT) has been widely adopted to increase the security of authentication and authorization scenarios. However, how to manage the JWT key during its lifecycle is rarely mentioned in the standards of JWT, which opens the door for developers with inadequate cryptography experience to implement cryptography incorrectly. Moreover, no effort has been devoted to checking the security of cryptographic usage in JWT applications. In this paper, we design and implement *JWTKey*, a static analysis detector leveraging program slicing technique to automatically identify cryptographic vulnerabilities in JWT applications. We derive 15 well-targeted cryptographic rules coupled with potential JWT key threats for the first time, and customized analysis entries and slicing criteria are identified accurately based on the observation of diversified JWT implementations, thus achieving balance between precise detection and overhead. Running on 358 open source JWT applications from GitHub, *JWTKey* discovered that 65.92% of the JWT applications have at least one cryptographic vulnerability. The comparative experiments with CryptoGuard demonstrate the effectiveness of our design. We disclose the findings to the developers and collect their feedback. Our findings highlight the poor cryptographic implementation in the current JWT applications.

Keywords: JWT · Key management · Cryptographic vulnerability

1 Introduction

JSON Web Token (JWT) is a compact claims representation format to be transferred between two parties [23]. As the advantages of being less verbose, more compact, smaller size, and easy to be parsed, JWT has been deeply coupled with various standard and non-standard access delegation and single sign-on (SSO) applications. Multiple indispensable parameters of standard protocols (e.g., OAuth [21,

© The Author(s), under exclusive license to Springer Nature Switzerland AG 2024
G. Tsudik et al. (Eds.): ESORICS 2023, LNCS 14346, pp. 263–282, 2024.
https://doi.org/10.1007/978-3-031-51479-1_14

22] and OpenID Connect (OIDC) [43]) are either supported (e.g., *authorization grant, client credentials,* and *access token*) or explicitly mandatory required (e.g., *ID token*) to be transmitted in the format of JWT. Moreover, various JWT-based self-defined authentication/authorization schemes have been proposed in multifarious scenarios, such as web services [20], cloud SaaS applications [13], multi-agent systems [42] and software-defined networking [50].

The key insights of JWT are as follows: the claims need to be digitally signed or integrity protected with a Message Authentication Code (MAC) and/or encrypted in the format of JSON Web Signature (JWS) or JSON Web Encryption (JWE) [23]. This ensures the integrity and authenticity of the claims. According to Kerckhoff's principle [34], a cryptographic system should be designed to be secure, even if all its details, except for the key, are publicly known. Therefore, the security of JWT applications is based on the proper management of cryptographic keys throughout their lifecycle (e.g., generation, storage, transmission, and use). Otherwise, severe consequences could be provoked. For example, a vulnerability was disclosed in the "View As" feature of Facebook, making attackers could obtain the access tokens of the users [19]. This exposes the fact that there are many risks of token leaks and attacks in various application scenarios. Moreover, some vulnerabilities (e.g., CVE-2022-35540 [8] and CVE-2022-36672 [9]) have been disclosed in popular projects (e.g., Novel-Plus and AgileConfig) due to hard-coded keys in their JWT usage, allowing attackers create a custom user session or gain administrator access.

Many efforts on the security of cryptographic applications have been proposed, while they are all limited in detecting cryptographic vulnerabilities of JWT applications. Firstly, previous JWT related studies either devote to extending the range of JWT applications [18,33,46] or try to check anti-protocol flaws at the protocol level (e.g., OAuth [2,14,41,53] and OIDC [15,18]), which only consider the correctness of the JWT-based parameters (e.g., *access token* and *ID token*), and do not consider the vulnerabilities from the aspect of JWT cryptographic usage. Secondly, the existing cryptographic misuse detectors commonly focus on the application security of APIs in underlying cryptographic libraries (e.g., JCA and OpenSSL) by using a program analysis method to check if an application respects the predefined cryptographic rules [31]. However, JWT applications typically do not invoke cryptographic libraries directly, but indirectly invoke them by third-party JWT libraries (e.g., java-jwt [4] and jose.4.j [6]), which encapsulate JWT cryptographic implementations by providing JWT generation and verification related APIs. Previous detectors treat JWT libraries as their "applications", whose diversified implementation details make the true upper applications (i.e., JWT applications) need to pass key-related parameters through multiple methods, classes, field variables, or conditional statements of the APIs in JWT libraries. The above complicated orthogonal invocations cannot be handled by the existing detectors as the refinements of clipping orthogonal explorations [40], thus resulting in prevalent false negatives [1].

In this paper, we tackle the above limitations and introduce *JWTKey*, a static analysis detector, which leverages static program slicing technique, achieving automated analysis of cryptographic vulnerabilities in JWT applications. Our design relies on several key insights: 1) To provide precise cryptographic vulnerability detection in JWT applications, we derive 15 well-targeted rules by taking an in-depth analysis of the potential security threats throughout a JWT key lifecycle; 2) To obtain precise detection outcomes with acceptable overhead, we determine analysis entries and slicing criteria based on the observation of diversified implementations of JWT applications and JWT libraries; 3) Based on the specific stated cryptographic rules, both backward/forward program slicing and properties file feature analysis are performed to track the APIs and arguments in the intermediate representation of the detected applications.

To demonstrate the effectiveness of *JWTKey*, we carry out a large-scale evaluation based on 358 popular Java-based JWT applications crawled from GitHub. *JWTKey* report 417 alerts for the 358 applications, and our manual analysis confirms 410 alerts, achieving an accuracy of 98.32%. We identify that 65.92% of the JWT applications have at least one cryptographic vulnerability. The large number of alerts indicates a widespread misunderstanding of how to properly manage keys in JWT applications. We also utilize CryptoGuard [40] (the detector with the highest precision [1]) for comparative experiments, while it only report 49 cases of JWT cryptographic vulnerabilities, leaving 361 cases undiscovered. We report our security findings to the corresponding developers of JWT applications and JWT libraries, some of which have been indeed patched (see Sect. 7). In summary, we make the following contributions:

- We study the security of JWT applications from a brand-new perspective (i.e., cryptographic vulnerabilities). We conduct an in-depth study on the potential security threats throughout a JWT key lifecycle and derive 15 cryptographic rules coupled with JWT implementation cryptographic APIs. The purpose of this research is to cover as many vulnerabilities as possible to guide developers to use cryptography securely on large JWT applications.
- We design and implement a static analysis detector, *JWTKey*[1]. With accurate identification of analysis entries and slicing criteria based on the observation of diversified implementations of JWT applications and JWT libraries, *JWTKey* achieves balance between precise detection and overhead.
- Our evaluation on 358 JWT applications and the comparative experiments with CryptoGuard demonstrate the effectiveness of our design in discovering cryptographic vulnerabilities of JWT applications.

2 Background

2.1 JWT Structure

JWTs encode claims to be transmitted as a JSON object that is used as the payload of a JSON Web Signature (JWS) [25] or as the plaintext of a JSON Web Encryption (JWE) [26], enabling the claims to be digitally signed or integrity protected with a Message Authentication Code (MAC) and/or encrypted. A

---

[1] Available at https://github.com/JWTKeyIIE/JWTKey.

JWT is represented as a sequence of URL-safe parts separated by period ('.') characters. Each part contains a base64url-encoded value. Specifically, a JWS consists of three parts (i.e., JSON object signing and encryption (JOSE) header, payload and signature) and a JWE consists of five parts (i.e., JOSE header, encrypted key, initialization vector, ciphertext and authentication tag).

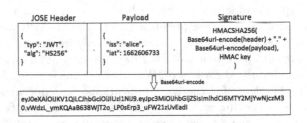

Fig. 1. A simple JWT instance with JWS structure.

Figure 1 presents a simple JWT instance with JWS structure. The first part is a JOSE header, whose contents describe the cryptographic operations applied to the corresponding JWT claims set. The "alg" (algorithm) parameter, which is required in the JOSE header, identifies the cryptographic algorithm (e.g., HMAC, ECDSA, AES-128) used to secure the JWT. Several optional parameters are also provided in the JOSE header, such as "jwk" (JSON web key), which is the public key that corresponds to the key used to sign the JWS or encrypt the JWE; "jku" (JWK set URL), which is a URI that refers to a resource for a set of JWK public keys; "kid" (key ID), which is a hint indicating which key was used to secure the JWS/JWE; "x5c" (X.509 certificate chain), which is the X.509 public key certificate or certificate chain corresponding to the key used to sign the JWS or encrypt the JWE; "x5u" (X.509 URL), which is a URI that refers to a resource for the public key certificate or certificate chain; "p2s" (PBES2 salt input), which is a salt value used for password-based encryption (PBE); "p2c" (PBES2 count), which is an iteration count used for PBE.

2.2 Static Program Slicing

Static program slicing is a decomposition technique that extracts program parts from program statements relevant to a particular computation [56]. As a static method, static program slicing does not require the execution of programs (e.g., JWT applications). They scale up to a large number of programs, cover a wide range of security rules, and are unlikely to have false negatives [40]. A program slice is the result of slicing which consists of a subset statements of a program that potentially affect or be affected by the slicing criterion. A slicing criterion consists of a pair $\langle p, V \rangle$. Specifically, p is a program point and V is a subset of program variables. Commonly speaking, there are two main types of static program slicing methods: backward slicing and forward slicing. Backward slicing is used to compute the set of instructions that affect the variables in V at program point p, and forward slicing is used to compute the set of instructions affected by the variables in V at program point p. It is worth to mention that a system dependence graph (i.e., SDG) is commonly built to identify the minimal set of program statements and variables which are necessary to produce a particular output. In particular, a SDG is a directed graph that represents the program statements as nodes and represents the dependencies between them as edges. Control dependence edges represent the flow of control in the program, while data dependence edges represent the flow of data between different statements.

3 Related Work

In recent years, researchers have shown significant interest in the problem of vulnerability detection on various kinds of applications. However, how to detect cryptographic vulnerabilities in JWT applications is still an open question.

JWT-Related Studies. Since JWT is deeply coupled with authentication and authorization protocols, many works related to protocol security have been proposed (e.g., OAuth [2,14,41,53] and OIDC [15,18]). In the case of OAuth, Wang et al. [53] proposed a tool that combines static analysis and network analysis to identify OAuth bugs on Android platform. Fett et al. [14] carried out a formal analysis of the OAuth 2.0 standard in an expressive web model. Rahat et al. [2] developed OAUTHLINT, which incorporates a query-driven static analysis to check anti-protocol programs of OAuth client-side. More recently, Rahat et al. [41] proposed Cerberus, which aims to find logical flaws and identify vulnerabilities in the implementation of OAuth service provider libraries. In the case of OIDC, Fett et al. [15] developed a formal model of OIDC based on the Dolev-Yao style model of the web infrastructure (FKS model). Ghasemisharif et al. [18] investigated the security implications of SSO, offered an analysis of account hijacking on the modern Web and proposed an extension to OIDC based on JWT revocation token. However, all the above previous researches mainly focus on checking anti-protocol flaws at the protocol level, and do not consider the diversified cryptographic implementation details of JWT applications. Differently, in this work, we aim to provide deeper insights into how to securely implement JWT from a foremost cryptographic security perspective.

Cryptographic Misuse Detectors. Recently, many cryptographic misuse detectors have been proposed. Their key insights are using static methods (e.g., program slicing and taint analysis) or dynamic methods (e.g., fuzzing and logging) to check if an application respects the predefined cryptographic rules [31]. For example, in Java, Egele et al. [12] proposed CryptoLint, which performed a study to measure cryptographic misuse in Android applications with only 6 rules. Krüger et al. [30] developed CrySL, which provided higher precision than CryptoLint [30] by designing a set of cryptographic rules for the JCA library. Wen et al. [54] proposed MUTAPI to discover API misuse patterns via mutation analysis. However, it cannot discover misuse patterns which require specific values (e.g., *javax.crypto.Cipher("DES")*). More recently, CryptoGuard [40] performed data-flow analysis based on forward/backward slicing methods for Java Projects. Piccolboni et al. [38] implemented CryLogger to detect cryptographic misuses dynamically. Ami et al. [3] presented the MASC framework, which enables a systematic and data-driven evaluation of cryptographic detectors using mutation testing. In C/C++, Rahaman et al. [39] proposed TaintCrypt, which adopted taint analysis to check projects issues using C/C++ cryptographic libraries (e.g., OpenSSL). Zhang et al. [57] implement CryptoRex to identify cryptographic misuse of firmware in IoT devices. In Python, Wickert et al. [55] designed LICMA, which adopted hybrid static analysis to discover cryptographic misuses in applications written in Python and C. Frantz et al. [16] proposed Cryptolation, which is a static analysis tool to discover Python cryptographic misuses.

The above detectors commonly focus on the library-level cryptographic implementation issues in cryptographic libraries (e.g., JCA, JCE and JSSE in Java, OpenSSL in C/C++, M2Crypto and PyCrypto in Python). Differently, in this work, we aim to fill the gap of inaccurate identification of cryptographic misuses at JWT applications by proposing JWT-oriented cryptographic rules and detection methods.

4   Threat Model and Cryptographic Rules

4.1   Threat Model

In this paper, we focus on the cryptographic vulnerabilities of JWT application during the lifecycle of key management. We assume that even developers with rich cryptography experience may bring insecure behaviors when handling JWT related keys. Adversaries aim to obtain resources or privileges of JWT applications by constructing forged JWTs with obtained key information. We consider two types of adversaries in this work. First, for the system adversaries who have physical or remote access to the physical devices (e.g., client or server devices), they could obtain or infer the symmetric key or private key of JWT applications during key generation, storage or use stages by reverse engineering [37] or privilege escalation [49]. Second, for the network adversaries, they can intercept and modify network traffics between JWT issuers and verifiers. They can also launch common TLS attacks (e.g., TLS stripping, rogue TLS certificate) to decrypt the HTTPS traffic [52] where the JWT application implements TLS problematically. Therefore, the network adversaries could exploit the insecure behaviors during key transmission or key use stages to infer the JWT key, or mislead the JWT verifiers to accept a forged JWT with a replaced key [11].

4.2   Cryptographic Rules

Based on our threat model, we take an in-depth analysis on the arguments of APIs in the JWT libraries, and summarize all the potential threats of a key throughout its lifecycle discussed by JWT specifications [24–26] and current security best practices [3,44], thus concluding the cryptographic rules in Table 1.

Table 1. JWT-oriented cryptographic rules derived form the APIs of JWT libraries and applications throughout a key lifecycle. ($\Leftarrow$: backward slicing; $\Rightarrow$: forward slicing; $\diamond$: feature analysis in properties files)

ID	Cryptographic Rules	Key Lifecycle	Method	Reference
R-01	Do not use insecure PRNG or predictable PRNG seeds	Generation	$\Leftarrow$, $\Rightarrow$	[29,39]
R-02	Do not use keys with insufficient length		$\Leftarrow$, $\Rightarrow$	[5,24]
R-03	Do not use hard-coded symmetric/private key	Storage	$\Leftarrow$	[5,40]
R-04	Do not use predictable/constant passwords for PBE		$\Leftarrow$	[5,24]
R-05	Do not use predictable/constant passwords for KeyStore		$\Leftarrow$, $\Rightarrow$	[5,40]
R-06	Do not store symmetric/private key in properties files		$\Leftarrow$, $\diamond$	[5,10]
R-07	Do not store private key in plaintext files		$\Leftarrow$, $\diamond$	[5,10]
R-08	Do not use HTTP URL connections for key transmission	Transmission	$\Leftarrow$, $\diamond$	[25,26]
R-09	Do not verify certificates or host names in SSL/TLS in trivial ways during key transmission		$\Leftarrow$, $\Rightarrow$	[31,40]
R-10	Do not use "jwk" and "jku" for key transmission		$\Leftarrow$	[43,45]
R-11	Do not use JWT public key before validating the certificate or certificate chain	Use	$\Leftarrow$, $\Rightarrow$	[25,26]
R-12	Do not use static IVs in cipher operation modes (e.g., CBC and GCM)		$\Leftarrow$	[7,40]
R-13	Do not use PBE with fewer than 1,000 iterations		$\Leftarrow$	[24,40]
R-14	Do not use static salts for PBE		$\Leftarrow$	[24,40]
R-15	Do not use deprecated insecure APIs		$\Rightarrow$	[11,24]

Vulnerabilities in Key Generation. HMAC, digital signature algorithms and symmetric/asymmetric encryption algorithms may be used in JWS or JWE (Sect. 2.1). *R-01* requires that the keys used in the cryptographic algorithms should be derived from a cryptographically secure random number generator. Insecure pseudo-random number generator (PRNG) should not be used (e.g., *java.util.Random*), meanwhile, predictable seeds should not be provided to the PRNG for key generation [39]. Otherwise, the generated key may be easily reversed by an attacker [29]. *R-02* emphasizes the security of information protected by cryptography directly depends on the strength of the keys [5]. However, keys with insufficient length are allowed to be supplied to the cryptographic algorithm APIs of JWT libraries, which may result in inputting keys with insufficient length for developers and thus are vulnerable to brute force attacks [28,40]. For example, RSA-1024 (with less than 112 bits security strength) should not be used to generate a JWT [24], and the key length of HS256 (i.e., HMAC using SHA-256) should be equal or over 256 bits.

Vulnerabilities in Key Storage. Confidentiality shall be provided for all secret key information [5], otherwise, the adversary may easily obtain or infer the key of JWT. However, there are various insecure key storage methods in JWT applications. *R-03* prohibits using hard-coded keys in the program codes. *R-04* and *R-05* forbid using predictable/constant passwords for password-based encryption (PBE) [24] and KeyStore, respectively. For example, though an application can only access its own KeyStore in Android, privilege escalation attacks can bypass this restriction if an insecure password is utilized [40,49]. The following two rules focus on the insecure ways of storing the key information at rest, i.e., in properties files (*R-06*) and plaintext files (*R-07*) [10].

Vulnerabilities in Key Transmission. There are many cases of key transmission in JWT applications, for example, the symmetric HMAC key and the public key in the case of JWS, the key encryption key (KEK) and the public key in the case of JWE. The protocol used to transmit the key must provide security protection, and thus secure TLS must be used for key transmission [25, 26]. Correspondingly, *R-08* forbids using HTTP URL connections for key transmission. *R-09* requires JWT applications to properly verify certificates and host names in SSL/TLS during key transmission to avoid man-in-the-middle attacks [31, 40]. *R-10* forbids using "jwk" and "jku" for key transmission, and additional verification is required (e.g., by matching the URL to a whitelist of allowed locations and ensuring no cookies are sent in the GET request) [43]. This is because JWT provides "jwk" and "jku" header parameters to refer to a resource for a set of public keys, however, blindly trusting the header parameters, which may contain an arbitrary URL, could result in server-side request forgery (SSRF) attacks [45].

Vulnerabilities in Key Use. Before using the public key to which the JWE is encrypted (or the key used to verify the JWS), the recipient must validate the corresponding certificate or certificate chain [25, 26]. *R-11* focuses on the validity of the obtained certificates (e.g., in the "x5c" or "x5u") in JWT, and the public key should be considered as invalid if any validation failure occurs, otherwise, SSRF attacks may occur [45]. As inappropriate settings of other parameters (e.g., IV, salts) may also pose a threat to JWT applications, we involve the following rules in *JWTKey*. Specifically, as JWT supports AES CBC mode and GCM mode to encrypt JWT content, *R-12* emphasizes that static IVs should not be used in CBC mode (to avoid chosen-plaintext attacks [40]) and GCM mode (to avoid forbidden attacks [7]). *R-13* focuses on that at least 1,000 iterations are required for PBE and *R-14* forbids using static salts for PBE, which may result in dictionary attacks [24, 40]. At last, *R-15* prohibits the use of deprecated insecure APIs of JWT libraries. For example, in java-jwt library, both private and public keys are allowed to simultaneously transmit to the *require* API in *Verification* class to verify tokens. Moreover, as RSAES-PKCS1-v1_5 algorithm may be vulnerable to certain attacks (e.g., Bleichenbacher million message attack [11]), thus it is not recommended for new applications [24].

5   Design

5.1   Overview

Figure 2 shows an overview of *JWTKey*, which leverages static program slicing [56] to detect cryptographic vulnerabilities of JWT applications. *JWTKey* takes Java source files (maven or gradle project), *.class* files, *.jar* files, *.war* files or *.apk* files as input, and outputs reports with the identified vulnerabilities.

5.2   Construct System Dependence Graph

Given a JWT application program, *JWTKey* first converts Java source code or byte-code into an intermediate representation (IR) format (i.e., Jimple) by

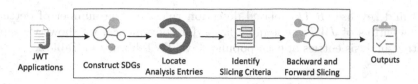

Fig. 2. Overview of *JWTKey*.

taking advantage of Soot [47] framework. Moreover, we use Soot to construct intra-procedural data-dependencies, which can be used to build system dependence graphs (SDGs). For inter-procedural analysis, *JWTKey* uses class-hierarchy analysis to determine the calling relationship between all the methods, thus building a caller-callee relationship of all the methods of the application. The calling relationship can be used to build control dependency edges in the SDG. Moreover, by processing the *AssignStmt* statements defined in Jimple, *JWTKey* adds field influence as a control dependency to the SDG for inter-procedural analysis.

As the original SDG is obtained by stitching all control flow graphs from the program methods, to improve the efficiency and accuracy, *JWTKey* confines the analysis by keeping track of the methods relevant to JWT implementations. Namely, we track the cryptographic related information to pinpoint a sub-callgraph during the whole key lifecycle. Since the sub-callgraph is typically small, its corresponding SDG will also be small.

5.3 Analysis Entries and Slicing Criteria

JWTKey adopts static program slicing to identify cryptographic vulnerabilities in JWT applications. In particular, we take the APIs, which are provided by the JWT libraries to generate or verify JWT, as analysis entries.

Analysis Entries. *JWTKey* locates the starting point of key related operations in JWT libraries and divides the analysis-entry-APIs from JWT libraries into the following two categories. First, the key specification APIs for JWT generation. JWT libraries provide APIs to set key related parameters for JWT generation and support developers to specify the algorithm and the corresponding key for signing or encrypting. *JWTKey* uses this kind of APIs as analysis entries to detect rules related to key generation (*R-01* and *R-02*), key storage (*R-03* to *R-07*), and key use (*R-12* to *R-15*). For example, *JWTKey* utilizes the *sign-With (Key key, SignatureAlgorithm alg)* method in *JWTBuilder* provided by jjwt library [27] as analysis entry and takes the key as the parameter of interest to perform slice analysis for different rules detection. Second, another category of analysis entries comprises the key specification APIs for JWT verification. For example, the *setVerificationKey(Key key)* method in the *JwtConsumerBuilder* class of Jose4j library [6]. *JWTKey* takes the key as the parameter of interest to perform analysis of key storage (*R-03* and *R-06*), key transmission (*R-08* to

272   B. Xu et al.

R-10) and key use (*R-11*) related detection rules. As the number of detected analysis entries of *JWTKey* is quite large, for convenience, we show two representative analysis entries of each popular Java JWT library in Table 2.

Table 2. The representative analysis entries APIs of the top 7 most popular Java JWT libraries (i.e., java-jwt, jjwt, jose.4.j, Nimbus-JOSE-JWT, Spring Security OAuth, FusionAuth JWT and Vert.x Auth JWT).

No.	Analysis Entry
1.1	com.auth0.jwt.algorithms.Algorithm HMAC256(**java.lang.String**)
1.2	com.auth0.jwt.algorithms.Algorithm RSA256(**java.lang.String**)
2.1	io.jsonwebtoken.JwtBuilder signWith(io.jsonwebtoken.SignatureAlgorithm,**byte[]**)
2.2	io.jsonwebtoken.JwtParser setSigningKey(**java.lang.String**)
3.1	org.jose4j.keys.HmacKey void < init>(**byte[]**)
3.2	org.jose4j.keys.AesKey void <init>(**byte[]**)
4.1	com.nimbusds.jose.crypto.MACSigner void <init>(**byte[]**)
4.2	com.nimbusds.jose.crypto.DirectEncrypter void <init>(**javax.crypto.SecretKey**)
5.1	org.springframework.security.jwt.crypto.sign.RsaSigner: void <init>(**java.lang.String**)
5.2	org.springframework.security.jwt.crypto.sign.EllipticCurveVerifier: void <init> (**java.security.interfaces.ECPublicKey**, java.lang.String)
6.1	io.fusionauth.jwt.hmac.HMACSigner: void <init>(io.fusionauth.jwt.domain.Algorithm,**byte[]**,java.lang.String, io.fusionauth.security.CryptoProvider)
6.2	io.fusionauth.jwt.rsa.RSASigner: void <init>(io.fusionauth.jwt.domain.Algorithm,**java.security.PrivateKey**, java.lang.String, io.fusionauth.security.CryptoProvider)
7.1	io.vertx.ext.auth.PubSecKeyOptions setPublicKey(**java.lang.String**)
7.2	io.vertx.ext.auth.PubSecKeyOptions setSecretKey(**java.lang.String**)

Slicing Criteria. Note that insecure key storage behaviours (i.e., *R-03, R-06* and *R-07*) can be detected by the corresponding analysis entries, while the others need more rounds of program slicing. For the other rules, starting from the analysis entries, the propagation paths of the parameter of interest tracks with the slicing criterion APIs. Similarly, as the number of slicing criterion APIs is quite large, we show partial representative APIs in Table 5 (in the Appendix). The slicing criterion APIs can be divided into two groups: APIs in JWT libraries and APIs in Java cryptographic libraries. First, the APIs in JWT libraries are used to detect the rules related to JWT-specific properties. For example, in *R-08, JWTKey* determines the APIs used to retrieve keys from URI provided by JWT libraries (e.g., the *retrieveKeysFromJWKS* method provided by Fusion-Auth JWT [17]). Then *JWTKey* uses these APIs as slicing criteria to perform a new round of backward slicing to determine whether there is an insecure HTTP connection. For *R-10, R-13, R-14, JWTKey* detects the header parameter setting and getting methods provided by JWT libraries, and performs backward slicing on the parameters of these related methods to analyze the insecure use of "jwk", "jku", "p2c", "p2s" header parameters. *JWTKey* detects IV setting methods in JWT libraries for *R-12*. Second, as only a few of JWT libraries provide APIs to generate random values (e.g., key, random number, salt value), thus a large part of JWT application developers still tend to use the APIs of cryptographic libraries to generate random values. Therefore, *JWTKey* also detects the misuse of the underlying Java cryptographic libraries APIs for different algorithms based on the slicing result of the analysis entries. For example, to detect *R-02*, *JWTKey* identifies the use of the *initialize* method in *KeyPairGenerator* class and the *init* method in *SecretKeySpec* class to check the key size.

5.4   Execute Specific Slicing for Different Rules

We break down the detection of rules into one or more steps and perform backward and/or forward slicing for each step (the fourth column of Table 1).

Backward Slicing. Backward slicing in *JWTKey* consists of intra-procedural and inter-procedural analysis. *JWTKey* leverages the Soot framework to perform def-use analysis to compute slices for intra-procedural backward slicing. For inter-procedural backward analysis, *JWTKey* analyzes the upward inter-propagation of the slicing criterion such as method invocation and indirect field access realized by orthogonal methods based on the intra-procedural backward slicing. For example, in *R-03*, *JWTKey* executes a single round of backward slicing based on key parameters from the analysis entries and locates hard-coded keys by analyzing the assignment statement and *Constant* object (defined by Soot) included in invocation statements of slices. *JWTKey* also checks the length of the hard-coded key for *R-02*. For the rules related to the misuse of APIs in cryptographic libraries (e.g., *R-01*, *R-05*), *JWTKey* performs one or more rounds of backward slicing. *JWTKey* first locates the detected APIs, and then determines the relationship between the APIs and the key lifecycle by analyzing the SDG and the slicing results of the analysis entry. For *R-01*, we detect PRNGs that contain a hard-coded seed value. When *JWTKey* analyzes the call of an insecure API (e.g., *init(byte[])* method in *SecureRandom* class) and determines that the API is related to JWT key generation, it will use the API as a slicing criterion, and execute backward slicing with the *byte[]* parameter. For *R-05*, we detect predictable KeyStore password by performing backward slicing with the parameters of *load*, *store*, *getKey* methods in *java.security.KeyStore* class and *getKeyPair* method in *KeyStoreKeyFactory* class provided by Spring Security OAuth [48] as the slicing criteria.

Forward Slicing. For example, we detect *getPublicKey* method in *X509Certificate* class. As shown in Listing 5.1, r12 is an object of *Certificate* class, where its fields are accessed indirectly with the orthogonal method (i.e., *getPublicKey*), and r13 is an object of *PublicKey* class. We design a forward slicing for *R-11* to detect the object of *PublicKey* class, which is used to verify a JWT. In addition, we perform inter-procedural forward analysis on methods invoking r12 object, and analyze whether these methods include certificate validity verification methods (e.g., *verify* method and *checkValidity* method in *java.security.cert.X509Certificate*) and certificate chain verification methods (e.g., *validate* method in *java.security.cert.CertPathValidatorResult* class).

```
1   r12 = (java.security.cert.X509Certificate) $r11;
2   ......
3   r13 = virtualinvoke r12.<java.security.cert.X509Certificate: java.security.PublicKey
        getPublicKey()>();
```

Listing 5.1. A converted IR of getting the public key from certificate in *R-11*.

Properties File Analysis. A myriad of JWT applications are based on Spring framework [48], which simplifies authentication and authorization implementations [32]. We observe that such applications commonly use properties file to externalize user configuration (e.g., key, password and URI). As static analysis methods commonly cannot capture the full semantics of features (e.g., the injection from properties file) [41], therefore, we conduct a special analysis on the processing of properties files in Spring framework. To detect the symmetric/private key, private key path and insecure HTTP URL in properties file (e.g., *R-06*, *R-07* and *R-08*), *JWTKey* analyzes the annotation of the assignment statement for specifying value, path, or URL of key used to process JWT, searches the *@Value* annotation and parses the corresponding property name, and then retrieves the properties files to obtain the corresponding property value. We analyze the property value injection methods provided by the Spring framework, and add corresponding analysis of *@Configuration*, *@EnableAuthorizationServer*, and *@Autowired* annotations, which are used to configure JWT related values from properties file.

6   Implementation and Evaluation

6.1   Implementation

We implemented *JWTKey* with around 12,403 lines of Java code. *JWTKey* is realized based on the Soot framework [47], which provides compilation and analysis for Java applications. We use the intra-procedural data-flow and def/use analysis provided by Soot to construct SDGs and utilize the worklist algorithm of Soot to process the orthogonal method during slicing. In *JWTKey*, we select and support the top seven most popular JWT libraries (i.e., java-jwt [4], jjwt [27], Nimbus-JOSE-JWT [35], jose.4.j [6], FusionAuth JWT [17], Vert.x Auth JWT [51] and Spring Security OAuth [48]). Note that 99% Java-based JWT applications that we crawled from GitHub are developed based on the above selected libraries.

6.2   Experimental Setup

We select our data-set from GitHub as follows: 1) we determined several key-words (e.g., authorization, authentication, OAuth, OIDC, microservice and mobile application) as the topics where JWT is most widely used to obtain popular open-source applications with JWT usage; 2) in each topic, we filtered by language Java and sorted by the number of stars that are more than 50 stars. Finally, we crawled 358 open source Java-based JWT applications in total. We deployed *JWTKey* on a PC with Intel Core i7-4500U (1.80GHZ CPU and 12GB RAM). The average runtime was 1.34 s per thousand LoC (Line of Code).

6.3 Security Findings in JWT Applications

The detailed evaluation results are shown in Table 3. *JWTKey* reported a total of 417 alerts for the 358 detected JWT applications. Out of the 358 applications, 236 applications (65.92%) have at least one JWT cryptographic vulnerability and 116 applications (32.40%) have at least two related vulnerabilities. Our careful manual source-code analysis (conducted by two Ph.D. students under the guidance of a professor from the area of applied cryptography) confirmed that 410 alerts are true positives, resulting in the accuracy as 98.32%. The 7 false positives are due to the path insensitivity and clipping detection depth when dealing with some complex semantic cases (See Sect. 7). Note that in terms of precision, CryptoGuard outperforms CrySL [1], and CrySL outperforms CryptoLint [30], therefore, we prove the effectiveness of *JWTKey* by making comparative experiments with CryptoGuard [40]. Note that *JWTKey* adopts JWT-oriented cryptographic rules, while some of the rules (e.g., *R-06*, *R-07*, *R-10*, *R-11* and *R-15*) are not supported by CryptoGuard, thus resulting in its direct false negatives.

Table 3. Accuracy comparison between *JWTKey* and CryptoGuard of 358 JWT applications. (TP: True Positives; FN: False Negatives; "-": Not supported. Note that the TP and FN of CryptoGuard are counted with the cryptographic rules of *JWTKey*.)

ID	JWTKey				CryptoGuard [40]	
	# Applications	# Alerts	# TP	Accuracy	# TP	# FN
R-01	1(0.28%)	1(0.24%)	1	100.00%	1	0
R-02	118(32.96%)	125(29.98%)	120	96.00%	4	116
R-03	105(29.33%)	109(26.14%)	109	100.00%	28	81
R-04	1(0.28%)	1(0.24%)	1	100.00%	1	0
R-05	17(4.75%)	17(4.08%)	17	100.00%	13	4
R-06	98(27.37%)	126(30.22%)	126	100.00%	-	126
R-07	3(0.84%)	3(0.72%)	3	100.00%	-	3
R-08	14(3.91%)	17(4.08%)	17	100.00%	1	16
R-09	0(0.00%)	0(0.00%)	0	0.00%	0	0
R-10	1(0.28%)	1(0.24%)	1	100.00%	-	1
R-11	11(3.07%)	11(2.64%)	9	81.82%	-	9
R-12	0(0.00%)	0(0.00%)	0	0.00%	0	0
R-13	1(0.28%)	1(0.24%)	1	100.00%	1	0
R-14	1(0.28%)	1(0.24%)	1	100.00%	1	0
R-15	4(1.12%)	4(0.96%)	4	100.00%	-	4
Total	N/A	417	410	98.32%	50	360

Vulnerabilities in Key Generation. For *R-01*, both *JWTKey* and Crypto-Guard identified 1 case (in GCAuth) using insecure PRNG (i.e., *random* method in *java.lang.Math* class) to generate a JWT key. For *R-02*, *JWTKey* reported 125 alerts, and we confirmed 120 of them. The false positives mainly come from path insensitivity. For example, in wetech-admin, the generated short HMAC key will be combined with other parameters (e.g., user ID) as the final HMAC key. As CryptoGuard detected insecure asymmetric ciphers (e.g., RSA and ECC), thus it can identify the 4 cases of insecure RSA short key pairs (e.g., spring-boot-api-seedling), while it cannot identify the rest 116 cases of short HMAC key (e.g., in restheart and micronaut-microservice).

Vulnerabilities in Key Storage. For *R-03*, *JWTKey* identified 109 cases, 2 of them are hard-coded AES symmetric keys and the rest 107 cases are hard-coded HMAC keys. For example, both litemall (6.7k forks, 17.3k stars) and lamp-cloud (1.2k forks, 4.4k stars) utilize a hard-coded HMAC key to sign and verify JWTs. We also detected that a hard-coded HMAC key is used in Novel-Plus, which has been defined as CVE-2022-36672 [9]. For *R-04*, both *JWTKey* and CryptoGuard reported 1 case of using hard-coded PBE password (i.e., azure-activedirectory). For *R-05*, *JWTKey* identified 17 cases of hard-coded KeyStore password. As CryptoGuard adopts refinements after clipping orthogonal explorations, it missed 81 cases and 4 cases in *R-03* and *R-05*, respectively. The accurate identification of analysis entries and slicing criteria of *JWTKey* shortens the analysis paths and avoids the false negatives of CryptoGuard. Moreover, *JWTKey* reported 126 alerts (e.g., eladmin and Sa-Token) and 3 alerts (e.g., stormpath-sdk-java) for *R-06* and *R-07*, respectively, however, CryptoGuard missed the above two cases due to lacking of feature analysis in properties files.

Vulnerabilities in Key Transmission. For *R-08*, *JWTKey* identified 17 cases of insecure HTTP URL for key transmission (e.g., happyride). However, CryptoGuard missed 16 cases due to a lack of feature analysis in properties files. For *R-09*, note that a JSSE provider (i.e., SunJSSE) is preinstalled and preregistered with JCA, which provides an implementation of secure SSL/TLS protocols [36] for key transmission without the need of self-configuration, thus no alert is reported by *JWTKey* and CryptoGuard. For *R-10*, *JWTKey* identified 1 case of using "jwk" parameter for key transmission in devdojo-microservices.

Vulnerabilities in Key Use. For *R-11*, *JWTKey* identified 11 cases of insecure certificate/chain validation, while we confirmed 9 of them. The 2 false positives come from path insensitivity or clipping detection depth when dealing with self-implemented certificate verification methods with inter-procedural forward analysis. For example, as shown in Listing 6.1, *JWTKey* raised an alert for *R-11* because the application obtains a public key from "x5c" parameter without certificate validity verification. However, this is a false positive due to the *setX5C* is set as false, making the path from line 4 to line 6 unreachable. As a path-insensitive static detector, *JWTKey* cannot handle such conditional execution paths.

```
1    boolean sendX5C;
2    ......//Setting sendX5C as false
3    if(setX5C){
4        List<cert> certs = new ArrayList<>();
5        for (String cert : credential.getEncodedPublicKeyCertificateChain()){
6            certs.add(new Base64(cert));}}
7    ......//cert get from KeyStore
```

Listing 6.1. A false positive example due to path insensitivity for *R-11*.

For *R-12*, no alert is reported by *JWTKey* and CryptoGuard due to the fact that rare applications are based on JWE in the wild. For *R-13* and *R-14*, both *JWTKey* and CryptoGuard reported 1 alert of fewer than 1,000 iterations and static salts for PBE (i.e., azure-activedirectory), respectively. For *R-15*, *JWTKey* identified 4 alerts of using deprecated insecure APIs (e.g., Dashboard uses *require* API to transmit both private and public keys to verify tokens). *JWTKey* identified no use case of RSAES-PKCS1-v1_5 algorithm in our data-set. Note that if a JWT application uses RSAES-PKCS1-v1_5 algorithm, it may not be directly vulnerable to an attack (e.g., Bleichenbacher attack [11]), thus more manual detection efforts should be taken to verify whether it is a vulnerability.

Table 4. Insecure functions provided in JWT libraries. (Lib 1–7 corresponds to java-jwt, jose.4.j, Nimbus-JOSE-JWT, jjwt, FusionAuth JWT, Vert.x Auth JWT and Spring Security OAuth, respectively. $\checkmark$: secure; $\times$: insecure; $\checkmark^{}$: provide insecure functions in previous versions; \: not supported.)

Functions	Lib-1	Lib-2	Lib-3	Lib-4	Lib-5	Lib-6	Lib-7
HMAC key length restriction	$\times$	$\checkmark$	$\checkmark$	$\checkmark^{}$	$\times$	$\times$	$\checkmark^{}$
RSA key length restriction	$\times$	$\checkmark$	$\checkmark$	$\checkmark$	$\checkmark$	$\times$	$\checkmark$
PBE parameters restriction	\	$\times$	$\checkmark$	\	\	\	\
Restrict HTTP for key transmission	$\times$	$\times$	$\times$	\	$\times$	\	\
Certificate verification before obtaining JWT public key	\	$\times$	$\times$	\	$\times$	\	$\times$

6.4 Security Findings in JWT Libraries

As Table 4 shows, *JWTKey* also discovered several vulnerabilities which are due to the insecure functions provided in the JWT libraries. Specifically, some JWT libraries adopt loose policy of key length restriction. For example, java-jwt, FusionAuth JWT, Vert.x Auth JWT, jjwt (before v0.10.0) and Spring Security OAuth (before v2.5.1) allow the use of HMAC keys with insufficient length. Java-jwt and Vert.x Auth JWT allow the use of RSA key pairs with less than 2048 bits. In the case of PBE, certain JWT libraries do not provide PBE functions (e.g., java-jwt and jjwt), while jose.4.j allows users to use less than 1,000 iterations and provides an interface to specify static salts during JWT generation. In the case of key transmission, java-jwt, jose.4.j, Nimbus-JOSE-JWT and FusionAuth JWT provide APIs to obtain keys used to verify signatures from an insecure

HTTP URL. At last, jose.4.j, Nimbus-JOSE-JWT, FusionAuth JWT and Spring Security OAuth provide APIs to obtain the public key from a certificate. However, none of the JWT libraries provide certificate validity verification functions before obtaining JWT public key, leaving this burden to the developers of JWT applications.

7   Limitations and Discussion

As a static analysis detector, same with previous methods [31,40], there still exist some avenues for future improvements for *JWTKey*.

Accuracy. As a static analysis detector, *JWTKey* has several inherent limitations. Firstly, *JWTKey* currently focuses on the APIs provided by the top 7 most popular Java-based JWT libraries, which may incur false negatives in the case of invocation of API from other JWT libraries. Secondly, since the detection is based on data- and control-flow, the limited depth of clipping detection makes it unable to handle certain complex semantics (e.g., determining the final HMAC key length, certificate verification). Thirdly, *JWTKey* can only cover the data stored in program files and properties files. However, if a vulnerable cryptographic argument (e.g., key, and IV) is generated dynamically (e.g., by manual inputting), *JWTKey* cannot detect such cases.

Responsible Disclosure. We contacted 236 developers of JWT applications with cryptographic vulnerabilities to disclose all the confirmed alerts reported in Table 3. We respected the disclosure policies of the companies we contacted. Unfortunately, only 42 developers provided useful feedback on our findings. Specifically, 32 developers acknowledged and fixed the JWT key security management vulnerabilities (e.g., *R-02*, *R-03* and *R-06*) in their applications (e.g., Solon, Admin3, JWT, and Sureness). Some developers (e.g., practical-microservices-architectural-patterns) explained that they support the insecure certificate verification option (*R-11*) by the reason for simplifying implementations. 3 vulnerabilities (e.g., hard-coded key) from 3 JWT applications (i.e., Lilishop, Saas_IHRM, and CWA_Warn) have been declared as non-issue, declaring that the current implementation will not cause specific attacks on their entire systems. We also contacted the developers of JWT libraries to disclose the security findings reported in Table 4, three of them provided feedback on key length and PBE parameter restriction. Firstly, the developer of java-jwt declared that the insufficient key length in HMAC and RSA will not have a specific effect on the users. Secondly, the developer of jose.4.j approved our disclosure, and promised to add a check of iteration count. Thirdly, the developer of Fusion-Auth JWT explained that the responsibility to ensure secure implementations belongs to the users rather than the library, and the restrictions on key length may limit the applicability of the JWT library. We have submitted a series of CVE ID requests to disclose the acknowledged and fixed vulnerabilities (e.g., *R-03*, *R-06*, *R-11* and *R-13*) in popular JWT applications. More details of the responsible disclosure will be provided on the homepage of *JWTKey*.

8 Conclusion

We propose *JWTKey* to detect cryptographic vulnerabilities of JWT applications. *JWTKey* leverages static program slicing technique, along with 15 cryptographic rules strongly coupled with JWT key potential security threats. The evaluation results on 358 JWT applications and the comparative experiments with CryptoGuard demonstrate the effectiveness of our design. Our work highlights a lack of appreciation for the principle of key management in real-world cryptographic deployments, which brings to the surface weaknesses not only in JWT applications, but also in other cryptographic implementations. With respect to the future work, the cryptographic vulnerability detection efforts would be expanded to other typical cryptographic application areas (e.g., blockchain, PKI system, and industrial control system).

Acknowledgements. We would like to thank the anonymous reviewers for their careful reading of our manuscript and their many insightful comments and suggestions. We are grateful to Prof. Juraj Somorovsky for helping us to improve our paper. This work is supported in part by National Natural Science Foundation of China No.62272457, National Key R&D Plan of China under Grant No.2020YFB1005800.

Appendix

Table 5. Partial representative slicing criterion APIs of JWT libraries and Java cryptographic libraries. ($\Leftarrow$: backward slicing; $\Rightarrow$: inter-procedural forward slicing; $\Rightarrow*$: intra-procedural forward slicing)

No.	API	Method
1.1	java.util.Random: int nextInt(int)	$\Rightarrow$
1.2	java.util.Random: double nextDouble()	$\Rightarrow$
1.3	java.security.SecureRandom: void <init>(**byte[]**)	$\Leftarrow$
1.4	java.security.SecureRandom: void setSeed(**byte[]**)	$\Leftarrow$
2.1	java.security.KeyPairGenerator: KeyPairGenerator getInstance(java.lang.String)	$\Rightarrow*$
2.2	java.security.KeyPairGenerator: KeyPairGenerator getInstance(String,String)	$\Rightarrow*$
2.3	java.security.KeyPairGenerator: void initialize(**int**)	$\Leftarrow$
2.4	javax.crypto.spec.SecretKeySpec: void <init>(**byte[]**,String)	$\Leftarrow$
4.1	org.jose4j.jwe.kdf.PasswordBasedKeyDerivationFunction2: byte[] derive(**byte[]**,byte[],int,int)	$\Leftarrow$
4.2	com.nimbusds.jose.crypto.PasswordBasedEncrypter: void <init>(**java.lang.String**,int,int)	$\Leftarrow$
5.1	org.springframework.security.oauth2.provider.token.store.KeyStoreKeyFactory: void <init>(org.springframework.core.io.Resource,**char[]**)	$\Leftarrow$
5.2	java.security.KeyStore: void load(InputStream,**char[]**)	$\Leftarrow$
8.1	com.auth0.jwk.UrlJwkProvider: void <init>(**java.lang.String**)	$\Leftarrow$
8.2	org.jose4j.jwk.HttpsJwks: void <init>(**java.lang.String**)	$\Leftarrow$
8.3	com.nimbusds.jose.jwk.source.RemoteJWKSet: void <init>(**java.net.URL**)	$\Leftarrow$
8.4	io.fusionauth.jwks.JSONWebKeySetHelper: java.util.List retrieveKeysFromJWKs(**java.lang.String**)	$\Leftarrow$
9.1	javax.net.ssl.HostnameVerifier: boolean verify(String,SSLSession)	$\Rightarrow$
9.2	javax.net.ssl.SSLSocketFactory: SocketFactory getDefault()	$\Rightarrow*$
10.1	com.nimbusds.jose.JWSHeader: com.nimbusds.jose.jwk.JWK getJWK()	$\Leftarrow$
10.2	com.nimbusds.jose.JWEHeader: java.net.URI getJWKURL()	$\Leftarrow$
11.1	java.security.cert.X509Certificate: void verify	$\Rightarrow*$
11.2	java.security.cert.X509Certificate: void checkValidity	$\Rightarrow*$
12.1	javax.crypto.spec.IvParameterSpec: void <init>(**byte[]**)	$\Leftarrow$
12.2	javax.crypto.spec.IvParameterSpec: void <init>(**byte[]**,int,int)	$\Leftarrow$
13.1	org.jose4j.jwe.kdf.PasswordBasedKeyDerivationFunction2: byte[] derive(byte[],byte[],**int**,int,java.lang.String)	$\Leftarrow$
13.2	com.nimbusds.jose.crypto.PasswordBasedEncrypter: void <init>(java.lang.String,int,**int**)	$\Leftarrow$
14.1	org.jose4j.jwe.kdf.PasswordBasedKeyDerivationFunction2: byte[] derive(byte[],**byte[]**,int,int)	$\Leftarrow$
14.2	org.jose4j.jwe.kdf.PasswordBasedKeyDerivationFunction2: byte[] derive(byte[],**byte[]**,int,int,java.lang.String)	$\Leftarrow$
15.1	com.auth0.jwt.interfaces.Verification require(com.auth0.jwt.algorithms.Algorithm)	$\Rightarrow$
15.2	com.nimbusds.jose.crypto.impl.RSA1_5: void <init>()	$\Rightarrow$

References

1. Afrose, S., Xiao, Y., Rahaman, S., Miller, B., Yao, D.D.: Evaluation of static vulnerability detection tools with java cryptographic API benchmarks. IEEE Trans. Softw. Eng. **49**, 485–497 (2022)
2. Al Rahat, T., Feng, Y., Tian, Y.: OAUTHLINT: an empirical study on OAuth bugs in android applications. In: 2019 34th IEEE/ACM International Conference on Automated Software Engineering (ASE), pp. 293 304. IEEE (2019)
3. Ami, A.S., Cooper, N., Kafle, K., Moran, K., Poshyvanyk, D., Nadkarni, A.: Why crypto-detectors fail: a systematic evaluation of cryptographic misuse detection techniques. In: 2022 IEEE Symposium on Security and Privacy (SP), pp. 614–631. IEEE (2022)
4. Auth0: Java jwt. A Java implementation of JSON Web Token (JWT) - RFC 7519 (2017). https://github.com/auth0/java-jwt
5. Barker, E.: Nist special publication 800–57 part 1 revision 5, recommendation for key management, part 1-general. NIST Spec. Publ. **800–57**, 1–171 (2020)
6. Bitbucket: Welcome to jose4j (2015). https://bitbucket.org/b_c/jose4j/wiki/Home
7. Böck, H., Zauner, A., Devlin, S., Somorovsky, J., Jovanovic, P.: {Nonce-Disrespecting} adversaries: practical forgery attacks on {GCM} in {TLS}. In: 10th USENIX Workshop on Offensive Technologies (WOOT 16) (2016)
8. Cve-2022-35540 (2022). https://nvd.nist.gov/vuln/detail/CVE-2022-35540
9. Cve-2022-36672 (2022). https://nvd.nist.gov/vuln/detail/CVE-2022-36672
10. CWE-260: Password in configuration file (2022). https://cwe.mitre.org/data/definitions/260.html
11. Detering, D., Somorovsky, J., Mainka, C., Mladenov, V., Schwenk, J.: On the (in-) security of javascript object signing and encryption. In: Proceedings of the 1st Reversing and Offensive-oriented Trends Symposium, pp. 1–11 (2017)
12. Egele, M., Brumley, D., Fratantonio, Y., Kruegel, C.: An empirical study of cryptographic misuse in android applications. In: Proceedings of the 2013 ACM SIGSAC Conference on Computer and Communications Security, pp. 73–84 (2013)
13. Ethelbert, O., Moghaddam, F.F., Wieder, P., Yahyapour, R.: A JSON token-based authentication and access management schema for cloud SaaS applications. In: 2017 IEEE 5th International Conference on Future Internet of Things and Cloud (FiCloud), pp. 47–53. IEEE (2017)
14. Fett, D., Küsters, R., Schmitz, G.: A comprehensive formal security analysis of OAuth 2.0. In: Proceedings of the 2016 ACM SIGSAC Conference on Computer and Communications Security, pp. 1204–1215 (2016)
15. Fett, D., Küsters, R., Schmitz, G.: The web SSO standard openID connect: In-depth formal security analysis and security guidelines. In: 2017 IEEE 30th Computer Security Foundations Symposium (CSF), pp. 189–202. IEEE (2017)
16. Frantz, M., Xiao, Y., Pias, T.S., Yao, D.D.: Poster: Precise detection of unprecedented python cryptographic misuses using on-demand analysis. The Network and Distributed System Security (NDSS) Symposium (2022)
17. FusionAuth: Fusionauth jwt (2016). https://github.com/fusionauth/fusionauth-jwt
18. Ghasemisharif, M., Ramesh, A., Checkoway, S., Kanich, C., Polakis, J.: O single sign-off, where art thou? an empirical analysis of single sign-on account hijacking and session management on the web. In: 27th USENIX Security Symposium (USENIX Security 18), pp. 1475–1492 (2018)

19. Guy Rosen: Facebook security update (2018). https://about.fb.com/news/2018/09/security-update/

20. Haekal, M., et al.: Token-based authentication using JSON web token on SIKASIR restful web service. In: 2016 International Conference on Informatics and Computing (ICIC), pp. 175–179. IEEE (2016)

21. Hammer-Lahav, E.: RFC 5849: The OAuth 1.0 protocol. Tech. rep., Internet Engineering Task Force (2010)

22. Hardt, D.: RFC 6749: The OAuth 2.0 authorization framework. Tech. rep., Internet Engineering Task Force (2012)

23. Jones, M., Bradley, J., Sakimura, N.: RFC 7519: JSON web token (JWT). Tech. rep, Internet Engineering Task Force (2015)

24. Jones, M.: RFC 7518: JSON web algorithms (JWA). Tech. rep, Internet Engineering Task Force (2015)

25. Jones, M., Bradley, J., Sakimura, N.: RFC 7515: JSON web signature (JWS). Tech. rep, Internet Engineering Task Force (2015)

26. Jones, M., Hildebrand, J.: RFC 7516: JSON web encryption (JWE). Tech. rep, Internet Engineering Task Force (2015)

27. Jwtk: Jjwt. Java JWT: JSON Web Token for Java and Android (2016). https://github.com/jwtk/jjwt

28. Kleinjung, T., et al.: Factorization of a 768-bit RSA modulus. In: Rabin, T. (ed.) CRYPTO 2010. LNCS, vol. 6223, pp. 333–350. Springer, Heidelberg (2010). https://doi.org/10.1007/978-3-642-14623-7_18

29. Krawczyk, H.: How to predict congruential generators. In: Brassard, G. (ed.) CRYPTO 1989. LNCS, vol. 435, pp. 138–153. Springer, New York (1990). https://doi.org/10.1007/0-387-34805-0_14

30. Krüger, S., Späth, J., Ali, K., Bodden, E., Mezini, M.: CrySL: an extensible approach to validating the correct usage of cryptographic APIs. IEEE Trans. Software Eng. 47(11), 2382–2400 (2019)

31. Li, W., Jia, S., Liu, L., Zheng, F., Ma, Y., Lin, J.: CryptoGO: automatic detection of go cryptographic API misuses. In: Annual Computer Security Applications Conference, pp. 318–331 (2022)

32. Meng, N., Nagy, S., Yao, D., Zhuang, W., Argoty, G.A.: Secure coding practices in java: challenges and vulnerabilities. In: Proceedings of the 40th International Conference on Software Engineering, pp. 372–383 (2018)

33. Michaelides, M., Sengul, C., Patras, P.: An experimental evaluation of MQTT authentication and authorization in IoT. In: WiNTECH'21: Proceedings of the 15th ACM Workshop on Wireless Network Testbeds, Experimental evaluation & CHaracterization, New Orleans, LA, USA, 4 February 2022, pp. 69–76. ACM (2021)

34. Mousa, A., Hamad, A.: Evaluation of the rc4 algorithm for data encryption. Int. J. Comput. Sci. Appl. 3(2), 44–56 (2006)

35. Nimbusds: Nimbus-jose-jwt (2016). https://bitbucket.org/connect2id/nimbus-jose-jwt/src/master/

36. Oracle: Java secure socket extension (jsse) reference guide (2018). https://docs.oracle.com/javase/8/docs/technotes/guides/security/jsse/JSSERefGuide.html#StandardAPI

37. OWASP: reverse engineering (2023). https://owasp.org/www-project-mobile-top-10/2016-risks/m9-reverse-engineering

38. Piccolboni, L., Di Guglielmo, G., Carloni, L.P., Sethumadhavan, S.: CRYLOGGER: detecting crypto misuses dynamically. In: 2021 IEEE Symposium on Security and Privacy (SP), pp. 1972–1989. IEEE (2021)

39. Rahaman, S., Cai, H., Chowdhury, O.H., Yao, D.D.: From theory to code: identifying logical flaws in cryptographic implementations in C/C++. IEEE Trans. Dependable Secure Comput. **19**, 3790–3803 (2021)
40. Rahaman, S., et al.: CryptoGuard: high precision detection of cryptographic vulnerabilities in massive-sized java projects. In: Proceedings of the 2019 ACM SIGSAC Conference on Computer and Communications Security, pp. 2455–2472 (2019)
41. Rahat, T.A., Feng, Y., Tian, Y.: Cerberus: query-driven scalable vulnerability detection in oauth service provider implementations. In: Proceedings of the 2022 ACM SIGSAC Conference on Computer and Communications Security, pp. 2459–2473 (2022)
42. Sabir, B.E., Youssfi, M., Bouattane, O., Allali, H.: Authentication and load balancing scheme based on JSON token for multi-agent systems. Proced. Comput. Sci. **148**, 562–570 (2019)
43. Sakimura, N., Bradley, J., Jones, M., De Medeiros, B., Mortimore, C.: OpenID connect core 1.0. The OpenID Foundation, p. S3 (2014)
44. Sharif, A., Carbone, R., Sciarretta, G., Ranise, S.: Best current practices for OAuth/OIDC native apps: a study of their adoption in popular providers and top-ranked android clients. J. Inf. Secur. Appl. **65**, 103097 (2022)
45. Sheffer, Y., Hardt, D., Jones, M.: RFC 8725: JSON web token best current practices. Tech. rep, Internet Engineering Task Force (2020)
46. Singh, J., Chaudhary, N.K.: OAuth 2.0 : architectural design augmentation for mitigation of common security vulnerabilities. J. Inf. Secur. Appl. **65**, 103091 (2022)
47. Soot-oss: Soot - a framework for analyzing and transforming java and android applications (2022). https://soot-oss.github.io/soot/
48. Spring: Spring security OAuth (2016). https://github.com/spring-attic/spring-security-oauth
49. van der Veen, V., et al.: Drammer: deterministic Rowhammer attacks on mobile platforms. In: Proceedings of the 2016 ACM SIGSAC Conference on Computer and Communications Security, pp. 1675–1689 (2016)
50. Varalakshmi, P., Guhan, B., Dhanush, T., Saktheeswaran, K., et al.: Improvising JSON web token authentication in SDN. In: 2022 International Conference on Communication, Computing and Internet of Things (IC3IoT), pp. 1–8. IEEE (2022)
51. Vertx: Vert.x jwt auth (2019). https://vertx.io/docs/vertx-auth-jwt/java/
52. Wang, H., Zhang, Y., Li, J., Gu, D.: The achilles heel of OAuth: a multi-platform study of OAuth-based authentication. In: Proceedings of the 32nd Annual Conference on Computer Security Applications, pp. 167–176 (2016)
53. Wang, H., et al.: Vulnerability assessment of OAuth implementations in android applications. In: Proceedings of the 31st Annual Computer Security Applications Conference, pp. 61–70 (2015)
54. Wen, M., Liu, Y., Wu, R., Xie, X., Cheung, S.C., Su, Z.: Exposing library API misuses via mutation analysis. In: 2019 IEEE/ACM 41st International Conference on Software Engineering (ICSE), pp. 866–877. IEEE (2019)
55. Wickert, A.K., Baumgärtner, L., Breitfelder, F., Mezini, M.: Python crypto misuses in the wild. In: the 15th ACM/IEEE International Symposium on Empirical Software Engineering and Measurement (ESEM), pp. 1–6 (2021)
56. Xu, B., Qian, J., Zhang, X., Wu, Z., Chen, L.: A brief survey of program slicing. ACM SIGSOFT Softw. Eng. Notes **30**(2), 1–36 (2005)
57. Zhang, L., Chen, J., Diao, W., Guo, S., Weng, J., Zhang, K.: CryptoREX: large-scale analysis of cryptographic misuse in IoT devices. In: RAID, pp. 151–164 (2019)

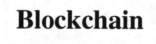

Blockchain

When is Slower Block Propagation More Profitable for Large Miners?

Zhichun Lu[1] and Ren Zhang[1,2(✉)]

[1] Cryptape Co. Ltd., Hangzhou, China
zhichunlu@cryptape.com
[2] Nervos, Hangzhou, China
ren@nervos.org

Abstract. For years, Bitcoin miners put little effort into adopting several widely-acclaimed block acceleration techniques, which, as some argued, would secure their revenues. Their indifference inspires a theory that slower block propagation is beneficial for some miners. In this study, we analyze and confirm this counterintuitive theory. Specifically, by modeling inadvertent slower blocks, we show that a mining coalition that controls more than a third of the total mining power can earn unfair revenue by propagating blocks slower to outsiders. Afterward, we explore the strategies of an attacker that consciously exploits this phenomenon. The results indicate that an attacker with 45% of the total mining power can earn 58% of the total revenue. This attack is alarming as it is equally fundamental but more stealthy than the well-known selfish mining attack. At last, we discuss its detection and defense mechanisms.

Keywords: blockchain · slow block attack · selfish mining

1 Introduction

Nakamoto consensus (NC), implemented in Bitcoin [22] and hundreds of subsequent digital currencies [19], is the first and most influential protocol to maintain an inalterable ledger without relying on any prior knowledge of the participants' identities. The ledger, called the *blockchain*, is organized as a chain of *blocks*; each block contains a set of transactions. NC's participants, called *miners*, compete for the right to extend the ledger by solving a cryptographic puzzle, generated from the blockchain's latest block and a group of new transactions. The puzzle-solving process is called *mining*. A successful miner broadcasts the puzzle solution and the transactions as a new block, hoping that other miners would accept the block in their blockchains, so that the miner is entitled to a fixed *block reward*. When a block is mined during another one's propagation, these blocks may extend the same "latest block" and the blockchain thus *forks* into multiple chains. During a fork, NC prescribes miners to work on the *main chain*, which is the most computationally challenging one to produce—usually the longest one. When several chains are of equal "length", miners should work on the *first-received* one. We

G. Tsudik et al. (Eds.): ESORICS 2023, LNCS 14346, pp. 285–305, 2024.
https://doi.org/10.1007/978-3-031-51479-1_15

call this situation a *tie*. Eventually, all miners would adopt the same longest chain, and blocks outside the chain are called *orphaned* and receive no reward.

Intuitively, the first-received policy incentivizes *all* miners to accelerate the propagation of their own blocks, because an accelerated block (1) is less likely to encounter a tie, and thus is less likely to be orphaned, and (2) could reach more miners before a slower competitor, and thus is more likely to win a tie. This intuition is stated or implicitly acknowledged in several early [1,2] and recent [18, 27] studies. Bitcoin developers also released Fast Internet Bitcoin Relay Engine (FIBRE) [10] in 2016 to help the miners distribute blocks as fast as possible among each other.

However, contrary to the common expectation, a significant proportion of Bitcoin's mining power did not embrace FIBRE to avoid ties. This can be seen from the stable 0.2% *orphan rate*, i.e., the percentage of orphaned blocks, between 2015 and mid-2017 [4,24]. The orphan rate dropped rapidly afterward thanks to the efforts of the network participants, i.e., *nodes*, rather than the miners. Specifically, in July 2017, the majority of nodes upgraded their clients to advocate their unwillingness for Bitcoin to split into multiple cryptocurrencies [16]. Such a massive-scale upgrade coincidentally deployed Compact Blocks [9], a network-level block propagation acceleration technique, which lowers the 3-second average latency for a new block to propagate to 50% of nodes to 500 ms [11]. As a result, orphaned blocks were reduced from one every three to four days to several per year [4].

Maxwell [20] and several other researchers [7,24] proposed a theory to explain the inconsistency between the miners' presumed rationale to accelerate their blocks' propagation and their indifference in reality. In this theory, slower block propagation might benefit larger miners, as they enjoy a headstart in finding the next block. This theory is not only *counterintuitive*—miners who accelerate their blocks may find themselves in a more disadvantageous situation—but also *subversive* to our understanding of NC's security—a system may be experiencing systemic unfairness even without any observable attacks. However, without a quantitative analysis of this phenomenon, whether or when can these seemingly inadvertent slow blocks profit their miners remains inconclusive.

In this paper, we address this situation by formally modeling the propagation of these slow blocks. We start by confirming this possibly inadvertent but systemic unfairness and computing its boundary conditions with a Markov process (MP), and then integrate Bitcoin's network parameters into the MP and evaluate against the boundary conditions. Further, we model a strategic adversary who consciously exploits this phenomenon for profit with a Markov decision process (MDP), which reveals more intricacies of NC's security.[1] In particular, our contributions include:

Confirming the Systemic Unfairness Caused by Slow Blocks. To confirm Maxwell's theory, we model the mining and block propagation process with some blocks slower than others with an MP. The MP is simple: the slow blocks' miner,

---

[1] Code available at https://github.com/Mitsuhamizu/delayed-miner-reward.

termed *D-miner* for "delay", does not employ any strategic behavior based on the status of the blockchain. Such a simple MP allows us to test the possibility of systemic unfairness even when all miners are benign.

The results show that slow blocks do raise D-miner's revenue share within a certain range of parameters. Specifically, a D-miner with a mining power share ρ can gain an unfair profit when $\rho > (1-\gamma)/(2-\gamma)$, where γ is the proportion of other mining power that works on the slow block during a tie. The profitable threshold $(1-\gamma)/(2-\gamma)$ is less than 0.5 as long as $\gamma > 0$, contradicting the intuition that all miners should accelerate their blocks. Moreover, in line with the selfish mining attack [15], the D-miner's unfair profit grows superlinearly with ρ, which incentivizes rational miners to join their forces and form a coalition, damaging the network's decentralized structure, just like Maxwell predicted [20].

Evaluating the Boundary Conditions with Bitcoin's Network Parameters. As the key parameter γ in our MP is not directly measurable, our MP cannot be plugged right into reality and answer questions regarding the inadvertent D-miner with a given ρ, including (1) whether it should produce slow blocks (or propagate its blocks slower), and (2) what is the optimal delay. We thus extend our model so that γ can be "dissected" and computed from measurable data. This extension allows us to incorporate the measurement results from the Bitcoin network [17,24], and thus answer the aforementioned questions.

The extended model indicates that in the pre-Compact-Block Bitcoin, a D-miner profits more by delaying its blocks with $\rho > 0.33$. The optimal additional delay grows roughly linearly from 0 when $\rho = 0.33$ to 6.8 s when $\rho = 0.49$.

Quantifying the Damage of Deliberate Attacks. Given that an inadvertent D-miner can make an unfair profit, likely, a *strategic* D-miner can further raise the profit by acting upon the blockchain's status. Rather than waiting for the slow blocks to propagate naturally like an inadvertent D-miner, here the adversary may push the blocks to the receivers when convenient. A fundamental difference between this *slow block attack* and selfish mining, where the adversary delays broadcasting the blocks as long as necessary to invalidate as many other miners' blocks as possible, is that our adversary never "delays" a block longer than a fixed maximum duration. In other words, the natural block propagation delay caps the delay time of all adversary blocks. Although such a constraint lowers the adversary's revenue, it also renders the attack undetectable via the traditional indicators of selfish mining [14], and thus does not risk causing a drop in the cryptocurrency's price. Therefore, we can regard the slow block attack as a stealthier, hence "safer" alternative to selfish mining.

We model the slow block attack with an MDP, where the adversary can choose what to do when one or more blocks are mined before a slow block finishes propagation. When $\rho < 0.42$, the optimal strategies output by our MDP are either honest or *naive*, i.e., to publish enough blocks to cause a tie with the honest public chain whenever possible. For $\rho \geq 0.42$, the strategy becomes more aggressive: the adversary may keep mining on its chain even when it is several blocks shorter than the honest chain. We also observe a rapid increase in the unfair profit in this region. When $\rho = 0.45$, the adversary gains revenue 2% to 26% higher than mining honestly, depending on the maximum delay.

Discussing Countermeasures. At last, we discuss how to detect and/or prevent the slow block attack. All the technical solutions require the collective effort of the nodes and the miners. Therefore the core issue at hand is to raise awareness of the stealthiness and fundamentality of the attack. Consequently, we call for the community to rethink the implicit assumption that an NC system, or any other system, is fair and safe when there is no observable attack, and to replace the widely-believed "universal" 50% security threshold with a value matching the system's actual network condition.

2   Block Propagation: The Faster, the Better?

2.1   Nakamoto Consensus

NC is among the most influential and actively studied consensus protocols since the inception of Bitcoin. It is implemented in hundreds of subsequent cyptocurrencies [19], including Ethereum, the cryptocurrency with the second largest market capitalization, before it switches to another protocol in September 2022. Henceforth we use Ethereum to denote the cryptocurrency before the switch.

Each block in NC contains (1) its *height*—distance from the hard-coded *genesis block*, (2) the hash value of the *parent block*, (3) a set of transactions, (4) a timestamp when the block is mined, and (5) a nonce. Embedding the parent hash ensures that a miner chooses which chain to mine on before starting to mine. To construct a valid block, miners work on finding the right nonce so that the block hash is smaller than the *difficulty target*. In Bitcoin, this target is adjusted every 2016 blockchain blocks so that on average one block is appended to the blockchain in ten minutes. In Ethereum, the target is slightly adjusted per block, leading to an average block interval of 13 s [13].

NC prescribes miners to publish blocks the moment they are found. Blocks of the same height are *competing blocks*. Eventually, all but one of the competing blocks are *orphaned*, i.e., discarded by all miners, and receive no reward.

2.2   Selfish Mining

The most influential attack against NC is *selfish mining*, first analyzed by Eyal and Sirer [15] and later generalized to a family of strategies [23,25,28]. In these attacks, a *selfish miner* keeps discovered blocks secret and mines on top of them, hoping to gain a larger lead on the public chain of *honest blocks* mined by other miners. The selfish miner publishes the secret chain when the public chain catches up, or right before that, to invalidate as many honest blocks as possible.

Selfish mining is one of the most fundamental attacks against NC as it allows the attacker to gain a higher percentage of block rewards than its mining power share. As the attacker's revenue rises superlinearly with the mining power, rational miners are incentivized to attack collectively for higher profits. This situation not only damages the system's decentralized structure but also raises the success rates of various other attacks.

Luckily, the community generally believes that selfish mining has never happened in Bitcoin as it is easily detectable [14]. Essentially, as the attacker cannot predict when the next honest block will be mined—hence when the secret block should be released, a secret block's timestamp is usually inconsistent with its releasing time, which would expose the attacker. As we shall see, the slow block attack undermines NC's security in the same way but is more difficult to detect.

2.3 Two Conflicting Opinions

The absence of selfish mining is often attributed to its detectability, as visible attacks on a cryptocurrency often cause sharp declines in its price, resulting in a financial loss larger than the attacker's gain. This argument is termed *exchange rate rationality* by Bonneau et al. [5]. Given that rational miners would not risk being detected to mine selfishly, whether due to exchange rate rationality or some other reasons, people disagree on whether all miners are incentivized to accelerate the propagation of their own blocks.

On the one hand, it is a general belief that although it might be irrational to propagate *other* miners' blocks, all miners would accelerate their *own* blocks' propagation, to avoid ties or to raise the probability of winning potential ties by being the first-received ones. This argument is first proposed by Babaioff as early as 2012 [1] and has echoed for a decade [2,18,27].

On the other hand, observing the slow adoption of FIBRE, Maxwell mentioned in a talk in 2017 that slower block propagation might benefit larger miners [20]. He further suspected that this phenomenon, as in selfish mining, would drive miners to form a coalition that propagates blocks immediately to insiders but slower to outsiders. Likewise, Neudecker and Hartenstein [24] speculated that "the block propagation delay gives the miner of the last block an advantage in finding the subsequent block, until other miners have received the block." Cao et al. also mentioned in [7] that a slower block may cause some miners to "waste hashing power on an already solved cryptographic puzzle".

The conflict between these two opinions has profound implications for NC's security. If the former is true, as long as no mining coalition controls more than half of the mining power, NC systems are seemingly incentive compatible in the absence of detectable selfish mining. Otherwise, we need to reevaluate the commonly-believed 50% security threshold and the effectiveness of exchange rate rationality in securing the network. We aim to resolve these conflicting views by quantitatively analyzing the slower block propagation behavior.

3   Modeling the Inadvertent D-Miner

Our analysis starts with the simplest case, where the slow blocks' miner, despite the (possibly inadvertent) delay, strictly follows NC. First, we discuss the potential causes of such a delay. We then introduce our threat model and how we model such a D-miner with an MP, whose results confirm the systemic unfairness.

3.1 The Potential Causes of the Longer Block Propagation Delay

The delay may reside in multiple phases in a block's lifecycle.

Pre-propagation. Before broadcasting a block, the miner processes it internally. Such processing includes (1) combining the puzzle solution with the transactions and (2) sending the block to the "guard nodes" [21], who are in charge of the broadcast. Both steps may be time-consuming when the guard nodes crash or when the mining pool communication software does not behave as expected.

In-propagation. Two reasons may lead to in-propagation delay. First, the miner may broadcast from some poorly-connected nodes, with few connections and low bandwidth. Second, the block itself may take longer to synchronize, perhaps because it is larger than the other blocks. Note that Compact Blocks (CBs), which hope to reduce the propagation latency by optimistically not transferring the transactions by default, do not eliminate the second case. This is because CBs accelerate a block's propagation only when all its transactions are already synchronized when the block is mined. If some transactions are new, or only known to the block miner, for each hop of the block's propagation, an extra round trip is required to query these transactions [9].

Post-propagation. After receiving a new block, miners should verify the validity of its transactions before starting to work on it, to avoid wasting time on an invalid block. This can be time-consuming when some transactions refer to a large number of previous transactions stored physically distantly from each other on the hard disk [6].

An inadvertent delay may happen at any phase. However, for a malicious D-miner, pre-propagation is the most convenient phase, because it does not require a large or slow-to-verify block, allowing the attacker to, when convenient, stop the delay and push the block to the receivers before the competing blocks.

3.2 The Threat Model for Our MP

We choose a weak yet realistic threat model to showcase that systemic unfairness exists even without any sophisticated attacks. Time is continuous and mining is modeled as a Poisson process with an average block interval T. Accordingly, the probability that all miners find exactly n blocks in t seconds is $(t/T)^n/n! \cdot e^{-t/T}$. There is only one D-miner with mining power share $\rho < 1$, whose blocks are delayed up to D seconds. We do not prescribe $\rho < 0.5$ to cover the case that several large mining pools propagate blocks quickly among each other but slowly to the outside world. All other miners, who control mining power share μ (where

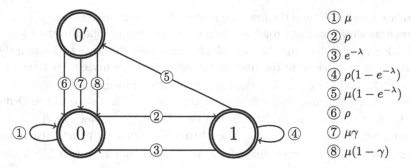

Fig. 1. Markov model with an inadvertent D-miner. The double-circled nodes denote the blockchain's states. The directed edges denote the transitions, whose probabilities are written on the right.

$\mu + \rho = 1$) broadcast their blocks immediately, which cannot be delayed by the D-miner. Since there is no need to distinguish these other miners, we use the singular form "the undelayed miner" for simplicity. Both ρ and μ remain unchanged throughout the process. All miners follow the longest chain rule, and each fork lasts at most one block. This assumption is reasonable because all Bitcoin forks measured by Neudecker and Hartenstein [24] are one-block long. We neglect transaction fees and only consider block reward in this paper, as the former only makes up 1% of the miners' rewards in Bitcoin [3].

3.3 Our Markov Process

MP is commonly used to model the mining process without any strategic behaviors. In line with previous work [15], the blockchain's statuses are encoded as *states*, i.e., the double-circled nodes in Fig. 1, whose transitions are triggered by two kinds of events: (1) a new block is mined, or (2) D seconds has passed.

There are three states, named after the D-miner's lead to the undelayed miner. In state 0, both miners work on the same block. In state 1, the D-miner has just found a block and is delaying it. Here the D-miner is the only one working on this latest block. In state 0', the blockchain is forked, and the undelayed mining power may be split: some, with a proportion γ, works on the D-miner's block, while the other $1 - \gamma$ works on the latest block mined by the undelayed miner.

We now describe the transitions, starting from state 0. If the undelayed miner finds a block (with probability μ, hereafter referred to as "w.p."), the system stays at state 0, and the undelayed miner gets a block reward (①). Otherwise, the next block is mined by the D-miner (w.p. ρ), who starts the delay and the system enters state 1 (②).

Three transitions may happen at state 1. If no block is mined in D seconds, the D-miner releases the block, gets a block reward, and then the state returns to 0 (③). As mining is modeled as a Poisson process, ③ happens with probability $e^{-\lambda}$, where $\lambda = D/T$ is the expected number of blocks mined in these D seconds.

If there are new blocks and the first one is mined by the D-miner (w.p. $\rho(1-e^{-\lambda})$), the previous slow block is broadcast immediately, issuing one reward to the D-miner, which starts delaying the new block, transiting the state to 1 again (④). If there are new blocks and the first one is mined by the undelayed miner (w.p. $\mu(1 - e^{-\lambda})$), the blockchain is forked and the state transits to 0' (⑤).

Three transitions may happen at state 0'; all end with state 0. If the D-miner finds the next block (w.p. ρ), it wins the tie, claiming two rewards (⑥). If the undelayed miner finds a block on the D-miner's block (w.p. $\mu\gamma$), each miner gets one reward (⑦). Otherwise, if the undelayed miner finds a block on the undelayed block (w.p. $\mu(1 - \gamma)$), the undelayed miner gets two rewards (⑧).

3.4   State Probabilities and Relative Revenues

Stationary Distribution. We derive the following equations from Fig. 1, where p_0, p_1, and $p_{0'}$ are the stationary probability of states 0, 1, and 0', respectively:

$$\begin{cases} p_0 = p_0\mu + p_1 e^{-\lambda} + p_{0'} \\ p_1 = p_0\rho + p_1(1 - e^{-\lambda}\rho) \\ p_{0'} = p_1(1 - e^{-\lambda})\mu \\ 1 = p_0 + p_{0'} + p_1 \end{cases} \tag{1}$$

Solving Eq. (1) gives us these probabilities:

$$\begin{aligned} p_0 &= (\mu + \rho e^{-\lambda})/(1 + \mu\rho + \rho^2 e^{-\lambda}) , \\ p_{0'} &= \rho\mu(1 - e^{-\lambda})/(1 + \mu\rho + \rho^2 e^{-\lambda}) , \\ p_1 &= \rho/(1 + \mu\rho + \rho^2 e^{-\lambda}) . \end{aligned} \tag{2}$$

Relative Revenue. The revenues for the D-miner and the undelayed miner, denoted r_d and r_u, can be computed from the transition probabilities among the states and their corresponding rewards:

$$\begin{aligned} r_d &= 2p_{0'}\rho + p_{0'}\mu\gamma + p_1(1 - e^{-\lambda})\rho + p_1 e^{-\lambda} , \\ r_u &= p_0\mu + 2p_{0'}\mu(1 - \gamma) + p_{0'}\mu\gamma . \end{aligned} \tag{3}$$

Combining Eq. (2) and (3) allows us to compute the *relative revenue*, i.e., the proportion of the D-miner's revenue among all the rewards:

$$R_d = \frac{r_d}{r_d + r_u} = \rho(e^{-\lambda} + (1 - e^{-\lambda})(\rho^2\gamma - 2\rho^2 - 2\rho\gamma + 3\rho + \gamma)) . \tag{4}$$

Equation (4) shows that R_d is a function of three inputs ρ, γ, and λ. We define the *unfair revenue* as $R_d - \rho$, i.e., the difference between R_d and the D-miner's fair reward share, and plot how it varies with these inputs in Fig. 2.

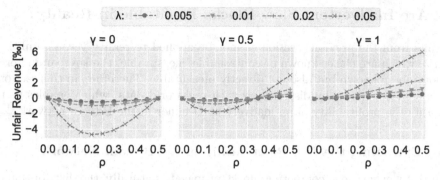

Fig. 2. Overview of unfair revenue for the D-miner

Analysis. Here are three patterns from Fig. 2 and their underlying reasons.

Observation 1. *The D-miner earns unfair revenue with a large enough ρ.*

This confirms the systemic unfairness, that propagating blocks slower can be more profitable than mining honestly, despite that the forks are no more than one block long. Even when $\gamma = 0$, i.e., no undelayed mining power works on the D-miner's block in a tie, the D-miner can still earn an unfair profit with $\rho > 0.5$.

Essentially, the unfair revenue comes from orphaning the undelayed miner's blocks in ties. The D-miner earns a profit if more than μ percentage of orphaned blocks are mined by the undelayed miner, but suffers a loss otherwise.

Observation 2. *Whether the D-miner earns unfair revenue depends only on ρ and γ, not on λ.*

To quantify when the D-miner earns an unfair profit, we solve the inequality $R_d > \rho$, leading to the condition $\rho > (1 - \gamma)/(2 - \gamma)$. Interestingly, this condition does not involve the delay duration λ, because here the D-miner's profitability depends only on the *probability of winning ties*, which further relies on ρ and γ, but not on the *frequency of ties*, which relies on ρ and λ.

The multifunctionality of ρ also explains why when γ and λ are fixed, the D-miner's unfair revenue first decreases, and then increases with a growing ρ. Specifically, when ρ is small, the D-miner loses almost all ties, thus increasing ρ results in a higher loss as it raises the frequency of ties; when ρ grows larger, the D-miner wins more ties, thus profiting more from the ties.

Observation 3. *When γ and ρ are fixed, the D-miner's profit/loss amplifies with a larger λ.*

A larger λ means a higher frequency of ties, amplifying the D-miner's profit/loss.

4   Are Inadvertent Slow Blocks Profitable in Reality?

Results from the previous section cannot be applied to reality yet, as, unlike ρ and λ, which are either known or controllable/measurable, the key parameter γ is not only unknown but also not directly measurable. Therefore, in this section, we extend our model by dissecting γ with real-world data, which enables us to quantify the profitability of an inadvertent D-miner in the Bitcoin network.

4.1   Extracting the D-γ Relationship in the Bitcoin Network

Intuitively, when both competing blocks propagate naturally, the distribution of mining power working on each block—other than their own miners—is mainly decided by the interval between their announcements. This intuition guides us to express γ as a function of D, which consists of two tasks: (1) express γ as a function of the *headstart*, i.e., the (equivalent) announcement interval, (2) express the headstart as a function of D.

Headstart to γ. We can only learn the relation between the headstart t_{hs} and γ from a series of (t_{hs}, γ) data points, where t_{hs} measures how long the block is announced *before* its competitor, in seconds. We fetch the t_{hs} values directly from Neudecker and Hartenstein's measurement study [24], which covers all Bitcoin forks between 2015 and 2017. Although γ is not directly measurable, we can estimate it by extending our model. According to [24], a miner wins a tie with probability $P_{win} = 3.07 \times 10^{-5}t_{hs} + 0.63$. On the other hand, $P'_{win} = \rho + \gamma(1 - \rho)$ in our model, which is the combination of transitions ⑥ and ⑦ in Fig. 1. Assuming $P'_{win} = P_{win}$, we have $\gamma = (3.07 \times 10^{-5}t_{hs} + 0.63 - \rho)/(1 - \rho)$. By inputting the miners' then-mining-power share—fetched from IntoTheBlock [17]—as ρ into this equation, we now have the estimated γ for each data point.

To fit these (t_{hs}, γ) data into a curve, we introduce an additional heuristic that $\gamma = 0.5$ when $t_{hs} = 0$. This is reasonable as two simultaneously-announced competing blocks should have an equal chance to be selected by a third party. Not surprisingly, a linear equation $\gamma(t_{hs}) = 6.37 \times 10^{-2}t_{hs} + 0.5$ for $t_{hs} \in [-7.8, 7.8]$, learned via the least squares method, already gives us a good estimation: the root-mean-square deviation (RMSD) is as low as 0.12.

This (t_{hs}, γ) relation implies that $\gamma = 1$ when $t_{hs} = 7.8$, meaning that it takes 7.8 s for a block to be propagated to all the miners. This result justifies the reasonableness of our model as it is consistent with the measured data: blocks propagated to 90% of nodes in 5 to 20 s [24].

We further verify this relation with Ethereum's data. Specifically, we fetch 236 553 fork instances, group those with similar ρ and t_{hs}, and compare each (ρ, t_{hs}) group's estimated $P'_{win} = \rho + \gamma(t_{hs}) \cdot (1 - \rho)$ and the actual P_{win}. The results confirm the accuracy of our model, whose details are in Appendix A.

D to Headstart. A stable delay D does not imply a stable t_{hs}, as the competing block may be announced anytime during D. If the undelayed competing block

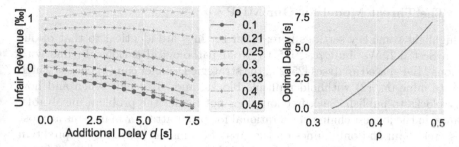

Fig. 3. Extra revenue varies with d and ρ.

Fig. 4. The optimal delay d

is mined in the first $d = D - 7.8$ s, the undelayed block may enjoy a headstart, i.e., $t_{\text{hs}} \leq 0$. Otherwise, the slow block enjoys a headstart and $t_{\text{hs}} > 0$.

We now solve how d, i.e., the slow block's delay in addition to the natural propagation latency, affects the probability distribution of t_{hs}. As mining is a Poisson process, the interval between the slow block's and the undelayed block's mining, denoted t_{in}, follows an exponential distribution, whose density function is $f(t_{\text{in}}) = \mu/600 \times e^{-(\mu/600)t_{\text{in}}}$ for $t_{\text{in}} \in (0, \infty)$, where $\mu/600$ is the expected number of undelayed blocks mined in a second. We compute the probability density function of t_{hs} from $f(t_{\text{in}})$ via two post-processing steps. First, $t_{\text{hs}} = t_{\text{in}} - d$ as the slow block's announcement is delayed for d seconds. Second, the density function is normalized by dividing $1 - e^{-(\mu/600)(d+7.8)}$ to exclude the situation that no undelayed blocks are mined during the slow block's propagation.

Finally, by linking these two relations, we can estimate γ with a given d: $\gamma = 0.748 - 0.0318d$ when $d \ll 600$. We omit the detailed process as it is relatively straightforward compared to the previous two steps.

4.2 Applying the Extended Model to the Bitcoin Network

We instantiate our MP in Sect. 3.3 with $\lambda = D/T = (d + 7.8)/600$ and $\gamma = 0.748 - 0.0318d$. We plot how d and ρ affect the unfair revenue $R_d - \rho$ in Fig. 3 and the most profitable additional delay d in Fig. 4.

Two thresholds—0.21 and 0.33—are identifiable from Fig. 3. Miners with $\rho > 0.21$ gain unfair revenue with no additional delay beyond the universal 7.8 s. Miners with $\rho > 0.33$ can increase their earnings by intentionally delaying block propagation. The optimal—most profitable—additional delay grows roughly linearly, from 0 when $\rho = 0.33$ to 6.8 s when $\rho = 0.49$.

5 Modeling the Strategic D-Miner

We now analyze how and how much a strategic D-miner can profit from the systemic unfairness by modeling its decisions with an MDP. We name the output strategy the *slow block attack*.

5.1   The Threat Model for Our MDP

We highlight some key settings here; other settings are identical to that of our MP in Sect. 3.2. We limit $\rho < 0.5$ to avoid pathological actions. In line with previous MDP-based analyses [25,28], the strategic D-miner can (1) choose which block to mine on, (2) withhold multiple blocks, and (3) decide when and how many blocks to publish. Such freedom does not render the problem unsolvable, because, in the longest chain rule, a rational for-profit attacker maintains at most one secret chain and only mines on the tips of chains, as proved by Sapirshtein et al. [25]. Their proof applies to our model. Henceforth we use *undelayed blocks* to denote "blocks mined by the undelayed miner" for brevity. Our model differs from previous analyses in that the D-miner must broadcast a secret block within every D seconds. This constraint adds a type of transition "delay" to our MDP, which models the passage of time and thus complicates the modeling due to the continuity of time. Consequently, we limit the attacker's actions when accurate modeling is infeasible, so that our MDP outputs achievable strategies and lower bounds on the D-miner's profitability, demonstrating the severity of the attack.

5.2   Our Markov Decision Process

Modeling Mining Processes as MDPs. An MDP models decision-making in situations where outcomes are partly random and partly under the control of a strategic player. Formally, an MDP is a four-element tuple (S, A, P, R). S is the *state space*, encoding all status and history information that might influence the player's decision. A is the *action space*, which includes all possible rational choices in an arbitrary state. P is the *transition matrix*, which encodes all possible outcome states for each (*state*, *action*) pair and their probability distribution. R is the *reward matrix*, which records a *reward* for every (*state*, *action*, *new_state*) transition; the reward is used to compute the final utility.

MDP is commonly employed in modeling mining processes [25,28]. We summarize Sapirshtein [25]'s selfish mining MDP here as the baseline of our design. In their MDP, a state transition is triggered by a mining event, and the attacker makes decisions at the beginning of a state. Blocks accepted or abandoned by both miners are *settled*, whose corresponding rewards are allocated to the miners. Settled blocks are removed from the state encoding, as they do not affect the attacker's decisions. Specifically, a state is a 3-tuple $(l_d, l_u, fork)$ where l_d and l_u represent the lengths of the unsettled attacker chain and the public chain, respectively, and *fork* indicates the latest block's miner and whether the attacker has the option to Match, which is defined next. There are at most four available actions at any moment: Adopt to throw away the attacker chain and mine on the public chain, Override to publish until the $(l_u + 1)$-th attacker block to invalidate the public chain, Match to publish until the l_u-th attacker block to cause a tie, which is available only when the honest miner has just mined a block and the attacker has a competing secret block, and Wait to keep mining on the attacker chain. We omit the reward distribution and the state transition matrices here.

Overview. Our MDP differs from previous works as we introduce a new type of transition called *delay*: the passage of D seconds. When the D-miner chooses not to publish all withheld blocks, the next transition must be a delay.

Formalizing these transitions is highly nontrivial as both the D-miner and the undelayed miner may mine blocks during the delay, and it is infeasible to encode all information that might influence the D-miner's decision. For example, the D-miner may make decisions based on the time of the first undelayed block: to Override if the block is mined at the beginning of D, and to Match if it is mined at the end. However, we cannot encode time into the state, as time is continuous, and the number of states must be finite. Dividing D into several slots and recording the mining sequence in each slot is also impractical, as in that case, the number of states is too large to be solvable.

To address this challenge, we prescribe the D-miner's strategy during the delay so that the system's state after the delay only depends on the pre-delay state and the number of blocks mined by each miner during the delay. Through careful engineering of the state space S and the action space A, the number of states becomes solvable after this simplification, yet our MDP still reveals a series of insights into the slow block attack. Next, we describe our MDP design.

State Space. A state is a four-element tuple $(l_d, l_w, l_u, fork)$. The lengths of the D-miner's and the undelayed miner's chains are encoded as l_d and l_u, respectively. Note that the common ancestors are not counted in l_d or l_u as they are settled. The variable l_w is the number of withheld blocks, which satisfies $l_w \leq l_d$ as these blocks are a suffix of the D-miner's chain. The variable *fork* indicates whether some undelayed mining power is working on the D-miner's chain, which is meaningful only in a tie, i.e., $l_d - l_w = l_u$. It has two possible values:

- Active. The l_u-th D-miner's block is published *along with* the last undelayed block, so some undelayed mining power may work on the D-miner's chain.
- Inactive. The l_u-th D-miner's block is published *after* the last undelayed block, so all undelayed mining power works on the undelayed chain.

There are two differences between our state space and that of [25]. First, we encode l_w explicitly so that the D-miner can learn/decide whether the next transition is a delay, and how many such delays to look forward to. Second, our *fork* has only two options, because the D-miner never needs to explicitly choose the Match action, whose reason is explained next.

Action Space. There are only three actions Adopt, Override, and Wait in our MDP. The definitions of Adopt and Override are identical to their counterparts in [25]. The Wait and Match actions in [25] are merged into our Wait action:

- Wait. If there are no withheld blocks, the D-miner keeps mining on its chain until the next block generation event. Otherwise, i.e., during a delay, the D-miner mines on its chain until the delay ends, and publishes enough blocks to cause a tie, i.e., "Match", when the undelayed chain "catches up from behind" and reaches the D-miner's *pre-delay* chain length l_d.

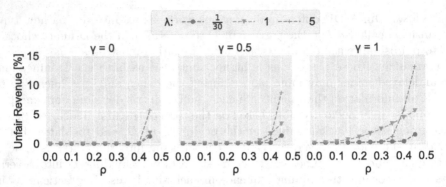

Fig. 5. The ϵ-optimal unfair revenue

To understand this change, we first introduce *how* we prescribe the D-miner's strategy during the delay. Given that a fixed strategy is necessary to avoid an overwhelming number of states, we want a strategy that is simple enough to be computationally feasible, yet still reasonable for the D-miner. A naive strategy is to force the D-miner to keep mining on its chain without publishing anything throughout the delay. This strategy causes a significant loss when the undelayed chain *overtakes*—catches up from behind and surpasses—the D-miner's chain during the delay, as the D-miner loses its entire chain with a high probability. A better strategy is to prescribe the D-miner to publish the entire chain at the exact moment when the undelayed chain catches up. However, as both miners may find blocks during the delay, it is difficult to predict *when* the catch-up happens unless we encode the full sequence of mining events during the delay into the MDP, which is computationally infeasible. Therefore, we choose a middle ground between these two strategies and prescribe the D-miner to cause a tie when the undelayed chain catches up to the D-miner's pre-delay chain length, which is reasonable as it lowers the attacker's risk of losing the whole chain, yet still manageable as there is no need to enumerate all possible mining sequences.

As an unexpected benefit of this "middle-ground" strategy, the D-miner never needs to explicitly choose Match. If the last undelayed block is mined during a delay, Match is automatic; otherwise, i.e., outside delays, the D-miner has no secret block by our threat model, thus cannot choose Match.

Transition and Reward Matrices. We leave the full matrices to Appendix B and provide a detailed description in the online extended version[2], while here, we briefly overview how we compute the post-delay transitions. We denote the number of blocks mined by the D-miner and undelayed miners during the delay as n_d and n_u. They are independent and follow the Poisson distribution, their joint probability distribution of the resulting states $(l_d + n_d, l_w + n_d, l_u + n_u, \text{inactive})$.

---

[2] https://ia.cr/2023/891.

Solving the MDP. We define the utility as the D-miner's relative revenue and solve the MDP with the *RelativeValueIteration* method of pymdptoolbox [8]. The stopping criterion is set to $\epsilon < 10^{-4}$. The upper bound for l_d and l_u is set to 60. We solve the MDP for all combinations of $\rho = \{0, 0.05, \cdots, 0.45\}$, $\gamma = \{0, 0.5, 1\}$, and $\lambda = \{1/30, 1, 5\}$.

5.3   Unfair Revenues and Profitable Thresholds

Relative Revenues. We visualize the D-miner's unfair revenue under various λ, γ, and ρ in Fig. 5, and notice two patterns:

Observation 4. *The strategic D-miner's unfair revenue increases with λ.*

This is consistent with our intuition: a longer delay upper bound gives the D-miner larger room for malicious manipulation, thus increasing the unfair revenue. Also, the unfair revenue never goes below zero, as the D-miner has the honest strategy as a safe choice.

Observation 5. *The unfair revenue rockets when $\rho \geq 0.42$ for all γ and λ.*

We locate the reason by examining the optimal strategies. For $\rho < 0.42$, the unfair revenue mainly comes from winning ties; the D-miner chooses Abandon if its chain is shorter than the undelayed chain. For $\rho \geq 0.42$, the optimal strategy becomes more aggressive: it keeps mining on its own chain even when it is two to four blocks behind. Admittedly, this also makes the attack detectable. We list the full strategy when $\rho = 0.45$, $\gamma = 1$ in Table 1. This strategy is counterintuitive given that $\rho < \mu$. We attribute this to the D-miner's higher risk tolerance than the undelayed miner: the D-miner gives up its chain at its chosen time, but the undelayed miner gives up as soon as it is one block behind. Indeed in the gambler's ruin problem, if one gambler has two to four coins and a 45% one-time winning rate, and the other one has only one coin but a 55% one-time winning rate, the latter is 1.48 to 2.47 times more likely to bankrupt than the former.

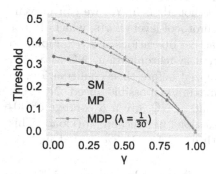

Fig. 6. Comparison of thresholds

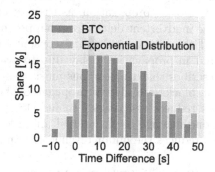

Fig. 7. The time difference

Profitable Thresholds. We compare the profitable thresholds of our MP $((1-\gamma)/(2-\gamma))$, MDP, and selfish mining $((1-\gamma)/(3-2\gamma)$, from [15]) in Fig. 6. The results show that the threshold of the strategic D-miner resides between that of the inadvertent D-miner and the selfish miner.

6   Detection and Defense

Detecting via the Timestamp-Announcement Difference. As mentioned in Sect. 2.2, it is long known that selfish mining can be detected by measuring the difference between the blocks' timestamp and their announcement time. Unfortunately, it is difficult to apply the same trick to detect the slow block attack, at least in Bitcoin, due to the miners' long timestamp updating cycle. We plot Bitcoin's timestamp-announcement difference distribution in Fig. 7 (blue bars), whose data are provided by Grundmann, the maintainer of a Bitcoin monitoring site [11]. There are 33 453 blocks from January 1 to August 20, 2020, and 93% of their differences are within $[-10, 50]$ s. The distribution is far from ideal, where all data concentrate at 0. Instead, it is close to the exponential distribution with an expectation of 30 s (orange bars). We speculate that this is because mining pools use specialized software, e.g., P2Pool [26], to assign tasks and collect shares among individual miners, which updates the timestamp roughly every 30 s. Consequently, as long as the D-miner keeps the delay within 30 s, e.g., $\lambda < 1/20$, it is difficult, if not impossible, to detect the slow block attack from the timestamp-announcement difference.

Detecting via the Orphan Rate. Most mining pools nowadays publish the blocks they mined for transparency, enabling us to compute a pool's percentage of blocks that have competing blocks. A mining pool encountering block races more often than the others is a strong indicator of systemic unfairness. Also, a rise in the overall orphan rate may indicate network issues or malicious behaviors.

Eliminating the Inadvertent Delays from the Protocol Level. Our analysis shows that we cannot expect the miners, especially large ones, to accelerate their blocks' propagation, as their incentive is not aligned. Yet we can prevent these inadvertent delays from happening via protocol-level efforts, which do not need the miners' individual consent or proactive operations. For example, to avoid in-propagation delay due to transaction synchronization, NC-Max [29] prescribes that transactions must be synchronized before their confirmation, so that blocks are always propagated at the maximum possible speed. NC-Max thus reduces the latency to just 18.7% of that in NC, given a context of 40-second average block interval and 100 transactions per second workload. This also reduces the unfair revenue of miners with $\rho = 0.4$ to 19.2% of that in NC.

Modifying the Tie-Breaking Mechanism. When a delayed block is forced to be broadcast due to the announcement of a competing block, its timestamp is usually inconsistent with its announcement time. This is because the

D-miner cannot predict when the competing block will be mined. This phenomenon inspires us to propose a new tie-breaking mechanism, which favors the block with a more accurate timestamp. This new mechanism only works if all undelayed miners synchronize their clocks and keep updating their blocks' timestamps. We leave the detailed threshold and rule of this mechanism to future work.

7 Conclusion

Despite numerous efforts from the Bitcoin community, many miners refused to accelerate their blocks' propagation, as revealed by the slow adoption of FIBRE and Compact Blocks. In this paper, we confirmed Maxwell's theory that slower propagation could be more profitable. These seemingly-benign slow blocks lead to systemic unfairness, which could be deliberately exploited for higher revenue. The slow block attack fundamentally undermines NC's security just like the selfish mining attack, yet is more difficult to detect. To mitigate this unfairness and deter such inadvertent or malicious behaviors, we call on the community to (1) keep accelerating block propagation on the protocol and the network layer, (2) synchronize the clocks and update the block timestamp more frequently, and (3) modify the protocol to defend against this attack. Most importantly, we must explicitly address it via proactive actions, rather than hoping that the miners' incentive will be spontaneously aligned.

This attack is another example that our attack detection metrics are limited by existing security analyses—most formal analyses of NC assume a fixed block propagation latency. Therefore, we—researchers—should keep looking for attacks folded into the assumptions of these analyses.

A Verifying the headstart-γ Relation in Ethereum

We apply the (ρ, t_{hs}) relation we learned in Sect. 4.1 to Ethereum network's data to test its accuracy. We obtain 236 553 fork instances from Etherscan [12], ranging from 2015 to 2022, which includes the then mining power of the competing blocks' miners. Since t_{hs} is not available, we approximate it as the difference between the competing blocks' timestamps. We then group these fork instances by ρ in steps of 0.05, and t_{hs} in steps of one second. We exclude groups with less than 1000 instances to reduce stochastic errors. At last, we plot each group's estimated win rate $P'_{win} = \rho + \gamma(t_{hs}) \cdot (1 - \rho)$ and the actual P_{win}, which is the number of winning cases divided by the total number of cases, in Fig. 8.

The results show that P'_{win} and P_{win} not only follow the same pattern but are also numerically close, confirming the (ρ, t_{hs}) relation we learned, except for two differences. First, P_{win} escalates faster with an increasing t_{hs}. We think this is because the network condition is improved in Ethereum's data, measured until 2022, compared with Bitcoin's pre-compact-block data [24]. When blocks propagate faster, the same positive t_{hs} yields a stronger advantage than before.

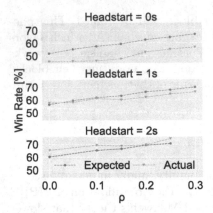

Fig. 8. The win rate about forks in Ethereum

Table 1. The optimal actions

l_d \\ l_u	0	1	2	3	4	5	6	7	8
0	A	W	A	A	A	A	A	A	A
1	W	W	W	W	A	A	A	A	A
2	W	O	W	W	W	W	A	A	A
3	W	W	O	W	W	W	W	A	A
4	W	W	W	O	W	W	W	W	W
5	W	W	W	W	O	W	W	W	W
6	W	W	W	W	W	O	W	W	W
7	W	W	W	W	W	W	O	W	W
8	W	W	W	W	W	W	W	O	W

Second, for groups with $t_{hs} = 0$, P'_{win} overestimates P_{win} by roughly 9%. We provide two possible explanations here. First, the P'_{win} formula overestimate the win rate as it ignores the producer of the competing block. In reality, the competing block's producer always works on its own block, rather than with γ probability. Secondly, 5.3% of ties in Ethereum involve three or more blocks, causing P_{win} to be lower than P'_{win} as the latter only covers the two-block case. These phenomena are not significant when $t_{hs} > 0$ as their effects are mitigated by the advantage of the early announcement.

B   The State Transition and Reward Matrices of MDP

The transition and reward matrices are defined in Table 2. The transition matrix describes the candidate states and corresponding probabilities for a given *state* × *action* combination, and the reward is a two-element tuple (r_u, r_d). Beside, we list an optimal strategy in Table 1, where $\rho = 0.45$, $\gamma = 0$, $l_d, l_u \leq 8$, fork = inactive and $l_w = l_d$. A, W, and O stand for Adopt, Wait, Override respectively.

B.1   Pruning Our MDP

Our model differs from selfish mining MDP [25] in that it introduces a new type of transition called "delay". The "delay" transition depends on the number of blocks mined by both parties. Given the number of mined blocks can be infinite, the MDP's transitions and states become unlimited, making it unsolvable. To overcome this while ensuring accuracy, we prune low-probability transitions.

Based on the probability calculation given in Sect. 3.2, we use ρ_n to denote the probability of a miner with mining power ρ to mine n blocks during the delay. Then, we set a cutoff n^* and approximate mining n blocks as n^* when $n > n^*$, with n^* being the maximum n where $\rho_n \geq \times 10^{-9}$. We will reset n^* to $60 - n$ if the fork length limitation is reached first. Besides, we use n_d^+, n_u^+ to denote positive n_d, n_u to identify cases where a party has mined blocks.

Table 2. State transition and reward matrices of MDP

State × Action	Condition	State	Probability	Reward
$(l_d, l_w, l_u, \cdot)$, adopt		$(1,1,0,i)$	ρ	$(0, l_u)$
		$(0,0,1,i)$	μ	
$(l_d, l_w, l_u, \cdot)$, override[a]	$l_d = l_u + 1$	$(1,1,0,i)$	ρ	$(l_u + 1, 0)$
		$(0,0,1,i)$	μ	
	$l_d > l_u + 1$	$(l_d - l_u - 2 + n_d,\, l_d - l_u - 2 + n_d,\, 0,\, i)$	$\rho n_d \mu 0$	$(l_u + 2, 0)$
		$(l_d - l_u - 1 + n_d,\, l_d - l_u - 2 + n_d,\, n_u^+,\, i)$	$\rho n_d \mu_{n_u}^+$	$(l_u + 1, 0)$
(l_d, l_w, l_u, i), wait	$l_w = 0$	$(l_d + 1,\, l_w + 1,\, l_u,\, i)$	ρ	$(0,0)$
		$(l_w,\, l_u,\, l_u + 1,\, i)$	μ	
	$l_w > 0$ && $(l_d \le l_u \,\|\, l_d > l_u + n_u^+)$ && $l_u = l_d - l_w$	$(l_w - 1 + n_d,\, l_w - 1 + n_d,\, 0,\, i)$	$\rho n_d \mu 0$	$(l_u + 1, 0)$
	$l_w > 0$ && $(l_d \le l_u \,\|\, l_d > l_u + n_u^+)$ && $l_u > l_d - l_w$	$(l_d + n_d,\, l_w + n_d - 1,\, l_u + n_u^+,\, i)$	$\rho n_d \mu_{n_u}^-$	$(0,0)$
		$(l_d + n_d,\, n_d,\, l_u + n_u^+,\, a)$	$\rho n_d \mu_{n_u}$	$(0,0)$
	$l_w > 0$ && $l_u < l_d \le l_u + n_u^+$ && $l_d = l_u + n_u^+$	$(n_d,\, n_d,\, l_u + n_u^+,\, i)$	$\rho n_d \mu_{n_u}^+$	$(0,0)$
	$l_w > 0$ && $l_u < l_d \le l_u + n_u^+$ && $l_d < l_u + n_u^+$	$(l_d + n_d,\, n_d,\, l_u + n_u^+,\, i)$	$\rho n_d \mu_{n_u}^+ \gamma$	$(l_d, 0)$
		$(l_d + n_d,\, n_d,\, l_u + n_u^+,\, i)$	$\rho n_d \mu_{n_u}^+ (1 - \gamma)$	$(0,0)$
(l_d, l_w, l_u, a), wait[b]	$l_w = 0$	$(l_d + 1,\, 1,\, l_u,\, a)$	ρ	$(0,0)$
		$(0,0,1,i)$	$\mu \gamma$	$(l_u, 0)$
		$(l_d,\, 0,\, l_u + 1,\, i)$	$\mu(1 - \gamma)$	$(0,0)$
	$l_w > 0$ && $(l_d \le l_u \,\|\, l_d > l_u + n_u^+)$	$(l_w - 1 + n_d,\, l_w - 1 + n_d,\, 0,\, i)$	$\rho n_d \mu 0$	$(l_u + 1, 0)$
		$(l_w + n_d,\, l_w + n_d - 1,\, l_u + n_u^+,\, i)$	$\rho n_d \mu_{n_u}^+ \gamma$	$(l_u, 0)$
		$(l_d + n_d,\, l_w - 1 + n_d,\, l_u + n_u^+,\, i)$	$\rho n_d \mu_{n_u}^+ (1 - \gamma)$	$(0,0)$
	$l_w > 0$ && $l_u < l_d \le l_u + n_u^+$ && $l_d = l_u + n_u^+$	$(l_w + n_d,\, n_d,\, l_w,\, a)$	$\rho n_d \mu_{n_u}^+ \gamma$	$(l_u, 0)$
		$(l_d + n_d,\, n_d,\, l_u + n_u^+,\, a)$	$\rho n_d \mu_{n_u}^+ (1 - \gamma)$	$(0,0)$
	$l_w > 0$ && $l_u < l_d \le l_u + n_u^+$ && $l_d < l_u + n_u^+$	$(n_d,\, n_d,\, l_u + n_u^+,\, i)$	$\rho n_d \mu_{n_u}^+ \gamma^2$	$(l_d, 0)$
		$(l_w + n_d,\, n_d,\, n_u^+,\, i)$	$\rho n_d \mu_{n_u}^+ (\gamma - \gamma^2)$	$(l_u, 0)$
		$(n_d,\, n_d,\, l_u - l_w,\, i)$	$\rho n_d \mu_{n_u}^+ (\gamma - \gamma^2)$	$(l_d, 0)$
		$(l_d + n_d,\, n_d,\, l_u + n_u^+,\, i)$	$\rho n_d \mu_{n_u}^+ (1 - \gamma)^2$	$(0,0)$

[a] feasible only when $l_d > l_u$
[b] feasible only when $l_d \ge l_u$

References

1. Babaioff, M., Dobzinski, S., Oren, S., Zohar, A.: On bitcoin and red balloons. In: 13th ACM Conference on Electronic Commerce, pp. 56–73. ACM (2012)
2. Bahack, L.: Theoretical Bitcoin attacks with less than half of the computational power (draft). arXiv preprint arXiv:1312.7013 (2013).http://arxiv.org/pdf/1312.7013.pdf
3. Blockchain: Bitcoin block explorer (2017). http://blockchain.info/
4. Blockchain Luxembourg S.A.: Orphaned blocks - blockchain.info (2019). http://www.blockchain.com/btc/orphaned-blocks
5. Bonneau, J., Miller, A., Clark, J., Narayanan, A., Kroll, J.A., Felten, E.W.: SoK: research perspectives and challenges for Bitcoin and cryptocurrencies. In: IEEE Symposium on Security and Privacy (S&P), pp. 104–121. IEEE (2015)
6. Buterin, V.: The limits to blockchain scalability (2021). http://vitalik.ca/general/2021/05/23/scaling.html
7. Cao, T., Decouchant, J., Yu, J., Esteves-Verissimo, P.: Characterizing the impact of network delay on bitcoin mining. In: 2021 40th International Symposium on Reliable Distributed Systems (SRDS), pp. 109–119. IEEE (2021)
8. Chadès, I., Chapron, G., Cros, M.J., Garcia, F., Sabbadin, R.: Mdptoolbox: a multi-platform toolbox to solve stochastic dynamic programming problems. Ecography **37**(9), 916–920 (2014)
9. Corallo, M.: Compact block relay (2016). http://github.com/bitcoin/bips/blob/master/bip-0152.mediawiki
10. Corallo, M.: Public highly optimized fibre network (2019). http://bitcoinfibre.org/public-network.html
11. DNS Research Group, KASTEL @ KIT: Bitcoin network monitor (2019). http://dsn.tm.kit.edu/bitcoin/
12. Etherscan: Ethereum ETH blockchain explorer (2019). http://etherscan.io/
13. Ethstats: Ethereum network status (2020). http://ethstats.net/
14. Eyal, I., Sirer, E.G.: How to detect selfish miners (2014). http://hackingdistributed.com/2014/01/15/detecting-selfish-mining/
15. Eyal, I., Sirer, E.G.: Majority is not enough: bitcoin mining is vulnerable. In: Financial Cryptography and Data Security, pp. 436–454. Springer, Heidelberg (2014)
16. Fry, S.: Mandatory activation of segwit deployment. http://github.com/bitcoin/bips/blob/master/bip-0148.mediawiki. Accessed 01 Sept 2022
17. IntoTheBlock: intotheblock. http://www.intotheblock.com. Accessed 01 Sept 2022
18. Mao, Y., Venkatakrishnan, S.B.: Less is more: fairness in wide-area proof-of-work blockchain networks (2022). https://doi.org/10.48550/ARXIV.2204.02461. http://arxiv.org/abs/2204.02461
19. mapofcoins: Map of coins: BTC map (2018). http://mapofcoins.com/bitcoin
20. Maxwell, G.: Advances in block propagation (2017). http://www.youtube.com/watch?v=EHIuuKCm53o
21. Miller, A., et al.: Discovering bitcoin's public topology and influential nodes (2015). http://www.cs.umd.edu/projects/coinscope/coinscope.pdf
22. Nakamoto, S.: Bitcoin: a peer-to-peer electronic cash system (2008). http://www.bitcoin.org/bitcoin.pdf
23. Nayak, K., Kumar, S., Miller, A., Shi, E.: Stubborn mining: generalizing selfish mining and combining with an eclipse attack. In: IEEE European Symposium on Security and Privacy (EuroS&P), pp. 305–320. IEEE (2016)

24. Neudecker, T., Hartenstein, H.: Short paper: an empirical analysis of blockchain forks in bitcoin. In: Goldberg, I., Moore, T. (eds.) FC 2019. LNCS, vol. 11598, pp. 84–92. Springer, Cham (2019). https://doi.org/10.1007/978-3-030-32101-7_6
25. Sapirshtein, A., Sompolinsky, Y., Zohar, A.: Optimal selfish mining strategies in bitcoin. In: Grossklags, J., Preneel, B. (eds.) FC 2016. LNCS, vol. 9603, pp. 515–532. Springer, Heidelberg (2017). https://doi.org/10.1007/978-3-662-54970-4_30
26. Voight, F.: P2Pool. http://p2pool.in. Accessed 09 Sept 2022
27. Xiao, Y., Zhang, N., Lou, W., Hou, Y.T.: Modeling the impact of network connectivity on consensus security of proof-of-work blockchain. In: IEEE INFOCOM 2020-IEEE Conference on Computer Communications, pp. 1648–1657. IEEE (2020)
28. Zhang, R., Preneel, B.: Lay down the common metrics: evaluating proof-of-work consensus protocols' security. In: 40th IEEE Symposium on Security and Privacy (S&P), pp. 1190–1207. IEEE (2019)
29. Zhang, R., Zhang, D., Wang, Q., Wu, S., Xie, J., Preneel, B.: NC-Max: breaking the security-performance tradeoff in Nakamoto consensus. In: The Network and Distributed System Security (NDSS) Symposium (2022)

Bijack: Breaking Bitcoin Network with TCP Vulnerabilities

Shaoyu Li[1]([✉]), Shanghao Shi[1], Yang Xiao[2], Chaoyu Zhang[1], Y. Thomas Hou[1], and Wenjing Lou[1]

[1] Virginia Polytechnic Institute and State University, Blacksburg, VA, USA
{shaoyuli,shanghaos,chaoyu,thou,wjlou}@vt.edu
[2] University of Kentucky, Lexington, KY, USA
xiaoy@uky.edu

Abstract. Recent studies have shown that compromising Bitcoin's peer-to-peer network is an effective way to disrupt the Bitcoin service. While many attack vectors have been uncovered such as BGP hijacking in the network layer and eclipse attack in the application layer, one significant attack vector that resides in the transport layer is largely overlooked. In this paper, we investigate the TCP vulnerabilities of the Bitcoin system and their consequences. We present Bijack, an off-path TCP hijacking attack on the Bitcoin network that is able to terminate Bitcoin connections or inject malicious data into the connections with only a few prior requirements and a limited amount of knowledge. This results in the Bitcoin network topology leakage, and the Bitcoin nodes isolation.

We measured the real Bitcoin network and discovered that more than 1700 (27%) of the reachable Bitcoin nodes are vulnerable to our attack whose physical locations are spread across the world. We evaluated the efficiency and impacts of the Bijack attack in real-world settings, and the results show that Bijack successfully realizes several fatal Bitcoin attacks without too much effort.

Keywords: Bitcoin · TCP · Network security

1 Introduction

With a market capitalization of more than 534 billion US dollars (May 9th, 2023), Bitcoin is among the most successful cryptocurrencies. The fundamental appeal of Bitcoin stems from its underlying design, the blockchain system, which is characterized as a fully decentralized architecture [33] that relies on a unique consensus protocol to ensure its security and immutability. Within this large and decentralized system, tens of thousands of Bitcoin nodes have formed a global peer-to-peer network overlaying upon the Internet. This peer-to-peer network, commonly referred to as the Bitcoin network, enables Bitcoin nodes to transmit transactions and blocks to each other and is critical to the fundamental consensus security of Bitcoin [46].

© The Author(s), under exclusive license to Springer Nature Switzerland AG 2024
G. Tsudik et al. (Eds.): ESORICS 2023, LNCS 14346, pp. 306–326, 2024.
https://doi.org/10.1007/978-3-031-51479-1_16

As a global and public infrastructure, the Bitcoin network has attracted various attacks from different perspectives that aim to disrupt the security and performance of the Bitcoin system. For example, the eclipse attack aims to dominate a victim node's communication with the main network in order to isolate it from the consensus [29,43]. The topology inference attack seeks to extract the connection profiles of targeted nodes to manipulate their consensus status [5,32,36]. Other network-based Bitcoin attacks include delay attacks [7,22] and deanonymization attacks [2,5], for which Sect. 8 provides a detailed discussion. In order to realize these network-based attacks, the attacker needs to manipulate the P2P connections of the victim, which ultimately requires tampering with the Internet functions that underpin the P2P network. To this regard, the BGP hijacking attack [3] and its stealthier variant [43] exploit the vulnerabilities of the BGP protocol to allow an autonomous system (AS)-level attacker to redirect all traffic from/to a victim toward its malicious routers. More recent connection manipulation attacks [15,16] leverage the positional advantage of the routing-level attackers to eavesdrop, monitor, and tamper with specific Bitcoin traffic.

Limitation of On-Path Attacks. The aforementioned connection manipulation attacks are predominantly performed by an *on-path* attacker. This assumption is impractical and often does not yield an attack reward comparable to the potential cost. On-path attackers, who can intercept, monitor, and modify network traffic trespassing them, are classified into two categories: routing-level attackers, such as switches or routers, and AS-level attackers. However, in the case of specific connection attacks, routing-level attackers are unlikely to cause a significant impact on the overall network because they can only disrupt the traffic passing through them, which affects only a small fraction of Bitcoin nodes. As for AS-level attackers, although they have the ability to monitor and tamper with a large volume of network traffic, they often refrain from doing so due to the need to carefully weigh the costs and potential reputation impact of their malicious actions against the potential gains of the attack. These large actors may face serious commercial and regulatory consequences when they are detected. Moreover, the open and dynamic nature of the Bitcoin network, whose topology is subject to constant change, imposes an additional cost for the on-path attacker to adapt and re-launch the attack.

Another commonality among existing network-based attacks is the overlook of Transport Layer vulnerabilities of the Bitcoin network. Like most connection-oriented network applications, Bitcoin relies on the TCP protocol for end-to-end data transmission between nodes, utilizing TCP connections established through the TCP three-way handshake. However, TCP itself has no authentication mechanism to build up secure channels between Bitcoin nodes and cannot verify the integrity of transmitted Bitcoin data. This creates an opportunity for attackers to manipulate Bitcoin connections by compromising the TCP connections and substituting legitimate data with malicious data. Worse yet, the Bitcoin protocol stack naturally transmits all traffic in plaintext, and Bitcoin does not employ TLS (Transport Layer Security, [13]) to guarantee the security of the TCP connections as in normal web apps like email and VoIP (Voice over Internet Protocol, [27]). Therefore, anybody in the network is able to eavesdrop, capture, and analyze the TCP traffic of the victim nodes, opening up opportunities for *off-path* attackers to conduct TCP-based manipulation attacks on the Bitcoin network.

Our Work. In this paper, we propose Bijack, a new off-path Bitcoin TCP hijacking attack against the Bitcoin network. As an off-path attack, Bijack does not require the attacker to have knowledge of on-path communication traffic between Bitcoin peers, nor need any information about the internal operating information of Bitcoin nodes. We exploit a TCP protocol vulnerability of the Linux system [17,18,37] to devise our attack, which is based on a security flaw of the mixed IPID assignment method in some versions of the Linux kernel. Our attack can be conducted in three phases. First, the attacker discovers the victim node by a flaw detection mechanism to identify whether the node is subject to the TCP vulnerability we have mentioned. Second, the attacker identifies the Bitcoin connections between the victim node and its peers. The Bitcoin connections will be tricked into downgrading the IPID assignment method from the per-packet-based method to the globally 2048 hash-based method and a side channel method based on the globally hash-based IPID assignments is utilized to infer the three-tuple [victim node's port number, peer's IP address, peer's port number]. The attacker completely hijacks the connections by inferring the sequence and acknowledgment numbers of the victim connections. After a successful hijack, the attacker can terminate the TCP connections by sending a forged TCP RST segment or injecting malicious Bitcoin data into the connections to disrupt the Bitcoin system. As a result, the attacker can take over the Bitcoin connections and send malicious transactions or blocks to the victim nodes to break the Bitcoin consensus.

To show the potential impact of Bijack, we demonstrate two Bitcoin network attacks mentioned earlier—the topology inference attack and the eclipse attack—for which an off-path attacker can perform based on Bijack. For the topology inference attack, the attack goal is to know the Bitcoin network topology around the victim nodes. The victim nodes are tricked by the attacker to send the known addresses to the attacker, helping it to detect the potential connections. Bijack allows the off-path attacker to build connections with the victim nodes and send forged network packets, and then infer the other connections of victim nodes. For the eclipse attack, the attacker aims to isolate the victim node from the rest of the Bitcoin network by surrounding it with malicious nodes, effectively controlling all incoming and outgoing connections of the victim. With Bijack, the off-path attacker who controls a swarm of malicious nodes (similar to the Sybil attack) can continuously disrupt the benign connections established by the victim until all of the victim's connections are established with the malicious nodes.

Evaluation. We provided global network-wide measurement and surprisingly found out that more than 27% of the total Bitcoin nodes are vulnerable to our attack as of May 2023. We also implemented the Bijack attack in the real world and evaluated the efficiency and impacts of the Bijack attack. For the topology inference attack, when given the address list of 46262 potential peers, the attacker was able to infer all connected peers of the victim node in 25.68 h. When performing the eclipse attack, the attacker discovered all initial ten outbound connections of the victim node in 168 min and successfully isolated the victim node in 11.6 h. Finally, we propose practical countermeasures (Sect. 7.2) from the perspective of the network and Bitcoin system to detect and defend against the Bijack attack.

In summary, we make the following contributions:

- To the best of our knowledge, this is the first work that focuses on the TCP vulnerabilities of the Bitcoin network. We identify this unique attack vector and its security impacts imposed on the Bitcoin network.
- We propose Bijack, an off-path Bitcoin TCP attack that only requires very little prior knowledge of the victim nodes. The attack can be launched by any malicious party within the Bitcoin network, resulting in a complete hijacking of the communication session between victim nodes. Bijack can lead to further catastrophes results including topology leakage, eclipse, and even double-spending.
- We measured all the reachable nodes from the Bitcoin network and found that more than 27% of them are vulnerable to our attack, calling for an urgent need to fix this vulnerability. We implemented Bijack attack in real Bitcoin networks by performing the topology inference and eclipse attack, and the experiment results confirm the efficiency and effectiveness of our attack.

2 Background

2.1 Bitcoin Network Formation

As a peer-to-peer network, Bitcoin requires each node to maintain a list of IP addresses of potential peers. This list stored in the local addresses database is initially acquired from a public DNS server, and additional addresses are exchanged among connected peers. Each Bitcoin node pseudo-randomly selects peers from the list to build unencrypted TCP connections with them. By default, each Bitcoin node establishes 10 outbound connections (including 2 block-relay connections) and accepts up to 117 inbound connections on TCP port 8333.

Nodes request connected peers' known addresses by sending GETADDR messages and the peer responds with ADDR messages containing up to (but necessarily) 1000 known node addresses. In addition, most nodes will unsolicitedly propagate their own addresses in ADDR messages to their peers when building new connections. Currently, in order to avoid topology leakage, each node can only propagate at most 1000 addresses per day [34].

2.2 TCP Vulnerability

The TCP vulnerability revealed in 2020 [37] enables an off-path attacker to monitor TCP connections of the victim hosts when they run the Linux kernels prior to version 5.17 [17, 18]. In this attack, the attacker first pretends to be a router and sends a forged ICMP "Fragmentation Needed" error message [38] to the victim node in order to trigger it to downgrade the IPID assignment of the victim connection from the per-socket-based method to the insecure hash-based method. For the hash-based method, the node uses a total of 2048 (11 bits) IPID counters determined by $IPID_{counter} = HASH(sourceIP, destIP, protocol, Boot\_key)$ to assign IPIDs for its IP packets. However, this method has been shown to be insecure [17] as the hash collision space is too small and an attacker is able to use many IP addresses and its desired protocol to trigger a hash collision. For example, the attacker can achieve this by using ICMP protocol and trying different destination IP addresses, as shown in Eq. (1):

$$hash(victim\_node\_IP, peer\_IP, TCP, Boot\_key)$$
$$= hash(victim\_node\_IP, attacker\_IP, ICMP, Boot\_key) \qquad (1)$$

In practice, the attacker can send ICMP echo request messages with its IP addresses and observe the IPID of the returned ICMP echo reply messages. If one IP address collides with the targeted TCP connection, the attacker can observe a non-linear IPID increment in its received ICMP messages because the victim connection and the attacker's ICMP connection are using the same IPID counter. As a result of this hash collision, the attacker is able to monitor the IPID changes in the victim's TCP connection by monitoring its own ICMP connection. More details about IPID can be found in Appendix A.1.

3 Bijack: Hijacking Bitcoin TCP Connections

3.1 Attack Model

The goal of our Bijack attack is to hijack the Bitcoin connections of the victim node. Figure 1 shows the attack model of Bijack, in which three types of nodes are involved, including the victim node V, the list of peers connected to the victim $P = \{p_1, p_2, \cdots, p_n\}$, and an off-path attacker A.

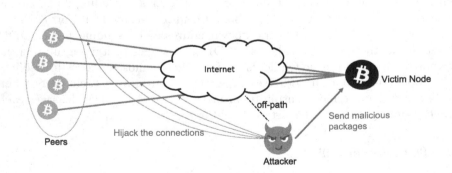

Fig. 1. The off-path attack model

We assume the off-path attacker is unable and does not necessarily need to monitor any inbound or outbound network traffic of the victim node. The attacker also has no information about any internal operating parameters and configurations of the victim node except the victim node's IP address, which is used as the public identifier of the victim node. We assume the attacker is able to craft and send malicious IP packets to the network, as well as possessing many IP addresses, following the convention of the existing Bitcoin network attacks [19]. We assume attacker A has the ability to send forged TCP segments, ICMP messages, and Bitcoin messages to victim V, without needing to manipulate the ASes (Autonomous Systems) to relay the forged packets, as over a quarter of ASes do not discard packets with spoofed source addresses in their networks [31]. In practice, any node in the Bitcoin network, such as a Bitcoin mining node or a light node, can become an attacker.

3.2   Detailed Procedures of Bijack

Phase-1: Victim Detection. Discovering vulnerable Bitcoin nodes that deploy a vulnerable Linux kernel is necessary for an off-path attacker to perform both node-level and network-level attacks because the attacker aims to detect the Bitcoin connections of the vulnerable nodes. Figure 2 illustrates the workflow of detecting the vulnerable nodes from the Bitcoin network.

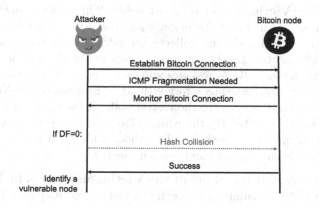

Fig. 2. Discovering a victim node

The attacker first establishes a Bitcoin connection with the target node to test if it is vulnerable. The attacker attempts to downgrade the IPID assignment method of the Bitcoin connection by sending an ICMP "Fragmentation Needed" message to the tested node. Only the **vulnerable** Bitcoin node will reply to the attacker with Bitcoin messages whose DF field changed from one to zero. After monitoring this, the attacker conducts the hash-collision as we have described in Sect. 2.2, and if it succeeds, it confirms that the current node is a vulnerable one.

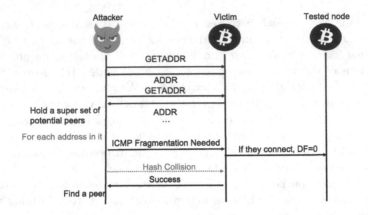

Fig. 3. Finding the victim's peer IP address

Phase-2: Connection Detection. For each victim node, the attacker attempts to reveal the details of the victim's existing Bitcoin connections established with peers. Each Bitcoin connection can be treated as a four-tuple vector, i.e., [**victim node's IP address, victim node's port number, peer's IP address, peer's port number**]. The attacker only knows the victim node's IP and it will infer the other three components.

Step 1: Finding Victim's Peer IP Addresses. The workflow of this IP detection process is shown in Fig. 3. To begin with, the attacker sends GETADDR messages to the victim node and collects the addresses in the replied ADDR messages, which may contain the connected peers as described in Sect. 2.1. Then each IP address in the ADDR messages will be tested to see if it connects to the victim nodes. The attacker sends a forged ICMP "Fragmentation Needed" message with the tested IP address to the victim node. If the victim node does have a connection with the tested IP, the connection will be triggered to downgrade the IPID assignment to the hash-based method, which will be detected by the attacker through hash-collision mentioned in Sect. 2.2.

Step 2: Inferring Port Numbers of the Victim and Peers. In this step, the attacker infers the port numbers between the victim and its peers. The attacker will first assume one node uses the destination port (typically 8333, while it can be detected by network scanning) and infer the other one's port number. If unsuccessful, swap the assumption. As a bonus, after the port inferring process, the attacker obtains knowledge about whether the current Bitcoin connection is inbound or outbound.

The workflow of port inference is illustrated in Fig. 4. For each of the identified peers, the attacker starts with continuous monitoring of the IPID increment between the victim node and the peer. The attacker can do so by continuously sending hash-collided ICMP messages (already succeed in the previous phase) to

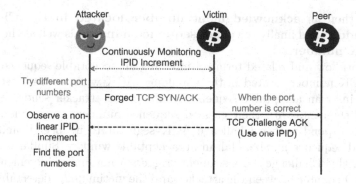

Fig. 4. Inferring the port numbers between the victim and its peer

the victim and observing the returned messages. To infer the port number, the attacker sends forged TCP SYN/ACK segments to victim nodes with different port numbers across the range (from 1024 to 65535). When the port number is correct, the victim will send a TCP Challenge ACK segment [41] to the peer, and if not, the victim responds with a TCP RST segment to the peer with a 0 value of the IPID [1,30]. Because this TCP Challenge ACK segment uses one or more additional IPIDs shared between the victim and attack connections, the attacker can observe a non-linear IPID increment, which is the indicator of the success of our inferring process. Note that this inferring process can be finished in a short time, we do assume there is no other TCP connection between the victim and its peer.

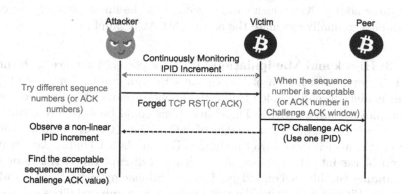

Fig. 5. Inferring acceptable sequence and ACK numbers

Step 3: Inferring Sequence Number and Acknowledgment Number. The attacker infers the exact sequence number and acceptable acknowledgment number in order to gain full knowledge of the victim's connection. The attacker achieves this in serial steps including first inferring an **acceptable sequence**

number, then an **acknowledgment number located in the Challenge ACK window,** and finally the **exact sequence number** as well as the **acceptable ACK number.**

The workflow and related terms of inferring an acceptable sequence number and an ACK number located in the Challenge ACK window are illustrated in Fig. 5. To infer an acceptable sequence number, the attacker sends the forged TCP RST segments with their guessed sequence numbers to the victim node, which will respond with a Challenge ACK segment to its peer if and only if the guessed sequence numbers fall in an acceptable window. Similar to the previous step, this Challenge ACK segment triggers a non-linear increment on the shared IPID counter between the attacker and the victim node, detectable by the attacker as the signal of finding an acceptable sequence number. Then with this acceptable sequence number, the attacker can infer an ACK number located in the Challenge ACK window (ranging from 1G to 2G [6,9,10]) by sending forged ACK segments and monitoring the IPID increment in the same fashion [41]. After that, the attacker infers the exact sequence number with a well-known method [17] as to sending forged ACK segments to the victim with decreasing sequence numbers from the acceptable sequence number and monitoring the reply rate of the TCP segments (or the IPID non-linear incremental rate). In the beginning, there is a burst of challenge ACK segments sent by the victim at the limited speed of 500 ms per segment by the protocol design of TCP. Once the sequence number reaches the lower bound, the sequence number is the exact one and the victim nodes will send ACK segments to its peer without any speed limitation. When inferring the acceptable ACK number, the lower bound of the challenge ACK window can be inferred in the same way and then the attacker uses it to calculate the *sequence number of the first unacknowledged octet* (the lower bound value adding 2G), which can be used with the known *typical size of the send window* to finally calculate the acceptable ACK number.

Phase-3: Hijack and Manipulation. With the correct inference of the underlying TCP layer information of the victim's Bitcoin connections, the off-path attacker is able to send spoofed traffic to the victim nodes to influence the victim's normal Bitcoin activities. The connections could be forcefully terminated by the attacker, using the knowledge of either the TCP or Bitcoin protocol. Moreover, the attacker can inject malicious Bitcoin data including fake transactions and blocks into the connections, which will disrupt the victim node from understanding the blockchain ledger, further influencing the integrity and stability of the Bitcoin consensus. We will explore these vulnerabilities in the next two sections.

4   Compromising Bitcoin Network Nodes

Hijacking Bitcoin connections can pose significant security risks to both Bitcoin nodes and the Bitcoin network. In this section, we have demonstrated two Bitcoin node manipulation attacks based on Bijack: (i) Bitcoin topology inference and (ii) eclipse attack. We will demonstrate how they are launched and their consequences on the Bitcoin network.

4.1 Bitcoin Topology Inference

Compared to the previous Bitcoin topology inference attack [5,12,28,32,36], Bijack can directly infer the inbound and outbound connections of the victim node through message feedback directly obtained from the network traffic without the requirement of collecting and analyzing detailed Bitcoin transactions or blocks. The attacker can detect all or at least most of the inbound and outbound connections of a targeted node.

In practice, to infer more connections, the attacker can repeatedly request ADDR messages as long as it does not exceed the limitation set by the Bitcoin system to gain as many potential peer IP addresses as possible. This allows the attacker to build up a superset of all the IP addresses it receives, up to 1,000 addresses per day. According to Bitcoin's design rules, the victim will randomly select peers to establish connections from their known IP addresses, which are highly likely to be within the IP superset, provided that the superset is large enough.

The attacker acquires the topology information of the victim nodes by launching this attack, which can be further exploited to conduct more severe Bitcoin attacks. For example, the attacker can identify the most connective nodes as the key or super nodes, and place corrupted nodes in these key locations or attack the super nodes to disrupt data transmission in the network. The attacker may even infer the complete topology of a local (e.g. in a certain network domain) or global Bitcoin network through mathematical modeling and analyzing the inbound and outbound relationships of the nodes [32], leaving space for the attacker to conduct the eclipse attack that isolates the victims. Moreover, the attacker is able to perform the 0-confirming double-spending attacks on the victim. After inferring the connections of the victim merchant, the attacker sends the double-spend transaction only to the victim's peers and sends others the legal transaction. The merchant will confirm the double-spending transaction after receiving it from most of its peers, while the legal transaction will be selected in the blockchain.

4.2 Eclipse Attack

The eclipse attack is a severe Bitcoin attack that aims to isolate the victim nodes from the rest of the network. It can render the victim nodes vulnerable to a double spending attack because the attacker controls the propagation of transactions to the victim nodes. It can also waste the mining power by manipulating the victim's view of the blockchain. Moreover, if the attacker is able to isolate a large number of Bitcoin nodes, the whole Bitcoin network may be partitioned. Unfortunately, Bijack can help the attacker to accomplish this in the following way.

The attacker first continuously sends Bitcoin ADDR messages to the victim node with multiple malicious IP addresses controlled by it. Because the current Bitcoin protocol lets the node accept all the received IP addresses without any verification, the attacker can gradually pollute the local IP database of the victims by increasing the portion of malicious IP addresses, from where the victim nodes establish outbound connections. In practice, to increase the number of nodes stored in the victim's database, the attacker can inject IP addresses with different prefixes to circumvent the built-in address discarding mechanism in the database—the database allocates a limited quota for IP addresses with the same prefix, and any exceeding ones will be discarded [29,43].

After this, the attacker attempts to manipulate all the victim node's connections through the Bijack. Once the attacker finds that the victim node is shut down and restarted, it immediately occupies all the inbound connections with its controlled IP addresses. This is achievable because the Bitcoin system does not specify its nodes to verify or authenticate the inbound connection requests. Moreover, existing work has shown that the Bitcoin nodes may restart for several reasons such as software updating, power failure, and DDoS attacks [11,40,42,44]. For the outbound connections, even if the attacker has polluted the local addresses database of the victim node, the benign IP addresses still constitute a large fraction and the victim may still establish connections with them. To terminate these benign connections and allow the attacker to fully control the victim's connections, the attacker needs to first detect and hijack all the benign connections with Bijack. The attacker then impersonates the corresponding peers of these connections to disrupt them by either sending forged TCP RST segments to trigger connection termination or sending malicious Bitcoin messages to the victim nodes, which causes ban scores of the benign peers to increase until they reach 100, resulting in a one-day blacklisting [15,16].

As a result, the attacker disconnects all the benign nodes from the victims and fully controls all their inbound and outbound connections, accomplishing the eclipse attack.

5   How Vulnerable Is Bitcoin to Bijack?

Evaluating the impact of our Bijack attack requires a good knowledge of the vulnerable nodes in the Bitcoin network. In this section, we conduct a measurement of the Bitcoin network to explore the number of vulnerable nodes as well as their mining power in the network and analyze Bijack potential impact.

5.1   Measurement on Real Bitcoin Network

We utilized one scanner Bitcoin node running Bitcoin Core version v24.99.0, with the IP address of *38.68.237.175*. Our scanner node was installed with Ubuntu 18.04 (Linux kernel version 4.15) and was capable of sending ICMP messages to other nodes using spoofed IP addresses with the Python Scapy package.

The victim detection phase (following Sect. 3.1) was carried out on the entire Bitcoin network for 10 days, from April 27th, 2023, to May 7th, 2023 (the detailed procedure is shown in Appendix A.2). During this time period, we discovered and successfully established Bitcoin connections with 6405 Bitcoin nodes and we found that 27.14% of connected nodes (1738 nodes) are vulnerable to the Bijack. We show our experiment results in Table 1, in which we present the geo-location, the number of vulnerable and reachable nodes, as well as the total scanning time.

Table 1. The top ten countries with the highest number of vulnerable nodes

Location	Victim Clients	Total Clients	Scan Time (min)
USA	332	1200	711.5
Germany	300	726	396.9
Netherlands	119	264	142.3
France	102	266	148.4
Finland	95	210	113.1
Canada	65	195	111.6
Singapore	53	114	61.0
United Kingdom	46	137	80.6
Japan	43	83	43.8
Switzerland	43	135	78.5

We measured the vulnerable mining nodes from the Bitcoin network during the same time period. We collected all the nodes that first relay new blocks, considering them as gateways of mining pools. We also collected the IP addresses of the mining devices by scanning the IPv4 network. We found that over 90% of the vulnerable nodes are associated with mining activities, with approximately 40% being mining nodes and the remaining portion belonging to mining pool gateways.

5.2   Bitcoin Impact Analysis

Our measurement found more than 27% Bitcoin nodes are vulnerable to our attack, spreading across different geographical locations. Therefore, these nodes are directly exposed to the threats we have mentioned in the previous section such as topology leakage, eclipse, and even double-spending. From the network's perspective, the attacker can cause more severe consequences as it can **partition** the whole Bitcoin network considering that 27% is a considerably large fraction and over 90% of the detected victim nodes belong to the mining nodes or mining pool nodes. These nodes possess a significant amount of computational power within the Bitcoin system. After partitioning the network, the attacker gains control over these nodes, and its computation power increases significantly, giving him a huge advantage to perform the selfish-mining attacks [14,21,35], in which the attacker may strategically conceal and release newly mined blocks to realize unfair mining gain when the attacked-controlled mining power exceeds a certain threshold β. Assuming the attacker's released block wins the fork competition of 50% chance, the threshold β becomes 25%. There is a non-negligible chance that the mining power of the 27% victim population may well exceed 25% of the total.

6   Experiment and Evaluation

We conducted the **topology inference attack** and **eclipse attack** on the real Bitcoin network to evaluate the effectiveness of Bijack. By launching the topology inference attack, we can infer **all** of the connected peers of the victim nodes (from the list of 46262 potential peers) in **25.68 h**. By launching the eclipse attack, we isolate the victim node in **11.6 h**.

Ethical Considerations. In order to prevent any potential harm or negative repercussions on the Bitcoin network and market, we only conduct the vulnerable detection phase of our attack without the following steps, which will jeopardize the operation of Bitcoin. For these steps that may cause actual harmful consequences, we implemented them only on our own machines. Our experimental activities do not pose any threat to other Bitcoin nodes. We did not send a large number of IP packets in the public Bitcoin network in order to not increase the burden on the network, and we maintain confidentiality regarding the list of nodes that are susceptible to the vulnerability.

6.1   Experiment Setup

We deployed one victim node with Bitcoin Core version v24.99.0 on the Amazon cloud by using an AWS EC2 virtual machine with Ubuntu 20.04 (Linux kernel version 5.5) located in the US East. Before our experiment, we ran the victim Bitcoin client on the node for 65 days to get it to fit into the environment of the Bitcoin system. We deployed twenty attacker nodes with Bitcoin Core version v24.99.0 equipped with Ubuntu 20.04 (kernel version 5.5). The prefix of the IP addresses for these nodes is 38.68.237.0/24. We own over 5000 addresses with the prefix of 71.178.0.0/16, 96.231.0.0/16, and 38.68.160.0/20 for hash collision and eclipse attack.

6.2   Experimental Results

Bitcoin Topology Inference Attack. We first conducted a 110-day experiment to evaluate the effectiveness of our peer detection process, i.e., the number of victim's connections that can be inferred from the address list collected from the ADDR messages. In our experiment, we continuously sent GETADDR messages to the victim node each day and collected the addresses returned by the victim nodes. The experimental results are shown in Fig. 6. Our experiment shows that after collecting addresses for a continuous period of 110 days, the attacker obtains the list that contains over 70% of the victim's outbound connected peers and over 50% of inbound connected peers. In total, the list contains 46242 addresses and 57 of them are connected peers. Subsequently, we executed our attack based on the list collected before and assessed the efficiency of the Bijack-based topology inference attack. The experimental results are shown in Fig. 6(b). In total, it took us 25.68 h to find all 57 connections from the 46242 addresses. More specifically, the average time cost to examine one address in the list was 39.98 s and the average time cost to discover one connected peer was 23.94 s.

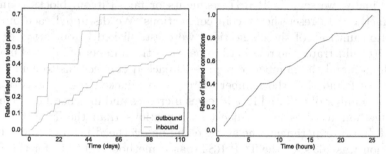

(a) Ratio of connected peers in the list to all connected peers

(b) Ratio of inferred connections in topology inference attack

Fig. 6. Topology Inference Attack Results

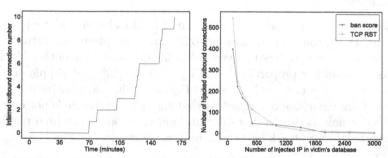

(a) Number of inferred outbound connections in eclipse attack

(b) The relationship between injected address and the hijacked connections

Fig. 7. Eclipse Attack Results

Eclipse Attack. We first scanned the whole Bitcoin network and found 5222 active nodes on May 10th, 2023. Then we checked each node to detect if the victim node built a connection with it. We used 5000 addresses (controlled by us) to conduct the hash-collision with each node and if we fail, we consider that node does not have a connection with the victim node. The average time cost of checking an unconnected node is 39.98 s by attempting all the 5000 addresses. For connected nodes, we utilized an average of 3461 addresses to discover their connection with a time cost of 27.40 s. In total, we spent 168 min finding all ten outbound connections of the victim, and Fig. 7 illustrates the results of discovering all outbound connections.

Afterward, we kept sending ADDR messages to the victim nodes to inject the malicious IP addresses into the victim's database. Each time we sent 1000 IP addresses to the victim node in 6 TCP segments with a total payload of 17495 bytes. Finally, we sent TCP RST segments or fake Bitcoin blocks (ban-score-based method) to reset the Bitcoin connections. We disrupted each outbound connection until all of the connections were established to our attacker nodes. Figure 7(b) illustrates the relationship between the number of injected malicious IP addresses and the number of required hijacked connections to complete the attack. We found that the number of required hijacked connections decreases when the number of polluted IP addresses increases and in general the ban-score-based method requires fewer hijacked connections than the TCP RST-based method. In our experiment, the average timing overhead for resetting a Bitcoin connection was 163 s for the TCP RST-based method and 247 s for the Bitcoin ban-score-based method. Specifically, when 200 IP addresses were injected into the database, we used 11.6 h to break the required 248 connections to accomplish our attack by sending TCP RST segments.

7   Discussion and Countermeasures

7.1   Discussion

The Bitcoin system transmits transactions and blocks in plaintext with the underlying TCP protocol and does not offer any encryption and authentication mechanism in order to reduce the payload of the network. Many other blockchain networks have similar properties including Litecoin [39], and Ripple [4]. Unfortunately, this makes them vulnerable to Bijack as the prerequisite requirement for successfully launching our attack is that the network traffic is not encrypted. For the blockchain networks that offer authenticated and encrypted traffic such as Ethereum [8], our attack fails to break their systems.

7.2   Countermeasures

The Bitcoin system may use the following feasible countermeasures to defend itself against Bijack.

Deploy a Customized Designed Intrusion Detection System. Bijack introduces some extra abnormal traffic to the system that can be detected by an intrusion detection system (IDS). For example, the IDS can monitor the IPID increment of the Bitcoin connections, or carefully check the ICMP "Fragmentation Needed" messages.

Refuse Unsolicited ADDR Messages. The node could choose to refuse the unsolicited ADDR messages with a large number of IP addresses, especially from incoming peers. This will prevent attackers from polluting the victim's address database, making it difficult to carry out an Bijack-based eclipse attack.

Encrypt the Traffic. If Bitcoin traffic is transmitted using encryption, our attack's impact will be significantly reduced. It would be challenging for attackers to send spoofed messages. Considering the impact of encryption on network performance, we can allow nodes to choose whether to encrypt based on their own circumstances.

Using Tor Network. Our attack cannot target the Tor network because our attack is based on the IPv4 network and we first need to identify the victim's IP address. Tor is anonymous by design and most existing Bitcoin attacks are not effective against the Tor network. Therefore, using the Tor network can mitigate network attacks.

8   Related Work

Bitcoin Network Attacks. The security of the Bitcoin network has gained a lot of attention from the academic community. The well-known eclipse attack [20, 29] exploits the vulnerabilities of Bitcoin's built-in peer-selecting procedure by injecting the address database of victims with the attacker-controlled to isolate the victim Bitcoin nodes from the major Bitcoin network. BGP hijacking attack [3] and EREBUS attack [43] exploits the advantage of an AS-level attacker to delay messages received by nodes or partition nodes. The Topology Inference attacks [5, 12, 28, 32, 36] infer connections by analyzing the transmitted Bitcoin data or timestamps. On-path Bitcoin network attacks [15, 16] hijack the Bitcoin connections to disrupt the operation of the system. The delay attack [7, 22, 45] exploits network timing as the attack vector and impedes the reception time of certain Bitcoin messages of the victim nodes. The data received and stored by the victim node differs from that of the remaining nodes in the network within a certain period, resulting in wasted computing power and defaming the victim node to be susceptible to double-spending attackers. Lastly, the deanonymization attack [2, 5] reveals the real IP addresses of the victim nodes by analyzing the Bitcoin traffic, making every transaction associated with the victim's IP address public.

Off-Path TCP Vulnerabilities. Side-channel attack in the challenge ACK mechanism [9, 10] can infer the TCP utilization for one specific connection and then hijack it by inferring its sequence numbers and ACK numbers. Global IPID counter vulnerability is exploited to infer TCP connections and help attackers inject malicious data into the TCP connections to poison the HTTP and Tor traffic [23–26]. Mixed IPID assignment off-path attack [17,18] leverages a new side channel vulnerability to downgrade the TCP connections of IPID assignment to the 2048-hash-based method, which helps the attacker infer the source port number and the destination port number of the connection, inferring the sequence numbers and the acknowledge numbers to hijack the TCP connection.

9   Conclusion

In this paper, we propose Bijack, a new off-path Bitcoin TCP hijacking attack against the Bitcoin network by exploiting a TCP protocol vulnerability of the Linux system. We also demonstrate two Bitcoin network attacks—the topology inference attack and the eclipse attack—to show the impact of our attack on the Bitcoin network. We measure the number of vulnerable nodes in the real Bitcoin network and analyze the influence of our attack. We evaluate the efficiency of our attacks. Our experiments show that the off-path attackers can successfully carry out the topology inferring attack and eclipse attack effectively.

Acknowledgement. This work was supported in part by the US National Science Foundation under grants 2247560, 2154929, 1916902, and 2247561.

A   Appendix

A.1   IPID Assignment

IPID Assignment. The identification field (IPID) in the Internet Protocol (IP) serves as a unique identifier for each IP packet and it occupies 16 bits in the IP packet. The IPID is assigned by the sender to aid in assembling the fragments of a datagram because IP datagrams may be fragmented into multiple fragments for transmission over the network during the transmission process. The generation of the IPID can employ different algorithms or strategies, but it must be unique within the sender's context. In certain versions, Linux employs a mixed IPID assignment method for packets [1]. There are two fundamental IPID assignment policies: the per-socket-based IPID assignment method and the 2048-globally-hash-based IPID assignment method, the former being specific to socket-based protocols such as TCP and UDP.

Per-Socket-Based IPID Assignment. This policy is specifically used for socket-based protocols such as TCP and UDP. A unique random value is initialized for each connection, and the counter is incremented by 1 each time it is used for transmitting a packet. This random counter makes it difficult for off-path attackers to infer the IPID value.

Hash-Based IPID Assignment. It involves assigning the IPID based on a hash counter. Linux has a total of 2048 hash counters, and the IPID is selected from one of these counters based on the hash value of four variables: the source IP address, destination IP address, the protocol number of the packet, and a random value generated by the Linux system. After the IPID value is copied from the selected counter, the counter is incremented by a uniform distribution value between 1 and the number of system ticks that have elapsed since the last packet transmission using the same counter.

Linux uses the Don't Fragment (DF) flag in the IP protocol to differentiate between the two methods. Normally the TCP and UDP use per-socket-based IPID assignment and the DF's value is one. For other network protocols (like ICMP), the DF is set as 0. For TCP, DF is set as 1 for TCP non-RST segments, enabling the MTU discovery (PMTUD) mechanism and signaling the use of the per-socket-based IPID assignment method, which is considered more secure. The IP examines the DF flag value set by the TCP protocol. If DF is 0, the hash-based IPID assignment method is used. If DF is 1 and the packet is not for a TCP SYN/ACK segment with both SYN and ACK flags set to 1 (assigned IPID of 0), the IP assigns the IPID using the per-socket-based method.

A.2   Bitcoin Network Measurement Procedure

We first scan all connectable nodes in the network based on the method in [47]. Then, we establish Bitcoin connections with these nodes for further testing. To reduce the bandwidth load on our node, we test only one Bitcoin node at a time and establish a connection with only that one Bitcoin node. Initially, we send malicious ICMP "Fragmentation Needed" messages to attempt to clear the DF flag. As for hash collision, we first observe the average rate m at which the tested node sends Bitcoin information to our node and the average IPID increment k between each message. Then, our scanner node sends forged ICMP messages with different source IP addresses to the tested node. For each source IP address, we will send the forged packets at a rate of $n * m$ for the time period of $1/m$. If we found that the IPID of a received Bitcoin message increased by $n * m + k$ compared to the most recent previous one, we considered the tested node collided. To minimize errors caused by network latency or the randomness of the IPID increment, when we observe the IPID increment value in the range of $n * m + k$, we repeat the test with the source IP address used for the collision to verify whether the collision really occurred.

References

1. Alexander, G., Espinoza, A.M., Crandall, J.R.: Detecting TCP/IP connections via IPID hash collisions. Proc. Priv. Enhancing Technol. **2019**, 4 (2019)
2. Apostolaki, M., Maire, C., Vanbever, L.: PERIMETER: a network-layer attack on the anonymity of cryptocurrencies. In: Borisov, N., Diaz, C. (eds.) FC 2021, Part I 25. LNCS, vol. 12674, pp. 147–166. Springer, Heidelberg (2021). https://doi.org/10.1007/978-3-662-64322-8_7
3. Apostolaki, M., Zohar, A., Vanbever, L. Hijacking bitcoin: routing attacks on cryptocurrencies. In: 2017 IEEE Symposium on Security and Privacy (SP), pp. 375–392. IEEE (2017)

4. Armknecht, F., Karame, G.O., Mandal, A., Youssef, F., Zenner, E.: Ripple: overview and outlook. In: Conti, M., Schunter, M., Askoxylakis, I. (eds.) Trust 2015. LNCS, vol. 9229, pp. 163–180. Springer, Cham (2015). https://doi.org/10.1007/978-3-319-22846-4_10

5. Biryukov, A., Khovratovich, D., Pustogarov, I.: Deanonymisation of clients in bitcoin P2P network. In: Proceedings of the 2014 ACM SIGSAC Conference on Computer and Communications Security, pp. 15–29 (2014)

6. Borman, D., Braden, B., Jacobson, V.: RFC 7323: TCP extensions for high performance (2014)

7. Boverman, A.: Timejacking & Bitcoin. Culubas Blog (2011)

8. Buterin, V., et al.: A next-generation smart contract and decentralized application platform. White Paper 3, 37, 2–1 (2014)

9. Cao, Y., Qian, Z., Wang, Z., Dao, T., Krishnamurthy, S.V., Marvel, L.M.: Off-path TCP exploits: global rate limit considered dangerous. In: USENIX Security Symposium, pp. 209–225 (2016)

10. Cao, Y., Qian, Z., Wang, Z., Dao, T., Krishnamurthy, S.V., Marvel, L.M.: Off-path TCP exploits of the challenge ack global rate limit. IEEE/ACM Trans. Netw. 26(2), 765–778 (2018)

11. BitcoinCore: CVE-2018-17144. https://bitcoincore.org/en/2018/09/20/notice/. Accessed May 2023

12. Delgado-Segura, S., Bakshi, S., Pérez-Solà, C., Litton, J., Pachulski, A., Miller, A., Bhattacharjee, B.: TxProbe: discovering bitcoin's network topology using orphan transactions. In: Goldberg, I., Moore, T. (eds.) FC 2019. LNCS, vol. 11598, pp. 550–566. Springer, Cham (2019). https://doi.org/10.1007/978-3-030-32101-7_32

13. Dierks, T., Allen, C.: RFC 2246: the TLS protocol version 1.0 (1999)

14. Eyal, I., Sirer, E.G.: Majority is not enough: bitcoin mining is vulnerable. Commun. ACM 61(7), 95–102 (2018)

15. Fan, W., Chang, S.-Y., Zhou, X., Xu, S.: ConMan: a connection manipulation-based attack against bitcoin networking. In: 2021 IEEE Conference on Communications and Network Security (CNS), pp. 101–109. IEEE (2021)

16. Fan, W., Wuthier, S., Hong, H.-J., Zhou, X., Bai, Y., Chang, S.-Y.: The security investigation of ban score and misbehavior tracking in bitcoin network. In: 2022 IEEE 42nd International Conference on Distributed Computing Systems (ICDCS), pp. 191–201. IEEE (2022)

17. Feng, X., Fu, C., Li, Q., Sun, K., Xu, K.: Off-path TCP exploits of the mixed IPID assignment. In: Proceedings of the 2020 ACM SIGSAC Conference on Computer and Communications Security, pp. 1323–1335 (2020)

18. Feng, X., Li, Q., Sun, K., Fu, C., Xu, K.: Off-path TCP hijacking attacks via the side channel of downgraded IPID. IEEE/ACM Trans. Netw. 30(1), 409–422 (2021)

19. Franzoni, F., Daza, V.: SoK: network-level attacks on the bitcoin P2P network. IEEE Access 10, 94924–94962 (2022)

20. Gervais, A., Karame, G.O., Capkun, V., Capkun, S.: Is bitcoin a decentralized currency? IEEE Secur. Priv. 12(3), 54–60 (2014)

21. Gervais, A., Karame, G.O., Wüst, K., Glykantzis, V., Ritzdorf, H., Capkun, S.: On the security and performance of proof of work blockchains. In: Proceedings of the 2016 ACM SIGSAC Conference on Computer and Communications Security, pp. 3–16 (2016)

22. Gervais, A., Ritzdorf, H., Karame, G.O., Capkun, S.: Tampering with the delivery of blocks and transactions in bitcoin. In: Proceedings of the 22nd ACM SIGSAC Conference on Computer and Communications Security, pp. 692–705 (2015)

23. Gilad, Y., Herzberg, A.: Off-path attacking the web. In: WOOT, pp. 41–52 (2012)
24. Gilad, Y., Herzberg, A.: Spying in the dark: TCP and Tor traffic analysis. In: Fischer-Hübner, S., Wright, M. (eds.) PETS 2012. LNCS, vol. 7384, pp. 100–119. Springer, Heidelberg (2012). https://doi.org/10.1007/978-3-642-31680-7_6
25. Gilad, Y., Herzberg, A.: Off-path TCP injection attacks. ACM Trans. Inf. Syst. Secur. (TISSEC) 16(4), 1–32 (2014)
26. Gilad, Y., Herzberg, A., Shulman, H.: Off-path hacking: the illusion of challenge-response authentication. IEEE Secur. Priv. 12(5), 68–77 (2013)
27. Goode, B.: Voice over internet protocol (VoIP). Proc. IEEE 90(9), 1495–1517 (2002)
28. Grundmann, M., Neudecker, T., Hartenstein, H.: Exploiting transaction accumulation and double spends for topology inference in bitcoin. In: Zohar, A., et al. (eds.) FC 2018. LNCS, vol. 10958, pp. 113–126. Springer, Heidelberg (2019). https://doi.org/10.1007/978-3-662-58820-8_9
29. Heilman, E., Kendler, A., Zohar, A., Goldberg, S.: Eclipse attacks on bitcoin's peer-to-peer network. In: 24th {USENIX} Security Symposium, {USENIX} Security 2015, pp. 129–144 (2015)
30. John, P.: Transmission control protocol. RFC 793 (1981)
31. Luckie, M., Beverly, R., Koga, R., Keys, K., Kroll, J.A., Claffy, K.: Network hygiene, incentives, and regulation: deployment of source address validation in the internet. In: Proceedings of the 2019 ACM SIGSAC Conference on Computer and Communications Security, pp. 465–480 (2019)
32. Miller, A., et al.: Discovering bitcoin's public topology and influential nodes (2015)
33. Nakamoto, S.: Bitcoin: a peer-to-peer electronic cash system. Decentralized Bus. Rev., 21260 (2008)
34. Naumenko, G.: Pr 18991: cache responses to Getaddr 3420 to prevent topology leaks. https://github.com/bitcoin/bitcoin/pull/18991. Accessed May 2020
35. Nayak, K., Kumar, S., Miller, A., Shi, E.: Stubborn mining: generalizing selfish mining and combining with an eclipse attack. In: 2016 IEEE European Symposium on Security and Privacy (EuroS&P), pp. 305–320. IEEE (2016)
36. Neudecker, T., Andelfinger, P., Hartenstein, H.: Timing analysis for inferring the topology of the bitcoin peer-to-peer network. In: 2016 International IEEE Conferences on Ubiquitous Intelligence & Computing, Advanced and Trusted Computing, Scalable Computing and Communications, Cloud and Big Data Computing, Internet of People, and Smart World Congress (UIC/ATC/ScalCom/CBDCom/IoP/SmartWorld), pp. 358–367. IEEE (2016)
37. National Institute of Standards and Technology: CVE-2020-36516. https://nvd.nist.gov/vuln/detail/CVE-2020-36516. Accessed May 2023
38. Postel, J.: Internet control protocol. RFC 792 (1981)
39. Litecoin Project: Litecoin. https://litecoin.org. Accessed May 2023
40. Raikwar, M., Gligoroski, D.: DoS attacks on blockchain ecosystem. In: Chaves, R., et al. (eds.) Euro-Par 2021: Parallel Processing Workshops, Euro-Par 2021. LNCS, vol. 13098, pp. 230–242. Springer, Cham (2022). https://doi.org/10.1007/978-3-031-06156-1_19
41. Ramaiah, A., Stewart, R., Dalal, M.: RFC 5961: improving TCP's robustness to blind in-window attacks (2010)
42. Schuba, C.L., Krsul, I.V., Kuhn, M.G., Spafford, E.H., Sundaram, A., Zamboni, D.: Analysis of a denial of service attack on TCP. In: Proceedings of the 1997 IEEE Symposium on Security and Privacy (Cat. No. 97CB36097), pp. 208–223. IEEE (1997)

43. Tran, M., Choi, I., Moon, G.J., Vu, A.V., Kang, M.S.: A stealthier partitioning attack against bitcoin peer-to-peer network. In: 2020 IEEE Symposium on Security and Privacy (SP), pp. 894–909. IEEE (2020)

44. Vasek, M., Thornton, M., Moore, T.: Empirical analysis of denial-of-service attacks in the bitcoin ecosystem. In: Böhme, R., Brenner, M., Moore, T., Smith, M. (eds.) FC 2014. LNCS, vol. 8438, pp. 57–71. Springer, Heidelberg (2014). https://doi.org/10.1007/978-3-662-44774-1_5

45. Walck, M., Wang, K., Kim, H.S.: TendrilStaller: block delay attack in bitcoin. In. 2019 IEEE International Conference on Blockchain (Blockchain), pp. 1–9. IEEE (2019)

46. Xiao, Y., Zhang, N., Lou, W., Hou, Y.T.: A survey of distributed consensus protocols for blockchain networks. IEEE Commun. Surv. Tut. **22**(2), 1432–1465 (2020)

47. Yeow, A. Bitnodes. https://bitnodes.io/nodes/#network-snapshot. Accessed April 2023

Syntax-Aware Mutation for Testing the Solidity Compiler

Charalambos Mitropoulos[1], Thodoris Sotiropoulos[2], Sotiris Ioannidis[1], and Dimitris Mitropoulos[3]([envelope])

[1] Technical University of Crete, Chania, Greece
cmitropoulos@isc.tuc.gr, sotiris@ece.tuc.gr
[2] ETH Zurich, Zürich, Switzerland
theodoros.sotiropoulos@inf.ethz.ch
[3] University of Athens, Athens, Greece
dimitro@uoa.gr

Abstract. We introduce FUZZOL, the first syntax-aware mutation fuzzer for systematically testing the security and reliability of solc, the standard Solidity compiler. FUZZOL addresses a challenge of existing fuzzers when dealing with structured inputs: the generation of inputs that get past the parser checks of the system under test. To do so, FUZZOL introduces a novel *syntax-aware mutation* that breaks into three strategies, each of them making different kind of changes in the inputs. Contrary to existing mutations, our mutation is able to change constructs, statements, and entire pieces of code, in a fine-grained manner that conforms to the syntactic rules of the Solidity grammar. Moreover, to explore new paths in the compiler's codebase faster, we introduce a *mutation strategy prioritization algorithm* that allows FUZZOL to identify and apply only those mutation strategies that are most effective in exercising new interesting paths. To evaluate FUZZOL, we test 33 of the latest solc stable releases, and compare FUZZOL with (1) *Superion*, a grammar-aware fuzzer, (2) *AFL-compiler-fuzzer*, a text-mutation fuzzer and (3) two grammar-blind fuzzers with advanced test input generation schedules: *AFLFast* and *MOPT-AFL*. FUZZOL identified 19 bugs in total (7 of which were previously unknown to Solidity developers), while the other fuzzers missed half of these bugs. Also, FUZZOL outperforms all fuzzers in terms of line, function, and branch coverage (from 3.75% to 408.8% improvement), while it is the most effective one when it comes to test input generation. Finally, our experiments indicate that our prioritization algorithm makes FUZZOL explore new paths roughly one day ($\sim$24 h) faster.

Keywords: Fuzzing · compilers · smart contracts · Solidity

1 Introduction

Smart contracts are programs that are stored on a distributed ledger (i.e., blockchain), and are used for automating the execution of agreements and transactions between crypto-currency parties. *Solidity* [5] is an object-oriented programming language designed for developing smart contracts that run on several

G. Tsudik et al. (Eds.): ESORICS 2023, LNCS 14346, pp. 327–347, 2024.
https://doi.org/10.1007/978-3-031-51479-1_17

blockchain platforms [1,2], including the *Ethereum*'s EVM (Ethereum Virtual Machine) [50]. Ethereum is an open-source blockchain with *Ether* being its native crypto-currency, which is the second-largest by market capitalization [16].

Although there are several research endeavors to identify bugs in smart contracts written in Solidity [15,24,27,30,46], there are no thorough studies focusing on solc, the *standard* Solidity compiler. solc is a relatively new compiler that counts ~100 releases since 2015 [5]. Given the intricate nature of Solidity, solc offers various special constructs related to smart contract functionalities including formal software verification and inline assembly. Due to this complexity, solc has exhibited a variety of bugs related to data structure mishandling, inadequate sanity checks, and unsound optimizations [6].

For the last two decades, *fuzzing* has become a standard technique for assessing software reliability and security [14,25,26]. Fuzzing has been used to identify bugs in miscellaneous entities such as system libraries [35], web and cloud applications [10], data-oriented systems [39,40], and compilers [19,34,48].

When it comes to programs whose inputs follow specific grammars (e.g. compilers), grammar-blind fuzzers (such as AFL [37]) struggle to get past syntax checks and explore deeper code. To this end, researchers have introduced a number of grammar-based fuzzing strategies [9,43,44], and have applied them to various domains, from PHP and Lua interpreters to JavaScript engines.

However, current grammar-based fuzzers have a number of disadvantages. For instance, *Superion* [44], performs some mutations that fail to preserve a correct syntax for the test cases it generates. In addition, many of these fuzzers produce test inputs completely from scratch without considering any promising and interesting language features.

Syntax-Aware Mutation. We introduce *syntax-aware mutation* for fuzzing the Solidity compiler. Unlike other grammar-based techniques, our mutation processes test inputs (seeds) without breaking the syntax rules. Our mutation comes with three different strategies operating on the Abstract Syntax Tree (AST) of a smart contract written in Solidity. We apply our strategies to the programs found in the compilers' test suite. Such programs are interesting and complex, as they exercise different language features and functionalities. Our mutations then result in valid programs by making small changes to the existing, complex seeds. This helps exercise new behaviors in the compiler while preserving much of the structure and characteristics of the given seed programs. The first strategy aims to change the control-flow of the input program by mutating statements, operators and data types. To combine diverse characteristics coming from different test inputs, our second strategy selects two contracts and performs permutations on their AST leafs. Finally, our third strategy detects parts written in inline assembly and changes them in a way that stresses solc's inline optimizer.

Mutation Strategy Prioritization. Based on syntax-aware mutation, we have realized FUZZOL, a practical AFL-based fuzzer. Notably, FUZZOL also incorporates existing grammar-blind and grammar-aware strategies. We further boost the effectiveness of FUZZOL by leveraging the insight that only a *small* number of mutation strategies is effective in exploring new paths [31]. To this end, FUZZOL comes with a novel *mutation strategy prioritization* algorithm that identifies and applies only those strategies that are effective for a particular seed. Given a seed smart contract c, our algorithm associates every strategy with an *effectiveness* score. The next time when FUZZOL processes c, our algorithm picks and executes only those strategies whose effectiveness score is greater than a specific threshold value, which is updated and computed dynamically.

Testing Campaign. We evaluate FUZZOL by testing 33 of the latest solc releases (>5,5M LoC). Further, we compare FUZZOL against Superion [44], a grammar-based fuzzer, *AFL-compiler-fuzzer* [28], a text-mutation fuzzer that has been used to test solc among other compilers, and two grammar-blind fuzzers with advanced seed-generation schedules: *AFLFast* [13] and *MOPT-AFL* [35]. Our results indicate that our approach is effective in finding bugs in solc. Specifically, our method led to the identification of 19 unique bugs, in total, 7 of which were related to previously unknown issues to the Solidity developers. Also, our campaign helped the developers to identify two performance issues [3, 4]. Notably, the other three fuzzers failed to identify half of the bugs (10/19) found by FUZZOL. Our findings also show that FUZZOL outperforms the other four fuzzers both in terms of bug-revealing capability, code coverage, and test input generation. Moreover, FUZZOL achieves higher levels of coverage on average: FUZZOL was able to cover ×1.05 more LoC than Superion, ×1.08 more LoC than AFL-compiler-fuzzer, ×4.49 more LoC than AFLFast, and ×5.80 more LoC than MOPT-AFL. Finally, our prioritization algorithm makes FUZZOL exercise new compiler code-base, significantly faster (∼24 h) compared to the-state-of-the-art.

Contributions. We make the following contributions.

- We introduce a novel syntax-aware mutation with three distinct strategies that performs fine-grained changes within an input program by taking into account the nature and rules of a corresponding grammar.
- We design a prioritization algorithm that is able to distinguish the most effective strategies for each seed, and speed up the fuzzing process.
- We implement our approach in an AFL-based greybox fuzzer, which we call FUZZOL. We provide in-depth evaluations for understanding the effectiveness of FUZZOL (and its key components) when compared to four state-of-the-art fuzzers in the context of a large-scale study including 33 releases of solc.

2   Background

We provide a brief overview of the Solidity compiler and present a number of illustrative examples of solc bugs that our approach can help reveal. Furthermore, we discuss the limitations of previous approaches in the context of compiler testing.

2.1   The Solidity Compiler

solc [7] is the standard Solidity smart contract compiler. To handle variables and function arguments, Solidity employs particular mechanisms such as *storage* (a persistent memory that every Ethereum account incorporates), and *memory* (a byte-array that holds the data until the execution of the function terminates).

Important components of `solc` include an *Application Binary Interface (ABI)*, the built-in *formal verification module*, and an *inline assembler*. ABI is a standard way to interact with contracts in the Ethereum ecosystem. Interactions can be both external (i.e., from outside of the blockchain) and contract-to-contract. Note that data is always encoded according to its type, as described in the specification of ABI. Further, the encoding is not self-describing and as a result, it requires a schema to decode. The verification module of `solc` utilizes Microsoft's Z3 theorem prover [8,23]. Specifically, `solc` translates a contract into an SMT (Satisfiability Modulo Theory) formula, and then it attempts to prove the correctness of the contract and warn users about potential arithmetic overflows, unreachable code and more. Finally, through the inline assembler, Solidity provides a way for contracts to interact with EVM at a low level.

2.2   Bugs in the Solidity Compiler

To motivate the design of our fuzzing approach, we discuss two indicative bugs.

Bug in SMTChecker. To enable formal verification within `solc`, developers must include the `SMTChecker` via the **pragma** keyword at the beginning of their contract (in general, the **pragma** keyword can be used to employ diverse compiler features or checks). To verify a given contract and detect property violations, `solc` applies *Bounded Model Checking (BMC)* [22] to all contract functions, including **free** functions. Free functions are defined at a file-level and are not part of a contract. As a result, they cannot directly access state variables and internal functions of contracts. Nevertheless, they can call other contracts, emit events and send Ether. When BMC (through the `SMTChecker` module, line 1) examines the following simple, free function, `solc` produces an internal compiler (version 0.7.3) error:

```
1  pragma experimental SMTChecker;
2  function f() { }
```

This happens because the `SMTChecker` implementation does not reason about **free** functions–f in our case (a known issue among several 0.7.x versions).

Bug in Array Handling. The Solidity compiler may also contain bugs related to the way it handles its various structures such as arrays. Consider the code fragment below:

```
1  contract C {
2     uint[7**90][500] ids;
3  }
```

Contract C defines an array of integers named `ids`. Note that the size of arrays in Solidity have an upper bound. When `solc` (v0.6.0) compiles this contract an internal error occurs. This is because the compiler fails to catch that the size of `ids` is beyond the maximum size and produce a corresponding error message to the developer. As a result, the compiler crashes notably at a later stage (i.e., code generation) when trying to statically allocate memory for `ids`.

2.3 Limitations of State-of-the-Art Fuzzers

A grammar-aware fuzzer, could affect both the parsing phase and the semantic analysis process of the compiler. For this reason, grammar-aware mutation strategies have been utilized to test scripting languages [9,44]. However, previous grammar-aware strategies fail to form well-structured inputs efficiently.

Consider two recent mutations: the *enhanced dictionary-based* mutation, employed by Superion [44], and the *tree-based* mutation, used by both Superion and the grammar-aware fuzzer *NAUTILUS* [9]. The basic concept behind the enhanced dictionary-based mutation strategy is a dictionary containing a list of tokens, e.g., reserved identifiers, coming from a specified grammar. Initially, the fuzzer will tokenize the test input. After locating the token boundaries, the mutation either places a new token from the dictionary in between two others, or overwrites an existing one with another also coming from the dictionary. This procedure takes place for each token in the dictionary. Unfortunately, the resulting test cases do not always conform to the syntax of the grammar. We provide an illustrative example later on, in Sect. 3.

The tree-based mutation strategy selects two test inputs and attempts to parse them and generate the corresponding ASTs based on the target grammar. Note that in case of a parsing error the strategy stops. The strategy collects all sub-trees coming from both inputs and stores them in a set (S). Given the AST of the first test case, the strategy replaces every sub-tree with a random sub-tree taken from S. Each replacement leads to a new test case. By design, the tree-based mutation strategy respects the grammar of the language, as it is based on actions that process AST sub-trees. However, as we noted above, there are many cases where parsing will fail. This is going to happen if other mutations have already changed the test input that the tree-based strategy currently handles in a way that it does not conform to the grammar rules.

The AFL-compiler-fuzzer [28] offers a *text-mutation* strategy that detects specific string instances in a test case and replaces it with new text taken from an existing set. Also, it can add specific code fragments inside a program in an arbitrary manner (e.g. include a generic if statement such as if(0==1)). Such changes can be made in test cases written in different programming languages and explore compilers in a unified manner. Nevertheless, they will not be able to take into account the specifics of the language and exercise the different components of a compiler such as Solidity.

3 Fuzzing Approach

We introduce a syntax-aware mutation that aims to reveal complex bugs in solc. Our mutation consists of three strategies operating on the AST of a smart contract written in Solidity (Sect. 3.1). To further boost the effectiveness of fuzz testing, we present a prioritization algorithm that identifies and applies the strategies that are most effective in exploring new interesting paths for a specific seed program (Sect. 3.2). Finally, we explain some technical details behind FUZZOL, the implementation of the proposed approach (Sect. 3.3).

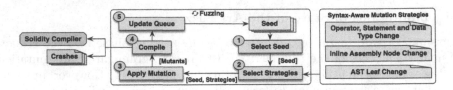

Fig. 1. Overview of our fuzzing approach for testing the Solidity compiler.

Figure 1 presents the overview of our approach. The input of our approach is a set of test programs written in Solidity. Our initial corpus consists of small test cases coming from the test suites of various Solidity releases. Notably, these test cases are designed to exercise all the different compiler features. First, we select a test input (seed) from the fuzzing queue. Then, our approach applies both grammar-blind strategies (such as *bit/byte flips* [37]) and our syntax-aware mutation to the selected seed. This *syntax-aware mutation* comes with three different mutation strategies. Each strategy has a different role in exercising Solidity's codebase. In particular, the first strategy performs changes to the control-flow of the input program by updating statements, operators and data types found in each smart contract. Our second strategy selects a random leaf from a contract's AST and place it in another contract. In this manner, we combine different characteristics (e.g. variable names) stemming from multiple contracts to create seeds that are more likely to trigger bugs. The third strategy detects the parts of a given AST written in inline assembly and replaces assembly code opcode arguments with other opcodes. The main goal of this strategy is to yield programs that contain more complicated inline assembly operations, and consequently involve more opportunities for `solc`'s inline optimizer.

To make our approach faster and explore deeper code, when a seed is selected from the queue, we employ a *mutation strategy prioritization* algorithm. As a result, we are able to identify, select, and apply the strategies that are most effective in exploring new paths for that specific seed. Our algorithm relies on an *effectiveness function* that leverages details from previous iterations of the fuzzing process (Sect. 3.2).

3.1   Syntax-Aware Mutation

Our syntax-aware mutation consists of different strategies. In the following, we analyze the proposed strategies. Given a smart contract c, each strategy performs a different change in c's AST altering the contract's behavior accordingly.

3.1.1   Operator, Statement and Data Type Change Strategy   Our first strategy applies changes in either an operator, a statement, or a data type of a given contract's AST. To do so, it replaces the selected item with another node of the same type (e.g., an operator is substituted by another operator). Thus, the strategy does not violate the syntax of the contract even though its behaviour and control flow can be significantly changed.

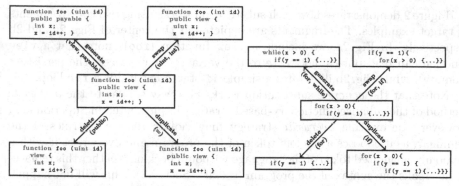

(a) Substitutions performed on operators (b) Substitutions performed on statements.
and data types.

Fig. 2. Example of substitutions applied to operators, statements and data types.

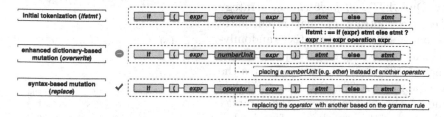

Fig. 3. The *overwrite* substitution of the *enhanced dictionary-based* strategy can potentially break the syntax rules. This is not the case in our *operator, statement, and data
type change* strategy.

Definition 1 (Operator, Statement and Data Type change). *Let c be a
smart contract and let a ∈ {ops, stm, datatype} be a node in c's AST that is either
an operator, a statement or a data type. Given a node a' ∈ {ops, stm, datatype},
we say that mut(c) = c[mut(a)] = c[a'/a] is an operator, statement and data
type change of the contract c that substitutes either an operator, a statement or
a datatype node with another similar node, preserving the syntax of the language.*

Specifically, a substitution $c[a'/a]$ may involve (1) the replacement of a token
(operator, datatype) or a statement a with another token/statement a' found in
the AST, or (2) the generation or deletion (i.e., represented by an empty node ϵ)
of valid tokens and program statements. Specifically, our strategy employs four
distinct types of substitutions namely: *generate, swap, delete,* and *duplicate.* By
performing such substitutions on Solidity tokens is of particular importance.
This is because Solidity has a number of special tokens related to smart contract
functionalities such as Ether units (e.g., `finney`, `wei` and `szabo`) and payment
addresses (e.g., `address`) that can change the course of compilation. For each
substitution we make sure that we maintain a correct grammar syntax. Note
that if a substitution violates the syntax we abort it.

Figure 2 demonstrates how each substitution works using two code fragments as target examples. The fragments are depicted at the center of Figs. 2a and 2b respectively. In Fig. 2a, we include a `view` function (`foo`) (note that a `view` function can read but cannot write to the variables that process the persistent memory), while Fig. 2b illustrates a simple `if` statement inside a `for` loop.

Note that the *generate* substitution works in a way similar to the *overwrite* method of the enhanced dictionary-based strategy implemented in Superion [44]. However, the existing *overwrite* strategy may violate the syntax rules of the grammar, as it chooses a random token of the program and overwrites it with a randomly-generated token of the language without checking whether this replacement breaks the syntax of the program (see also Sect. 2.3). This will not happen with our *generate* method because the strategy will enforce a correct syntax. Figure 3, highlights The distinct difference between *overwrite* and *generate*.

3.1.2 AST Leaf Node Change Strategy

Our *AST leaf node change* strategy takes the contract c_1 that is currently first on the queue, and another randomly-selected contract c_2 from the queue. Then, it parses the contracts and generates the corresponding ASTs. Given an AST leaf node of the first contract, the strategy replaces it with a random leaf node that stems from the second contract. Such a replacement leads to a new test case that involves unexpected characteristics (e.g., variable names), which in turn examine new compiler behaviours. Notably, the

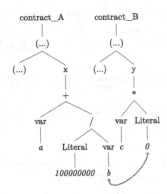

Fig. 4. *AST leaf node change.*

strategy considers changes only in the tree leafs and not in the sub-trees, making our strategy efficient and fast. This is because moving sub-trees across ASTs leads to large test cases that slow down the process.

Definition 2 (AST Leaf Node Change). *Let c_1 and c_2 be two contracts and let l_1 be a leaf node of c_1, and l_2 be a leaf node of c_2. Then the we say that $mut(c_1) = c_1[l_2/l_1]$ is an AST leaf node change of the contract c_1 that replaces a leaf l_1 with another leaf l_2 from another AST c_2, preserving language syntax.*

This strategy again results in well-formed programs because l_2 of c_2 will replace l_1 of c_1, only if this change respects the grammar rules of the language. An example is depicted in Fig. 4. Contract A, contains the following expression: `x = a + (100000000 / b)` while contract B includes: `y = c * 0`. Our strategy takes the leaf node 0 from contract A and replaces it with the leaf node b from contract B. Such a change can produce unexpected behaviours, e.g., triggering the compiler check that verifies whether the program is free from divisions by zero. Note that the strategy is designed to preserve the syntax, contrary to the tree-based strategy discussed in Sect. 2.3.

Algorithm 1: Mutation Strategy Prioritization

```
 1  Function Prioritization(t, strategies, scores, k, bound):
 2      if scores = nil then // first time we process t
 3          for s ∈ strategies do
 4              apply strategy s
 5              scores_s ← eff(s, t)
 6          bound ← GetKthScore(scores, k)
 7      else
 8          for s ∈ strategies do
 9              if scores_s ≥ bound then
10                  apply strategy s
11                  scores_s ← eff(s, t)
12                  if scores_s ≤ bound then
13                      bound ← scores_s
14          bound ← GetKthScore(scores, k)
15      return bound
16  End Function
```

3.1.3 Inline Assembly Node Change Strategy

In the context of Solidity, developers are able to employ blockchain-specific opcodes only available through inline assembly. However, malformed inline assembly code can affect the optimizations that can be applied to programs by the compiler, leading to crashes [18]. Our *inline assembly node change* strategy identifies inline assembly nodes, and makes changes in the corresponding assembly's opcodes depth.

Definition 3 (Inline Assembly Node Change). *Let c be a smart contract, $o_1 \in opcodes$ be an opcode node of c, and n be a child node of o_1. Given another opcode $o_2 \in opcodes$, we say that $mut(c) = c[o_1[o_2/n]/o_1]$ is an inline assembly node change of the contract c that replaces an argument of an opcode with another opcode according to the grammar rules of the language. This change increases the depth of the opcodes in the AST.*

Consider the following example. In a smart contract A that involves the opcode $o = \text{add}(x, y)$, the strategy operates as follows: First, it selects a random opcode o' (e.g.., mul) from the set of available *opcodes* supported by the Solidity's inline assembly language. Then, it chooses a random child node of the initial opcode o (i.e., either x or y) and replaces it with the new opcode o' with the same arguments as o's (e.g. add(mul(x, y), y)).

Overall, the *inline assembly node change* strategy produces complicated code and makes it hard for the compiler to solve some formulas used for verifying program correctness. Further, changing the inline assembly code can lead to discrepancies among the optimized code and the regular one. The reason behind this is that a program that manifests more complex opcodes in inline assembly triggers more paths in the solc's inline assembly optimizer, as the code now involves more optimization opportunities.

3.2 Mutation Strategy Prioritization

The key idea of our algorithm is that for every seed, instead of applying all strategies in a deterministic manner (as all AFL-based fuzzers do), we choose to perform *only* the top-k strategies that are most effective in producing test cases that explore new paths. In this way, testing does *not* waste time and resources in applying strategies that are deemed to be ineffective for a particular seed.

To achieve this, we introduce a function that evaluates the *effectiveness* of a strategy s on a test case t based on the fraction of the number of new explored paths (*#newpaths*) and the number of times the strategy s is applied to t (*#executions*).

$$eff(s, t) = \frac{\#newpaths}{\#executions}$$

Intuitively, the greater the $eff(s, t)$ is, the more effective the mutation strategy s is on this test case.

Algorithm 1 summarizes the details of the concept. The inputs of the algorithm are: (1) one seed program (t), (2) the set of mutation strategies that can be potentially applied to t, (3) an integer constant k indicating the number of top strategies exploring new paths, (4) the effectiveness scores of the strategies from the last time the t was processed, and (5) a *bound* value. Based on these inputs, our algorithm operates as follows. If it is the first time we process the given test case (which indicates that we do not have the effectiveness scores from previous runs, i.e., *scores* = **nil**, line 1), the algorithm applies all available strategies and computes their scores (lines 2–4). Then, the algorithm computes the *bound* value, which is used as an indicator of whether a strategy should be selected or not the next time we will process the seed. This bound value is the result of the `GetKthScore` function, which sorts the list of effectiveness scores in a descending order and then returns the score of the kth strategy.

If the given test case has been previously processed, the algorithm iterates all mutation strategies and applies only those whose effectiveness score is greater or equal to the bound (line 8). Practically, this means that the algorithm performs the top-k mutation strategies with the greatest effectiveness scores as computed in the previous run of the given seed. To prevent our algorithm from applying the same top-k strategies all the time, when the current effectiveness score $eff(s, t)$ of an executed mutation strategy is lower than the value of *bound*, the algorithm updates *bound* as *eff(s, t)* (lines 12–13). Conceptually, updating and lowering *bound* gives the opportunity to other strategies to take the place of a strategy currently included the top-k list (assuming the condition at line 9 holds).

3.3 FUZZOL

We have implemented FUZZOL, an AFL-based fuzzer to test the Solidity compiler. Our fuzzer is available as open-source software at https://github.com/chamitro/Fuzzol. We have developed our novel syntax-aware mutation together with its three distinct strategies in C/C++. Furthermore, we have adapted Superion's [44] tree-based and enhanced dictionary-based mutation strategies (also written in C/C++) to handle smart contracts and included them in our implementation. Beyond that, FUZZOL also employs other common grammar-blind strategies [37] such as *bit/byte flips* and *interesting values*. Finally, FUZZOL follows our prioritization algorithm to identify and apply strategies that are effective for a particular seed in the way we discussed in the previous section.

We built the Solidity grammar using ANTLR 4. Even though an ANTLR grammar for Solidity exists, it is incomplete and does not support the latest versions of the Solidity compiler. Thus, we have enriched the grammar adding more than 200 lines of code containing new grammar rules.

4 Evaluation

We evaluate FUZZOL by examining multiple releases of the Solidity compiler, seeking answers to the following research questions:

RQ1 Is FUZZOL effective in finding bugs in the Soldity compiler?
RQ2 How effective is our syntax-aware mutation when compared to grammar-blind strategies?
RQ3 How effective is FUZZOL when compared to the state-of-the-art fuzzers?
RQ4 Does our prioritization algorithm speed up the fuzzing process?

4.1 Evaluation Setup

We focused on the last 33 Solidity versions, i.e., from solc-v0.5.11 to solc-v0.8.17. We excluded solc-v0.8.1, solc-v0.8.2, and solc-v0.8.14 because we were not able to properly set them up due to configuration problems. Each compiler version contains 230k LoC on average.

Our initial corpus of seeds was populated by the test cases coming from the aforementioned versions. We extracted small test cases (less than 1 kB – recall that using small and targeted seeds is preferred in compiler testing [42]) that explore all the different functionalities from every version we tested. We gathered 1.5k test cases in total, each containing 10 LoC on average.

4.2 RQ1: Discovering Bugs

FUZZOL triggered several crashes. We examined the crashes to identify their source and find potential bugs in the Solidity compiler. Table 1 summarizes our results. FUZZOL identified 19 bugs in total, which we reported to the development team of Solidity. The team was already aware of some bugs. For the unknown bugs (enlisted in Appendix A), there were prompt fixes (~6 h after our report). Note also, that our testing campaign helped identify two performance issues [3, 4]. We further classified the discovered bugs based on their root cause. In the following, we describe the categories that we have identified.

Table 1. Total bugs discovered in all `solc` versions by FUZZOL. Bugs are grouped in categories based on their root cause.

Category	Total	Fixed	Confirmed (Unfixed)
Verification	5	5	0
ABI encoding	2	2	0
Inline assembly	3	3	0
Data structures & functions	8	7	1
Optimization	1	0	1
Total	**19**	17	2

Verification-Related Bugs. As we discussed in Sect. 2.1, `solc` enables formal verification through the `SMTChecker` module. We have found that several contracts that invoke this module can lead to compiler crashes. By examining these cases we have identified five distinct bugs. As an example of this bug category, consider again the first issue discussed in Sect. 2.2.

ABI Encoding Bugs. Using the `ABIEncoder` module, `solc` encodes and decodes various elements of a contract (e.g., structs) into other formats such as JSON. FUZZOL was able to identify two bug instances related to ABI encoding. As an example, consider the following test case:

```
1  function f() public {
2     mapping(uint=>uint)public memory x;
3  }
```

This test case calls the `mapping` function, which can be used to store data in the form of key-value pairs (both `uint` in our case). Our *AST leaf node change* strategy replaced the second leaf of `uint` with a new leaf `uint[1000000]`, which comes from another contract. The corresponding mutant triggered a *"mapping used outside of storage"* error in `solc`. This happens because when the `ABIEncoder` attempts to encode the elements of the contract, it does not prevent the processing of an out-of-bounds array.

The bug above highlights that combining individual characteristics of two contracts (i.e., through the *AST leaf node change* strategy) can result in test cases with unique features that are more likely to trigger bugs. For example, it is highly unlikely for a generator to produce the construct `uint[1000000]`.

Inline Assembly-Related Errors. As discussed in Sect. 2.1, contracts can have direct access to the EVM through `solc`'s inline assembler. In Solidity, inline assembly is marked by the `assembly { ... }` statement. Inside the curly braces, developers can utilize variable declarations, literals, opcodes and more. We observed that in three occasions the compiler did not handle such features in a correct manner. As an example, consider a contract that assigns one integer variable to another in inline assembly:

```
1  assembly {
2    uint x;  uint y;
3    x := y
4  }
```

Our *operator, statement and data type change* strategy, changed the type of x from uinit into a `calldata` type. When `solc` versions 0.6.4 and 0.6.8 attempted to compile the code above they both crashed. This is because there was a bug in the assignment implementation of the `calldata` types.

Bugs in Data Structures and Functions. We have discovered eight bugs in the implementations of various Solidity data structures and modules.

We have already discussed one of theses issues in Sect. 2.2. (bug in array handling). Our *AST leaf node change* strategy helped reveal this bug in the following manner. It collected a large integer number from a leaf of another contract and substituted the boundary of the array with this number. When processing the corresponding test case during the code generation stage, the compiler crashed because there were no checks regarding array limits.

Optimization Bugs. We identified one bug related to compiler optimizations. The code that led to the identification of the issue contained a *hex* value, that was replaced with another, large, *hex* value, i.e., `hex"344383800E6110`.... In this case, our *AST Leaf Node Change* strategy replaced the leaf node of the *hex* value, and replaced it with another *hex* value node, existed in another contract.

4.3   RQ2: Comparing Syntax-Aware and Grammar-Blind Strategies

We compare our strategies (described in Sect. 3.1) with standard grammar-blind strategies. We focus on the state-of-the-art strategies offered by AFL, namely: *bit/byte flips, arithmetics* and *interesting values*. To do so, we compare the number of unique test cases each strategy generates, i.e., the test cases that trigger new paths, over a 48 h window. Note that comparing test cases is a standard way to evaluate strategies [31,36,47]. Also, collecting seeds for 48 h is consistent with previous work where the time window for the experiments was roughly 24 h [13,35]. Furthermore, we compare the strategies in terms of effectiveness. We define the effectiveness of a mutation strategy as the ratio of unique test cases to the total number of test cases it generates [9,31,32].

Figure 5 presents the evolution of the generated test cases by each strategy for `solc` v0.8.16. We observed very similar trends in other compiler versions and omit the corresponding results for brevity. Our results indicate that all mutation strategies show a linear growth with different coefficients. Our *operator, statement and data type change* strategy turns out as the most productive one at all times. Notably, after 48 ours it has generated 250 test cases more than the *bit/byte flips* strategy (the second most productive), and 1000 more than the *arithmetics* strategy (the least productive). Our two other syntax-aware strategies come in the third and fourth place respectively.

Our results indicate that our strategies offer an increasing rate of producing interesting test cases. Another observation is that grammar-blind strategies can

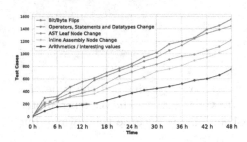
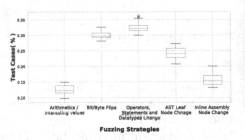

Fig. 5. Test cases produced for `solc` 0.8.13 by each strategy.

Fig. 6. The ratio of interesting test cases per fuzzer to the total number of generated test cases.

be productive when fuzzing a compiler, an observation made also by the authors of Superion [44], who examined different interpreters.

Focusing on effectiveness we observed that our *operator, statement and data type change* strategy is the most effective one. Figure 6 shows box-plots that present the effectiveness of each strategy for all 32 `solc` versions. The green line inside every box plot indicates the corresponding median value. The *operator, statement and data type change* strategy has the highest ratio overall (30–40%). Then, *bit/byte flipping* is the second best strategy with an overall ratio of 28–32%. Our *AST leaf node change* strategy has a (23–28%) ratio, and the *inline assembly node change* strategy comes next with a 15–20% ratio. Finally, the *arithmetic* strategy ratio is the lowest (10–15%).

4.4   RQ3: Comparison with State-of-the-Art Fuzzers

We compare FUZZOL with four AFL-based fuzzers, namely: Superion [44], the AFL-compiler-fuzzer [28], AFLFast [13] and MOPT-AFL [35]. Appendix B presents the design differences between FUZZOL and the fuzzers above. Unfortunately, given the time restrictions, we were not able to compare FUZZOL with other grammar-aware fuzzers, such as NAUTILUS [9], *IFuzzer* [43], *GRIMOIRE* [11]. This is because these fuzzers are not AFL-based, thus it requires much engineering effort and sufficient time to make them run for Solidity.

To perform our comparison we focus on two dimensions: (1) the bug finding capabilities of each tool and (2) code coverage. To gather our results, we run all fuzzers for 48 h. All experiments were run on a machine with an Intel Xeon CPU E5-2650v3 2.30GHz processor with 6 logical cores and 64 GB of RAM.

Figure 7 presents the bugs discovered by each tool for the last 12 `solc` versions. From versions 0.8.0 to 0.8.7, all tools reported crashes related to existing bugs. In all cases, FUZZOL found more bugs than any other fuzzer. From versions 0.8.8 to 0.8.13 there are no bugs found by the fuzzers. While in versions v0.8.15 and v0.8.16 FUZZOL identified one optimization issue, while the other four fuzzers were not able to detect any bugs.

We measured how much code is exercised by each tool by examining three `solc` versions. To do so, we used *afl-cov* [38]. Table 2 presents the line, function,

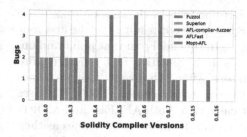

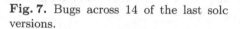

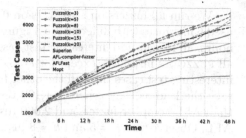

Fig. 7. Bugs across 14 of the last solc versions.

Fig. 8. The ratio of interesting test cases per strategy to the total number of generated test cases.

and branch coverage per fuzzer – version. Overall, we found that on average, FUZZOL was able to cover ×1.05 (i.e., 5.4% code coverage improvement) more lines than Superion, ×1.08 (i.e., 8.5% code coverage improvement) more lines than AFL-compiler-fuzzer, ×4.40 more lines than AFLFast (i.e., 230.6% code coverage improvement) and ×5.80 more lines than MOPT (i.e., 408.8% code coverage improvement). Notably, given the compiler's large codebase, an 1% code coverage improvement translates to covering 2,220 more lines of code. The situation is similar in the case of functions and branches where FUZZOL outperformed all fuzzers. In particular, our results show that on average, FUZZOL invoked ×1.04 more functions than Superion, ×1.08 more functions than AFL-compiler-fuzzer, ×2.4 more than AFLFast and MOPT. Finally, in terms of branch coverage, FUZZOL was ×1.03 better than Superion, ×1.07 better than AFL-compiler-fuzzer, ×2.56 better than AFLFast and ×3.2 better than MOPT.

All the above clearly indicate that the techniques implemented in FUZZOL lead to better results compared to the-state-of-the-art, in terms of both bug-finding capabilities and code coverage improvement.

4.5   RQ4: Mutation Strategy Prioritization Algorithm

To evaluate our mutation strategy prioritization algorithm (Sect. 3.2), we run different FUZZOL instances with different settings, i.e., we tried out different values of k, which is an input of our algorithm. Recall that k indicates the number of top strategies exploring new paths (see Sect. 3.2). Focusing on performance, we examined the number of unique test cases generated over time. Further, we compared FUZZOL's performance against the corresponding ratios of the other four tools mentioned earlier.

Apart from the three strategies discussed in Sect. 3, FUZZOL also incorporates all grammar-blind strategies of AFL and the grammar-based strategies implemented in Superion [44], namely, *enhanced dictionary-based* mutation and *tree-based* mutation, counting 20 strategies in total. Therefore, running our algorithm with $k = 20$ is equivalent to running FUZZOL with the default, AFL-based prioritization algorithm, i.e., running all the strategies in the same order.

We run all fuzzers on `solc` version 0.8.16 for 48 h. In the case of FUZZOL we used 6 instances with different k's. Figure 8 illustrate our results. For the first four hours, all fuzzers add interesting test cases in the queue. From that point and on, all FUZZOL 's instances, except for FUZZOL 's instance with $k = 3$, generate more interesting test cases than all the other fuzzers. After 24 h, five FUZZOL instances take the lead as they generate 1,100 test cases than Superion, 1,500 test cases than AFL-compiler-fuzzer, and 2,000 test cases than both AFLFast and MOPT-AFL. Observe that $k = 5$ and $k = 8$ instances are the most effective ones as they yield 1,100 more test cases than the baseline, i.e., $k = 20$. We observed similar trends in all the remaining compiler versions.

Table 2. Line, function and branch coverage for three of the latest `solc` versions.

Tool	Line Coverage (%)			Function Coverage (%)			Branch Coverage (%)		
	v0.8.16	v0.8.15	v0.8.13	v0.8.16	v0.8.15	v0.8.13	v0.8.16	v0.8.15	v0.8.13
FUZZOL	48.1	48.3	48.0	21.6	21.8	21.1	28.5	28.5	28.3
Superion [44]	46.3	45.0	46.1	20.6	20.5	20.6	28.1	28.0	27.5
AFL-compiler-fuzzer [28]	45.2	44.3	45.6	19.6	20.5	20.1	25.7	26.1	26.5
AFLFast [13]	15.2	15.0	15.4	<10	<10	<10	11.2	<10	11.3
MOPT [35]	<10	<10	<10	<10	<10	<10	<10	<10	<10

Our results indicate that our prioritization algorithm further boosts the fuzzing process. First, as we observe in Fig. 8 the baseline FUZZOL instance (the black thick line) is faster than all the other fuzzers, something that is consistent with our RQ3 findings (Sect. 4.4). However, it is slower than the instances that employ the algorithm (except the one with $k = 3$). This indicates that when our algorithm is used with values of k that are neither too high nor too low (e.g., $k = 5$, $k = 8$), there is a significant benefit in the performance of the fuzzing process, because FUZZOL produces unique test cases much faster.

5   Related Work

Grammar-Aware Mutation and Generation. We have already discussed the basic limitations of the strategies employed by Superion [44] in Sect. 2.3. *IFuzzer* [43] is a grammar-aware fuzzer that uses genetic programming [45] to compose new seeds for the JavaScript interpreter. Holler et al. [29] have proposed a similar approach. Specifically, they extract code fragments form sample code and use them to mutate test cases. On the grammar-aware generation front, *NAUTILUS* [9] can generate seeds containing valid code and then perform tree-based mutations on them (see also Sect. 2.3). Then, the corresponding mutants can be used to test languages such as PHP and JavaScript. Notably, NAUTILUS works without an initial set of test cases and generates inputs from scratch without taking into account different language characteristics. Recall that utilizing the existing test cases of a compiler helps exercising interesting compiler features (see Sect. 3). *GRIMOIRE* [11] extends NAUTILUS adding more mutations including string replacements, recursive replacements, and more.

Compared to this body of work, FUZZOL is the first fuzzer for the Solidity language, which implements novel syntax-aware strategies that takes into account Solidity's grammar and syntax rules.

Testing Compilers. Compiler testing approaches have been extensively surveyed [21]. We enumerate a number of methods related to our work. *Csmith* [49] automatically generates C programs that are free from undefined behavior. Randomized differential testing has also been used to examine production compilers such as GCC and Clang [34,41]. The AFL-compiler-fuzzer [28] uses a text-based mutation to test different compilers, including `solc` (as we discussed in Sect. 2.3). Our evaluation indicated that our approach is more effective and achieves better results in terms of both bug-finding capabilities and code coverage improvement than the AFL-compiler-fuzzer.

Advanced Scheduling. There are several approaches that provide more dynamic and effective power schedules for seeds prioritization. MOPT [35] employs a modified *particle swarm optimization* algorithm to make an effective use of the mutation scheduler. To further improve scheduling, *Cerebro* [33] takes into account elements such as coverage, and execution time. Furthermore, Cha et al. [17] employ symbolic analysis on execution traces to maximize effectiveness. *AFLGo* [12] and *Hawkeye* [20] introduce power schedules able to direct the fuzzing process towards specific locations of a programs (*directed* fuzzing), based on distance metrics. AFLFast [13] and *fair-fuzz* [32], include a scheduling algorithm that prioritizes rarely-exercised branches to achieve higher coverage.

FUZZOL implements a novel prioritization algorithm that is able to identify mutations that can achieve better results in terms of exploring new paths. Conceptually, our algorithm instead of prioritizing seeds, it prioritizes mutations.

6   Conclusion

We have presented FUZZOL, a greybox fuzzer for the Solidity compiler. FUZZOL comes with two key components for boosting the effectiveness of Solidity compiler fuzzing: (1) a syntax-aware mutation for producing syntactically-valid mutants that get past the syntactic checks of the compiler (and thus exploring deeper code), and (2) a mutation strategy prioritization algorithm that treats each seed differently, according to the mutations that are most suitable for that specific seed. Our in-depth evaluation on 33 compiler releases indicates that FUZZOL is superior to four state-of-the-art fuzzers in terms of bug-finding capability, improved code coverage, and test input generation. Finally, our prioritization algorithm makes FUZZOL generate unique test inputs almost one day faster.

Acknowledgments. We thank the anonymous reviewers and the shepherd for their constructive feedback. This work was supported by the European Union programme under grant agreements No. 82735 (Cybersecpro) and No. 82886 (Sentinel).

A   Bugs Previously Unknown to Solidity Developers

In the table below, we enumerate all bugs that (1) FUZZOL identified and (2) were unknown to Solidity developers.

Table 3. Category and references of the bugs that were unknown to Solidity developers.

Category	URL
Data structures & functions	github.com/ethereum/solidity/issues/11677
Data structures & functions	github.com/ethereum/solidity/issues/10502
Data structures & functions	github.com/ethereum/solidity/issues/7550
Inline assembly	github.com/ethereum/solidity/issues/9936
Inline assembly	github.com/ethereum/solidity/issues/11680
Verification	github.com/ethereum/solidity/issues/10798
Verification	github.com/ethereum/solidity/issues/7546

B   Differences Between FUZZOL and Fuzzers Included in Our Evaluation

In the following table, we present the main design differences between FUZ-ZOL and the related fuzzers included in our evaluation. Note that all fuzzers are AFL-based.

Table 4. Point-to-point comparison between FUZZOL and the fuzzers included in our evaluation. GB: grammar-blind, GA: grammar-aware, TM: text-mutation

Fuzzer	Mutation	Advanced Schedule	Target Program
Superion [44]	GA, GB	✗	JavaScript interpreter
AFL-compiler-fuzzer [28]	TM	✗	Solidity, Move, Fe, Zig
AFLFast [13]	GB	✓	Binaries
MOPT [35]	GB	✓	Binaries
FUZZOL	GA, GB	✓	Solidity

References

1. The Counterparty financial platform. https://counterparty.io/. Accessed 15 Jan 2023

2. Hedera hashgraph. Accessed 15 Jan 2023
3. Optimized contract crash. https://github.com/ethereum/solidity/issues/12840. Accessed 05 Jan 2023
4. Optimized contract freeze. https://github.com/ethereum/solidity/issues/12848. Accessed 03 Jan 2023
5. Solidity. https://docs.soliditylang.org/en/v0.8.0/. Accessed 03 Jan 2023
6. Solidity compiler - issues catalog. https://github.com/ethereum/solidity/issues. Accessed 15 Jan 2023
7. The Solidity contract-oriented programming language Github repository. https://github.com/ethereum/solidity. Accessed 05 Jan 2023
8. Z3 GitHub repository (2021). https://github.com/Z3Prover/z3. Accessed 20 Jan 2023
9. Aschermann, C., Frassetto, T., Holz, T., Jauernig, P., Sadeghi, A., Teuchert, D.: NAUTILUS: fishing for deep bugs with grammars. In: Proceedings of the 26th Annual Network and Distributed System Security Symposium (NDSS) (2019)
10. Atlidakis, V., Godefroid, P., Polishchuk, M.: Restler: stateful rest API fuzzing. In: Proceedings of the 41st International Conference on Software Engineering, ICSE 2019, pp. 748–758. IEEE Press (2019)
11. Blazytko, T., et al.: Grimoire: synthesizing structure while fuzzing. In: Proceedings of the 28th USENIX Conference on Security Symposium, pp. 1985–2002. USENIX Association, USA (2019)
12. Böhme, M., Pham, V.T., Nguyen, M.D., Roychoudhury, A.: Directed greybox fuzzing. In: Proceedings of the 2017 ACM SIGSAC Conference on Computer and Communications Security, CCS 2017, pp. 2329–2344. Association for Computing Machinery, New York (2017)
13. Böhme, M., Pham, V.T., Roychoudhury, A.: Coverage-based greybox fuzzing as Markov chain, CCS 2016, pp. 1032–1043. Association for Computing Machinery, New York (2016)
14. Bounimova, E., Godefroid, P., Molnar, D.: Billions and billions of constraints: whitebox fuzz testing in production. In: Proceedings of the 2013 International Conference on Software Engineering, ICSE 2013, pp. 122–131. IEEE Press (2013)
15. Brent, L., Grech, N., Lagouvardos, S., Scholz, B., Smaragdakis, Y.: Ethainter: a smart contract security analyzer for composite vulnerabilities. In: Proceedings of the 41st ACM SIGPLAN Conference on Programming Language Design and Implementation, PLDI 2020, pp. 454–469. Association for Computing Machinery, New York (2020)
16. Browne, R.: Ether, the world's second-biggest cryptocurrency, is closing in on an all-time high (2021). https://www.cnbc.com/2021/01/19/bitcoin-ethereum-eth-cryptocurrency-nears-all-time-high.html. Accessed 20 Jan 2023
17. Cha, S.K., Woo, M., Brumley, D.: Program-adaptive mutational fuzzing. In: Proceedings of the 2015 IEEE Symposium on Security and Privacy, SP 2015, pp. 725–741. IEEE Computer Society, USA (2015)
18. Chaliasos, S., Gervais, A., Livshits, B.: A study of inline assembly in solidity smart contracts. Proc. ACM Program. Lang. 6(OOPSLA2) (2022)
19. Chaliasos, S., Sotiropoulos, T., Spinellis, D., Gervais, A., Livshits, B., Mitropoulos, D.: Finding typing compiler bugs. In: Proceedings of the 43rd ACM SIGPLAN International Conference on Programming Language Design and Implementation, PLDI 2022, pp. 183–198. ACM, New York (2022)
20. Chen, H., et al.: Hawkeye: towards a desired directed grey-box fuzzer. In: Proceedings of the 2018 ACM SIGSAC Conference on Computer and Communications

Security, CCS 2018, pp. 2095–2108. Association for Computing Machinery, New York (2018)

21. Chen, J., et al.: A survey of compiler testing. ACM Comput. Surv. **53**(1), 1–36 (2020)

22. Cordeiro, L., Fischer, B., Marques-Silva, J.: SMT-based bounded model checking for embedded ANSI-C software. In: Proceedings of the 2009 IEEE/ACM International Conference on Automated Software Engineering, ASE 2009, pp. 137–148. IEEE Computer Society, USA (2009)

23. de Moura, L., Bjørner, N.: Z3: an efficient SMT solver. In: Ramakrishnan, C.R., Rehof, J. (eds.) TACAS 2008. LNCS, vol. 4963, pp. 337–340. Springer, Heidelberg (2008). https://doi.org/10.1007/978-3-540-78800-3_24

24. Ghaleb, A., Pattabiraman, K.: How effective are smart contract analysis tools? Evaluating smart contract static analysis tools using bug injection. In: Proceedings of the 29th ACM SIGSOFT International Symposium on Software Testing and Analysis, ISSTA 2020, pp. 415–427. ACM, New York (2020)

25. Godefroid, P.: Fuzzing: hack, art, and science. Commun. ACM **63**(2), 70–76 (2020)

26. Godefroid, P., Levin, M.Y., Molnar, D.: Sage: whitebox fuzzing for security testing: Sage has had a remarkable impact at Microsoft. Queue **10**(1), 20–27 (2012)

27. Grech, N., Kong, M., Jurisevic, A., Brent, L., Scholz, B., Smaragdakis, Y.: Madmax: analyzing the out-of-gas world of smart contracts. Commun. ACM **63**(10), 87–95 (2020)

28. Groce, A., van Tonder, R., Kalburgi, G.T., Le Goues, C.: Making no-fuss compiler fuzzing effective. In: Proceedings of the 31st ACM SIGPLAN International Conference on Compiler Construction, CC 2022, pp. 194–204. Association for Computing Machinery, New York (2022)

29. Holler, C., Herzig, K., Zeller, A.: Fuzzing with code fragments. In: Proceedings of the 21st USENIX Conference on Security Symposium, Security 2012, p. 38. USENIX Association, USA (2012)

30. Jiang, B., Liu, Y., Chan, W.K.: Contractfuzzer: fuzzing smart contracts for vulnerability detection. In: Proceedings of the 33rd ACM/IEEE International Conference on Automated Software Engineering, ASE 2018, pp. 259–269. Association for Computing Machinery, New York (2018)

31. Klees, G., Ruef, A., Cooper, B., Wei, S., Hicks, M.: Evaluating fuzz testing. In: Proceedings of the 2018 ACM SIGSAC Conference on Computer and Communications Security, CCS 2018, pp. 2123–2138. Association for Computing Machinery, New York (2018)

32. Lemieux, C., Sen, K.: Fairfuzz: a targeted mutation strategy for increasing greybox fuzz testing coverage. In: Proceedings of the 33rd ACM/IEEE International Conference on Automated Software Engineering, ASE 2018, pp. 475–485. Association for Computing Machinery, New York (2018)

33. Li, Y., et al.: Cerebro: context-aware adaptive fuzzing for effective vulnerability detection. In: Proceedings of the 2019 27th ACM Joint Meeting on European Software Engineering Conference and Symposium on the Foundations of Software Engineering, ESEC/FSE 2019, pp. 533–544. ACM, New York (2019)

34. Livinskii, V., Babokin, D., Regehr, J.: Random testing for C and C++ compilers with YARPGen. Proc. ACM Program. Lang. **4**(OOPSLA) (2020)

35. Lyu, C., et al.: MOPT: optimized mutation scheduling for fuzzers. In: Proceedings of the 28th USENIX Conference on Security Symposium, pp. 1949–1966. USENIX Association, USA (2019)

36. Lyu, C., et al.: EMS: history-driven mutation for coverage-based fuzzing. In: 29th Annual Network and Distributed System Security Symposium (2022)

37. Zalewski, M.: American fuzzy lop (2013). https://lcamtuf.coredump.cx/afl/. Accessed 13 Jan 2023
38. Rash, M.: AFL-COV - AFL fuzzing code coverage (2021). https://github.com/mrash/afl-cov. Accessed 06 Jan 2023
39. Rigger, M., Su, Z.: Testing database engines via pivoted query synthesis. In: 14th USENIX Symposium on Operating Systems Design and Implementation (OSDI 2020), pp. 667–682. USENIX Association (2020)
40. Sotiropoulos, T., Chaliasos, S., Atlidakis, V., Mitropoulos, D., Spinellis, D.: Data-oriented differential testing of object-relational mapping systems. In: 2021 IEEE/ACM 43rd International Conference on Software Engineering (ICSE), pp. 1535–1547 (2021)
41. Sun, C., Le, V., Su, Z.: Finding and analyzing compiler warning defects. In: Proceedings of the 38th International Conference on Software Engineering, ICSE 2016, pp. 203–213. Association for Computing Machinery, New York (2016)
42. Sun, C., Le, V., Zhang, Q., Su, Z.: Toward understanding compiler bugs in GCC and LLVM. In: Proceedings of the 25th International Symposium on Software Testing and Analysis, ISSTA 2016, pp. 294–305. Association for Computing Machinery, New York (2016)
43. Veggalam, S., Rawat, S., Haller, I., Bos, H.: IFuzzer: an evolutionary interpreter fuzzer using genetic programming. In: Askoxylakis, I., Ioannidis, S., Katsikas, S., Meadows, C. (eds.) ESORICS 2016. LNCS, vol. 9878, pp. 581–601. Springer, Cham (2016). https://doi.org/10.1007/978-3-319-45744-4_29
44. Wang, J., Chen, B., Wei, L., Liu, Y.: Superion: Grammar-aware greybox fuzzing. In: Proceedings of the 41st International Conference on Software Engineering, ICSE 2019, pp. 724–735. IEEE Press (2019)
45. Weimer, W., Nguyen, T., Le Goues, C., Forrest, S.: Automatically finding patches using genetic programming. In: Proceedings of the 31st International Conference on Software Engineering, ICSE 2009, pp. 364–374. IEEE, USA (2009)
46. Wüstholz, V., Christakis, M.: Harvey: a greybox fuzzer for smart contracts. In: Proceedings of the 28th ACM Joint Meeting on European Software Engineering Conference and Symposium on the Foundations of Software Engineering, ESEC/FSE 2020, pp. 1398–1409. Association for Computing Machinery, New York (2020)
47. Yan, S., Wu, C., Li, H., Shao, W., Jia, C.: Pathafl: path-coverage assisted fuzzing. In: Proceedings of the 15th ACM Asia Conference on Computer and Communications Security, ASIA CCS 2020, pp. 598–609. Association for Computing Machinery, New York (2020)
48. Yang, X., Chen, Y., Eide, E., Regehr, J.: Finding and understanding bugs in C compilers. SIGPLAN Not. **46**(6), 283–294 (2011)
49. Yang, X., Chen, Y., Eide, E., Regehr, J.: Finding and understanding bugs in c compilers. In: Proceedings of the 32nd ACM SIGPLAN Conference on Programming Language Design and Implementation, PLDI 2011, pp. 283–294. Association for Computing Machinery, New York (2011)
50. Zubairy, R.: Create a blockchain app for loyalty points with Hyperledger Fabric Ethereum Virtual Machine (2018). Accessed 06 Jan 2023

Efficient Transparent Polynomial Commitments for zk-SNARKs

Sungwook Kim[1] , Sungju Kim[2] , Yulim Shin[3] , Sunmi Kim[3] ,
Jihye Kim[4]([⊠]) , and Hyunok Oh[3]([⊠])

[1] Seoul Women's University, Seoul, Republic of Korea
kim.sungwook@swu.ac.kr
[2] Zkrypto Inc., Seoul, Republic of Korea
sungjukim@zkrypto.com
[3] Hanyang University, Seoul, Republic of Korea
{smkim2164,hoh}@hanyang.ac.kr
[4] Kookmin University, Seoul, Republic of Korea
jihyek@kookmin.ac.kr

Abstract. This paper proposes a new efficient transparent polynomial commitment scheme. In a polynomial commitment scheme, a prover commits a polynomial and a verifier sends a random point to the prover. The prover then evaluates the polynomial on the given point with generating a proof that the evaluated value is correctly computed according to the committed function. Our construction is based on the polynomial commitment scheme (the DARK compiler) proposed by Bünz, Fisch, and Szepieniec in EUROCRYPT 2020. The approach of DARK is that a prover recursively generates 2 group elements as the proof for a polynomial with a halved degree and a verifier indirectly verifies them at each recursion. In our construction, a prover commits all the reduced polynomials across recursions at once, and then generates a single aggregated proof for them. By aggregating commitments from recursive steps in DARK, the proposed scheme reduces the proof size by half, and provides better performance in the proof generation and the proof verification compared to DARK. By adopting the proposed scheme, the efficiency of transparent SNARKs from polynomial IOPs can be significantly improved.

Keywords: Polynomial commitment scheme · Transparent · zk-SNARKs · Groups of unknown order

1 Introduction

Zero-Knowledge Succinct Non-interactive Arguments of Knowledge (zk-SNARKs) are non-interactive proof systems that validate NP statements with a short and efficiently verifiable proof without revealing any information other than the correctness of the statements. Due to their strong privacy guarantee and efficient verification of (possibly delegated) computations, zk-SNARKs have

© The Author(s), under exclusive license to Springer Nature Switzerland AG 2024
G. Tsudik et al. (Eds.): ESORICS 2023, LNCS 14346, pp. 348–366, 2024.
https://doi.org/10.1007/978-3-031-51479-1_18

received much attention as a cutting edge solution for real-world applications, in particular, blockchain systems for privacy and scalability; Zerocash [3] showed how to effectively apply zk-SNARKs to a distributed ledger payment system to enhance privacy; off-chain systems [20,21] that utilize zk-SNARKs for verifiable computation improve blockchain scalability by enabling a significant amount of computation of on-chain nodes to be replaced by verification of the correctness of execution. In line with their rapid and extensive adoption, there have been a variety of proposals of zk-SNARKs: Aurora [4], Hyrax [35], Ligero [1], Marlin [17], Plonk [23], and Sonic [31], to name a few.

Recent constructions of zk-SNARKs [17,23,31] show that polynomial interactive oracle proof (IOP) is a powerful tool to transform a constraint system for a statement (circuit) to zk-SNARKs. The main ingredient for zk-SNARKs from polynomial IOPs is a polynomial commitment scheme. A polynomial commitment scheme enables for a prover to commit a low-degree polynomial $f(X)$ and later convinces a verifier that $f(X)$ is correctly evaluated at $X = z$ chosen randomly by a verifier. In real-world applications, a desirable class of zk-SNARKs is those that do not require a trusted-setup (i.e. transparent zk-SNARKs). Transparency of zk-SNARKs from polynomial IOP exactly depends on that of the underlying polynomial commitment scheme.

We are interested in efficient transparent polynomial commitment schemes. By "efficient", we mean that the proof size and verification cost are logarithmic in the degree of a given polynomial. In this line of research, notable prior works include the DARK compiler (DARK) [13,16][1] and Dory [29]. DARK has been constructed over groups of unknown order. It obtains a logarithmic proof size by recursively arguing the correctness of evaluation of an input polynomial that is randomly updated by a verifier with halved degree at each iteration. Dory has been proposed as a generalized inner-product argument system. It bases on a pairing group and obtains an efficient transparent polynomial commitment scheme via ideas in [14,35].

1.1 Contributions

In this paper, we propose an efficient transparent polynomial commitment scheme based on groups of unknown order. Our construction, motivated by DARK, significantly reduces its proof size. While its asymptotic complexities are the same as DARK, it actually performs better on the computations of the prover and the verifier respectively. We summarize our contributions as follows:

New Construction. We develop a new polynomial commitment scheme motivated by DARK. The heart of DARK is to perform recursive arguments, where the degree of a polynomial becomes half at each recursive call. At each iteration, a DARK prover generates 3 commitments, i.e., two to the left- and right-hand sub-polynomials and one to *proof of correct exponentiation* (PoE) [36]. In the view of argument of knowledge, DARK guarantees that a prover should know the committed polynomial at the first place and all reduced polynomials obtained

---

[1] The original DARK [13] has security flaw, which is addressed in [16].

Table 1. Efficiency comparison with existing transparent polynomial commitment schemes with logarithmic proof size and verification cost

$\mathbb{G}_U$: a group of unknown order; $(\mathbb{G}_1, \mathbb{G}_2, \mathbb{G}_T)$: a pairing group with a bilinear map $P : \mathbb{G}_1 \times \mathbb{G}_2 \rightarrow \mathbb{G}_T$; $\mathbb{F}$: a prime field $\mathbb{Z}_p$; d: the maximum degree of polynomials defined in the schemes; $\mu := \lceil \log_2 (d+1) \rceil$; $\mathbb{Z}(b)$: an integer between $-b$ and b, where $\log_2 b \approx \mu\lambda$ for a security parameter λ.

Elements of sets in the second ($|\pi|$), fifth ($|\mathsf{pp}|$), and sixth ($|\mathsf{pp}|$ pre-comp.) columns denote their sizes. In the column $|\mathsf{pp}|$, we ignore a group description (e.g., RSA modulus). Elements of sets and P in the third (the prover $\mathcal{P}$) and forth (the verifier $\mathcal{V}$) columns denote the corresponding cost of operations, where the superscript exp denotes a group exponentiation. DARK (opt.) refers to its optimized version.

	$|\pi|$	$\mathcal{P}$	$\mathcal{V}$	$|\mathsf{pp}|$	$|\mathsf{pp}|$ pre-comp.
This work	$(\mu+1)\,\mathbb{G}_U + 2\mu\,\mathbb{F} + \mathbb{Z}(b)$	$O(d)\,\mathbb{G}_U^{\mathsf{exp}}$	$O(\mu)\,\mathbb{G}_U^{\mathsf{exp}}$	$(\mu+1)\,\mathbb{G}_U$	$d(\mu/2+1)\,\mathbb{G}_U$
DARK [13,16]	$3\mu\,\mathbb{G}_U + 2\mu\,\mathbb{F} + \mathbb{Z}(b)$			$\mathbb{G}_U$	$d\,\mathbb{G}_U$
DARK (opt.)	$2\mu\,\mathbb{G}_U + \mu\,\mathbb{F} + \mathbb{Z}(b)$				
Dory [29]	$(3\mu+7)\,\mathbb{G}_T +$ $(1.5\mu+3)\,(\mathbb{G}_1 + \mathbb{G}_2) + 8\,\mathbb{F}$	$O(d)\,(\mathbb{G}_1^{\mathsf{exp}} + P)$	$O(\mu)\,\mathbb{G}_T^{\mathsf{exp}}$	$(\sqrt{d}+2)\,(\mathbb{G}_1 + \mathbb{G}_2) +$ $(1.5\mu+4)\,\mathbb{G}_T$	

Table 2. Comparison of proof size with 128-bit security [bytes]

An RSA-3072 group is taken for ours and DARK. For DORY, the curve BLS12-381 [10] is used as in their paper. For all cases we set $\mathbb{F} := \mathbb{Z}_p$ for a 128-bit prime p.

Degree	2^{10}	2^{11}	2^{12}	2^{13}	2^{14}	2^{15}	2^{16}
This work	4,576	4,992	5,408	5,824	6,240	6,656	7,072
DARK (opt.)	8,016	8,816	9,616	10,416	11,216	12,016	12,816
Dory	9,824	10,616	11,408	12,200	12,992	13,784	14,576

during recursion steps. Roughly speaking, the approach of DARK is to independently (and indirectly) check the prover's knowledge of a polynomial at every step, where PoE is used for the efficient verification of the proof. While our construction is similar with DARK in a way that it recursively reduces a polynomial to a constant, it takes a different approach to provide knowledge soundness. We observe that knowledge of polynomials can be checked in an aggregated way by adopting *proof of knowledge of representation* (PoKRep) [7]. More precisely, instead of checking the knowledge at every step, the prover in our construction first commits to all the polynomials generated during recursion, and later provides a single proof that the prover knows them. We show that our polynomial commitment scheme has knowledge-soundness (witness-extended emulation) as an argument of knowledge under the strong RSA assumption.

Communication-Efficient Polynomial Commitment. Our polynomial commitment scheme reduces the size of proof by one third and a half compared to those of DARK and its optimized version, respectively. This advantage directly comes from the adoption of PoKRep for knowledge of polynomials. As described previously, a proof of each iteration consists of 3 group elements in

DARK. PoKRep in our construction provides a way to aggregate the part of PoE commitments in DARK. Our construction, thus, only requires a single commitment at each recursion and another single commitment for PoKRep after the polynomial reduction part ends. Consequently, our polynomial commitment scheme reduces the proof size from $2 \log_2 \deg f(X)$ or $3 \log_2 \deg f(X)$ in [13, 16] to $\log_2 \deg f(X)$. We compare the efficiency of the proposed commitment scheme to prior transparent polynomial commitment schemes in Table 1. Table 2 concretely compares the proof sizes of the proposed polynomial scheme with Dory [29] and DARK over 128-bit security. Table 2 shows that the proof size of our construction is half as small as the existing schemes.

Implementation. We evaluate the performance of the proposed scheme in an RSA-2048 group. The estimation shows that the ratio of the proof size in our construction to DARK is about 0.4 almost independently of the degree of a polynomial. For the optimized DARK, the ratio is about 0.6. We implement our polynomial commitment scheme and DARK over an RSA-2048 group. We perform experiments to measure the proof generation and verification time by varying the degree of a polynomial (2^{10}–2^{16}). Experimental results show that the proof generation in our construction is about 3 times faster than DARK. The verification performance gain becomes significant as the degree of a polynomial increases.

1.2 Organization

The remainder of this paper is organized as follows. In Sect. 2, we provide the background groups of unknown order, arguments of knowledge, and the syntax of a polynomial commitment scheme. In Sect. 3, we present our construction of a polynomial commitment scheme. In Sect. 4, we evaluate the proposed scheme over an RSA-2048 group in comparison with DARK. We review related works in Sect. 5.

2 Preliminaries

Notations. Throughout the paper, λ denotes the security parameter written in unary. $\mathsf{negl}(\lambda)$ is a negligible function of the security parameter λ. We write $\log_2$ as $\log$. For a set S, we use $e \xleftarrow{\$} S$ to denote that an element e is sampled uniformly at random from S. For a probabilistic algorithm A, we write $y \leftarrow A(x)$ to denote that y is returned as the result of A on input x together with a randomness picked internally. $\mathsf{Primes}(\lambda)$ is the set of primes less than 2^λ. $GGen(\lambda)$ is a randomized algorithm that generates a group of unknown order. For integers a and b, $[a, b] = \{i \in \mathbb{Z} : a \leq i \leq b\}$. For a set $\mathbb{S}$ and $\mu \in \mathbb{N}$, $\mathbb{S}[\mu]$ denotes the set of μ-variate multilinear polynomials with coefficients from $\mathbb{S}$. By convention, $\mathbb{S} = \mathbb{S}[0]$. For a μ-variate multilinear polynomial f over $\mathbb{Z}$, $\|f\|_\infty$ denotes the maximum over the absolute values of all coefficients of f. $a \bmod n$ denotes the remainder when we divide a by n. $a = b \pmod{n}$ means a and b are congruent to modulo n.

2.1   Groups of Unknown Order

A variety of cryptographic primitives are constructed over groups of unknown order such as delay functions [36], accumulators [7], and polynomial commitment schemes [13]. Our construction is inspired by the polynomial commitment scheme (the DARK compiler), which is built over groups of unknown order in [13,16]. The use of groups of unknown order requires two cryptographic assumptions for security, i.e., the r-Strong RSA Assumption [2] and the Adaptive Root Assumption [36]. In the r-Strong RSA Assumption, the adversary is hard to compute an arbitrary root (except the power of r) of a random group element. In the Adaptive Root Assumption, the adversary is infeasible to compute a random root of an arbitrary group element. We note that the above two assumptions hold in the generic group model for groups of unknown order [7,18].

Definition 1 (r-Strong RSA Assumption). *The r-Strong RSA Assumption states that an efficient adversary cannot compute l-th roots for a given random group element, if l is not a power of r. Specifically, it holds for GGen if for any probabilistic polynomial time (poly-time) adversary $\mathcal{A}$:*

$$\Pr\left[u^l = g \wedge l \neq r^k, k \in \mathbb{N} \; : \; \begin{array}{c} \mathbb{G} \xleftarrow{\$} GGen(\lambda), \; g \xleftarrow{\$} \mathbb{G}, \\ (u,l) \in \mathbb{G} \times \mathbb{N} \leftarrow \mathcal{A}(\mathbb{G},g) \end{array}\right] \leq \mathsf{negl}(\lambda).$$

When $r = 1$, the r-strong RSA assumption is exactly the standard strong RSA assumption.

2.2   Arguments of Knowledge

Let $\mathcal{R} \subset \mathcal{X} \times \mathcal{W}$ be a poly-time decidable binary relation. $x \in \mathcal{X}$ and $w \in \mathcal{W}$ are called a statement and a witness, respectively. The language of $\mathcal{R}$ ($L_{\mathcal{R}}$) is defines as the set $\{x \in \{0,1\}^* : \exists w \in \{0,1\}^*$ such that $(x,w) \in \mathcal{R}\}$. An argument system for an NP relation $\mathcal{R}$ in the common random string model consists of three probabilistic poly-time algorithms (Setup, $\mathcal{P}, \mathcal{V}$), where we call algorithms $\mathcal{P}$ and $\mathcal{V}$ a prover and a verifier, respectively. Setup takes the security parameter λ, a some set of parameters param depending on the relation $\mathcal{R}$, and returns public parameters pp. For a triple (pp, $x \in \mathcal{X}, w \in \mathcal{W}$), interactive algorithms $\mathcal{P}(\mathsf{pp}, x, w)$ and $\mathcal{V}(\mathsf{pp}, x)$ are called a prover and a verifier, respectively. We denote the transcript produced by $\mathcal{P}$ and $\mathcal{V}$ when interacting by tr $\leftarrow \langle \mathcal{P}(\mathsf{pp}, x, w), \mathcal{V}(\mathsf{pp}, x)\rangle$ After interaction with $\mathcal{P}$, $\mathcal{V}$ accepts or rejects tr. We denote the final decision returned by $\mathcal{V}$ by $\langle \mathcal{P}(\mathsf{pp}, x, w), \mathcal{V}(\mathsf{pp}, x)\rangle = b$, where $b = 1$ if $\mathcal{V}$ accepts and $b = 0$ if $\mathcal{V}$ rejects. One can transform public coin interactive argument systems to non-interactive systems by applying the Fiat–Shamir heuristic [22].

Definition 2 (Argument of Knowledge). *We call the triple (Setup, $\mathcal{P}, \mathcal{V}$) an argument of knowledge for a relation $\mathcal{R}$ if it satisfies:*

- *(Completeness)* For all $(x, w) \in \mathcal{R}$

$$\Pr\left[\langle \mathcal{P}(\mathsf{pp}, x, w), \mathcal{V}(\mathsf{pp}, x)\rangle = 1 \ : \ \mathsf{pp} \leftarrow \mathsf{Setup}(1^\lambda, \mathsf{param})\right] = 1.$$

- *(Knowledge Soundness)* For all poly-time adversaries $\mathcal{A}_1$ there exists a poly-time extractor $\mathcal{E}$ such that for all poly-time adversaries $\mathcal{A}_0$

$$\Pr\left[\begin{matrix} \langle \mathcal{A}_1(\mathsf{pp}, x, \mathsf{state}), \mathcal{V}(\mathsf{pp}, x)\rangle = 1 \\ \wedge \ (x, w) \notin \mathcal{R} \end{matrix} : \begin{matrix} \mathsf{pp} \leftarrow \mathsf{Setup}(1^\lambda, \mathsf{param}), \\ (x, \mathsf{state}) \leftarrow \mathcal{A}_0(\mathsf{pp}), \\ w \leftarrow \mathcal{E}(\mathsf{pp}, x, \mathsf{state}) \end{matrix}\right] = \mathsf{negl}(\lambda).$$

DARK [13,16] and SPARTAN [34] extend a polynomial commitment scheme to an argument of knowledge. Those constructions strengthened the knowledge soundness by adopting the property witness-extended emulation [30]. We note that Lindell also proved that any every knowledge sound protocol also satisfies witness-extended-emulation [30].

Definition 3 (Witness-extended Emulation [24,30]). *A public coin argument* $(\mathsf{Setup}, \mathcal{P}, \mathcal{V})$ *has witness-extended emulation if for every deterministic polynomial-time prover* $\mathcal{P}^*$ *there exists an expected polynomial-time emulator* $\mathcal{E}$ *such that for all non-uniform polynomial-time adversaries* $\mathcal{A}$, *the difference between the following two probabilities is at most* $\mathsf{negl}(\lambda)$:

$$\Pr\left[\mathcal{A}(\mathsf{tr}) = 1 \ : \ \begin{matrix} \mathsf{pp} \leftarrow \mathsf{Setup}(1^\lambda, \mathsf{param}), \\ (x, \mathsf{state}) \in \mathcal{A}(\mathsf{pp}), \\ \mathsf{tr} \leftarrow \langle \mathcal{P}^*(\mathsf{pp}, x, \mathsf{state}), \mathcal{V}(\mathsf{pp}, x)\rangle \end{matrix}\right] \quad and$$

$$\Pr\left[\begin{matrix} \mathcal{A}(\mathsf{tr}) = 1 \ \wedge \\ if \ \mathsf{tr} \ is \ accepting, \ then \ (x, w) \in \mathcal{R} \end{matrix} : \begin{matrix} \mathsf{pp} \leftarrow \mathsf{Setup}(1^\lambda, \mathsf{param}), \\ (x, \mathsf{state}) \in \mathcal{A}(\mathsf{pp}), \\ (\mathsf{tr}, w) \leftarrow \mathcal{E}^{\langle \mathcal{P}^*(\mathsf{pp}, x, \mathsf{state}), \mathcal{V}(\mathsf{pp}, x)\rangle}(\mathsf{pp}, x) \end{matrix}\right],$$

where $\mathcal{E}$ *has access to a transcript oracle* $\langle \mathcal{P}^*(\mathsf{pp}, x, \mathsf{state}), \mathcal{V}(\mathsf{pp}, x)\rangle$ *that can be rewound to a particular round and run again with* $\mathcal{V}$ *using fresh randomness.*

2.3 Polynomial Commitment Scheme

We adopt the syntax of a polynomial commitment scheme which allows interactive evaluation proofs, following DARK [13,16] and SPARTAN [34]. A polynomial commitment scheme is a tuple of protocols $\mathsf{PC} = (\mathsf{Setup}, \mathsf{Commit}, \mathsf{Open}, \mathsf{Ver})$ for μ-variate multilinear polynomials $f(X_1, \ldots, X_\mu)$ over a field $\mathbb{F}$:

- $\mathsf{pp} \leftarrow \mathsf{PC.Setup}(1^\lambda, \mu, \mathbb{F})$ generates a public parameter pp with taking a security parameter λ, the maximum number of variables, and the field $\mathbb{F}$.
- $C \leftarrow \mathsf{PC.Commit}(\mathsf{pp}, f; \tau)$ takes as input pp, $f(X_1, \ldots, X_\mu) \in \mathbb{F}[\mu]$, and the randomness τ used in the computation. It returns a commitment C. If τ is not used, we write $\mathsf{PC.Commit}(\mathsf{pp}, f)$. We call (f, τ) the opening of C.

- $(y, \pi) \leftarrow$ PC.Open(pp, $C, \vec{z}, f; \tau$) is a public coin interactive protocol between a probabilistic poly-time prover $\mathcal{P}$ and a verifier $\mathcal{V}$. $\mathcal{P}$ takes as input C, a point $\vec{z} = (z_1, \ldots, z_\mu) \in \mathbb{F}^\mu$, and τ used in PC.Commit. After interaction with $\mathcal{V}$, $\mathcal{P}$ returns an evaluation $y = f(\vec{z}) \in \mathbb{F}$ and a proof of its correctness π, i.e., $y = f(\vec{z})$ for a witness polynomial f of C. If τ is not used, we write PC.Open(pp, $C, \vec{z}, f$).
- $b \in \{0, 1\} \leftarrow$ PC.Ver(pp, $C, \vec{z}, y, \pi$) takes as input pp, C, $\vec{z}$, y, and π. It returns 1 if it accepts the proof and 0 otherwise.

Recent SNARKs from polynomial IOPs require that a polynomial commitment scheme is extractable, i.e., interactive evaluation proofs is an argument of knowledge for the relation

$$\mathcal{R}_{\mathsf{PC}} = \{((C, \vec{z}, y), f) : f \in \mathbb{F}[\mu] \wedge y = f(\vec{z}) \wedge \mathsf{PC.Ver}(\mathsf{pp}, C, \vec{z}, y, \pi) = 1\}.$$

Definition 4. *A polynomial commitment scheme* PC = (Setup, Commit, Open, Ver) *for μ-variate multilinear polynomials over a field $\mathbb{F}$ is extractable if the following properties holds:*

- *(Binding) For all probabilistic poly-time adversaries $\mathcal{A}$*

$$\Pr\left[\begin{array}{c} f_0 \neq f_1 \wedge \\ \mathsf{PC.Commit}(\mathsf{pp}, f_0; \tau_0) \\ = \mathsf{PC.Commit}(\mathsf{pp}, f_1; \tau_1) \end{array} : \begin{array}{c} \mathsf{pp} \leftarrow \mathsf{PC.Setup}(1^\lambda, \mu), \\ (f_0, f_1, \tau_0, \tau_1) \leftarrow \mathcal{A}(\mathsf{pp}) \end{array}\right] \leq \mathsf{negl}(\lambda).$$

- *(Completeness) For all μ-variate multilinear polynomials $f \in \mathbb{F}[\mu]$ and all points $\vec{z} \in \mathbb{F}^\mu$*

$$\Pr\left[b = 1 : \begin{array}{c} \mathsf{pp} \leftarrow \mathsf{PC.Setup}(1^\lambda, \mu), C \leftarrow \mathsf{PC.Commit}(\mathsf{pp}, f; \tau), \\ (y, \pi) \leftarrow \mathsf{PC.Open}(\mathsf{pp}, C, \vec{z}, f; \tau), b \leftarrow \mathsf{PC.Ver}(\mathsf{pp}, C, \vec{z}, y, \pi) \end{array}\right] = 1.$$

- *(Witness-extended emulation)* PC *has witness-extended emulation as a public coin argument of knowledge for the relation $\mathcal{R}_{\mathsf{PC}}$.*

3   Our Construction

3.1   Integer Encoding of μ-Variate Multilinear Polynomials

We employ an encoding method in DARK [16] that presents a polynomial as an integer. For a non-negative real number b, let $\mathbb{Z}(b) := \{x \in \mathbb{Z} : |x| \leq b\}$. Given a polynomial $f(X) \in \mathbb{Z}(b)[X]$ an encoding function ρ_q is defined as $\rho_q(f(X)) \to f(q) \in \mathbb{Z}$ where q is parameterized in b and $\deg f(X)$. To encode polynomial $f(X) \in \mathbb{Z}_p$, we take a representative of $f(X) \in \mathbb{Z}_p$ as an integer polynomial with coefficients from $[0, p-1]$, thus, $f(X) \in \mathbb{Z}(p-1)[X]$. The decoding map ρ_q^{-1} is also given in DARK for integers in certain range.

Lemma 1 ([16, Fact 1]). *Let q be an odd integer. For any $-\frac{q^{d+1}}{2} < z < \frac{q^{d+1}}{2}$, there is a unique degree d integer polynomial $f(X) \in \mathbb{Z}(\frac{q}{2})[X]$ such that $f(q) = z$.*

Algorithm 1. Protocol PoKRep (Proof of knowledge of representation)

Public Parameter $pp := (\mathbb{G}, \vec{G}) \leftarrow \mathsf{PoKRep.Setup}(1^\lambda, t)$
Inputs: $G \in \mathbb{G}$; Witness: $(x_1, ..., x_t) \in \mathbb{Z}^t$; Claim: $G = \prod_{i=1}^t G_i^{x_i}$

1. $\mathcal{V}$ samples $\ell \overset{\$}{\leftarrow} \mathsf{Primes}(\lambda)$ and sends ℓ to $\mathcal{P}$.
2. $\mathcal{P}$ computes $\pi := (\vec{r} \in \mathbb{Z}^t, Q \in \mathbb{G}) \leftarrow \mathsf{PoKRep.Open}(pp, \ell, (x_1, ..., x_t))$ and sends π to $\mathcal{V}$.
3. $\mathcal{V}$ returns $b \leftarrow \mathsf{PoKRep.Ver}(pp, \ell, G, \pi)$.

$\mathsf{PoKRep.Setup}(1^\lambda, t)$:

  1: $\mathbb{G} \overset{\$}{\leftarrow} GGen(\lambda)$
  2: $\vec{G} := (G_1, \ldots, G_t) \overset{\$}{\leftarrow} \mathbb{G}^t$
  3: return $(\mathbb{G}, \vec{G})$

$\mathsf{PoKRep.Open}(pp, \ell, (x_1, \ldots, x_t))$:

  1: **for** $i = 1$ **do** t
  2:     compute $r_i \leftarrow x_i \bmod \ell$
  3: **end for**
  4: $\vec{r} := (r_1, \ldots, r_t)$
  5: compute $Q \leftarrow \prod_{i=1}^t G_i^{\lfloor \frac{x_i}{\ell} \rfloor}$
  6: return $\pi := (\vec{r}, Q)$

$\mathsf{PoKRep.Ver}(pp, \ell, G, \pi)$:

  1: parse π as $(\vec{r}, Q)$
  2: compute $G' \leftarrow Q^\ell \cdot \prod_{i=1}^t G_i^{r_i}$
  3: **if** $G = G'$ **then**
  4:     $b \leftarrow 1$
  5: **else**
  6:     $b \leftarrow 0$
  7: **end if**
  8: return b

There exists a 1-1 correspondence between the set of univariate polynomials of degree d and the set of μ-variate multilinear polynomials, where $\mu := \lceil \log(d+1) \rceil$. More precisely, let $X_i := X^{2^{i-1}}$ for $i = 1, ..., \mu$. For $0 \le j \le d$, we consider its binary representation $j = \sum_{i=0}^{\mu-1} b_i 2^i$, where $b_i \in \{0, 1\}$. We then have $X^j = X^{\sum_{i=0}^{\mu-1} b_i 2^i} = \prod_{i=1}^{\mu} X_i^{b_i}$. Under this correspondence ρ encodes a μ-variate multilinear polynomial $f(X_1, ..., X_\mu) \in Z(\frac{q}{2})[\mu]$ as an integer by $\rho_q(f) = f(q, ..., q^{2^{\mu-1}})$. Lemma 1 holds analogously for $f \in \mathbb{Z}(\frac{q}{2})[\mu]$ such that $f(q, q^2, \ldots, q^{2^{\mu-1}}) = z$ for $-\frac{q^{2^{\mu-1}}}{2} < z < \frac{q^{2^{\mu-1}}}{2}$.

3.2 Proof of Knowledge of Representation

Let $\mathbb{G}$ be a group of unknown order. For public parameters $\mathbb{G}$ and $G_1, \ldots G_t \in \mathbb{G}$, Boneh, Bünz, and Fisch [7] introduced an argument of knowledge for the relation

$$\mathcal{R}_{\mathsf{Rep}} = \left\{ (G \in \mathbb{G}, (x_1, \ldots, x_t) \in \mathbb{Z}^t) : G = \prod_{i=1}^t G_i^{x_i} \right\}$$

called "Proof of knowledge of representation (PoKRep)". The protocol has knowledge soundness under the strong RSA assumption. We present the protocol PoKRep in Algorithm 1. The protocol PoKRep plays an important role in our construction of a polynomial commitment scheme.

3.3 The Proposed Polynomial Commitment Scheme

Algorithm 2. Polynomial Commitment Scheme

PC.Setup($1^\lambda, \mu, p$):
1: $(\mathbb{G}, (G, \vec{R})) \leftarrow$ PoKRep.Setup($1^\lambda, 1 + \mu$), where $\vec{R} := (R_1, \ldots, R_\mu)$
2: $b \leftarrow (p-1)p^\mu; q \leftarrow 2 \cdot p^{2\mu+1}$;
3: return pp $:= (1^\lambda, \mathbb{G}, (G, \vec{R}), b, q)$

PC.Commit(pp; $f(X_1, \ldots, X_\mu) \in \mathbb{Z}(p-1)[X_1, \ldots, X_\mu]$):
1: $C \leftarrow G^{\hat{f}}$ where $\hat{f} := f(q, q^2, \ldots, q^{2^{\mu-1}}) \in \mathbb{Z}$
2: return C

PC.Open(pp, $C \in \mathbb{G}, \vec{z} \in \mathbb{Z}_p^\mu, f(X_1, \ldots, X_\mu) \in \mathbb{Z}(p-1)[X_1, \ldots, X_\mu]$)):
1: $\mathcal{P}$ sends C to $\mathcal{V}$
2: $\mathcal{P}$ initializes $g_1(X_1, \ldots, X_\mu) \leftarrow f(X_1, \ldots, X_\mu)$ // $g_1 = f_1$
3: **for** $i = 1$ **do** μ
4:     $\mathcal{P}$ computes $g_{i,L}(X_1, \ldots, X_{\mu-i})$ and $g_{i,R}(X_1, \ldots, X_{\mu-i})$ such that
    $g_i(X_1, \ldots, X_{\mu-i+1}) = g_{i,L}(X_1, \ldots, X_{\mu-i}) + X_{\mu-i+1} \cdot g_{i,R}(X_1, \ldots, X_{\mu-i})$
         // Operations on polynomials are performed over $\mathbb{Z}[\mu - i + 1]$
5:     $\mathcal{P}$ computes $D_i \leftarrow R_i^{\hat{g}_{i,R}}$ where $\hat{g}_{i,R} = g_{i,R}(q, \ldots, q^{2^{\mu-i}}) \in \mathbb{Z}$ and sends D_i to $\mathcal{V}$
6:     $\mathcal{P}$ computes $y_{i,R} \leftarrow g_{i,R}(z_1, \ldots, z_{\mu-i})$ mod p and sends $y_{i,R}$ to $\mathcal{V}$
7:     $\mathcal{V}$ samples $\alpha_i \xleftarrow{\$} [0, p-1]$ and sends α_i to $\mathcal{P}$
8:     $\mathcal{P}$ computes $g_{i+1}(X_1, \ldots, X_{\mu-i}) \leftarrow g_{i,L}(X_1, \ldots, X_{\mu-i}) + \alpha_i \cdot g_{i,R}(X_1, \ldots, X_{\mu-i})$
         // Operations on polynomials are performed over $\mathbb{Z}[\mu - i]$
9: **end for**
10: $\mathcal{P}$ sends $g_{\mu+1} \in \mathbb{Z}$ to $\mathcal{V}$
11: $\vec{g} \leftarrow (\hat{g}_{1,R}, \ldots, \hat{g}_{\mu,R}) \in \mathbb{Z}^\mu, \vec{D} \leftarrow (D_1, \ldots, D_\mu) \in \mathbb{G}^\mu$, and $\vec{y} \leftarrow (y_{1,R}, \ldots, y_{\mu,R}) \in \mathbb{Z}_p^\mu$
12: $\mathcal{V}$ samples $\ell \xleftarrow{\$}$ Primes(λ) and sends ℓ to $\mathcal{P}$
13: $\mathcal{P}$ computes $((r, \vec{s}), Q) \leftarrow$ PoKRep.Open($(\mathbb{G}, (G, \vec{R})), \ell, (\hat{f}, \vec{g})$)
14: $\pi \leftarrow (g_{\mu+1}, \vec{D}, \vec{y}, r, \vec{s}, Q)$ // $r = \hat{f} = \hat{g}_1$ mod $\ell, s_i = \hat{g}_{i,R}$ mod $\ell, Q = G^{\lfloor \hat{f}/\ell \rfloor} \cdot \prod_{i=1}^\mu R_i^{\lfloor \hat{g}_{i,R}/\ell \rfloor}$
15: $\mathcal{P}$ returns $(y := f(\vec{z}), \pi)$

PC.Ver(pp, $C \in \mathbb{G}, \vec{z} \in \mathbb{Z}_p^\mu, y \in \mathbb{Z}_p, \pi$):
1: parse $\pi = (g_{\mu+1}, \vec{D}, \vec{y} = (y_{1,R}, \ldots, y_{\mu,R}), r, \vec{s} = (s_{1,R}, \ldots, s_{\mu,R}), Q)$
2: assert that $|g_{\mu+1}| \leq b$
3: assert that PoKRep.Ver($(\mathbb{G}, (G, \vec{R})), \ell, C \cdot \prod_{i=1}^\mu D_i, ((r, \vec{s}), Q)$) = 1
4: $s_1 \leftarrow r$ mod ℓ
5: $y_1 \leftarrow y$ mod p
6: **for** $i = 1$ **do** μ
7:     $s_{i,L} \leftarrow s_i - q^{2^{\mu-i}} \cdot s_{i,R}$ mod ℓ
8:     $s_{i+1} \leftarrow s_{i,L} + \alpha_i \cdot s_{i,R}$ mod ℓ
9:     $y_{i,L} \leftarrow y_i - z_{\mu-i+1} \cdot y_{i,R}$ mod p
10:     $y_{i+1} \leftarrow y_{i,L} + \alpha_i \cdot y_{i,R}$ mod p
11: **end for**
12: assert that $g_{\mu+1} = s_{\mu+1}$ (mod ℓ)
13: assert that $g_{\mu+1} = y_{\mu+1}$ (mod p)
14: return 1 if all checks pass, otherwise 0

We describe the proposed polynomial commitment scheme to μ-variate multilinear polynomial over $\mathbb{Z}_p$ with a λ-bit prime p. In PC.Commit, $\mathcal{P}$ first commits the starting μ-variate multilinear polynomial $g_1(X_1, \ldots, X_\mu])$ using the same basic DARK commitment scheme by $C := G^{\hat{g}_1}$, where $\hat{g}_1 := g_1(q, q^2, \ldots, q^{2^{\mu-1}})$.

The complete description is given in Algorithm 2. Similarly to DARK, our polynomial commitment scheme executes arguments of knowledge on the polynomial $g_1(X_1, \ldots, X_\mu) \in \mathbb{Z}[\mu]$ recursively (Line 3–9 in PC.Open). Note that $(\mu - i + 1)$-variate multilinear polynomial $g_i \in \mathbb{Z}[\mu - i + 1]$ splits to two parts, one for terms without the variable $X_{\mu-i}$ as a factor and the other with it, hence, one can writes $g_i = g_{i,L}(X_1, \ldots, X_{\mu-i}) + X_{\mu-i+1} \cdot g_{i,R}(X_1, \ldots, X_{\mu-i})$ (Line 4 in PC.Open). At ith iteration for $i = 1, \ldots, \mu$, a $(\mu - i + 1)$-variate multilinear polynomial g_i is reduced to $(\mu - i)$-variate multilinear polynomial $g_{i+1} \in \mathbb{Z}[\mu - i]$ (Line 8 in PC.Open), hence, μ recursive calls are required.

What crucially differentiates our scheme from DARK is that the proof of our polynomial commitment scheme at each iteration includes a single group element D_i in PC.Open, whereas DARK requires additional group element(s). This benefit comes from the employment of PoKRep (Algorithm 1) on the integer encoding of a vector of multilinear polynomials $(g_1, g_{1,R}, g_{2,R}, \ldots, g_{\mu,R})$ as follows: 1) $\mathcal{P}$ is asked to send entire commitments $\vec{D}$ to updated polynomials $g_{i,R}$'s across iterations with respect to distinct commitment keys $\vec{R}$ (Line 5 in PC.Open), 2) $\mathcal{V}$ next sends a random prime ℓ (Line 12 in PC.Open), and 3) $\mathcal{P}$ then generates a single proof using PoKRep.Open in the product form $C \cdot \prod_{i=1}^\mu D_i$ with the corresponding commitment keys $(G, \vec{R})$ (Line 13 in PC.Open). The evaluation $y = g(z_1, \ldots, z_\mu)$ is analogously transformed and $y_{i,R}$'s are computed by $\mathcal{P}$ and sent to $\mathcal{V}$ as a part of evaluation proof.

The verification of the proof also works in a different way with DARK. $\|g_{i+1}\|_\infty$ grows by a factor of p over $\|g_i\|_\infty$ since $g_{i+1} = g_{i,L} + \alpha_i g_{i,R}$ for $\alpha_i \in [0, p-1]$. Thus, the last polynomial $g_{\mu+1}$ should lie in the range $[0, (p-1)p^\mu]$, which is verified first (Line 2 in PC.Ver). $\mathcal{V}$ checks the knowledge of polynomials $(g_1, g_{1,R}, g_{2,R}, \ldots, g_{\mu,R})$ from PoKRep.Ver (Line 3 in PC.Ver). $\mathcal{V}$ proceeds to reconstruct $(\hat{g}_1, \hat{g}_2, \hat{g}_3, \ldots, \hat{g}_\mu, g_{\mu+1})$ modulo ℓ (Line 4–11 in PC.Ver) and checks if the reconstructed $g_{\mu+1}$) equals to the received $g_{\mu+1}$ modulo ℓ (Line 12 in PC.Ver). The evaluation is analogously reconstructed and checked modulo p (Line 13 in PC.Ver).

3.4 Security Analysis

We show the security of our polynomial commitment scheme according to Definition 4. Since our PC.Commit in Algorithm 2 is identical to that of DARK [13], the binding property immediately holds, thus, we omit the proof of Theorem 1.

Theorem 1 (Binding [13, Lemma 3]). *PC.Commit in Algorithm 2 is binding for μ-variate multilinear polynomials in $\mathbb{Z}(b)[\mu]$ for $b < \frac{q}{2}$ if the strong RSA assumption holds.*

Theorem 2 (Completeness). *The proposed polynomial commitment scheme of Algorithm 2 is complete for μ-variate multilinear polynomials in $\mathbb{Z}(p-1)[\mu]$ if $q > 2b$.*

The proof of Theorem 2 is relegated to Appendix. The encoding parameter q can be chosen large enough so that $q > 2b$ for the completeness. Witness-extended emulation, however, requires q to be much larger than $2b$ due to a knowledge extractor algorithm. In the case of DARK, an extracting process should handle rational polynomials with bounded numerators and denominators. The issue involves *Multilinear Composite Schwartz-Zippel Lemma* [15]. This leads to increasing the size of q by approximately $\lambda \log \mu$ bits for DARK. Our polynomial commitment scheme, however, avoids the issue of handling rational polynomials since ours directly exploits a knowledge extractor of PoKRep. Thus, the size of q is significantly smaller than that of DARK, which decreases the computation overhead of $\mathcal{P}$. The Theorem 3 states that Algorithm 2 has witness-extended emulation. The proof is relegated to Appendix.

Theorem 3 (Witness-extended emulation). *The proposed polynomial commitment scheme of Algorithm 2 for μ-variate polynomials in $\mathbb{Z}(b)[\mu]$ with λ-bit challenge and $\log q \geq (2\mu + 1)\lambda + 1$ has witness extended emulation if the strong RSA assumption holds.*

4 Performance Evaluation

We evaluate our polynomial commitment scheme. For convenience, we implement our polynomial commitment scheme and DARK over univariate polynomials of degree d for performance analysis. By the 1-1 correspondence in Sect. 3.1, a μ-variate multilinear polynomial $f(X_1, \ldots, X_\mu)$ are identified as a univariate polynomial $f(X)$ of degree $d = 2^\mu - 1$ and $\rho_q(f) = f(q)$.

4.1 Optimization

Encoding Parameter q. Since q is large, computing $\rho_q = f(q)$ is somewhat burdensome. q is a parameterized value in the maximum degree of polynomials d and the field size p of λ bits. q is chosen so that $\mathbb{Z}(p-1)[X]$ and the range $\left(-\frac{q^{d+1}}{2}, \frac{q^{d+1}}{2}\right)$ is bijective under the map $\rho_q(f(X)) = f(q)$. In fact, we can choose a lager value for q since we only require an injective ρ_q. Thus, if we choose q as a power of 2 as long as ρ is injective, we can replace a part of necessary multiplications for computing $f(q)$ with bit-shift operations, which saves computation cost. Thus we set $\log q := 2\mu(\lambda + 1) + 1$ in ours. In the case of DARK, $\log q := \lambda(2\mu + \log \mu + 6) + 32\mu^2 + 5$.

Pre-computation. In the proposed polynomial commitment scheme, the computation bottleneck for a prover is to compute $G^{f(q)}$ for a group element $G \in \mathbb{G}$ and a polynomial $f(X)$. As in DARK, a group exponentiation by $f(q)$ can be efficiently performed using pre-computation. Let $d := \deg f$ and $\mu := \lceil \log (d+1) \rceil$.

Table 3. Size of public parameter, commitment, and proof for RSA-2048 [bytes]

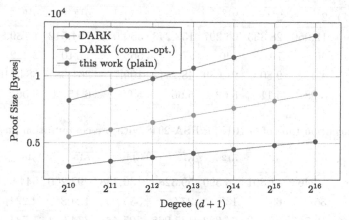

Degree $(d+1)$		2^{10}	2^{11}	2^{12}	2^{13}	2^{14}	2^{15}	2^{16}
$|pp|$	**DARK**	528	528	528	528	528	528	528
	This work	3,088	3,344	3,600	3,856	4,112	4,368	4,624
$|C|$	**DARK**	256	256	256	256	256	256	256
	This work							
$|\pi|$	**DARK**	8,176	8,996	9,808	10,624	11,440	12,256	13,072
	DARK (opt.)	5,456	6,000	6,544	7,088	7,632	8,176	8,720
	This work	3,238	3,632	3,936	4,240	4,544	4,848	5,152

While DARK requires a single group element for the commitment key, our polynomial commitment scheme has $\mu + 1$ group elements as the commitment key. More precisely, for the commitment key G and $\vec{R} = \{R_1, \ldots, R_\mu\}$, one precomputes $\{G^q, \ldots, G^{q^d}\}$ and $\{R_i^q, \ldots, R_i^{q^{\lceil (d+1)/2 \rceil - 1}}\}$ for $i = 1, \ldots, \mu$. Note that for the case of R_i's, we compute powers up to $\lceil \frac{d+1}{2} \rceil - 1$ because the highest degree of reduced polynomials has the half degree of an input polynomial.

4.2 Proof Size

We evaluate and compare the proof sizes of ours and DARK. For the concrete evaluation, we estimate the sizes of public parameters pp, commitment C, and proof π for an RSA-2048 group that offers 112-bit security. We take a 128-bit prime p for $\mathbb{F} = \mathbb{Z}_p$. For pp, we only include an RSA modulus N, common reference strings (CRS), and p for $\mathbb{F}$. Note that one can just store the size of q instead of q as discussed previously.

We present the sizes of pp, C, and π across various degrees ($2^{10} \leq d+1 \leq 2^{16}$) of a polynomial in Table 3. As shown in the table, the size of pp in our construction is about $\frac{2+\log \deg f(X)}{2} = \frac{\mu+2}{2}$ times lager than that of DARK, which

Table 4. Execution time of ours for RSA-2048 with pre-computation [ms]

Degree $(d+1)$	2^{10}	2^{11}	2^{12}	2^{13}	2^{14}	2^{15}	2^{16}
Pre-Compute	12,050	28,335	66,297	153,243	350,046	794,512	1,789,869
Commit	36	70	140	278	555	1,110	2,222
Prove	4,454	9,803	21,689	48,261	109,778	261,981	684,516
Verify	5.08	5.11	5.62	5.66	5.99	6.15	6.56

Table 5. Execution time of DARK for RSA-2048 with pre-computation [ms]

Degree $(d+1)$	2^{10}	2^{11}	2^{12}	2^{13}	2^{14}	2^{15}	2^{16}
Pre-Compute	5,246	11,801	26,590	59,328	130,738	292,260	644,854
Commit	35	69	138	277	555	1,108	2,224
Prove	12,793	28,749	64,623	145,965	325,481	774,651	1,784,460
Verify	15	19	23	34	55	101	209

Table 6. Size of encoding parameter $(\log q)$ [bits]

Degree $(d+1)$	2^{10}	2^{11}	2^{12}	2^{13}	2^{14}	2^{15}	2^{16}
This work	2,689	2,945	3,201	3,457	3,713	3,969	4,225
DARK	7,045	7,973	8,965	10,021	11,141	12,325	13,573

is approximate ratio between the sizes of pp of two schemes. When ignoring the description of the underlying group, the ratio becomes approximately μ (see Table 1). For the size of the commitment, two schemes have exactly the same size, which is only a single group element.

For the proof size, our construction shows promising results. The main factor is the required number of group elements, where μ, 2μ, and 3μ for our construction, DARK, and its communication-efficient version, respectively. Table 3 shows that the proof size of ours is quite compact, that is, it is only about one-third and one-half of those of DARK and its optimized version, respectively. The figure above Table 3 plots the proof size of each scheme in the table. In the figure, the slope of each line corresponds to the required number of group elements in the proof over log-scale of degrees.

4.3   Experiment Results

We implemented the proposed polynomial commitment scheme and DARK to assess and compare the proof generation and verification time. All experiments are performed on Apple M1 Pro CPU with 32 GB RAM and single-thread. The program language is C using the Flint2 library [26].

We use an RSA-2048 group as a base group and set $\mathbb{F} := \mathbb{Z}_p$ for a 128-bit prime p. We take $\log q$ as $2\mu(\lambda+1)+1$ for ours and $\lambda(2\mu+\log\mu+6)+32\mu^2+5$ for DARK. For convenience, we choose the prover's input polynomial whose coefficients are 32-bit integers. We measure the execution time of pre-computation, proof generation with pre-computation, proof verification over degrees 2^{10}–2^{16} in this setting.

Table 4 and Table 5 present execution time of our construction and DARK, respectively. Recall that our construction has the commitment key G and $\vec{R} = \{R_1, \ldots, R_\mu\}$. Our scheme pre-computes $\{G^q, \ldots, G^{q^d}\}$ and $\{R_i^q, \ldots, R_i^{q^{\lceil\frac{d+1}{2}\rceil-1}}\}$ for $i = 1, \ldots, \mu$. In DARK, pre-computation consists of only $\{G^q, \ldots, G^{q^d}\}$. Thus, the storage overhead for pre-computation in our case is about $\mu/2$ larger than that in DARK (Table 1). The computation cost for pre-computation depends on not only the number of commitment keys but also the size of q. As presented in Table 6, the size of q is about 3 times smaller than that of DARK when $2^{10} \le d + 1 \le 2^{16}$. Thus, the total computation cost for pre-computation in ours is about $\mu/6$ times larger than that in DARK. However, we note that the extended commitment key from pre-computation is universal CRS and requires only one-time generation at off line.

For proof generation with pre-computation, the execution time of ours is about 3 times smaller than that of DARK. This result comes from the ratio between q sizes in two schemes. Namely, proof generations for PoKRep and PoE are time-consuming parts (over 90%) in ours and DARK, respectively. Their time complexities depends on the size of input exponents, which grows in $d \log q$.

In the case of verification, the required number of group exponentiations of ours is about one third of that of DARK ($\mu+2$ and 3μ, respectively). The verifier of PoE, however, needs to compute the reminder r of an input integer q^d divided by a prime ℓ where d is the degree of a polynomial and ℓ is previously chosen by the verifier. Thus, the time to compute r exponentially grows in d and becomes time-consuming part for the DARK verification. We empirically observe this from Table 4 and Table 5, where the verification time of DARK exponentially increases over $d > 2^{13}$.

5   Related Work

Kate et al. first constructed an efficient and succinct polynomial commitment scheme (KZG) for univariate polynomials [27]. It employees bilinear pairings and requires a trusted setup. The KZG has been extended to the multivariate version in [32,38] with a trusted setup. There are also numerous works to propose transparent polynomial commitment schemes. Bootle et al. [8] constructed a transparent polynomial commitment scheme in the discrete log setting with $O(\sqrt{d})$ proof size where d is a degree of a polynomial. Wahby et al. proposed a transparent polynomial commitment scheme [35] for multilinear polynomials under the discrete log assumption with $O(\sqrt{d})$ proof size. Ben-Sasson et al. [5] introduced the Fast Reed Solomon IOP of Proximity (FRI) which implicitly yields a transparent polynomial commitment scheme. A method for obtaining polynomial commitment schemes from FRI was presented in [28,37] whose proof size is $O(\log^2 d)$. DARK [13] and Dory [29] archived $O(\log d)$ proof size with linear proof generation cost and logarithmic verification cost. Block et al. [6] found the security flaw in the originally proposed DARK and proposed a modification of DARK using the theory of integer lattices. Recently, Bünz et al. [16] also address the security flaw by extending integer polynomials to rational polynomials in the knowledge extraction together with the notion of almost-special-soundness.

Recent SNARKs such as Marlin [17], Plonk [23], and Sonic [31] take a framework to convert an NP-hard problem of satisfiability of an arithmetic circuit into evaluations of low-degree polynomials by employing polynomial commitment schemes. This framework, called polynomial IOPs, is formalized by Chiesa et al. [17] and Bünz et al. [13]. Bünz et al. also have obtained Supersonic by employing their polynomial commitment scheme (DARK) to Sonic.

Groups of unknown order are used for the construction of valuable cryptographic primitives such as delay functions [36], accumulators [7], and polynomial commitment schemes [13]. There are two candidates of groups of unknown order for most cryptographic constructions: RSA groups [33] and ideal class groups of imaginary quadratic fields (class groups) [12]. An RSA group is a multiplicative group $\mathbb{Z}_N^*$, where N is a product of two large primes. Since computing $|Z_N^*|$ is as hard as factoring N, the use of an RSA group requires one-time trusted setup for the generation of an RSA modulus N. In RSA groups, the Adaptive Root Assumption does not hold because the order of -1 is trivially 2. Thus, we instead work on the set of quadratic residues QR_N. A class group $Cl(\Delta)$ is determined by the discriminant Δ, where $\Delta = 1 \pmod 4$ and $-\Delta$ is prime. [11,25] suggested a class group with 1665-bit negative fundamental discriminant for 128-bit security. [19] reported that a 1665-bit discriminant only provides 55-bit security, hence, a 6656-bit discriminant is desirable. In class groups, one can efficiently compute square roots of any given group elements [9]. This forces us to use the 2-Strong RSA Assumption for class groups.

6   Conclusion

This paper introduces a new efficient transparent polynomial commitment scheme over groups of unknown order. For a μ-variate multilinear polynomial (or a univariate polynomial of degree $2^\mu - 1$ equivalently), the proposed polynomial commitment scheme meets logarithmic verification cost and requires only $\mu + 1$ group elements in the proof. This is the smallest proof size when compared to existing transparent polynomial commitment schemes with logarithmic verifier, such as DORY (3μ) and DARK (2μ). We have implemented the proposed scheme and rigorously estimated the proof size over an RSA-2048 group, demonstrating its efficiency. The extension to batch processing for multiple polynomials or points is left as future work.

Acknowledgement. This work was supported by Institute of Information & communications Technology Planning & Evaluation (IITP) grant funded by the Korea government (MSIT) (No. 2021-0-00727, A study on cryptographic primitives for SNARK,

50%; No. 2021-0-00518, Blockchain Privacy preserving techniques based on data encryption, 50%). J. Kim and H. Oh are co-corresponding authors.

Appendix

Proof of Theorem 2

Proof. We show that an honest commiter passes all check in PC.Ver of Algorithm 2. We first show that $g_{\mu+1} = s_{\mu+1} \pmod{\ell}$. By construction, $s_1 = r = \hat{g}_1 \pmod{\ell}$ and $s_{i,R} = \hat{g}_{i,R} \pmod{\ell}$ for $i = 1, ..., \mu$. We then have that $s_{i,L} = s_i - q^{2^{\mu-i}} s_{i,R} \pmod{\ell} = \hat{g}_i - q^{2^{\mu-i}} \hat{g}_{i,R} \pmod{\ell} = \hat{g}_{i,L} \pmod{\ell}$ and $s_{i+1} = s_{i,L} + \alpha_i s_{i,R} \pmod{\ell} = \hat{g}_{i,L} + \alpha_i \hat{g}_{i,R} \pmod{\ell} = \hat{g}_{i+1} \pmod{\ell}$ for $i = 1, ..., \mu$. This proves $g_{\mu+1} = s_{\mu+1} \pmod{\ell}$. With similar argument, it holds that $g_{\mu+1} = y_{\mu+1} \pmod{p}$.

Next we show that $|g_{\mu+1}| \leq b = (p-1)p^\mu$. Note that $f \in \mathbb{Z}(p-1)[\mu]$. Let $b_1 = p - 1$. Suppose, for each i, there exists a bound b_i such that $\|g_i\|_\infty \leq b_i$. Since $\alpha_i \in [0, p-1]$, we have $\|g_{i+1}\|_\infty = \|g_{i,L} + \alpha_i g_{i,R}\|_\infty \leq b_i p = (p-1)p^i$ for $i = 1, ..., \mu$. Finally, PoKRep.Ver returns 1 because

$$C \cdot \prod_{i=1}^{\mu} D_i = G^{\hat{f}} \cdot \prod_{i=1}^{\mu} R_i^{\hat{g}_{i,R}} = G^{\left\lfloor \frac{\hat{f}}{\ell} \right\rfloor \ell + \hat{f} \bmod \ell} \cdot \prod_{i=1}^{\mu} R_i^{\left\lfloor \frac{\hat{g}_{i,R}}{\ell} \right\rfloor \ell + \hat{g}_{i,R} \bmod \ell} = Q^\ell \cdot G^r \cdot \prod_{i=1}^{\mu} R_i^{s_{i,R}}.$$

Sketch of Proof for Theorem 3

Lemma 2 ([16, Lemma 6]). *For any μ-variate multilinear polynomial f over $\mathbb{Z}$ and $p \geq 2$, $\Pr_{\vec{\alpha} \xleftarrow{\$} [0,p-1]^\mu}[|f(\vec{\alpha})| \leq \frac{1}{p^\mu} \cdot \|f\|_\infty] \leq \frac{3\mu}{p}$.*

Proof Sketch. We prove that the proposed polynomial commitment scheme is knowledge sound, thus, has witness-extended emulation [30]. We first define the series of bounds $B_{\mu+1} \leq \cdots \leq B_1$ by $B_i := (p-1)p^{2\mu-i+1}$ for $i = \mu+1, ..., 1$. Note that $B_{\mu+1}$ is equal to the bound parameter b in the proposed polynomial commitment scheme. We describe the extractor $\mathcal{E}_{PC}$. The extractor $\mathcal{E}_{PC}$ employs a poly-time knowledge extractor $\mathcal{E}_{PoKRep}$ of the protocol PoKRep. The description of $\mathcal{E}_{PoKRep}$ is given in [7, proof of Theorem 7]. $\mathcal{E}_{PoKRep}$ receives a polynomial in λ (denoted as $\mathsf{poly}(\lambda)$) number of accepting PoKRep–transcripts and extracts an input integer vector. Let $\mathsf{tr}_{PC} = \{C, (D_i, y_{i,R}, \alpha_i)_{i=1,...,\mu}, g_{\mu+1}, Q, (\ell, (r, \vec{s}))\}$ be an accepting transcript that $\mathcal{P}$ and $\mathcal{V}$ generate by executing PC.Commit, PC.Open, and PC.Ver. Algorithm $\mathcal{E}_{PC}$ works as follows:

1. on input $U := C \prod_{i=1}^{\mu} D_i$, call PoKRep $\mathsf{poly}(\lambda)$ times, sampling fresh randomness ℓ for $\mathcal{V}$, and obtain $\mathsf{poly}(\lambda)$ number of accepting transcripts $T := \{(\ell_i, Q_i, (r_i, \vec{s}_i))\}_{i=1,...,\mathsf{poly}(\lambda)}$ of PoKRep.
2. run $\mathcal{E}_{PoKRep}$ on input T and obtain a witness integer vector $(\hat{g}_1'', \hat{g}_{i,R}', \ldots, \hat{g}_{\mu,R}')$ such that $U = G^{\hat{g}_1'} \prod_{i=1}^{\mu} R_i^{\hat{g}_{i,R}'}$.

3. set $\hat{g}'_{\mu+1} \leftarrow g_{\mu+1}$ and compute $\hat{g}'_i \leftarrow (\hat{g}'_{i+1} - \alpha_i \cdot \hat{g}'_{i,R}) + q^{2^{\mu-i}} \hat{g}'_{i,R}$ from $i = \mu$ to 1. If $\|g''_1(X_1, \ldots, X_\mu)\| := \rho_q^{-1}(\hat{g}''_1)\|_\infty > B_1$ or $\|g'_i(X_1, \ldots, X_{\mu-i+1})\|_\infty > B_i$ for some $i \in [1, \mu]$, then return to Step 1.
4. if $\hat{g}'_1 = \hat{g}''_1$ and $g'_1(\vec{z}) = y \pmod{p}$, output g'_1 and stop.
5. return to Step 1.

We argue that $\mathcal{E}_{\mathsf{PC}}$ succeeds with overwhelming probability in a $\mathsf{poly}(\lambda)$ number of rounds. We first claim that Step 3 of $\mathcal{E}_{\mathsf{PC}}$ successfully outputs integers $\hat{g}''_1$ and $\hat{g}'_i$'s for $i = 1, \ldots, \mu$ such that $\|\rho_q^{-1}(\hat{g}''_1)\|_\infty \leq B_1$ and $\|\rho_q^{-1}(\hat{g}'_i)\|_\infty \leq B_i$ with overwhelming probability. Suppose we have $\hat{g}'_i$ such that $\|\rho_q^{-1}(\hat{g}'_i)\|_\infty > B_i$ from an accepting transcript. Then, by Lemma 2, we have $\Pr[|g'_i(\alpha_\mu, \ldots, \alpha_i)| \leq B_{\mu+1}] = \Pr[|g'_i(\alpha_\mu, \ldots, \alpha_i)| \leq B_i/p^{\mu-i+1}] \leq \Pr[|g'_i(\alpha_\mu, \ldots, \alpha_i)| \leq \|g'_i\|_\infty/p^{\mu-i+1}] \leq \frac{3(\mu-i+1)}{p} \leq \frac{3\mu}{p}$, where $(\alpha_\mu, \ldots, \alpha_i) \overset{\$}{\leftarrow} [0, p-1]^{\mu-i+1}$. Thus, the probability that Step 3 fails to output integers is less than or equal to $\frac{3\mu^2}{p} \approx \frac{3\mu^2}{2^\lambda}$, which is negligible.

We now claim that Step 4 of $\mathcal{E}_{\mathsf{PC}}$ successfully outputs a witness polynomial. We argue that $\hat{g}'_1 = \hat{g}''_1$ holds with overwhelming probability. From Step 3, we have $\hat{g}'_1 = \hat{g}'_{\mu+1} + \sum_{i=1}^{\mu}(q^{2^{\mu-i}} - \alpha_i)\hat{g}'_{i,R}$. Then, by the $\mathsf{PC.Ver}$, it holds that $\hat{g}'_1 = s_{\mu+1} + \sum_{i=1}^{\mu}(q^{2^{\mu-i}} - \alpha_i)\hat{s}_{i,R} = r = \hat{g}''_1 \pmod{\ell}$. Because the verifier sends a randomly selected λ-bit prime ℓ to the prover after the verifier receives all commitments made by the prover, the probability that $\hat{g}'_1 \neq \hat{g}''_1$ is negligible. Finally, we show that $g'_1(\vec{z}) = y$. Note that $g_{\mu+1} = y + \sum_{i=1}^{\mu}(\alpha_i - z_{\mu+1-i})y_{i,R} \pmod{p}$ from $\mathsf{PC.Ver}$. We also have that $g_{\mu+1} = g'_1(z_1, \ldots, z_\mu) + \sum_{i=1}^{\mu}(\alpha_i - z_{\mu+1-i})g'_{i,R}(z_1, \ldots, z_{\mu-i}) \pmod{p}$ from $\mathcal{E}_{\mathsf{PC}}$. Thus, $y + \sum_{i=1}^{\mu}(\alpha_i - z_{\mu+1-i})y_{i,R} = g'_1(z_1, \ldots, z_\mu) + \sum_{i=1}^{\mu}(\alpha_i - z_{\mu+1-i})g'_{i,R}(z_1, \ldots, z_{\mu-i})$ $\pmod{p}$ for $\vec{z} = (z_1, \ldots, z_{\mu-i})$ and randomly selected $(\alpha_1, \ldots, \alpha_\mu)$ in $\mathsf{PC.Open}$. This means that $g'_1(\vec{z}) = y \pmod{p}$, $g'_{i,R} = y_{i,r} \pmod{p}$ for $i = 1, \ldots, \mu$ with overwhelming probability.

References

1. Ames, S., Hazay, C., Ishai, Y., Venkitasubramaniam, M.: Ligero: lightweight sublinear arguments without a trusted setup. In: ACM CCS 2017, pp. 2087–2104. ACM (2017)
2. Barić, N., Pfitzmann, B.: Collision-free accumulators and fail-stop signature schemes without trees. In: Fumy, W. (ed.) EUROCRYPT 1997. LNCS, vol. 1233, pp. 480–494. Springer, Heidelberg (1997). https://doi.org/10.1007/3-540-69053-0_33
3. Ben-Sasson, E., et al.: Zerocash: decentralized anonymous payments from bitcoin. In: IEEE Symposium on Security and Privacy 2014, pp. 459–474. IEEE (2014)
4. Ben-Sasson, E., Chiesa, A., Riabzev, M., Spooner, N., Virza, M., Ward, N.P.: Aurora: transparent succinct arguments for R1CS. In: Ishai, Y., Rijmen, V. (eds.) EUROCRYPT 2019. LNCS, vol. 11476, pp. 103–128. Springer, Cham (2019). https://doi.org/10.1007/978-3-030-17653-2_4

5. Ben-Sasson, E., Goldberg, L., Kopparty, S., Saraf, S.: DEEP-FRI: sampling outside the box improves soundness. In: ITCS 2020, LIPIcs, pp. 5:1–5:32. Schloss Dagstuhl - Leibniz-Zentrum für Informatik (2020)
6. Block, A.R., Holmgren, J., Rosen, A., Rothblum, R.D., Soni, P.: Time- and space-efficient arguments from groups of unknown order. In: Malkin, T., Peikert, C. (eds.) CRYPTO 2021. LNCS, vol. 12828, pp. 123–152. Springer, Cham (2021). https://doi.org/10.1007/978-3-030-84259-8_5
7. Boneh, D., Bünz, B., Fisch, B.: Batching techniques for accumulators with applications to IOP's and stateless blockchains. In: Boldyreva, A., Micciancio, D. (eds.) CRYPTO 2019. LNCS, vol. 11692, pp. 561–586. Springer, Cham (2019). https://doi.org/10.1007/978-3-030-26948-7_20
8. Bootle, J., Cerulli, A., Chaidos, P., Groth, J., Petit, C.: Efficient zero-knowledge arguments for arithmetic circuits in the discrete log setting. In: Fischlin, M., Coron, J.-S. (eds.) EUROCRYPT 2016. LNCS, vol. 9666, pp. 327–357. Springer, Heidelberg (2016). https://doi.org/10.1007/978-3-662-49896-5_12
9. Bosma, W., Stevenhagen, P.: On the computation of quadratic 2-class groups. J. de Théorie des Nombres de Bordeaux **8**(2), 283–313 (1996)
10. Bowe, S.: BLS12-381: new zk-SNARK elliptic curve construction. https://electriccoin.co/blog/new-snark-curve/
11. Buchmann, J., Hamdy, S.: A survey on IQ cryptography. In: Public Key Cryptography and Computational Number Theory, pp. 1–15 (2001)
12. Buchmann, J., Williams, H.C.: A key-exchange system based on imaginary quadratic fields. J. Cryptol. **1**(2), 107–118 (1988)
13. Bünz, B., Fisch, B., Szepieniec, A.: Transparent SNARKs from DARK compilers. In: Canteaut, A., Ishai, Y. (eds.) EUROCRYPT 2020. LNCS, vol. 12105, pp. 677–706. Springer, Cham (2020). https://doi.org/10.1007/978-3-030-45721-1_24
14. Bünz, B., Maller, M., Mishra, P., Tyagi, N., Vesely, P.: Proofs for inner pairing products and applications. In: Tibouchi, M., Wang, H. (eds.) ASIACRYPT 2021. LNCS, vol. 13092, pp. 65–97. Springer, Cham (2021). https://doi.org/10.1007/978-3-030-92078-4_3
15. Bünz, B., Fisch, B.: Schwartz-Zippel for multilinear polynomials mod N. Cryptology ePrint Archive, Paper 2022/458 (2022). https://eprint.iacr.org/2022/458
16. Bünz, B., Fisch, B., Szepieniec, A.: Transparent snarks from dark compilers. Cryptology ePrint Archive, Paper 2019/1229 (2019). https://eprint.iacr.org/2019/1229
17. Chiesa, A., Hu, Y., Maller, M., Mishra, P., Vesely, N., Ward, N.: Marlin: preprocessing zkSNARKs with universal and updatable SRS. In: Canteaut, A., Ishai, Y. (eds.) EUROCRYPT 2020. LNCS, vol. 12105, pp. 738–768. Springer, Cham (2020). https://doi.org/10.1007/978-3-030-45721-1_26
18. Damgård, I., Koprowski, M.: Generic lower bounds for root extraction and signature schemes in general groups. In: Knudsen, L.R. (ed.) EUROCRYPT 2002. LNCS, vol. 2332, pp. 256–271. Springer, Heidelberg (2002). https://doi.org/10.1007/3-540-46035-7_17
19. Dobson, S., Galbraith, S.D.: Trustless groups of unknown order with hyperelliptic curves. IACR Cryptology ePrint Archive (2020)
20. Eberhardt, J., Tai, S.: ZoKrates - scalable privacy-preserving off-chain computations. In: 2018 IEEE International Conference on Blockchain, pp. 1084–1091. IEEE (2018)
21. ethereum.org. Zero-knowledge rollups. https://ethereum.org/en/developers/docs/scaling/zk-rollups/

22. Fiat, A., Shamir, A.: How to prove yourself: practical solutions to identification and signature problems. In: Odlyzko, A.M. (ed.) CRYPTO 1986. LNCS, vol. 263, pp. 186–194. Springer, Heidelberg (1987). https://doi.org/10.1007/3-540-47721-7_12

23. Gabizon, A., Williamson, Z.J., Ciobotaru, O.: PLONK: permutations over lagrange-bases for oecumenical noninteractive arguments of knowledge. Technical report, Cryptology ePrint Archive, Report 2019/953 (2019)

24. Groth, J., Ishai, Y.: Sub-linear zero-knowledge argument for correctness of a shuffle. In: Smart, N. (ed.) EUROCRYPT 2008. LNCS, vol. 4965, pp. 379–396. Springer, Heidelberg (2008). https://doi.org/10.1007/978-3-540-78967-3_22

25. Hamdy, S., Möller, B.: Security of cryptosystems based on class groups of imaginary quadratic orders. In: Okamoto, T. (ed.) ASIACRYPT 2000. LNCS, vol. 1976, pp. 234–247. Springer, Heidelberg (2000). https://doi.org/10.1007/3-540-44448-3_18

26. Hart, W., Johansson, F., Pancratz, S.: FLINT: fast library for number theory (2013)

27. Kate, A., Zaverucha, G.M., Goldberg, I.: Constant-size commitments to polynomials and their applications. In: Abe, M. (ed.) ASIACRYPT 2010. LNCS, vol. 6477, pp. 177–194. Springer, Heidelberg (2010). https://doi.org/10.1007/978-3-642-17373-8_11

28. Kattis, A., Panarin, K., Vlasov, A.: RedShift: transparent snarks from list polynomial commitment IOPs. IACR Cryptology ePrint Archive (2019)

29. Lee, J.: Dory: efficient, transparent arguments for generalised inner products and polynomial commitments. In: Nissim, K., Waters, B. (eds.) TCC 2021. LNCS, vol. 13043, pp. 1–34. Springer, Cham (2021). https://doi.org/10.1007/978-3-030-90453-1_1

30. Lindell, Y.: Parallel coin-tossing and constant-round secure two-party computation. J. Cryptol. **16**(3), 143–184 (2003)

31. Maller, M., Bowe, S., Kohlweiss, M., Meiklejohn, S.: Sonic: zero-knowledge snarks from linear-size universal and updatable structured reference strings. In: ACM CCS 2019, pp. 2111–2128. ACM (2019)

32. Papamanthou, C., Shi, E., Tamassia, R.: Signatures of correct computation. In: Sahai, A. (ed.) TCC 2013. LNCS, vol. 7785, pp. 222–242. Springer, Heidelberg (2013). https://doi.org/10.1007/978-3-642-36594-2_13

33. Rivest, R.L., Shamir, A., Wagner, D.A.: Time-lock puzzles and timed-release crypto. Technical report, Massachusetts Institute of Technology (1996)

34. Setty, S.: Spartan: efficient and general-purpose zkSNARKs without trusted setup. In: Micciancio, D., Ristenpart, T. (eds.) CRYPTO 2020. LNCS, vol. 12172, pp. 704–737. Springer, Cham (2020). https://doi.org/10.1007/978-3-030-56877-1_25

35. Wahby, R.S., Tzialla, I., Shelat, A., Thaler, J., Walfish, M.: Doubly-efficient ZKSNARKs without trusted setup. In: IEEE Symposium on Security and Privacy 2018, pp. 926–943. IEEE (2018)

36. Wesolowski, B.: Efficient verifiable delay functions. In: Ishai, Y., Rijmen, V. (eds.) EUROCRYPT 2019. LNCS, vol. 11478, pp. 379–407. Springer, Cham (2019). https://doi.org/10.1007/978-3-030-17659-4_13

37. Zhang, J., Xie, T., Zhang, Y., Song, D.: Transparent polynomial delegation and its applications to zero knowledge proof. In: IEEE Symposium on Security and Privacy 2020, pp. 859–876. IEEE (2020)

38. Zhang, Y., Genkin, D., Katz, J., Papadopoulos, D., Papamanthou, C.: vSQL: verifying arbitrary SQL queries over dynamic outsourced databases. In: IEEE Symposium on Security and Privacy 2017, pp. 863–880. IEEE (2017)

n-MVTL Attack: Optimal Transaction Reordering Attack on DeFi

Jianhuan Wang[1]($\boxtimes$), Jichen Li[1,2], Zecheng Li[1], Xiaotie Deng[2], and Bin Xiao[1]

[1] Department of Computing, The Hong Kong Polytechnic University,
Hong Kong, Hong Kong
{21122251r,jichen.li,zecheng.li,csbxiao}@connect.polyu.hk
[2] School of Computer Science, Peking University, Beijing, China
xiaotie@pku.edu.cn

Abstract. Decentralized finance (DeFi) is a global and open financial system built on the blockchain technology, typically using Ethereum smart contracts. Decentralized exchanges (DEXs) are very important sectors in the DeFi ecosystem, with billions of USD trading volume daily. Unfortunately, the transparency of pending pools can be exploited by attackers and DEXs are vulnerable to *transaction reordering attacks*, allowing attackers to gain miner extracted value (MEV). Previous transaction reordering attacks aim at exploiting the vulnerability of a single victim transaction, such as sandwich attack and dagwood sandwich attack.

In this paper, we propose a novel transaction reordering attack named n-multiple-victim-transaction-layer (n-MVTL) attack to exploit the overall vulnerability among multiple victim transactions. Such advanced design can significantly expand the victim transaction search space and bring more profits to attackers. Given a set of ordered victim transactions, we propose an optimal algorithm to identify the optimal solution for n-MVTL attacks, which aims to maximize the profit of the attack strategy. This algorithm supports a trade-off between time efficiency and attack profit, making the attack algorithm more practical. Our simulations show that the n-MVTL attack can yield an average extra daily profit of 940 USD from the top 2 most popular liquidity pools in Uniswap V2 from Mar. 2021 to Apr. 2023, compared with the sandwich attack.

Keywords: Decentralized Finance (DeFi) · Miner Extractable Value (MEV) · Decentralized Exchange (DEX) · DeFi Attack · Blockchain

1 Introduction

In recent years, DeFi as a supplement to traditional finance has become an enormous ecosystem with a total locked value of 47 billion USD in May 2023 [5]. Within the DeFi ecosystem, *Automated Market Makers (AMMs)* play a crucial role by providing real-time asset pricing for user transactions in DeFi. AMMs-based exchange platforms (e.g., Uniswap [11] and Pancakeswap [8]) handle swap transactions with a total volume of several billions of USD per day [4].

© The Author(s), under exclusive license to Springer Nature Switzerland AG 2024
G. Tsudik et al. (Eds.): ESORICS 2023, LNCS 14346, pp. 367–386, 2024.
https://doi.org/10.1007/978-3-031-51479-1_19

However, the feature of Ethereum prioritizing transaction ordering based on gas fees rather than time sequence makes AMMs susceptible to *transaction reordering attacks*. These attacks are defined as the manipulation of transaction order within blocks by miners, with the aim of extracting *miner/maximum extracted value (MEV)* [3]. One of the most common transaction reordering attacks is *sandwich attack*, which was formalized and quantitatively analyzed for attack profitability by Zhou *et al.* [15]. As shown in Fig. 1(a), the sandwich attack strategy involves the execution of a malicious front-running transaction and a malicious back-running transaction aimed at a victim transaction. Then, the attacker profits from the discrepancy between the execution prices of the front and back-running transactions. One extension work of the sandwich attacks is the dagwood sandwich attack [1] which targets multiple victim transactions simultaneously by utilizing front-running attacks on each victim transaction separately as shown in Fig. 1(b). The sandwich attack has a single-victim-transaction layer and the dagwood sandwich attack has several single-victim-transaction layers. We refer to these attacks as n-single-victim-transaction-layer (n-SVTL) attacks.

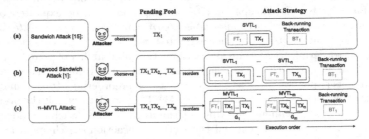

Fig. 1. Visualization of n-SVTL attacks and n-MVTL attack.

Previous studies in the field of defense mechanisms of transaction reordering attacks focus on limiting transaction parameters [7,14–16]. Due to the simple structure of n-SVTL attack, the attack profit gain from each layer is strongly influenced by the trading amount and tolerable price slippage of the victim transaction. DeFi users can prevent n-SVTL efficiently by two defenses (i.e., limited trading volume [14–16] and limited slippage [7,15]). We refer to transactions that utilize these two defenses as *un-sandwichable transactions*. In light of the aforementioned advancements in defense mechanisms against n-SVTL attacks, an important question arises: *Do the existing defenses offer adequate security for transactions of DeFi users? Are there other kinds of transaction reordering attacks that can bypass these defenses?*

To address this question, we propose the utilization of a more flexible structure termed n-MVTL (details provided in Sect. 4). Unlike the approach of employing n front-running transactions to attack n victim transactions in n-SVTL attack, we split the n victim transactions into m ($m \leq n$) different layers, with only one front-running transaction used to attack the victim transactions in each layer, as illustrated in Fig. 1(c). Note that the n-SVTL structure is a typical sub-class of the n-MVTL structure. By adopting the n-MVTL structure instead of the n-SVTL structure, we can explore additional potential attack strategies.

Furthermore, we observe that the transaction reordering attack employing the *n*-MVTL structure, hereafter referred to as *n*-MVTL attack, can detect the overall vulnerability among multiple un-sandwichable transactions, enabling attacks on un-sandwichable transactions. To comprehensively evaluate the severity of the *n*-MVTL attack, we provide a formalized description of this novel attack and quantify its associated risks. To the best of our knowledge, we are the first to explore the feasibility and profitability of transaction reordering attack that exploit the overall risk of multiple transactions. The contributions of our research can be summarized as follows:

- **Novel Transaction Reordering Attack.** We propose the *n*-MVTL attack, a novel transaction reordering attack in Sect. 4, which can compromise the traditional defense mechanisms in DeFi. This attack consists of two components: a transaction selecting algorithm, which aims to identify the largest subset of transactions that can be targeted, and an optimal algorithm to find the best strategy to attack them and maximize the attacker's profit. Compared to the dagwood sandwich attack, the *n*-MVTL attack can exploit multiple swap transactions simultaneously in a general market environment with no assumption about the real price of tokens. Our algorithm also considers an important cost factor, *AMM swap fees*, which is not included in most existing attacks.
- **Optimal Analysis of Attack.** We present an algorithmic analysis of our optimal algorithm, showcasing its ability to find an approximate optimal attack strategy when provided with a set of vulnerable transactions. We also evaluated the profit ratio of our algorithm compared to the maximum profit achievable for attackers and conducted an analysis of the algorithm's time complexity. Details as discussed in Sect. 5.
- **Implementation.** We implement a prototype of our proposed *n*-MVTL attack to discover the time efficiency of our attack algorithms. Experimental results show that our algorithms are efficient and practical for generating attack strategies against constant product market markers (CPMMs) even with a personal computer (e.g., Macbook Pro).
- **Validation of Attacks on Historical Transactions.** In Sect. 6, we validate the *n*-MVTL attack strategies on a simulation system that implements the swap formula of Uniswap V2. We find that *n*-MVTL attack yields an extra profit of 656,972 USD compared to the sandwich attack from block height 12,000,000 to 17,000,000 in Ethereum. We demonstrate that *n*-MVTL attack can spot more attack opportunities than sandwich attacks.

1.1 Paper Organization

The remainder of this paper is organized as: Sect. 2 reviews related literature. We describe how to encode AMM protocols into state transition models in Sect. 3. We propose *n*-MVTL attack in Sect. 4. We conduct a comprehensive analysis of the optimal attack algorithm in Sect. 5. We evaluate our algorithms and validate our attack strategies in Sect. 6. Section 7 concludes our paper.

2   Background and Related Work

2.1   Reordering Transactions

There are three types of reordering transactions that are used to emit transaction reordering attacks: (I) **Front-running transaction (FT)**: If a transaction runs before a victim transaction and its parameters are carefully set by an attacker to prevent the victim transaction from failing to swap the tokens, we classify this transaction as an FT. (II) **Fatal front-running transaction (FFT)**: If a transaction runs before a victim transaction and its parameters are maliciously set by the attacker to cause the failure of the victim transaction's execution, we classify this transaction as an FFT. This type of malicious transaction results in more losses for DeFi users as they must pay gas fees even if their transactions fail to swap the tokens; (III) **Back-running transaction (BT)**: If a transaction runs after a victim transaction, we classify this transaction as a BT.

2.2   Sandwich Attack

The most common transaction reordering attack is the sandwich attack, formalized by Zhou *et al.* [15]. Due to the transparency of DeFi, transaction information in the pending pool can be obtained by attackers. We consider a victim transaction TX_1, whose information is observed by an attacker. Then, the attacker emits a front-running transaction FT_1 and a back-running transaction BT_1 to launch a sandwich attack as shown in Fig. 1(a). These malicious transactions aim to trigger the largest price slippage of TX_1. The gas prices of malicious transactions are carefully set to ensure that the execution order will be: FT_1, TX_1, BT_1. Then, the attacker gains attack profit from the difference of execution prices of FT_1 and BT_1. Zhou *et al.* demonstrated that the sandwich attack yields a total profit of 174.34M USD from block 6,803,256 to 12,965,000 in Ethereum.

To further strengthen the attack capability, Bartoletti *et al.* [1] proposed a multi-layer dagwood sandwich attack which can attack several victim transactions simultaneously. The idea of this attack is to repetitively launch a front-running attack on each transaction, targeting every transaction individually. This approach, however, disregards the overall vulnerability among victim transactions, making it susceptible to resistance from conventional defense mechanisms [7,13,16]. Furthermore, the dagwood sandwich attack relies on two unrealistic assumptions: (I) *Stable price assumption.* The author employs the stable price assumption for facilitating the calculation of attack profit. However, this assumption is hard to guarantee in the real market, attackers may incur losses due to fluctuations in real prices of tokens. (II) *No AMM swap fees.* The authors introduce the assumption that no AMM swap fees are charged by the liquidity pool. This assumption enables the use of a remarkably convenient property (i.e., the liquidity of the liquidity pool is always constant) to determine the maximum loss state for each victim transaction. However, almost all of the DEXs (e.g., Uniswap [11] and Pancakeswap [8]) charge AMM swap fees. In summary, the two assumptions of the dagwood sandwich attack make it difficult to apply it to the real DeFi market.

2.3   Defense Strategies

Many researchers have focused on defense strategies against sandwich attack [7,13,16]. Zhou *et al.* [15] proposed two primary protection possibilities that could be adopted for DeFi users to prevent sandwich attacks: Limit Slippage and Limit Trading Volume.

- *Limit Slippage.* A DeFi user can set her transaction slippage as small as possible to reduce the attack profit from a sandwich attack. To extend this defense method, Heimbach *et al.* [7] introduced the sandwich game to analyze sandwich attacks analytically and provided traders with a simple and extremely effective algorithm for setting the valid slippage tolerance.
- *Limit Trading Volume.* A DeFi user can set her transaction's trading amount below a minimum profitable victim input to resist sandwich attacks. To extend this defense, Züst [16] proposed a strategy that splits a sandwichable transaction into several transactions with limited trading amounts.

3   Model

In this section, we formally describe a state transition model for AMM protocols. Then we describe the profit and strategy space of our *n*-MVTL attack.

3.1   AMM Model

AMM are fundamental protocols that enable the automated trading of tokens for DeFi. Given a pair of tokens, an AMM will create a liquidity pool (LP), which state changes upon the execution of transactions, and it can set prices automatically based on a specific rule. In this paper, we focus on the CPMM [12], wherein the product of tokens in a pair remains constant before and after a transaction is conducted, and it represents a widely adopted subclass of AMMs.

- **Liquidity Pool State.** Given a liquidity pool LP with two types of tokens, τ_x and τ_y, the state $S = (X \in \mathbb{N}^+, Y \in \mathbb{N}^+)$ denotes the state of the LP, where X and Y denote the amount of τ_x and τ_y in this LP, respectively. The total liquidity of the LP can be derived as $K = X \cdot Y$.
- **Transactions.** In this paper, we only focus on *swap* transactions. We use $TX^d : swap(ax \in \mathbb{N}_0^+, ay \in \mathbb{N}_0^+)$ to denote the collection of swap transactions, where $d \in \{x \to y, y \to x\}$ is the swap direction. For example, when $d = x \to y$, then this transaction means that the user wants to swap ax of τ_x for at least ay of τ_y, and vice versa.
- **Constant Product Pricing Rule.** Given a transaction $TX^{x \to y}:swap$ (ax,ay) and the state (X_0, Y_0) of an Pool $\mathcal{LP}$, the execution price p of this transaction can be calculated by Formula 1, where f indicates the AMM swap fee rate set by $\mathcal{LP}$ (e.g., 0.3% in Uniswap [11]). The end (post-execution) state of $\mathcal{LP}$ after executing $TX^{x \to y}$ can be derived as $(X_0 + \Delta x, \ Y_0 - \Delta y)$. When this transaction is successfully executed, the user should pay $\Delta x \cdot f$ of τ_x as a transaction swap fee to $\mathcal{LP}$, which will add some liquidity to $\mathcal{LP}$.

$$\Delta x = ax, \ \Delta y = \lfloor Y_0 - K_0/(X_0 + (1-f) \cdot \Delta x) \rfloor, \ p = \Delta x/\Delta y \qquad (1)$$

In the following attack modeling, we assume that all victim transactions' swap directions are $x \to y$. To simplify notation, we write $TX(ax, ay)$ for $Tx^{x \to y}(ax, ay)$. We use $FT \subset TX^{x \to y}$ and $BT \subset TX^{y \to x}$ to denote the collections of FTs and BTs, respectively. Since we assume the attackers have the power to manipulate the order of transactions, they need not care about the tolerable slippage of FT and BT. To simplify notation, we write $FT(ax)$ and $BT(ay)$ for $FT^{x \to y}(ax, 0)$ and $BT^{y \to x}(0, ay)$, respectively.

- **AMM Transition Functions.** We define a swap transition function as $\mathcal{F}((X_i, Y_i), TX_{i+1}, f) \to S_{i+1}$, which outputs the next state S_{i+1} after executing TX_{i+1} on the state S_i, where f is the transaction fee rate set by the LP $\mathcal{LP}$. We also define a swap amount calculating function based on Formula 1 as $\mathcal{F}_A((X_i, Y_i), TX_{i+1}, f) \to y_{i+1}$, which outputs the amount of swapped τ_y after executing transaction TX_{i+1}. We represent the state change of $\mathcal{LP}$ upon the execution of TX_{i+1} as $(X_i, Y_i) \xrightarrow{TX_{i+1}} (X_{i+1}, Y_{i+1})$.

- **Slope Point.** We introduce a crucial auxiliary concept, called the *slope point*, which plays a significant role in the transaction reordering attacks. Given a state of a liquidity pool (X_0, Y_0) and a transaction $TX_i(ax_i, ay_i)$, we aim to identify a transition $(X_{i-1}, Y_{i-1}) \xrightarrow{TX_i} (X_i, Y_i)$ (where $X_i \cdot Y_i = X_0 \cdot Y_0$) that maximizes the execution price of the transaction (i.e., $TX_i.p$), up to its maximum tolerable price (i.e., ax_i/ay_i). We can calculate (X_i, Y_i) by Formula 2. We define $sp_i = X_i$ as the *slope point* of TX_i.

$$sp_i = X_i = (ax_i + \sqrt[2]{ax_i^2 + 4 \cdot X_0 \cdot Y_0 \cdot ax_i/ay_i \cdot (1-f)})/2, Y_i = X_0 \cdot Y_0/X_i \quad (2)$$

3.2 Attack Model

Attack Structure. Given an LP (τ_x/τ_y) and multiple victim transactions $\{TX_i\}_{i=1}^N$, the attacker can devise an attack strategy consisting of a series of malicious and victim transactions. We assume that the attacker has the authority to alter the execution order of the victim transactions in order to maximize the attack profit. In addition, as shown in Fig. 1(c), the attacker inserts m FTs, denoted as $\{FT_i\}_{i=1}^m$, into these victim transactions, where $m \leq n$. These FTs ensure that the victim transactions are executed in the state envisioned by the attacker. By employing these FTs, the attacker can swap τ_x for τ_y at relatively lower prices. Towards the end of the attack, the attacker emits a back-running transaction BT_1 to swap all swapped τ_y back to τ_x. Note that the execution price of this BT is relatively higher, allowing the attacker to gain profits.

Transaction Selection. We prioritize the selection of transactions for attack based on their slope points. Transactions exhibiting higher slope points are given higher precedence for n-MVTL attack. This preference is rooted in the observation that transactions with larger slope points inherently show greater vulnerability, as they allow BT emitted by the attacker to swap back τ_x at higher prices. Moreover, preserving transactions with larger slope points allows for more flexibility in subsequent optimization algorithms, providing additional room for adjustments of attack strategies.

Attack Profit. According to the structure of n-MVTL attack strategy, we define the attack profit by $R = \mathcal{F}_\mathcal{A}(S_n, BT, f) - \Sigma_{i=1}^m FT_i.ax$, where S_n is the post-execution state of LP after executing the last victim transaction; BT and $\{FT_i\}_{i=1}^m$ are the malicious transactions emitted by the attacker. Attackers can use this formula to precompute the potential profit from the attack strategy.

4 n-MVTL Attack

Given an initial state (X_0, Y_0) of an LP and a list of victim transactions $\{TX_i\}_{i=1}^N$ with the same swap direction $x \rightarrow y$ in the pending pool, we find the optimal attack strategy using two algorithms: **Transaction Selecting** algorithm and **Optimal Attack** algorithm. We first provide a transaction selecting algorithm to identify the largest subset of vulnerable transactions $\{TX_i\}_{i=1}^n$. Then, we provide an optimal attack algorithm to calculate an approximate optimal attack strategy, thereby yielding maximum attack revenue. Our attack process can be represented as follows:

$$\{Tx_i\}_{i=1}^n \leftarrow \texttt{TransactionSelecting}((X_0, Y_0), \{TX_i\}_{i=1}^N), \tag{3}$$

$$\mathcal{ST} \leftarrow \texttt{OptimalAttack}((X_0, Y_0), \{Tx_i\}_{i=1}^n). \tag{4}$$

4.1   Transaction Selecting

We present an iterative approximation algorithm designed for selecting victim transactions. To maximize the space for inserting transactions within the strategy, we strive to place transactions as close as possible to the price that triggers their maximum tolerable price. In our algorithm, as the number of iterations increases, the execution price of victim transactions becomes increasingly closer to their maximum tolerable price. The algorithm considers *AMM swap fees*, which are not considered in most existing attack designs. In practice, an LP charges AMM swap fees from DeFi users for conducting their swap transactions. Therefore, the liquidity of the LP will increase after each transition. We use $EK_i \in \mathbb{N}^+$ to represent the estimated liquidity of the LP after executing TX_i. As illustrated in Fig. 2, **Transaction Selecting** involves three phases: (1) *Initial Phase*; (2) *Iteration Phase*; and (3) *Final Phase*.

Initial Phase. We initialize the parameter required for the iterative algorithm. We assign K_0 for all EK_i, $i \in [N]$.

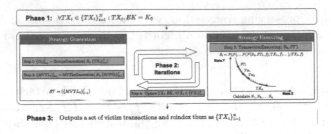

Phase 3: Outputs a set of victim transactions and reindex them as $\{TX_i\}_{i=1}^n$

Fig. 2. Overview of Algorithm **Transaction Selecting**.

Iteration Phase. We execute two processes for each iteration in the iteration phase: transaction generating and transaction executing. We first use the transaction generating function to generate the attack transactions FTs between victim transactions $\{TX_i\}_{i=1}^N$ in the LP (in Step 1–3). Then, by transaction executing, we can calculate the post-execution states $\{(X_i, Y_i)\}_{i=1}^N$ for $\{TX_i\}_{i=1}^N$ (in Step 4), and then use $\{(X_i, Y_i)\}_{i=1}^N$ to update $\{EK_i\}_{i=1}^N$ (in Step 5).

Step 1: Transaction Group Generation. A transaction group G is defined as a sequential of victim transactions that can be successfully executed consecutively, where the last victim transaction meets its slope point. To facilitate the description of the following steps, we define SS_j and ES_j as the expected start and end states of transaction group G_j, respectively. We represent the state change of the LP upon the execution of G_j as $SS_j \xrightarrow{G_j} ES_j$.

We split the victim transactions $\{TX_i\}_{i=1}^N$ into several transaction groups by **Group Generating Algorithm**. In each group, the end state of the last victim transaction triggers at its slope point corresponding to its maximum tolerable prices, while the end state of each other victim transaction is the start state of its next victim transaction.

Building Block: Group Generating Algorithm. Given an input $\{(X_0, Y_0), \{TX_i\}_{i=1}^N\}$, the algorithm output a list of $\{G_j\}_{j=1}^m$. In this algorithm, for each TX_i, we first use its estimated attribute EK_i instead of $X_0 \cdot Y_0$ and the transaction swap fee rate f to calculate its estimated slope point by Formula 2. Then, we traverse all victim transactions by their estimated slope point in reverse order and place transactions into groups as follows:

1. For the first transaction TX_N that has the largest slope point, we create the first group G_1 and place TX_N into it. We set $SS.X = sp_N - ax_N$, and $ES.X = sp_N$, respectively (where $SS.X$ and $ES.X$ are the values of τ_x in the start and end states of the current group, respectively).

2. For other $TX_i \in \{TX_i\}_{i=1}^{N-1}$, if $SS.X \leq sp_i$, we insert TX_i to the front of the current G_j, since it can be executed successfully with the subsequent victim transactions (i.e., will not exceed its slope point) in this group. Then we update $SS.X = SS.X - ax_i$. Otherwise, if $SS.X > sp_i$, we finish the transaction group G_j and create a new G_{j+1} (G_{j+1} becomes the current group). Then we place TX_i into this group and reset $SS.X$ and $ES.X$ to $sp_i - ax_i$ and sp_i, respectively.

Note that when attempting to place TX_i into an G_j, if $SS.X - ax_i \leq X_0$, the operation of adding TX_i to G_j will be aborted, and the next iteration will proceed. Ultimately, only a subset of the victim transactions may be placed into groups. We reverse the index the transaction group as $\{G_i\}_{i=1}^{m}$, and denote the selected transaction subset as $\{TX_i\}_{i=1}^{n}$.

- **Step 2: Multiple-Victim-Transactions Layers (MVTLs) Generation.**
An MVTL $MVTL_j$ is defined as a combination of a front-running transaction FT_j and a transaction group G_j (cf. Figure 1(c)). FT_j is used to let the last victim transaction in G_j trigger at its slope point, thereby maximizing the victims' loss.
After we split the victim transactions into $\{G_j\}_{j=1}^{m}$, there are some state change gaps among them. For each G_j, we generate FT_j to fill the state change gap before G_j by Formula 5 and then combine it with G_j into $MVTL_j$. The process of creating FT_j is:

$$FT_j = \begin{cases} FT(SS_j.X - X_0), & j = 1 \\ FT(SS_j.X - ES_{j-1}.X), & 1 < j \leq m \end{cases} \quad (5)$$

- **Step 3: Strategy Executing.** We input a strategy ST (i.e., $\{MVTL_j\}_{j=1}^{k}$) and (X_0, Y_0) to the function `TransactionExecuting` to calculate the states $\{(X_i, Y_i)\}_{i=1}^{n}$ after executing $\{TX_i\}_{i=1}^{n}$, respectively.
- **Step 4: Parameters Updating.** Based on the calculated states $\{(X_i, Y_i)\}_{i=1}^{n}$ from Step 3, we update the estimated liquidity ES_i for each transaction $TX_i \in \{TX_i\}_{i=1}^{n}$ by the formula: $EK_i = X_i \cdot Y_i$ and go to the next iteration.

Final Phase. After several iterations in the iteration phase, the algorithm outputs the set of victim transactions $\{TX_i\}_{i=1}^{n}$ extracted from the MVTLs of the last iteration.

4.2 Optimal Attack Algorithm

Our optimal attack algorithm hinges upon a fundamental observation: as transactions are executed, the price of token pair τ_x/τ_y continuously decreases. Consequently, strategically inserting the front-running transaction as early as possible can maximize the attacker's revenue. This observation forms the basis of our optimal attack algorithm, which utilizes two critical building blocks: the **Front-running algorithm** and the **Backward algorithm**.

Building Block: Front-Running Algorithm. Given the current state of the LP and the set of victim transactions, this algorithm calculates an optimal front-running attack, assuming that victim transactions don't have slope points.

- **Input**: The algorithm gets $\{(X,Y), \{TX_i\}_{i=1}^{n}, s_y\}$ as inputs, where (X,Y) is the current state of the LP, $\{TX_i\}_{i=1}^{n}$ is the set of victim transactions, and s_y is the amount of τ_y hold by the attacker.
- **Output**: The algorithm outputs an optimal front-running attack $FT(\Delta x)$.

Although directly calculating Δx is difficult, we can obtain the range of Δx based on Theorem 1. After inserting an attack transaction $FT(\Delta x)$, the attacker's will have $s'_y = s_y + (Y - \frac{X \cdot Y}{X+(1-f)\Delta x})$ of τ_y, and the current state (X_1, Y_1) of the LP becomes $X_1 = X + \Delta x$, $Y_1 = \frac{X \cdot Y}{X+(1-f)\Delta x}$.

To simplify the notation, let's denote the trading amounts in $\{TX_i\}_{i=1}^n$ by $\{x_i\}_{i=1}^n$, $V_x = \sum_{i=1}^n x_i$ and $t = 1 - f$. Then the new state (X_2, Y_2) of the LP after executing all victim transactions satisfied:

$$X_2 = X + \Delta x + V_x, \quad Y_2^{min} \le Y_2 \le Y_2^{max}.$$

$$Y_2^{min} = \frac{X_1 \cdot Y_1}{X_1 + tV_x} = \frac{(X + \Delta x)(X \cdot Y)}{(X + t\Delta x)(X + \Delta x + tV_x)},$$

$$Y_2^{max} = \frac{(X + \Delta x)(X \cdot Y)}{t^{n-1}(X + t\Delta x)(X + \Delta x + V_x)},$$

where Y_2^{min} and Y_2^{max} come from Theorem 1. The attack profit after BT is:

$$P_x = X_2 - X_2 \cdot Y_2/(Y_2 + (1 - f)s'_y) - \Delta x. \tag{6}$$

According to Eq. 6, we find that P_x and $\frac{dP_x}{d\Delta x}$ are strictly decreasing when Y_2 is increasing. Therefore, we can obtain the Δx range by taking the derivative $\frac{dP_x}{d\Delta x} = 0$. The result of $\Delta x \in [\Delta x^{min}, \Delta x^{max}]$ is:

$$\Delta x^{max} = \frac{X(s_y(t-1)tX - XY + t^2(V_x + X)Y) + \sqrt{B^{max}}}{(t-1)(s_y t(tV_x - X) + (t^2 V_x - X - tX)Y)}$$

$$B^{max} = t^2 V_x^2 X(s_y(t-1) + tY)$$
$$\times (s_y(t-1)t(t(V_x + X) - X) + (X - t^2(V_x + X) + t^3(V_x + X))Y)$$

$$\Delta x^{min} = \frac{X(s_y(t-1)t^n X - XY + t^{1+n}(V_x + X)Y) + \sqrt{B^{min}}}{(t-1)s_y t^n(tV_x - X) + (t^{2+n} V_x + X - t^{1+n}(V_x + X))Y}$$

$$B^{min} = t^{1+n} V_x^2 X(s_y(t-1) + tY)$$
$$\times (s_y(t-1)t^n(-X + t(V_x + X)) + (X - t^{1+n}(V_x + X) + t^{2+n}(V_x + X))Y)$$

Building Block: Backward Algorithm. Given the current state of the LP and the set of victim transactions, this algorithm calculates a maximized FT attack while ensuring the last victim transaction can be successfully executed. We consider the maximum tolerable prices in this algorithm.

- **Input:** The algorithm gets $\{(X, Y), \{TX_i\}_{i=1}^k\}$ as input, where (X, Y) is the current state of the LP, $\{TX_i\}_{i=1}^k$ is the set of victim transactions.
- **Output:** The algorithm output a maximized front-running attack $FT(\Delta x)$.

We also calculate the range of Δx based on Theorem 1. To simplify the notation, we denote the number of tokens in $\{TX_i\}_{i=1}^k$ by $\{x_i\}_{i=1}^k$, $V_x = \sum_{i=1}^{k-1} x_i$ and $t = 1 - f$. Then the post-executing state of FT is $X_0 = X + \Delta x$, $Y_0 = \frac{XY}{X+(1-f)\Delta x}$. The state $\{X_{k-1}, Y_{k-1}\}$ after executing $\{TX_i\}_{i=1}^{k-1}$ is:

$$X_{k-1} = X_0 + \Delta x + V_x, \ Y_{k-1}^{min} \leq Y_{k-1} \leq Y_{k-1}^{max},$$
$$Y_{k-1}^{min} = (X_0 \cdot Y_0)/(X_0 + tV_x) = (X + \Delta x)(X \cdot Y)/(X + t\Delta x)/(X + \Delta x + tV_x),$$
$$Y_{k-1}^{max} = (X + \Delta x)(X \cdot Y)/(t^{n-1}(X + t\Delta x)(X + \Delta x + V_x)).$$

Then TX_k can get y_k of τ_y:

$$y_k = Y_{k-1} - X_{k-1} \cdot Y_{k-1}/(X_{k-1} + tx_k) = t \cdot Y_{k-1}x_k/(X_{k-1} + tx_k). \tag{7}$$

According to Eq. 7, we know that y_k is strictly decreasing when Y_{k-1} is increasing. Therefore we can obtain the range of $\Delta x \in [\Delta x^{min}, \Delta x^{max}]$ by solve Eq. 7:

$$\Delta x^{min} = (-\frac{1+t}{2})V_x - X - \frac{tx_k}{2} + \sqrt{\frac{tXx_kY}{yk} + \frac{((1-t)(V_x - x_k) + x_k)^2}{4}},$$
$$\Delta x^{max} = t^{1-k}\Delta x^{min}.$$

Attack Algorithm. Given a start state (X_0, Y_0) of the LP and a sequence of sorted victim transactions $\{TX_i\}_{i=1}^n$, the attack algorithm outputs an attack strategy $\mathcal{ST}$, which maximizes the attacker's revenue.

The algorithm runs in n rounds. In each round $k \in [n]$, the algorithm attack transactions $\{TX_i\}_{i=k}^n$. At the beginning of each round, the algorithm initializes parameters $s_y = 0$, $X = X_0$, $Y = Y_0$, and $l = k$, where s_y is the amount of τ_y the attacker have got, and l is the index of victim transaction. In each round, the algorithm runs in two steps:

1 The algorithm runs **Front-running Algorithm**$(X, Y, \{TX_i\}_i^n, sy = 0)$, receives an interval $\{\Delta x^{min}, \Delta x^{max}\}$ containing the optimal trading amount of the front-running attack. Then the algorithm runs **Binary Search** d times to search an FT approximated with the optimal attack transaction.

2 The algorithm executes FT from state (X, Y), then try to execute victim transactions $\{TX_i\}_{i=l}^n$.
   - All transactions are executed successfully: The algorithm should record the attack strategy and move to the next round.
   - When executing transactions, a transaction TX_j exceeds its slope point: Now for all $k \in [j, n]$, the algorithm should run **Backward Algorithm** $((X, Y), \{TX_i\}_{i=l}^k)$, and receive intervals $\{\Delta x_k^{min}, \Delta x_k^{max}\}_{k=j}^n$. By calculating $\Delta x^{min} = \min_{k \in [j,n]} \Delta x_k^{min}$ and $\Delta x^{max} = \max_{k \in [j,n]} \Delta x_k^{max}$, the algorithm gets the interval which containing optimal FT attack. Then employing **Binary Search** d times, the algorithm can find an approximate maximum FT attack x which swaps for y of τ_y. Assume the transaction $Tx_{j'}$ reaches its slope point in the attack x, the resulting state after executing transactions FT and $\{TX_i\}_{i=l}^{j'}$) is denoted as $(X_{j'}, Y_{j'})$. Subsequently, the algorithm updates $s_y = s_y + y$, $X = X_{j'}$, $Y = Y_{j'}$, $l = j' + 1$ and proceeds to run step 1.

Finally, the algorithm compares all the revenues in n rounds and chooses the attack strategy $\mathcal{ST}$ with the largest revenue.

Each step of the algorithm runs binary search at most d times in which the algorithm should execute at most n transactions. Meanwhile, the algorithm should calculate the interval at most n times. Hence the algorithm runs at most $O(nd + n)$ time in each step. As the algorithm runs each step at most n times in each round, and there are n total rounds, the time complexity of the optimal attack algorithm is $O(n^3(d + 1))$.

4.3   Implementing Attacks on Blockchain

We consider an Ethereum-like blockchain where many DeFi users initiate their transactions on the pending pool. We consider a rational attacker $\mathcal{A}$ who observes the pending pool's transactions in real-time. When $\mathcal{A}$ detects one or more victim transactions that interact with the same LP and have the same swap direction, $\mathcal{A}$ can use n-MVTL attack algorithms to find an optimal attack strategy $\mathcal{ST}$ to attack these victim transactions. After that, if $\mathcal{A}$ is a miner (or builder in ETH 2.0), he can include $\mathcal{ST}$ in a new block and broadcast it to Ethereum on his own if $\mathcal{A}$ is a miner. Otherwise, $\mathcal{A}$ can send $\mathcal{ST}$ as a bundle with an auction fee to an honest miner (or builder) via an MEV relay (e.g., flashbots [3], Eden Network [6]). If $\mathcal{A}$ wins the auction, the honest miner (or builder) will then include $\mathcal{ST}$ in a new block and broadcast it to Ethereum.

The n-MVTL attack surpasses prior works by overcoming three limitations: (I) *No stable price assumption.* The attack profit obtained by the n-MVTL attack are positive amount of τ_x, hence ensuring positive gains without the stable price assumption. (II) *Consider AMM swap fees.* The liquidity of an LP is not constant when considering AMM swap fees. In our algorithm, we take this factor into account to generate attack strategies. This increases the computational complexity, but it makes our generated attack strategies more practical. (III) *Hard to defend.* We employ a structure n-MVTL to exploit the vulnerability among multiple victim transactions, making it difficult for DeFi users to resist n-MVTL attacks using conventional methods. We show how the novel structure works in Appendix B.

5   Analysis

In this section, we first proved the upper and lower bounds of the LP's state after executing re-ordered transactions. Then, we provide a comprehensive analysis of the revenue of the optimal attack algorithm.

5.1   Post-execution State Analysis

The greatest difficulty when analyzing the revenue of the algorithm is determining the post-execution reserve of τ_y in the LP because it is according to the transaction order. To estimate the reserve of τ_y in the LP after n transactions, we prove the following theorem:

Theorem 1. *Given a start state (X_0, Y_0) of the LP and a set of transactions $\{TX_i\}_{i=1}^n$ in which the trading amounts are $\{x_i\}_{i=1}^n$. Then post-executing state (X_n, Y_n) satisfied:*

$$X_n = X_0 + V_x, \frac{X_0 Y_0}{X_0 + (1-f)V_x} < Y_n < \frac{X_0 Y_0}{X_0 + (1-f)V_x} * (1-f)^{1-n},$$

where f is the rate of transaction swap fee, and $V_x = \sum_{i=1}^n x_i$.

The proof is in Appendix A. With Theorem 1, we can estimate the output in **Front-running Algorithm** and **Backward Algorithm**.

Corollary 1. *In Front-running algorithm (or Backward algorithm) with d times of Binary search, the trading amount Δx in the output attack transaction and the trading amount Δx_{opt} for the optimal attack transaction are satisfied:*

$$\frac{\Delta x_{opt} - \Delta x}{\Delta x_{opt}} \leq \frac{(1-f)^{1-n} - 1}{2^d}, \tag{8}$$

where n is the number of input victim transactions in the algorithm.

Proof. Because $\Delta x_{max} \leq (1-f)^{1-n} \Delta x_{min}$, we have:

$$(\Delta x_{opt} - \Delta x)/\Delta x_{opt} \leq (\Delta x_{max} - \Delta x_{min})/2^d \Delta x_{min} = ((1-f)^{1-n} - 1)/2^d. \tag{9}$$

5.2 Revenue Analysis

Meanwhile, we notice that when the total number of τ_x in the FTs is fixed, the attacker can get more revenue by inserting as many front-running transactions as possible in the front. This statement can be written into the following lemma.

Lemma 1. *Given a starting state (X_0, Y_0), a victim transactions TX_1 and two attacking transaction $FT_1 = FT(\Delta x_1)$ and $FT_2 = FT(\Delta x_2)$, the attack sequence $\{FT(\Delta x_1 + \Delta x_2), TX_1\}$ can earn more τ_y than sequence $\{FT_1, TX_1, FT_2\}$, if TX_1 do not exceed its slope point.*

The proof is straightforward as the price of τ_y is a monotone increase while executing transactions. Then according to Corollary 1 and Lemma 1, we have the following theorem:

Theorem 2. *Given a set of ordered victim transactions $\{TX_i\}_{i=1}^n$, assume the revenue of our attack is P_{n-MVTL}, the maximum revenue by any attack strategy is P_{max}, we have the following lower-bound:*

$$P_{n-MVTL} > (1 - ((1-f)^{1-n} - 1)/2^d)^2 P_{max}. \tag{10}$$

The proof is in Appendix A. This theorem shows that for any ϵ, the algorithm with parameter $d > \log_2 \frac{(1-f)^{1-n}-1}{\epsilon}$ can receive at least $(1-\epsilon)$ of the maximum revenue. Therefore, the attack strategy of the algorithm is an approximate optimal attack strategy.

6   Evaluation

We first implement a prototype of an attack system in Python 3.8.0. We test the implementation of the critical method $\mathcal{F}$ in our attack system to ensure it aligns with the real smart contract, minimizing discrepancies caused by different rounding method implementations. We use real-world data to test the accuracy of our calculations, where test data is extracted from `Sync event`[1] initiated by the Uniswap V2 smart contract to obtain the state of the liquidity pool before and after each transaction, and `Swap event`[2] initiated by the Uniswap V2 smart contract to obtain the amount of τ_x spent by the user in the transaction and the amount of τ_y obtained. We test 10,000 historical transactions by executing them based on their pre-execution states, and the post-execution states calculated by our attack system are consistent with the post-execution states in history.

Then, we conduct a series of experiments on a machine with Quad-Core Intel Core i5 (1.4 GHz) and 16 GB memory, including: (a) evaluating the time efficiency of attack algorithms, (b) validating the profitability of attack strategies, and (c) conducting the trade-off analysis for **Optimal Attack**.

6.1   Time Complexity

To evaluate the time efficiency of our algorithms, we record the time taken to perform each step in our algorithms. We set the state at $(10^{27}, 10^{24})$ in the experiments since it exceeds the current size of any liquidity pool. Victim transactions were randomly generated in the experiments as the veracity of the transactions will not influence the time efficiency of our algorithms. We set the number of iterations utilized in **Transaction Selecting** to 10. We do not limit the number of iterations of **BSA** utilized in **Optimal Attack**. As we can see from Table 1, the time cost of **Transaction Selecting** rises nearly linearly in all cases as the number of random transactions increases, while the time cost of **Optimal Attack** has cubic growth. In total, it takes around 4 s to build an optimal attack strategy when the number of random transactions is 100. Note that the average number of executed transactions per block is 154.8, and the average block generation time is 12.2 s on April 20, 2023, in Ethereum [2]. The results show that our algorithms are feasible in the current Ethereum.

6.2   Attack Strategy Validation

We evaluate the profitability of n-MVTL attack on historical blockchain data from block 12,000,000 to block 17,000,000 over a total of 699 days. We locally deploy the Uniswap V2 Router02 smart contract[3] using Foundry[4], a popular

---

[1] Topic0 of Sync events: 0x1c411e9a96e071241c2f21f7726b17ae89e3cab4c78be50e062b03 a9fffbbad1.

[2] Topic0 of Swap events: 0xd78ad95fa46c994b6551d0da85fc275fe613ce37657fb8d5e3d13 0840159d822.

[3] https://github.com/Uniswap/v2-periphery/blob/master/contracts.

[4] https://github.com/foundry-rs/foundry.

Table 1. Time Cost of Attack Algorithms.

Algorithms	# of TXs			
	10	20	50	100
Transaction Selecting	0.014 s	0.024 s	0.051 s	0.120 s
Optimal Attack	0.042 s	0.171 s	0.888 s	4.018 s
All	0.056 s	0.195 s	0.939 s	4.138 s

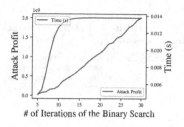

Fig. 3. Average time cost and attack profit of attacks.

EVM development platform, and interact with the deployed smart contracts to execute all malicious and victim transactions. We compute the actual profits based on the transaction execution results in Foundry. We focus on the transactions of the top 2 most popular liquidity pools in Uniswap v2 (i.e., ETH/USDC and ETH/USDT). Our attack solely targeted successfully executed transactions recorded on the blockchain. Each attack is specifically directed towards transactions with the same swap direction that are present within a single block. We set the number of iterations utilized in **Transaction Selecting** to 10. We do not limit the number of iterations of **BSA** utilized in **Optimal Attack**. To measure the performance of n-MVTL attack on extracting extra profits compared to sandwich attacks, we establish a comparison group as a baseline by launching sandwich attacks on victim transactions. As shown in Table 2, n-MVTL attack can extract extra profits in all cases compared to the baseline. In total, n-MVTL attack can yield 656,976 (i.e., 295,608 + 361,368) USD of extra attack profit from 5,006 (i.e., 2,498 + 2,508) profitable victim transactions since n-MVTL attack can only attack victim transactions in one swap direction at the same time. The overall profits from the n-MVTL attack increased by 13.7% compared to the sandwich attack, rising from 4,786,556 USD (i.e., 3,555,817 USDC + 1,230,739 USDT) to 5,443,532 USD (i.e., 3,851,425 USDC + 1,592,107 USDT).

To eliminate the influence of private pending pools on n-MVTL attacks, we did not attack against failed and pending transactions. Our attacks are restricted to transactions that were successfully executed within the same block in the historical blockchain. These transactions were inevitably witnessed by one miner, regardless of whether these transactions originated from private pools. Thus, if the miner possesses malicious intent, he can launch an n-MVTL attack against these transactions. As the number of transactions attacked in this validation is less than the number of real attackable transactions in history. Therefore, the profit statics only represent lower bounds on the severity of n-MVTL attack.

6.3 Trade-Off Analysis of Time Cost and Profit

We employ historical transactions of the LP (ETH/USDT) for trade-off analysis. We re-run the attack on transactions in the USDT-¿ETH swap direction by varying the limits on the number of iterations of **BSA** utilized in **Optimal**

Table 2. Estimated attack profit of SVTL attack and MVTL attack.

LP and swap direction		Profitable TXs / total TXs	Attack profit of 1-SVTL attack	Attack profit of n-MVTL attack	# of n-MVTL attacks	Extra profit (token)	Extra profit (USD)
ETH/USDC (Uniswap V2)	ETH -> USDC	1,965/1,481,222	562.24 ETH	616.40 ETH	592	54.16 ETH	103,066 USD
	USDC -> ETH	2,498/1,373,080	3,555,817 USDC	3,851,425 USDC	790	295,608 USDC	295,608 USD
ETH/USDT (Uniswap V2)	ETH -> USDT	2,564/1,387,482	677.27 ETH	718.76 ETH	782	41.49 ETH	78,955 USD
	USDT -> ETH	2,508/1,472,498	1,230,739 USDT	1,592,107 USDT	798	361,368 USDT	361,368 USD

Attack. Figure 3 illustrates the interplay between time cost, attack profit, and the corresponding iteration limits in **BSA**. As the iteration limits increase, the time cost exhibits a linear growth, while the attack profit demonstrates exponential growth when the number of iterations is below 15. Remarkably, the profit nearly converges to that of attacks with no limit when the number of iterations reaches 15. In a real-world setting, the attackers can adjust the iteration limits within **BSA** to strike a trade-off between time cost and profitability.

7   Conclusion

In this paper, we propose a novel transaction reordering attack, n-MVTL attack, to attack against multiple transactions in DeFi. Unlike traditional transaction reordering attacks, n-MVTL attacks enable attacks on un-sandwichable transactions and consider *AMM swap fees*. In addition, we provide an optimal algorithm to generate an optimal n-MVTL attack strategy with maximum attack profit. This algorithm strikes a balance between time efficiency and attack profit, enhancing the practicality of the attack algorithm. We also validate the attack strategies on historical blockchain data. The result shows that the n-MVTL attack can generate an average daily more profit of 940 USD compared to the sandwich attack. Our new attack can offer attackers more profit and thus cause more loss to normal users in DeFi. Compared with the sandwich attack, n-MVTL attack is more difficult to defend against and harmful to DeFi users. We hope our research raises awareness of this unresolved MEV risk and engenders future work on defense mechanisms against MEV.

Acknowledgments. This work was supported in part by HK RGC GRF under Grant PolyU 15209822 and NSFC/RGC Joint Research Scheme (2022/23), N_PolyU529/22. We would like to thank our anonymous reviewers for their insightful feedback.

A   Proof

Proof for State Analysis. The proof of the **lower bound** and **upper bound** for Y_n comes from the following claims.

Claim. Given two transactions $TX_1(x_1), TX_2(x_2)$ and a transaction $TX(x_1+x_2)$, the reserve of τ_y in the LP after running transaction TX is lesser than running transactions TX_1 and TX_2.

Proof. Assume the state of the LP is (X_0, Y_0). Let $(X_0, Y_0) \xrightarrow{TX} (X_1, Y_1)$, and $(X_0, Y_0) \xrightarrow{TX_1, TX_2} (X_2, Y_2)$. Then, we have: $\frac{Y_1}{Y_2} = \frac{(X_0+(1-f)x_1)(X_0+x_1+(1-f)x_2)}{(X_0+x_1)(X_0+(1-f)(x_1+x_2))}$. Notice that $(X_0 + x_1) + (X_0 + (1-f)(x_1+x_2)) = (X_0 + (1-f)x_1) + (X_0 + x_1 + (1-f)x_2)$ and $(X_0 + (1-f)x_1) < (X_0 + x_1)$, $(X_0 + (1-f)(x_1 + x_2)) < (X_0 + x_1 + (1-f)x_2)$. With average inequality, we have $\frac{Y_1}{Y_2} < 1$, thus $Y_1 < Y_2$.

With this claim, we can get the **lower bound** by merging all the victim transactions into one transaction TX, in which $V_x = \sum_{i=1}^{n} x_i$. Thus we have:

$$Y_n > X_0 Y_0 / (X_0 + (1-f)V_x).$$

Claim. Given the start state (X_0, Y_0), two transactions TX_1 and TX_2 such that the trading amount satisfied $x_1 + x_2 = T$. Then when $x_1 = \sqrt{X_0 T} - X_0$, the LP has a maximum reserve of τ_y after executing two transactions.

Proof. Assume the number of τ_y after executing is Y, we have:

$$Y = \frac{(X_0 + x_1)(X_0 + T)X_0 Y_0}{(X_0 + (1-f)x_1)(X_0 + x_1 + (1-f)(T - x_1))},$$

$$\frac{dY}{dx_1} = \frac{f(1-f)X_0 Y_0(X_0 + T)(X_0 T - 2X_0 x_1 - x_1^2)}{(X_0 + (1-f)x_1)^2(X_0 + x_1 + (1-f)(T - x))^2}.$$

Notice that $\frac{dY}{dx_1} > 0$ when $x_1 < \sqrt{X_0 T} - X_0$, and $\frac{dY}{dx_1} < 0$ when $x_1 > \sqrt{X_0 T} - X_0$. Thus Y is maximum when $x_1 = \sqrt{X_0 T} - X_0$.

With this claim, we know that the maximum Y_n when V_n is given is when $X_i^2 = X_{i-1} \cdot X_{i+1}$ for each $i \in [n-1]$. Thus the maximum Y_n is:

$$Y_n \leq \frac{X_0 Y_0}{X_n} \prod_{i=1}^{n} \frac{X_i}{fX_{i-1} + (1-f)X_i} = \frac{X_0 Y_0}{X_n} \prod_{i=1}^{n} \frac{(X_0 + V_x)^{\frac{1}{n}}}{\left(fX_0^{\frac{1}{n}} + (1-f)(X_0 + V_x)^{\frac{1}{n}}\right)}$$

$$= \frac{X_0 Y_0}{X_n} \frac{(1-f)^{-n}}{(1 + \frac{fX_0^{1/n}}{(1-f)(X_0 + V_x)^{1/n}})^n} \leq \frac{X_0 Y_0}{(1-f)^{n-1}(fX_0 + (1-f)(X_0 + V_x))},$$

$$= \frac{X_0 Y_0}{X_0 + (1-f)V_x} \cdot (1-f)^{1-n}.$$

Proof for Profit. Due to the page limit, we only give a proof of sketch. Firstly, if the output of the Front-running and Backward algorithms is the optimal solution, we prove that our algorithm can get the maximum attack profit.

Proof. Assuming there is an optimal strategy consisting of $\{FT_i, G_i\}_{i=1}^{k}$. According to Lemma 1, the last transaction of G_i, $1 \leq i \leq k - 1$ must reach its slope point (Otherwise, removing a part of FT in the front can get more revenue). This is exactly what our Backward algorithm is working for. Also, for the last FT FT_k, it should consider BT to maximize its profit, which is exactly the result of our Front-running algorithm. Thus, our algorithm can get the maximum profit.

However, our Front-running and Backward algorithms have a little loss in the output, which can be bounded according to Corollary 1. We now calculate the total loss in the attack. Assume there are k front-running transactions $\{FT_i\}_{i=1}^k$ in our attack. By Sect. 3, we know that the first $k-1$ FT is calculated by Backward algorithm. Assume the trading amount of the transaction FT_i is Δx_i, and $V_{FT} = \sum_{i=1}^{k-1} \Delta x_i$, by Corollary 1 we have the inequality 11. As the price of τ_y is monotone increasing, the profit of Backward algorithm P_{BW} satisfied the inequality 12.

$$(V_{FT}^{opt} - V_{FT})/V_{FT}^{opt} \le ((1-f)^{1-n} - 1)/2^d. \tag{11}$$
$$P_{BW} \ge (1 - ((1-f)^{1-n} - 1)/2^d)P_{BW}^{opt}. \tag{12}$$

Then, we calculate the loss of FT_k. Because of backward algorithm loss, the input state Y_n is bigger than the exactly Y_n^{max} and satisfied the inequality 13. And according to Corollary 1, the gap between the output Δx of the algorithm and the optimal output Δx_{max} in FT_k also satisfied the inequality 14. So the profit of Front-running algorithm P_{FR} satisfied the inequality 15. As there are only two types of loss in the algorithm, we finish the proof of Theorem 2.

$$Y_n/Y_n^{opt} \le V_{FT}^{opt}/V_{FT} \le 1/(1 - ((1-f)^{1-n} - 1)/2^d) \tag{13}$$
$$(\Delta x_{opt} - \Delta x)/\Delta x_{opt} \le ((1-f)^{1-n} - 1)/2^d \tag{14}$$
$$P_{FR} \ge (1 - ((1-f)^{1-n} - 1)/2^d)^2 P_{FR}^{opt}. \tag{15}$$

B   Examples

Example 1 (A Typical 1-MVTL Attack). As shown in Fig. 4, we assume that a user $\mathcal{U}$ wants to swap 120,000 of τ_x for at least 800 of τ_y. If $\mathcal{U}$ initiates a transaction with 120,000 token X, this transaction is prone to sandwich attack (cf. (1) of Fig. 4). Suppose $\mathcal{U}$ uses the limiting volume defense strategy [16] that splits her transaction into four small transactions to defend against sandwich attack (cf. (2a) of Fig. 4). Then, each small transaction only has a small trading volume (30,000 of τ_x) so that none of the split transactions can be attacked by the sandwich attack (cf. (2b) of Fig. 4). In contrast, the n-MVTL attack can identify the overall vulnerability among the victim transactions. In this case, the large state change provided by these split transactions is one form of overall vulnerability, which is prone to n-MVTL attack. As shown in (3) of Fig. 4, the attack profit of the n-MVTL attack is 27,621 of τ_x.

Example 2 (An n-MVTL Attack with Optimization). When the real price of a cryptocurrency increases or decreases dramatically, there might be a large number of arbitrage transactions in the pending pool with the same swap direction. We assume that the current state of an LP is (10,000,000, 1,000,000), and the real price of this token pair is 11.0. The pending pool has 11 arbitrage transactions, as illustrated in Fig. 5. To attack these victim transactions, we use **Transaction Selecting** (cf. Section 4.1) to find the largest set of victim transactions

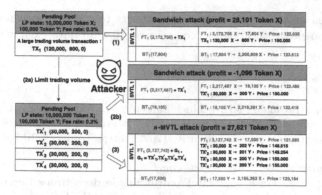

Fig. 4. Example 1. A 1-MVTL attack strategy.

$\{TX_i\}_{i=2}^{11}$ that can be attacked together, and these transactions can be grouped into five MVTLs. In each MVTL, there exists one FT and one or more victim transactions. Then, we optimize the attack strategy by **Optimal Attack**. The algorithm's results indicate that we can maximize the attack profit when we only attack against $\{TX_i\}_{i=5}^{11}$. The strategy optimization increases the attack profit from 4,621 of τ_x to 7,042 of τ_x.

We observe that TX_1 and TX_2 have the ability to defend against sandwich attacks since they are set with small slippages (only 1%). However, they still face the risk of n-MVTL attack. In the optimal n-MVTL attack strategy, TX_1 and TX_2 are not executed intentionally by $\mathcal{A}$. We can regard that TX_1 and TX_2 suffer a fatal front-running attack that makes the users fail to swap their tokens.

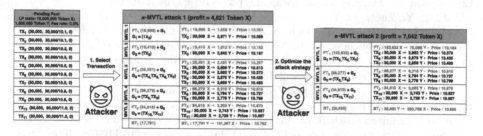

Fig. 5. Example 2. An optimal n-MVTL attack strategy.

C   Potential Defense

The premise for launching transaction reordering attacks is that attackers can analyze transaction parameters (e.g., trading amounts) based on the input data of transactions. One potential defense mechanism involves strengthening the protection of transaction information through cryptographic protocols. Currently, in other areas of DeFi, there have been efforts to enhance privacy-preserving using zero-knowledge technology (i.e., mixers [10] and data exchanges [9]).

References

1. Bartoletti, M., Chiang, J.H.y., Lluch-Lafuente, A.: Maximizing extractable value from automated market makers. In: 2022 International Conference on Financial Cryptography and Data Security (2022). https://doi.org/10.1007/978-3-031-18283-9_1
2. Bitinfocharts. https://bitinfocharts.com/
3. Daian, P., et al.: Flash boys 2.0: Frontrunning in decentralized exchanges, miner extractable value, and consensus instability. In: 2020 IEEE Symposium on Security and Privacy (SP), pp. 910–927. IEEE (2020). https://doi.org/10.1109/SP40000.2020.00040
4. DeFi Tracker. https://defiprime.com/dex-volume
5. DeFi Llama. https://defillama.com/
6. Eden Network. https://www.edennetwork.io/
7. Heimbach, L., Wattenhofer, R.: Eliminating sandwich attacks with the help of game theory. In: Proceedings of the 2022 ACM on Asia Conference on Computer and Communications Security (ACM ASIACCS), pp. 153–167 (2022). https://doi.org/10.1145/3488932.3517390
8. Pancakeswap. https://pancakeswap.finance/
9. Song, R., Gao, S., Song, Y., Xiao, B.: ZKDET: a traceable and privacy-preserving data exchange scheme based on non-fungible token and zero-knowledge. In: 2022 IEEE 42nd International Conference on Distributed Computing Systems (ICDCS), pp. 224–234. IEEE (2022). https://doi.org/10.1109/ICDCS54860.2022.00030
10. Tornado. http://tornado.cash/
11. Uniswap. https://www.uniswap.org
12. Uniswap v1. https://docs.uniswap.org/protocol/V1/introduction
13. Wang, Y., Zuest, P., Yao, Y., Lu, Z., Wattenhofer, R.: Impact and user perception of sandwich attacks in the DeFi ecosystem. In: CHI Conference on Human Factors in Computing Systems, pp. 1–15 (2022). https://doi.org/10.1145/3491102.3517585
14. Zhou, L., Qin, K., Gervais, A.: A2mm: mitigating frontrunning, transaction reordering and consensus instability in decentralized exchanges. arXiv preprint arXiv:2106.07371 (2021). https://doi.org/10.48550/arXiv.2106.07371
15. Zhou, L., Qin, K., Torres, C.F., Le, D.V., Gervais, A.: High-frequency trading on decentralized on-chain exchanges. In: 2021 IEEE Symposium on Security and Privacy (SP), pp. 428–445. IEEE (2021). https://doi.org/10.1109/SP40001.2021.00027
16. Züst, P.: Analyzing and Preventing Sandwich Attacks in Ethereum (2021). https://pub.tik.ee.ethz.ch/students/2021-FS/BA-2021-07.pdf

Miscellaneous

stoRNA: Stateless Transparent Proofs of Storage-time

Reyhaneh Rabaninejad[1]($\boxtimes$), Behzad Abdolmaleki[2], Giulio Malavolta[3], Antonis Michalas[1,4], and Amir Nabizadeh[1,2,3,4]

[1] Tampere University, Tampere, Finland
{reyhaneh.rabbaninejad,antonios.michalas}@tuni.fi
[2] University of Sheffield, Sheffield, UK
behzad.abdolmaleki@sheffield.ac.uk
[3] Max Planck Institute for Security and Privacy, Bochum, Germany
giulio.malavolta@mpi-sp.org
[4] RISE Research Institutes of Sweden, Gothenburg, Sweden

Abstract. Proof of Storage-time (PoSt) is a cryptographic primitive that enables a server to demonstrate non-interactive continuous availability of outsourced data in a publicly verifiable way. This notion was first introduced by Filecoin to secure their Blockchain-based decentralized storage marketplace, using expensive SNARKs to compact proofs. Recent work [2] employs the notion of trapdoor delay function to address the problem of compact PoSt without SNARKs. This approach however entails statefulness and non-transparency, while it requires an expensive pre-processing phase by the client. All of the above renders their solution impractical for decentralized storage marketplaces, leaving the stateless trapdoor-free PoSt with reduced setup costs as an open problem. In this work, we present *stateless* and *transparent* PoSt constructions using probabilistic sampling and a new Merkle variant commitment. In the process of enabling adjustable prover difficulty, we then propose a multi-prover construction to diminish the CPU work each prover is required to do. Both schemes feature a fast setup phase and logarithmic verification time and bandwidth with the end-to-end setup, prove, and verification costs lower than the existing solutions.

1 Introduction

Storage-as-a-Service, including cloud storage services and, more recently, Decentralized Storage Networks (DSNs) [15,22], has attracted extensive interest and caused big data migration from local storage systems to storage servers, as it offers efficient and scalable services at a lower cost. However, after outsourcing, the data owner has no physical control over the data. Hence, continuous data availability is an important trait that highly-reliable service providers [5] should guarantee to protect users against downtime, whatever its cause, and ensure that data owners can retrieve their data files at any time. Continuous data availability is becoming increasingly critical as it provides global ceaseless access to online

© The Author(s), under exclusive license to Springer Nature Switzerland AG 2024
G. Tsudik et al. (Eds.): ESORICS 2023, LNCS 14346, pp. 389–410, 2024.
https://doi.org/10.1007/978-3-031-51479-1_20

business data and business-to-business applications. The existing notion of Proof of Storage (PoS) [1, 10] ensures data integrity and availability at a specific time point (i.e., the time the challenge is issued). A naive approach to certify continuous data availability consists of using PoS and performing frequent checks over time. However, this requires that clients be online when sending sequential challenges to the storage server. Moreover, in DSNs such as Filecoin [15], where proofs are verified by the blockchain network, this method causes communication complexities and, eventually, leads to network bottlenecks.

1.1   Proof of Storage-time

Ateniese *et al.* [2] formalized the notion of Proof of Storage-time (PoSt) to address the issue of continuous availability guarantees for outsourced data, and proposed two constructions in the random oracle model. Informally, a PoSt protocol enables storage servers to efficiently convince a verifier that data is continuously available and retrievable via generating chained sequential challenge-responses over a specified time interval. Consider D as the time period during which a specific data file is deposited in the server. D is divided into time slots of length T, where T is the audit frequency parameter – the prover is challenged once in every time slot T, while the verifier is not required to remain online. This helps approximating continuous data availability throughout a D time range with discretized frequent auditing, where a smaller T provides a superior availability guarantee. The measure of time here is the number of unit steps of the Turing machine. Let *timer* be a global (verification) timer initiated by the data owner, but public (with the timer the verification algorithm can check whether the final proof is received on time). A PoSt consists of a tuple of four algorithms PoSt = (Setup, Store, Prove, Verify), as defined below.

- Setup($1^\lambda, T, D$) → (par, sk): Inputs security parameter λ, audit frequency parameter T, D and outputs the public parameters par and secret key sk.
- Store(F^*, sk, par, T, D) → (F, tg): Takes as input an original data file F^*, a secret key sk, an audit frequency parameter T, and a deposit time D and generates an encoded file F. It also outputs tag tg as necessary information to run PoSt.Prove and PoSt.Verify algorithms.
- Prove(par, *chal*, tg, F) → π: Inputs encoded file F, tag tg, public parameters par, and challenge seed *chal* issued by a verifier at the outset of the deposit period, and outputs proof π promptly after the deposit period ends.
- Verify(par, sk, tg, *chal*, π, *timer*) → {*accept*, *reject*}: Inputs par, secret key sk, tag tg, challenge *chal*, proof π, and *timer* to check timely reception of the final proof . It outputs a bit b to designate *accept* or *reject*.

PoSt schemes may present the following core features:

Public Verifiability. A smart contract or any third party (not just the clients) are able to audit continuous data availability by verifying the output from PoSt.Prove algorithm. To this end, the verification algorithm PoSt.Verify should not take any secret sk as input.

Statelessness. An unbounded (polynomial) number of verifications are supported without requiring the verifier to maintain the protocol state. If a PoSt protocol is stateful, when the number of verifications reaches a pre-determined fixed bound, the protocol stops and no further audits are possible, unless the data owner retrieves outsourced files and relaunches the PoSt.Store algorithm.

Dynamic. Efficient updates on outsourced data are enabled at any time without the need for an expensive setup.

Transparency. A PoSt scheme may import a one-time trusted setup run by an honest client with a publicly published setup output to all entities. However, a PoSt scheme is transparent if its setup does not involve any secret sk.This property is necessary in DSNs where provers may also be clients and prevents *generation attack*– that is, a malicious client-prover output a valid proof at the time a challenge is issued by generating data *on-the-fly* to collect network rewards, without really reserving storage.

Compactness. Low verification cost is enabled independent of the file size and deposit length.

   Additionally, a PoSt scheme must present the following security properties:

Completeness. For all files $F^* \in \{0,1\}^*$, all (par, sk) values output by $\mathsf{Setup}(1^\lambda, T, D)$, and all (F, tg) output by $\mathsf{Store}(F^*, \mathsf{sk}, T, D)$, a proof π generated by honest prover in $\mathsf{Prove}(\mathsf{par}, chal, \mathsf{tg}, F)$ on the challenge $chal$ will cause $\mathsf{Verify}(\mathsf{par}, \mathsf{sk}, \mathsf{tg}, chal, \pi, timer)$ to always output *accept*.

Soundness. This property guarantees that if a prover is able to convince an honest verifier that it has stored a file throughout the specified deposit time then there is an extractor Ext,that given a subset of prover configurations and the code of the transition function (i.e the random-coin r of the prover) can extract data via interacting with the prover[1]. Formally, a PoSt scheme is sound, if for any PPT adversary $\mathcal{A}$ for a file F, there is an extractor $\mathsf{Ext}_\mathcal{A}$ s.t for all λ and all files $F^* \in \{0,1\}^*$,

$$\Pr \left[\begin{array}{l} (\mathsf{par}, \mathsf{sk}) \leftarrow \mathsf{Setup}(1^\lambda, T, D); (F, \mathsf{tg}) \leftarrow \mathsf{Store}(F^*, \mathsf{sk}, T, D); \\ (\pi || \hat{F}) \leftarrow (\mathcal{A} || \mathsf{Ext}_\mathcal{A})(\mathsf{par}, chal, \mathsf{tg}, F; r) : \\ \mathsf{Verify}(\mathsf{par}, \mathsf{sk}, \mathsf{tg}, chal, \pi, timer) \wedge \hat{F} \neq F \end{array} \right] \approx_\lambda 0$$

Here, $chal$ is the verifier challenge and tg is a tag corresponding to file F.

Ateniese's et al. Construction in a Nutshell: The work in [2] presents two different constructions of PoSt. The first warm-up protocol is based on the intuition proposed in the Filecoin whitepaper [15]: the prover generates sequential Proofs of Retrievability (PoRs), where each PoR proof is computed based on

---

[1] The data should be extracted from the configuration corresponding to any specific time and the transition function.

a challenge derived from the PoR proof in a previous iteration. As a result, the verifier merely provides the first challenge and can then go offline. The scheme leverages the notion of Verifiable Delay Function (VDF) [6] to guarantee a specific amount of delay between two successive PoR proofs, even if the prover uses parallel processors. In every time slice, the prover evaluates VDF by feeding a priori PoR proof as its input and generates a challenge by hashing the VDF output. The prover returns all sequential challenge-proof pairs along with the respective VDF proofs, to be inspected all at once by the verifier. The verification procedure of this warm-up construction however is very expensive since the verifier must audit all proofs one-by-one, and the communication cost is high.

The second protocol follows a different approach based on the Trapdoor Delay Function (TDF). The client executes a pre-processing phase to generate a tag, producing the same sequence of challenge-proof pairs as the prover, but with faster TDF evaluations due to the trapdoor. Nevertheless, in this compact scheme the client relies on a trapdoor to run the setup phase and generate challenges, thus it does not provide public verifiability. Moreover, this protocol is stateful and static. Besides, the soundness of the compact scheme assumes the holder of the trapdoor is honest. This signifies that contrary to what is stated by the authors, the construction cannot be directly used in the DSNs as is the case with Filecoin. Authors have pointed several aspects that remain unresolved such as: (i) support for dynamic data updates, (ii) stateless and transparent PoSt constructions (without trapdoors), and (iii) setup cost reduction.

In light of these issues we ask the following question: *Can we have a Proof of Storage-time for continuous availability monitoring of dynamic data at storage providers in a transparent, stateless, yet efficient manner?*

1.2   Our Contributions

This work makes significant progress in answering the above question. We propose stoRNA, a new stateless PoSt protocol with a fast setup for light clients, aiming to outsource their data to a storage network for a deposit period. A public verifier can verify continuous data availability with computation and communication overheads logarithmic in the length of the deposit period. The construction can be instantiated from any stateless publicly verifiable PoR and invokes Proof of Elapsed-time (PoEt) proposed in [7] as a trust-less proxy for time.

Commitment and Random Sampling. We present a new commitment graph inspired by the Directed Acyclic Graph (DAG) introduced in [7], where every single graph node is efficiently updated in sequential time slots, based on the notion of the Merkle Mountain Range, and takes external inputs from the proofs generated at said time slot. The constant-size root of this graph plays as a commitment over the whole PoSt sequence generated by the prover. This commitment mechanism enables the verifier to randomly sample and verify only a logarithmic number of proofs from the PoSt sequence. Inclusion proofs of the commitment graph aid the verifier to check if the proofs returned by the prover are bound to challenged positions of the PoSt sequence.

Stateless-Transparent-Dynamic Construction. Since the client does not rely on any trapdoor, stoRNA is *transparent* and copes with malicious clients. Moreover, it provides unbounded use: when number of verifications reaches an a priori bound (deposit period ends), the client can extend it with no computation (*deposit-extendability*). This is possible due to the incremental nature of the proof chain: the prover can keep up the chain from the last state to append further PoRs at agreed frequency. stoRNA also enables dynamic updates on outsourced files at marginal costs (*file-extendability*).

Multi-prover Setting. stoRNA is in single-prover setting: the prover hosting the data and providing storage proofs also proves the passage of time between successive storage proofs. We next extend stoRNA to a multi-prover PoSt construction, mstoRNA, which differs as regards prover resources. Any arbitrary number of provers can join the decentralized market by providing their preferred resources: (i) *Time Nodes*, who mainly spend CPU work by continuously running PoEt and periodically publishing the publicly verifiable state, and (ii) *Storage Nodes* who provide storage-time by renting out disk-space over time to the clients. A PoSt sequence generated by a prover in this construction is like a public storage-ledger that any one in public can verify, while it can migrate to any other prover, who may continue the ledger where previous prover left off. This aspect is particularly important when considering the rapid-changing distributed nature of DSNs with real nodes susceptible to failure.

1.3 Technical Overview

Consider a data owner wishing to outsource its data to the storage provider(s) and verify continuous data availability without remaining online. Additionally, at a later time, the data owner may extend the deposit time or update its outsourced files without relaunching the entire setup or adding much cost to the verification algorithm. stoRNA enables any light client to do so: the client only requires to perform an efficient Store algorithm to generate necessary information for the prover and public verifier. Each storage provider, participating in the stoRNA protocol, stores the data file for a specific deposit period. To prove "storage-time" i.e., continuous availability of the specified storage over the specified deposit time, the storage provider sequentially generates PoRs during the entire storage period. To compel a specific amount of delay between successive PoRs generated by the prover, the protocol leverages the concept of publicly verifiable PoEt.

In order to enable efficient verification procedure with low communication, the verifier randomly samples and verifies a logarithmic number of proofs from the chain. However, with this probabilistic sampling approach, a dishonest prover can fool the verifier by sending correctly-generated proofs from *arbitrary* time slots in response to the verifier's challenge. Hence, sampling fails to catch continuous data availability with high probability.

One way to enforce the prover to send storage proofs at the *precise* challenged time slots on the chain, is to have him *commit* to the entire chain before random slots are sampled. As a result, the verifier can use the commitment to check

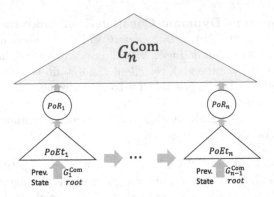

Fig. 1. Structure of stoRNA.

whether the returned responses belong to the challenged slots. To commit to the whole chain of sequential proofs, the prover updates a graph G_n^{Com} based on a variation of the Merkle commitment with some extra edges as illustrated in Fig. 2, across all PoRs generated up to the current time. This commitment graph G_n^{Com} is inspired by the elegant DAG proposed in [7], but with subtle modifications to be discussed in Sect. 4. At each time slot i, the prover efficiently updates the G_n^{Com} by appending the hash of the most recent PoR and PoEt proofs to the labels of the parents of node i and uses the new tree root as a statement to run the next PoEt (Fig. 1). Consequently, the tree root at each time slot i, plays as a commitment over the whole chain up to that slot.

At the end of deposit period, the prover returns the root label of latest G_n^{Com} as a commitment to the entire series of proofs generated within the whole period. Upon receiving the commitment, the verifier challenges a randomly sampled subset of time slots (this can be made non-interactive using the Fiat-Shamir heuristic [9] – i.e., the prover can generate challenge slots himself by hashing the commitment). For every sampled time slot, the prover provides the corresponding PoR, PoEt proofs together with the logarithmic size Merkle opening. The verifier, first checks whether returned proofs are located at the challenged positions of the chain previously committed by , which is made possible via the position-binding guarantee in the Merkle proofs. Next, it checks the correctness of the PoR, PoEt proofs. If the PoR, PoEt proofs or the Merkle opening of any sampled slot is invalid, the verifier will reject. Else, the verifier is convinced that the commitment is computed *mostly* correct. Figure 1 depicts a schematic overview of our construction, named stoRNA since the single strand built by the prover can be viewed as a **storage RNA**[2] that carries information about client data: the extractor algorithm of the underlying PoR scheme can use PoRs appended over time to the chain, to extract the client file with high probability.

Multi-prover PoSt Construction. The above construction, seems to provide all desirable features at once:

---

[2] RNA is a single strand biological molecule essential in coding, decoding, and expression of genes.

- *Fast setup and transparency.* The client only requires to perform the Store algorithm of the underlying PoR scheme on the data files before outsourcing without relying on any trapdoors. Hence, the scheme is transparent.
- *Logarithmic verification time and bandwidth.* The verifier algorithm can audit continuous data availability with high probability in time and communication logarithmic in the length of the deposit period.
- *Statelessness and unbounded use.* When the number of verifications reaches the a priori bound (deposit period ends), the client can easily extend the deposit period without relaunching the Store algorithm. The prover can keep up the PoSt sequence from the last state to append further PoRs at the agreed frequency.
- *Dynamic.* Assuming the underlying PoR scheme supports dynamic databases, the client can update its outsourced files at any time without a re-computation of the entire initialization algorithm. The client only requires to perform fast setup *on the modified data blocks* and outsources them to be updated at the storage server. The verifier needs to use the new PoR tags for auditing the chain from the point update takes place.

However, there is still a challenge to be addressed: Even the honest prover algorithm requires heavy inherently sequential CPU computations. More precisely, the prover participating in the network, needs to spend two distinct resources: (i) storage-time (storage resources over time) and (ii) CPU work (CPU power over time). The first one is natural in PoSt mechanisms as the prover has to dedicate a specified amount of disk-space over time. But the CPU work is due to the use of PoEt in the protocol to guarantee a delay between storage proofs and prevent the prover from generating all required proofs at once and discarding the data. This CPU work is a major deterrent to renting out storage by storage providers or leads to increased storage fees in decentralized storage markets.

Our second construction, mstoRNA (shown in appendix B for space constraint), is based on division of CPU work and storage-time resources between "Time Nodes" and "Storage Nodes". Time Nodes participate in the decentralized market by continuously running PoEt algorithm. At each time slot, the Time Node advertises the PoEt state and waits for Storage Nodes to submit PoR proofs generated based on the challenge derived from the freshly advertised PoEt state and the signature of each individual Storage Node. The wait time is specified based on the network roundtrip time (RTT). Next, the Time Node (i) creates a Merkle tree with the PoRs collected from Storage Nodes, (ii) inputs the Merkle root together with PoEt proof to update G_n^{Com}, and (iii) timestamps the updated commitment into the PoEt sequence by appending the most recent G_n^{Com} root into the shared PoEt state. At the end of the deposit period, the Time Node, acting as the main prover interacting with the verifier in this network, returns the root-label of the latest commitment graph as a commitment to all proofs from all Storage Nodes sequentially generated during the deposit period. Upon receiving the commitment, the verifier simply opens some of the committed labels to verify both storage and time proofs included in those labels. In Table 1, we give a high-level comparison of our constructions over compact PoSt [2].

Table 1. Comparison of our constructions over compact PoSt [2]. $N = \frac{D}{T}$ denotes number of iterations during the deposit period D, $t = \log \frac{T}{2}$, $n = \log \frac{N}{2}$, and m denotes the number of Storage Nodes connected to a Time Node in mstoRNA construction.

	Features			Overhead		
	stateless	transparent	dynamic	setup	verification	proof size
cPoSt [2]	✗	✗	✗	$O(N)$	$O(1)$	$O(1)$
stoRNA	✓	✓	✓	$O(1)$	$O(tn)$	$O(tn)$
mstoRNA	✓	✓	✓	$O(1)$	$\frac{O(tn)}{m}$‡	$\frac{O(tn)}{m}$‡

‡ These are with respect to a single Storage Node.

1.4 Application Domain

Here, we exemplify applications our stoRNA construction could be beneficial to.

Blockchain History Expiry. Hard disk storage is one of the biggest bottlenecks in L1 blockchain scalability. For example, the Ethereum chain will become gigantic in the coming years, making storage infeasible for individuals. The idea of History expiry is to obviate the need for all, full nodes to download the entire chain from genesis. Instead, only the most recent historical blocks would be held and served by the core blockchain protocol. Older blocks would be stored by external storage providers, which can minimize requirements for node hard drive space, paving the way for further decentralization. Many Decentralized Applications (DApps) are already removing data from blockchains for efficiency. However, since being an immutable trustless record is one of the principal features of blockchain, long term availability of older blocks should be guaranteed. Using our method one can publicly verify long term continuous availability of large historical blocks.

Decentralized Storage Networks. DSN is a decentralized algorithmic market based on blockchain made up of various nodes rewarded for storing and maintaining data availability. The network controls the accessible disk space, disperses client data across nodes, audits the integrity and retrievability of data, restores possible failures and rewards honest nodes. The stateless and transparent nature of stoRNA makes it suitable for audit purposes in DSNs.

2 Related Work

Proofs of Storage (PoS) schemes enable clients to outsource files to a server, and later in an interactive audit phase, verify the integrity of the stored data. A verifier, repeatedly challenges the server and checks the returned proof that the server is still storing the client's file intact. The term verifier refers to the client, who originally outsourced the file (privately verifiable PoS), or any third party (publicly verifiable PoS).These protocols are also known as Provable Data Possession (PDP) [3]. Proofs of Retrievability (PoR) schemes [10] are similar to PDP, but they additionally guarantee data retrievability, achieved by an extractor that reconstructs the client file from the proofs returned by the prover.

The extensive research on PDP/PoR schemes covers various advanced features including dynamic data updates [16], shared data files [17], and proof of replicated storage [18].

Proofs of Space (PoSpace) schemes enable a prover to convince a verifier certain disk space is dedicated. PoSpace schemes can be used as an alternative to the blockchain Proof of Work (PoW) consensus mechanism, where instead of the CPU computation, disk-space is expended [8]. PoSpace can also be viewed as a PoS scheme, where the prover shows that it is storing *incompressible* data demonstrating the allocation of a lower-bound amount of resources.

Proofs of Space-time (PoSt) proposed by Moran and Orlov [14], is in a sense PoSpace over time. However, [14] only guarantees the dedication of space resources, not the stored data retrievability. In other words, the server only stores a randomly-generated string with no external utility to guarantee space dedication. The Filecoin project [15] introduced a PoSt scheme, where the server stores real data that can be used outside the protocol. Due to this important shift resource-wasting PoW schemes were replaced by a useful storage service. In [15], the prover executes sequential auditings, where each challenge is deterministically derived from the proof at a previous iteration and an input from a trusted randomness beacon. The prover chains the sequential challenges and proofs and compresses this chain using zk-SNARK , to be publicly inspected by the verifier. However, zk-SNARK is a heavy cryptographic machinery [4] entailing expensive computational/memory costs on the prover side, thus detering storage providers from renting storage to clients. Ateniese *et al.* [2] constructed a compact PoSt scheme based on TDF to obviate the need for zk-SNARKs.

3   Preliminaries

3.1   Merkle Tree and Merkle Mountain Range

A Merkle tree MT is a balanced binary tree with $n = 2^i$ leaves, such that every leaf holds the hash of a data block and every inner node is labelled with a hash of its children [13]. The inclusion of any data block in the tree can be proved only with a number of logarithmic hashes in the number of leaf nodes. A Merkle Mountain Range MMR [20], is a variant of Merkle tree that can be seen either as a list of perfectly balanced binary trees or a single binary tree truncated from the top right. Specifically, a MMR with root r is defined as a tree with $n = 2^i + j$ leaves, such that $i = \lfloor \log_2(n - 1) \rfloor$. The left sub-tree $r.left$ can be seen as a MT with 2^i leaves, and the right sub-tree $r.right$ as a MMR with j leaves.

3.2   Proofs of Sequential Work

Proofs of Sequential Work (PoSW) first introduced by Mahmoody et al. [12] is a protocol between a prover P and a verifier V, where P can generate a proof convincing V that some computation took place for N time steps, since some statement χ was received. The protocol is defined by algorithms PoSW, Open, and Verify as described below. P and V commonly input security parameters $w, c \in \mathbb{N}$ and a time parameter $N \in \mathbb{N}$. All parties have access to a random oracle $\mathsf{H} : \{0,1\}^* \to \{0,1\}^w$.

- PoSW: V samples a random statement $\chi \leftarrow \{0,1\}^w$ and sends it to P. P makes N sequential queries to H and computes a proof $(\phi, \phi_P) := \mathsf{PoSW}^{\mathsf{H}}(\chi, N)$, where ϕ is sent to V and ϕ_P is stored locally.
- Open: P computes $\tau := \mathsf{Open}^{\mathsf{H}}(\chi, N, \phi_P, \gamma)$ in response to random challenge $\gamma \leftarrow \{0,1\}^{c \cdot w}$ sampled by V. τ is then forwarded to V. The challenge can be generated non-interactively by the prover using the Fiat-Shamir [9].
- Verify: V outputs $\mathsf{Verify}^{\mathsf{H}}(N, \phi, \gamma, \tau) \in \{accept, reject\}$.

For a prover P and a verifier V honestly following the protocol's specifications, a complete PoSW protocol will output *accept* with probability 1. Soundness requires that even in the case of resourceful adversaries with parallel processing ability, a malicious prover cannot output a valid proof in time less than N. Cohen and Pietrzak [7] propose a simple PoSW construction based on a Merkle tree variant with added edges that connect the left siblings of a leaf's path to the root with the leaf itself in order to compute a leaf label. This graph is used for both sequential work enforcement and commitment purposes. In this paper, we use the terms PoET and PoSW interchangeably, since a PoSW protocol proves that N time has *elapsed* after χ was received.

3.3   Proof of Retrievability

Proof of Retrievability (PoR) schemes [10,19] are a Proof of Storage category of protocols where a prover simultaneously ensures both possession and retrievability of a data file. PoR schemes consist of four algorithms (KeyGen, Store, Prove, Verify):

- KeyGen$(1^\lambda) \to (\mathsf{sk}, \mathsf{pk})$: Inputs λ and outputs secret/public key pair $(\mathsf{sk}, \mathsf{pk})$.
- Store$(F^*, \mathsf{sk}) \to (F, \mathsf{tg})$: Takes original data file F^*, secret key sk, and generates encoded file F. It also outputs tag tg as necessary information to run PoR.Prove and PoR.Verify algorithms.
- Prove$(\mathsf{pk}, chal, \mathsf{tg}, F) \to \pi$: Inputs file F, tag tg, public key pk, and challenge $chal$ issued by a verifier, and outputs proof π corresponding to the $chal$.
- Verify$(\mathsf{sk}, \mathsf{pk}, \mathsf{tg}, chal, \pi) \to \{accept, reject\}$: Inputs secret/public key pair $(\mathsf{sk}, \mathsf{pk})$, tag tg, $chal$, proof π. Outputs a bit b to designate *accept* or *reject*.

The completeness property of a PoR scheme ensures that the protocol outputs *accept* with a probability of 1 for a prover and verifier honestly following the protocol's specifications. Loosely speaking, soundness requires an extractor algorithm that will recover the data through interaction with any prover that can pass the verification with overwhelming probability [19]. In other words, for any adversary $\mathcal{A}$ generating a valid proof π in the PoR protocol, there is an extractor algorithm $\mathsf{PoR.Ext}_{\mathcal{A}}(\mathsf{pk}, \mathsf{sk}, \mathsf{tg}; r)$ having as input pk, sk, the file tag tg, and the description r of $\mathcal{A}$ (the random coin of $\mathcal{A}$), outputs the file F. PoR schemes also satisfy the *unpredictability* property ensuring that the prover cannot guess a valid response before it sees the corresponding challenge.

4   stoRNA Design

Now, we present our stoRNA, a stateless transparent PoSt protocol.

Ingredients and Notation. stoRNA uses the following primitives:

- Collision-resistant hash function H with the output range of size w.
- Publicly verifiable PoEt = (Prove, Verify) in [7] as a proxy for time (non-interactive version).
- Publicly verifiable stateless PoR = (KeyGen, Store, Prove, Verify) scheme.

We denote concatenation of bit-strings by $\|$. For $x \in \{0, 1\}^*$, $x[i \ldots j]$ and $|x|$ denote concatenation of all bits from i^{th} bit to j^{th}, and bit-length of x, respectively.

Given PoR.Store algorithm outputs (processed file F and tag tg), a random seed rs, deposit time D, and audit frequency parameter T, stoRNA output is proof π that ensures a public verifier: (i) F is continuously available over time D, (ii) the prover did not learn the stoRNA output until D time after receiving F. The measure of time here is the number of sequential CPU hash invocations. We prove the following theorem.

Theorem 1. *Let* PoR *be a stateless PoR scheme with ϵ-soundness and unpredictability. Let* PoEt *be a PoEt scheme with δ-evaluation time. The time cost of* PoR *and hash function evaluation are negligible w.r.t. T. The time cost of s_0 sequential steps on the server processor is T'. If $T' + 2\delta D < T$, the proposed* PoSt *scheme (Algorithm 1) is stateless, complete, and ϵ-sound.*

4.1   Construction

The stoRNA scheme described in Algorithm 1 formally consists of three algorithms: stoRNA.Store, stoRNA.Prove, and stoRNA.Verify. In stoRNA.Store algorithm, the client only performs PoR.Store on an erasure encoded file F^* and outputs processed file F and tag tg to a prover. In the stoRNA.Prove algorithm, for every T time unit, the PoEt.Prove state will serve as the PoR challenge to generate a fresh PoR in PoR.Prove. Next, in order to commit to the whole chain of sequential (PoEt, PoR) proofs, the prover efficiently updates a graph as illustrated in Fig. 2 and Algorithm 2.

This graph is based on the special DAG introduced in [7] with a number of modifications. Let $G_n^{\mathsf{Com}} = (V, E)$ be the commitment DAG, where each node in V is indexed by a bit string with a length at most n, while the root node is indexed by the empty string ϵ. Also, let $E = E' \cup E''$, where sub-graph (V, E') is a complete Merkle tree of depth n, with edges directed from the leaves coming up to the root. Index of each node in depth $i < n$ of the tree is made up of the common bits of its parents. E.g., two parents indexed by $u = v \| 0$ and $u = v \| 1$ form a child indexed by v (Algorithm 2, line 5). Moreover, for all leaves $v \in \{0, 1\}^n$, E'' consists of an edge (u, v) for any u that is a left node sibling on the path from v to the root ϵ (Algorithm 2, line 6).

Algorithm 1. stoRNA Construction

1: <u>stoRNA.Store</u>
2: input data file F^* and $(\mathsf{PoR.sk}, \mathsf{PoR.pk})$
3: $(F, \mathsf{tg}) \leftarrow \mathsf{PoR.Store}(\mathsf{PoR.sk}, \mathsf{PoR.pk}, F^*)$
4: sample random seed $rs \leftarrow_\$ \{0,1\}^w$
5: output (rs, F, tg)
6: <u>stoRNA.Prove</u>
7: input processed file F, tag tg, random seed rs, deposit time D, and audit frequency
   T
8: set $i \leftarrow 0$ and $et \leftarrow 0$ ▷ i:number of audit iterations, et: elapsed time
9: set $\mathsf{st} \leftarrow rs$
10: **while** $et \le D$ **do**
11:     $\mathsf{st} \leftarrow \mathsf{PoEt.Prove}(T, \mathsf{st})$
12:     $i \leftarrow i + 1$
13:     $h_i \leftarrow \mathsf{st}$
14:     $c_i \leftarrow \mathsf{H}(h_i)$
15:     $\pi_i \leftarrow \mathsf{PoR.Prove}(\mathsf{PoR.pk}, F, \mathsf{tg}, c_i)$
16:     $l_\epsilon \leftarrow G_n^{\mathsf{Com}}.\mathsf{Update}(v = i, \mathcal{V} = h_i \,\|\, \pi_i)$ ▷ Algorithm 2
17:     $\mathsf{st} \leftarrow \mathsf{H}(\mathsf{st} \,\|\, l_\epsilon)$ ▷ update the state by appending the new G_n^{Com} root
18:     $et \leftarrow et + T$
19: $N \leftarrow i$
20: $H_{FNL} \leftarrow \mathsf{st}$
21: output $\mathsf{Com} = (H_{FNL}, l_\epsilon)$
22: <u>stoRNA.Verify</u>
23: input commitment Com, tag tg, seed rs, public key $\mathsf{PoR.pk}$
24: generate random $c-$element subset $I^* \subset [1, N]$ and send it to the prover.
25: wait to receive $\pi = \{h_i, \pi_i, \{l_k\}_{k \in \Delta_i}\}_{i \in I^*}$, where $\Delta_i = \{i[1, j-1] \,\|\, 1 - i[j]\}_{j \in [1,n]}$
      ▷ Δ_i contains the index of all siblings of the nodes on the path from
      leaf i to the root as in Merkle tree commitment opening
26: **for all** $i \in I^*$ **do**
27:     $c_i \leftarrow \mathsf{H}(h_i)$
28:     **if** $\mathsf{PoR.Verify}(\mathsf{PoR.pk}, \mathsf{tg}, \pi_i, c_i) = false$ **then** return false
29:     **if** $\mathsf{PoEt.Verify}(T, h_i) = false$ **then** return false
30:     **if** $l_i \ne \mathsf{H}(i, \pi_i, l_{p_1}, \ldots, l_{p_d})$, where $(p_1, \ldots, p_d) = \mathsf{Parents}(i)$ **then** return false
31:     **if** $\exists j \in \Delta_i : l_j \ne \mathsf{H}(j, l_{j\|0}, l_{j\|1})$ **then** return false   ▷ verify G_n^{Com} opening
32: return true

At iteration i, the prover updates the graph G_n^{Com} similarly to a Merkle mountain range described in Subsect. 3.1, also including additional E'' edges as described above. Besides, the label of node i is updated by appending the hash of the most recent $(\mathsf{PoEt}, \mathsf{PoR})$ proofs to the labels of parents of node i. After an update to the commitment graph, the new root label l_ϵ is mixed into the state for the next PoEt execution. At the end of the deposit period, stoRNA.Prove algorithm outputs the latest root label l_ϵ together with the final PoEt state as a commitment to the chain of proofs sequentially generated during the entire period.

Algorithm 2. G_n^{Com}.Update

1: input index $v \in \{0,1\}^n$ and value $\mathcal{V}$, and DAG $G_n^{\mathsf{Com}} = (V, E)$, where $E = E' \cup E''$, sub-graph (V, E') is a Merkle tree, and E'' contains, for all leaves $v \in \{0,1\}^n$ an edge (u, v) for any u that is a left sibling of node on the path from v to the root ϵ.

2: $\mathsf{node_{count}} \leftarrow G_n^{\mathsf{Com}}$.GetNodeCount   ▷ get total number of graph nodes

3: **if** $v > \mathsf{node_{count}}$ **then**

4:     $V \leftarrow V \cup v$ ▷ add leaf v to the tree

5:     $E' \leftarrow E' \cup \{(x \,\|\, b, x) : b \in 0, 1, |x| < n\}$ ▷ update Merkle tree edges starting from new leaf $v = x \,\|\, b$ to the root

6:     $E'' \leftarrow E'' \cup \{(i, v) : v = a \,\|\, 1 \,\|\, a', i = a \,\|\, 0\}$

7:     $l_v = \mathsf{H}(\mathcal{V}) \,\|\, \mathsf{H}(v, l_{p_1}, \ldots, l_{p_d})$, where $(p_1, \ldots, p_d) = \mathsf{Parents}(v)$

8:     $\forall i \in V, |i| < n : l_i = \mathsf{H}(i, l_{p_1}, l_{p_2})$, where $(p_1, p_2) = \mathsf{Parents}(i)$ ▷ recursively update all labels up to root

9: **else**

10:     go to lines 7-8 to update labels

11: output l_ϵ

Upon receiving the commitment, in stoRNA.Verify algorithm, (i) the verifier challenges a randomly sampled subset of time slots, (ii) for every challenged time slot, the prover provides a Merkle opening together with all the $(\mathsf{PoEt}, \mathsf{PoR})$ proofs on the path from this challenged node to the root, (iii) the verifier, uses the commitment to check whether the returned proofs are located at the correct positions of the chain, and (iv) runs $\mathsf{PoEt.Verify}, \mathsf{PoR.Verify}$ algorithms to respectively verify the returned $\mathsf{PoEt}, \mathsf{PoR}$ proofs.

High Level of Security Proof. For the soundness property, we need to prove that the largest time between two PoRs is less than T. Thus, for an honest prover P, any successive configurations of any time slot with a T length must contain at least a PoR proof. Then, following the soundness definition of PoR in 3.3, one can use the PoR extractor to recover the data from the partial configurations and the transition function. To recover the sequence of each computation epoch and feed it to an extractor, we use programability of random oracle. To this aim, we force PoSt provers inevitably query the random oracle, the challenge (except the first one) and response (except the last one) for each PoR via querying the random oracle H. Thus, the extractor can invoke a PoR extractor to extract the data by controlling H. We note that, our soundness proof exploits unpredictability of the random oracle[3]. Finally, we argue about the sequenciality of the scheme that follows the proof of sequentiality of Cohen and Pietrzak [7]. A malicious prover PoSt.P', making the verifier accept (in relation to G_n^{Com} in Algorithm 2) with high probability must have queried H "almost" N times sequentially. We use the outputs of PoR.Prove as the input nodes of the specified tree construction of [7]. We defer the proof of Theorem 1 to appendix A.

---

[3] The unpredictability of the random oracle is important in the malicious prover case, as it is hard to let the extractor access each PoR's challenge and response.

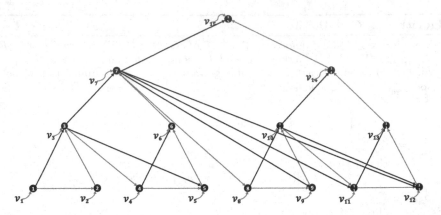

Fig. 2. A complete G_3^{Com} achieved after $N = 15$ iterations. Red lines show the traversing order of the tree with node numbers from 1 to $N = 2^{n+1} - 1$ for a tree of depth n and node i updated at iteration i. Also, $\mathcal{V}_i = (\mathsf{PoEt}, \mathsf{PoR})$ (Algorithm 1, line 16) shown in blue is input to $G_n^{\mathsf{Com}}.\mathsf{Update}$ algorithm at iteration i. (Color figure online)

5   Efficiency Analysis and Experimental Results

Implementation and Experimental Setup. We implement a prototype of the prover and the verifier in Golang[4]. Our testbed consisted of a MacBook Pro with 16 GB 3.22 GHz memory and a 2.06 GHz Intel Core i10 CPU with M1 (ARM based) chipset and Mac OS monterey as operating system. We implemented the scheme of [19] as our underlying stateless publicly verifiable PoR for randomly generated files of different sizes and relied on SHA-256 for all hash implementations. Following what presented in [7], here T and D are measured as the amount of sequential CPU steps. We refer to [21] for discussions on how it translates to real-world time. The results were averaged over 10 runs.

Setup Cost. stoRNA computation for the client solely includes running the PoR.Store algorithm once, no matter how long the deposit length D is. This cost is ignorable as compared with the setup cost of [2] which equals $1 \cdot \mathsf{PoR.Store} + N \cdot (\mathsf{TDF.TrapEval} + \mathsf{PoR.Prove})$, and $N = \frac{D}{T}$ denotes number of iterations during the deposit period D. As an example, the setup algorithm of [2] for a file of size 256 MB, stored for 5 months and checked on a 1-hour basis, takes about 200 min on a client machine. This time is prolonged for larger files or longer deposit lengths. Our stoRNA.Store algorithm can be accomplished in a constant time $1 \cdot \mathsf{PoR.Store}$, independent of the deposit length.

Prover Cost. stoRNA.Prove algorithm makes a total of N sequential queries to PoEt, which is an intrinsically sequential process with overall steps proportional to the deposit length D. In mstoRNA.Prove, the average computational complexity per prover algorithm regarding PoEt computations is divided by m, assuming

---

[4] Code will be open-sourced soon and is available upon request.

Table 2. Proof sizes at various $t = \log \frac{T}{2}$ and $n = \log \frac{N}{2}$, with $N = \frac{D}{T}$. We assume $w = 256$ bits and $c = 150$, which guarantees 2^{-50} security.

D	t, n	Proof Size (MB)
2^{50}	29, 19	2.7930
	34, 14	2.3940
	39, 9	1.7550
2^{60}	29, 29	4.2630
	34, 24	4.1040
	39, 19	3.7050
	44, 14	3.0660
	49, 9	2.1870
2^{70}	29, 39	5.7330
	34, 34	5.8140
	39, 29	5.6550
	44, 24	5.2560
	49, 19	4.6170

m as the number of Storage Nodes connected to a Time Node. Therefore, as m increases, the overall computational complexity of prover algorithm diminishes.

Verifier Cost. We now evaluate how our scheme verification time changes as the deposit period D grows. We fix the audit frequency parameter T to 2^{40} and vary the deposit period from 2^{50} to 2^{70} CPU steps. Since the results on various file sizes was roughly the same, we report the mean over all data files of sizes 64 MB, 128 MB, and 256 MB, with 10 experiments each. Figure 3a shows the results. As deposit length increases by $2^{20} \times$, the verification time grows from 1.64 min to 5.29 minutes, an increase of only $3 \times$. This is because the number of nodes in each of c openings that the verifier algorithm checks their consistency is equal to the depth of the commitment graph, which grows logarithmically with the deposit length. We also explore how the change in audit frequency parameter T affects the verification time. For this experiment, we fix the deposit period D to 2^{60} vary T from 2^{30} to 2^{50} CPU steps. For each configuration, we run 10 tournaments and measure the average of the verification time. Figure 3b shows the results. When $T = 2^{50}$, the verification time reaches the lowest, at 2.07 minutes. We also note that the verification algorithm is parallelizable, where nodes can be checked concurrently using verifier CUDA cores. In this prototype we have not implemented such parallelism and the results reflect the whole verification time without parallelism. mstoRNA construction shown in appendix B further optimizes the overall verification cost in the sense that PoEt sequence is inspected once for all m Storage Nodes connected to a Time Node.

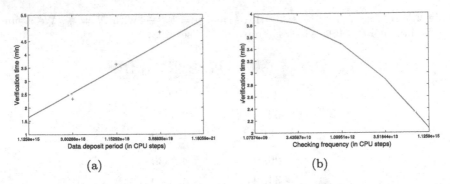

Fig. 3. stoRNA.Verify algorithm time cost for $c = 150$. Solid lines show the trend. (a) Verification time when varying the deposit period D and audit frequency parameter $T = 2^{40}$. The overall verification cost is the same for all file sizes and logarithmic in the deposit length. (b) Verification time when varying audit frequency parameter T and deposit period $D = 2^{60}$.

Proof Size. The proof consists of the $\mathsf{Com} = (H_{FNL}, l_e)$ and c openings, each including n tuples of the form $\{h_k, \mathsf{PoEt}_k, \pi_k, l_k\}_{k \in \Delta_i}$, where $\Delta_i = \{i[1, j-1] \,\|\, 1 - i[j]\}_{j \in [1,n]}$. Table 2 report the results on proof sizes when varying deposit period D and audit frequency parameter T. With $w = 256$ bits, $c = 150$, which guarantees 2^{-50} security, $t = 39$ (i.e., over 10^{12} steps), and $n = 9$ (1024 total iterations), the proof size is approximately 1.7 MB.

Discussion. Our construction is slower to verify and has larger proofs than the compact solution in [2]. This is the cost we pay for stateless and transparent features. Nonetheless, our *end-to-end* setup, proof, and verification costs are smaller than [2]. In Table 1, we give a high-level comparison with compact PoSt [2]. On top of potential parallelism possible in the verification mentioned earlier, there are potential ways of further optimizing performance: In addition to full-node verifiers inspecting the entire PoSt sequence, light client verification approaches like [11] are possible in stoRNA. Concretely, by adding intermediate "checkpoints" during the PoSt sequence computation, where each checkpoint includes the hash of the previous, a light client can verify directly through consecutive checkpoints and skip the validation of every time slot in PoSt sequence. Therefore, it is possible to audit data availability only for a specific time and not for the whole chain (*point verification*).

Acknowledgments. This work was funded by the HARPOCRATES EU research project (No. 101069535) and the Technology Innovation Institute (TII), UAE, for the project ARROWSMITH. Giulio Malavolta was partially funded by the German Federal Ministry of Education and Research (BMBF) in the course of the 6GEM research hub under grant number 16KISK038 and by the Deutsche Forschungsgemeinschaft (DFG, German Research Foundation) under Germany's Excellence Strategy - EXC 2092 CASA - 390781972.

A   Theorem 1 Proof

(*i: Completeness*): Directly follows from the completeness of the PoR and PoEt schemes.

(*ii: Soundness*): Let an adversary $\mathcal{A}$ be against the soundness of the stoRNA scheme. Let the extractor PoSt.Ext $= (\text{Ext}_{\text{PoSt},1}, \text{Ext}_{\text{PoSt},2})$ recover the data F from the prover. Where $\text{Ext}_{\text{PoSt},1}$ on input the description of the prover, outputs the configurations, the epoch (a randomly chosen time slot) and the transition function, and $\text{Ext}_{\text{PoSt},2}$ is a PoR extractor that recovers the data from the configurations, the epoch and the transition function. Intuitively, we first show that the prover executes "one PoR" in a randomly chosen epoch and then by invoking the PoR extractor, we recover the data from the configurations the epoch and the transition function (extraction phase).

We first argue about the sequenciality in Algorithm 1. A potentially malicious prover PoSt.P', making the verifier accept (in relation to G_n^{Com} in Algorithm 2) with high probability must have queried H "almost" N times sequentially. The proof of sequentiality follows Cohen and Pietrzak [7]. We use the outputs of PoR.Prove as the input nodes of the specified tree construction of [7]. Thus, the sequentiality proof of Algorithm 1 follows the sequentiality proof of [7]. Formally we have that,

Lemma 1. [Theorem 1 of [7]]. Consider the scheme in Algorithm 1, with parameters c, w, N and a "soundness gap" $\alpha > 0$. If PoSt.P' makes at most $(1 - \alpha)N$ sequential queries to H, and at most q queries in total, then PoSt.V will output reject with probability $1 - (1 - \alpha)^c - (2 \cdot n \cdot w \cdot q^2)/2^w$.

Where N is assumed to be number of sequential steps of the form $N = 2^{n+1} - 1$ for an integer $n \in \mathbb{N}$, and c is a statistical security parameter (the size of the subset I^* in which the larger the c the better the soundness), and w is the output range of H, which we need to be collision-resistant and sequential. $w = 256$ is a typical value. The proof follows the proof of Theorem 1 in [7].

In general, the verification algorithm of the stoRNA requires the prover to compute all PoR challenges and responses and evaluate the PoEts. Thus the PoR responses are valid and the PoEt are evaluated as expected with probability $(1 - \alpha)^c - (2 \cdot n \cdot w \cdot q^2)/2^w$ based on Lemma 1. Because of the unpredictability of PoR and the sequentiality of PoEt, the PoR proofs must be generated sequentially.

Let D_0 and D_k be the start and end time points for running $\mathcal{A}$. For i from 1 to $k - 1$, we set each time point D_{i+1} to be the first time when $\mathcal{A}$ queries the random oracle H on $(\text{st} \| l_e)$ (Alg.1 step 17). Similarly, we set each time point $\hat{D}_i$ as the start when $\mathcal{A}$ queries the H on st (Alg.1 step 13). Then we prove that the random time epoch with length $T > T' + 2\delta D$ chosen by $\text{Ext}_{\text{PoSt},1}$ must contain at least one interval $[D_i, \hat{D}_i)$ for some i. To this aim, we prove the following lemmas 2, 3, 4, and 5:

Lemma 2. The time point D_i must precede D_{i+1}.

Proof. we show that each PoEt's output st_{i-1} must be firstly queried to the random oracle H before st_i. To prove it we use the contradiction in a way that, if not, then $\mathcal{A}$ must be able to either generate the PoEt output st_i before st_{i-1}, which violates the sequentiality of PoEt; or generate the PoEt input st_{i-1} before the output of H (step 17, Algorithm 1), which violates the unpredictability of the random oracle H; or generate the PoR challenge c_i before st_{i-1}, which violates the unpredictability of the random oracle H (step 13, Algorithm 1); or generate the PoR response π_i before c_i, which violates the unpredictability of PoR;

Lemma 3. T' is shorter than the length of each time slot $[D_i, D_{i+1})$.

Proof. By the unpredictability of the random oracle, the output of the PoEt, st_i must be generated before the time point D_{i+1}. On the other hand, the PoR response π_i must be generated via the PoR on the challenge st_i after the time point D_i. Thus, a PoEt function must be evaluated within the time slot $[D_i, D_{i+1})$. By the sequentiality of PoEt, the length of $[D_i, D_{i+1})$ must be longer than T'.

Lemma 4. $T' + \delta D$ is bigger than the length of each time slot $[D_i, D_{i+1})$.

Proof. Let D' be the execution time of PoSt.P'. By the correctness of the verification algorithm, $D' < (1 + \delta)D$. Based on the result of Lemma 3 , we have that the length of each time slot $[D_i, D_{i+1})$ is longer than T', thus, the longest slot should be shorter than $(1 + \delta)D - (k - 1)T' = \delta D + T'$.

Lemma 5. Each $\hat{D}_i \in [D_i, D_{i+1})$ and the time slot $[D_i, \hat{D}_i)$ is shorter than δD.

Proof. Finally, we show the PoEt response st_i must be queried to the random oracle H (Algorithm1 step 13) within this time slot $[D_i, D_{i+1})$ and that the time slot $[D_i, \hat{D}_i)$ is shorter than δT. The output of the PoR π_i is queried at the time point D_{i+1}, hence the input of the PoR, c_i must be generated by PoSt.P' before the time D_{i+1} according to the sequentiality of PoR. Due to the unpredictability of the random oracle, H must be queried on input st_i before the time D_{i+1}. On the other hand, according to the unpredictability of PoEt, PoSt.P' can not figure out the PoEt proof st_i before the time point D_i, when the PoEt input is generated. Given this, st_i must be queried to the random oracle H in time slot $[D_i, D_{i+1})$. Furthermore, since the maximum length of $[D_i, D_{i+1})$ and the evaluation time of PoEt is longer than T', the slot $[D_i, \hat{D}_i) < \delta D$.

Extraction Phase. In this phase, we show that given the bunch of configurations for PoSt.P' for time slot $[D_i, \hat{D}_i)$ (or $[D_{i-1}, \hat{D}_{i-1})$) and the code of the transition function, c_i and st_i can be accessed by the PoSt.Ext. Indeed, since both random oracles H are maintained by the extractor, a cheating prover of PoR.P' can be constructed by manipulating the output of the random oracle H (step 13, Algorithm 1) as the PoR challenge, rewinding the part of the PoSt.P' corresponding to time segment $[D_i, \hat{D}_i)$ and collecting the queries of the random oracle H (step 17, Algorithm 1) as the PoR response. Since there is a PoR extractor to recover the storage data from PoR.P′, the soundness proof of PoSt is complete.

B   Stateless Multi-prover PoSt Construction

In this section we show improvement options to the concrete efficiency of prover algorithm by proposing an extended multi-prover PoSt construction mstoRNA = (Store, Prove, Verify) (see Algorithm 3 for details). More precisely, we assume any arbitrary number of "Time Nodes" and "Storage Nodes" can freely join the DSN by respectively providing "CPU work" and "storage-time" resources to the network. mstoRNA.Store algorithm is executed to output file F_j and tag tg_j which are outsourced to Storage Node j. In stoRNA.Prove algorithm, (i) Time Node, every T time units, shares the PoEt state and waits for a time gap determined by network latency. (ii) Storage Node j hosting file F_j, generates a challenge based on the freshly advertised PoEt state, serving as the PoR challenge, and submits $\pi_{ij} \leftarrow$ PoR.Prove. (iii) Time Node collects all PoR proofs from all Storage Nodes and creates a Merkle tree MT_i with root r_i. (iv) Time Node inputs r_i together with PoEt proof to update the commitment graph G_n^{Com}, and (v) Time Node timestamps the updated G_n^{Com} root, l_ϵ, into the shared PoEt state for the next PoEt execution. At the end of the deposit period D, the Time Node returns l_ϵ together with the final PoEt state as a commitment to all proofs sequentially generated during D. Upon receiving the commitment, in mstoRNA.Verify algorithm, (i) the verifier challenges a randomly sampled subset of time slots (ii) for every challenged time slot, the Time Node provides openings for both G_n^{Com} and Merkle tree MT_i together with all the (PoEt, PoR) proofs on the path from this challenged node to the root, (iii) the verifier, verifies commitment openings of both MT_i and G_n^{Com}, and (iv) runs PoEt.Verify, PoR.Verify algorithms to respectively verify the returned PoEt, PoR proofs. As the number of Storage Nodes connected to a Time Node increases, the overall computational complexity of the prover algorithm diminishes. This enables even personal resource-constrained devices to partake in DSNs by dedicating some amount of disk-space, resulting in more decentralization. Besides, a PoSt sequence in mstoRNA can migrate to any other Time Node, who can continue where the previous prover left off. This is particularly important considering real nodes susceptible to Failure.

Algorithm 3. mstoRNA Construction

mstoRNA.Store
input data file F^* and (PoR.sk, PoR.pk)
$(F, \text{tg}) \leftarrow$ PoR.Store(PoR.sk, PoR.pk, F^*)   ▷ repeat this for different files outsourced to m storage nodes
sample random seed $rs \leftarrow^\$ \{0,1\}^w$
output (rs, F, tg)

mstoRNA.Prove
Time Node
input random seed rs, deposit time D, and audit frequency T
set $i \leftarrow 0$ and $et \leftarrow 0$
set st $\leftarrow rs$
while $et \leq D$ **do**
   st $\leftarrow$ PoEt.Prove(T, st)
   advertise st
   $i \leftarrow i + 1$
   $h_i \leftarrow$ st
   wait to receive PoR proofs from storage nodes   ▷ wait time is determined based on average network roundtrip time (RTT)
   for all $j \in [1, m]$ **do**
      $r_i \leftarrow$ MT.AppendLeaf(π_{ij}) ▷ create a Merkle tree with PoRs received from Storage Nodes
   $l_e \leftarrow G_n^{\text{Com}}$.Update($v = i, \mathcal{V} = h_i \parallel r_i$)   ▷ Algorithm 2
   st $\leftarrow$ H(st $\parallel l_e$)
   $et \leftarrow et + T$
$N \leftarrow i$
$H_{FNL} \leftarrow$ st
output Com $= (H_{FNL}, l_e)$

Storage Node
node j input processed file F_j, tag tg_j, deposit time D, and audit frequency T
periodically input advertised state st
$c_i \leftarrow$ H(st)
$\pi_{ij} \leftarrow$ PoR.Prove(PoR.pk, F_j, tg_j, c_i)
output π_{ij}

mstoRNA.Verify
input commitment Com, tag $\{\text{tg}_j\}_{j \in [1,m]}$, seed rs, public key PoR.pk
generate random $c-$element subset $I^* \subset [1, N]$ and send it to all provers.
wait to receive $\{h_i, r_i, \pi_{ij}, \{l_k\}_{k \in \Delta_i}\}_{i \in I^*}$, where $\Delta_i = \{i[1, j-1] \parallel 1 - i[j]\}_{j \in [1,n]}$
                    ▷ Δ_i contains commitment openings for both G_n^{Com} and MT_i
for all $i \in I^*$ **do**
   $c_i \leftarrow$ H(h_i)
   for all $j \in [1, m]$ **do**
      if MT.Verify(r_i, π_{ij}) $= false$ **then** return false   ▷ verify MT_i opening
      if PoR.Verify(PoR.pk, $\text{tg}_j, \pi_{ij}, c_i$) $= false$ **then** return false
   if $l_i \neq$ H($i, r_i, l_{p_1}, \ldots, l_{p_d}$), where $(p_1, \ldots, p_d) =$ Parents(i) **then** return false
   if $\exists j \in \Delta_i : l_j \neq$ H($j, l_{j\parallel 0}, l_{j\parallel 1}$) **then** return false   ▷ verify G_n^{Com} opening
   if PoEt.Verify(T, h_i) $= false$ **then** return false
return true

Theorem 2. *Let* PoR *be a stateless PoR scheme with ϵ-soundness and unpredictability. Let* PoEt *be a PoEt scheme with δ-evaluation time. The time cost of* PoR *and hash function evaluation are negligible w.r.t. T. The time cost of s_0 sequential steps on the server processor is T'. If $T' + 2\delta D < T$, the proposed* mstoRNA *scheme in Algorithm 3 is stateless, complete, and ϵ-sound.*

References

1. Ateniese, G., et al.: Provable data possession at untrusted stores. In: Proceedings of the 14th ACM Conference on Computer and Communications Security, pp. 598–609. ACM (2007)
2. Ateniese, G., Chen, L., Etemad, M., Tang, Q.: Proof of storage-time: Efficiently checking continuous data availability. In: NDSS (2020)

3. Ateniese, G., Di Pietro, R., Mancini, L.V., Tsudik, G.: Scalable and efficient provable data possession. In: Proceedings of the 4th International Conference on Security and Privacy in Communication Netowrks. ACM (2008)

4. Ben-Sasson, E., Chiesa, A., Tromer, E., Virza, M.: Succinct non-interactive zero knowledge for a von neumann architecture. In: 23rd USENIX Security (2014)

5. Bertrand Portier: Always on: Business considerations for continuous availability. http://www.redbooks.ibm.com/redpapers/pdfs/redp5090.pdf, 2014

6. Boneh, D., Bonneau, J., Bünz, B., Fisch, B.: Verifiable Delay Functions. In: Shacham, H., Boldyreva, A. (eds.) Advances in Cryptology – CRYPTO 2018: 38th Annual International Cryptology Conference, Santa Barbara, CA, USA, August 19–23, 2018, Proceedings, Part I, pp. 757–788. Springer International Publishing, Cham (2018). https://doi.org/10.1007/978-3-319-96884-1_25

7. Cohen, B., Pietrzak, K.: Simple proofs of sequential work. In: Nielsen, J.B., Rijmen, V. (eds.) Advances in Cryptology – EUROCRYPT 2018: 37th Annual International Conference on the Theory and Applications of Cryptographic Techniques, Tel Aviv, Israel, April 29 - May 3, 2018 Proceedings, Part II, pp. 451–467. Springer International Publishing, Cham (2018). https://doi.org/10.1007/978-3-319-78375-8_15

8. Dziembowski, S., Faust, S., Kolmogorov, V., Pietrzak, K.: Proofs of Space. In: Gennaro, R., Robshaw, M. (eds.) CRYPTO 2015. LNCS, vol. 9216, pp. 585–605. Springer, Heidelberg (2015). https://doi.org/10.1007/978-3-662-48000-7_29

9. Fiat, A., Shamir, A.: How to prove yourself: practical solutions to identification and signature problems. In: Odlyzko, A.M. (ed.) CRYPTO 1986. LNCS, vol. 263, pp. 186–194. Springer, Heidelberg (1987). https://doi.org/10.1007/3-540-47721-7_12

10. Juels, A., Kaliski Jr, B.S.: Pors: proofs of retrievability for large files. In: Proceedings of the 14th ACM Conference on Computer and Communications Security, pp. 584–597. ACM (2007)

11. Light Clients and Proof of Stake: https://blog.ethereum.org/2015/01/10/light-clients-proof-stake/

12. Mahmoody, M., Moran, T., Vadhan, S.: Publicly verifiable proofs of sequential work. In: Proceedings of the 4th conference on Innovations in Theoretical Computer Science, pp. 373–388 (2013)

13. Merkle, R.C.: Protocols for public key cryptosystems. In: IEEE Symposium on Security and Privacy 1980, pp. 122–122. IEEE (1980)

14. Moran, T., Orlov, I.: Simple proofs of space-time and rational proofs of storage. In: Boldyreva, A., Micciancio, D. (eds.) Advances in Cryptology – CRYPTO 2019: 39th Annual International Cryptology Conference, Santa Barbara, CA, USA, August 18–22, 2019, Proceedings, Part I, pp. 381–409. Springer International Publishing, Cham (2019). https://doi.org/10.1007/978-3-030-26948-7_14

15. Protocol Labs: Filecoin: A decentralized storage network (2018)

16. Rabaninejad, R., Attari, M.A., Asaar, M.R., Aref, M.R.: Comments on a lightweight cloud auditing scheme: Security analysis and improvement. J. Netw. Comput. Appl. **139**, 49–56 (2019)

17. Rabaninejad, R., Attari, M.A., Asaar, M.R., Aref, M.R.: A lightweight auditing service for shared data with secure user revocation in cloud storage. IEEE Trans. Serv. Comput. **15**(1), 1–15 (2019)

18. Rabaninejad, R., Liu, B., Michalas, A.: Port: non-interactive continuous availability proof of replicated storage. In: Proceedings of the 38th ACM/SIGAPP Symposium on Applied Computing, pp. 270–279 (2023)

19. Shacham, H., Waters, B.: Compact proofs of retrievability. In: Pieprzyk, J. (ed.) ASIACRYPT 2008. LNCS, vol. 5350, pp. 90–107. Springer, Heidelberg (2008). https://doi.org/10.1007/978-3-540-89255-7_7
20. Todd, P.: Merkle mountain range. https://github.com/opentimestamps/opentimestamps-server/blob/master/doc/merkle-mountain-range.md
21. Wesolowski, B.: Efficient verifiable delay functions. In: Annual International Conference on the Theory and Applications of Cryptographic Techniques (2019)
22. Wood, G., et al.: Ethereum: a secure decentralised generalised transaction ledger. Ethereum project yellow paper 151, 1–32 (2014)

Secure Approximate Nearest Neighbor Search with Locality-Sensitive Hashing

Shang Song, Lin Liu$^{(\boxtimes)}$, Rongmao Chen$^{(\boxtimes)}$, Wei Peng$^{(\boxtimes)}$, and Yi Wang

College of Computer Science and Technology, National University of Defense
Technology, Changsha, China
{songshang19,liulin16,chromao,wpeng,wangyi14}@nudt.edu.cn

Abstract. Ensuring both security and efficiency in Nearest Neighbor
Search (NNS) on large datasets remains a formidable challenge, as it
often leads to substantial computation and communication costs due to
the resource-intensive nature of ciphertext computations. To date, there
have been some solutions that are capable of handling privacy-preserving
NNS queries on big datasets. However, these approaches either impose
significant communication and computational burdens or compromise
security. In this paper, we introduce a novel framework, namely Secure-
ANNS, for secure approximate nearest neighbor search in the semi-honest
setting. Our approach begins by enhancing the building blocks of secure
NNS, specifically the multiplexer and comparison operations, through
oblivious transfer. We then adapt the plaintext Locality-Sensitive Hashing algorithm to select a smaller subset, reducing the need for extensive two-party computation. Finally, we introduce a new bucket retrieval
algorithm for efficient subset retrieval. Experimental results on various
datasets demonstrate that our SecureANNS achieves a speedup of 4×
and 14× compared to two state-of-the-art methods respectively.

Keywords: Nearest neighbor search · Privacy protection ·
Locality-sensitive hashing

1 Introduction

Nearest Neighbor Search (NNS) is a fundamental algorithmic problem widely
applied in fields such as recommendation systems [11], intrusion detection [30],
and network traffic analysis [51]. It involves finding the closest data point to
a query point under specific distance metrics (e.g., Euclidean or Hamming distance). However, in privacy-preserving scenarios, this seemingly simple query
becomes complex. Firstly, ensuring the privacy of the service provider's dataset
is paramount, as it is a valuable asset to the provider. Moreover, users' queries
and query results may also contain sensitive information, necessitating robust
data protection measures to gain user trust. Additionally, data leakage may result
in legal violations, such as the General Data Protection Regulation (GDPR) [52]
and the Health Insurance Portability and Accountability Act (HIPAA) [26].

© The Author(s), under exclusive license to Springer Nature Switzerland AG 2024
G. Tsudik et al. (Eds.): ESORICS 2023, LNCS 14346, pp. 411–430, 2024.
https://doi.org/10.1007/978-3-031-51479-1_21

Ideally, both dataset owners and query users might seek to enjoy high-quality service without revealing any information about their data to each other. Early attempts at achieving this goal were based on linear scanning which turns out to be impractical for large datasets containing millions or billions of data points [40,45]. As a result, there has been a surge of research on Approximate Nearest Neighbor Search (ANNS) algorithms that prioritize efficiency over exact accuracy [14,49,50,58]. In ANNS, query results consist of neighbors close enough to the query point without the need to examine all data points exhaustively. However, while efforts have been made to secure ANNS in large datasets [14,49], several performance and security challenges remain to be addressed:

- Performance limitations in current secure two-party computation (2PC) functions, such as secure comparison.
- Low efficiency in existing subset retrieval algorithms, especially when dealing with large-sized subsets.
- Concerns about concrete efficiency in traditional Oblivious RAM (ORAM) protocols, despite favorable asymptotic complexity.
- Potential extraction of distance information from query results by users.

1.1 Our Contributions

To tackle the challenges mentioned above, in this paper, we present SecureANNS, a novel protocol for securely performing approximate nearest neighbor searches in the semi-honest adversary setting. Our main contributions are as follows:

New Multiplexer and Comparison Algorithms. We introduce a novel batching technique for correlated oblivious transfer (COT), enabling participants to batch COTs with different choice bits based on correlation. As depicted in Table 1, this advancement leads to the development of a secure multiplexer algorithm with optimal communication complexity compared to previous works [37,43,47,48]. Additionally, we improve secure comparison protocols by designing optimized methods for correlated bit triple generation, achieving optimal communication and computation costs (see Table 2 for a detailed comparison).

Modified LSH-Based NNS Algorithm. We modify the standard Locality-sensitive hashing (LSH)-based plaintext ANNS algorithm [34] to meet the security and performance requirements in the privacy-preserving scenario. Our modified LSH algorithm includes a new retrieval algorithm that reduces the number of calls of the most time-consuming ciphertext computations and results in smaller subset datasets, consequently enhancing SecureANNS's performance.

Private Bucket Retrieval. We optimize the implementation of private bucket retrieval adopted by [49] in several ways, including reducing the distributed point function (DPF) domain, introducing early termination optimization via Boolean sharing and Boolean-to-Arithmetic conversion, and leveraging the AVX2 instruction set for faster computation. These optimizations significantly reduce the cost of the private bucket retrieval module, improving overall system efficiency.

In summary, our SecureANNS presents advancements in multiplexer and comparison algorithms, a modified LSH-based NNS algorithm, and an optimized private bucket retrieval module. Our theoretical analyses and experimental results demonstrate that SecureANNS achieves substantial speed improvements over state-of-the-art methods while preserving privacy.

Related Works. Prior privacy-preserving nearest neighbor search schemes have typically struggled with small-scale datasets due to performance limitations. Some designs, such as those utilizing homomorphic encryption [50,58], have achieved favorable communication rounds but suffer from significant computational overhead. Even with parallelization across multiple cores, processing only a few thousand feature vectors can take hours. Secure multi-party computation-based designs offer reduced computational requirements, but the use of oblivious transfer and garbled circuits introduces substantial communication overhead, limiting scalability. Notably, there are two schemes capable of handling million-level datasets. One approach [14] employs clustering for dataset preprocessing and combines various techniques for subset extraction and computation. Another recent work [49] offers malicious security using locality-sensitive hashing (LSH), but its comparison-free technique results in a certain level of information leakage. Further details of both protocols can be found in Sect. 4.

1.2   System Model and Thread Model

System Model. As illustrated in Fig. 1, this work assumes the two non-colluding server setting just like [49]. Two servers each obtain a copy of the dataset from the data provider in the setup phase. After receiving query shares from clients, these servers cooperate with each other to do secure two-party computation and return shares of NNS results to the

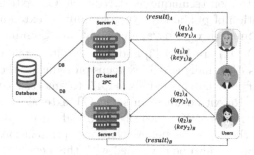

Fig. 1. System Model

clients. We remark that such a distributed trust model is acceptable not only in the research community [1,7,18] but also in practice [22].

Threat Model. We assume all parties in our design are semi-honest (a.k.a. honest-but-curious), which means they strictly follow the protocol but may attempt to infer additional information from others. Specifically, our security guarantees can be summarized as follows:

- *Data Privacy.* Ensuring that the dataset details are not disclosed to clients.
- *Query Privacy.* Preventing cloud servers from revealing the client's query.
- *Result privacy.* Restricting access to query results to only the legitimate user.
- *Access Pattern Privacy.* Ensuring that cloud servers cannot infer relevant information about queries from memory access patterns.

2 Preliminaries

2.1 Arithmetic Secret Sharing

For the 2-out-of-2 arithmetic secret sharing [6] used in this work, a value x is split into random shares $\langle x \rangle_0^t$ and $\langle x \rangle_1^t$ in the ring $\mathbb{Z}_t$ with the only constrain that $\langle x \rangle_0^t + \langle x \rangle_1^t \equiv x \bmod t$. For simplicity, we omit the superscript if t is clear from the context.

2.2 Oblivious Transfer

Our protocol relies heavily on oblivious transfer (OT) for 2-party computation on the candidate set, especially 1-out-of-2 correlated OT and 1-out-of-k OT. In 1-out-of-k OT functionality [10], denoted by $\binom{k}{1}$-OT_l, a sender inputs k l-bit strings $m_0, ..., m_{k-1} \in (0,1)^l$ and the receiver inputs an index $j \in [k]$. Then the receiver obtains m_j and the sender gets no output. In addition, general 1-out-of-2 OT [27,46] is a special case of $k = 2$. 1-out-of-2 correlated OT (COT) [3], denoted by $\binom{2}{1}$-COT_l, is frequently used in our batching scenarios. $\binom{2}{1}$-COT_l generates correlated outputs for 2 parties, a sender inputs a value Δ and receiver inputs a choice bit c, at the end the function outputs a random value $r \in \mathbb{Z}_{2^l}$ to the sender and $-r + c\Delta$ to the receiver.

Ishai et al. proposed OT extension [35] (hereafter, we will refer to this OT extension technique as IKNP-style OT extension) to reduce the heavy computation of public key cryptography by extending a few base OT instances with symmetric cryptographic operations. Communication required for $\binom{2}{1}$-COT_l and $\binom{k}{1}$-OT_l are $\lambda + l$ [3] and $2\lambda + kl$ [36], excluding setup cost for base OT phase. As l is usually small, we focus on reducing the number of OT instances by using different batching skills [44,47] to amortize communication.

Recent advances in silent-OT extension [20,54] show us a new direction for designing MPC protocols. Although such a pre-processing model is not our focus in the paper, we believe that our optimizations utilized in IKNP-style OT extension can also be combined with this new technique.

2.3 Distributed Point Function

Previous work such as SANNS [14] uses Floram [25] to retrieve subsets of data points securely. Despite the use of symmetric cipher with less number of AND gates to reduce communication, the bandwidth of this part is still a big burden. In this paper, we utilize the distributed point function to hide access patterns when retrieving buckets. DPF is also called the function secret sharing scheme for point functions. We briefly introduce the scheme with several definitions.

Definition 1 (Function Secret Sharing, FSS). Unlike previous secret sharing schemes for individual elements, function secret sharing [8,9] split function f into separate keys. Each party evaluates its own key with input x and generates a secret share of $f(x)$. Note that parties can not infer any information about function f only from their own keys.

Definition 2 (Point Function). A point function $f_{\alpha,\beta} : \{0,1\}^n \rightarrow \{0,1\}^m$ is defined as follows:

$$f_{\alpha,\beta}(x) = \begin{cases} \beta, & \text{if } x = \alpha \\ 0, & \text{otherwise} \end{cases}$$

Here we only discuss the special case of $\beta = 1$.

Definition 3 (Distributed Point Function, DPF). A two-party distributed point function [8,32] is a function secret sharing scheme for such point function class and consists of two Probabilistic Polynomial Time (PPT) algorithms:

1. Key generation algorithm $\mathbf{Gen}(1^\lambda, (\alpha, 1))$ inputs security parameter λ and point function $f_{\alpha,1}$, then outputs a pair of DPF keys $\langle key \rangle_0$ and $\langle key \rangle_1$.
2. Evaluation algorithm $\mathbf{Eval}(\langle key \rangle_b, x)$ inputs P_b's DPF key $\langle key \rangle_b$, $b \in \{0,1\}$, and evaluation on point $x \in \{0,1\}^n$, then outputs a value y_b^x which satisfies $f_{\alpha,\beta}(x) = y_0^x + y_1^x$.

The security of DPF depends on two properties, correctness and privacy. We recommend [8,9,32] for more details.

2.4 Locality-Sensitive Hashing

Locality-sensitive hashing (LSH) is an efficient method for approximate nearest neighbor search. The key idea of LSH is to hash data points close to each other into the same buckets with high probability. For a dataset $P \subset \mathbb{R}^d$ and output space X, we formally describe LSH as:

Definition 4 (Locality-Sensitive Hashing). A hash family $\mathcal{H} = \{h : \mathbb{R}^d \rightarrow X\}$ is called (R, cR, p_1, p_2)-sensitive if for any two points $v, q \in \mathbb{R}^d$

- if $q \in \boldsymbol{B}(v, R)$ then $\Pr_{\mathcal{H}}[h(q) = h(v)] \geq p_1$,
- if $q \notin \boldsymbol{B}(v, cR)$ then $\Pr_{\mathcal{H}}[h(q) = h(v)] \leq p_2$.

where $c > 1$, $p_1 > p_2$ and $\boldsymbol{B}(v, R)$ denotes the ball of radius R centered at v.

An LSH family is often combined with a universal hash function $\mathcal{H}_u = \{h : X \rightarrow U\}$ to fix the output range to U [21] ($\mathbb{Z}_{2^n}$ for example). However, such $\mathcal{H}_u$ may introduce fake collisions if n is too small, that is, data points with different LSH collide because of the random collision caused by universal hashing. We emphasize in advance that the discussion on the choice of n is an important part of this paper to achieve performance improvement.

Definition 5 ((c, r)-Approximate Near Neighbor Search Problem). Given a distance scale $r > 0$ and an approximation factor $c > 1$, build a data structure that if $\boldsymbol{B}(q, r) \cap P \neq \emptyset$ holds for a query q, return a point $p' \in P$ such that $p' \in \boldsymbol{B}(q, cr)$.

LSH can be used to solve the (c, r)-NN problem: Choose a family of (r, cr, p_1, p_2)-sensitive hash functions and store each point $v \in P$ in the bucket

$h(v)$ in the preprocessing phase, then compare the query with points in bucket $h(q)$ to return a point within distance cr. The data structure can be further used to solve the nearest neighbor problem by brute-force comparison with all the points in bucket $h(q)$ and returning the closest one.

Certain optimizations can be made to get better searching efficiency, including multiple hash tables, multi-probing [42], and amplification [2].

3   Building Blocks for Exact NNS with Oblivious Transfer

Secure exact NNS problem has been widely studied in the research community [15,40,53,57]. It requires the query to scan all points in the database and obtain the nearest neighbor without approximation. We point out that such an exact search algorithm is an important part of our sublinear protocol as we still need to do a linear scan on the final candidate dataset. The exact NNS algorithm consists of distance computation and Top 1 selection (calculate the ID of the closest point), the latter can be further divided into comparison and multiplexer.

We optimize the Top 1 selection using oblivious transfer only. Throughout our optimizations, we make extensive use of batching techniques of COT to narrow bandwidth. So we first introduce a batching method used in previous works in Sect. 3.1. Then we illustrate our batching idea in the context of multiplexer in Sect. 3.2. We propose our improved comparison algorithm in Sect. 3.3. In addition, our sub-protocols can be combined with a newly popular silent OT extension in the pre-processing model.

Table 1. Communication for Π^l_{MUX}

Protocol	Imple.	Func.	Comm.
GC [37]	[38] [56]	Full	$2\lambda l$
OT [48]	$2 \times \text{GOT}_l$	$y = 0$	$2\lambda + 4l$
OT [47]	$2 \times \text{COT}_l$	$y = 0$	$2\lambda + 2l$
OT [43]	$4 \times \text{COT}_l$	Full	$4\lambda + 4l$
This work	$2 \times \text{COT}_{2l}$	Full	$2\lambda + 4l$

Table 2. Communication for Π^l_{CMP}

Protocol	Comm.	Rounds
GC [38,56]	$2\lambda l$	2
GMW [29]	$\approx 6\lambda l$	$\log l + 3$
OT [19](SC3)	$> 3\lambda l$	$\approx \log^* l$
OT [48]$(m = 4)$	$< (\lambda l + 14l)$	$\log l$
This work(SC1)	$< (\lambda l + 6l)$	$\log l$
This work(SC2)	$< (\lambda l + 4l)$	$\log l$

3.1   Revisiting COT Batching in Previous Works

Considering the problem of multiplying two integers s and t in the ring $\mathbb{Z}_l$, we parse s as $s[l]||...||s[1]$. As Gilboa et al. [31] first observed COT can be used to compute the product of two values. In a high level, two parties invoke l instances of COT_l where $f(x_i) = x_i + t \cdot 2^{i-1} \bmod 2^l$ is the sender's correlation function and $s[i]$ is the receiver's choice bit in the ith COT_l. To further improve efficiency, authors of [23] find that the last i bits will be cut off in the ith COT_l. Therefore, the length of ith COT can be reduced to $l - i$.

Later in [44], multiplication of a $|B| \times d$ matrix $\mathbf{A}$ and a d-dimensional vector $\mathbf{B}$ is discussed. They leverage the matrix structure as follows. Since each element b_j in $\mathbf{B}$ is multiplied by a column of elements, the same choice bit $b_j[i]$ will be used in $|B|$ COTs. However, they pack those $|B|$ instances of COT_{l-i} into $\lceil \frac{(l-i) \cdot |B|}{128} \rceil$ instances of COT_{128}. Recent work [47] further batches them into a single COT of length $|B| \cdot (l - i)$, in which the mask of this COT can be extended using a PRG. We call this method the same choice bit COT batching (scbCB).

3.2   Batched Multiplexer

Secure multiplexer is a widely used nonlinear tool in MPC [37, 40, 43], as summarized in Table 1. It takes choice bit c and two l-bit values x and y as inputs, all in secret shared form, and returns y if $c = 0$ or x otherwise. We represent the functionality as $z = c \cdot x + \bar{c} \cdot y$.

Observation. Due to the following correlation $c \oplus \bar{c} = (\langle c \rangle_0 \oplus \langle \bar{c} \rangle_0) \oplus (\langle c \rangle_1 \oplus \langle \bar{c} \rangle_1) = 1$, each party could deduce the XOR of two bits hold by the other from the XOR of two bits hold by itself. For example, P_0 can get correlation of $\langle c \rangle_1$ and $\langle \bar{c} \rangle_1$ from $\langle c \rangle_1 \oplus \langle \bar{c} \rangle_1 = 1 \oplus (\langle c \rangle_0 \oplus \langle \bar{c} \rangle_0)$. Utilizing this property, each party could batch 2 instances of COT_l into 1 instance of COT_{2l} as the OT sender to reduce the number of OT instances. We further explain our design in detail.

[47] rewrites $c \cdot x = (\langle c \rangle_0 + \langle c \rangle_1 - 2\langle c \rangle_0 \cdot \langle c \rangle_1) \cdot (\langle x \rangle_0 + \langle x \rangle_1) = \langle c \rangle_0 \cdot \langle x \rangle_0 + \langle c \rangle_1 \cdot (\langle x \rangle_0 - 2\langle c \rangle_0 \cdot \langle x \rangle_0) + \langle c \rangle_1 \cdot \langle x \rangle_1 + \langle c \rangle_0 \cdot (\langle x \rangle_1 - 2\langle c \rangle_1 \cdot \langle x \rangle_1) \bmod 2^l$. Parties can compute the two terms $\langle c \rangle_0 \cdot \langle x \rangle_0$ and $\langle c \rangle_1 \cdot \langle x \rangle_1$ locally and other two cross terms with 2 instances of COT_l. In particular, to calculate $\langle c \rangle_0 \cdot (\langle x \rangle_1 - 2\langle c \rangle_1 \cdot \langle x \rangle_1)$, COT sender P_1 inputs correlation function $f(v) = v + \langle x \rangle_1 - 2\langle c \rangle_1 \cdot \langle x \rangle_1 \bmod 2^l$ and receiver P_0 inputs choice bit $\langle c \rangle_0$. Similarly, other two COT_l instances are needed when calculating $\langle \bar{c} \rangle_0 \cdot (\langle y \rangle_1 - 2\langle \bar{c} \rangle_1 \cdot \langle y \rangle_1)$ and $\langle \bar{c} \rangle_1 \cdot (\langle y \rangle_0 - 2\langle \bar{c} \rangle_0 \cdot \langle c \rangle_0)$ of $\bar{c} \cdot y$.

We take a close look at those two COT_l instances in which P_0 plays the role of OT sender, namely $\langle c \rangle_1 \cdot (\langle x \rangle_0 - 2\langle c \rangle_0 \cdot \langle x \rangle_0)$ and $\langle \bar{c} \rangle_1 \cdot (\langle x \rangle_0 - 2\langle \bar{c} \rangle_0 \cdot \langle x \rangle_0)$. We denote $\langle x \rangle_j - 2\langle \bar{c} \rangle_j \cdot \langle x \rangle_j$ as Δ_j for simplicity. Since P_0 could deduce $\langle c \rangle_1 \oplus \langle \bar{c} \rangle_1$ from its $\langle c \rangle_0$ and $\langle \bar{c} \rangle_0$, we discuss the following two situations. If $\langle c \rangle_0 \oplus \langle \bar{c} \rangle_0 = 1$, which means $\langle c \rangle_1 = \langle \bar{c} \rangle_1$, then P_0 can batch its two inputs into one instance of COT_{2l} with the scbCB method described in Sect. 3.1. Otherwise $\langle c \rangle_1 = \langle \bar{c} \rangle_1 \oplus 1$, we illustrate how to construct such batched COT next and call our method different choice bit COT batching (dcbCB).

Suppose we already have an OT_{2l} instance, generated from random OT extension and derandomization for example, where P_0 is the sender with inputs (r_0, r_1) and P_1 is the receiver with choice bit $\langle c \rangle_1$ as input and $r_{\langle c \rangle_1}$ as output. P_0 parses its inputs as $r_0 = r_0[l] || r_0[r]$ and $r_1 = r_1[l] || r_1[r]$, P_1 parses its input as $r_{\langle c \rangle_1} = r_{\langle c \rangle_1}[l] || r_{\langle c \rangle_1}[r]$. Recall that the bandwidth saving of COT comes from setting the first message to be sent as 0. So if $\langle c \rangle_1 = 0$, we set the random value of our batched COT_{2l} equal to r_0. At this time, two parties should obtain secret-shared 0 and Δ_1 from the batched COT, so we set P_0's

---

Algorithm 1. Multiplexer, Π_{MUX}^l

Input: For $b \in \{0,1\}$, P_b holds c_b, $\bar{c}_b$, x_b and y_b.
Output: For $b \in \{0,1\}$, P_b learns z_b s.t. $z = x$ if $c = 1$, else $z = y$.
1: P_0 sets $c' = 1 - (c_0 \oplus \bar{c}_0)$, $\Delta_0 = (x_0 - 2c_0 *_l x_0)$, $\Delta_1 = (x_0 - 2\bar{c}_0 *_l x_0)$.
2: If $c' = 0$, P_0 and P_1 invoke an instance of COT_{2l} using scbCB.
3: Else, P_0 and P_1 invoke an instance of COT_{2l} using dcbCB, where P_0 is the sender with correlation function $f(x_1||x_2) = ((x_1 + \Delta_0)||(x_2 - \Delta_1))$ and P_1 is the receiver with input c_1 and output tmp_1. P_0 gets tmp_0 from function $f(x_1||x_2) = ((-x_1)||(\Delta_1 - x_2))$.

---

output as $-r_0[l]||(\Delta_1 - r_0[r])$. Else $\langle c \rangle_1 = 1$, two parties should obtain secret-shared Δ_0 and 0, which means the only message P_0 receive from the COT is $((r_0[l] + \Delta_0)||(r_0[r] - \Delta_1)) \oplus r_1$. Our batched multiplexer algorithm is provided in Algorithm 1.

3.3   Correlated Bit Triples for Comparison

Secure comparison Π_{CMP}, also known as millionaires' problem [55], is another fundamental building block of many algorithms. Naive comparison protocols take two l-bit values x and y as inputs and output $1\{x < y\}$ in secret shared form. In this section, we propose two different methods for generating correlated bit triples, which can be applied later in achieving a more efficient comparison protocol than state-of-the-art [48]. Considering that inputs in our scenario are also secretly shared, we use a reduction lemma from [19] to non-interactively reduce our problem into the naive one.

We give a brief introduction to comparison protocol in [48]:

1) Two parties split their inputs into m-bit blocks x_i and y_i. Then they compute equality and comparison on those blocks, denoted $\text{eq}_i = 1\{x_i = y_i\}$ and $\text{lt}_i = 1\{x_i < y_i\}$ separately, using $\lceil l/m \rceil$ instances of $\binom{2^m}{1}$-OT_2.
2) Comparison of longer strings can be achieved according to the following property first noticed in [29]: $\text{lt} = \text{lt}_1 \oplus (\text{eq}_1 \wedge \text{lt}_0)$, where $x = x_1||x_0$ and $y = y_1||y_0$. In addition, two parties also need to compute $\text{eq}_1 \wedge \text{eq}_0$ to get eq on intermediate nodes of the evaluation tree. [48] observes that eq_1 are used twice in bit multiplication and uses one instance of $\binom{8}{1}$-OT_2 to generate correlated bit triples.

Correlated bit triples are two-bit triples [4] of the form $ab = c$ and $ad = e$. We use two different kinds of OTs to optimize those triple generations for saving bandwidth.

First, we further extend the $\binom{N}{1}$-OT method. [48] utilizes this correlation to reduce one instance of $\binom{16}{1}$-OT_2 [24] to one $\binom{8}{1}$-OT_2 and gets an amortized communication of $\lambda + 8$ bits per triple. However, if we batch four-bit triples into two correlated bit triples, which can be instantiated with an instance of $\binom{64}{1}$-OT_4, then our communication cost is $2\lambda + 64 \cdot 4$ bits. As a result, our amortized communication can be reduced to λ per triple. Although this approach obtains optimal communication cost, the use of $\binom{64}{1}$-OT_4 also introduces a large number of correlation robust function calls (instantiated with re-keyed AES [23, 24] for example, more clock cycles required than fixed-key AES [5, 33]), leading to a significant increase in computation overhead [14].

Second, we expand the formulas into $a_0 b_0 + a_1 b_1 + a_0 b_1 + a_1 b_0$ and $a_0 d_0 + a_1 d_1 + a_0 d_1 + a_1 d_0$. After computing local terms, the remaining cross-terms could be divided into two groups $(a_0 b_1, a_0 d_1)$ and $(a_1 b_0, a_1 d_0)$. The scbCB method can be adopted here again with 2 instances of COT_2 and gives us an amortized cost of $\lambda + 2$ bits per triple. Although the extra 2 bits are needed, this approach replaces those re-keyed AES with only 3 calls to fixed-key AES.

Besides, our goal is to calculate $eq_1 \wedge lt_0$ and $eq_1 \wedge eq_0$, we find that the 2 COT approach above can be used to do the computation directly without the help of those bit triples. As a result, the 6 additional bits are not needed any more and we achieve a new secure comparison algorithm SC2 with optimal computation and communication, Table 2 shows comparison with different designs.

3.4 Distance Computation

As described in Sect. 3.1, we follow the idea of [23] and combine it with batch COT to implement our distance computation Π_{DIS}. It should be noted that [47] also proposes a method to perform matrix multiplication with non-uniform bitwidths, which further reduces the communication overhead. However, in order to achieve such communication optimization, it extensively utilizes Π_{CMP} from [48] to implement the wrap function for overflow, introducing additional computational cost and communication rounds, thus significantly increasing end-to-end latency. Nevertheless, if parallelization can be utilized in specific scenarios to reduce amortized latency, we consider [47] as an alternative.

4   Sublinear Approximate NNS Protocol with LSH

As two state-of-the-art privacy-preserving approximate NNS schemes that scale to million-level size, [14] and [49] design their systems with different ideas.

The underlying plaintext ANNS algorithm of [14] is clustering, the server first preprocesses the dataset using the k-means algorithm [41] to construct balanced clusters. Later in the query phase, a client obliviously retrieves points from closest clusters to form a candidate set and then performs a brute force search in this smaller set by using two-party computation. Even if the massive overhead of preprocessing is not considered, a single query generates more than 1GB of communication and takes several seconds to process in a fast network for datasets with 1 million elements. We believe that the cost of their scheme is huge due to three main reasons. 1) Large candidate set. 120K points are chosen from dataset SIFT (1M points), which is not satisfying. 2) Expensive retrieval method. Floram consumes half of the bandwidth and processing time. 3) Costly 2PC overhead.

BFV [28] based distance computing and garbled circuit-based Top-k selection generate a big amount of computation and communication separately.

[49] adopts a creative design to avoid oblivious comparison using LSH. They generate the LSH data structure on a series of increasing neighbor radii R_i and bound the probability of false positive very low, which means if two points are hashed into the same bucket at radius R_i, then they have a high probability of being cR_i near neighbors. Therefore, they can select a point randomly from the first non-empty candidate set to meet the requirements, instead of brute-force comparison like trivial LSH approaches. Although this method achieves better performance than [14] in parallel, it is still possible to improve in the following aspects. 1) **Extra leakage.** Their design leaks more information than baseline leakage which only reveals the ANN to the client. 2) **Large universal hash range.** In order to reduce the accuracy loss caused by a random collision in the universal hashing phase, the universal hash range is set quite large, leading to the result that total processing time is dominated by private point retrieval using DPF.

4.1   Modified Plaintext Algorithm with LSH

Our plaintext ANNS idea is inspired by [49], we modify their method to adapt to our idea of brute-force comparison within subset and fix their leakage issue.

In order to eliminate costly oblivious comparison, [49] uses amplification to bound the probability of false-positive in the candidate set very low, namely (r, cr, p_1, p_2)-sensitive hash family $\mathcal{H}$ with a small p_2. As a result, points hashed into the same bucket are most likely within distance cr. Another problem is how to set the distance scale r without knowing the exact closest distance between the query and points in the database before utilizing the idea above. They use a series of increasing neighbor radii in a range, obtained from the distribution of closest distance on real datasets, to construct their data structure and choose randomly from the first non-empty candidate set.

We design our data structure in a similar way, but add some changes according to the following observation: in order to make the distance between every point selected randomly from the first non-empty candidate set and the query within cr with high probability (95% for example), [49] sets universal hashing range $\mathbb{Z}_{2^n}$ very large to bound the probability of fake collisions introduced by universal hashing, which is the main reason of false-positive. But in our design, a smaller n will not affect the number of true positives and the newly introduced fake collisions only increase the size of our candidate set. Therefore, we can carefully tune the LSH parameters to achieve a balance between less private bucket retrieval cost determined by DPF range $\mathbb{Z}_{2^n}$ and more oblivious comparison overhead caused by a larger candidate set size. Details are as follow.

Setting New Universal Hashing Range. To protect client privacy, Private Information Retrieval (PIR) [16] is used to obtain buckets from hash tables. In this paper, the universal hash range $\mathbb{Z}_{2^n}$, also as DPF domain, has a great impact on the performance of DPF-based two-server PIR and our plaintext LSH scheme allows a smaller n. On this basis, we further optimize the implementation of DPF to reduce the number of PRGs required. We discuss this problem in Sect. 4.2 and provide specific values with experimental results.

Bounding Capped Size for Hash Buckets. More collisions may occur with the narrowing of the universal hashing range, resulting in different bucket sizes. It's a regular method to fix the bucket size to prevent leakage caused by size information. In addition, DPF-based PIR also requires the same size for each data block. We choose different parameters and test their performances.

Tuning Number of Tables and Probes. In practice, multiple hash tables and probes are used in constructing the LSH data structure for better accuracy and query time. Although amplification expands the gap between p_1 and p_2, it also increases the number of tables required. We test the number of tables and probes needed to achieve specific accuracy on different datasets through experiments.

We present our plaintext ANNS data structure and query method in Algorithm 2 and Algorithm 3.

Algorithm 2. Construct LSH Data Structure

Input: Database $\mathcal{DB}$ with N points, L LSH families $\mathcal{H}_i$ corresponding to radius r_i, capped size cp.
Output: L hash functions h_i and hash tables T_i, query q.
1: **for** $i \leftarrow 1$ to L **do**
2:    Sample h_i from $\mathcal{H}_i$ randomly.
3:    **for** $j \leftarrow 1$ to N **do**
4:       Hash point v_j into bucket $\mathcal{B}_{h_i(v_j)}$.
5:    **end for**
6:    Construct hash table T_i by capping all non-empty buckets: if bucket size $|\mathcal{B}| < cp$, add $cp - |\mathcal{B}|$ dummy points to the bucket; if $|\mathcal{B}| > cp$, sample $|\mathcal{B}|$ points randomly from the bucket.
7:    Output LSH hash function h_i and hash table T_i.
8: **end for**

Algorithm 3. Query NN from LSH Hash Tables

Input: L hash functions h_i and corresponding hash tables T_i.
Output: IDs of the nearest neighbor.
1: **for** $i \leftarrow 1$ to L **do**
2:    Compute l bucket numbers via multi-probing: $(\alpha_1, ..., \alpha_l) \leftarrow \text{multiprobe}(h_i, q)$.
3:    **for** $j \leftarrow 1$ to l **do**
4:       Retrieve bucket $\mathcal{B}_{\alpha_j}$ from T_i.
5:    **end for**
6:    Set sub candidate set $\mathcal{C}_L := \mathcal{B}_{\alpha_1} \cup ... \cup \mathcal{B}_{\alpha_l}$.
7: **end for**
8: Set final candidate set $\mathcal{C} := \mathcal{C}_1 \cup ... \cup \mathcal{C}_L$.
9: Output the ID of the closest point after computing the distance between q and all points in the final candidate set.

4.2   Private Bucket Retrieval with DPF

The goal of our private retrieval algorithm is to extract data blocks used for subsequent exact NNS. We have described DPF in Sect. 2, which has been used to construct two-server private information retrieval (PIR) [16,17] in [8,9]. Now we use it as a tool to design our private bucket retrieval (PBR) algorithm.

Parameters: number of hash tables L, number of probes l.
Server Input: Database $\mathcal{DB}$.
Client Input: query q.

Setup
1. The servers compute L radii R_i from distribution of the closest distances and generate L LSH families $\mathcal{H}_1, ..., \mathcal{H}_L$ corresponding to $R_1, ..., R_L$.
2. The servers run Algorithm 2, send returned L hash functions to the client and store L hash tables.
3. Two servers agree on common randomness used later.

Step1: Client-side
1. for $i \in \{1, ..., L\}$:
1.1. Compute l probes $(\alpha_{i1}, ..., \alpha_{il})$ with multiprobe(h_i, q).
1.2. for $j \in \{1, ..., l\}$:
$(\langle key_{i,j}\rangle_0, \langle key_{i,j}\rangle_1) \leftarrow$ DPF.GEN$(1^\lambda, (\alpha_{i,j}, 1)))$.
2. $\langle \mathbf{K}\rangle_0 \leftarrow (\langle key_{1,1}\rangle_0, ..., \langle key_{L,l}\rangle_0)$ and $\langle \mathbf{K}\rangle_1 \leftarrow (\langle key_{1,1}\rangle_1, ..., \langle key_{L,l}\rangle_1)$.
3. Send $\langle \mathbf{K}\rangle_0$ and $\langle \mathbf{K}\rangle_1$ to cloud servers respectively.

Step2: Server-side
1. Parse $\langle \mathbf{K}\rangle = (\langle key_{1,1}\rangle, ..., \langle key_{L,l}\rangle)$.
2. for $i \in \{1, ..., L\}$ and for $j \in \{1, ..., l\}$:
2.1 $\alpha_{i,j} \leftarrow$ bucket key for table i, probe j.
2.2 $\mathcal{B}_{\alpha_{i,j}} \leftarrow \sum_1^m \oplus(Eval(\langle key_{i,j}\rangle, \alpha_{i,j}) \cdot \mathcal{B}_{i,j})$ retrieve bucket by keyword from table i with DPF.
3. $\mathcal{C}_b \leftarrow \mathcal{B}_{\alpha_{i,j}}$ combine all those buckets to get boolean share of the candidate set.
4. Perform B2A conversion to get the arithmetic share of the candidate set.
5. Perform secure distance computation on the secret shared candidate set.
6. Perform Top 1 selection in the form of a binary tree, involving the composition of secure comparison and multiplexer.
7. Return the share of NN's ID to the client.

Step3: client-side
Reconstruct NN's ID.

Fig. 2. Private NNS Protocol with LSH

In DPF-based two-server PIR, each server has an identical copy of the dataset divided into m buckets $\mathcal{B}$ of equal length. Suppose a client wants to retrieve the data bucket with index i, he generates DPF keys $\langle key\rangle_0$ and $\langle key\rangle_1$ for point function $f_{i,1}$ and send them to two servers. Then the servers evaluate all indexes

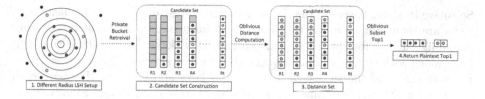

Fig. 3. Visualization of our algorithm

on their own key $\langle key \rangle_b$ and multiply each of them with the corresponding value. The sum of all those results is a secret share of $\mathcal{B}_i$. We call the above approach PIR with full domain DPF and illustrate it with the formula 1.

$$\sum_{j=1}^{m}(Eval(\langle key \rangle_b, j) \cdot \mathcal{B}_j) = \sum_{j=1, j \neq i}^{m}(\langle 0 \rangle_b \cdot \mathcal{B}_j) + \langle 1 \rangle_b \cdot \mathcal{B}_i = \langle \mathcal{B}_i \rangle_b. \qquad (1)$$

Recent advances in function secret sharing [8,9] further reduce the communication cost of DPF to $\lceil \sqrt{m} \rceil (\lambda + 2)$ bits, which greatly saves bandwidth when DPF domain is large. In addition, keyword-based DPF only calculates a part of the indexes within the DPF domain, which has much less computation cost than full domain DPF because the number of keywords is usually much smaller.

Compared with communication, the computation cost becomes the performance bottleneck of DPF-based PIR. We divide it into two parts: generation of bit array and sum of buckets. Because the retrieval algorithm aims to obtain data points in arithmetic sharing for two-party computation later, some designs use DPF in arithmetic sharing. In those works, they first generate arithmetic shared bit arrays and operate addition and multiplication over some integer ring. However, take [49] as an example, DPF cost for generating the bit array takes more than 1 s and becomes the main bottleneck. Obviously, such an efficiency imbalance has greatly affected the overall performance. To tackle this problem, we use the original XOR-based DPF to generate the bit array in Boolean shared first, which provides the possibility of reducing computation by amortizing the cost. The advantage of such a design is that it can greatly reduce the number of length-doubling PRGs required for DPF evaluation by utilizing early termination [9] as an optimization, thus greatly reducing computation. Then, we can use Boolean to Arithmetic conversion (B2A) [48] to convert the PIR output into arithmetic shares. This part together with computation in the candidate set are the extra costs of our amortized design.

4.3   Putting It All Together

With all those building blocks described before, we now give a high-level summary of our secure sublinear NNS protocol. Figure 3 provides a visual illustration.

First, the service provider sets the number of tables and probes corresponding to certain accuracy requirements and preprocesses the dataset with Locality-

Sensitive Hashing based on the distribution of nearest distances. The hash functions are then sent to users. Users use these hash functions to calculate corresponding buckets for the query and generate DPF keys. Users return the DPF keys, along with the secret shared query, to the cloud servers. The servers retrieve Boolean shares of the subset with those DPF keys and perform 2PC with each other using OT to determine the ID of the nearest data point. Finally, users reconstruct query results after receiving shares from cloud servers, completing the query process. We provide a description of the query procedure in Fig. 2.

4.4   Security Proofs

Theorem 1. The SecureANNS protocol is secure against semi-honest adversaries.

First we define the leakage collection $\mathcal{L}(P, \mathbf{q}) = (\text{dim}, \text{siz})$, where dim and siz are formally defined as follows:

- Dimension of a point (dim). $\text{dim} = |p_i|$, where $p_i \in P$ and $|x|$ is denoted as the length of x.
- Size of a dataset (siz). $\text{siz} = |P|$ denotes the number of points in dataset P.

Then, we prove the security of our SecureANNS in the framework of the simulation paradigm [12,39]. For the ease of explanation, we prove the secure comparison protocol Π_{CMP} for illustration.

Theorem 2. The Π_{CMP} protocol is $\mathcal{L}$-secure if both $\binom{M}{1}$-OT_1 and COT_2 are semantically secure.

Proof. Let $\mathcal{S}$ be a simulator and $\mathcal{A}$ be any probability polynomial time (PPT) adversary, we want to proof that the outputs of two games $Real_{\mathcal{A}}(\lambda)$ and $Idea_{\mathcal{A},\mathcal{S}}(\lambda)$ are computationally indistinguishable.

In the game $Real_{\mathcal{A}}(\lambda)$, given inputs x and y, Server B receives n/m bits $\langle \Pi_{\text{CMP}}^m \rangle_1^B$ via n/m $\binom{M}{1}$-OT_1. Then Server A and Server B gets their share of $\langle \Pi_{\text{CMP}}^n \rangle_1^B$ by several calls to COT_2. In the game $Idea_{\mathcal{A},\mathcal{S}}(\lambda)$, $\mathcal{S}$ simulates inputs as (r_1, r_2), runs protocol Π_{CMP}^n and gets the result $\langle s' \rangle$. Based on the simulator $\mathcal{S}$, no probability polynomial-time (PPT) adversary can distinguish the outputs of $Real_{\mathcal{A}}$ and $Idea_{\mathcal{A},\mathcal{S}}$ because of the security guarantee of $\binom{M}{1}$-OT_1 and COT_2. In addition, since inputs of Server A to n/m $\binom{M}{1}$-OT_1 are masked by random values, intermediate results in Π_{CMP}^n are obscured and indistinguishable to $\mathcal{A}$.

To sum up, $\mathcal{A}$ cannot distinguish views in $Real_{\mathcal{A}}(\lambda)$ and $Idea_{\mathcal{A},\mathcal{S}}(\lambda)$. Namely,

$$|Pr[Real_{\mathcal{A}}(\lambda) = 1] - Pr[Idea_{\mathcal{A},\mathcal{S}}(\lambda) = 1]| \leq negl(\lambda) \tag{2}$$

Similarly, Π_{MUX}, Π_{DIS}, Π_{PBR} can be proved secure under semi-honest (non-colluding) adversaries.

Composition Theorem [12]. Given a protocol Π consists of some sub-protocols, if all the sub-protocols are secure and all the intermediate results are random or pseudorandom, then protocol Π is secure.

Finally, we give the proof of Theorem 1 as follow: based on Theorem 2, we get the conclusion that each sub-protocol in the SecureANNS protocol is secure. Simultaneously, the security of our SecureANNS protocol follows directly according to the Composition Theorem.

5   Evaluations

5.1   Experiment Setup

We implement SecureANNS and perform experiments on several datasets. Accuracy tests of plaintext NNS algorithm is written in GO and secure computation algorithms are written in C and C++ based on open-source libraries [13, 22]. We deploy cloud servers with two Openbayes instances (2.2 GHz, 30 cores, and 50 GB of RAM each) and simulate the client with a laptop device (2.6 GHz, 6 cores and 32 GB of RAM). Network latency between cloud servers is 0.05 ms.

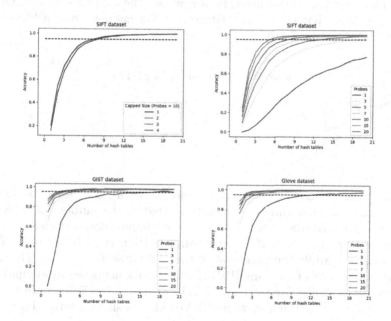

Fig. 4. Accuracy

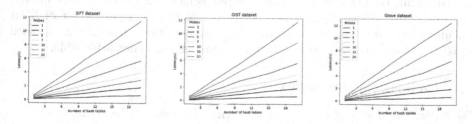

Fig. 5. Latency

Three NNS datasets are selected for our evaluation. SIFT is an image descriptor dataset (n = 1000000, d = 128). GIST is a dataset of features representing the global spatial information of images (n = 1000000, d = 960). GloVe is a dataset of vector representation for words (n = 1183514, d = 100). We reduce the dimensionality of dataset Gist to 128 and quantize each element of the three datasets to an 8-bit unsigned integer representation.

5.2 Performance Results

Accuracy. Accuracy is defined as what fraction of ANNs found are within c-times to the true closest distance. First, we perform tests with different capped sizes, and Fig. 4 shows the results on SIFT. It can be observed that different capped sizes only lead to minor differences in accuracy. Therefore, when aiming for a 95% accuracy, increasing this value only provides a limited improvement, but leads to larger data buckets, which further increases the performance bottleneck, namely retrieval overhead. Hence, we set the capped size to 1. On this basis, Fig. 4 shows that for all three datasets, 95% accuracy can be achieved with less than 10 tables and 7 probes.

Table 3. Comparison with SOTAs

	Preprocessing	OT Phase	Distance	Top1	Retrieval	Query Time	Multi Cores	Dataset Leakage
[14]	12.6 s 484 MB	0.35 s 156 MB	2.21 s 56.7 MB	1.96 s 645 MB	3.85 s 1.06GB	8.06 s 1.77GB	1.55 s (5.2 ↑)	No
[49]	Almost None	None	None	None	28.2 s 1.5 MB	28.2 s 1.5 MB	1.1 s (25.6 ↑)	Yes
This work	Almost None	None	0.02 s 3.4 MB	0.05 s 2.7KB	1.95 s 1.16 MB	2.02 s 4.56 MB	0.71 s (2.85 ↑)	No

Performance. We show the latency of SecureANNS in Fig. 5. It can be observed that the time cost in 1 thread is linearly related to the number of tables and probes. The main reason is that, although the computational efficiency of PBR has been improved greatly, the performance bottleneck still lies in DPF and XOR operations, while the time cost of the OT phase is minimal. This aligns with our expectation of reducing PBR time by introducing secure computation. The time cost is similar for SIFT and GIST (about 2 s for 95% accuracy with n = 25, 10 tables, and 7 probes), while GloVe exhibits slightly larger latency due to a larger dataset size.

Multi-thread. Our parallel optimization primarily aims to reduce the time cost of PBR, while the OT phase is still computed using a single thread. Only limited improvement (2.85 times) has been achieved due to the large amount of XOR calculation in our multi-thread setting. We believe that resource contention, such as I/O, is one of the reasons why further improvement is not achievable.

5.3 Comparison with SOTA

We report the results of our comparison with two state-of-the-art in Table 3.

Comparison with [14]. SecureANNS is 4 and 2.18 times faster in single-thread and multi-thread respectively, even without considering preprocessing and OT precomputation. Our modified LSH algorithm is more efficient compared to the clustering method, and the subset size for 2PC computation is much smaller. As a result, the communication cost between computation servers is significantly lower than [14]. Therefore, in application scenarios where slow networks need to be considered, the impact on [14] will be much greater than ours.

Comparison with [49]. SecureANNS greatly reduces the number of AES in DPF, resulting in 14 times faster in a single-threaded environment. Specifically, [49] sets n = 35 which consumes nearly 2^{25} AES for each table. On the other hand, by combining early termination with n = 25, we only need to compute 2^{18} AES. Additionally, our protocol avoids the leakage issue that occurred in [49].

Acknowledgements. This work is supported by the National Natural Science Foundation of China (Grant No. 62122092, No. 62032005).

References

1. Addanki, S., Garbe, K., Jaffe, E., Ostrovsky, R., Polychroniadou, A.: Prio+: privacy preserving aggregate statistics via Boolean shares. In: Galdi, C., Jarecki, S. (eds.) SCN 2022. LNCS, vol. 13409, pp. 516–539. Springer, Cham (2022). https://doi.org/10.1007/978-3-031-14791-3_23
2. Andoni, A., Indyk, P., Razenshteyn, I.: Approximate nearest neighbor search in high dimensions. In: Proceedings of the International Congress of Mathematicians: Rio de Janeiro 2018, pp. 3287–3318. World Scientific (2018)
3. Asharov, G., Lindell, Y., Schneider, T., Zohner, M.: More efficient oblivious transfer and extensions for faster secure computation. In: Proceedings of the 2013 ACM SIGSAC Conference on Computer & Communications Security, pp. 535–548 (2013)
4. Beaver, D.: Efficient multiparty protocols using circuit randomization. In: Feigenbaum, J. (ed.) CRYPTO 1991. LNCS, vol. 576, pp. 420–432. Springer, Heidelberg (1992). https://doi.org/10.1007/3-540-46766-1_34
5. Bellare, M., Hoang, V.T., Keelveedhi, S., Rogaway, P.: Efficient garbling from a fixed-key blockcipher. In: 2013 IEEE Symposium on Security and Privacy, pp. 478–492. IEEE (2013)
6. Blakley, G.R.: Safeguarding cryptographic keys. In: International Workshop on Managing Requirements Knowledge, p. 313. IEEE Computer Society (1979)
7. Boneh, D., Boyle, E., Corrigan-Gibbs, H., Gilboa, N., Ishai, Y.: Lightweight techniques for private heavy hitters. In: 2021 IEEE Symposium on Security and Privacy (SP), pp. 762–776. IEEE (2021)
8. Boyle, E., Gilboa, N., Ishai, Y.: Function secret sharing. In: Oswald, E., Fischlin, M. (eds.) EUROCRYPT 2015. LNCS, vol. 9057, pp. 337–367. Springer, Heidelberg (2015). https://doi.org/10.1007/978-3-662-46803-6_12
9. Boyle, E., Gilboa, N., Ishai, Y.: Function secret sharing: improvements and extensions. In: Proceedings of the 2016 ACM SIGSAC Conference on Computer and Communications Security, pp. 1292–1303 (2016)
10. Brassard, G., Crepeau, C., Robert, J.-M.: All-or-nothing disclosure of secrets. In: Odlyzko, A.M. (ed.) CRYPTO 1986. LNCS, vol. 263, pp. 234–238. Springer, Heidelberg (1987). https://doi.org/10.1007/3-540-47721-7_17

11. Cai, R., Zhang, C., Zhang, L., Ma, W.Y.: Scalable music recommendation by search. In: Proceedings of the 15th ACM International Conference on Multimedia, pp. 1065–1074 (2007)

12. Canetti, R.: Security and composition of multiparty cryptographic protocols. J. Cryptol. **13**, 143–202 (2000)

13. Chandran, N., Gupta, D., Rastogi, A., Sharma, R., Tripathi, S.: EZPC: programmable and efficient secure two-party computation for machine learning. In: 2019 IEEE European Symposium on Security and Privacy (EuroS&P), pp. 496–511. IEEE (2019)

14. Chen, H., Chillotti, I., Dong, Y., Poburinnaya, O., Razenshteyn, I., Riazi, M.S.: {SANNS}: scaling up secure approximate {k-Nearest} neighbors search. In: 29th USENIX Security Symposium (USENIX Security 2020), pp. 2111–2128 (2020)

15. Chen, K., Liu, L.: Privacy preserving data classification with rotation perturbation. In: Fifth IEEE International Conference on Data Mining (ICDM 2005), pp. 4-pp. IEEE (2005)

16. Chor, B., Gilboa, N., Naor, M.: Private Information Retrieval by Keywords. Citeseer (1997)

17. Chor, B., Kushilevitz, E., Goldreich, O., Sudan, M.: Private information retrieval. J. ACM (JACM) **45**(6), 965–981 (1998)

18. Corrigan-Gibbs, H., Boneh, D., Mazières, D.: Riposte: an anonymous messaging system handling millions of users. In: 2015 IEEE Symposium on Security and Privacy, pp. 321–338. IEEE (2015)

19. Couteau, G.: New protocols for secure equality test and comparison. In: Preneel, B., Vercauteren, F. (eds.) ACNS 2018. LNCS, vol. 10892, pp. 303–320. Springer, Cham (2018). https://doi.org/10.1007/978-3-319-93387-0_16

20. Couteau, G., Rindal, P., Raghuraman, S.: Silver: silent VOLE and oblivious transfer from hardness of decoding structured LDPC codes. In: Malkin, T., Peikert, C. (eds.) CRYPTO 2021. LNCS, vol. 12827, pp. 502–534. Springer, Cham (2021). https://doi.org/10.1007/978-3-030-84252-9_17

21. Datar, M., Immorlica, N., Indyk, P., Mirrokni, V.S.: Locality-sensitive hashing scheme based on p-stable distributions. In: Proceedings of the Twentieth Annual Symposium on Computational Geometry, pp. 253–262 (2004)

22. Dauterman, E., Feng, E., Luo, E., Popa, R.A., Stoica, I.: Dory: an encrypted search system with distributed trust. In: Proceedings of the 14th USENIX Conference on Operating Systems Design and Implementation, pp. 1101–1119 (2020)

23. Demmler, D., Schneider, T., Zohner, M.: ABY-a framework for efficient mixed-protocol secure two-party computation. In: NDSS (2015)

24. Dessouky, G., Koushanfar, F., Sadeghi, A.R., Schneider, T., Zeitouni, S., Zohner, M.: Pushing the communication barrier in secure computation using lookup tables. Cryptology ePrint Archive (2018)

25. Doerner, J., Shelat, A.: Scaling ORAM for secure computation. In: Proceedings of the 2017 ACM SIGSAC Conference on Computer and Communications Security, pp. 523–535 (2017)

26. Edemekong, P.F., Annamaraju, P., Haydel, M.J.: Health insurance portability and accountability act (2018)

27. Even, S., Goldreich, O., Lempel, A.: A randomized protocol for signing contracts. Commun. ACM **28**(6), 637–647 (1985)

28. Fan, J., Vercauteren, F.: Somewhat practical fully homomorphic encryption. Cryptology ePrint Archive (2012)

29. Garay, J., Schoenmakers, B., Villegas, J.: Practical and secure solutions for integer comparison. In: Okamoto, T., Wang, X. (eds.) PKC 2007. LNCS, vol. 4450, pp. 330–342. Springer, Heidelberg (2007). https://doi.org/10.1007/978-3-540-71677-8_22

30. Garcia-Teodoro, P., Diaz-Verdejo, J., Maciá-Fernández, G., Vázquez, E.: Anomaly-based network intrusion detection: techniques, systems and challenges. Comput. Secur. **28**(1–2), 18–28 (2009)

31. Gilboa, N.: Two party RSA key generation. In: Wiener, M. (ed.) CRYPTO 1999. LNCS, vol. 1666, pp. 116–129. Springer, Heidelberg (1999). https://doi.org/10.1007/3-540-48405-1_8

32. Gilboa, N., Ishai, Y.: Distributed point functions and their applications. In: Nguyen, P.Q., Oswald, E. (eds.) EUROCRYPT 2014. LNCS, vol. 8441, pp. 640–658. Springer, Heidelberg (2014). https://doi.org/10.1007/978-3-642-55220-5_35

33. Guo, C., Katz, J., Wang, X., Yu, Y.: Efficient and secure multiparty computation from fixed-key block ciphers. In: 2020 IEEE Symposium on Security and Privacy (SP), pp. 825–841. IEEE (2020)

34. Indyk, P., Motwani, R.: Approximate nearest neighbors: towards removing the curse of dimensionality. In: Proceedings of the Thirtieth Annual ACM Symposium on Theory of Computing, pp. 604–613 (1998)

35. Ishai, Y., Kilian, J., Nissim, K., Petrank, E.: Extending oblivious transfers efficiently. In: Boneh, D. (ed.) CRYPTO 2003. LNCS, vol. 2729, pp. 145–161. Springer, Heidelberg (2003). https://doi.org/10.1007/978-3-540-45146-4_9

36. Kolesnikov, V., Kumaresan, R.: Improved OT extension for transferring short secrets. In: Canetti, R., Garay, J.A. (eds.) CRYPTO 2013. LNCS, vol. 8043, pp. 54–70. Springer, Heidelberg (2013). https://doi.org/10.1007/978-3-642-40084-1_4

37. Kolesnikov, V., Sadeghi, A.-R., Schneider, T.: Improved garbled circuit building blocks and applications to auctions and computing minima. In: Garay, J.A., Miyaji, A., Otsuka, A. (eds.) CANS 2009. LNCS, vol. 5888, pp. 1–20. Springer, Heidelberg (2009). https://doi.org/10.1007/978-3-642-10433-6_1

38. Kolesnikov, V., Schneider, T.: Improved garbled circuit: free XOR gates and applications. In: Aceto, L., Damgård, I., Goldberg, L.A., Halldórsson, M.M., Ingólfsdóttir, A., Walukiewicz, I. (eds.) ICALP 2008. LNCS, vol. 5126, pp. 486–498. Springer, Heidelberg (2008). https://doi.org/10.1007/978-3-540-70583-3_40

39. Lindell, Y.: How to simulate it – a tutorial on the simulation proof technique. In: Lindell, Y. (ed.) Tutorials on the Foundations of Cryptography. ISC, pp. 277–346. Springer, Cham (2017). https://doi.org/10.1007/978-3-319-57048-8_6

40. Liu, L., et al.: Toward highly secure yet efficient KNN classification scheme on outsourced cloud data. IEEE Internet Things J. **6**(6), 9841–9852 (2019)

41. Lloyd, S.: Least squares quantization in PCM. IEEE Trans. Inf. Theory **28**(2), 129–137 (1982)

42. Lv, Q., Josephson, W., Wang, Z., Charikar, M., Li, K.: Multi-probe LSH: efficient indexing for high-dimensional similarity search. In: Proceedings of the 33rd International Conference on Very Large Data Bases, pp. 950–961 (2007)

43. Mohassel, P., Rosulek, M., Trieu, N.: Practical privacy-preserving k-means clustering. Cryptology ePrint Archive (2019)

44. Mohassel, P., Zhang, Y.: SecureML: a system for scalable privacy-preserving machine learning. In: 2017 IEEE Symposium on Security and Privacy (SP), pp. 19–38. IEEE (2017)

45. Qi, Y., Atallah, M.J.: Efficient privacy-preserving k-nearest neighbor search. In: 2008 The 28th International Conference on Distributed Computing Systems, pp. 311–319. IEEE (2008)

46. Rabin, M.O.: How to exchange secrets with oblivious transfer. Cryptology ePrint Archive (2005)
47. Rathee, D., et al.: SIRNN: a math library for secure RNN inference. In: 2021 IEEE Symposium on Security and Privacy (SP), pp. 1003–1020. IEEE (2021)
48. Rathee, D., et al.: CrypTFlow2: practical 2-party secure inference. In: Proceedings of the 2020 ACM SIGSAC Conference on Computer and Communications Security, pp. 325–342 (2020)
49. Servan-Schreiber, S., Langowski, S., Devadas, S.: Private approximate nearest neighbor search with sublinear communication. In: 2022 IEEE Symposium on Security and Privacy (SP), pp. 911–929. IEEE (2022)
50. Shaul, H., Feldman, D., Rus, D.: Secure k-ish nearest neighbors classifier. arXiv preprint arXiv:1801.07301 (2018)
51. Su, M.Y.: Using clustering to improve the KNN-based classifiers for online anomaly network traffic identification. J. Netw. Comput. Appl. **34**(2), 722–730 (2011)
52. Voigt, P., Von dem Bussche, A.: The EU General Data Protection Regulation (GDPR). A Practical Guide, 1st edn., vol. 10, no. 3152676, p. 10–5555 Springer, Cham (2017)
53. Wong, W.K., Cheung, D.W., Kao, B., Mamoulis, N.: Secure KNN computation on encrypted databases. In: Proceedings of the 2009 ACM SIGMOD International Conference on Management of Data, pp. 139–152 (2009)
54. Yang, K., Weng, C., Lan, X., Zhang, J., Wang, X.: Ferret: fast extension for correlated OT with small communication. In: Proceedings of the 2020 ACM SIGSAC Conference on Computer and Communications Security, pp. 1607–1626 (2020)
55. Yao, A.C.C.: How to generate and exchange secrets. In: 27th Annual Symposium on Foundations of Computer Science (SFCS 1986), pp. 162–167. IEEE (1986)
56. Zahur, S., Rosulek, M., Evans, D.: Two halves make a whole. In: Oswald, E., Fischlin, M. (eds.) EUROCRYPT 2015. LNCS, vol. 9057, pp. 220–250. Springer, Heidelberg (2015). https://doi.org/10.1007/978-3-662-46803-6_8
57. Zhu, Y., Xu, R., Takagi, T.: Secure k-NN computation on encrypted cloud data without sharing key with query users. In: Proceedings of the 2013 International Workshop on Security in Cloud Computing, pp. 55–60 (2013)
58. Zuber, M., Sirdey, R.: Efficient homomorphic evaluation of k-NN classifiers. Proc. Priv. Enhancing Technol. **2021**(2), 111–129 (2021)

ConGISATA: A Framework for Continuous Gamified Information Security Awareness Training and Assessment

Ofir Cohen(✉)⬤, Ron Bitton⬤, Asaf Shabtai⬤, and Rami Puzis⬤

Software and Information Systems Engineering and Cyber@BGU,
Ben-Gurion University of the Negev, Beer-Sheva, Israel
{cofir,ronbit}@post.bgu.ac.il, {shabtaia,puzis}@bgu.ac.il

Abstract. The incidence of cybersecurity attacks utilizing social engineering techniques has increased. Such attacks exploit the fact that in every secure system, there is at least one individual with the means to access sensitive information. Since it is easier to deceive a person than it is to bypass the defense mechanisms in place, these types of attacks have gained popularity. This situation is exacerbated by the fact that people are more likely to take risks in their passive form, i.e., risks that arise due to the failure to perform an action. Passive risk has been identified as a significant threat to cybersecurity. To address these threats, there is a need to strengthen individuals' information security awareness (ISA). Therefore, we developed ConGISATA - a continuous gamified ISA training and assessment framework based on embedded mobile sensors; a taxonomy for evaluating mobile users' security awareness served as the basis for the sensors' design. ConGISATA's continuous and gradual training process enables users to learn from their real-life mistakes and adapt their behavior accordingly. ConGISATA aims to transform passive risk situations (as perceived an individual) into active risk situations, as people tend to underestimate the potential impact of passive risks. Our evaluation of the proposed framework demonstrates its ability to improve individuals' ISA, as assessed by the sensors and in simulations of common attack vectors.

Keywords: Information Security Awareness · Social Engineering · Human Factors · Gamification · Cybersecurity Training · Mobile Devices

1 Introduction

Defense mechanisms are deployed to prevent attackers from performing malicious activities such as hacking into networks, accessing sensitive information, and compromising computerized systems. Social engineering (SE) refers to techniques

© The Author(s), under exclusive license to Springer Nature Switzerland AG 2024
G. Tsudik et al. (Eds.): ESORICS 2023, LNCS 14346, pp. 431–451, 2024.
https://doi.org/10.1007/978-3-031-51479-1_22

aimed at manipulating people into performing actions that help an attacker bypass state-of-the-art defense mechanisms [1]. The ease with which the human factor can be exploited has resulted in numerous cyberattacks caused by human error [2,20]. For mobile users, SE is one of the main attack vectors [24], and given the prevalence of smartphones today, SE poses a significant threat to society.

Approaches for mitigating the risk posed by cybersecurity attacks utilizing SE techniques consist of two essential components: assessing information security awareness (ISA) and improving it.

Various methods can be used to assess ISA, the most common being questionnaires [13,14,23]. However, questionnaires require users' active involvement and collaboration; moreover, they are subjective and prone to bias, as they rely on self-reported behavior [25]. Despite their widespread use, questionnaires have been shown to be an unreliable measurement tool for ISA [11].

Challenges involving simulations of common attacks are also used to measure ISA. The primary advantage of this type of assessment is that it measures users' ability to handle real-life attack scenarios. However, challenges also have a major limitation: they do not consider users' context (e.g., opening an email from home versus opening an email at work). Since human behavior often depends on the context, these methods are inherently less accurate [26].

To address the limitations of existing ISA assessment methods, Bitton *et al.* [8,11] proposed a taxonomy for mobile users' security awareness that defines a set of measurable criteria organized by technological focus areas. These criteria are measured by a mobile agent that collects data from sensors on the users' devices. The sensors are mapped to the taxonomy's criteria, and a final passive ISA score is produced by aggregating their outputs. This ISA score can be changed dynamically based on continuous sensor readings. In this research, we use this sensor-based approach, along with challenges associated with three common attack vectors, to assess ISA.

Typically, ISA is improved by participating in security awareness programs (workshops) or performing challenges with feedback. However, the previously mentioned limitation also applies when challenges are used to improve ISA. In many cases, efforts aimed at improving ISA evoke fear, which has been shown to be counterproductive at times; such efforts also result in 'security fatigue,' in which people tire of being presented with security procedures and processes [3].

Gamification is a technique often used to overcome the limitations described above. Deterding *et al.* [4] defined gamification as "the use of game design elements in non-game contexts", and Hamari *et al.* [5] reviewed many gamification studies and concluded that this method works well in various fields, particularly for improving learning and training sessions. As a result, the use of gamification to increase ISA has grown, leading to the development of various gamified solutions for this purpose [16–18].

Nevertheless, standard gamification alone is insufficient. A literature review performed by Böckle *et al.* [27] highlighted the problem of the "one size fits all" approach, which may result in declining engagement and loss of interest in overly simple challenges. To overcome this, the authors suggested using adaptive gamification that dynamically re-engages users. Our approach for improving ISA utilizes adaptive gamification through a personalized feedback loop tailored to the outputs of the sensors.

A behavioral aspect that was not considered in previously proposed gamified solutions is passive/active risk-taking. Studies have classified risks as either active or passive risks [9,10]. Active risk describes actions people take that put them at risk, while passive risk is "*risk brought on or magnified by inaction or avoidance*". One example from the cybersecurity domain is the risk of having malware on your mobile device. In its active form, this risk derives from the possibility of unknowingly downloading a malicious file, whereas in its passive form, it stems from failing to install anti-malware software on the device in advance. These studies showed that passive risks are perceived as being less risky than equivalent active risks. Therefore, our framework aims to reduce passive risk-taking (PRT), by transforming passive risks into active risks. By deducting game points from users who fail in a passive-risk-related scenario, we impose an immediate punishment on passive behaviors. By doing so, we can help users gradually overcome the human tendency to overlook passive risks.

In this research, we propose ConGISATA, a continuous gamified ISA training and assessment framework, which addresses the problems of existing gamification-based methods described above. Our approach is implemented by a mobile agent (an app) that collects data from the set of sensors used in the taxonomy and assessment method of Bitton *et al.* [8,11]. The app has a graphical user interface with the key components of a gamified system: a detailed home screen, a leaderboard, and a learning screen. The learning screen is composed of sections, one for each criterion in the taxonomy. For each criterion, there is a score and a link to an article or blog post that should help users improve their behavior with regard to the criterion. The scores on this screen are updated daily according to the sensors' readings and highlight the areas in which the user needs to improve. Challenges are also presented throughout the learning process to help assess users' ISA as they progress.

To evaluate the proposed framework, we performed an extensive experiment involving 70 subjects, each of whom installed our mobile app on their smartphone and used ConGISATA for a period of five weeks. We compared our method with a baseline method inspired by methods commonly used in academia and industry today. In the baseline method, users were provided personalized articles/blog posts based on their performance in the challenges, without taking the sensor data into account. Our results show that users who were trained using the ConGISATA framework had greater improvement than those trained using the baseline method for almost all criteria of the ISA taxonomy. In addition, a significant correlation between the use of our app and users' ISA improvement was observed. Importantly, by using simulations of three common attack vectors, we found that ConGISATA helps users deal with real-life SE scenarios.

Our contributions can be summarized as follows: (1) We propose a novel framework for improving and assessing mobile users' ISA. (2) To the best of our knowledge, we are the first to take continuous sensor readings and show their impact on improving ISA in an adaptive gamification setting. (3) We empirically demonstrate the importance of considering passive risk-taking in the ISA training domain.

2 Background

Active Versus Passive Risk-Taking: Keinan *et al.* [9] established passive risk as a unique and separate construct. The authors provide the following explanation:*"People are often held less responsible for their omissions than for their commissions. This lack of perceived responsibility may lower the motivation to act. People are usually less likely to do something if they believe they will not be held accountable for failing to do it. However, risk aversion often increases with personal accountability, since accountability stimulates self-critical forms of thought and increases awareness of one's own judgment processes. It seems plausible that once people feel accountable they process information better, realize that they are in a risky situation, and be motivated to act to avoid risk."*

A follow-up paper [10] showed that a passive risk is judged as less risky than a completely equivalent active risk. For example, the following scenario was presented in both active and passive forms: actively parking your car in a restricted zone or not moving your car once you realize it is parked in a restricted zone. When asked to rate scenarios by risk level, in its active form this scenario was rated as riskier than in its passive form.

The authors suggest that *"this inferior ability to devote attention to the absence of events leads to passive risks being less available to our consciousness, to be underestimated, and thus to be perceived as less risky. We need to be motivated to devote attention to passive risks."* The authors add the following recommendation: *"The findings of the current research suggest stressing people's personal responsibility for complying with recommended preventive measures may raise risk perception and increase preventive action."*

Finally, Arend *et al.* [19] examined how self-reported passive risk behavior predicts cybersecurity behavioral intentions and their relation to actual cybersecurity behavior. This series of three studies showed that passive risk had a notable impact on cybersecurity intentions, meaning that high passive risk scores were associated with low adherence to safe cybersecurity behavior. It was also shown that behavioral choices related to cybersecurity are highly correlated with a tendency to take passive risks. Overall, these studies established that passive risk tendencies are an important factor in the context of cyber behavior.

3 Related Work

Every gamified approach for mitigating the risk posed by SE attacks consists of two essential components: measuring ISA and improving it.

Questionnaires are the most common means of measuring ISA, with the vast majority of prior studies on this topic relying on them [6,12,15,29–32]. Despite their widespread use, they tend to be an unreliable measurement tool for behavior because of their subjective nature. Additionally, they are prone to bias, as they rely solely on self-reported behavior [25].

A more advanced method of evaluating ISA is to use attack simulations (also referred to as challenges). Despite their inability to consider users' context, the employment of challenges to assess ISA during security awareness training is extremely valuable, as it provides important insights into authentic user behavior. Their application in the literature, however, has been limited [22]. Our framework utilizes three different types of challenges: phishing, permission attacks, and impersonation. When using our framework, users do not know when or how they are presented with these challenges; this ensures that the challenges are as natural and objective as possible. Additionally, the framework collects data from sensors in users' everyday environments to examine aspects of their ISA in real-life settings, outside of controlled laboratory conditions.

When it comes to improving ISA using gamification, two core elements distinguish current gamified solutions: training duration and personalization of the content. Most of the gamified training mentioned in the literature was performed for a single brief session and utilized a physical board/card game, which is a difficult requirement for long-term training (over a period of weeks) [12,15]. We only identified one paper with a longer training process – that of Alahmari et al., where the training took place for two weeks [28]. Our framework is designed to achieve long-term behavioral change through continuous learning over several weeks or months, without requiring physical attendance at training sessions.

Böckle et al. [27] highlighted the problem of the "one size fits all" approach in gamified solutions for improving ISA and suggested the use of personalization. Heid et al. [33] created a gamified prototype that poses questions related to security and privacy issues associated with apps installed on the user's smartphone. A quiz engine providing multiple choice questions regarding known vulnerabilities and app properties was implemented using Appicaptor, a mobile application analysis platform that performs static and dynamic app tests. The question engine automatically generates questions from Appicaptor's database content, which are personalized for the users based on the apps installed on their smartphones. However, this work is limited, because only one sensor served as a source of information, the proposed method was only tested within the research group, and it relies on an external data source that is not publicly available, preventing its reproducibility.

Our literature review failed to identify any other papers utilizing personalization besides the work of Heid et al. mentioned above. Our framework generates scores for each user based on their weaknesses, as measured using multiple sensors. We evaluated the framework's impact in a comprehensive experiment spanning several weeks. All the materials used are publicly available and presented in the appendix. Furthermore, our gamified solution is the only method that demonstrates how passive risks can be transformed into active ones, which is a key contribution of our research.

A summary of the related work is provided in Table 1.

Table 1. Summary of related work

Paper	Platform	Personalization	Considers PRT	Continuous Learning	Questionnaires	Attack Simulations	Sensors
Newbould *et al.* [12], 2009	Board game	✗	✗	✗	✓	✗	✗
Denning *et al.* [15], 2013	Tabletop card game	✗	✗	✗	✓	✗	✗
Gjertsen *et al.* [6], 2017	Exercises	✗	✗	✗	✓	✗	✗
Scholefield *et al.* [30], 2019	Mobile (Android) game	✗	✗	✗	✓	✗	✗
Dincelli *et al.* [29], 2020	Interactive storytelling	✗	✗	✗	✓	✗	✗
Heid *et al.* [33], 2020	Multiple choice quizzes	✓	✗	✓	✗	✗	✓
Omar *et al.* [31], 2021	Educational quizzes	✗	✗	✗	✓	✗	✗
Wu *et al.* [32], 2021	Multiple choice quizzes	✗	✗	✗	✓	✗	✗
Alahmari *et al.* [28], 2022	Mobile app	✗	✗	✓	✓	✗	✗
Canham *et al.* [22], 2022	Phishing simulations	✗	✗	✗	✓	✓	✗
Our method, 2023	Mobile (Android) game	✓	✓	✓	✗	✓	✓

4   Proposed Method

In this section, we present ConGISATA. First we provide a high-level description of the framework (illustrated in Fig. 1a), and then we elaborate on each component.

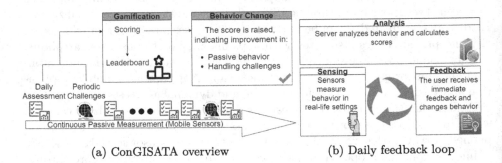

(a) ConGISATA overview   (b) Daily feedback loop

Fig. 1. The ConGISATA security awareness training and assessment framework

In the framework, the following steps are performed in a process aimed at raising ISA:

Calibration Period: For each user, the game starts with a calibration period in which the user's initial security awareness score is assessed for each criterion in the taxonomy. This assessment does not require the user to interact with the game, as it is performed using the mobile sensors and challenges described in Sect. 4.1. Following this evaluation, the initial overall ISA score is presented to the user on the game's home screen, and a score for each criterion is presented on the learning screen.

Training: In this step, the user starts to interact with the framework in an attempt to gradually improve their behavior and raise their ISA scores. Sensor measurement and challenges still occur in the background, resulting in daily changes to the user's ISA scores, which are presented to them. Training is performed cyclically, through a daily feedback loop, as follows:

Sensing - Each day, the different aspects of the users' behavior are measured by obtaining the sensor values.

Updating Scores - The application's learning screen is always accessible and displays the users' scores for each criterion in the ISA taxonomy, along with their overall ISA score. At midnight, these scores are updated to reflect the previous day's performance. The learning screen also presents the score delta for each criterion, which is the change in the score between two consecutive days. The score deltas enable the user to identify specific behavioral weaknesses (criteria with a negative score delta) and take corrective action.

Articles and Blog Posts - When the user is faced with a low score or a negative score delta for a criterion, they can obtain additional information about that specific focus area via the learning screen, which provides a link to an external, predetermined, and comprehensive article or blog post (for convenience, we refer to them as articles in the rest of the paper) on that subject.

Behavior Change - Upon reading the articles, the user will modify their behavior accordingly, improving their score over time, and climb the leaderboard.

Figure 1b illustrates the daily feedback loop of passive ISA.

4.1 Assessing Mobile Users' ISA

To generate an overall ISA score for each user, we measure two aspects of their behavior: active and passive. The active side refers to the user's ability to handle situations in which immediate action is required, as when facing an attack. Our framework measures this aspect using SE challenges. The passive side refers to ongoing elements of the user's behavior that do not result in an immediate punishment if not performed, such as using a lock screen or deleting unused apps to avoid malware. In our framework, we adapt the method proposed by Bitton *et al.* [8,11] to generate a passive ISA score. Instead, we generate an overall ISA score, which reflects both aspects, active and passive, as follows:

Assessing ISA Using Attack Simulations (Challenges): Each user is regularly presented with challenges derived from three attack vectors. These challenges assess the user's ability to handle real-life attack scenarios and ensure that this capability is also reflected in their overall ISA score. The challenges are presented in a randomized manner (in terms of both time and order) throughout the training process, to prevent detectable patterns. The active score denotes the user's performance on SE challenges and is based on a scale of zero to 100. The score is derived from a moving window of the last X challenges, where X is determined based on the training duration. Each challenge is individually scored between zero, assigned for a failure to make the correct decision, and $100/X$, assigned for successful decision making. For example, for $X = 5$, each challenge can contribute at most $100/5 = 20$ points to the overall active score. Some challenges may involve two decision points, in which case the score assigned is $(100/X)/2$ if the user makes the correct decision at just one of the decision points. For example, a phishing challenge may include two decision points; the first is clicking on the unknown link to enter the phishing website, and the second is providing sensitive details such as login credentials. In such a case, if a user only clicks on the unknown link but does not provide any details, $(100/5)/2 = 10$ points will be added to the overall active score.

Assessing ISA Using Sensor Measurements: Bitton *et al.* [8] developed a taxonomy to measure mobile users' ISA that classifies criteria by technological focus areas and psychological dimensions. Each focus area is further divided into sub-focus areas, and each of these sub-focus areas encompasses several security topics. For instance, the "Applications" focus area is bifurcated into "Application Installation" and "Application Handling" sub-focus areas, with "Untrusted Sources" as a security topic under "Application Installation". The intersection of this security topic with the "Confronting Behavior" psychological dimension leads to a specific criterion: *"Installs applications solely from trusted sources"*.

Bitton *et al.* [11] also proposed a framework for evaluating ISA, which employs a mobile agent with embedded sensors, a network traffic monitor, and cybersecurity challenges. Their framework, which is based on the ISA taxonomy, enables the computation of ISA scores at any given point. The study found that there was a difference between users' self-reported behavior and their actual behavior, highlighting the significance of monitoring real-life user behavior instead of relying solely on questionnaires.

In order to gain a deeper understanding of users' behavior in real-life scenarios, we included sensors based on the ISA taxonomy in our mobile application. These sensors periodically perform a thorough scan of users' devices and actions. By analyzing the resulting data, we can compute a user's passive ISA score and an individual score for each criterion, and identify their potential weaknesses. This knowledge allows us to provide the user with personalized feedback about their ISA scores and offer guidance on how to improve their security practices.

In the paper, we describe ConGISATA's use in training a group of users, which we believe is the more common scenario. The framework can be easily adapted to train individuals, however we do not discuss that in the paper. The process of computing the passive score begins with a calibration period, during which each user's initial passive ISA score is obtained, without any prior training. After this period, the mean and standard deviation of the entire user group are calculated for each criterion in the taxonomy. During training, a new z-score (standard score) is computed daily for each user for each criterion, using the mean and standard deviation derived in the calibration period. The new z-scores are then averaged for each of the taxonomy's focus areas and are subsequently averaged again to obtain a final passive score for each user. Since the z-score is not meaningful to users, the cumulative probability function of the normal distribution is used to transform the z-score to a 0–100 scale.

Computing the Overall Score: The overall ISA score is the average of the active and passive scores.

4.2 Gamification

To increase user engagement and optimize the effectiveness of training, we have incorporated essential gamification elements into our framework. Table 2 lists some of these key elements, along with their rationale, and explains how they have been implemented in ConGISATA.

Table 2. ConGISATA's gamification elements

Element	Explanation
Continuous Learning	Dunlosky *et al.* [21] provided a comprehensive review of study techniques and assessed their effectiveness. One of the techniques covered is continuous learning, which was termed *distributed practice* and defined as *"implementing a schedule of practice that spreads out study activities over time"*. Based on prior research, distributed practice was one of just two techniques to be rated by the authors as having high utility. It was assessed that distributed practice *"works across students of different ages, with a wide variety of materials, on the majority of standard laboratory measures, and over long delays"*. Focusing on the cybersecurity domain, the findings of Kumaraguru *et al.* [7] align with those of Dunlosky *et al.*, demonstrating the benefits of extended security training over condensed single sessions. Based on these findings, we designed our game as a continuous learning process, unlike the common approach found in the literature of a single-session game
Considers PRT	Following the research presented in Sect. 2, we implemented a penalty mechanism to discourage PRT, whereby users that fail to take preventive measures will face penalties, resulting in point deductions. This approach transforms PRT into active risk-taking, where users are held accountable for their inaction shortly after it occurs, regardless of whether or not any damage was incurred. For instance, if our sensors detect that certain users have not installed anti-malware software, they will have points deducted, even if no malware has exploited this vulnerability on their devices. Furthermore, users will continue to face daily penalties until they address and fix the issue by installing anti-malware software, further discouraging avoidance behavior
Levels/Progression	It is crucial to provide players with a clear indication that they are acquiring knowledge and advancing through the training process. We achieve this through a ranking system comprised of two elements: points and levels. Players earn points (reflected in their ISA score) by exhibiting good security practices, and as they accumulate more points, they move up to higher levels. Our framework assigns users to one of three levels based on their ISA score: "beginner", "intermediate", and "pro". These levels do not change the difficulty of training and are only used to give the users the feeling that they are advancing
Competition	Competition is a fundamental aspect of nearly every game, in contexts including security. Healthy competition can significantly enhance engagement and enjoyment among players and encourage individuals to surpass their previous performance. Our game incorporates competition through (1) a leaderboard that ranks players by points, providing insight into their standing relative to others; and (2) the points and levels mentioned above, promoting competition among players
Adaptive Gamification Through Personalized Feedback/Guidance	Immediate personalized feedback is important to prevent player confusion and maintain their engagement in the game. Further guidance helps players progress and improve as the game continues. Immediate feedback in our game is in the form of the learning screen. Each event that causes points to be earned or deducted, such as a sensor discovering poor application handling behavior, is presented on the learning screen on the day on which the event occurred. Additional guidance is possible through a dedicated article on the event's topic. In addition, each user's scores appear on their learning screen, highlighting the areas requiring improvement
Conciseness	The game's exercises should be brief and not take much of the players' time. In our game, the feedback is succinct and highlights the topics pertinent to each player. This approach reduces the time commitment for players and avoids redundant review of familiar material

5   Evaluation

To evaluate the proposed framework, we performed a long-term experiment involving 70 undergraduate and graduate students who use their smartphones regularly. The subjects' ages ranged from 21 to 31, with a mean age of 25 and a median age of 26. The experiment involved the collection of sensitive personal information from subjects for a long period of time, including their browsing patterns. We took measures to preserve the subjects' privacy and reduce any privacy risks associated with participating in the experiment. The experiment was approved by the Institutional Review Board (IRB), provided that: (1) The subjects participated in the experiment, freely, at their own will. The subjects received course credit in exchange for their participation. The subjects were fully aware of the type of data that would be collected and were allowed to withdraw from the study at any time. (2) The data was encrypted before being transmitted between the server and the mobile app. (3) The server was within the university domain, with restricted access and organizational defenses. (4) When possible, the sensitive data itself was not transmitted to the server (such as SMS contents), only the meta-data was (such as the number of SMS messages containing URLs). During the experiment, we measured the subjects' behavior while operating their smartphones and exposed them to three types of SE attacks in 15 attack simulations. We then compared each subject's initial and final ISA scores, measuring the improvement achieved. We also examined how the participants' performance in responding to the challenges evolved during the training process. This section provides a detailed description of the evaluation process and results.

5.1   Mobile Sensors

To evaluate the passive aspects of subjects' behavior, we implemented multiple sensors using Android APIs and used them to assess various criteria from the taxonomy of Bitton *et al.* We did not assess all of the criteria for reasons of simplicity and privacy. The criteria and the way they were assessed are presented in Table 3. In some cases, we found that the corresponding sensor did not work well for a large number of subjects or the sensor had no influence on the score; for example, for criterion OS2, we found that all of our subjects did not root their device before or during the experiment. In such cases, we omitted these sensors and the criteria that correspond to them, and they are not included in our analysis of the results. In addition, 10 out of the 70 subjects either had a technical problem with their smartphone which prevented them from participating, did not use the app, or decided to withdraw from the study. These subjects were omitted from the results analysis as well. Finally, while a higher z-score usually indicates better performance, some of the criteria represent bad behaviors (such as criterion AI1). In such cases, indicated in Table 3 by having "(lower is better)" in their means of assessment, we multiplied their z-score by -1, changing positive numbers into negative progression indicators.

Table 3. List of criteria assessed for the experiment

Criterion	Means of assessment
AI1: Downloads apps from trusted sources	An app was considered trusted if it was downloaded from an official app store (such as Google Play). The score for this criterion is the number of untrusted apps found on the subject's device (lower is better)
AI2: Does not install apps that require dangerous permissions	The score for this criterion is the number of apps on the subject's device which require dangerous permissions, as classified by Android (lower is better)
AI3: Does not install apps with a low rating	We considered a low rating to be less than three and a half stars (out of five) in the Google Play store. The score for this criterion is the number of apps with a low rating found on the subject's device (lower is better)
AH1: Regularly updates apps	Google Play features the last date on which an app was updated. The score for this criterion is the number of apps that are not up-to-date found on the subject's device (lower is better)
AH3: Properly manages running/installed apps	An app is considered unused if the subject did not use the app for more than two weeks. The score for this criterion is the number of unused apps found on the subject's device (lower is better)
B1: Does not enter malicious domains	A domain is considered malicious if Google's safebrowsing API has classified it as such. The score for this criterion is the number of malicious domains the subject has entered in the last seven days (lower is better)
VC1: Does not open messages received from unknown senders	We monitored two message inboxes for each subject - SMS and Gmail's spam inbox. An SMS is considered to be from an unknown sender if the sender of the SMS is not in the subject's contact list. The SMS score is the percentage of how many unknown SMSs the subject has opened in the last seven days. Likewise, the Gmail score is the percentage of emails classified as spam by Gmail that were opened in the last 30 days. The final score for this criterion is the average of the SMS and Gmail scores (lower is better)
VC2: Does not click on links received from unknown senders	We considered an event to be of the 'clicking on links received from unknown senders' type if the following three conditions were met: (1) the subject opened a message from an unknown sender, as defined in VC1, (2) the message that was opened contained a URL, and (3) we also identified a transition between the SMS/Gmail apps and the browser app (Google Chrome), suggesting the subject has clicked on that URL. The score for this criterion is the number of times a subject has clicked on URLs from unknown senders in the last seven days (lower is better)
A2: Uses two-factor authentication mechanisms	A subject was considered to be using two-factor mechanisms if either a two-factor authentication app or an SMS (from the last seven days) indicating two-factor use was found on their device. The score for this criterion is one if the subject uses two-factor mechanisms and otherwise zero (higher is better)
A3: Uses password management services	The subject was considered to be using password management services if a password-managing app was found on their device. The score for this criterion is one if the subject uses password management services and otherwise zero (higher is better)
OS2: Does not root or jailbreak the device	We used a dedicated Android package (rootBeer) that implements various heuristics to determine whether or not a device is rooted. The score for this criterion is one if the subject has not rooted the device and otherwise zero (higher is better)
SS2: Uses anti-virus application regularly to scan the device	The score for this criterion is one if the subject has an anti-virus app installed on the device and otherwise zero (higher is better)
SS5: Uses PIN code, pattern, or fingerprint	A device was considered secured if a lock-screen was enabled. The score for this criterion is one if the subject's device is secured and otherwise zero (higher is better)
N1: Does not connect to unencrypted networks	A network was considered encrypted if a security protocol was enabled (such as WPS, WPA2). The score for this criterion is the number of unencrypted networks the subject has connected to in the last seven days (lower is better)
N3: Uses VPN services on public networks	The subject was considered to be using VPN services if a VPN app was found on their device. The score for this criterion is one if the subject uses VPN services and otherwise zero (higher is better)
PC1: Disables connectivity when not in use	The score for this criterion is the number of times in the last seven days that a connectivity channel (i.e., Bluetooth, Wi-Fi, NFC) was enabled for more than five minutes, without being connected (lower is better)

5.2   Social Engineering Challenges

To evaluate ConGISATA's influence on behavior in active risk situations, we implemented three types of challenges: phishing, impersonation, and permission attacks. The challenges were presented weekly, with one challenge of each type per week, resulting in three challenges every week and a total of 15 challenges. The order of the challenges presented during the week, as well as the day and hour in which they were presented, was randomized. Examples of the challenges are provided in Fig. 2. The challenges were designed as follows.

Phishing: Phishing is the most prevalent SE attack vector. In our experiment, this attack involved creating a web page that emulates a login page from a pre-designed template, typically for student services. The attack was initiated by emailing the subjects and enticing them to click on an attached link to authenticate themselves for a supposed university-related event. The link directed them to one of three domains that we purchased for the experiment, which resemble the actual university domain. The email was sent by a familiar sender, like 'student administration,' who is known to the subjects as a legitimate email source for university administration. The email was sent during the academic semester when administrative emails from the university are expected. Although the phishing email appears genuine, there are several indications that it was a phishing attack. First, it was not sent from the university's mail system; second, the link provided was not associated with the university's domain: and third, the phishing web page did not employ the HTTPS protocol. To safeguard the subjects' privacy, authentication information was not transmitted to the server. In this challenge, we evaluated the subject twice. First, we determined whether they clicked on the link and accessed the website. If they did, we then determined if they entered login details. The following phishing templates were used:

(1) Facebook security: An email was sent, informing subjects that they violated Facebook's code of conduct and their profile was at risk of deletion. Subjects were urged to log in to their account and appeal, via a link provided in the email.

(2) Moodle - new grade: Moodle is a learning platform that the university uses to upload course materials and students use to submit assignments. An email was sent to subjects telling them a grade was assigned to them on the Moodle platform, providing a link to log in and view it.

(3) Organizational password change: Students are required to change their organizational password periodically. An email was sent to students asking them to change their password via the link provided or their account would be locked.

(4) New appeal response: In the subjects' university, students can make an appeal about the way in which their test was reviewed and graded. During the exam period, an email was sent to subjects informing them of a response to an appeal they made regarding a specific exam, followed by a link to the appeal system.

(5) New exam scan: In the exam period, an email was sent to subjects telling them that an exam they took had been graded and the results were published. A link to the exam website was provided, enabling the subject to see the grade.

Permission Attack: Malicious applications can trick unaware subjects into granting dangerous permissions during runtime. In each variant of this challenge, the device requested the granting of a dangerous permission to an app that does not need that permission. The mobile agent triggered the attack scenario when the subject used the phone and appeared on the screen using the Android permission requests' UI. The subject could reject or approve the request; a subject who granted privileges to the app was considered vulnerable to the attack.

The experiment included the following permission request templates: The Calculator requests camera permissions, WhatsApp requests calender permissions, Camera requests SMS permissions, and Gmail requests SMS permissions.

Impersonation: Fraudulent apps can deceive people in order to gain possession of their credentials. In this challenge, we simulated a malicious application that sends a push notification while impersonating a legitimate service. The user interface of the notification exhibited a characteristic indicative of a phishing attack, which is the appearance of our mobile agent's name, along with the impersonated app name. Upon clicking the notification, our application launched, presenting a replica of the login screen of a well-known and trusted app. To assess the subjects' performance in this attack, we classified them into two categories: half-vulnerable if they clicked the notification but did not complete the login process, and fully vulnerable if they both clicked the notification and completed the login process. To ensure the privacy of the subjects, the authentication information was not transmitted to the server. The experiment included an app impersonating Facebook, Instagram, and the university's official app.

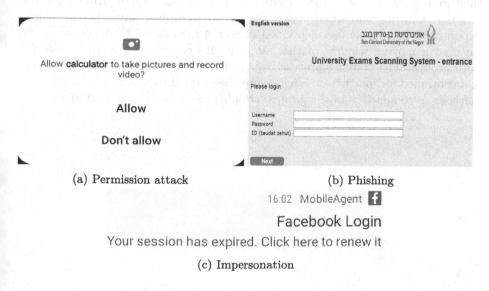

(a) Permission attack   (b) Phishing

(c) Impersonation

Fig. 2. Illustration of the different challenges

5.3   Articles and Blog Posts

Prior to the experiment, we searched the web for publicly available relevant educational articles and blog posts. We looked for two types of items: items about each focus area in the ISA taxonomy (meaning only about passive aspects) for the ConGISATA group and items about each of the three types of SE challenges (meaning only about active aspects) for the baseline group. After a thorough review, we found 32 items (16 per group) and labeled them by topic. Additionally, for the baseline group, each item was manually assigned a comprehensiveness grade, reflecting its depth and complexity on a scale from one (denoting basic and intuitive content) to five (indicating comprehensive and technical material). This grade determined the order in which the items were provided to subjects in the baseline group, as described in Sect. 5.4. In the ConGISATA group, the order of the items was predetermined and fixed for the entire training process. There was one item about each focus area in the ISA taxonomy. The list of articles and blog posts is presented in Table 5 in the appendix.

5.4   Experiment Setup

Each subject was assigned randomly to one of two groups, ConGISATA and baseline, each of which initially had 35 subjects. All subjects were asked to install our mobile app on their smartphones and keep it for the next five weeks. As mentioned in Sect. 4, we first needed to calculate an initial score for each subject in a calibration period. All subsequent scores in the training process were relative to this initial score and used for personalization and later analysis. For both groups, the calibration period consisted of the first week of the experiment. During this period, the mobile sensors monitored the subjects' behavior, and they were presented with three challenges (one of each type). Afterward, the sensor monitoring and three weekly challenges continued until the end of the experiment. In addition, as mentioned in Sect. 4.1, to compute the active score, we used a moving window of the last X challenges. We set X to be five for both groups. The training process began at the end of the calibration period and continued for four weeks. Each group was trained using one of two different methods; a comparison of the groups' training processes is provided in Table 4.

5.5   Results

In this study we address the following three research questions:

RQ1: Can our framework improve users' passive ISA score, as measured by the mobile ISA taxonomy? If so, how does it compare to the baseline method? First, we analyzed the passive score deltas and examined each criterion individually. Figure 6 (in the appendix) shows the delta in the score for each of the criteria as a function of the number of days since the experiment started. An increase

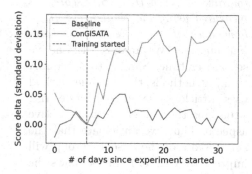

Fig. 3. Average passive score deltas per group over time

in the score was observed for all but one criterion. Furthermore, our framework resulted in a more notable improvement in the group's performance relative to that of the baseline group. We also examined the total passive ISA score for each group, calculated as the average across the focus areas of the various criteria. As seen in Fig. 3, the use of our framework improved the passive ISA score, whereas no improvement was observed for the baseline group.

Table 4. Comparison of the groups' training processes

Group	Subject of Articles	# Articles	Gamification	Personalization	Timing
ConGISATA	Passive risk related	16	✓	The collection of articles is fixed. Low scores or negative score deltas direct subjects to articles related to focus areas that need improvement.	All articles were available from the second week.
Baseline	Active risk related	8 are chosen personally, from a pool of 16	✓	Articles are selected based on the subject's performance in challenges. Their comprehensiveness increases with repeated failures in the same attack vector.	Starting from the second week, articles were incrementally provided twice a week and remained accessible until the experiment's conclusion, with notifications sent to subjects' devices.

RQ2: Does ConGISATA help users improve their active ISA score, as measured using the challenges? If so, how does it compare to the baseline method? We analyzed the active score over time. Similar to other ISA training methods, the baseline method uses articles related to active risk situations thereby emphasizing active aspects. Thus, we anticipate that the active score of the baseline group will improve over time. Figure 4 shows the change in score throughout the exper-

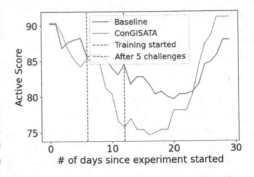

Fig. 4. Active score over time

iment. Initially, both groups experienced a decrease in their scores for two reasons: Firstly, during the first week (to the left of the red dotted line), the groups received no training. Secondly, the initial active score was calculated after day 13 (indicated by the green dotted line), after a sufficient number of challenges were presented – a minimum of five challenges with at least one challenge from each one of the three attack vectors (see Sect. 5.4). After day 13 both groups demonstrated notable improvement, with the ConGISATA group exhibiting slightly better performance. This result emphasizes that the training for secure passive behavior received by the ConGISATA group also reinforces active behavior.

RQ3: Does increased use of our framework correlate with greater improvement in passive behavior?

We logged every view of each of the app's screens and looked for a correlation between views and behavioral change. As expected, the most significant Pearson correlation was found between the number of views of the learning screen and the total delta in the passive score ($r = 0.72$, $p = 3.41e{-}5$), as seen in Fig. 5. A similar result was obtained when checking for a correlation between the number of days in which a subject viewed the learning screen and the passive score

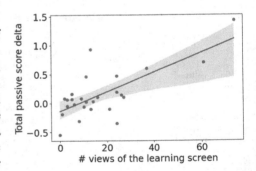

Fig. 5. Correlation between the number of views of the learning screen and passive score delta

delta. However, one of our learning screen's main advantages is its continuous nature, allowing users to see up-to-date details on each focus area with respect to their passive behavior. Going through the entire screen thoroughly may require more than one view per day so we chose to report the number of views and not the number of days, to differentiate subjects who viewed the learning screen multiple times a day from those who did not.

6 Conclusion

This study introduces ConGISATA - a continuous gamified ISA training and assessment framework that collects data from various sensors in users' everyday environments to examine aspects of ISA in real-life settings. The sensor readings are integrated into the framework, which generates a feedback loop. This continuous feedback mechanism helps users learn from their mistakes and improve their resilience against prevalent security risks. The use of sensors and challenges also provides a more reliable ISA assessment than the commonly used self-reported questionnaires. Our results confirm that ConGISATA improves passive behavior, while the baseline method does not. Moreover, although ConGISATA only provides articles on passive behavior, it helps users improve their ability to handle active attack scenarios. ConGISATA can be used in a corporate environment, in new employee training or as a regularly performed periodic procedure. Adapting the framework to new threats should be relatively easy, and may include these steps: (1) adding a new type of challenge simulating the new threat; (2) implementing additional sensors to measure related real-life behaviors; and (3) collecting (or creating) educational articles about the new threat. The number of subjects in this study does not allow meaningful analysis of the contribution of timing and personalization to ConGISATA's ability to improve ISA. This limitation can be addressed in more extensive experiments, including an ablation study performed with a large group of users, which we plan for future work.

Appendix

List of Articles and Blog Posts

As described in Sect. 5.3, we collected 32 publicly available relevant educational articles and blog posts to use in the experiment (the blog posts and articles are listed in Table 5). The items for the ConGISATA group are listed first, with their corresponding ISA taxonomy criterion ID, and do not include a comprehensiveness grade. The items for the baseline group, which include a comprehensiveness grade, are listed after the bold horizontal line.

Table 5. The articles and blog posts used in the experiment

	Topic	Links	Comprehensiveness Grade
ConGISATA	Account (A2)	link	–
	Account (A3)	link	–
	Browser (B1)	link	–
	Virtual Communication (VC1)	link	–
	Virtual Communication (VC2)	link	–
	Network (N1)	link	–
	Network (N3)	link	–
	Application Installation (AI1)	link	–
	Application Installation (AI2)	link	–
	Application Installation (AI3)	link	–
	Application Handling (AH1)	link	–
	Application Handling (AH3)	link	–
	Security Systems (SS2)	link	–
	Security Systems (SS5)	link	–
	Physical Connectivity (PC1)	link	–
	Operating System (OS2)	link	–
Baseline	Impersonation Attacks	link	2
	Impersonation Attacks	link, link, link, link	3
	Impersonation Attacks	link	5
	Permission Attacks	link, link	2
	Permission Attacks	link, link	3
	Permission Attacks	link	5
	Phishing Attacks	link, link, link, link, link	1

Passive Score Delta by Criterion

Figure 6 shows the average score deltas for the groups per criterion, as a function of the number of days since the experiment started.

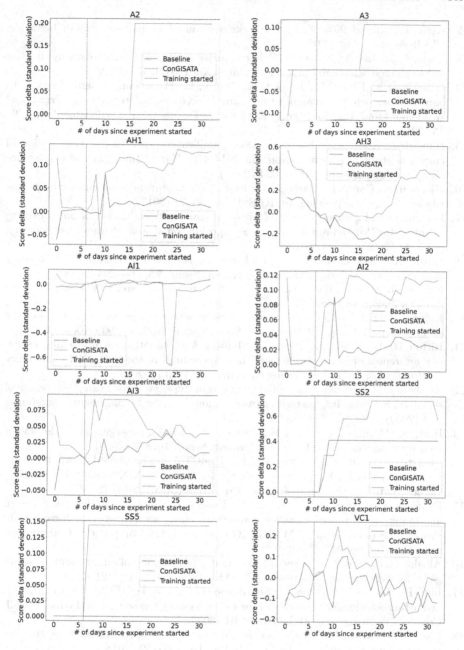

Fig. 6. Average score deltas for the groups per criterion, as a function of the number of days since the experiment started.

References

1. Kumar, A., Chaudhary, M., Kumar, N.: Social engineering threats and awareness: a survey. Eur. J. Adv. Eng. Technol. **2**, 15–19 (2015)

 2. Kelly, R.: Almost 90% of cyber attacks are caused by human error or behavior. ChiefExecutive. Net (2017)
 3. Bada, M., Sasse, A., Nurse, J.: Cyber security awareness campaigns: why do they fail to change behaviour? arXiv Preprint arXiv:1901.02672 (2019)
 4. Deterding, S., Dixon, D., Khaled, R., Nacke, L.: From game design elements to gamefulness: defining "gamification". In: Proceedings of the 15th International Academic MindTrek Conference: Envisioning Future Media Environments, pp. 9–15 (2011)
 5. Hamari, J., Koivisto, J., Sarsa, H.: Does gamification work?–a literature review of empirical studies on gamification. In: 2014 47th Hawaii International Conference on System Sciences, pp. 3025–3034 (2014)
 6. Gjertsen, E., Gjære, E., Bartnes, M., Flores, W.: Gamification of information security awareness and training. In: ICISSP, pp. 59–70 (2017)
 7. Kumaraguru, P., et al.: School of phish: a real-world evaluation of anti-phishing training. In: Proceedings of the 5th Symposium on Usable Privacy and Security, pp. 1–12 (2009)
 8. Bitton, R., Finkelshtein, A., Sidi, L., Puzis, R., Rokach, L., Shabtai, A.: Taxonomy of mobile users' security awareness. Comput. Secur. **73**, 266–293 (2018)
 9. Keinan, R., Bereby-Meyer, Y.: "Leaving it to chance"–passive risk taking in everyday life. Judgment Decis. Making **7** (2012)
10. Keinan, R., Bereby-Meyer, Y.: Perceptions of active versus passive risks, and the effect of personal responsibility. Pers. Soc. Psychol. Bull. **43**, 999–1007 (2017)
11. Bitton, R., Boymgold, K., Puzis, R., Shabtai, A.: Evaluating the information security awareness of smartphone users. In: Proceedings of the 2020 CHI Conference on Human Factors in Computing Systems, pp. 1–13 (2020)
12. Newbould, M., Furnell, S.: Playing safe: a prototype game for raising awareness of social engineering. In: Australian Information Security Management Conference, p. 4 (2009)
13. Hart, S., Margheri, A., Paci, F., Sassone, V.: Riskio: a serious game for cyber security awareness and education. Comput. Secur. 101827 (2020)
14. Chapman, P., Burket, J., Brumley, D.: PicoCTF: a game-based computer security competition for high school students. In: 2014 USENIX Summit on Gaming, Games, and Gamification in Security Education (3GSE 2014) (2014)
15. Denning, T., Lerner, A., Shostack, A., Kohno, T.: Control-Alt-Hack: the design and evaluation of a card game for computer security awareness and education. In: Proceedings of the 2013 ACM SIGSAC Conference On Computer & Communications Security, pp. 915–928 (2013)
16. Alqahtani, H., Kavakli-Thorne, M.: Design and evaluation of an augmented reality game for cybersecurity awareness (CybAR). Information **11**, 121 (2020)
17. Luh, R., Temper, M., Tjoa, S., Schrittwieser, S., Janicke, H.: PenQuest: a gamified attacker/defender meta model for cyber security assessment and education. J. Comput. Virol. Hacking Tech. **16**, 19–61 (2020)
18. Yasin, A., Liu, L., Li, T., Fatima, R., Jianmin, W.: Improving software security awareness using a serious game. IET Softw. **13**, 159–169 (2018)
19. Arend, I., Shabtai, A., Idan, T., Keinan, R., Bereby-Meyer, Y.: Passive-and not active-risk tendencies predict cyber security behavior. Comput. Secur. 101929 (2020)
20. Selvam, V.: Human error in IT security. arXiv Preprint arXiv:2005.04163 (2020)
21. Dunlosky, J., Rawson, K., Marsh, E., Nathan, M., Willingham, D.: Improving students' learning with effective learning techniques: promising directions from cognitive and educational psychology. Psychol. Sci. Public Interest **14**, 4–58 (2013)

22. Canham, M., Posey, C., Constantino, M.: Phish derby: shoring the human shield through gamified phishing attacks. Front. Educ. **6**, 536 (2022)
23. Jaffray, A., Finn, C., Nurse, J.: SherLOCKED: a detective-themed serious game for cyber security education. In: International Symposium on Human Aspects of Information Security and Assurance, pp. 35–45 (2021)
24. Sophos Sophos 2023 Threat Report (2022). https://assets.sophos.com/X24WTUEQ/at/b5n9ntjqmbkb8fg5rn25g4fc/sophos-2023-threat-report.pdf
25. Redmiles, E., Zhu, Z., Kross, S., Kuchhal, D., Dumitras, T., Mazurek, M.: Asking for a friend: evaluating response biases in security user studies. In: Proceedings of the 2018 ACM SIGSAC Conference on Computer and Communications Security, pp. 1238–1255 (2018)
26. Solomon, A., et al.: Contextual security awareness: a context-based approach for assessing the security awareness of users. Knowl.-Based Syst. **246**, 108709 (2022)
27. Böckle, M., Novak, J., Bick, M.: Towards adaptive gamification: a synthesis of current developments (2017)
28. Alahmari, S., Renaud, K., Omoronyia, I.: Moving beyond cyber security awareness and training to engendering security knowledge sharing. Inf. Syst. E-Bus. Manag. 1–36 (2022)
29. Dincelli, E., Chengalur-Smith, I.: Choose your own training adventure: designing a gamified SETA artefact for improving information security and privacy through interactive storytelling. Eur. J. Inf. Syst. **29**, 669–687 (2020)
30. Scholefield, S., Shepherd, L.A.: Gamification techniques for raising cyber security awareness. In: Moallem, A. (ed.) HCII 2019. LNCS, vol. 11594, pp. 191–203. Springer, Cham (2019). https://doi.org/10.1007/978-3-030-22351-9_13
31. Omar, N., Foozy, C., Hamid, I., Hafit, H., Arbain, A., Shamala, P.: Malware awareness tool for internet safety using gamification techniques. In: Journal of Physics: Conference Series, vol. 1874, p. 012023 (2021)
32. Wu, T., Tien, K., Hsu, W., Wen, F.: Assessing the effects of gamification on enhancing information security awareness knowledge. Appl. Sci. **11**, 9266 (2021)
33. Heid, K., Heider, J., Qasempour, K.: Raising security awareness on mobile systems through gamification. In: Proceedings of the European Interdisciplinary Cybersecurity Conference, pp. 1–6 (2020)

Tactics for Account Access Graphs

Luca Arnaboldi[1(✉)], David Aspinall[2], Christina Kolb[2], and Saša Radomirović[3]

[1] University of Birmingham, Birmingham, UK
l.arnaboldi@bham.ac.uk
[2] University of Edinburgh, Edinburgh, UK
david.aspinall@ed.ac.uk, c.kolb@utwente.nl
[3] University of Surrey, Guildford, UK
s.radomirovic@surrey.ac.uk

Abstract. Account access graphs have been proposed as a way to model relationships between user credentials, accounts, and methods of access; they capture both multiple simultaneous access routes (e.g., for multi-factor authentication) as well as multiple alternative access routes (e.g., for account recovery). In this paper we extend the formalism with state transitions and tactics. State transitions capture how access may change over time as users or adversaries use access routes and add or remove credentials and accounts. Tactics allow us to model and document attacker techniques or resilience strategies, by writing small programs. We illustrate these ideas using some attacks against mobile authentication and banking applications which have been publicised in 2023.

Keywords: account access graphs · tactics · security · Android · iOS

1 Introduction

As the connections between online services we use in our daily lives increase, so do the possibilities for an attacker to exploit them. By chaining a series of access escalations, often using recovery or fallback methods, an attacker can take over more and more of a user's accounts. A prominent example of such an account takeover attack was in 2012 when the Wired journalist Mat Honan's Twitter account was compromised in a sequence of steps in which an attacker took control of his Amazon account, Apple account, Google account and eventually the coveted Twitter account [10]. Several analogous attacks have arisen over the years following similar procedural steps [6,13,15]. Attacks that abuse a particular constellation of user accounts are difficult to eliminate because different users have different and continuously changing account ecosystems.

Attackers use multiple strategies and build complex attacks by combining smaller steps. To understand and prevent attacks it helps to catalogue vulnerabilities and reduce complex attacks to their constituent building blocks. This approach is seen elsewhere. For software vulnerabilities, for example, the Metasploit Framework [11] provides a scripting language so penetration testers can combine known exploits with scanning tools.

In this paper we provide ways to model and catalogue account takeover attacks and their defences. To do this we propose a generic language of attack and defence actions based on tactics, which are small programs in a domain specific language. The actions act on Account Access Graphs [9] which capture connections between users' devices, credentials and accounts. They were developed to help assess security of a user's account ecosystem. While the original account access graphs have been successful in visualising account ecosystems and analysing static security properties, they are insufficient to model account takeover attacks in which an attacker disconnects a device or account from the user's account ecosystem, thus modifying the user's account access graph in the process. We overcome this limitation here by considering account access graphs as states in a state transition system. We then introduce tactics to transition from one account access graph to another.

To demonstrate our approach, we consider two notable case studies where the attacker's goal is to gain access to and lock out the user from an account of central importance to many users: the Apple ID account for iPhone users and the Google account for Android device users. We compare the attacks in the two cases and we discuss countermeasures for each of them.

Contributions. We provide the following key contributions: (1) The extension of account access graphs to include state and a transition system; (2) the introduction of tactics for the development and exploration of state based account access graphs; and (3) the demonstration of this new formalism across two case studies showcasing their efficacy and flexibility.

Structure. The paper is structured as follows. Section 2 introduces the original account access graphs and the new extension with state. Section 3 introduces the properties of account access graphs with state, the changes to account access graphs, the tactics, and account access graph requirements. In Sect. 4 we present our case studies to showcase the effectiveness of tactics to explore attacks. In Sect. 5 we discuss related work in the area and in Sect. 6 we conclude this work and present ideas for future work.

2   Account Access Graphs with State

The initial underlying structure of account access graphs was first defined in [9] to formally model a user's account ecosystem.

Definition 1 (Account Access Graph [9]). *An account access graph is a directed graph $G = (V_G, E_G, C_G)$, where V_G are vertices, C_G are colours and $E_G \subseteq V_G \times V_G \times C_G$ are directed coloured edges.*

An example of an account access graph that represents a standard way to unlock a modern mobile phone is shown in Fig. 1(a). The graph consists of four vertices, namely a Phone, a PIN, a Face, and a Locked_Phone vertex. The graph shows two alternative ways to access the Phone vertex. One way is to have access to both, the Locked_Phone and the PIN and the other way is to have access to the Locked_Phone and the Face vertex.

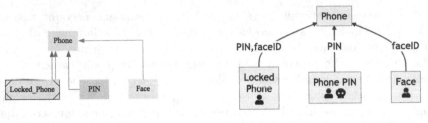

(a) Account Access Graph   (b) Account Access Graph with State

Fig. 1. Illustration of Definitions 1 and 2

Two natural threats to a user's account are account compromise and loss of access. In order to capture the evolution of users' account access graphs which includes, for example, the addition of new accounts, changed credentials, loss of access, and compromise, we start by extending the definition of account access graphs to include information on which accounts and credentials are (presently) accessed by which parties. We add state to the account access graph by including a map which assigns a, possibly empty, set of parties to each vertex.

Our account access graph with state has an underlying account access graph equivalent to Definition 1. However, in our definition we replace an account access graph's multiple, coloured edges from one vertex to another by a single edge to which we assign a set of labels. The cardinality of the assigned set in our definition is equal to the number of edges between the same vertices in the original definition of the graph. Figure 1(b) shows an account access graph with state whose underlying account access graph is equivalent to the graph shown in Fig. 1(a). In addition, the graph in Fig. 1(b) shows that the user 🧑 presently has access to the LockedPhone, the PIN, and the Face, but not to the Phone. That is, the user's phone is currently not in the unlocked state. The adversary 💀 has presently only access to the PIN. In this state, the user would be able to unlock the phone, while the adversary would not. Formally, let $\mathcal{V}$ be a countably infinite set of vertices (representing, e.g., accounts, devices, credentials), ranged over by (possibly indexed) variables u and v. Let $\mathcal{L}$ be a countably infinite set of labels (for access methods) ranged over by l and $\mathcal{A}$ be a set of participants, typically a user and an attacker, ranged over by a. In this paper, $\mathcal{A}$ will contain the user 🧑 and the attacker 💀.

Definition 2 (Account Access Graphs with State). *An account access graph with state is a triple $G = (V, E, A)$ where $V \subset \mathcal{V}$ is a finite set of vertices, $E : (V \times V) \to 2^{\mathcal{L}}$ is a map labelling pairs of vertices with finite sets of access methods, pairs of vertices labelled with a non-empty set of access methods are edges, and $A : V \to 2^{\mathcal{A}}$ is a map labelling vertices with a finite set of participants.*

The vertices of account access graphs with state represent accounts, passwords, access tokens, etc. For every pair of vertices, the edge function $E(u, v)$ gives a set of labels. If the set is non-empty, the pair (u, v) is an edge of the graph.

A label shared between n edges $(u_1, v), \ldots, (u_n, v)$ models an n-ary multi-factor route for access to the target vertex v. Alternative routes for access have different labels. Identity of labels only matters locally, i.e., for edges with identical target vertex. The map A labels vertices with sets of participants who have current access to the vertices and represents the state of the account access graph.

3   A Transition System

We now build a transition system for account access graphs with state to capture the changes that can occur in an account access graph as a consequence of a participant's (i.e., a user's or adversary's) actions. First we introduce properties which describe the shape of the graph; these can be used to build up precise statements of requirements or outcomes.

3.1   Properties of Account Access Graphs with State

A property on an account access graph G is a predicate over (V, E, A). Such a property takes into account the structure of the graph as well as the user's and adversary's current access to vertices in the graph. To define a simple logic of properties, we use basic assertions on the account access graph, and allow propositional combinations. Expressions in the logic are given by the grammar:

$$\phi ::=$$
$$\begin{array}{ll} is\_account(v) & \textit{account } v \textit{ exists in graph} \\ |\ has\_access_a(v) & \textit{user } a \textit{ is accessing account } v \\ |\ could\_access_a(v) & \textit{user } a \textit{ has a way to access } v \\ |\ uses\_method_l(u, v) & v \textit{ is accessible from } u \textit{ using label } l \\ |\ \phi_1 \wedge \phi_2\ |\ \phi_1 \vee \phi_2\ |\ \neg\phi\ |\ true \end{array}$$

Definition 3 (Validity).   *The validity of assertions is defined inductively, starting from atomic propositions:*

- $\langle V, E, A \rangle \models is\_account(v)$ *if* $v \in V$.
- $\langle V, E, A \rangle \models has\_access_a(v)$ *if* $v \in V$ *and* $a \in A(v)$.
- $\langle V, E, A \rangle \models could\_access_a(v)$ *if* $v \in V$ *and* $\exists l, u. l \in E(u, v) \wedge \forall x \in V . l \in E(x, v) \implies a \in A(x)$.
- $\langle V, E, A \rangle \models uses\_method_l(u, v)$ *if* $u, v \in V$ *and* $l \in E(u, v)$.
- $\langle V, E, A \rangle \models \phi_1 \wedge \phi_2$ *if* $\langle V, E, A \rangle \models \phi_1$ *and* $\langle V, E, A \rangle \models \phi_2$.
- $\langle V, E, A \rangle \models \phi_1 \vee \phi_2$ *if* $\langle V, E, A \rangle \models \phi_1$ *or* $\langle V, E, A \rangle \models \phi_2$.
- $\langle V, E, A \rangle \models \neg\phi$ *if it does not hold that* $\langle V, E, A \rangle \models \phi$.
- $\langle V, E, A \rangle \models true$ *always.*

It would be natural to extend the assertion language to include forms of quantification over vertices, labels and participants, such as existential or universal choice (selection). For simplicity we restrict to propositional forms here; for particular fixed settings talking about known sets of users, accounts and access methods, we can use finitary expansions. For example, if $V = \{\text{pwd}, \text{phone}\}$, $A = \{\text{👤}, \text{💀}\}$ then $\exists v, a.\ could\_access_a(v)$ stands for the expansion

$$could\_access_{👤}(\text{pwd}) \lor could\_access_{💀}(\text{pwd}) \lor$$
$$could\_access_{👤}(\text{phone}) \lor could\_access_{💀}(\text{phone}).$$

To be clear, when we use quantification below it is in the metalogic.

3.2   Changes to Account Access Graphs

Next we give a transition relation which allows users or attackers to change their current access to vertices in the graph or the graph itself. To this end, we give seven operations in Definition 4 below.

The first three operations (GAIN, DISC, LOSE) modify the state of the account access graph, i.e., the access map, without changing the graph structure. These model users accessing accounts via access links already in the graph, attackers discovering access "out of thin air" and users or attackers losing or dropping access. The next four operations, CREATE, DELETE, ADD and the two remove variants (REMOVE1, REMOVE2), change the graph structure by adding or removing vertices and edges in ways that might be possible by a user or attacker.

Definition 4 (Account Access Graph Operations). *An account access graph with state can be modified with the following seven operations. We use α to range over these operations.*

$$\frac{\langle V, E, A \rangle \models could\_access_a(u)}{\langle V, E, A \rangle \overset{gain\_access_{a,v}}{\rightsquigarrow} \langle V, E, A[v \mapsto a] \rangle} \quad (\text{GAIN})$$

$$\langle V, E, A \rangle \overset{disc\_access_{a,v}}{\rightsquigarrow} \langle V, E, A[v \mapsto a] \rangle \quad (\text{DISC})$$

$$\langle V, E, A \rangle \overset{lose\_access_{a,v}}{\rightsquigarrow} \langle V, E, A[v \setminus a] \rangle \quad (\text{LOSE})$$

The notation $A[v \mapsto a]$ means A updated to add a into the access set of v, i.e. the updated map A' given by

$$A'(x) = \begin{cases} A(v) \cup \{a\} & \text{when } x = v \\ A(x) & \text{otherwise.} \end{cases}$$

Similarly, $A[v \setminus a]$ means A updated to remove a from the set of accesses $A(v)$.

$$\langle V, E, A \rangle \overset{create\_account_{a,v}}{\rightsquigarrow} \langle V \uplus \{v\}, E, A[v \mapsto a] \rangle \quad (\text{CREATE})$$

$$\frac{\langle V, E, A \rangle \models has\_access_a(v)}{\langle V, E, A \rangle \overset{del\_account_{a,v}}{\rightsquigarrow} \langle V \setminus \{v\}, E \setminus v, A|_{V \setminus \{v\}} \rangle} \quad (\text{DELETE})$$

$$\frac{\langle V, E, A \rangle \models has\_access_a(v) \qquad E'(x,y) = \begin{cases} \{l\} & \text{if } x \in \{u_1, \ldots, u_n\} \text{ and } y = v \\ \{\} & \text{otherwise.} \end{cases}}{\langle V, E, A \rangle \overset{add\_access_{a, \{u_1, \ldots, u_n\}, v, l}}{\rightsquigarrow} \langle V, E \uplus E', A \rangle}$$

$$(\text{ADD})$$

$$\frac{\langle V, E, A \rangle \models has\_access_a(v)}{\langle V, E, A \rangle \overset{rem\_access_{a,v,l}}{\rightsquigarrow} \langle V, E[(\_, v) \setminus \{l\}], A \rangle} \quad (\text{REMOVE1})$$

$$\frac{\langle V, E, A \rangle \models has\_access_a(v) \qquad \langle V, E, A \rangle \models uses\_method_l(v, u)}{\langle V, E, A \rangle \overset{rem\_access_{a,u,l}}{\rightsquigarrow} \langle V, E[(\_, u) \setminus \{l\}], A \rangle} \quad (\text{REMOVE2})$$

Here the notation $E \setminus v$ denotes the edge function E updated to remove any edges that have v as source or target, i.e., E' such that:

$$E'(u_1, u_2) = \begin{cases} \{\} & \text{if } u_1 = v \text{ or } u_2 = v \\ E(u_1, u_2) & \text{otherwise.} \end{cases}$$

Similarly, the notation $E[(\_, v) \setminus \{l\}]$ means the update of E to remove the access method l to vertex v from E.

We give an example to illustrate these operations which demonstrates how the extension increases the expressivity of the formalism.

Example 1. Access to SMS previews on a locked phone was previously identified as a vulnerability because the phone's theft could allow an attacker to escalate their access to online accounts that use SMS as a recovery method. The security advice reported, e.g., in [8], was to disable the display of messages on the lock screen. However, this may not be sufficient. Figure 2(a) shows a state where an attacker has stolen a phone, but does not know the phone's PIN. In this graph the adversary cannot gain access to the SMS vertex.

By having physical access to the phone, the attacker can physically access the victim's SIM card to be inserted into a phone controlled by the attacker. Formally, a *gain_access* ☠,SIM card transition followed by a *create_account* ☠,2nd Phone transition. The resulting state is shown in Fig. 2(b).

Next, the attacker removes the SIM card from the victim's phone which leads to the phone's loss of ability to receive SMS. The attacker inserts the SIM card into their own phone to gain access to SMS messages delivered to that SIM card on the second phone. The result is shown in Fig. 2(c). This is possible since, as modelled in this graph, the SIM card is not protected by its own PIN. This is particularly likely to be the case in countries where SIM cards are sold without a preset, unique PIN. The state transitions to reach the last state from the graph in Fig. 2(b) are: *rem_access* ☠,SIM card,phys (by REMOVE1), *rem_access* ☠,Phone SMS,SIMapp (by REMOVE2), *add_access* ☠,2nd Phone,SIM card,phys, *gain_access* ☠,SIM key, *create_account* ☠,2nd Phone SMS, and *add_access* ☠,S,D,l for $S = \{$2nd Phone, SIM card, SIM key$\}$, $D = $ 2nd Phone SMS and $l = $ SMSapp.

The countermeasure to this attack is to lock the SIM card with a PIN code as shown in Fig. 2(d). This prevents the adversary's access to the SIM key and thus access to SMS messages.

The discovery and explanation of this attack require reasoning about the adversary's actions to carry out the attack, notably, stealing the phone, removing the SIM card and inserting it into a second phone controlled by the adversary. As shown in Fig. 2(c), these actions not only change the access map A, but also the underlying account access graph (V, E).

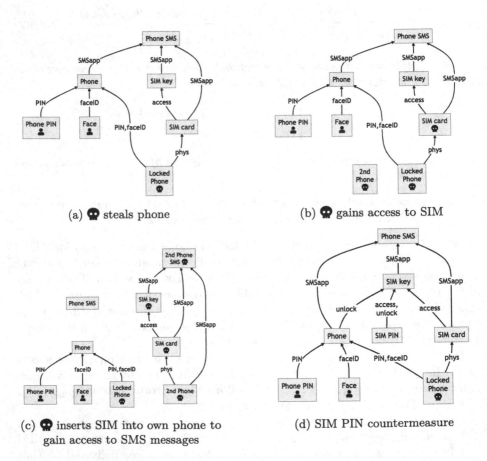

(a) ☠ steals phone

(b) ☠ gains access to SIM

(c) ☠ inserts SIM into own phone to gain access to SMS messages

(d) SIM PIN countermeasure

Fig. 2. Three states in the evolution of an attack (a)–(c) and a mitigating measure against the attack (d).

3.3 Tactics

A tactic is a short, abstract program with a well-defined semantics which applies the operations α in Definition 4 to achieve a given goal. The idea is borrowed from interactive theorem proving where tactics are used to generate proofs in a logic. Here, tactics capture the way attacks or defensive techniques (or system operations) execute.

To define tactics we start with syntactic expressions for composing operations α in certain orders, with testing to check properties and alternation to try alternatives. For simplicity we give the language a deterministic semantics, treating both sequencing (;) and alternation ($\|$) sequentially, although generalisation to parallel forms would be possible. The language includes $\top$ which is the tactic for successful termination and $\bot$ which is the failure tactic. We use b to range over the constants $\top, \bot$.

$$t ::= \quad \alpha \mid b \mid t \; ; \; t \mid t \parallel t \mid \mathsf{CHECK}(\phi)$$

Next we give a semantics as evaluation rules for tactics. The tactic semantics defines a tactic as a function on states σ, although its definition does not depend on the form of the state; changes on the state are made only by the primitive graph operations. The states σ are our account access graphs with state (V, E, A).

We define the big-step semantics for the tactic operations by extending the transition relation given earlier, to give a relation $\langle \sigma \rangle t \; \Downarrow \; b \langle \sigma' \rangle$, where $b \in \{\top, \bot\}$. Executing a tactic either succeeds or fails, giving a possibly updated state.

Definition 5 (Tactics for Account Access Graph Operations). *The following list of rules inductively defines tactic evaluation for account access graphs.*

$$\frac{\langle \sigma \rangle \xrightarrow{\alpha} \langle \sigma' \rangle}{\langle \sigma \rangle \, \alpha \; \Downarrow \; \top \langle \sigma' \rangle} \qquad\qquad \textit{(AX-T)}$$

$$\langle \sigma \rangle \, b \; \Downarrow \; b \langle \sigma' \rangle \qquad\qquad \textit{(CONST)}$$

$$\frac{\langle \sigma \rangle \, t_1 \; \Downarrow \; \bot \langle \sigma' \rangle}{\langle \sigma \rangle \, t_1 \; ; \; t_2 \; \Downarrow \; \bot \langle \sigma' \rangle} \qquad\qquad \textit{(SEQ-B)}$$

$$\frac{\langle \sigma \rangle \, t_1 \; \Downarrow \; \top \langle \sigma' \rangle \qquad \langle \sigma' \rangle \, t_2 \; \Downarrow \; b \langle \sigma'' \rangle}{\langle \sigma \rangle \, t_1 \; ; \; t_2 \; \Downarrow \; b \langle \sigma'' \rangle} \qquad\qquad \textit{(SEQ-T)}$$

$$\frac{\langle \sigma \rangle \, t_1 \; \Downarrow \; \bot \langle \sigma' \rangle \qquad \langle \sigma \rangle \, t_2 \; \Downarrow \; b \langle \sigma'' \rangle}{\langle \sigma \rangle \, t_1 \parallel t_2 \; \Downarrow \; b \langle \sigma'' \rangle} \qquad\qquad \textit{(OR-B)}$$

$$\frac{\langle \sigma \rangle \, t_1 \; \Downarrow \; \top \langle \sigma' \rangle}{\langle \sigma \rangle \, t_1 \parallel t_2 \; \Downarrow \; \top \langle \sigma' \rangle} \qquad\qquad \textit{(OR-T)}$$

$$\frac{\langle \sigma \rangle \models \phi}{\langle \sigma \rangle \ \mathsf{CHECK}\phi \ \Downarrow \ \top \ \langle \sigma \rangle} \qquad (\text{CHECK-T})$$

$$\frac{\neg\langle \sigma \rangle \models \phi}{\langle \sigma \rangle \ \mathsf{CHECK}\phi \ \Downarrow \ \bot \ \langle \sigma \rangle} \qquad (\text{CHECK-F})$$

Note that tactic evaluation can get stuck and not terminate in $\bot$ or $\top$. Specifically, the rule AX-T can fail if one of the account access graph operations rules given in Definition 4 cannot be applied. However, where tactic evaluation terminates, it is deterministic.

Proposition 1 (Tactic Determinism). *If $\langle \sigma \rangle\, t \ \Downarrow \ b\,\langle \sigma' \rangle$ then b and σ' are the unique such b and σ'.*

Proof. We can use induction on the structure of t, noting that the evaluation rules are mutually exclusive. In the case of operations α, we notice from Definition 4 that the new state σ' is uniquely determined by α.

The next example shows tactic evaluation and introduces an account access graph that we will also discuss, from an attacker perspective, in the case study.

Example 2. Consider a state σ where a user has an iPhone with an associated Apple ID, but (for simplicity) no biometric authentication method registered on the phone. Figure 3(a) shows the corresponding account access graph.

If the user applies the tactic

$$t = create\_account_{\textbf{⚫},iCloud}; \ add\_access_{\textbf{⚫},\{AppleID\},iCloud,icloud};$$
$$create\_account_{\textbf{⚫},ApplePay}; \ add\_access_{\textbf{⚫},\{Phone\},ApplePay,pay}$$

to first add iCloud to their Apple ID and then Apple Pay to their Phone, then the original account access graph would change to the graph shown in Fig. 3(b). The tactic evaluation would proceed as follows. Rule (AX-T) is applied to create the iCloud account. This leads to a state transition where a new vertex named iCloud is generated and assigned to ⚫ . Since this transition was successful, the (SEQ-T) rule (as opposed to the (SEQ-B) rule) is applied for the sequential operator;. Next the (AX-T) rule is applied to add the iCloud vertex to vertex AppleID, followed by the (SEQ-B) rule. The four rule applications are then repeated for the addition of ApplePay to the user's account ecosystem.

Observe that $\mathsf{CHECK}\phi$ turns a property into a tactic. We can use this to define a condition by guarding *both* branches. Indeed, it is handy to use some shorthand notation for conditional branching by letting IF ϕ THEN t_1 ELSE t_2 stand for $(\mathsf{CHECK}\phi \ ; \ t_1) \ || \ (\mathsf{CHECK}\neg\phi \ ; \ t_2)$. Note that in case t_1 fails in the THEN branch, the guard $\neg\phi$ makes sure the ELSE branch t_2 is not taken.

Relatedly, we can define a shorthand notation for repeating tactics over several vertices. We may write FORALL x IN $[v_1, \ldots, v_n]$ DO t where t uses a metavariable x as a vertex name. Then

$$\mathsf{FORALL} \ x \ \mathsf{IN} \ [\mathsf{pwd, phone}] \ \mathsf{DO} \ \mathsf{CHECK} \ could\_access_{\textbf{☠}}(x)$$

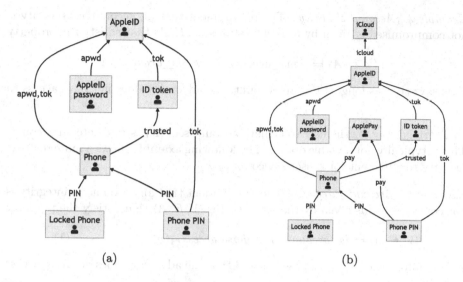

(a)   (b)

Fig. 3. Initial account access graph (left) and resulting account access graph after addition of iCloud and ApplePay.

stands for the sequence of two checks. To iterate the alternation operation instead, we write FORONE x IN $[v_1, \ldots, v_n]$ TRY t which expands to $t[x \mapsto v_1] \parallel \cdots \parallel t[x \mapsto v_n]$. These can be combined with the corresponding expansion of properties.

3.4   Account Access Graph Requirements

The purpose of tactics is to reach some goal. To evaluate whether a user's or adversary's tactics are successful, we define requirements on our account access graphs with state. The user's goal is usually to satisfy a security requirement while the adversary's goal is to break a security requirement.

Formally, an *account access graph requirement* r is a set of states $\sigma = \langle V, E, A \rangle$. We say that a state σ satisfies a requirement r if $\sigma \in r$. We give several examples of security requirements.

Example 3 (Multifactor Authentication). A multifactor authentication requirement for an account v is given by the set of states $\langle V, E, A \rangle$ in which there are distinct vertices u and u' and an access method l such that

$$\langle V, E, A \rangle \models \mathit{uses\_method}_l(u, v) \wedge \mathit{uses\_method}_l(u', v) \vee \neg \mathit{is\_account}(v).$$

The Multifactor Authentication requirement is a structural requirement on the account access graph that has been used to discuss the overall security of users' account access graphs [1,8]. The following examples show standard security requirements that depend on the state map and thus necessitate account access graphs with state.

Example 4 (Account Security). The requirement that an account v's security is not compromised is given by the set of states $\langle V, E, A \rangle$ that satisfy the property

$$\langle V, E, A \rangle \models \neg has\_access_{\skull}(v) \lor \neg is\_account(v).$$

This says that as long as v is an account, the adversary does not have access to it.

A trivial way for the user to achieve account security is to delete an account. This is typically not a viable option. The following example shows a more realistic security requirement for a user's account.

Example 5 (Account Integrity). The requirement that an account v's integrity is not compromised is given by the set of states $\langle V, E, A \rangle$ that satisfy the property

$$\langle V, E, A \rangle \models is\_account(v) \land \neg has\_access_{\skull}(v). \tag{1}$$

This requires that the account exists and that the adversary does not have access to it.

The account integrity property concerns unauthorised access and modification (deletion) of an account, but it does not consider whether the user has access to the account. The following example considers accessibility.

Example 6 (Account Access). The requirement that the user has access to account v is given by the set of states $\langle V, E, A \rangle$ that satisfy the property

$$\langle V, E, A \rangle \models is\_account(v) \land has\_access_{\text{\tiny user}}(v). \tag{2}$$

The preceding examples are typical security goals for users. A standard goal for the adversary is account compromise, i.e., the negation of account security.

Example 7 (Account Compromise). The requirement that an account v is compromised is given by the set of states $\langle V, E, A \rangle$ that satisfy the property

$$\langle V, E, A \rangle \models is\_account(v) \land has\_access_{\skull}(v).$$

We will use requirements (1) and (2) in our case study in the next section.

4   Case Study

We demonstrate the use of tactics to explore the ways an attacker can compromise a user's account ecosystem on the following scenario that is based on a recently published article in The Wall Street Journal [15]: *Thieves target iPhone users and observe them until they learn a victim's iPhone PIN. They then steal the iPhone and within minutes gain access to sensitive data and bank accounts. The thieves remove the victim's access from all their Apple devices to their data and steal money from their bank accounts.*

We use the basic template of phone and PIN to propagate the attack across accounts. We then analyse the same scenario on Android to assess the feasibility of success in this setting. We start by defining the relevant security requirements, the user and adversary capabilities.

4.1   Security Requirements, User Capabilities and Adversary Model

Based on the described scenario, we define concrete security requirements for an iPhone user with an account access graph as shown in Fig. 3(b). The two core properties we wish to enforce are Account Integrity and Account Access as defined in (1) and (2) in Examples 5 and 6, respectively, for the accounts AppleID, iCloud and ApplePay. Thus we have a total of six security requirements, two for each of the three accounts.

The defined security requirements would be meaningless if we allow the user and the adversary to make arbitrary use of the *disc_access* tactic. The user could magically regain access to accounts that they have been locked out of and the adversary could compromise any account and device at will. In the case study scenario, the user does not have magic abilities and the adversary is assumed to only have the ability to eavesdrop on the PIN and steal the phone. Therefore, we will analyse the security requirements under the assumption that no *disc_access* transitions occur, except for $disc\_access$ ☠,PIN and $disc\_access$ ☠,Phone.

4.2   Case Study 1: iPhone Tactics to Systematically Access Accounts

We formalise the attack tactics of a potential adversary and show how the attacker can systematically infringe on all the security properties the user wished to have for their protection.

1. We start with an account access graph for a user 👤 with device Phone that contains the graph shown in Fig. 3(b), and potentially includes further devices with a similar access relation to the AppleID and iCloud accounts, but no access to ApplePay.
2. The attacker's initial tactic is to discover the PIN of the user's iPhone while he observes the user entering the PIN into the iPhone. At a suitable moment, the attacker steals the iPhone and, together with the PIN, gains access to Phone and ApplePay. The user loses access to the phone and ApplePay. This violates the account integrity and account access requirements for ApplePay.

$$disc\_access\text{ ☠,PIN} ; disc\_access\text{ ☠,LockedPhone} ; gain\_access\text{ ☠,Phone} ;$$
$$gain\_access\text{ ☠,ApplePay} ; lose\_access\text{ 👤,LockedPhone} ; lose\_access\text{ 👤,ApplePay}$$

3. The attacker has access to the unlocked phone. Thus he gains access to the stored IDtoken on the phone. Together with the phone and the ID token, the attacker gains access to the AppleID account.

$$gain\_access\text{ ☠,IDtoken} ; gain\_access\text{ ☠,AppleID} ; gain\_access\text{ ☠,iCloud}$$

At this point the integrity requirement for AppleID and iCloud is violated, but the access requirement could still be satisfied through the user's access to other devices in their account access graph.

4. In the final step, the attacker removes the user's ability to access their AppleID and iCloud accounts by changing the AppleIDpassword and removing any devices from the Apple ID. The latter is achieved by invalidating the ID token stored on the device, i.e., deleting the corresponding vertex in the graph. We formulate a tactic where the attacker does not need to know the user's account access graphs in advance. Let n be the finite number of devices other than the phone the user could own and suppose ID tokens for these devices are IDtoken_1, . . . , IDtoken_n and their AppleID password access methods are labelled apwd_1, . . . , apwd_n. Then the attacker will employ the following tactic to remove all possible devices the user could have associated with their Apple ID:

$$create\_account\ _{\text{☻,AdvPassword}}\ ;\ rem\_access\ _{\text{☻,AppleID,apwd}}\ ;$$
$$add\_access\ _{\text{☻,\{Phone,AdvPassword\},AppleID}}\ ;$$
$$\text{FORALL } x \text{ IN } [\text{apwd\_1}, . . . , \text{apwd\_}n] \text{ DO } rem\_access\ _{\text{☻,AppleID},x}\ ||\ \top\ ;$$
$$\text{FORALL } x \text{ IN } [\text{IDtoken\_1}, . . . , \text{IDtoken\_}n] \text{ DO } del\_account\ _{\text{☠,}x}\ ||\ \top\ ;$$
$$\text{FORALL } x \text{ IN } [\text{iCloud, AppleID}] \text{ DO } lose\_access\ _{\text{♟,}x}\ ||\ \top\ ;$$

The tactic is to create a new password AdvPassword, remove the previous access method with the old password (from the phone) and add the new password with the same label apwd that was used for the old password. Then any password-based access method is removed by trying out all possible access labels. Next all possible devices are removed by trying to delete each possible ID token. Finally the user's access is removed from the iCloud and the AppleID account, if possible.

From here on, the user does not know the correct AppleIDpassword and does not have a device that has a trusted id stored for the Apple ID. Therefore the remaining two account access requirements are not satisfied thus fully breaking all the security requirements of the iPhone user. Since the user cannot discover access to their AppleID, there is no tactic for the user to regain access from this state.

In terms of countermeasures, although the Wall Street article suggests Apple's screen time feature as a potential defence measure, we find that through a simple sequence of steps, the attacker can bypass the screen time block (starting with "forgotten screen time password"). This is once again achievable by simply having access to the Phone and PIN. In a real-world attack this slows the attacker down a little.

The users' lack of viable options to protect their Apple ID against this type of attack is a well-known flaw [16].

4.3   Case Study 2: Android Security and Expansion with Tactics

The original Wall Street Journal Article speculated that the same attack was possible on Android (although no such crimes were reported). For reference this would mean we could take the same tactic that worked on the iPhone and apply it to Android. So we formulate the same set of properties for the Android device as we do for the iPhone, namely, that given the attacker has access to the phone and PIN he still cannot 1) cannot access the Google account, 2) cannot compromise the users access to the Google account, and 3) even if he has access to the Google account the user will retain access to his Google Cloud and AndroidPay. The same evolution of the account access graph for Android is displayed in Fig. 4.

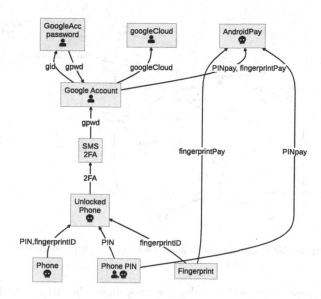

Fig. 4. Apple attack on Android (fails)

We can see that the same initial tactics steps from the iPhone apply to the Android device if we represent the Android phone in the same way with account access graph $G_0 = (V_0, E_0, A_0)$, as before. The initial tactic follows the same steps:

$$disc\_access_{\text{☠},\text{PIN}} \; ; \; disc\_access_{\text{☠},\text{LockedPhone}} \; ;$$
$$gain\_access_{\text{☠},\text{Phone}} \; ; \; lose\_access_{\text{♟},\text{LockedPhone}}$$

However this is the step where it changes as if we attempt to use tactics to test the feasibility of the next step using

CHECK($could\_access($ ☠, IDtoken$)$) || CHECK($could\_access($ ☠, GoogleAccount$)$)

we obtain ⊥ (**false**), for both checks, and according to the axioms of the language the tactic now terminates. The checks do not pass because the PIN is not enough to change the google account password. This is further empirically evaluated across Android, versions, and phone models. This Analysis was conducted from secondary evidence as well as across, 5 different devices 1) Motorola

G10 Android 11, 2) Lenovo YT-X705F Android 10, 3) Xiaomi Redmi Note Pro 10 Android 11, and 4) Samsung Galaxy Tab S6 Lite Android 13. Some of these devices had their own manufacturer accounts, namely Samsung and Xiaomi. They both suffered from the same limitation of Apple for those bespoke accounts. Although the Google account remains safe the bespoke accounts are compromised. This is depicted for the Samsung device in Fig. 5 (Xiaomi is the same).

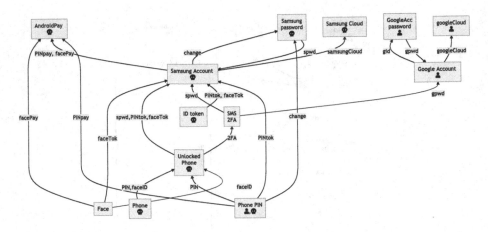

Fig. 5. Attack on bespoke manufacturer account on Android

Note that across all analysed devices they have the ability to individually lock apps behind further protection (Appendix A), making the success of this attack even less likely. Unlike Apple, Google always required a Google password to make any changes, so it is impossible (across all Android devices) to change the Google password in the way the Apple password can be changed.

These results show the efficacy of the formalism to explore attacks on access graphs and provide useful insights to a defender to improve security.

5   Related Work

Account access graphs were introduced in [9]. They were employed in user studies [1,8] to explore users' understanding of account security and the strategies users apply to keep themselves secure and used to enhance a password manager with a user-friendly dashboard for account dependency analysis [14]. In these works account access graphs are static objects used as a tool to visualise and analyse the security of a snapshot of a user's accounts. Account access graphs with state and transitions extend these works and allow for a security analysis with models of attacks, defences and mitigating measures.

In [17] new attacks on PIN protected SIM and eSIM cards are presented in scenarios where a known, preset PIN is used and scenarios where the attacker has access to the victim's phone to install malicious hardware or software. A variant of (static) account access graphs is then used to design and analyse the proposed improvements to the security of SIM and eSIM authentication and access control.

Tactics were introduced in interactive theorem proving, embodying a classical AI technique for goal-directed search [4, 7]. Tactics can decompose subgoals, and act in sequence, alternation, or parallel steps. They also allow repetition and exceptional failure to capture trying one thing, and then trying another if that fails (similarly to logic programming). Here we have used a simplified tactic language as a domain-specific language for modelling finitary account access graph construction and modifications, leaving more complex attack and defence examples to future work. As far as we are aware, this is a novel idea, although it is related to the use of dedicated formal languages to express security protocols (ProVerif [3], Tamarin [12] and many others) or scripting programming languages to combine software exploits. (e.g., Metasploit [11]).

6   Conclusions and Future Work

This work expanded on account access graphs by introducing state, transitions and tactics; these enable precise modelling and exploration of attacker behaviours. We demonstrated these on recently publicised attacks on iPhone users, allowing both the analysis of attacker strategies whilst simultaneously showing how to defend against it. Attempting similar attacks on Android showed an effective defence; we show conclusively that the attack on iPhones is not successful on Android thus disproving a supposition of the WSJ article.

This paper is a first foray in the possible applications of account access graphs with state; adding a tactic language enables several exciting new possibilities. One possibility is to explore trade-offs between security and safety and resilience in account access graphs. For example, providing recovery access to accounts (such as Apple designed for AppleID) enhances safety (account access) for the user but can ease the job of an attacker, potentially reducing security. Modelling and measuring this could help us to understand safety and security interactions within threat modelling [2,5]. Another topic to investigate is the use of more sophisticated tactics which can loop, to capture attacks such as repeatedly searching for vulnerable accounts or credentials. These could be accompanied by stronger logical properties expressing (non)-reachability requirements as goals and using first class variables rather than finitary expansions. Ultimately we can consider tactics used both by attackers and by defenders. To add verification of security to the setup then, we can introduce a program logic to prove properties of tactics. So we could state that applying a certain tactic always ensures some security (or safety) property of resulting access graphs.

Of course, to build up a useful, testable catalogue of attacks and defences (and perhaps even connect to real access systems), we also want to have an implementation. This seems desirable given the ongoing account takeover attacks and significant rise in fraud cases being publicised [6,13,15].

Acknowledgements. This work was partially funded by the UK EPSRC under grant number EP/T027037/1. We're grateful to Blair Walker and Sándor Bartha for discussions.

A   Application Security on Android

As discussed in the paper, the main point of weakness for the iPhone example is that the PIN allows access to several further accounts on the phone. Whilst iPhones have no way of further protection against this [16], Android allows locking of the applications so that even if the PIN is compromised, the attacker cannot access individual apps. This is available in one way or another across manufacturers.

A.1   Xiaomi/POCO/MI

These brands of phones provide the ability to lock individual apps by default. They allow choosing a custom PIN, however, with the limitation that one has to use the same pin for all the locked apps.

A.2   ONE Plus

ONE Plus phones give the ability to lock individual apps, each with a custom PIN, Password, or pattern.

A.3   Samsung

Samsung provides a "Secure Folder" feature, a folder locked by custom PIN, Password or pattern, where you can move all your private apps (Similar to Xiaomi/POCO/MI in terms of protection). We also note that this brand provides nice guidance on relative security of the three options.

A.4   Huawei/Honor/ASUS

These three brands allow for locking individual apps, each with custom PIN, Password, or pattern (as previous). This is done with an App called AppLock, which comes preinstalled on these devices.

A.5   ALL

Just like for Huawei, Honor and ASUS, we note that AppLock can be installed from the Google store, so any android device can achieve the same level of security. We note that the homonymous app on iPhones seems to have reduced functionality, i.e. only allows locking of photos and files. This is largely due to the sandboxing present on iOS devices.

References

1. Abraham, M., Crabb, M., Radomirović, S.: "I'm doing the best I can" - understanding technology literate older adults' account management strategies. In: Parkin, S.E., Viganò, L. (eds.) Socio-Technical Aspects in Security - 11th International Workshop, STAST 2021, Virtual Event, 8 October 2021, Revised Selected Papers. LNCS, vol. 13176, pp. 86–107. Springer, Cham (2021). https://doi.org/10.1007/978-3-031-10183-0_5

2. Arnaboldi, L., Aspinall, D.: Towards interdependent safety security assessments using bowties. In: Trapp, M., Schoitsch, E., Guiochet, J., Bitsch, F. (eds.) Computer Safety, Reliability, and Security. SAFECOMP 2022 Workshops: DECSoS, DepDevOps, SASSUR, SENSEI, USDAI, and WAISE Munich, Germany, 6–9 September 2022, Proceedings, pp. 211–229. Springer, Cham (2022). https://doi.org/10.1007/978-3-031-14862-0_16

3. Blanchet, B., Smyth, B., Cheval, V., Sylvestre, M.: ProVerif 2.00: automatic cryptographic protocol verifier, user manual and tutorial. Version from, pp. 05–16 (2018)

4. Boyer, R.S., Moore, J.S.: A Computational Logic Handbook: Formerly Notes and Reports in Computer Science and Applied Mathematics. Elsevier, New York (2014). https://doi.org/10.1016/C2013-0-10412-6

5. Budde, C.E., Kolb, C., Stoelinga, M.: Attack trees vs. fault trees: two sides of the same coin from different currencies. In: Quantitative Evaluation of Systems: 18th International Conference, QEST 2021, Paris, France, 23–27 August 2021, Proceedings, pp. 457–467. Springer, Cham (2021). https://doi.org/10.1007/978-3-030-85172-9_24

6. Cavaglieri, C.: Weak banking security is leaving customers vulnerable to fraud on stolen phones, Which? warns, May 2023

7. Gordon, M., Milner, R., Morris, L., Newey, M., Wadsworth, C.: A metalanguage for interactive proof in LCF. In: Proceedings of the 5th ACM SIGACT-SIGPLAN Symposium on Principles of Programming Languages, pp. 119–130 (1978). https://doi.org/10.1145/512760.512773

8. Hammann, S., Crabb, M., Radomirović, S., Sasse, R., Basin, D.A.: "I'm surprised so much is connected". In: Barbosa, S.D.J., et al. (eds.) CHI 2022: CHI Conference on Human Factors in Computing Systems, New Orleans, LA, USA, 29 April 2022–5 May 2022, pp. 620:1–620:13. ACM (2022). https://doi.org/10.1145/3491102.3502125

9. Hammann, S., Radomirović, S., Sasse, R., Basin, D.: User account access graphs. In: Proceedings of the 2019 ACM SIGSAC Conference on Computer and Communications Security, CCS 2019, pp. 1405–1422, New York, NY, USA. ACM (2019). https://doi.org/10.1145/3319535.3354193

10. Honan, M.: How Apple and Amazon Security Flaws Led to My Epic Hacking. Wired, August 2012

11. Rapid7 LLC. Metasploit framework. https://github.com/rapid7/metasploit-framework. Accessed 27 May 2023

12. Meier, S., Schmidt, B., Cremers, C., Basin, D.: The TAMARIN prover for the symbolic analysis of security protocols. In: Sharygina, N., Veith, H. (eds.) CAV 2013. LNCS, vol. 8044, pp. 696–701. Springer, Heidelberg (2013). https://doi.org/10.1007/978-3-642-39799-8_48

13. Palmer, A.: Here's how the recent Twitter attacks probably happened and why they're becoming more common, September 2019

14. Pöhn, D., Gruschka, N., Ziegler, L.: Multi-account dashboard for authentication dependency analysis. In: ARES 2022: The 17th International Conference on Availability, Reliability and Security, Vienna, Austria, 23–26 August 2022, pp. 39:1–39:13. ACM (2022). https://doi.org/10.1145/3538969.3538987

15. Stern, J., Nguyen, N.: A basic iPhone feature helps criminals steal your digital life. Wall Street J. (2023). https://www.wsj.com/articles/apple-iphone-security-theft-passcode-data-privacya-basic-iphone-feature-helps-criminals-steal-your-digital-life-cbf14b1a. Accessed 27 May 2023

16. u/AncientBlueberry42. Reddit thread (and comments) - WSJ: a basic iPhone feature helps criminals steal your entire digital life, February 2023. https://www.reddit.com/r/apple/comments/11awqv5/comment/j9uo56h/. Accessed 4 June 2023

17. Zhao, J., Ding, B., Guo, Y., Tan, Z., Lu, S.: SecureSIM: rethinking authentication and access control for SIM/eSIM. In: ACM MobiCom 2021: The 27th Annual International Conference on Mobile Computing and Networking, New Orleans, Louisiana, USA, 25–29 October 2021, pp. 451–464. ACM (2021). https://doi.org/10.1145/3447993.3483254

Machine-Checked Proofs of Accountability: How to sElect Who is to Blame

Constantin Cătălin Drăgan[1], François Dupressoir[2], Kristian Gjøsteen[3], Thomas Haines[4], Peter B. Rønne[5], and Morten Rotvold Solberg[3(✉)]

[1] University of Surrey, Guildford, UK
c.dragan@surrey.ac.uk
[2] University of Bristol, Bristol, UK
f.dupressoir@bristol.ac.uk
[3] Norwegian University of Science and Technology, Trondheim, Norway
{kristian.gjosteen,mosolb}@ntnu.no
[4] Australian National University, Canberra, Australia
thomas.haines@anu.edu.au
[5] CNRS, LORIA, Université de Lorraine, Nancy, France
peter.roenne@loria.fr

Abstract. Accountability is a critical requirement of any deployed voting system as it allows unequivocal identification of misbehaving parties, including authorities. In this paper, we propose the first game-based definition of accountability and demonstrate its usefulness by applying it to the sElect voting system (Küsters *et al.*, 2016) – a voting system that relies on no other cryptographic primitives than digital signatures and public key encryption.

We strengthen our contribution by proving accountability for sElect in the EasyCrypt proof assistant. As part of this, we identify a few errors in the proof for sElect as presented by Küsters *et al.* (2016) for their definition of accountability.

Finally, we reinforce the known relation between accountability and verifiability, and show that it is still maintained by our new game-based definition of accountability.

1 Introduction

A system is accountable if, when something goes wrong, it is possible to judge who is responsible based on evidence provided by the system participants. For a voting system, this means that if we do not accept the outcome of an election, the honest parties should be able to produce evidence that pinpoints who is to blame, in the sense that they have not followed the protocol. This is in principle trivial for some voting systems, such as the Helios voting system where each party proves their correct behaviour using zero knowledge arguments. This is, however, not trivial for every reasonable voting system, in particular voting systems with complex ballot submission procedures, such as the Swiss Post voting system [21];

G. Tsudik et al. (Eds.): ESORICS 2023, LNCS 14346, pp. 471–491, 2024.
https://doi.org/10.1007/978-3-031-51479-1_24

in the Swiss Post case the system involves a complicated protocol between half a dozen participants to decide if a ballot was cast by a valid voter and well-formed and hence should be counted.

The sElect voting system [17] is an interesting case for accountability. Unlike Helios, the system does not use any advanced cryptography, relying entirely on secure public key encryption. The system uses nested public key encryption to allow a very simple mixnet decryption. The voter creates a nested encryption of their ballot and a random check value, each layer encrypted with a mix server public key. Each mix server decrypts one layer of encryption, sorting the result lexicographically to effect mixing. The last mix server simply outputs decrypted ballots, together with the voter-specific check value. Voters verify that their ballot is included in the count by checking that the ballot appears together with the voter's check value.

Informally, the sElect system is accountable because voters can reveal the randomness used in the nested encryption, thereby enabling tracing of the encrypted ballot through the mixnet, which will pinpoint which mix server did not correctly decrypt.

Accountability might seem to be a fairly simple notion, but it is technically difficult to find a definition that both captures accountability and is easy to work with. This can be seen from the fact that no definition of accountability seems to have been broadly accepted in the community. Also, when Küsters *et al.* [17] apply the definition from [18] to sElect, there are a number of errors in the result they claim; we will discuss these in greater length in Sec. 1.2. These errors suggest that the existing accountability definitions are hard to work with. In other words, there is a need for a workable general definition of accountability.

The simplicity of sElect comes at a cost, which is that the system is only private for voters that accept the election outcome. This problem can be mitigated using the final cryptosystem trick from [12]; with this trick, "a sender first encrypts her message under the "final" public key and uses this encrypted message as an input to the protocol as described so far. This innermost encryption layer is jointly decrypted only if the protocol does not abort. If the protocol does abort, only the encrypted values are revealed and privacy is protected by the final layer of encryption." However, using this mitigation in sElect would require the voters' devices to check the mix before the result is decrypted which substantially complicates the protocol and delays the tally result, which would be unacceptable in most cases.

Privacy is of course essential for voting systems, but we note that we are not studying privacy in this paper, only accountability, since the privacy of sElect is well-understood.

1.1   Our Contribution

This paper contains two main contributions: The first game-based definition of accountability, and a proof of accountability for the sElect [17] voting system. A variant of the latter proof has been formalised in the EasyCrypt [3] proof assistant.

This game-based definition is significant because this style of definitions are often easier to understand and work with. For security proofs, ease of understanding and use is a significant factor in getting things right and later verifying that things are indeed correct. Further, it allows us to use existing tools for game-based proofs, specifically EasyCrypt, to formally verify security.

The accountability proof for sElect is significant, first because it demonstrates that our new definition of accountability works. Second, the sElect voting system is interesting because it is so simple, requiring no other primitives than digital signatures and public key encryption. Proving security properties for interesting voting systems is intrinsically interesting.

As we have seen, informal arguments sometimes contain errors. A proof formalised in EasyCrypt is significant, in that it ensures that we have no errors in arguments, making the overall security proof easier to verify.

In addition to the main contribution, we also make the relation between verifiability and accountability precise, in the sense that accountability implies verifiability (when suitably defined). This is a significant result, suggesting that future system designers should focus on achieving accountability.

1.2   Related Work

To the best of our knowledge, no game-based definition of accountability has been proposed earlier. However, several definitions of accountability (for general security protocols, not only electronic voting protocols) have been proposed in the symbolic model. Bruni *et al.* [5] propose a general definition amenable to automated verification. Künnemann *et al.* [16] give a definition of accountability in the decentralised-adversary setting, in which single protocol parties can choose to deviate from the protocol, while Künnemann *et al.* [15] give a definition in the single-adversary setting, where all deviating parties are controlled by a single, centralised adversary. Morio & Künnemann [19] combine the definition from [15] with the notion of case tests to extend the definition's applicability to protocols with an unbounded number of participants. Furthermore Küsters *et al.* [18] put forward quantitative measures of accountability both in the symbolic and computational model. Similar for all these definitions is that they clearly distinguish between *dishonest* parties and *misbehaving* parties. Even though a party is dishonest (controlled by an adversary), it does not necessarily deviate from the protocol and cause a violation of the security goal. In such cases, the party is not misbehaving and should not be held accountable for anything.

While no game-based definition of accountability has been proposed, game-based definitions for other voting-related security properties do exist in the literature. Some of these definitions have also been formalised in the proof assistant EasyCrypt [3], with related machine-checked proofs for a variety of voting protocols. Cortier *et al.* [6] formalise a game-based definition of ballot-privacy called BPRIV [4] in EasyCrypt and give a machine-checked proof that Labelled-MiniVoting [6] and several hundred variants of Helios [2] satisfy this notion of ballot privacy. Cortier *et al.* [7] build on work from [6] and also formalise a game-based definition of verifiability in EasyCrypt, in addition to giving a machine-checked proof that Belenios [9] is ballot-private and verifiable. Drăgan *et al.* [10] formalise the mb-BPRIV ballot privacy definition [8] in EasyCrypt and give a machine-checked proof that Labelled-MiniVoting and Belenios satisfy this definition. They also propose a new game-based ballot privacy definition called du-mb-BPRIV, which is applicable to schemes where voter verification can or must happen after the election result has been computed, and give a machine-checked proof that Labelled-MiniVoting, Belenios and Selene [20] all satisfy this definition.

Problems in the Küsters et al. [17] *Accountability Proof.* In carefully analysing sElect we became aware of two errors in the Accountability theorem which we detail below; to our knowledge these errors have not previously been documented in the literature. There is a significant complexity in the parameters used in Theorem 3 (Accountability) in the full version of sElect [17], but fortunately this is largely orthogonal to the points we need to discuss.

Ballot Stuffing The goal for which accountability is proven (see Definition 1 in [17]) somewhat implicitly requires that the multiset containing the election result contains at most n elements, where n is the number of voters. However, no argument is made in the proof that the judge will hold anyone accountable if there are more than n ballots. Both the pen-and-paper description and the implementation of sElect omit any checks which would catch the addition of ballots by the mix servers, and it seems that the authentication server could also stuff ballots though this would be more involved. As significant as this vulnerability is, it is easy to fix and we have done so in the version of sElect we prove accountability for.

Honest Nonce Collision A described above, the goal the theorem aims for uses multisets and hence if multiple honest voters vote for the same choice we expect to see at least that many copies of the choice in the output; this is somewhat complicated in sElect by the augmentation of voter choices with nonces. The mechanism which sElect uses to detect ballots being removed relies on the plaintext encrypted by the honest voters being unique; however, this does not happen when the nonces and choices of the honest voters collide. The chance of such collision should appear in the security bound of accountability for sElect unless it is explicitly negligible in the security parameter. Strangely, sElect will drop these votes even with no adversarial involvement since the protocol specifies that the final mix server (like all others) should filter its output for duplicates. We note that the probability of collisions does appear in the verifiability theorem and proof.

2   Game Based Accountability

In this section we present our game based definition of accountability for electronic voting protocols, and we start by presenting the parties and their roles.

2.1 Parties

We consider the following parties and their role in the election process.

Voting Authority VA that sets up the election process, generates public parameters, defines voter eligibility, etc. The election secret keys are managed by separate parties, called decryption and mixnet authorities.

Decryption and Mixnet Authorities $MS_i(msk_i, mpk_i)$ that manage together the decryption process, and each party has been allocated a part of the decryption key/election secret key. This is typically done by decryption or re-encryption together with shuffling of ballots/votes to break the link between recorded ballots and the votes.

Authentication Server AS(ask, apk) issues confirmation tokens that ballots were recorded as cast, typically under the form of signatures.

Judge J assigns blame to misbehaving parties based on publicly available data and voter reported evidence. We model this by having an algorithm Judge.

Voters id_i that cast their vote v_i. The voting process is facilitated by a voting supporting device VSD that builds ballots for the user and then casts them.

Bulletin board BB stores publicly verifiable information relevant to an election, e.g. ballots, mixnet outcomes, and election outcome. The bulletin board may be divided into subcomponents such as a list of submitted ballots or the election outcome.

2.2 Voting System

The election process is defined by the following tuple of algorithms.

Setup(): This algorithm produces the public election data pd and the secret election data sd. This is done by interaction between VA, $MS_0, \ldots, MS_k$, and potentially AS.

Vote(pd, v): This algorithm builds the ballot b based on the vote v and public data pd. Additionally, it produces the internal state of the voter, state, to facilitate the verification process later.

ASCreate(ask, b): This algorithm produces a token σ that the ballot b has been received and accepted by the authentication server AS(ask, apk).

ASVerify(pd, b, σ): This algorithm verifies if the token σ is valid for the ballot b and public data pd.

Tally(sd, BB): This algorithm models the sequence of calls to the mixnet and decryption authorities to produce the election outcome.

VSDVerify((state, b, σ), pd, BB): Checks if the system has followed the required processes for this user's vote and ballot, and it outputs $\perp$ if no misbehaving party has been identified. Otherwise, it returns the misbehaving party and the corresponding evidence.

Judge(pd, BB, E): It checks that the publicly available data is valid with respect to some predefined metrics and against the list of evidence E. It returns the error symbol $\perp$ if no misbehaving party has been identified; otherwise, it outputs the misbehaving party B. As all checks can be replicated publicly, it does not need to return evidence.

$\mathsf{Exp}_{\mathcal{A},\mathcal{V}}^{\mathsf{GBA}}(\lambda)$	$\mathcal{O}\mathsf{vote}(id, v)$
1: pd ← $\mathcal{A}()$;	1: (state, b) ← Vote(pd, v);
2: (BB, tL) ← $\mathcal{A}^{\mathcal{O}\mathsf{vote}}()$;	2: V[id] ← (state, b);
3: e_s ← true;	3: return b;
4: foreach $id \in V$:	
5: (state, b) ← V[id]; σ ← tL[id];	Verify()
6: if ASVerify(pd, b, σ) = $\bot$:	1: E = $\emptyset$;
7: e_s ← false; break;	2: foreach $id \in V$:
8: E ← Verify();	3: (state, b) ← V[id];
9: E ← E ∪ $\mathcal{A}$(E);	4: σ ← tL[id];
10: B ← Judge(pd, BB, E);	5: blame ← VSDVerify((state, b, σ), pd, BB);
11: e_f ← ($B \not\subseteq$ Bad(pd, BB, V, E));	6: if blame $\neq \bot$ then E ← E ∪ {blame};
12: e_c ← ($\neg(N_v \geq |\mathsf{BB}_{vote}| \geq |\mathsf{BB}_{dec}| \wedge V \subseteq \mathsf{BB}_{dec}) \wedge B = \bot$);	7: return E;
13: return $e_s \wedge (e_f \vee e_c)$;	

Fig. 1. The new game-based security notion for accountability. BB_{vote} and BB_{dec} denote different subcomponents of the bulletin board, respectively ballots submitted through $\mathcal{O}\mathsf{vote}$ and information produced by tallying.

The following algorithm is unbounded, but is only part of the security experiment and will not be run during an election.

Bad(pd, BB, E, V): This unbounded algorithm serves to provide a ground truth of which parties misbehaved. By the requirements of our definition, it always blames a party when the election result does not reflect the votes of voters - given the public data pd, the bulletin board BB, the list of evidence E, and the internal state of honest voters V. Optionally, it may detect whether a party has deviated from the protocol in a way which does not change the election result. It should never blame an honest party.

2.3 Accountability

We consider that the adversary has full control over all parties introduced in Sect. 2.1, except the Judge. The adversary can also incorporate their own evidence to Judge. If a party deviates from the protocol steps, then that party becomes *misbehaving* and could be identified and blamed by either Judge or Bad. However, if the party follows exactly the protocol steps we call that party *behaving*, independent of them being honest or dishonest (corrupted by the adversary).

The formal accountability definition is found in Fig. 1. The first step for the adversary is to start the election process and provide the public data pd. Then, the adversary runs the voting and tally phase and commits to the current state of the bulletin board BB, together with a list of all authentication tokens tL. During the voting phase, the adversary can make use of the oracle $\mathcal{O}\mathsf{vote}$ to replicate the behavior of behaving voters and build their ballot b and internal state state.

To capture the natural behavior of behaving and honest voters that would check their tokens and complain before the tally is provided, we incorporate an automatic lose condition for the adversary if any of the provided tokens for those voters cannot be verified by ASVerify; this approach is similar to that taken by Küsters *et al.* [17] in their (non-game based) accountability proof of sElect.

Verification is done as a two-stage process, first by collecting evidence E from all honest voters (those that used $\mathcal{O}$vote and whose internal states are stored in V) and from the adversary $\mathcal{A}(E)$; and secondary by calling Judge to check the public data together with that evidence. The Judge is responsible for providing either a misbehaving party B if there is enough evidence to do so, or $\perp$ if nothing could be detected. The adversary wins if one of the following happens:

Fairness: Judge wrongly blames a party B when it did not misbehave. This is checked by running the Bad algorithm to identify all misbehaving parties in the system and check whether B has been included, or

Completeness: the result is not consistent with the honest votes but no one is blamed. This is done by Judge producing $\perp$ when an honest voter's ballot was dropped, or there are more submitted ballots than there are voters, or more ballots in the election outcome than the number of ballots that were cast in the first place.

Definition 1 (Game-Based Accountability). *Let* V *be a voting system as defined in this section. We say that* $\mathcal{V}$ *satisfies* GBA *if for any efficient adversary* $\mathcal{A}$ *their advantage is negligible in* λ*:*

$$\mathsf{Adv}^{\mathsf{gba}}_{\mathcal{A},\mathcal{V}}(\lambda) = \Pr\left[\mathsf{Exp}^{\mathsf{GBA}}_{\mathcal{A},\mathcal{V}}(\lambda) = 1\right].$$

Our adversary winning conditions aligns our definition with the one from Küsters *et al.* [17], such that any voting system that satisfies our accountability definition will also satisfy the one by Küsters *et al.* [17] (with the goal used for sElect), with some possible caveats about the casting of schemes between the two definitions. We expand on this in Sect. 3.3.

3 sElect

In this section we introduce sElect [17] using the format of Sect. 2; we focus on the elements with are important for accountability and omit some orthogonal details. The formal description is in Fig. 2. We denote by $\mathsf{BB}_{vote}, \mathsf{BB}_{mix}$ and BB_{dec} the different subcomponents of BB: respectively the submitted ballots, data produced by the mixnet and the election outcome, which is a list of plaintext votes.

3.1 Cryptographic Primitives

The voting system sElect relies on two basic cryptographic primitives: an IND-CCA2 encryption scheme $E = (\mathsf{KeyGen}, \mathsf{Enc}, \mathsf{Dec})$ and an EU-CMA signature scheme $S = (\mathsf{KeyGen}, \mathsf{Sign}, \mathsf{SigVerif})$. To make the encryption scheme compatible with decryption mixnets it needs to allow nested encryptions. Typically, this is

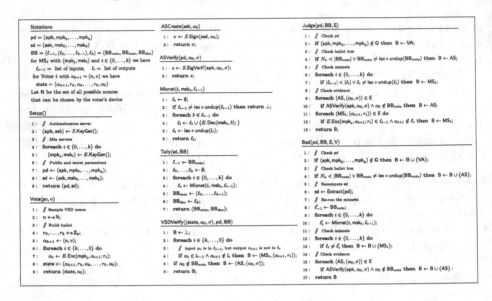

Fig. 2. Algorithms defining the sElect voting scheme with an IND-CCA2 secure public key encryption system $E = (\text{KeyGen}, \text{Enc}, \text{Dec})$ and an EU-CMA secure signature scheme $S = (\text{KeyGen}, \text{Sign}, \text{SigVerif})$.

done through a hybrid cryptosystem [1], by combining hybrid ElGamal and AES in a suitable mode such that each encryption contains an AES encryption of the message under a random AES key and an ElGamal encryption of the AES key.

As part of the formalisation for the shuffling done by the mixnet servers $\text{MS}_0, \ldots, \text{MS}_k$, we consider the operators lex for sorting a list in lexicographic order, and undup for removing duplicates. We additionally have that the authentication authority AS runs S.

3.2   sElect Algorithms

Setup(): The authentication server key pair (apk, ask) is generated by $S.\text{KeyGen}$, and the mixnet servers key pairs $(\text{mpk}_i, \text{msk}_i)$ are computed by $E.\text{KeyGen}$. The algorithm returns the public data $\text{pd} = (\text{apk}, \text{mpk}_0, \ldots, \text{mpk}_k)$ and secret data $\text{sd} = (\text{ask}, \text{msk}_0, \ldots, \text{msk}_k)$.

Vote(pd, v): The algorithm samples a supporting device verification code n such that it can be used later by the voter to ensure their vote was counted. sElect also considers a short voter verification code n_{voter} that has no security assumptions (for accountability); we have included that code together with the voter's candidate choices c as part of the vote $v = (n_{voter}, c)$. The algorithm sets $\alpha_{k+1} = (n, v)$ and uses a series of encryptions $\alpha_i \leftarrow \text{Enc}(\text{mpk}_i, \alpha_{i+1}, r_i)$ to build the ballot α_0 and internal state $\text{state} = (\alpha_{k+1}, \alpha_k, r_k, \ldots, \alpha_0, r_0)$, given some random coins $r_0, \ldots, r_k \in \mathbb{Z}_p$.

ASCreate(asd, α_0): It returns a signature σ by calling $S.\text{Sign}$ over the ballot α_0.

ASVerify($\mathsf{pd}, \alpha_0, \sigma$): This algorithm calls $S.\mathsf{SigVerif}$ to check if the signature σ is valid for the ballot α_0.

Tally(sd, BB): Given the ballot box $\ell_{-1} = \mathsf{BB}_{vote}$, this algorithm runs each mixnet MS_i over ℓ_{i-1} to produce ℓ_i, for $i \in \{0, \ldots, k\}$. Each mixnet MS_i, ensures first that the inputs are in lexicographic order and contain no duplicates, before decrypting all ciphertexts received as inputs, and finally outputting them in lexicographic order and without duplicates. The last mixnet server produces the election outcome $\mathsf{BB}_{dec} = \ell_k$. The algorithm returns the mixing info $\mathsf{BB}_{mix} = (\ell_0, \ldots, \ell_{k-1})$ and election outcome BB_{dec}.

VSDVerify($(\mathsf{state}, \alpha_0, \sigma), \mathsf{pd}, \mathsf{BB}$): Voters check the output of each mixnet server by using their internal state $(\alpha_{k+1}, \alpha_k, r_k, \ldots, \alpha_0, r_0)$. The voter blames a mixnet server MS_i if they see that their ciphertext α_{i+1} is in the input list of that server, but the ciphertext α_i is not in the output list. Recall that α_i has been created by encrypting α_{i+1} under that server's public key mpk_i: $\alpha_i \leftarrow \mathsf{Enc}(\mathsf{mpk}_i, \alpha_{i+1}, r_i)$; thus, (α_{i+1}, r_i) can be used as evidence of misbehaviour of MS_i. The voter also checks that their ballot α_0 has been included in the ballot box BB_{vote}, and blames the authentication server AS if that has not happened, using the signature σ the user received during voting as evidence. This step can be done at any point in the election if one considers an ideal bulletin board, or at the end of an election under weaker trust assumptions over the bulletin board [11].

Judge($\mathsf{pd}, \mathsf{BB}, \mathsf{E}$): This algorithm does an initial round of checks over the public data before evaluating the collected evidence E. The verification of public data consists of

 - Ensuring that the public data is valid - that is, the public keys are group elements. If this is not true, then the voting authority VA is blamed as it allowed the election to run.
 - Checking that the size of the ballot box does not exceed the number of voters and that the ballot box has been ordered lexicographically and duplicates have been removed. Otherwise, the authentication server AS is blamed.
 - Checking that each mixnet server output is in lexicographic order and has no duplicates, and that the size of the output list does not exceed the size of the input list. If these properties do not hold for mixnet server MS_i then the algorithm blames this mixnet server.

Once all the public data has been verified, the algorithm looks at the evidence collected by voters from their VSDVerify algorithm:

 - Evidence (α_0, σ) against AS. If the evidence contains a valid signature σ for a ballot α_0 not in the ballot box, then the authentication server AS is blamed.
 - Evidence (α_{i+1}, r_i) against MS_i. If the evidence shows that $\alpha_i \leftarrow \mathsf{Enc}(\mathsf{mpk}_i, \alpha_{i+1}, r_i)$ is in the input list of this server, but α_{i+1} is not in the output, then this mixnet server is blamed.

Bad($\mathsf{pd}, \mathsf{BB}, \mathsf{E}, \mathsf{V}$): This algorithm uses a computationally unbounded algorithm $\mathsf{sd} \leftarrow \mathsf{Extract}(\mathsf{pd})$ to obtain the secret keys of all authorities sd from their public data pd; similar to the vote extraction algorithm from [13,14]. Extract will never fail to return something as it will see any bitstring in the public data as a group element. However, it may not produce meaningful data or the real secret keys if these do not exist.

Bad uses the secret data from Extract to re-run the election tally and perform all verification steps to identify misbehaving parties. It looks at the validity of the public data pd and ballot box BB_{vote} using the same methods employed by Judge. Then, it re-creates for each mixnet server MS_i its estimated output ℓ'_i and blames that party if their estimated output ℓ'_i is different from the declared output ℓ_i. This type of check already includes the checks on the evidence submitted by voters against mixnet servers. Finally, it performs the checks on the evidence against the authentication server AS.

3.3 EasyCrypt Proof

Informally, we prove that the probability that the adversary is able to produce valid public data, a valid bulletin board and valid signatures, while at the same time violating either fairness or completeness, is negligible. We assume throughout the proof that the public key encryption scheme used to encrypt and decrypt ballots is perfectly correct, i.e. if we let $E = (\mathsf{KeyGen}, \mathsf{Enc}, \mathsf{Dec})$ be the (IND-CCA2 secure) PKE used in sElect, then we assume that for all key pairs $(\mathsf{pk}, \mathsf{sk})$ output by KeyGen and for all plaintexts m in the message space, we have $\mathsf{Dec}(\mathsf{sk}, \mathsf{Enc}(\mathsf{pk}, m)) = m$. As we assume that sElect is implemented with hybrid encryption of ElGamal and AES (cf. Section 3.1), this assumption holds. Under this assumption, the probability that the adversary violates the fairness aspect of accountability is in fact 0. The probability that the adversary violates the completeness aspect of accountability, is related to whether or not *nonce collisions* occur, i.e. whether or not the devices of two or more honest voters sample the same nonce.

Theorem 1. *Let* sElect(E, S) *be defined as in Fig. 2 for an IND-CCA2 encryption scheme E and an EU-CMA signature scheme S. Then, for all PPT adversaries $\mathcal{A}$ against* GBA*, we have*

$$\mathsf{Adv}^{\mathsf{gba}}_{\mathcal{A},\mathsf{sElect}}(\lambda) \leq \Pr[Col],$$

where Col is the event that a collision occurs in the nonces chosen by the voters' devices.

The proof sketch can be found in App. A.

Differences between our paper proof and EasyCrypt proof. The main difference in the above proof and the proof formalised in EasyCrypt[1] is that in EasyCrypt we let the adversary choose both the plaintext vote and the verification nonce and compress this into a single plaintext. Under the assumption that the choices made by the adversary are unique, this allows us to use sets rather than multisets

---

[1] The EasyCrypt code can be accessed from https://github.com/mortensol/acc-select.

in EasyCrypt which is technically easier. In some sense this is however also a stronger result than above since it proves accountability even in the case where the nonces are adversarially chosen, but still unique. What is not proven in Easy-Crypt is the probability of a collision happening, but for uniform distributions of nonces this is the well-known birthday paradox which is not interesting for the present paper to verify in EasyCrypt. Finally, keeping a general collision probability for the full plaintext consisting of device-generated nonce, voter-chosen nonce and plaintext vote is more general, and cannot be assumed to be uniformly random in practice, but can be bounded by the birthday probability on the device-generated nonces.

4 Relation to the Küsters et al. Definition

In this section we relate the above presented definition of accountability, GBA, to the one by Küsters et al. [18], which we denote Acc_{KTV}. More precisely, we sketch a proof that for the class of voting schemes expressible in our definition, if they satisfy GBA for a certain definition of Bad then they must be accountable under Acc_{KTV} with a standard goal.

Consider a voting scheme as defined in Sect. 2, consisting of a voting authority VA, decryption authorities DA, mixnet authorities MS, authentication server AS, voters id_i with voter supporting devices VSD_i, and bulletin board BB. We assume there are authenticated channels from the VSDs to the AS. We assume that each VSD has one authenticated and one anonymous channel to the BB. We assume that all communication is authenticated with signatures with the exception of the anonymous channel and for simplicity omit the description of this occurring from the exposition below.

4.1 Modeling

A voting scheme of this kind can be modeled in the framework of [18] in a straightforward way as a protocol $\mathcal{P}(n, m, q, \mu, p_{voter}^{verif}, p_{abst}^{verif})$. We refer to [18] for the notation used. We denote by n the number of voters and supporting devices, by m the number of mix servers, by q the number of decryption servers. By μ we denote the probability distribution on the set of candidates/choices, including abstention. We denote by p_{voter}^{verif} and p_{abst}^{verif} the probability that the voting voter will verify and an absenting voter will verify respectively.[2]

We define Φ_k as the accountability property consisting of the constraints:

$$\chi_i \rightarrow dis(id_i) \vee dis(AS), \quad \chi_i' \rightarrow dis(id_i) \vee dis(AS)$$
$$\neg\gamma_k \wedge \neg\chi \rightarrow dis(\mathsf{VA})|dis(\mathsf{AS})|dis(\mathsf{DA}_i)_{i=1}^{q}|dis(\mathsf{MS}_j)_{j=1}^{m}$$

where

---

[2] Absenting voters verify that their identifier is not included on the list published by the AS.

γ_k contains all runs of the protocol where at most n votes are in the result and where at most k of the honest votes are not included in the result. See [17] for a formal definition and discussion of this goal.

χ_i contains all the runs of $\mathcal{P}$ where the voter i complains they did not get a receipt.

χ_i' contains all the runs of $\mathcal{P}$ where the voter i complains they did not vote but a vote was cast on their behalf.

χ contains the union of all runs in χ_i and χ_i' for all $i \in [1, ..., n]$

4.2   Result

Let Bad be defined as follows: Bad returns all parties whose output is not in the co-domain of the honest algorithms. When parties are called multiple times on different algorithms and pass states, we take the co-domain over all possible states consistent with their early public output.

Let the Judge_{KTV} algorithm for Acc_{KTV} in [18] be constructed as follows:

(J1) first it runs Judge (from our definition) and if this outputs blame, then Judge_{KTV} blames the party returned by Judge.

(J2) If no valid complaints were made by the voters causing blame, the judge checks the complaints posted by the voters. If there is any such complaint then Judge_{KTV} blames (disjunctively) both the party accused and the voter accusing.

Definition 2 (Voter Verification Correct). *For a scheme π we say that it is voter verification correct if for all runs of the protocol the party blamed by* VSDVerify *is in the set output by* Bad *or it blames the* AS *after receiving an invalid confirmation.*

Theorem 2 (GBA implies Acc_{KTV}). *Let the judge Judge_{KTV} and algorithm* Bad *be defined as above. Then for any scheme which has* GBA *and voter verification correctness, Judge_{KTV} ensures $\left(\Phi_k, \delta^k(p_{voter}^{verif}, p_{abst}^{verif})\right)$-accountability for $\mathcal{P}(n, m, q, \mu, p_{voter}^{verif}, p_{abst}^{verif})$ where*

$$\delta^k(p_{voter}^{verif}, p_{abst}^{verif}) = (1 - \min(p_{voter}^{verif}, p_{abst}^{verif}))^{k+1}.$$

Due to space constraints, we detail this in App. A. The proof relies on analysing fairness and completeness for the two definitions.

5   Verifiability

In this section we show that our definition of accountability implies verifiability; a relation already shown in the framework of Küsters et al. [18]. To prove this implication here, we introduce a new game-based definition of verifiability, that we formalize via the experiment $\mathsf{Exp}_{\mathcal{A}}^{Ver}(\lambda)$ in Fig. 3.[3] Our definition of verifiability ensures individual verifiability and no ballot stuffing during tally, and is appropriate for lightweight voting systems like sElect. Our definition is modular, and can be enhanced to model stronger notions of verifiability (e.g., universal verifiability or no ballot stuffing at submission time); however, to achieve them voting systems will require heavier cryptographic primitives, likes zero-knowledge proofs for correct tallying or shuffling.

We consider $\mathcal{I}$ the set of eligible voter IDs, and we introduce algorithm VoterVerif that enables voters to verify their vote. We keep track of voters that successfully verified using the set Checked and we raise the flag Complain when verification fails. The adversary can choose which voters verify via the oracle $\mathcal{O}\mathsf{Verify}(id)$. Additionally, the adversary uses the vote oracle $\mathcal{O}\mathsf{Vote}$ to model honest voters (re-)casting their votes; we focus on the last vote counts policy, but this can easily be generalized for any policies.

The adversary also controls the bulletin board BB, however anyone can perform UniversalVerification(pd, BB) to universally verify this state. We further use ResultConsistency(BB, Checked, . . .) to model the consistency relations on the bulletin board, and can depend on the different subcomponents of BB: list of submitted ballots $\mathsf{BB}|_{submit}$, the election result $\mathsf{BB}|_{res}$ and extra info $\mathsf{BB}|_{extra}$.

Consider the election result function $\rho : \mathsf{Cand}^* \mapsto \mathsf{Res}$ as a symmetric function from the set of plaintext votes, chosen from the space of candidates Cand, to a given result set Res. Using $\mathsf{V}[S]$ the corresponding list of plaintext votes from the vote oracle, we model

- Individual Verifiability: Intuitively this should ensure that the verified votes are all included in the tally. Using the verification oracles $\mathcal{O}\mathsf{Verify}_i, i = 1, \ldots, k$ we denote the successful verifiers Checked. The constraint from ResultConsistency is $\exists v_1, \ldots, v_i \in \mathsf{Cand}, i + |\mathsf{Checked}| \leq |\mathcal{I}|$:

$$\rho(v_1, \ldots, v_i, \mathsf{V}[\mathsf{Checked}]) = \mathsf{BB}|_{res}$$

  where we have slightly abused notation for readability. We have included a constraint on the number of malicious votes since if the result function allows cancelling votes the inclusion of the honest votes would make little sense if the adversary can add malicious votes arbitrarily.
- No Ballot Stuffing at Tally Time: $|\mathcal{I}| \geq |\mathsf{BB}|_{submit}|$ and $\exists i \leq |\mathsf{BB}|_{submit}|$ $\exists v_1, \ldots, v_i \in \mathsf{Cand} : \rho(v_1, \ldots, v_i) = \mathsf{BB}|_{res}$, i.e. there is at most as many submitted ballots as eligible voters and the result is consistent with a number of votes that is less than or equal to the submitted ballots.

---

[3] In the game, we use the notation "Require" for **if** · · · **else return** $\perp$.

$\mathsf{Exp}_A^{Ver}(\lambda)$	$\mathcal{O}vote(id, v)$
1 : Complain = **false**;	1 : $(b, state) \leftarrow \mathsf{Vote}(pd, v)$;
2 : $pd \leftarrow \mathcal{A}()$;	2 : $\mathsf{V}[id] \leftarrow (state, b)$;
3 : $\mathsf{BB}, state_A \leftarrow \mathcal{A}^{\mathcal{O}vote}()$;	3 : **return** b;
4 : $\mathcal{A}(state_A)^{\mathcal{O}\mathsf{Verify}_i}$;	
5 : Require Complain = **false**;	$\mathcal{O}\mathsf{Verify}(id)$
6 : Require UniversalVerification(pd, BB);	1 : Require$(\exists \mathsf{V}[id])$;
7 : **return** $\neg$ResultConsistency$(\mathsf{BB}, \mathsf{Checked}, \ldots)$;	2 : $(state, b) \leftarrow \mathsf{V}[id]$;
	3 : **if** VoterVerif$((state, b), pd, \mathsf{BB})$;
	4 : $\mathsf{Checked} = \mathsf{Checked} \cup \{id\}$;
	5 : **else** Complain = **true**;

Fig. 3. Verifiability assuming uncorrupted vote-casting.

In the case of schemes where all the decrypted votes are displayed individually in $\mathsf{BB}|_{res}$, especially this holds for the mixnet-tally schemes, the slightly stronger statement can be made that

$$|\mathcal{I}| \geq |\mathsf{BB}|_{submit}| \geq |\mathsf{BB}|_{res}| \wedge \mathsf{V}[\mathsf{Checked}] \subseteq_{ms} \mathsf{BB}|_{res}, \tag{1}$$

where we use $\mathsf{V}[\mathsf{Checked}]$ and $\mathsf{BB}|_{res}$ as multisets.

We define verifiability given a chosen ResultConsistency if any efficient adversary has negligible advantage in $\mathsf{Exp}_A^{Ver}(\lambda)$. In particular, we define verifiability for voting systems with the result being the plaintext votes as:

Definition 3. *We say that a voting system $\mathcal{V}$, with result function being the set of votes, satisfies individual verifiability and no ballot stuffing at tally time if for any efficient adversary $\mathcal{A}$ their advantage $\mathsf{Adv}_{A,\mathcal{V}}^{ver}(\lambda) = \mathsf{Exp}_{A,\mathcal{V}}^{Ver}(\lambda)$ is negligible in λ, where ResultConsistency checks Eq. 1.*

We note that there are some verifiability properties that sElect does not fulfill but could be easily captured by the ResultConsistency or separate games, namely

- Tally Uniqueness: The adversary cannot produce two boards both satisfying UniversalVerification and individual verifications but with different tally results and having the same submitted ballots $\mathsf{BB}|_{submit}$.
- Universal Verifiability: Here ResultConsistency requires that the result is the same as the result from votes extracted from the valid ballots in $\mathsf{BB}|_{submit}$ given only that the board satisfies UniversalVerification(pd, BB).

5.1   Accountability Implies Verifiability

We will now prove that the GBA accountability definition implies verifiability for individual verifiability and no ballot stuffing as defined in Def. 3. However, in order to do so, we need to relate the Judge and the VSDVerify algorithms used in $\mathsf{Exp}_{\mathcal{A},\mathcal{V}}^{\mathsf{GBA}}(\lambda)$ with the algorithms UniversalVerification and VoterVerif used in $\mathsf{Exp}_{\mathcal{A},\mathcal{V}}^{Ver}(\lambda)$. Especially, the verifiability definition does not consider the authentication server AS and its signatures, since it is not relevant for defining verifiability. To this end we make the following definition for a voting system $\mathcal{V}$ fitting both the accountability and the verifiability framework:

Definition 4. *We call a voting system $\mathcal{V}$ accountability-verifiability-correct if the signature part for AS is an independent part that can be removed to give a reduced system valid for the verifiability framework, or correspondingly added. Further, the Judge will never output blame if all verification checks by the verifying voters using VSDVerify does not output blame and UniversalVerification $= \top$. Further, VSDVerify$((state, b, \sigma), \mathsf{pd}, \mathsf{BB}_{vote}, \mathsf{BB}_{mix}, \mathsf{BB}_{dec})$ will not output blame if ASVerify$(\mathsf{pd}, b, \sigma) = \top$ and VoterVerif$((state, b), \mathsf{pd}, \mathsf{BB}) = \top$.*

Theorem 3. *Given an accountability-verifiability-correct voting system, then accountability as defined in Definition 1 implies individual verifiability and no ballot stuffing at tally time as defined in Definition 3 assuming the AS signature scheme is perfectly correct and we have a constant number of voters. More precisely for any efficient adversary $\mathcal{A}$ against $\mathsf{Exp}_{\mathcal{A},\mathcal{V}_r}^{Ver}(\lambda)$ with advantage $\mathsf{Adv}_{\mathcal{A},\mathcal{V}_r}^{ver}(\lambda)$ in the reduced system $\mathcal{V}_r$ without signatures, we can construct an adversary $\mathcal{B}$ against $\mathsf{Exp}_{\mathcal{A},\mathcal{V}}^{\mathsf{GBA}}(\lambda)$ with advantage at least $\frac{1}{2^{|\mathcal{I}|}}\mathsf{Adv}_{\mathcal{A},\mathcal{V}_r}^{ver}(\lambda)$.*

Due to space constraints the full proof is in Appendix A.

It follows from Theorem 1 and Theorem 3 that sElect fulfills individual verifiability and no ballot stuffing at tally time as defined in Definition 3.

6   Concluding Remarks

We study notions of accountability for electronic voting, and produce the first *game-based* notion of accountability for mix-based electronic voting schemes. We relate our notion to Küsters et al's quantitative notion, arguing that they coincide at the extremes of the parameter range.

We demonstrate the value of such a game-based notion by formalising it in EasyCrypt, and produce a machine-checked proof of accountability-as we define it-for Küsters et al.'s sElect protocol, discussing issues with previous accountability results for sElect as we go. Finally, we use our new game-based definition of accountability to study the relationship between accountability, verifiability, demonstrating in particular that accountability implies verifiability.

Generalisation Beyond sElect. We framed our discussions, and our definitions, with sElect. However, our definitions would also somewhat trivially apply to other voting schemes. In particular, as mentioned in the introduction, any scheme making judicious use of sound zero-knowledge proofs for verifiability can be trivially argued to be accountable: an adversary who is able to break accountability with sound zero-knowledge proofs does so either by breaking soundness of the zero-knowledge proof systems, or by breaking accountability of a scheme in which verification for the zero-knowledge proofs is idealised to reject any proof that was not produced as is by the prover-relying then only on the correctness of the encryption scheme as in our sElect proof. Although this argument is easy to make on paper, formalising it in EasyCrypt on existing formal definitions for Helios (for example) would involve effort incommensurate to its scientific value as part of this specific paper.

Beyond Accountability. Capturing accountability as a game-based notion is not just useful to allow a more precise analysis of accountability. By doing so, we hope to open the way to the study of privacy and security properties of voting schemes *with dispute resolution*. Formally taking into account dispute resolution requires a precise understanding of the individual and overall guarantees offered by verifiability in terms of the accuracy of the election result.

Acknowledgment. T. Haines is the recipient of an Australian Research Council Australian Discovery Early Career Award (project number DE220100595). C. C. Drăgan is supported by EPSRC grant EP/W032473/1 (AP4L), EU Horizon grants 101069688(CONNECT) and 101070627 (REWIRE). P. Rønne received funding from the France 2030 program managed by the French National Research Agency under grant agreement No. ANR-22-PECY-0006.

Appendix A Sketch of Proof of Theorem 1

We now sketch the proof of Theorem 1. We begin by defining two new games: a fairness game G_f and a completeness game G_c. These games are almost identical to the original security game, with the exception that in G_f, we remove the variable e_c from the experiment and only consider the fairness aspect of accountability, while in G_c, we remove the variable e_f and only consider the completeness aspect of accountability. Let E_f resp. E_c be the event that the game G_f resp. G_c returns 1. It is straightforward to see that $\Pr\left[\mathsf{Exp}_{\mathcal{A},\mathsf{sElect}}^{\mathsf{GBA}}(\lambda) = 1\right] \leq \Pr[E_f] + \Pr[E_c]$. Thus, the adversary has two possibilities to win. Either Judge has blamed an innocent party, or it has blamed no one, but the result is inconsistent with the honest votes. We analyze the fairness and completeness aspects separately, and argue that the adversary has zero probability of winning the fairness game and negligible probability of winning the completeness game.

We begin with fairness. We will consider each way in which the judge may blame a party and show that it will never blame a party that did not misbehave.

Recall the various checks performed by the judge: The judge first checks that the public keys used by the authentication server and the mix servers are valid. If not, it will blame the voting authority as it allowed the election to run with invalid keys. Note that Bad will also blame the voting authority if the keys are invalid (but not otherwise), meaning that the voting authority will only be blamed by the judge if it indeed misbehaved. As invalid keys will result in the voting authority being blamed by both the judge and by Bad, we assume for the remainder of the proof that all the public keys are valid.

The judge then checks that the bulletin board BB_{vote} is valid, i.e. that it contains at most N_v elements and that its contents are in lexicographic order and duplicate-free. If this check fails, the judge blames the authentication server. If this is the case, the authentication server will also be blamed by Bad, ensuring that if AS is blamed for producing an invalid board, it must indeed have misbehaved. Next, the judge checks that the output of each mix server contains at most as many elements as in its received input and that the output of each mix server is duplicate free and in lexicographic order. Since an honest mixer filters out duplicates and sorts the output list, it will always pass this check.

The judge then checks, for all ciphertext and signature pairs in the evidence list whether or not there is a ballot with a valid signature that is not present on BB_{vote}. Since an honest authentication server only authenticates the first ballot from each voter, and posts all these on the bulletin board, it will always pass this check. Note that if a dishonest voter blames the authentication server with valid evidence, the Bad algorithm will also blame the authentication server, and thus the judge will not blame the authentication server unless it is also blamed by Bad. Finally, Judge checks, for any triple $(\mathsf{mpk}_i, \alpha_{i+1}, r_i)$, whether or not $\mathsf{Enc}(\mathsf{mpk}_i, \alpha_{i+1}; r_i)$ is in the input to the ith mix server, but α_{i+1} is not in its output. Since the encryption system is correct, $\mathsf{Enc}(\mathsf{mpk}_i, \alpha_{i+1}; r_i)$ will decrypt to α_{i+1} and since an honest mix server does not remove any ciphertexts other than duplicates, it will always pass this check. In summary, Judge will never blame an honestly behaving party, and thus, the adversary has zero probability of winning the fairness game.

We now move on to completeness and bound the adversarial advantage in the completeness game, i.e. that if extra ballots are added or honest voters' ballots are dropped, the judge will, with overwhelming probability, hold someone accountable. Fairness ensures that the blamed party actually misbehaved.

We begin with the first criterion for completeness, i.e. that the number of ballots on BB_{vote} is not greater than the number of eligible voters. This follows from the second check of the Judge algorithm, where it checks if the bulletin board is valid. The second criterion (that the number of votes on BB_{dec} is not greater than the number of cast ballots) follows from the judge checking that the output of each mix server contains at most as many elements as its input.

Now consider the criterion that says that all honest votes are in the multiset of votes output by the last mix server (i.e. BB_{dec}). Every honest voter checks, using VSDVerify, that their ballot appears in BB_{vote}. If not there, they output the token σ given to them by the authentication server. This, in turn, causes the authentication server to be blamed by the judge. If AS was not blamed, we know that all honest ballots were present in BB_{vote}. If any honest ballot is dropped by one of the mix servers, this will be detected by VSDVerify, which will output some evidence that this mix server misbehaved, which in turn causes this mix server to be blamed by the judge.

Now, the adversary has one possibility of winning the completeness game, namely if two (or more) voters have cast the same vote, and their sampled nonces happen to be equal. In this case, the adversary may drop all but one of these ballots without it being detected. To analyze this situation, we slightly modify the completeness game. We call the new game G'_c and let E'_c be the probability that G'_c returns 1. The difference from G_c to G'_c is that in G'_c, we keep track of the nonces that are sampled when the adversary calls the vote oracle, and only sample new nonces from the set of nonces that have not been used earlier. The two games are equivalent unless there is a collision in the first game, hence $|\Pr[E_c] - \Pr[E'_c]| \leq \Pr[Col]$.

In G'_c, as there are no collisions in the nonces, any ballot that is dropped by the adversary will be detected by VSDVerify, which in turns causes the judge to blame the misbehaving party. In other words, in G'_c, the adversary will have zero probability of winning, so $\Pr[E'_c] = 0$. Thus, the probability that the adversary wins the completeness game is bounded by $\Pr[Col]$. As the adversary has zero probability of winning the fairness game, and the probability of winning the accountability game is bounded by the sum of winning the fairness game and the completeness game, we arrive at the conclusion of Theorem 1 that the advantage is bounded by the collision probability. By the birthday paradox the collision probability is bounded by $\frac{q_v(q_v-1)}{2 \cdot |N|}$, where q_v is the number of queries vote oracle queries and N is the nonce space.

Appendix B Proof for Theorem 2

The proof of the theorem follows from analyzing Fairness and Completeness.

Lemma 1 (Fairness).   *The judge J is computationally fair in $\mathcal{P}(n, m, \mu, p_{voter}^{verif}, p_{abst}^{verif})$.*

Proof. The proof is essentially the same as for sElect in [17] for the voting phase but relies on GBA in the mixing and decryption phases.

Consider what happens if the voter makes a complaint and the judge blames both the party accused and the voter (J2). Since the bulletin board is honest and the channel is authenticated the voter must really have made the complaint. There are two cases. If the voter is dishonest the verdict is clearly true. If the voter is honest, the correctness of the verdict follows from the voter verification correctness of the protocol either because the person it blamed has misbehaved or because the authentication server did not send a valid confirmation. (J2) covers both the case where the voter's ballot is dropped and when it is added.

Case (J1) is covered by GBA. Since the scheme has GBA it follows that the adversary cannot make either of these conditions trigger when the party ran its honest program, otherwise GBA would not hold.

Lemma 2 (Completeness). *For every instance* π *of* $\mathcal{P}(n, m, \mu, p_{voter}^{verif}, p_{abst}^{verif})$, *we have*

$$Pr\left[\pi(1^l) \rightarrow \neg(J : \Phi_k)\right] \leq \delta^k(p_{voter}^{verif}, p_{abst}^{verif}) = \left(1 - \min\left(p_{voter}^{verif}, p_{abst}^{verif}\right)\right)^{k+1}$$

with overwhelming probability as a function of l.

Again, the proof is essentially the same as for sElect in the voting phase but relies on GBA in the mixing and decryption phases. We need to show that the following probabilities are bounded for every i: a) $Pr\left[\pi(1^l) \rightarrow (\chi_i \wedge \neg dis(v_i) \wedge \neg dis(AS))\right]$, b) $Pr\left[\pi(1^l) \rightarrow (\chi_i' \wedge \neg dis(v_i) \wedge \neg dis(AS))\right]$, c) $Pr\left[\pi(1^l) \rightarrow (\neg\gamma_k \wedge \neg\chi \rightarrow dis(\mathsf{VA})|dis(\mathsf{AS})|dis(\mathsf{DA}_i)_{i=1}^q|dis(\mathsf{MS}_j)_{j=1}^m)\right]$. The first two probabilities are equal to zero as noted in the sElect proof [17]. The last probability is δ^k bounded by the completeness component of GBA. This is immediate when p_{voter}^{verif} is equal to one since our definition assumes all honest voters vote and verify; when p_{voter}^{verif} is lower this is more complicated and requires guessing ahead of time which voters will verify. This can be achieved using standard techniques from complexity leveraging.

Appendix C Proof for Theorem 3

Proof. Consider an adversary $\mathcal{A}$ against $\mathsf{Exp}_{\mathcal{A},\mathcal{V}_r}^{Ver}(\lambda)$. We start by running $\mathcal{A}$ getting the output pd which we use for $\mathcal{B}$ in addition to an honestly generated signing keypair for AS. We then make a random guess about which voters $\mathcal{A}$ is going to ask to verify. The probability of guessing correctly is at least $1/2^{|\mathcal{I}|}$. Now, we keep running $\mathcal{A}$ to choose honestly cast votes and creating the bulletin board BB. Every time the vote oracle is called and we guessed the voter is going to verify, we let $\mathcal{B}$ query the same and forward the output to $\mathcal{A}$. If we guessed that the voter is not going to verify, we simply honestly generate the ballot and send it to $\mathcal{A}$ without $\mathcal{B}$ querying the vote oracle. We use the board BB output by $\mathcal{A}$ in addition to honestly generated signatures for AS. Since the signature scheme is perfectly correct, the signatures will verify in lines 4–7 of $\mathsf{Exp}_{\mathcal{A},\mathcal{V}}^{GBA}(\lambda)$.

We now run $\mathcal{O}\mathsf{Verify}$ for $\mathcal{B}$ which will call verification for all voters used in the oracle calls in $\mathsf{Exp}_{\mathcal{A},\mathcal{V}}^{GBA}(\lambda)$. We can use the outputs to $\mathcal{A}$'s calls to the verification oracle. Here we assume that we guessed the verifiers correctly and, further, in this case the two sets of verifying voters will be the same in the two experiments. For the sake of the proof, we will abort if they do not match, hence the degradation factor in the advantage. Now with probability $\frac{1}{2^{|\mathcal{I}|}}\mathsf{Adv}^{ver}_{\mathcal{A},\mathcal{V}_r}(\lambda)$ in $\mathsf{Exp}^{Ver}_{\mathcal{A},\mathcal{V}_r}(\lambda)$ we will have no complaints from the individual verification, the universal verification will be successful and we have $\neg(|\mathcal{I}| \geq |\mathsf{BB}|_{submit}| \geq |\mathsf{BB}|_{res}| \wedge \mathsf{V}[\mathsf{Checked}] \subseteq_{ms} \mathsf{BB}|_{res})$. Using that the scheme is accountability-verifiability-correct in $\mathsf{Exp}^{GBA}_{\mathcal{A},\mathcal{V}}(\lambda)$ all individual verification will also produce no blame since the signatures will verify by perfect correctness, and, finally, again by accountability-verifiability-correctness and successful universal verification, no blame will be output by Judge, i.e. $|B| = 0$. Since the votes from the verifying voters, $\mathsf{V}[\mathsf{Checked}]$, in $\mathsf{Exp}^{GBA}_{\mathcal{A},\mathcal{V}}(\lambda)$ exactly corresponds to the votes from the oracle vote calls in $\mathsf{Exp}^{GBA}_{\mathcal{A},\mathcal{V}}(\lambda)$ and $|\mathsf{BB}|_{submit}| = |\mathsf{BB}_{vote}|$ and $\mathsf{BB}|_{res} = \mathsf{BB}_{dec}$ we exactly get the winning condition $(\neg(n \geq |\mathsf{BB}_{vote}| \geq |\mathsf{BB}_{dec}| \wedge V \subseteq \mathsf{BB}_{dec}) \wedge B = \bot)$ in $\mathsf{Exp}^{GBA}_{\mathcal{A},\mathcal{V}}(\lambda)$.

References

1. Abdalla, M., Bellare, M., Rogaway, P.: DHIES: an encryption scheme based on the Diffie-Hellman problem. Contributions to IEEE P1363a (Sep 1998)
2. Adida, B.: Helios: web-based open-audit voting. In: van Oorschot, P.C. (ed.) USENIX Security 2008, pp. 335–348. USENIX Association (Jul / Aug 2008)
3. Barthe, G., Dupressoir, F., Grégoire, B., Kunz, C., Schmidt, B., Strub, P.-Y.: EasyCrypt: a tutorial. In: Aldini, A., Lopez, J., Martinelli, F. (eds.) FOSAD 2012-2013. LNCS, vol. 8604, pp. 146–166. Springer, Cham (2014). https://doi.org/10.1007/978-3-319-10082-1_6
4. Bernhard, D., Cortier, V., Galindo, D., Pereira, O., Warinschi, B.: A comprehensive analysis of game-based ballot privacy definitions. Cryptology ePrint Archive, Report 2015/255 (2015). https://eprint.iacr.org/2015/255
5. Bruni, A., Giustolisi, R., Schürmann, C.: Automated analysis of accountability. In: Nguyen, P.Q., Zhou, J. (eds.) ISC 2017. LNCS, vol. 10599, pp. 417–434. Springer, Heidelberg (Nov (2017)
6. Cortier, V., Dragan, C.C., Dupressoir, F., Schmidt, B., Strub, P.Y., Warinschi, B.: Machine-checked proofs of privacy for electronic voting protocols. In: 2017 IEEE Symposium on Security and Privacy, pp. 993–1008. IEEE Computer Society Press (May 2017). https://doi.org/10.1109/SP.2017.28
7. Cortier, V., Dragan, C.C., Dupressoir, F., Warinschi, B.: Machine-checked proofs for electronic voting: Privacy and verifiability for belenios. In: Chong, S., Delaune, S. (eds.) CSF 2018 Computer Security Foundations Symposium, pp. 298–312. IEEE Computer Society Press (2018). https://doi.org/10.1109/CSF.2018.00029
8. Cortier, V., Lallemand, J., Warinschi, B.: Fifty shades of ballot privacy: privacy against a malicious board. In: Jia, L., Küsters, R. (eds.) CSF 2020 Computer Security Foundations Symposium, pp. 17–32. IEEE Computer Society Press (2020). https://doi.org/10.1109/CSF49147.2020.00010
9. Cortier, V., Gaudry, P., Glondu, S.: Belenios: a simple private and verifiable electronic voting System, pp. 214–238 (04 2019). https://doi.org/10.1007/978-3-030-19052-1_14

10. Drăgan, et al.: Machine-checked proofs of privacy against malicious boards for selene & co. In: 2022 IEEE 35th Computer Security Foundations Symposium (CSF), pp. 335–347 (2022). https://doi.org/10.1109/CSF54842.2022.9919663

11. Hirschi, L., Schmid, L., Basin, D.A.: Fixing the achilles heel of E-voting: The bulletin board. In: Küsters, R., Naumann, D. (eds.) CSF 2021 Computer Security Foundations Symposium, pp. 1–17. IEEE Computer Society Press (2021). https://doi.org/10.1109/CSF51468.2021.00016

12. Khazaei, S., Moran, T., Wikström, D.: A mix-net from any CCA2 secure cryptosystem. In: Wang, X., Sako, K. (eds.) ASIACRYPT 2012. LNCS, vol. 7658, pp. 607–625. Springer, Heidelberg (2012). https://doi.org/10.1007/978-3-642-34961-4_37

13. Kiayias, A., Zacharias, T., Zhang, B.: End-to-end verifiable elections in the standard model. In: Oswald, E., Fischlin, M. (eds.) EUROCRYPT 2015. LNCS, vol. 9057, pp. 468–498. Springer, Heidelberg (2015). https://doi.org/10.1007/978-3-662-46803-6_16

14. Kiayias, A., Zacharias, T., Zhang, B.: Ceremonies for end-to-end verifiable elections. In: Fehr, S. (ed.) PKC 2017. LNCS, vol. 10175, pp. 305–334. Springer, Heidelberg (2017). https://doi.org/10.1007/978-3-662-54388-7_11

15. Künnemann, R., Esiyok, I., Backes, M.: Automated verification of accountability in security protocols. In: Delaune, S., Jia, L. (eds.) CSF 2019 Computer Security Foundations Symposium, pp. 397–413. IEEE Computer Society Press (2019). https://doi.org/10.1109/CSF.2019.00034

16. Künnemann, R., Garg, D., Backes, M.: Accountability in the decentralised-adversary setting. In: Küsters, R., Naumann, D. (eds.) CSF 2021 Computer Security Foundations Symposium, pp. 1–16. IEEE Computer Society Press (2021). https://doi.org/10.1109/CSF51468.2021.00007

17. Küsters, R., Müller, J., Scapin, E., Truderung, T.: sElect: a lightweight verifiable remote voting system. In: Hicks, M., Köpf, B. (eds.) CSF 2016 Computer Security Foundations Symposium, pp. 341–354. IEEE Computer Society Press (2016). https://doi.org/10.1109/CSF.2016.31

18. Küsters, R., Truderung, T., Vogt, A.: Accountability: definition and relationship to verifiability. In: Al-Shaer, E., Keromytis, A.D., Shmatikov, V. (eds.) ACM CCS 2010, pp. 526–535. ACM Press (Oct 2010). https://doi.org/10.1145/1866307.1866366

19. Morio, K., Künnemann, R.: Verifying accountability for unbounded sets of participants. In: Küsters, R., Naumann, D. (eds.) CSF 2021 Computer Security Foundations Symposium, pp. 1–16. IEEE Computer Society Press (2021). https://doi.org/10.1109/CSF51468.2021.00032

20. Ryan, P.Y.A., Rønne, P.B., Iovino, V.: Selene: voting with transparent verifiability and coercion-mitigation. In: Clark, J., Meiklejohn, S., Ryan, P.Y.A., Wallach, D., Brenner, M., Rohloff, K. (eds.) FC 2016. LNCS, vol. 9604, pp. 176–192. Springer, Heidelberg (2016). https://doi.org/10.1007/978-3-662-53357-4_12

21. SwissPost: Swiss post voting system. https://gitlab.com/swisspost-evoting (2022)

Author Index

© The Editor(s) (if applicable) and The Author(s), under exclusive license
to Springer Nature Switzerland AG 2024
G. Tsudik et al. (Eds.): ESORICS 2023, LNCS 14346, pp. 493–494, 2024.
https://doi.org/10.1007/978-3-031-51479-1

Printed in the United States
by Baker & Taylor Publisher Services